FiZZ, BUBBLE & FLASH!

Element Explorations & Atom Adventures for Hands-On Science Fun!

Anita Brandolini, Ph.D.

Illustrations by
Michael Kline

WILLIAMSON PUBLISHING • CHARLOTTE, VERMONT

Library of Congress Cataloging-in-Publication Data

Brandolini, Anita J., 1956-
  Fizz, bubble & flash! : element explorations and atom adventures for hands-on science fun! / Anita Brandolini.
      p. cm.
    "Williamson kids can! book."
    Includes index.
    Summary: Gives instructions for a variety of experiments that examine the characteristics of some of the common elements around us.
    ISBN 1-885593-83-X
    1. Chemical elements--Juvenile literature. 2. Science--Experiments--Juvenile literature.
[1. Chemical elements. 2. Science experiments. 3. Experiments.] I. Title: Fizz, bubble, and flash. II. Title.

QD466.B635 2003
546'.078--dc21   2003043096

Kids Can! ® **series editor:** Susan Williamson
Project editor: Emily Stetson
Interior design: Sarah Rakitin
Interior illustrations: Michael Kline
Cover design and illustrations: Michael Kline
Printing: Quebecor World

Photography: page 16: the *Hindenburg*, Kevin W. Pace collection; page 58: geodesic dome, Courtesy, the Estate of R. Buckminster Fuller.

Williamson Publishing Co.
P.O. Box 185
Charlotte, VT 05445
(800) 234-8791

Printed in Canada

10 9 8 7 6 5 4 3 2

Dedication
For George and Isabel

Acknowledgments
This book got its start years ago in discussions about chemistry exhibits at Liberty Science Center in Jersey City, New Jersey. It continued to grow through my participation in the public outreach activities of the North Jersey section of the American Chemical Society. Many friends and colleagues have helped with this project, contributing interesting tidbits about the elements and other ideas. Two people who deserve special mention are Joan Mara of Liberty Science Center and Valerie Kuck of the American Chemical Society; they encouraged me to actually assemble all these facts and ideas into a book. Many kids read over various versions of this work, and their feedback about what they liked (as well as what they found boring) was invaluable. The editorial staff at Williamson Publishing, particularly Emily Stetson and Susan Williamson, further helped me refine the early draft into something vastly more entertaining, without diluting the science. I have learned a great deal about writing for children from them.

Finally, I'd like to thank all the kids I've met over the years — at Liberty Science Center, through National Chemistry Week, and during school visits. Your excitement about science inspired me to write this book, and I hope that you enjoy it. Always remember that science is important and science is challenging, but above all, science is fun!

Table of Contents

Meet the Elements!

Take a look around you. Everything you see, and the many things you can't see, are made up of materials called *elements*. They are the building blocks that make up everything around us on earth, even *in* us, and out in space, too! Whether a gas (like the air we breathe), a liquid (water in the ocean), or solid (the clothes you're wearing, the house you live in, or a tree outside — even this book!), everything around you is made up of some combination or grouping of these 100–plus chemical building blocks. Important? You bet! Without them, the world as we know it just wouldn't exist! (And that means no CD players, no TVs, no food, no pets, no "us"!) So, let's have some fun, and find out what these awesome things we call *chemical elements* are all about.

It's elementary — elements are made of only one kind of atom. By themselves, or combined with other elements, they make up everything in the universe!

WHAT <u>IS</u> AN ELEMENT?
& OTHER QUESTIONS (WITH ANSWERS!)

Whether you know it or not, you're already familiar with many of these elements — like sodium, copper, silver, mercury, and aluminum. Others have strange-sounding names, such as neodymium and americium. (More about those *later!*) The helium in a party balloon, the gold in a necklace, and the carbon in charcoal are all elements — and so is the silicon in a computer memory chip and the iron in your fortified breakfast cereal!

BUT I THOUGHT THAT THE SMALLEST BITS OF SOMETHING WERE CALLED *ATOMS?*

And you're right! *Atoms* (AH-tums) are the smallest particles of an element that can exist and still be that element. Some of the things around you are made up of *atoms of the same element* — the helium in that balloon, the carbon in charcoal, the aluminum in aluminum foil, or the oxygen in the air you breathe. Think of them like various Lego creations made by connecting pieces of exactly the same shape, size, and color into combinations of atoms.

But you'd probably get pretty bored with your Legos if you could only build towers out of identical pieces. You probably like to mix them up! Well, atoms feel the same way, so most substances are made up of groups of two or more *different* types of atoms stuck together. These groups are called *molecules* or *compounds.* Our world would be awfully dull if everything were made only of pure element combinations. So it's a good thing that so many things are made up of molecules!

For example, a molecule of water has one oxygen and two hydrogen atoms (think of three Legos — one of one kind and two of another). Its chemical formula is H_2O: an H for hydrogen, with a little 2 to show there are two atoms of it in each molecule, and a single O for oxygen.

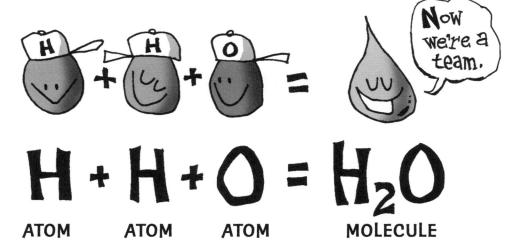

Now we're a team.

$$H + H + O = H_2O$$

ATOM   ATOM   ATOM   MOLECULE

There are small molecules, medium-sized ones, and even giant molecules with thousands of atoms! The cotton or nylon clothes we wear contain long, stringy molecules with strange-sounding names like *cellulose* (SELL-you-lowse) and *polyamide* (POL-ee-AM-id). Your body is made from thousands of different kinds of molecules — water, proteins, and fats, to name a few.

So, atoms are the smallest particles that are just one element, and molecules are combinations of atoms of the same or different elements. Either way, it's back to elements again!

WHO DISCOVERED THE ELEMENTS?

Humans have been discovering elements ever since they started exploring the world! The first elements were found so long ago, we don't know who discovered them. People have been using elements such as gold, iron, and copper for thousands of years. As humans started experimenting with the rocks and minerals they found around them, they uncovered other elements — tin from the mineral *cassiterite* (ka-SIT-er-ite), mercury from the mineral *cinnibar* (SIN-neh-bar), and carbon from burning wood. They didn't call them "elements" back then, though.

The discovery of elements really started to take off around 1700, when scientists started figuring out what kinds of stuff the world was made of. They were able to *isolate*, or separate out, the elements hidden in many common materials. Between 1700 and the early 1900s, most of the 90 natural elements were discovered. Then in the 1940s, scientists realized that they could create totally new elements in the laboratory. So far, scientists have discovered or created more than 112 elements, and they're still making more!

Fizz, Bubble & Flash!

Hey, could I discover an element?

We're not missing any natural elements, so you won't find any just lying around. If you want to help create a new element, you could study chemistry or physics in college and then go to work in one of the labs that creates new elements. But how about working with the elements we already have? *Chemists* are scientists who try to combine elements to make new molecules or to better understand the ones we already have. A new molecule might become a medicine that helps sick people, a detergent that cleans better, or a fuel that doesn't pollute the environment! And yes, you could create it!

SO, HOW DO SCIENTISTS KEEP ALL THESE ELEMENTS STRAIGHT?

To organize and keep track of all the different elements, scientists give each one a number and a nickname (like the H for hydrogen) and group them by similarities — a lot like the way different instruments are grouped in an orchestra.

With elements, though, the arrangement is called the *Periodic Table*. The particular spot that an element has is important, because elements in the same column, or *family*, are chemical cousins, and act in much the same way, just as the individual instruments in a musical family (woodwinds, brass, etc.) sit together and sound similar.

Together, these groupings form the orchestra of every element here on earth ... and beyond!

Presenting: The Periodic Table!

You've just learned that everything around you is built from about 100 different kinds of really small building blocks called *chemical elements*. Each of these elements gets its own special box on the Periodic Table. Each box usually shows the *symbol* (the short code or nickname for the element), the *atomic number* (a number identifying the element and determining where it sits at the table), and the *atomic mass* (how heavy it is). The atomic numbers start at the top left, beginning with H (#1), and read left to right, row by row — just like the lines in this book. Families of elements that *behave in similar ways* are grouped in columns. Some families are all metals, some all gases. Here's one element up close, and you can see how all the elements are arranged on page 10.

WHO FIRST THOUGHT OF THE PERIODIC TABLE?

For a long time, scientists realized that many elements seemed to be related to one another. But trying to organize this information was like trying to solve a jigsaw puzzle with a lot of pieces missing, when you don't even know what the picture is supposed to look like!

In 1869, a clever Russian chemist named Dmitri Mendeleev (duh–MEE–tree men–duh–LAY–uf) figured out some of the answers to the puzzle. He even predicted which elements were missing, and how they would behave. Scientists later filled in the blanks, and found that his predictions were right! (For the inside scoop on elements and some of these atom adventures, see page 122.)

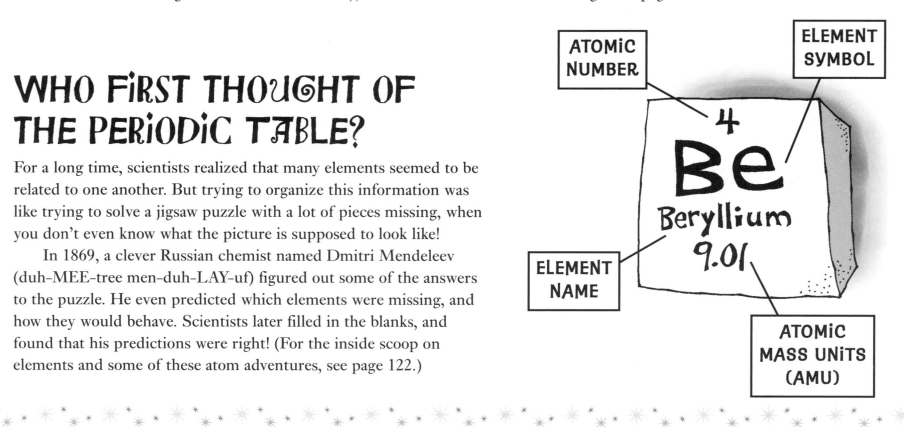

ATOMIC NUMBER

ELEMENT SYMBOL

ELEMENT NAME

ATOMIC MASS UNITS (AMU)

4
Be
Beryllium
9.01

THE NAME GAME

Gold's nickname is Au, lead's is Pb, and potassium's is K. What's up with that?

Usually the one- or two-letter nicknames (symbols) for the elements are easy to remember — N for nitrogen and O for oxygen, for example. Other elements are named after famous scientists (Es for einsteinium, named after Albert Einstein), after countries (Fr for Francium, named after France), or for the places where they were discovered (Yb for ytterbium, named after the town of Ytterby, Sweden).

There are some strange symbols that are harder to recognize, though, because the names come from other languages. Gold's symbol, Au, only makes sense if you know that the Latin word for this metal is *aurum*. The same is true of lead, whose symbol, Pb, is from the Latin *plumbum*. And sometimes the symbol refers to another name for the element, such as the W for tungsten, which is also called *wolfram*, from the mineral *wolframite*.

If you discovered an element, what would you call it? Can you turn your own name into one for an element? Try adding "ium" or just "um" to the end. You might end up with "Isabelium," "Stevenium," or "Georgium." Or, would you prefer to name a scientific discovery after your friends or members of your family, your town, or even your pet? Who knows, someday you just might get the chance!

I hear about "plutonium" and "uranium" in the news. How come?

Most of the atoms that make up the different elements are very *stable* — the little pile of protons and neutrons in the nucleus (see Elements: The Inside Scoop, page 122) will stick around forever. But the atoms of some elements are *unstable* — they have trouble holding themselves together. These atoms fall apart, losing or gaining more protons. This can give off a lot of energy — and changes them into a different element altogether! (You can check out how this works on page 111.)

Scientists call such atoms *radioactive* (page 113), and the energy they give off can be very powerful, even dangerous when used in certain ways. One of the uses of plutonium and uranium, for example, is in nuclear weapons. But many radioactive elements are very helpful to us when used carefully. Doctors and dentists, for example, use X rays from radioactive compounds to help diagnose medical problems — like checking for cavities in your teeth!

THE PERIODIC TABLE

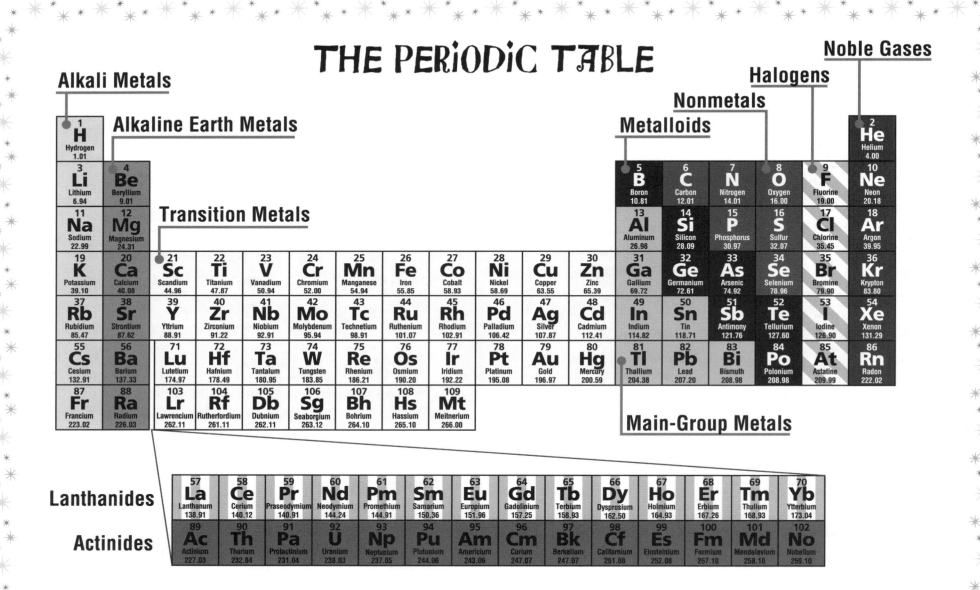

Alkali Metals

Alkaline Earth Metals

Transition Metals

Metalloids

Nonmetals

Halogens

Noble Gases

Main-Group Metals

1 H Hydrogen 1.01																	2 He Helium 4.00
3 Li Lithium 6.94	4 Be Beryllium 9.01											5 B Boron 10.98	6 C Carbon 12.01	7 N Nitrogen 14.01	8 O Oxygen 16.00	9 F Fluorine 19.00	10 Ne Neon 20.18
11 Na Sodium 22.99	12 Mg Magnesium 24.31											13 Al Aluminum 26.98	14 Si Silicon 28.09	15 P Phosphorus 30.97	16 S Sulfur 32.07	17 Cl Chlorine 35.45	18 Ar Argon 39.95
19 K Potassium 39.10	20 Ca Calcium 40.08	21 Sc Scandium 44.96	22 Ti Titanium 47.87	23 V Vanadium 50.94	24 Cr Chromium 52.00	25 Mn Manganese 54.94	26 Fe Iron 55.85	27 Co Cobalt 58.93	28 Ni Nickel 58.69	29 Cu Copper 63.55	30 Zn Zinc 65.39	31 Ga Gallium 69.72	32 Ge Germanium 72.61	33 As Arsenic 74.92	34 Se Selenium 78.96	35 Br Bromine 79.90	36 Kr Krypton 83.80
37 Rb Rubidium 85.47	38 Sr Strontium 87.62	39 Y Yttrium 88.91	40 Zr Zirconium 91.22	41 Nb Niobium 92.91	42 Mo Molybdenum 95.94	43 Tc Technetium 98.91	44 Ru Ruthenium 101.07	45 Rh Rhodium 102.91	46 Pd Palladium 106.42	47 Ag Silver 107.87	48 Cd Cadmium 112.41	49 In Indium 114.82	50 Sn Tin 118.71	51 Sb Antimony 121.76	52 Te Tellurium 127.60	53 I Iodine 126.90	54 Xe Xenon 131.29
55 Cs Cesium 132.91	56 Ba Barium 137.33	71 Lu Lutetium 174.97	72 Hf Hafnium 178.49	73 Ta Tantalum 180.95	74 W Tungsten 183.85	75 Re Rhenium 186.21	76 Os Osmium 190.20	77 Ir Iridium 192.22	78 Pt Platinum 195.08	79 Au Gold 196.97	80 Hg Mercury 200.59	81 Tl Thallium 204.38	82 Pb Lead 207.20	83 Bi Bismuth 208.98	84 Po Polonium 208.98	85 At Astatine 209.99	86 Rn Radon 222.02
87 Fr Francium 223.02	88 Ra Radium 226.03	103 Lr Lawrencium 262.11	104 Rf Rutherfordium 261.11	105 Db Dubnium 262.11	106 Sg Seaborgium 263.12	107 Bh Bohrium 264.10	108 Hs Hassium 265.10	109 Mt Meitnerium 266.00									

Lanthanides

57 La Lanthanum 138.91	58 Ce Cerium 140.12	59 Pr Praseodymium 140.91	60 Nd Neodymium 144.24	61 Pm Promethium 144.91	62 Sm Samarium 150.36	63 Eu Europium 151.96	64 Gd Gadolinium 157.25	65 Tb Terbium 158.93	66 Dy Dysprosium 162.50	67 Ho Holmium 164.93	68 Er Erbium 167.26	69 Tm Thulium 168.93	70 Yb Ytterbium 173.04

Actinides

89 Ac Actinium 227.03	90 Th Thorium 232.04	91 Pa Protactinium 231.04	92 U Uranium 238.03	93 Np Neptunium 237.05	94 Pu Plutonium 244.06	95 Am Americium 243.06	96 Cm Curium 247.07	97 Bk Berkelium 247.07	98 Cf Californium 251.08	99 Es Einsteinium 252.08	100 Fm Fermium 257.10	101 Md Mendelevium 258.10	102 No Nobelium 259.10

The Periodic Table really should look like this:

But to fit that wide a table in a normal-sized book, you'd have to make the boxes tiny — too small to read! So the two wide rows (lanthanides and actinides) usually appear below the Table. They really belong between the second and third columns.

(Fizz, Bubble & Flash!)

A Periodic Poem

Each element has a spot on the Periodic Table,
Whether metal or gas, radioactive or stable.
You can find out its number, its symbol, its weight,
And from its position, its physical state.

Elements lined up in columns and rows,
The reason for this order, as each chemist knows,
Is that atoms are made up of still smaller bits,
(figuring this out tested scientists' wits!).

In the nucleus, protons and neutrons are found,
And a cloud of electrons is buzzing around.
First take one proton, put in its place;
Now you have hydrogen, the simplest case.

Add two neutrons and one more proton,
And suddenly, the hydrogen's gone!
Now you have helium, quite different stuff ...
You get the picture; I've said enough.

These tiny particles: they're like building blocks
That make people and buildings, flowers and rocks.
They create all of the elements we find
In everyday things of every kind!

Meet the Alkali Metals!

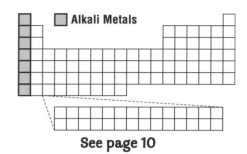

Alkali Metals

See page 10

The first column of the Periodic Table, way on the left, contains the elements called the *alkali* (AL-kah-lye) *metals*. All of them, except hydrogen, are *metals*. (Hydrogen's the littlest atom, and it doesn't exactly behave like any other element. But its electrons are arranged like the other alkali metals, so it's put here, too.) You know something about what metals are already: They're often shiny, even reflecting light, and they conduct heat — think of how a metal spoon gets warm if you leave it in hot cocoa. And, as you'll find out on page 14, metals also conduct electricity! Most metals are also *malleable*, which just means that they're easily bent, shaped, or molded — just like that metal spoon again.

You'll never find a spoon made of an alkali metal, though, or even run into one of these alkali metals on its own in nature. They just don't hang around long enough! This family of elements is the most *reactive* of all the metals — its members combine really fast with other elements. A piece of pure alkali metal reacts in the blink of an eye! When exposed to water or air, they can be pretty wild, bursting into flames and giving off lots of very bright light!

So what do alkali metals have to do with you? Well, they help you season your food, for one! You have plenty of alkali metals lurking around your house, combined with other elements. Check them out!

HYDROGEN

Hydrogen, the first element, is in old H₂O;
It's also the gas that caused the Hindenburg* to blow!
Look up at the stars — they're hydrogen, too,
And there's H in our bodies — in me and in you.

* page 16

FAIR SHARE

What holds the hydrogen and oxygen (page 68) atoms together in a water molecule? All atoms have a lot of electrons (page 122) whizzing around. When the hydrogens and the oxygen get close together, they share electrons. This sharing is called a *chemical bond*. And as you know, it's nice to bond and it's good to share!

HYDROGEN (HiGH-dro-jen)
* Symbol: H
* Number: 1
* Mass: 1.01 amu
* Discovery: In 1766, by Englishman Henry Cavendish

Meet the Alkali Metals!

Take a Water Break!

The next time you drink a glass of water, make a toast to hydrogen! Hydrogen and oxygen explode *(ka-boom!)* when they combine to make water, but you can break water molecules apart in a much quieter way.

Materials

- Ruler
- Two 6" to 8" (15 to 20 cm) pieces of insulated copper hookup wire (available from hardware stores)
- Four "alligator" clips
- Water
- Small glass or jar
- Two pencil "leads" (the type for mechanical pencils)*
- Tape
- 9-volt battery (the kind used in a smoke detector)

  *Pencil lead is made of carbon (page 54), not lead (page 32).

Make It Happen!

1. Strip $^1/_2$" (1 cm) of insulation from both ends of the wire pieces; attach a clip to each end of both wires.

2. Put about 2" (5 cm) of water into the glass. Place the pencil "leads" into the water, about 1" (2.5 cm) apart, and tape to the side of the jar as shown. The leads are your *electrodes* (ee-LEK-trodes).

3. Clip one end of each wire to the top of a lead. (The lead electrodes can break easily, so be careful!) Attach the other ends of the wires to the battery terminals. Now watch the electrodes closely. When you're finished observing, unhook the wires from the battery.

♦ Investigate hydrogen fuel cells. Do a display showing how they might be used in the future.

♦ Do a survey of how much water people of different ages drink each day. Graph your results and compare them with the recommendations of the American Medical Association.

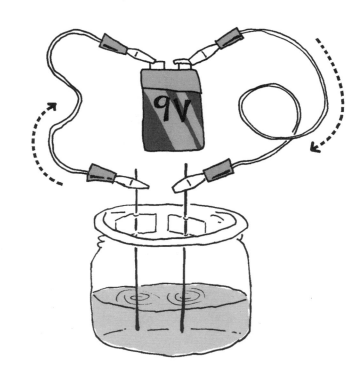

These current events sure seem electrifying! Water and carbon (the pencil "lead") both *conduct* electricity, providing a pathway along which it flows. When the wires are connected to the battery, electrons travel around and around in a circle from the battery, along one wire, through the lead, across the water, through the other lead and wire, and back into the battery. As this electrical *current* passes through the water, it breaks water — H_2O — into its elements, hydrogen and oxygen. Those bubbles you saw forming along the leads were gases — hydrogen along one; oxygen along the other! Cool, huh? This simple–yet–amazing process is called *electrolysis* (ee-leck-TROL-uh-suss). And you made it happen!

2 H's & an O

The *chemical formula* for water, H_2O, tells you a lot about its makeup. Each water molecule is made up of two atoms of hydrogen (H) and one atom of oxygen (O). These elements exist separately as something quite different from the molecule of water they form when they combine!

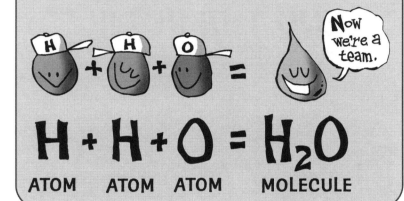

Now we're a team.

$$H + H + O = H_2O$$

ATOM   ATOM   ATOM   MOLECULE

ENVIRONMENTAL ALERT!

CARS OF YOUR FUTURE?

Someday you may drive a car powered by hydrogen! Scientists are trying to make nonpolluting automobile engines. Using hydrogen as a fuel instead of gasoline just may be the answer. These "clean engines" would combine hydrogen and oxygen from the air. So, instead of nasty air pollution, the only thing to come out of your car would be water! These engines are powerful, too. They are even used to launch rockets into space. Right now, they're too heavy and expensive to put in cars, but scientists are trying to make them lighter and less expensive.

THE BIG H ...

Hydrogen is not only the first element in the Periodic Table (page 10), but it's number one in quantity, too! There is more hydrogen in the universe than any other element. Stars are made of it, and hydrogen roams through the space between the stars as well. On earth, most hydrogen is found in water and other kinds of molecules, rather than by itself.

... AND THE BLIMP

We're lucky that most hydrogen atoms are tied up in compounds like H_2O, because hydrogen gas, by itself, is very explosive — a fact that made headlines all around the world in the early 1900s. Have you ever seen old photos or movies about the *Hindenburg* disaster? The *Hindenburg*, a hydrogen-filled passenger airship (a blimp), was the largest aircraft *ever* to fly (it was four times larger than the blimps you see today). On May 6, 1937, as the airship was trying to make a much-delayed landing in Lakehurst, New Jersey, it caught on fire and crashed, killing 35 of the 97 people aboard and one ground crew member.

Don't worry about the blimps you see today, though. They are full of lightweight helium (page 82) gas, which doesn't burn.

The German passenger airship *Hindenburg* on its way from Frankfurt to the Naval Air Station at Lakehurst, New Jersey, on May 6, 1937.

Fizz, Bubble & Flash!

SODIUM

Sodium streetlights have a warm, pleasing glow,
And sodium chloride melts the ice and the snow.
Sodium bicarbonate is important in cake,
Fluffs it up nicely while it continues to bake.

YOUR SODIUM-FILLED HOME

Sodium is found in many things around your house.

- You probably have a salt shaker in your kitchen that is full of *sodium chloride* (NaCl).

- *Sodium bicarbonate* ($NaHCO_3$), also called baking soda, makes cakes fluffy, because it gives off carbon dioxide gas (just as the yeast in the carbon experiment, page 56, does) when it's heated.

- Most laundry detergents contain *sodium carbonate* (Na_2CO_3), and bleach is *sodium hypochlorite* (NaOCl) that is mixed with water.

NA = SODIUM? HUH?

Why is the symbol for sodium Na, not S or So? Good question! Na is short for *natrium*, which is the Latin word for the chemical *sodium carbonate* (Na_2CO_3). Natrium was named for the Natron Valley in Egypt where it was first found. Ancient people used this chemical compound to make glass.

Element Essentials

SODIUM (SO-dee-um)
* Symbol: Na
* Number: 11
* Mass: 22.99 amu
* Discovery: In 1807, by Sir Humphry Davy of England

Meet the Alkali Metals!

All Eyes on Ions!

Did you notice that chemicals seem to have a first and a last name, like "sodium chloride"? The name tells you the elements that have combined to make the chemical. In this case, they're sodium and chlorine (page 77). Why does chlorine's name lose an "n" and gain a "d"? Check page 72 to find out!

Like many simple chemicals, sodium chloride is made of two *ions* (EYE-ons) — one positive and one negative. The molecule's first name is the name of the positive ion, and its last name is the negative ion. So, which is which in NaCl?

Can you spot the names of other negative ions in YOUR SODIUM-FILLED HOME on page 17? Of course, you can, because like a good scientist your eyes are on everything! *Chloride* is an ion that comes from a chlorine atom. The other ions are a little more complicated. Sometimes gangs of atoms get together to form ions. Some of these gangs are called *bicarbonate* (a hydrogen, a carbon, and three oxygens), *carbonate* (a carbon and three oxygens), and *hypochlorite* (an oxygen and a chlorine).

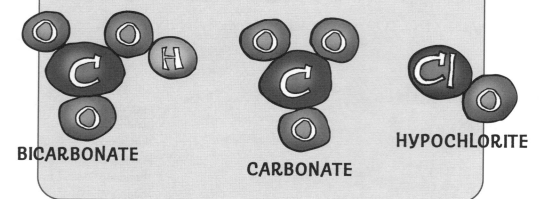

BICARBONATE

CARBONATE

HYPOCHLORITE

Water molecules Saltwater molecules

PLEASE DON'T FREEZE!

If you live in an area with cold winters, you probably know that salt melts ice. Throw some rock salt on icy steps and the ice will melt. Fresh water freezes at 32°F (or 0°C), but salty water has to be much colder to become a solid. (Go ahead and try it: Place plain water in one paper cup; salted water in another. Then leave them in the freezer for a few hours. Keep checking to see what happens!)

In liquid water, the molecules (H_2O) are bouncing around all over the place. As they get colder and begin to freeze, the water molecules line up in nice, neat rows and stop moving around so much. But when salt water tries to freeze, the sodium and chloride atoms get in the way of the water molecules, making it harder for them to line up.

Fizz, Bubble & Flash!

I Scream, You Scream ...

Here's a delicious experiment to prove that salt water is colder than plain water. A good rule that scientists follow is "Never eat the results of an experiment." This time it's OK — it's ice cream!

Materials

- ½ cup (125 mL) heavy cream
- ½ cup (125 mL) milk
- 2 teaspoons (10 mL) sugar
- ¼ teaspoon (1 mL) vanilla
- 1 quart (1 L) size zip-locking plastic freezer bag
- 2½ cups (625 mL) crushed ice
- 1 gallon (4 L) size zip-locking plastic freezer bag
- Dish towel or oven mitt
- ½ cup (125 mL) kosher or rock salt

Make It Happen!

1. Combine the cream, milk, sugar, and vanilla in the quart bag and zip it closed. Shake to mix.

2. Put the ice into the gallon bag. Now put the smaller bag into the bigger one and close the whole thing up. Shake both bags together for 10 to 15 minutes. (Hold the bags with the towel or oven mitt if they feel too cold.) Notice anything?

3. Next, open the bigger bag and add the salt to the ice. Close everything up again and shake for another 10 to 15 minutes. Notice anything?

4. Empty the smaller bag and enjoy your experiment!

Curious Minds want to know...?

Why can't I make ice cream with just ice water?
In order to make yummy ice cream, you have to freeze the fat in the milk and the cream, and they must be really cold to turn solid. Plain old ice water just isn't chilly enough to do the trick. But if you add salt, your snack will be ready in a jiffy!

"BUT YOU OWE ME THREE TABLESPOONS"

How would you like to have your allowance paid in salt instead of money? No way? Well, salt isn't worth much now, but long ago, salt was so valuable that it was used as money. Soldiers in ancient Rome were paid in salt. The Latin word for salt, *salarius,* later became the English word *salary.*

Why was salt so valuable? There were only a few places where lots of sodium chloride could be easily mined, and it was expensive to dig it up and move it to the cities. Wait a minute, you might be thinking, isn't there a lot of salt in the oceans? Why didn't they use that salt? The problem is that it takes a long time to collect sodium chloride by evaporating all the water away. It's still a lot faster to dig salt up from the ground.

Today, we do have some desalinization plants where salt is removed from ocean water. Unfortunately, the process still takes a long time!

Take It to the SCIENCE FAIR

🎗 **Just how cold is salt water?** Find a thermometer that goes down below 32°F (0°C) and see! Does it matter how much salt you add? Do other chemicals have the same effect? Try a salt substitute (such as *potassium chloride,* or KCl), baking soda (sodium bicarbonate) or sugar.

🎗 **So, salt makes it harder for water to freeze** — what effect does it have on making water *boil?* Experiment to find out. Put the same amount of water in two pots, and add 1 tablespoon (5 mL) salt to one pot. Turn on the heat (with adult supervision, of course) to the same level under both pots. Which pan boils more quickly? Can you figure out why?

🎗 **Make your own salt crystals by evaporation!** Dissolve some salt in water and put it in a warm place to evaporate. How long does it take for the water to disappear? Do the salt crystals look different from the ones you started with?

Answer: The water without the salt boils faster, and at a lower temperature. The water molecules are trying to float up into the air, but the salt gets in the way, keeping them from escaping. It may seem strange, but salt lowers the freezing temperature of water and raises its boiling temperature!

Fizz, Bubble & Flash!

ALL IN THE (ALKALI METALS) FAMILY

LITHIUM

7-Up soda originally contained **lithium** (Li) and was called "Bib-Label Lithiated Lemon-Lime Soda." Yum!

The *vacuums* (airless tubes) inside television and computer screens are protected from leaking by **rubidium** (Rb). It safely combines with any air that sneaks in.

RUBIDIUM

CESIUM

Since 1960, official time has been measured by the vibrations of **cesium** (Cs) atoms in atomic clocks.

POTASSIUM

What do orange juice, bananas, broccoli, raisins, and avocados have in common? They're all great sources of **potassium** (K).

Francium (Fr) is so rare, there's not even enough of it to allow scientists to study its chemistry!

SIGH...

FRANCIUM

Meet the Alkali Metals!

Meet the Alkaline Earths!

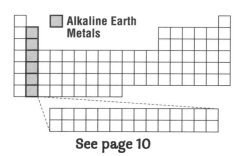

Alkaline Earth Metals

See page 10

The *alkaline earth metals* are close relatives of the alkali metals (page 12), and these metallic elements act much the same. You don't find them as elements in nature on their own, either, but their compounds are pretty common. Like the alkali metals, they also react with air and water but don't put on quite as exciting a show.

But why "earths"? Are they only found on our planet? No — some have even been found on the moon and Mars!

Before scientists really understood about atoms (pages 122 to 125), they named groups of elements after the places where they were discovered. Most of these elements can be found in the ground as rocks and minerals, so the old-time scientists called them "earths."

You probably drink a liquid that contains one of these "earths" every day to keep you healthy. Another alkaline earth element lets plants turn sunlight into food and still another even helps you celebrate the Fourth of July!

MAGNESIUM

A plant has magnesium in its green chlorophyll —
Whether palm tree, or rose, or spring daffodil.
In some parts, in autumn, this color does fade
And trees become brilliant with a more orangy shade.

GREEN MACHINES

Look out the nearest window. What do you see? If you spot any green plants, you are looking at very important magnesium-containing molecules — *chlorophyll* (KLOR-oh-fill). This green chemical helps plants convert water, air, and sunlight into food.

Element Essentials

MAGNESIUM (mag-NEEZE-ee-um)
* Symbol: Mg
* Number: 12
* Mass: 24.31 amu
* Discovery: In 1808, by Sir Humphry Davy of England

Get Your Fill of Chlorophyll!

What colors can you find hiding in leaves?

Materials

- Spinach or other dark green leafy vegetable
- Small jar or plastic cup
- Rubbing alcohol
- Metal spoon
- Aluminum foil
- Scissors
- Coffee filters
- Tape

Make It Happen!

Warning: Be sure to do this experiment outside or in a room with the windows open, so you get adequate ventilation from the alcohol fumes.

1. Tear up several leaves and put them into the jar. Pour the rubbing alcohol over the pieces, to just cover them. Use the spoon to mash the leaves until the alcohol turns green.

2. Cover the jar loosely with aluminum foil. Let the mixture stand for 1 hour, swirling it every 5 to 10 minutes.

3. Cut a strip of coffee filter paper. Remove the foil from the jar. Dip one end of the strip in the green solution. Tape the other end to the rim of the jar.

4. Watch for about 30 minutes. What colors do you see?

CURIOUS MINDS WANT TO KNOW...

Where did all those colors come from? Green chlorophyll isn't the only colorful molecule in leaves. Actually, there are two kinds of chlorophyll. One, called *chlorophyll a*, is blue-green. *Chlorophyll b* is yellow-green. Other molecules in leaves can be yellow, orange, red, or even purple!

Fizz, Bubble & Flash!

Take It to the
SCIENCE
FAIR

🎗 **What happens in the fall?** If you live in a place where the trees change color in autumn, try this experiment on their leaves at different times of the year. In autumn, does the green chlorophyll change into a red, orange, or yellow chemical? Or does the chlorophyll just cover up the other colors during spring and summer? (See answer at the bottom of the page to find out.) Make a poster that explains why leaves change color.

🎗 **Try this experiment with different colors of leaves.** Some plants have red or purple leaves, instead of green, even in the spring and summer. Is there any green chlorophyll hiding inside? Make a display showing your results.

Answer: The yellow, orange, and red chemicals are *always* present in the leaves. Most of the time, though, they're overpowered by the chlorophyll. When the chlorophyll production stops in the fall, the other colors appear in all their autumn glory!

SPARKLE POWER!

Have you ever waved a sparkler (with adult supervision, of course) on Independence Day or another holiday? That sparkle is another one of magnesium's surprises. Sparklers contain powdered magnesium. When they're lit, the magnesium burns, giving off a bright white light and showers of sparks.

Eat Your Veggies

Magnesium is one of the essential elements that keeps you strong. Without enough magnesium, you may feel weak, dizzy, shaky, and cranky. Luckily, it's easy to get plenty of this element — if you eat your veggies, that is. But be careful how you cook them! When you boil green vegetables too long, the magnesium atoms come out of the chlorophyll and end up in the cooking water. Not only are the veggies less healthy, but they also turn an icky greenish brown color. Yuck! Here's the trick for keeping them healthy and appetizing: Add a pinch of baking soda (sodium bicarbonate, page 17) to the water. The magnesium will stay put and you'll get vegetables that are a yummy bright green — and good for you!

Meet the Alkaline Earths!

CALCIUM

Calcium's found in the shells around eggs,
And the bones in your arms and bones in your legs.
Calcium sulfate in a cast made of plaster
Helps broken bones heal so much faster.

Element Essentials

CALCIUM (CAL-see-um)
* Symbol: Ca
* Number: 20
* Mass: 40.08 amu
* Discovery: In 1808, by Sir Humphry Davy of England

BUBBLE TROUBLE

Do you like bubble baths? Who doesn't? But in places where the local rocks contain a lot of calcium and magnesium (page 23), making a big tubful of soap bubbles is mighty tough! When it rains, these elements dissolve and wind up in rivers, lakes, and groundwater (the water trickling among the rocks deep underground). Water with a lot of dissolved minerals is called *hard water*. When these calcium and magnesium ions combine with soap, they make a scum that won't dissolve in water. Ugh! Not exactly what you want floating in your bath!

Fizz, Bubble & Flash!

These Suds Are Duds!

Learn firsthand what hard water is like.

Materials

- ☺ Marker
- ☺ Measuring cup and spoons
- ☺ 2 disposable cups of the same size
- ☺ Water
- ☺ Plaster of paris powder (from a craft or hardware store)
- ☺ 2 drinking straws
- ☺ Liquid soap (not detergent)

Make It Happen!

1. Label one cup "plain" and the other "hard." Pour $\frac{1}{2}$ cup (125 mL) of water into each.

2. Add $\frac{1}{4}$ teaspoon (1 mL) plaster of paris powder to the "hard" cup. Using a drinking straw, stir until most of it disappears.

3. Put 1 tablespoon (15 mL) of liquid soap into each cup; stir quickly. What do you notice about the bubbles that form?

4. Blow gently into each straw. (Don't suck any liquid into your mouth, though.) Are there more bubbles in one cup than in the other?

CURIOUS MINDS WANT TO KNOW...

What's with the plaster water?
Plaster is *calcium sulfate* ($CaSO_4$). When it dissolves, the calcium ions make the water "hard." When the soap is added, those ions combine with the soap, so there's less "free" soap to make bubbles.

← BLOW!

PLASTER OF PARIS

Hola! My name is Miguel, and I'm conducting a science fair survey...

Take It to the SCIENCE FAIR

🎗 **Repeat the experiment,** adding washing soda (available in the laundry aisle in your supermarket) to both cups. Washing soda, properly known as *sodium carbonate* (Na_2CO_3), softens water by removing the calcium and magnesium. Does it make a difference? Why would it be sold as a laundry product?

What other chemicals around your house make water hard? Some things to try are salt, sugar, salt substitute, Epsom salts, driveway deicer, and borax. Do the bubble test, and see what happens!

🎗 **Conduct a water taste test!** Many natural "bottled waters" contain a lot of dissolved ions. Buy a few different brands of bottled water and compare them to the water from your home faucet. To compare them to truly ion-free water, get a bottle of distilled water, too (available from the drugstore or supermarket). Invite some friends to taste each kind of water, but make sure they don't know which one is which. Do the waters taste different? Which water does your panel of tasters like best?

🎗 **Do a survey** around your neighborhood to find out how many households use water softeners, which remove the calcium, magnesium, and other mineral ions. Check out a water-hardness map from the U.S. Geological Survey at <http://water.usgs.gov/owq/Explanation.html> to find out if the water where you live is naturally hard or soft, and call your local water department to find out how your water is treated before you drink it.

CHALK, PEARLS & OTHER CALCIUM FEATS

What do the following things have in common: eggshells, seashells, coral, chalk, marble, limestone, and pearls? If you guessed that they are all made with calcium, you're exactly right! *Calcium carbonate* ($CaCO_3$), to be exact, which is very hard to dissolve in water. If you were a clam or an oyster protected by a $CaCO_3$ shell, you'd probably think that was a very good thing!

Examine the basements, roads, steps, and sidewalks where you live. Are any of them made with concrete? This building material was invented by the ancient Romans, who used it to make the famous Colosseum that still stands in Rome. Cement, the material that gives concrete its strength, is typically a mixture of calcium carbonate and calcium sulfate (page 27). And if any of the walls in your home are made of "plasterboard," "drywall," "Sheetrock," or "wallboard," well, they're held together by calcium sulfate — also called *plaster* or *gypsum* (JIP-sum). If you've ever broken a bone, the doctor probably put a plaster cast around the injured part to keep it from moving — calcium sulfate again! That calcium really gets around!

COW-cium?

Lots of COW-lories.

Good for you

Cow-cium?

Are adults always reminding you to drink your milk? Like cheese, yogurt, and other dairy products, milk contains lots of calcium, which your body needs for strong bones and teeth. As you grow, your bones and teeth grow, too — which means you need to keep on downing foods that have calcium!

ALL IN THE (ALKALINE EARTH METALS) FAMILY

BARIUM

BERYLLIUM

A mixture of **beryllium** (Be) and copper (page 88) is used to make tools that can be used around strong magnets and in situations where sparks from iron-based tools could cause an explosion.

With **barium** (Ba), doctors can get a clear picture of your body's "plumbing" from an X ray!

Years ago, clock dials were painted with **radium** (Ra) so they would glow in the dark. But the young women who made the clocks — the "Radium Girls" — were unknowingly poisoned by exposure to this radioactive element.

RADIUM

Bright red fire-works get their color from a **strontium** (Sr) compound.

STRONTIUM

Fizz, Bubble & Flash!

Meet the Main-Group Metals!

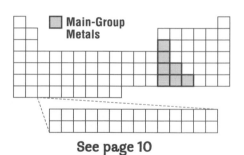

Main-Group Metals

See page 10

You probably know a metal when you see one, but *how* do you know? Think of some characteristics of metals: they're shiny, they get hot quickly, and electricity flows through them easily. They are also strong and can be used to make lots of things. How many metal objects can you see from where you're sitting? The atoms in this group aren't just used in their element form, though. You'll find their compounds in many unexpected places!

82?

82!

HEAVY METAL HISTORY!

Lead is a very heavy gray metal. Humans learned to make things with this metal about 6,000 years ago, because it is easy to melt and can be made into useful shapes. In ancient Rome, lead pipes carried water into homes and other buildings. In fact, the Roman word for lead, *plumbum*, eventually became the English word "plumbing." During the American Revolution, the colonists fought with long guns called muskets that fired small round balls made from lead.

Fizz, Bubble & Flash!

Ring-a-Ding!

When lead is added to glass, it makes *lead crystal*, which is much harder than ordinary glass. If you tap on lead crystal, you hear a ringing sound rather than a "thunk." That's because crystal vibrates, just like a bell. Use this property of lead crystal to make a musical instrument!

Mom, could I borrow some wineglasses?

Materials

- 8 thin wineglasses, preferably lead crystal (use with adult permission only, please)
- Water
- Small bowl

Make It Happen!

1. Fill each glass with a little more water than the one before it has. (Each glass will stand for one note of the *do-re-mi-fa-so-la-ti-do* musical scale.)

2. Pour a small amount of water into the bowl. Wet the tip of your index finger in the bowl and rub slowly around the rim of the first glass until you hear a ringing sound. (Hold the base of the glass so it doesn't tip over.)

3. Repeat with each glass. Adjust the water levels until your eight glasses sing (or rather, ring) the scale.

LEAD-WIG VAN BEETHOVEN?

At one time, no one understood how dangerous lead could be. Sugar was very expensive back then, so *lead acetate* was used to sweeten wine and fruit juices. People who drank a lot of wine suffered serious health problems, but no one knew why. The German composer Ludwig van Beethoven (1770–1827) wrote beautiful music, yet as he grew older, he often acted strangely and he eventually became deaf. It's believed that the lead in his wine caused these problems. Scientists have now measured the amount of lead in his hair. It had 100 times more than normal!

Play a Tune

See if you can play a song on your instrument! Fill glasses with increasing amounts of water from 1 (lowest amount) to 8 (highest amount) for the eight notes of the scale. Benjamin Franklin, the American patriot and scientist, invented a musical instrument much like your water-filled glasses. He called it the *armonica* (from the Italian word for harmony).

Fizz, Bubble & Flash!

PROTECT YOURSELF!

Lead is a good shield against dangerous radiation. When your dentist takes X rays of your teeth, what does she use to protect your body? That heavy apron you wear is made from lead.

ENVIRONMENTAL ALERT!

GeT THE LeaD OUT!

Houses don't have lead pipes in them now, like the ancient Romans used. They've long since been replaced with copper pipes or plastic tubing. But not so many years ago, gasoline contained a lead chemical that helped car engines run more smoothly. When this gasoline burned in an engine, the lead escaped into the atmosphere. Breathing lead isn't healthy, so our gas is now "unleaded," and we all breathe cleaner air.

Lead chemicals were also used in paints, and some old buildings still have lead paint inside or out. When this paint chips or peels, young children sometimes put small pieces of it into their mouths, and it makes them very sick, stunting their growth and affecting how they learn. If your home, school, or other buildings in your town were built before 1978, they should be checked for lead. Don't just scrape the old paint off yourself! This puts paint dust into the air, and you'll likely breathe in the lead it contains. Lead paint must be removed only by people who know how to do it safely. You can learn more about lead in the environment at <www.epa.gov/opptintr/lead/leadinfo.htm>.

Meet the Main-Group Metals!

BISMUTH

Bismuth in lipstick, eye shadow, and such
Gives a lustrous sheen that's admired so much.
It also helps cure your stomach upset,
And in fire alarm systems, it can make you quite wet!

BISMUTH BEAUTY

Scientists have known about the metal called bismuth for 500 years, but for half that time, they thought that it was just another form of tin (page 40) or lead (page 32), because these three elements are often found mixed together. Bismuth metal is very cool-looking — it can have a yellow, purple, or blue shine to it. In fact, some people like to *wear* it!

Today, some of bismuth's most common uses are in makeup and medicine. Pearly *bismuth oxychloride* (OX-ee-klor-ide, BiOCl) is added to lipstick, eye shadow, and nail polish to make them look frosted. The pink antacids you find in the drugstore also have bismuth. The next time you're at the store, see if you can find a brand whose name gives a clue as to its "elemental" ingredient!

Answer: Pepto-Bismol

Element Essentials

BISMUTH (BiZ-muth)
* Symbol: Bi
* Number: 83
* Mass: 208.98 amu
* Discovery: In 1753, by Claude Geoffroy of France

Fizz, Bubble & Flash!

The Art of Acid Indigestion

When you have an upset stomach, you may take an *antacid* to help settle it. Antacids (short for anti-acids) are *bases*, which neutralize or "balance" some of the acid in your stomach by reacting to form less upsetting molecules. Do your own kitchen-variety acid and base test, using cabbage, lemon juice, and baking soda!

Materials

- Red cabbage
- Bowl or pan
- Water
- Strainer
- Jar with lid
- Clear plastic cups
- Measuring cups and spoons
- Baking soda
- Lemon juice
- Marker
- Eyedropper or drinking straw
- Paper and crayons or colored pencils

Cabbage indicator **Water** **Lemon juice** **Baking soda & water**

Make It Happen!

1. Place five or six chopped red cabbage leaves in the bowl or pan with just enough water to cover them. Cook (with adult supervision) the cabbage in a microwave oven set on high for 5 minutes. The water will turn dark purple. (If you want to know why this smells so bad as it's cooking, check out the experiment on page 65!) Let the cabbage juice cool, then strain it and store it in the jar. This is your *indicator*, which will show you whether you have an acid or a base.

2. In one of the cups, dissolve 1 teaspoon (5 ml) of baking soda (a base) in $\frac{1}{2}$ cup (125 mL) water. Pour $\frac{1}{2}$" (1 cm) of lemon juice (an acid) into another cup, and water into a third. Label each cup.

3. Add five to six drops of red cabbage indicator to each cup. What color is the base? How about the acid? (If you don't have an eyedropper, dip one end of the drinking straw into the indicator until there's about $\frac{1}{2}$" (1 cm) of liquid in the straw. Cover the other end of the straw with your finger and lift it out of the indicator. The liquid will stay inside until you take your finger away.)

4. Add the baking soda solution, $\frac{1}{2}$ teaspoon (1 mL) at a time, to the lemon juice. After the bubbles settle down, check the color. When the color matches that of the cup with the water, you have neutralized the acid. How did the color change?

5. Keep adding the baking soda solution, $\frac{1}{2}$ teaspoon (1 mL) at a time, until the color of the lemon juice stops changing. Keep track of the results.

6. Repeat the experiment, but this time in reverse, adding lemon juice to your baking soda solution. Make a chart to show all the glorious colors of your cabbage-juice indicator!

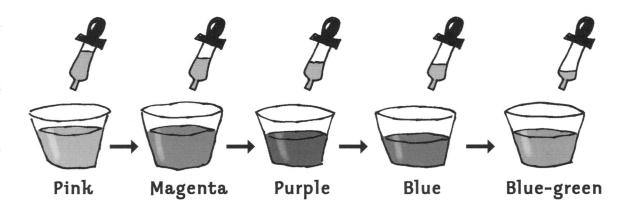

Pink → **Magenta** → **Purple** → **Blue** → **Blue-green**

Curious Minds Want to Know...

Where did all those colors come from? Red cabbage juice contains indicator molecules called *anthocyanins* (an-tho-SIGH-ah-nins), which are reddish orange in acids, and bluish green in bases. You can see the color gradually change as an acid (lemon juice) is neutralized by a base (baking soda or antacid).

What's a Base?

Bases are the opposite of acids. Acids are chemicals that *give up* hydrogen (page 13) atoms, while bases are chemicals that *grab up* these hydrogens. When both of these chemicals are in balance, the bases have snatched all the hydrogens that the acids gave up. This is called *neutralization* (NEW-tral-iz-ay-shun). One base you may have heard of is ammonia, which is used in cleaning products (you always know it's there — it's really smelly!). Most soaps, detergents, and other cleaners are bases, too.

Take It to the SCIENCE FAIR

🏅 **Do an antacid test.** Use your cabbage indicator to investigate the chemistry of different antacids. Compare various brands (dissolve the liquid or a tablet in water) by using them in place of the baking soda in the experiment on page 37. Which takes the least amount to neutralize the acid?

🏅 **Find other bases around your home.** Use cabbage juice to test orange juice, strong coffee, soda, egg whites, soaps, and window cleaners to find out which are acids, which are bases, and which are neutral.

INDOOR SHOWERS

An *alloy* (metal mixture) of bismuth, tin (page 40), lead, and cadmium (a transition metal) is called Wood's metal. Because it melts at a low temperature, Wood's metal is used in fire alarm and sprinkler systems. The smoke and heat created by a fire change the flow of electricity through the detector, melting the Wood's metal. This sets off the alarm and triggers a shower of water!

Meet the Main-Group Metals!

ALL IN THE (MAIN-GROUP METALS) FAMILY

Fizz, Bubble & Flash!

Meet the Metalloids!

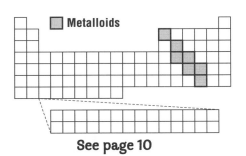

Metalloids

See page 10

OK, so you know what a "metal" is, but what's with the "oid"? Can you think of any other words that end in "oid"? How about an "android" — what is that? In science fiction, an android is a robot with a human form. Sometimes it acts like a robot, and at other times, like a person. So now what do you think a *metalloid* (MET-ah-loyd) is? Hmmm,

not a robot element, but an element whose characteristics are a little like a metal, but not completely. For example, metalloids conduct electricity, like a metal, but just a little bit. They're sometimes called *semiconductors*, and they're used in computers and all kinds of electronic gadgets. This small family is sure important in the modern world!

STATE-OF-THE-ART ANDROID?

CURRENTLY UNEMPL-OID.

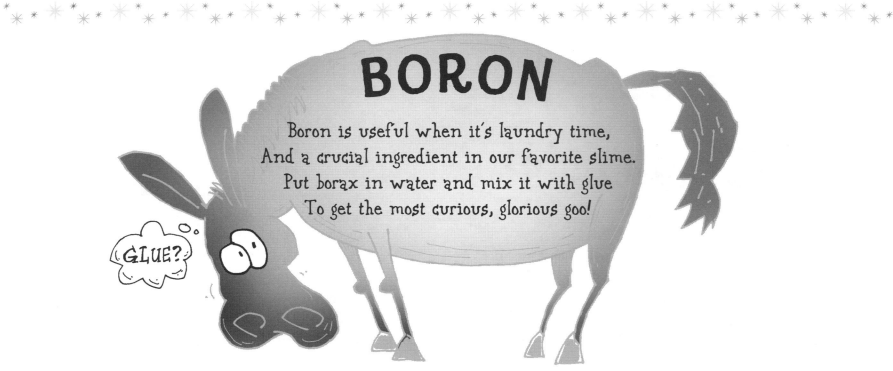

BORON

Boron is useful when it's laundry time,
And a crucial ingredient in our favorite slime.
Put borax in water and mix it with glue
To get the most curious, glorious goo!

GLUE?

OF MULES AND MEN — AND BORAX!

Most boron comes from the mineral *borax* (BORE-ax), which also contains sodium (page 17) and oxygen (page 68). Borax is useful because it makes glass stronger, and helps soaps clean better.

So, what do mules and the element boron have in common? Well, in 1870, a huge borax mine was discovered in the Mojave Desert in California. There was a problem, though: The nearest railroad was 165 miles (265 km) away, and there were no roads to it — just hot, sandy desert. How were the miners going to get the borax out? They hitched 20 mules to giant wagons. Each wagon weighed 32,000 pounds (16 tons/14.5 t), and its wheels were 7' (2.2 m) high! It took 10 days to make the trip. The town of Boron, California, was named after a borax mine. See if you can find Boron on a map.

Of course, they don't use mules to move borax anymore, but you can still see a picture of the mules on the box of 20 Mule Team Borax at the supermarket in the laundry aisle.

Element Essentials

BORON (BORE-on)
* Symbol: B
* Number: 5
* Mass: 10.81 amu
* Discovery: In 1808, by Sir Humphry Davy of England

Fizz, Bubble & Flash!

Slime Time!

Try this experiment, then tell all your friends, "I've been slimed!"

Materials

- Blue gel glue (available from drugstores)
- 2 plastic cups
- Water
- Plastic spoon
- Measuring spoons
- Borax laundry conditioner or "booster"
- Clear drinking glass or jar
- Small plastic bag

Make It Happen!

1. Pour about 1" (2.5 cm) of glue into one of the cups. Add the same amount of water; stir until mixed.

2. Place about 2 tablespoons (30 mL) of borax directly into the glass or jar. Fill the jar half full with water, then heat (with adult supervision) on high in the microwave oven until the water boils. Let the hot borax mixture cool to room temperature. You might see some white solids on the bottom.

3. Add the cooled borax to the glue mixture, 1 tablespoon (15 mL) at a time. Keep stirring. What do you see happening?

4. Take the slime out and play with it. You can keep the slime in a plastic bag for a few weeks, but if it starts to smell funny or gets black spots, throw it away. You can always make more, now that you know how!

Cool! What happened when I mixed these chemicals? The glue starts out as a sticky liquid. When you add borax, it turns into something slimy, sort of a solid and sort of a liquid. That's because glue is made of long, stringy molecules called *polyvinyl alcohol*. Borax links these strings together, forming a net. The water molecules get trapped inside, so the slime feels wet. Scientists call stuff like this a *gel*. Can you think of any other gels?

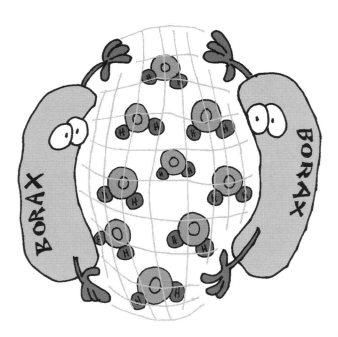

🎗 **Study "slimology"** by experimenting with different slime recipes.

What happens if you don't add any water to the glue? Or, try using even more water.

Try sliming with white glue instead of the blue kind. Is this stuff more or less slimy?

What does the slime feel like if you add more or less borax?

Can you explain what you see? The borax ties the polyvinyl alcohol strings together like knots in a net. And the more knots, the tighter the net!

BECOME A BORON SLEUTH

Boric acid (H_3BO_3) kills germs, and you can find it in many kinds of eye-drops. It can also be used to kill bugs. *Boron nitride* (BN) powder sparkles, and is sometimes added to makeup to make it shiny.

Look for boron-containing glass in your home or school. Regular glass without boron breaks easily, and can crack if it is heated or cooled too fast. But *borosilicate* (BORE-oh-SILL-uh-kate) glass is sturdy and temperature-proof, making it ideal for bowls, dishes, pans — even test tubes! — that need to take the heat or cold. Most borosilicate glass is called Pyrex. Is there any in your cupboards?

Fizz, Bubble & Flash!

SiLiCON

Silicon chips control toys of all sorts;
Silicon dioxide is sometimes called quartz.
Silicone putty is rubbery stuff,
It stretches a lot and is remarkably tough!

THE SiLiCON AGE?

You've probably heard about the Stone Age, the Iron Age, and the Bronze Age — those important stages of history from long ago. Well, students of the future may call *our* time the Silicon Age, because this element is so important in the electronic gadgets we use — all those computers, digital cameras, video games, and CD players. If you have an old, broken electronic gizmo, try taking it apart to see what's inside. (Get permission first, of course! Remove any batteries and make sure that the item is unplugged.) Many of the little chips and plastic electronic parts you see contain silicon, especially any ones that look like little black squares or rectangles.

Element Essentials

SiLiCON (SiLL-uh-con)
* Symbol: Si
* Number: 14
* Mass: 28.09 amu
* Discovery: In 1824, by Jöns Jacob Berzelius of Sweden

Nutty Putty

You've probably already played with this silicon-containing toy!

Materials

- ♻ Play putty (the kind that comes in an egg-shaped container)
- ♻ Ruler or measuring tape

Make It Happen!

1. Grab one end of the putty in each hand, and snap it quickly. What happens?

2. Now pull on the putty slowly, and use the ruler to measure how far it will stretch before it breaks.

3. Roll it into a ball, and see if it bounces.

4. Try to flatten the putty by smacking it with your fist, then by pushing gently with your fingers. Does it feel different?

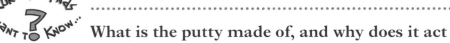

Curious Minds Want to Know...

What is the putty made of, and why does it act like this? Putty is a *silicone polymer* (POLL-uh-mer), long chains of silicon, oxygen (page 68), carbon (page 54), and hydrogen (page 13). It behaves in some strange ways because the molecules are so very long and stringy. To get the picture, watch spaghetti as it cooks. Carefully stir the pasta, and watch how the strands get tangled at first, then sort themselves out and line up. Well, in the same way, the silicone molecules get all mixed up, then arrange themselves neatly. When you push or pull on the putty quickly, the molecules don't have time to slide past one another, and the putty either breaks or feels hard. But if you pull or push slowly, the molecules can wriggle past one another. The putty stretches, staying in one piece.

A Silly Success

Now-famous Silly Putty was actually a failure at the start! Try as he might, chemist James Wright was never able to create rubber from silicon oil as he had hoped. When he added boric acid, the strange stuff bounced! Not exactly what he had in mind for making boots and tires.

Along came Peter Hodgson in 1949 with a whole new view of things. He stuck Wright's "failure" in a plastic egg, and it's been selling as Silly Putty ever since!

ROCK ON ...

Not only are we in the Silicon Age, but we also live on Planet Silicon! Almost all the rocks you see around you contain this element combined with oxygen (page 68), and maybe some others, such as calcium (page 26), magnesium (page 23), or chlorine (page 77). Silicon is the second most abundant element in the earth's crust (good old oxygen is first), so it's not surprising that sand, soil, and clays are also chock-full of silicon. Luckily, this common element has lots of practical uses, from bathroom caulk to computer chips!

Silicon dioxide (SiO_2), called *quartz* for short, contains crystals with silicon and oxygen atoms. Ever wonder why some watches say "quartz" on them? Quartz vibrates when an electrical current passes through it, and the buzz is so steady that tiny quartz crystals are used to run clocks and watches.

... AND ON!

Many jewels are also quartz-based, such as smoky quartz (brown), rose quartz (pink), and amethyst (purple). But quartz crystals are clear, so where do all these colors come from? Just a tiny smidgen of another element can change the color. Smoky quartz has a little aluminum (page 40); rose quartz, some titanium (page 100) and manganese (a transition metal element); and amethyst, a touch of iron (page 84).

Glass is another silicon compound you're familiar with. To make glass, sand is melted, then formed into the desired shape. This "liquid sand" is cooled quickly, so there's no time for the atoms to rearrange themselves back into a solid crystal. The result is clear and shiny, but easily broken. Glass behaves much differently from its starting material! (For more on glass, see page 44.)

Ohhh... Give me a break!

Take It to the SCIENCE FAIR

🎗 **Repeat the putty experiment** with Silly Putty (page 46) that has been in the refrigerator, in the freezer, or warmed with a hair dryer for a few minutes. How do your results change?

🎗 **Become a rock hound!** Pick up some stones and rocks around your neighborhood and try to identify them. Your library will have many books to help you. Many museums have rock and mineral collections, too. Check them out! You can also see pictures of many beautiful rocks at <www.nmnh.si.edu/minsci/images/gallery/gallery.htm>.

POLONIUM

Polonium's uses are somewhat dramatic
It really is helpful if you must control static.
Polonium spark plugs are no longer found,
They're radioactive — who wants them around?

MADAME MARIE

Polonium was discovered by the famous scientists Marie and Pierre Curie. Madame Marie's original name was Maria Sklodowska. She was born in Warsaw, Poland, but moved to France in 1891 to study math and science. At that time, women couldn't teach college in Europe, and most colleges didn't even want women around as students. (How unfair!) But that didn't stop Maria. In 1898, while still a student, she discovered the radioactive element polonium, and named it after her native country, Poland. Her work was so important that Marie Curie won a Nobel prize with her husband Pierre in 1903 for physics and one in 1911 for chemistry. She was the first woman to win any Nobel prize, and the first person, man or woman, to win two!

> **Element Essentials**
>
> POLONIUM (puh-LONE-ee-um)
> * Symbol: Po
> * Number: 84
> * Mass: 208.98 amu
> * Discovery: In 1898, by Marie Curie (Polish-born) and her husband, Pierre Curie, of France

Meet the Metalloids!

What Are the Nobel Prizes?

And why are they such a big deal? The prizes were started by Alfred Nobel, a Swedish inventor, chemist, and manufacturer. Every year, they're given for outstanding work in physics, chemistry, medicine, economics, literature, and peace. Keep your ears open to see who the next winners are (they are announced every year in October). Meanwhile, get to know the past winners at <www.nobel.se>.

Nobel Prize winner Marie Curie

An Ec-Static Experiment

Ever wonder how dust sticks to things? The particles are held in place by static electricity. Polonium to the rescue! It's in little brushes that remove static, for example, used for cleaning dust from film. Because polonium's radioactive, you can't work with it directly, but you can experiment with static electricity all you want to!

Materials
- Facial tissues
- Balloon
- Antistatic dryer sheet

Make It Happen!

1. Tear off about five small pieces of tissue paper about $\frac{1}{2}$" (1 cm) square.

2. Blow up the balloon and knot the end so that the air doesn't escape.

3. Rub the balloon on your hair for about 10 seconds, then place it near the tissue pieces. What happens?

4. Now rub the balloon with the dryer sheet, then place it near the tissues. Notice any difference?

5. Try "recharging" the balloon by rubbing it on your hair again. Can you get it to pick up the tissues?

Curious Minds Want to Know...

Why does the tissue paper jump around like that? And what's in that dryer sheet? When you rub the balloon on your hair, some of the electrons in your hair jump over to the balloon. This gives the balloon a negative charge. The tissue doesn't have a charge, and because uncharged things are attracted to charged ones (see page 73), the tissue sticks to the balloon.

The dryer sheet, on the other hand, contains ions that cancel out the extra electrons from the balloon. So the balloon loses its charge, and no longer attracts the tissue.

ZAP!

Zap!

In the past, some automobile spark plugs used polonium to help an electrical charge get things rolling. When a spark plug fires, the charge leaps between two small pieces of metal, making the spark. The spark zaps the gasoline in the engine, creating little explosions that make the engine parts move — and away you go! People are now concerned about the radioactivity in polonium, so you won't find this element under the hood of your car today.

ANTISTATIC FANATIC

Static electricity can really be annoying! Have you ever gotten zapped after you walked across a rug? Here's a trick: Keep a dryer sheet in your pocket, and wipe your hands with it every now and then. If your clothes stick to you, rubbing a dryer sheet on your clothes will loosen them. If your hair stands up when you brush it, smooth a sheet over your head, and your flyaway hair will come in for a landing!

ALL IN THE (METALLOIDS) FAMILY

Ancient beauties, such as the Egyptian queen Cleopatra, wore dark gray eye makeup made from the mineral *stibnite*, a compound of **antimony** (Sb) and sulfur (page 64).

ANTIMONY

TELLURIUM

Working with **tellurium** (Te) can make you very unpopular! Humans exposed to even tiny amounts of tellurium develop a garlic-like odor!

Germanium (Ge), found in electronic gadgets such as video games, cell phones, and computers, is used to make *diodes* (DIE-odes), which let electrical current flow in only one direction.

GERMANIUM

The small colored lights on electronic gadgets that show when the power is on, called LEDs *(light-emitting diodes)*, are made from a compound of **arsenic** (As) and gallium (page 40).

ARSENIC

Fizz, Bubble & Flash!

Meet the Nonmetals!

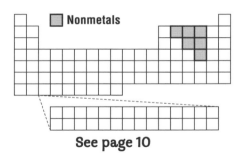

Nonmetals

See page 10

Remember the metalloids (pages 41 to 52), which can't make up their minds — sort of metal, sort of not? The *nonmetals* aren't at all confused — they know that they're nothing like a metal. In fact, some are even gases! The solid nonmetals are dull and don't let heat or electricity through. But that doesn't mean that they aren't important, because there are a lot of nonmetals in you, like carbon, nitrogen, oxygen, phosphorus, and sulfur. And they're in your dog, your cat, birds, plants, and every other living thing! All life on earth is based on nonmetals! While the metals are useful, they only form a few kinds of compounds. Nonmetals, though, know lots of bonding tricks, and they can be put together in millions and millions of ways, which makes them really interesting!

CARBON

Carbon is known as the element of life,
And also of diamonds that cut like a knife.
The lead found in pencils is carbon graphite,
And the carbon in charcoal makes barbecues bright.

CARBON – IT'S EVERYWHERE!

All of earth's living things are carbon-based — bacteria, plants, animals, and people. This means that almost all the molecules that are necessary for life contain carbon. These include the proteins, sugars, vitamins, fats, and DNA in your body. So, when you eat food, you are scarfing down carbon! Of course, when you breathe, you take in oxygen molecules (O_2) and some other gases. And then a pretty amazing thing happens when you *exhale* (breathe out): One atom of carbon combines with the two atoms of oxygen, and you end up with a molecule of CO_2, called *carbon dioxide*.

54

Is It Getting Hotter?

You may know that coal, oil, and natural gas come from the remains of animals and plants that died long, long ago, so these fuels — called *fossil fuels* — are carbon-based, too. When a carbon-containing fuel, like coal, oil, or wood, is burned, it gives off carbon dioxide (just as you do when you exhale). This gas builds up in the atmosphere, and many scientists believe it is making the climate on planet Earth hotter. This problem is called *global warming*. Think for a minute about all the houses that use oil and natural gas to stay warm, and all the cars and trucks on highways that burn gasoline each day. That's a whole lot of carbon dioxide entering the atmosphere! If earth does become much warmer, the weather could change. The trouble is, no one knows just how bad these changes might be. No wonder people are so worried about global warming!

If we are going to put less CO_2 into the atmosphere, we'll all have to live differently. We'll need to drive smaller cars, take buses and trains when we can, and use less electricity (this includes TV!). What do you think? Are you willing to do these things? You can find more information about global warming on the Internet at <www.epa.gov/globalwarming/kids/index.html>.

BUBBLES, BAUBLES & BRIQUETTES!

Lest you think that carbon is just a troublemaker, turn your thoughts to a loaf of homemade bread rising in the oven, glistening diamonds, and a summer picnic grilling over a wood or charcoal fire. Yes, you can thank carbon for those good things, too!

Need some more carbon, dad?

CHARCOAL

A Feast for Yeast

Yeast is a fungus (something like a mushroom) that is used to make bread. The little holes in bread are actually formed when CO_2 is exhaled by these yeasty beasties, as the dough is mixed. Do you like to eat sweets? Well, yeast does, too. If you feed it sugar, you can watch it give off CO_2!

Materials

- 1 tablespoon (15 mL) sugar
- Small water or soda bottle
- Warm (not hot) water
- Yeast packet (from grocery store)
- Small balloon

Make It Happen!

1. Put the sugar in the bottle and add warm water until the bottle is about three-fourths full. Add the package of yeast and shake. Do you see anything happening in the bottle?

2. Stretch the balloon over the mouth of the bottle.

3. Wait for an hour and watch what happens. Can you explain what you observe?

4. Now, experiment with some other kinds of food (maybe honey or salt) to see what other things yeasties like to eat.

Curious Minds want to know...

How did the balloon blow up, without any huffing and puffing? Yeast digests its food just as you do yours, changing the carbon in sugar into CO_2. Of course, yeast doesn't have a nose to exhale with, but it gives off the gas all the same. The bubbles you see, and the gas that fills the balloon, are CO_2. When you use yeast in bread, the bubbles get trapped by the sticky dough, causing the dough to rise up in a loaf shape and making the bread light and fluffy.

Fizz, Bubble & Flash!

PARDON ME!

Fizzy soft drinks are also full of CO_2 bubbles. That's why we sometimes call them *carbonated*. If you drink a soft drink too fast, a big bubble of CO_2 gas can form in your stomach. What happens when it comes rushing out of your mouth all of a sudden? You burp! Just remember to say, "Excuse my carbon dioxide!"

MEET THE COUSINS: PENCILS & DIAMONDS

The two most familiar forms of the element carbon are *diamond* and *graphite* (GRAFF-ite), which is found in pencil lead. Pencil lead is soft, gray, and dull, while a diamond is hard, clear, and beautiful. These two things may not seem to have much in common, but both are made of the same stuff — pure carbon! The difference between them is the way the carbon atoms are stacked up.

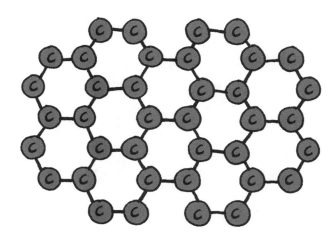

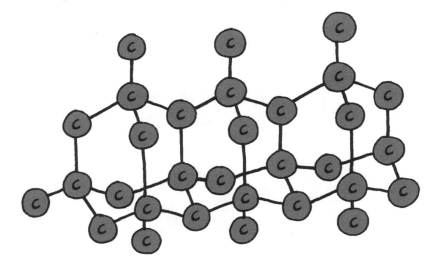

PENCIL LEAD (GRAPHITE)

The atoms in pencil lead are spread out in flat sheets that are stacked on top of one another. The piles aren't very strong because the sheets aren't bound together in any way. (You know how easy it is to push over a tall stack of loose papers!)

DIAMOND

In a diamond, all the carbon atoms are connected, as if all the papers in the stack were glued together. This makes a diamond very strong. In fact, it's one of the hardest substances on earth!

CHARCOAL AND SOCCER BALLS

Scientists know about two other kinds of carbon as well. After wood burns, what's left over? You have black, crumbly *charcoal*. Chunks of charcoal are used to barbecue. In some countries, people still use charcoal to heat their homes and cook their food. In charcoal, the carbon atoms are all jumbled up in a heap, not arranged neatly as they are in graphite or diamond.

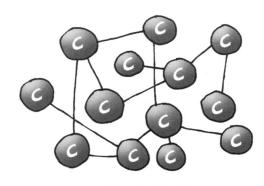

CHARCOAL

The last kind of carbon has the curious name of *buckminsterfullerene* (BUCK–min–stir–FULL–er–een). The carbon atoms are arranged like the shapes on a soccer ball! Scientists call this arrangement a *buckyball* for short. Buckyballs are very rare, and scientists are still looking for good uses for them. So, why the wacky name? They are named after R. Buckminster Fuller, an engineer and architect who built *geodesic* (jee–ah–DEH–sik) *domes*, which are light but strong structures shaped like buckyballs. You might want to do an Internet search to learn more about Mr. Fuller and his domes. A good place to start is at the Buckminster Fuller Institute's site at <www.bfi.org>.

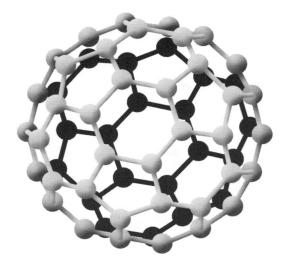

BUCKYBALL

Charcoal (above right) is made up of carbon atoms jumbled up in a heap, while the carbon in a buckyball (above) is arranged like the shapes on a soccer ball!

Buckminster Fuller's famous geodesic dome at the United States Pavilion at Montreal's Expo '67.

Fizz, Bubble & Flash!

Take It to the
SCIENCE FAIR

Get involved in global warming issues! This is a "hot" topic!

🎗 **Research the issue to learn more about global warming (page 55).** Not all scientists believe that it is really happening. Why don't they, and with whom do you agree?

🎗 **Do a questionnaire in your community** to figure out how many gallons (L) of gasoline are burned by the average family per week. How much gas would be saved by carpooling?

🎗 **Investigate new kinds of car engines** that get better gas mileage, such as electric motors or hybrids, and present a comparison.

🎗 **Discuss ways** that you and your family can save energy.

🎗 **Study the efforts** some countries around the world are making to help reduce CO_2 levels in the air.

Investigate the many shapes of carbon.

🎗 **Learn how the diamond** became such a precious gem with such high prices.

🎗 **Study the many uses** of diamonds.

🎗 **Build models of the carbon atom arrangements** in graphite, a diamond, and a buckyball. You can use foam balls and wooden sticks from an art-supply store, or even little marsh-mallows and toothpicks!

PHOSPHORUS

Phosphorus burns and phosphorus glows —
This chemical fact, each scientist knows.
Phosphorus white and phosphorus red —
Quickly set fire to tiny match heads.

We DO NOT want to play with you, so don't play with us!

Element Essentials

PHOSPHORUS (FOSS-for-us)
* Symbol: P
* Number: 15
* Mass: 30.97 amu
* Discovery: In 1669, by Hennig Brand of Germany

"PHREAKY" PHOSPHORUS

A lot of strange things have been done in the name of science, but this tale of phosphorus ranks right up there as "pretty gross"! German scientist Hennig Brand started with urine (yuck!) and let it sit around for two weeks (double yuck!). Then he boiled it for 24 hours. (Imagine how bad his laboratory must have smelled!) Brand saw a glowing gas rising from the boiling urine. After this gas cooled, it formed a solid that kept shining. This weird stuff even burst into flames when it touched air! Brand didn't know what he had made, but he knew that no one had ever seen anything like this before. He even thought that it was magical, but now we know better — it was phosphorus!

60

Make Your Pennies Shine!

When phosphorus is combined with other atoms, it becomes very useful. One of these chemicals is even found in a popular soft drink! What it can do is almost magical. See for yourself!

Materials

- Plastic or paper cup
- Can or bottle of dark cola like Coke or Pepsi
- Several dirty pennies

Make It Happen!

1. Fill the cup about halfway with cola. Drop in the pennies and let them sit overnight.

2. Fish the pennies out. What do they look like?

3. Pour the cola down the drain. *Warning: Do not drink it!* It contains copper ions, which are not good for you.

🎖 **Soda Shine?** Are there any other beverages that can shine your pennies? Try other sodas, coffee, tea, milk, or other drinks.

🎖 **Acid Attack.** There are other acids around your house. Do they dissolve the coating on old pennies? Try vinegar, lemon juice, and orange juice. If you're not sure whether a liquid is an acid, use the red-cabbage indicator (page 37) to check.

Why did the pennies change color? Cola contains *phosphoric acid* (H₃PO₄), which gives it a tangy flavor. New pennies, as you know, are brightly colored and shiny. As they get older, they turn dark brown and dull because the copper in the penny combines with oxygen in the air. The phosphoric acid breaks up the copper-oxygen compound, so the dull-and-dirty pennies come out shining like new!

I'M NOT HUNGRY RIGHT NOW...

MEET YOUR MATCH

Every time you light a match, thank Hennig Brand! The burning, glowing phosphorus he created (page 60) is called *white phosphorus*. There's another kind, *red phosphorus*, which just sits around and does nothing exciting. The difference between them (besides the color) is the way in which the phosphorus atoms are stacked up. The strip on the outside of a matchbox contains red phosphorus. When you rub a match against this strip, the heat created by *friction* (the rubbing) turns the red phosphorus into the white form, which immediately bursts into flame, setting fire to the match itself.

BRAIN FOOD?

It turns out that your brain has more phosphorus in it than the rest of your body. Back in the 1700s, doctors thought that you could become smarter just by eating foods rich in phosphorus! We now know that phosphorus has nothing to do with intelligence, but it does help your body produce energy. (Guess you'll just have to keep on studying hard!)

PHOSPHATES ON TRIAL

Years ago, laundry detergents contained a compound called *sodium phosphate* (Na_3PO_4), which made them clean better. But because laundry water was washed down the drain, phosphates ended up in many lakes and rivers. Around the same time, people noticed that the water in lakes and rivers was turning greener. Tiny plants called *algae* were growing out of control! These algae hogged the oxygen in the water, so the fish were suffocating. Many people thought that phosphates were to blame. In the 1970s, phosphates were taken out of detergents. Then, in the 1990s, scientists discovered that the phosphates weren't the problem after all! The real trouble was that other pollutants killed the organisms that normally ate the algae. *That's* why they were growing like crazy! Seems the phosphates were innocent all along. This story reminds us that the interrelationships in our environment are very complicated. Sometimes problems that look easy to solve turn out to be much tougher than they seem. But even so, you can always do your part to help the environment by picking up trash, conserving water, using less electricity, and recycling.

SULFUR

Many compounds of sulfur are terribly smelly,
(You can find lots of them inside a deli!)
Stinky onions, raw cabbage, turnips, and garlic,
Will give you bad breath — so pop a mint quick!

THE WORLD'S STINKIEST MOLECULES

Sulfur causes more bad smells than any other element! Some plants and animals use sulfur chemicals to protect themselves. What does a skunk do when it's frightened? It flips its tail into the air and sprays nasty-smelling stuff on some unsuspecting critter — or on you! I'm sure you can guess what element is found in all those skunk-smell molecules? Sulfur!

There's even a plant in South America with beautiful flowers that smell like rotting meat. Most animals (and people) leave it alone because of the sulfur stink. But there's one kind of bee that doesn't mind at all, so it can feed without being bothered by other creatures. The bee then carries pollen from one flower to another, helping the plant to reproduce. It appears that Mother Nature either likes to play tricks or wants to guarantee that this type of plant sticks around for a long time!

Element Essentials

SULFUR (SULL-fur)
* Symbol: S
* Number: 16
* Mass: 32.07 a.mu
* Discovery: Known since ancient times

Fizz, Bubble & Flash!

What's That Smell?

Many vegetables, like cabbage and Brussels sprouts, don't smell too bad when they're raw, but watch out while you're boiling them for dinner!

Materials

- ✪ Knife (use with adult supervision)
- ✪ Head of cabbage
- ✪ Saucepan
- ✪ 1 cup (250 mL) water
- ✪ Slotted spoon

Make It Happen!

1. Cut the cabbage in half. Cut one half into small pieces. Put the chopped half into the saucepan, and set the unchopped half aside as the *control* (the part of the experiment that remains unchanged). Smell both cut and uncut pieces — do they differ?

2. Add the water to the saucepan. Boil for 20 minutes, noting the odor of the cooking and the uncooked cabbage at about 5-minute intervals. How do they compare?

3. Using the slotted spoon, carefully lift the cooked cabbage out of the water and let it cool. Compare its odor to that of the uncooked portion. What do you notice?

Curious Minds Want to Know...

Why do they smell so bad? Many stinky chemicals have sulfur in them. Some vegetables, such as cabbage, onions, and Brussels sprouts, have a lot of sulfur in them, and they smell really bad when you boil them. Think about it: The hot water makes these sulfur-containing molecules leave the vegetables and float into the kitchen air. Ugh! Yet, after they're cooked, the vegetables don't smell nearly so bad because all of the sulfur chemicals have floated into the air!

CUTE CURLS

If you want curly hair but don't have it naturally, what can you do? You can get a *perm* (short for permanent wave). Yes, so, what does that have to do with sulfur? Well, some of the proteins in your hair contain sulfur atoms that are linked together. The first step in a perm is to break them apart using a special kind of chemical lotion. Next, the hair is twisted tightly around a curler, and another chemical is applied that reconnects all the sulfurs. What's the difference? Now the proteins have a curly shape, and so does the hair! (It's not really permanent, though. You have to redo it every few months.)

SULFUR IN SPACE?

Pure sulfur is a light yellow powder. On earth, it is often found on rocks near volcanoes and geysers. There are even some really weird bacteria around these hot spots that live on sulfur. Scientists know that many other planets also have volcanoes. Io, a moon of the planet Jupiter, has lots of volcanoes, and its surface is covered with sulfur. Might there also be sulfur-loving bacteria on Io? We don't know yet. Stay tuned for the answer!

ENVIRONMENTAL ALERT! ACID FROM THE SKY

Sulfur can also cause a serious environmental problem. Many kinds of coal contain lots of sulfur. When they are burned for fuel, the sulfur combines with water in the air to form *sulfuric* (sul-FYOUR-ick) *acid* (H_2SO_4). When it rains, this acid falls back to earth as *acid rain,* which contaminates water and harms plants, fish, the paint finish on cars, and even some buildings. Many ancient landmarks, such as the Great Sphinx in Egypt and the Greek Parthenon, were made from rocks that are now being damaged by acid rain. The pollution we create is destroying these remarkable world treasures! And here's the real rub: We *have* learned how to burn coal without making sulfuric acid. Now if only all the electric companies and factories would use what we know to reduce pollution!

Fizz, Bubble & Flash!

What's an Acid?

An acid is a special kind of molecule that usually contains a hydrogen atom. But, as you already know, you can't stereotype, even in science — not all molecules with hydrogen are acids! And not all acids are the same.

Strong acids, such as the sulfuric acid in a car battery, are very dangerous; they can seriously burn your skin and your eyes. Steer clear! There aren't many strong acids around the house, so you're not likely to run into them. *Weak acids* are much safer — many are so safe, in fact, you can eat them! Vinegar is actually *acetic acid* ($C_2H_4O_2$). Orange juice contains *citric acid* ($C_6H_8O_7$), and milk has *lactic acid* ($C_3H_6O_3$).

What makes some acids strong and some weak? Do some of them work out, or what? No, it has to do with hydrogen ions. (Yes, ions again!) When molecules of a strong acid dissolve in water, all the hydrogens break off, and there are lots of positive and negative ions floating around the solution. When weak acids dissolve, only a few molecules come apart. So, it's the number of hydrogen ions that makes an acid a hulk or a wimp. Scientists use a number called the *pH* to show how strong an acid is. The pH is related to the number of hydrogen ions. The lower the pH, the stronger the acid.

Take It to the
SCIENCE FAIR

🎗 **Become a chemical cook!** Try cooking cabbage for different amounts of time, and see if that changes the flavor. What about cutting it into different-sized pieces before boiling it?

🎗 **Try the vegetable experiment** with different vegetables. These pages list a bunch of sulfur-containing veggies, but what happens if you boil something like a carrot or lettuce that doesn't have any stinky molecules? Does the smell still change?

🎗 **Check out the effect of acid rain** on different kinds of building materials. Use vinegar as your acid, and drip it on wood, bricks, concrete, rocks, or anything else you want to test. What happens?

ALL IN THE (NONMETALS) FAMILY

NITROGEN

Liquid **nitrogen** (N) is *so* cool that it's positively frigid … at –321°F (–196°C)! Doctors sometimes use drops of liquid nitrogen to freeze warts.

Warts?

LIQUID NITROGEN

Nitrogen (N) can be a lifesaver! During the split second that a car is hit, *sodium azide* (NaN_3) molecules break apart to create lots of nitrogen gas, inflating the car's air bags.

Oxygen (O) is all around you — in the air, water, rocks, and soil. That's a good thing! Our bodies need oxygen to burn the food we eat for energy!

OXYGEN

SELENIUM

White flakes on your scalp? **Selenium** (Se) — a nonmetal element that resembles sulfur — can help! *Selenium sulfide* (SeS_2) is found in dandruff shampoos.

68

Meet the Halogens!

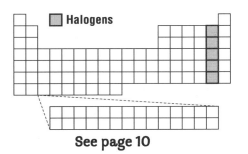

Halogens

See page 10

Meet the what? The *halogens* (HAL-o-jens). All the members of this family of elements behave in much the same way: They like to react — a lot! Some might even call them the thugs of the element world, because each of them likes to steal an electron from the other elements (see page 72).

Halogens particularly like to react with hydrogen to make acids. In fact, you have a halogen-containing acid in your stomach! *Hydrochloric acid* (HCl) helps you digest your food. If you breathe a little halogen gas like *bromine* (Br_2), you'll cough and get a sore throat. If you breathe too much, you'll have even bigger problems — it's poisonous! But in combination with many other elements, these irritating elements become nice and gentle. In fact, you brush your teeth with a halogen compound and put another one on your fries!

Waahh! He stole my electron!

35

FLUORINE

Fluorine (as fluoride) is found in toothpaste;
It helps stop decay, with a fresh, minty taste.
In waterproof clothing, it protects you from rain,
While fluorine in carpets resists dirty stains.

TOUGHER TEETH!

If you don't like having cavities filled by the dentist, make fluorine your friend! A form of this element, called *fluoride* (FLOOR-ide), is found in most toothpastes. It helps prevent cavities by changing the chemicals in your teeth. You see, saliva in your mouth turns the sugars in food into acid that slowly eats away the hard enamel covering your teeth. When you brush with fluoride toothpaste, the fluorines soak into your teeth, turning the enamel into a compound that is more difficult for the acids to dissolve. The happy result is that you get fewer cavities. Really makes you want to brush, doesn't it?

Element Essentials

FLUORINE (FLOOR-een)
* Symbol: F
* Number: 9
* Mass: 19.00 amu
* Discovery: In 1886, by Henri Moissan of France

Fizz, Bubble & Flash!

An Eggs-traordinary Eggs-periment

Check how well fluoride toothpaste works without risking any cavities yourself.

Materials

- Permanent marker
- 2 eggs
- 2 tablespoons fluoride toothpaste (check the label)
- Warm water
- Glass container large enough to hold both eggs
- White vinegar
- Aluminum foil

Make it happen!

1. Mark one egg with an X, so that you can tell them apart, and set aside.

2. Squeeze the toothpaste onto the other egg and smear it around until the egg's covered. Let the egg set for 24 hours, then wash the toothpaste off with warm water.

3. Place both eggs in the glass container and pour in enough vinegar (an acid) to cover them. (It's OK if the eggs float.) What do you notice after a short while?

4. Cover the jars loosely with foil so that the vinegar smell doesn't bother anyone. Check on the eggs every few hours for 12 hours (except while you're sleeping). Compare both eggs. Are you surprised at what you find?

Curious Minds Want to Know...

What happened to those eggshells? Vinegar is an acid that dissolves the chemical the eggshells are made of (see calcium, page 26). The fluoride in toothpaste combines with the calcium in the shell to make another chemical that isn't attacked by the vinegar. So, the shell of the egg without any protection disappears faster than the one with the fluoride. Your teeth and eggshells aren't made out of exactly the same stuff, but they're related.

How would you prefer your teeth to spend their time — protected by fluoride, or left all alone in your acidic saliva?

All Eyes on Ions!

You may have noticed that the experiment for this element talked about *fluoride*, yet the element's name is *fluorine*. What's going on here? Is this just a mistake, or are these really two different things?

Well, fluoride is just a special kind of fluorine. Fluorine atoms have this habit of snatching negatively charged electrons (page 122) away from other atoms. (In other words, they steal.) If a fluorine atom steals an electron from another kind of atom, it gets a negative charge, and the atom that loses the electron becomes positively charged. Any atom that either has extra electrons or is missing some electrons is called an *ion* (EYE-on). A fluorine atom that has an extra electron is called a *fluoride* ion. Changing the name is like hanging a sign on it that says, "I Am an Electron Thief!"

CURIOUS ROY

In 1938, a young chemist named Roy Plunkett was working in the lab. He opened a tank that should have been full of a chemical called *tetrafluoroethylene*, but nothing came out! Many people would have just thrown the tank away. But being a curious guy, Roy decided to take the tank apart to see what the problem was. The white powder he found inside turned out to be awesome! It felt very slippery. It wouldn't melt or burn. It didn't get stiff at freezing cold temperatures. Water didn't make it wet. Even acids had no effect on it! Take a guess at what Roy had found.

Fizz, Bubble & Flash!

Roy Plunkett had discovered Teflon, an amazing plastic with many uses. Cooked food doesn't stick to Teflon-lined pans. Clothes made with this plastic are waterproof, and carpets coated with it don't stain. Doctors can even make spare body parts from it — noses, knees, blood vessels, and heart valves. A chemical much like Teflon can be used as artificial blood. Teflon has even gone to the moon! The suits the astronauts wore were made with Teflon because the fabric stayed flexible even at the very cold temperatures in space.

So, when things don't work out the way you expect, don't give up. Ask more questions, try something else, put your brain to work, and maybe you'll discover something just as wonderful as curious Roy did!

OPPOSITES ATTRACT

You've heard that expression, I bet. Well, it applies to ions, too. Opposite charges *attract* each other, so positive and negative ions pair up to make molecules (combinations of atoms). The name of the positive ion comes first, followed by the name of the negative ion. If a fluorine atom steals an electron from a sodium atom, we call the resulting molecule *sodium fluoride*. It's found in most fluoride toothpaste. Lots of important chemicals are *ionic*.

Take It to the
SCIENCE
FAIR

Try different kinds of toothpaste in the egg experiment (page 71) to see which provides the best protection. Some toothpastes don't have fluoride. Check these out, too! Why do you think they still sell toothpaste without fluoride?

Explore the wondrous properties of Teflon. See what happens when you put water on it and stick it in the freezer. Try cooking (with adult supervision) something that can get sticky, like eggs, in a Teflon-lined pan, and in a regular one. Which is easier to use? Which is easier to clean up?

Meet the Halogens!

IODINE

Tincture of iodine helps heal scrapes and cuts;
It disinfects them — no ifs, ands, or buts!
It also turns purple on starches like bread,
And other good foods with which we're fed.

Element Essentials

IODINE (EYE-oh-dine)
* Symbol: I
* Number: 53
* Mass: 126.90 amu
* Discovery: In 1811, by Bernard Courtois of France

CRIME STOPPERS

If you try to buy something with a large bill, like $100, you may see the cashier write on it with a special pen. What is he or she doing? It's a simple test to see if the bill is real, and it involves iodine! Real money is printed on a special paper that has no *starch*, a long stringy molecule of many sugars joined together that is found in certain plants. (Normal paper is made from starch-containing plants.) The pen contains iodine, which turns blue when it touches starch. So, if the pen makes the paper blue, the bill's a fake!

Fizz, Bubble & Flash!

Bread's Got the Blues

Many foods also contain starch. Test out a few for yourself to see if they do.

Materials

- ❂ Knife (use with adult supervision)
- ❂ Potato
- ❂ Bread
- ❂ Pasta
- ❂ Apple
- ❂ Lettuce
- ❂ Plastic or paper plate
- ❂ Sugar
- ❂ Iodine tincture (not decolorized) or betadine solution (from the drugstore)

Make It Happen!

WARNING! Don't eat these foods after you've experimented with them!

1. Cut the solid foods into pieces, washing the knife between each use, and arrange them on the plate in different piles. Add a small pile of sugar on the side.

2. Put a drop of iodine solution onto each pile. What do you observe? Do the foods react differently?

CURIOUS MINDS WANT TO KNOW... **Why is some of my food turning blue?** Iodine combines with the starch in food to make a *complex* (two molecules stuck together that act like one) that is dark blue in color. So, starchy foods like potatoes, pasta, and bread turn blue, while nonstarchy foods like lettuce and apples don't change color.

Test other foods to see which have starch, and which don't. What do starchy foods have in common?

Chew a starchy food, then try the test again with the chewed food. (Just don't do this at the dinner table!) What happens? Your saliva changes the starch into sugar!

Keep warm

The *thyroid* (THIGH-royd) gland in your neck uses an iodine-containing compound to keep you warm and peppy. In the past, some people who didn't get enough iodine in their food developed ugly thyroid swellings in their necks called *goiters* (GOY-ters). Iodine doesn't show up in many foods, except for seafood and seaweed. Now, our table salt is usually *iodized* with *potassium iodide* (KI). So good-bye goiters!

Tincture of iodine kills bacteria, so it's good for disinfecting cuts and scrapes. Not many people use it anymore, though, because it stings so badly. (Ouch!)

Sublime Iodine

What happens if you leave an ice cube out on the counter? It melts, and turns into water. What if you leave the little puddle there? Eventually, it disappears because it *evaporates*, or turns into a gas (water vapor). Purple-black iodine crystals skip the liquid step, changing directly from a solid into a gas without melting first! Scientists call this process *sublimation* (SUB-lim-ay-shun).

There's probably sublimation going on in your freezer right now. No, not with iodine, but with good old water. Have you ever noticed that ice cubes get smaller if you leave them in there a long time? At the low temperature in the freezer, water sublimes, too, going straight to a gas with no puddles of water!

YEP! I remember the good old days...

76

ALL IN THE (HALOGENS) FAMILY

Pure **chlorine** (Cl) is a poisonous greenish yellow gas. But just a little added to water *kills* disease-causing germs and keeps a pool clean and clear!

CHLORINE

Astatine (At) is such a rare element, most people have never even heard of it. All the astatine on earth weighs about one ounce (25 g). Not very much, for sure!

astatine

BROMINE

Say "Cheese"! **Bromine** (Br) makes photography possible. Black–and–white film contains tiny bits of *silver bromide* (AgBr) spread over a plastic backing. When you snap a picture, the light changes the bromide into silver metal. When the film is developed, the unreacted silver bromide is washed away, leaving a negative. But when the photo is printed on paper, the dark and light areas get reversed, and the picture looks normal.

Meet the Noble Gases!

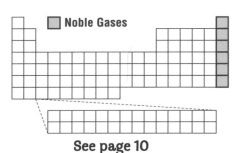

Noble Gases

See page 10

The *noble gases* are the snobbiest elements in the Periodic Table! Most elements are only too happy to combine with others, but these snooty elements don't like to react. For many years, scientists thought it was impossible to make noble–gas compounds, but now they know how. Xenon and krypton let you snap photos indoors; neon and argon are used in lights and signs; and helium, of course, is in party balloons. (Hopefully, you don't have much radon, the densest gas known, in your basement.)

Noble gases are found in the air, so you're breathing them in even as you read this! But because your body doesn't use them, you just blow them back out again. In fact, a scientist stumbled upon argon when he was trying to figure out just what gases are in the air. Once argon was found, xenon, neon, and krypton followed close behind. Helium was first discovered in rays of sunlight, while radon was found slowly leaking out of rocks.

I **love** being out in the fresh noble gases...

KRYPTON

All through the air, krypton atoms do roam
(Though this isn't the planet that's Superman's home!).
You find it in lightbulbs, their color light blue.
A measure of length — yes, that's krypton, too!

THE SUPERMAN ELEMENT!

You probably recognized the name of this element right away — it's the name of Superman's home planet. Why? Hard to say. Maybe Jerry Siegel and Joseph Shuster, the guys who created the first Superman comic books, just thought it sounded like something from outer space! By the way, there really isn't a chemical called kryptonite, so if you happen to be from Krypton, you can rest easy! To learn more about the science of superheroes, check out <www.bbc.co.uk/science/hottopics/superheroes>.

Meet the Noble Gases!

FLASH!

As one of the noble gases, krypton doesn't like to react with other elements, so it's sometimes used to fill lightbulbs to extend the life of the tungsten filaments (page 101). Most lightbulbs are filled with another noble gas, argon (page 82), which gives off a pale orange glow. The light from krypton-filled bulbs is much bluer and looks more like natural sunlight. You've seen krypton lights if you've ever flown in an airplane — they're the blue lights along the runway. (Good thing they're there!) Look for krypton-filled flashlights or floodlight bulbs in the hardware store. Camera flashes are filled with a mixture of krypton and xenon (page 82), which imitates sunlight.

Say Cheese!

All electric lights look white to our eyes, but to the eye of a camera, they look quite different! See for yourself!

Materials

- Film and camera (not digital) with a flash that can be turned off
- Roll of print (not slide) film
- Lamp with an incandescent lightbulb
- Lamp with a fluorescent lightbulb

Make It Happen!

1. Follow the instructions to turn off the flash on your camera.

2. Go outdoors on a bright, sunny day and snap a few pictures of your house, your friends, your pet, some flowers — anything you like.

3. After dark, turn on one or more *incandescent lights* (the kind with the regular round lightbulbs) and take a few photos. Hold the camera as still as possible.

4. Now go to a room with *fluorescent lights* (the kind with long, straight bulbs) and take some pictures there.

5. If your camera has a flash, turn it on and take a few more pictures indoors.

6. Have your film developed. How do your photos compare?

Huh? Why do some of these pictures look so odd? Because sometimes, believe it or not, your brain plays tricks on you! The light from a bulb has a color — orange from argon-filled incandescents, green from fluorescents. But your brain "knows" that light is supposed to be white (like sunlight), so that's how *you* see things indoors. The film in the camera isn't fooled, though! It records the colors that are actually there. Without the light of a flash, the oranges and greens tint the scene.

Most film is made to give the "right" colors outside on a sunny day. When the "artificial sunlight" of a krypton-xenon flash is used to light up an indoor scene, the film thinks it's outside, and the picture looks just fine!

How Long?

Most of the world measures using the metric system, in which lengths are based on the meter (about 39"). The original "meter stick" was a rod made of two elements that are transition metals, platinum and iridium (page 94). The problem was that the stick was stored in Paris, France, so anyone who wanted to use it had to travel there. In 1960, scientists decided to change the way they measured a meter. They used the wave-like vibrations of the krypton atom. These waves are really small — it takes 1,650,763 of them to make a meter! So scientists could make very accurate length measurements without traveling to France!

Take It to the
SCIENCE FAIR

🎗 **Balancing act.** Get "tungsten-balanced" film from a camera store. This is a special film that's made to be used indoors under photo lights. It erases most of the orange color from incandescents bulbs, which have tungsten filaments. The problem is, pictures taken outside with this film look really weird! Try it and see what happens!

Meet the Noble Gases!

ALL IN THE (NOBLE GASES) FAMILY

HELIUM

Have you ever seen a blimp floating through the air? It's a giant bag full of lighter–than–air **helium** (He) gas.

The bluish purple headlights you sometimes see are filled with **xenon** (Xe) gas, which gives off a brilliant light when electricity is passed through it.

XENON

ARGON

Argon (Ar) doesn't react with anything. In fact, its name comes from the Greek word *argos*, which means "lazy" — perfect for use in lightbulbs.

Neon (Ne) gas is usually colorless, but when electricity passes through it, the gas glows brightly – ideal for a bright red neon sign!

NEON

RADON

When the radioactive elements thorium and uranium decay, they give off a radioactive gas called **radon** (Rn). In some places, radon can build up inside basements. Check whether you live in a Radon Zone at <http://www.epa.gov/iaq/radon/zonemap.html >.

82

Meet the Transition Metals!

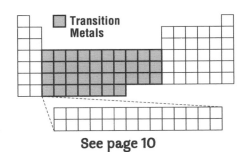

Transition Metals

See page 10

This is a really big family! In fact, more elements in the Periodic Table belong to the transition metals than any other group! Some of the elements you know best — iron, copper, gold, silver — are transition metals.

The transition metals inhabit the "sunken" section of the Periodic Table, between the alkaline earths to the left and the main-group metals and metalloids to the right. Aside from their position, how are the transition metals different from other types of metals? Unlike the softer alkali and alkaline earth metals, most of the transition metals are hard and have high melting points. Vanadium, for instance, is used to make steel tools that can take the heat, like saws for cutting and hot engines, and tungsten holds the Periodic Table's record for

melting points — it has to be heated to 6200°F (3410°C) before it melts! (How hot is that? Well, molten lava spilling out of a volcano is "only" 2200°F/1200°C — way too cool to melt tungsten!)

For the most part, though, you can't see the differences — aluminum (a main-group metal) looks a lot like titanium (a transition metal). What you *can* see in this big family is a lot of color. Ever heard of "cobalt blue" or "cadmium yellow"? Many of these elements form brightly colored compounds used in paint. Other transition-metal compounds are used for making hardworking tools, such as building supports, and to make your coins look shiny. Yes, this big family has a big impact on your daily life!

IRON

Weighty iron, wrought and cast,
Building things designed to last.
Iron in cereal, iron in bread,
Iron makes your blood dark red!

Good for You

Blood Red

Many foods, such as breads and breakfast cereals, boast that they contain extra iron. Why is this element so important for your health? Well, blood contains a molecule called *heme* (HEEM) that has an iron atom in the middle. Heme looks a little like chlorophyll (page 23). Its purpose is to carry the oxygen you breathe to every part of your body. If you don't have enough iron in your blood, you will look pale and feel tired. This sickness is called *anemia* (ah-NEEM-ee-ah), or "iron-poor blood." Taking iron supplements will cure it. That's why iron's one of the "essential elements"!

Fizz, Bubble & Flash!

A Breakfast "Fe-ast"

Adults usually tell you, "Don't play with your food!" but sometimes it's OK — like right now! Go ahead — play with your food as you separate the iron from your breakfast cereal!

Materials

- 1 cup (250 mL) iron-fortified cereal, such as Total
- Gallon-sized (4 L) plastic zip-locking bag
- Rolling pin
- Sheet of white paper
- Magnet (not the flexible type)

Make It Happen!

1. Seal the cereal in the plastic bag. Crush the cereal with your hands.

2. Put the bag down on a flat surface and carefully crush the cereal to a powder, using the rolling pin.

3. Pour a little cereal powder onto the white paper and spread it out. Hold the magnet under the paper and move it around. Do you see anything moving?

Curious Minds Want to Know...

What are those little black bits? Did you notice any little black specks in the cereal that moved when the magnet was near them? They're actually tiny pieces of iron metal added to the cereal to make it more nutritious!

Meet the Transition Metals!

85

IRON ABOVE AND IRON BELOW

Meteorites (particles of rock that enter our atmosphere from outer space) are always dusting the earth. Sometimes you can see them on a clear night — as shooting stars! Actually, they are just pieces of rock burning as they travel through our atmosphere. These space rocks usually have lots of iron in them, so we know that there is iron above our heads, up in space.

Way, way below your feet (we're talking 3,000 miles/4,800 km down!), there's also plenty of iron — in the earth's core. Scientists think that the core's temperature is about 9000°F (5000°C). It's hard to know for sure, because no one can go down to check!

ANCIENT IRONWORKERS

Humans have been making things from iron for a very long time. At first, they probably collected pieces of metal from meteorites they found. We know that the Egyptians made objects from meteorite iron more than 5,000 years ago. The Inuit people of the Arctic traveled to one large space rock that had landed on earth to collect iron for tools.

Are we there yet?

About 3,500 years ago, the Hittites, who lived in what is now Turkey, learned how to remove iron from rocks and minerals. The Hittites sold their iron to their neighbors and became very rich and powerful. They guarded their secret of iron-making, but eventually word leaked out. Soon many other ancient peoples were also producing iron and making things from it. In Delhi, India, there is a 20' (6 m) iron tower that was built 1,500 years ago!

STEEL: THE REAL DEAL

Iron is a very useful metal, but there's one big problem with it. If left outside, exposed to air and water, iron combines with oxygen and water, making reddish brown, crumbly rust. And rust makes the iron metal very weak. If a piece of iron is left out too long, it will rust away to iron dust!

Fortunately, people discovered that if you mix certain other elements, like carbon (page 54), vanadium (page 100), nickel (page 100), tungsten (page 101), and chromium (Cr), in with the iron, you get *steel* — which is much stronger than pure iron and doesn't rust! Which would *you* rather have for your bridge supports, car bodies, and building beams?

NO MORE GREEN EGGS?

Have you ever noticed a thin green film around the yolk of a hard-boiled egg? Actually, that's an iron compound! When you cook an egg, iron in the yolk can combine with sulfur (page 64) in the egg's proteins to make *iron sulfide* (FeS). If you don't want green yolks, cool the eggs quickly by adding cold water as soon as they're finished cooking. The cold water stops the chemical reaction between the iron and the sulfur.

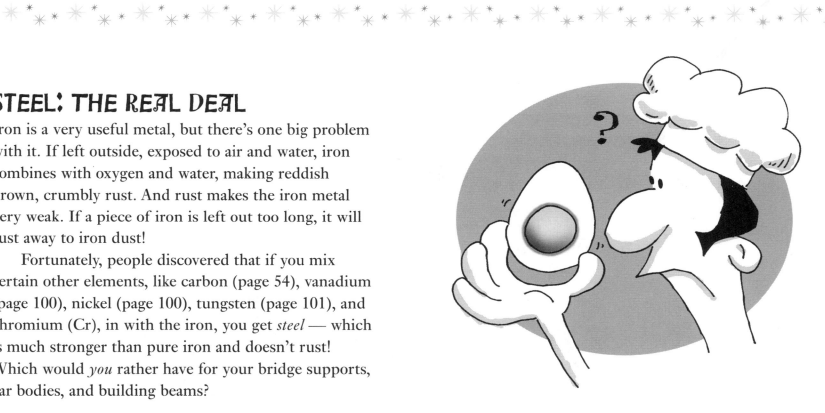

Take It to the
SCIENCE FAIR

🎖 **How fast does iron rust?** Take some iron nails and put them in different places: in a glass of water; outside where they can get wet; outside in a protected spot; inside the house. When do you start to see rust? Take pictures to show how the rust increases from week to week, or even day by day!

Do other metals rust faster or slower than iron? Try aluminum foil, stainless steel, copper, brass, or any others you can find. Keep track of what you observe.

COPPER

Pennies are brown from their thin copper coat,
But the inside is zinc — a good fact to note.
Copper's many uses, you can't help admiring:
Plumbing and plating, roofing and wiring.

A PENNY EARNED IS ...
A PENNY PLATED

A "copper" used to mean a coin made of copper, like a penny, which originally was copper all the way through. But now copper is too expensive to be used for the whole coin — it would cost more than one cent to make the penny! So all U.S. pennies made since 1982 have just a thin copper coating outside. The inside is made of another transition metal, zinc. This thin metal coating is called *plating*.

Fizz, Bubble & Flash!

Copper Topping

Give an ordinary iron nail a spiffy new copper coating!

Materials

- 2 lemons, or $1/4$ cup (50 mL) lemon juice
- Plastic or paper cup (throw away after the experiment)
- 10 to 20 dull pennies
- Salt
- 2 iron nails (*not* galvanized)
- Watch or clock with a second hand
- Steel wool scouring pad

Make It Happen!

1. Squeeze the lemons or pour the lemon juice into the cup.

2. Place the pennies in the juice. Add a pinch of salt. Wait 3 minutes. While you are waiting, rub one of the nails with the steel wool; then rinse it off. Put the other nail aside.

3. Drop the scoured nail into the cup; wait an hour.

4. Pour off the lemon juice and rinse off the bathed nail. Compare it to the other nail. Notice anything different?

CURIOUS MINDS WANT TO KNOW...

Why are the nails different colors? It's that ion thing again! The copper from the plated pennies dissolves in the lemon juice (an acid, page 67), producing copper ions. When the iron nail is put into the acid, the copper ions are attracted to the iron and build up, layer upon layer, until the nail gets a new coat. (See page 72 for more about ions.)

CALLING ALL ALLOYS!

Copper sure is a hardworking element! It has even more uses when it's mixed with other metals to make alloys. Gold-colored *brass* contains copper and zinc, and greenish brown *bronze* is made of copper and tin (page 40). *Sterling silver* is mostly silver (page 100), but there's a little copper mixed in to make it stronger. Which of these alloys can you find around your house?

The Lady in Green

Do you know a famous green woman? Here's a hint — she's on an island in New York Harbor! She's Lady Liberty, of course! The Statue of Liberty is made of copper. Copper doesn't rust by combining with oxygen, the way iron does, but it does react with other gases in the air to form *copper carbonate* ($CuCO_3$) and *copper sulfate* ($CuSO_4$). Both of these chemical compounds are light green in color. This coating is called a *patina* (pah-TEEN-ah). Some buildings have roofs made of copper, and they also eventually turn this lovely shade of green. Look around your town for buildings with copper roofs.

Take It to the
SCIENCE FAIR

🎖 **Go on a copper quest.**
Where else might you find copper? It's often used for plumbing pipes because it doesn't rust when water flows through it. Though many of the pipes in homes are made of plastic these days, some of them are still made of copper. You'll recognized copper piping by its color (a dull greenish tone or brighter copper color, depending on how old the pipes are). Copper is also one of the best metals to use for wires, because electricity moves through it easily (see page 14). And check out the kitchen, too: Some cooking pots and pans have copper bottoms because this ever-useful metal heats up quickly and evenly. Make a display or poster of your copper finds, showing off examples of this metal of many uses!

Fizz, Bubble & Flash!

ZIRCONIUM

Cubic zirconia glistens and gleams,
Looks just like a diamond — at least, so it seems.
Zirconium compounds help keep you dry
In the antiperspirants that some people buy!

A GEM OF AN ELEMENT (BUT NOT QUITE A DIAMOND)

For ages, people have admired the beautiful yellow stone called *zircon*, which can be polished into a jewel. (In fact, the name of both this stone and the element zirconium come from the Arabic word *zargun*, which means "gold-colored.") Scientists have learned how to make crystal-clear fake diamonds — the cubic zirconia stones you often see in inexpensive jewelry — from *zirconium oxide* (ZrO_2).

But zirconium is also used in totally different ways. The metal is very lightweight and can be used at high temperatures — perfect for space vehicles that get very hot as they reenter earth's atmosphere. Zirconium oxide is used to make artificial joints, such as knees and hips, because it's very strong. And a zirconium compound is even used to keep your underarms dry!

> **Element Essentials**
>
> **ZIRCONIUM (Zur-CONE-ee-um)**
> * Symbol: Zr
> * Number: 40
> * Mass: 91.22 amu
> * Discovery: In 1787, by Martin Heinrich Klaproth of Germany

Meet the Transition Metals!

No Sweat!

Curious kids want to know: How *do* those antiperspirants advertised on TV and in magazines really work? Well, with a little science sleuthing, you'll find the answer!

Materials

- Antiperspirant stick
- Aluminum foil
- Ruler
- Glass or metal bowl
- Water
- Ice

Make It Happen!

1. Rub antiperspirant on the foil, filling in a spot about an inch (2.5 cm) in diameter.

2. Fill the bowl halfway with cold water. Add enough ice to bring the water level about an inch (2.5 cm) below the rim.

3. Cover the bowl with the foil, with the antiperspirant spot facing up. (Don't let the foil touch the water or ice.)

4. Now watch and observe, particularly the area around the antiperspirant spot. What clue does that give you about how antiperspirants work?

92

Curious Minds WANT TO KNOW...?

Now you see it, now you don't! You probably noticed water forming on the foil. When the warmer air above the foil is cooled by the ice below, the moisture in the air *condenses* (changes from vapor to liquid) and collects on the foil. But what you observe happening on the antiperspirant spot itself is what you're interested in.

So, what do you see? Aha, NO sweat (or water) where the antiperspirant was applied! Something in the antiperspirant caused this — and that something just happens to contain the element zirconium. The zirconium compound in an antiperspirant soaks up water, so in your experiment, you don't see any condensing in that area.

Well, the same thing happens on your skin — the zirconium compound soaks up the water when you perspire, so you don't see the sweat (unless you're perspiring a lot).

... AND SPEAKING OF SWEATING

Can you guess why people don't rub antiperspirants over their entire bodies? Sweating is how your body cools itself. If you weren't able to sweat, you would get overheated, which can be very dangerous. Antiperspirants are meant to be applied to your underarms, where you are more likely to develop body odor because you have a concentration of sweat glands there. And don't forget about good old soap — the potassium (page 21) in it is great for keeping you clean!

Take It to the **SCIENCE FAIR**

🎀 **Try a few different kinds of antiperspirant** to see which absorb water best. What about the products called *deodorants?* Do they work as well? Set your experiments up so people at the fair can see the differences themselves.

Meet the Transition Metals!

93

IRiDiUM

Dinosaurs could not avoid
An iridium-heavy asteroid.
It kicked up dust, and that was that;
They went extinct in no time flat.

That has BAD DAY written all over it!

DINO-MANiA!

Iridium is not very common on earth, but asteroids contain a lot of it. When *paleontologists* (scientists who study fossils) examined the rocks that formed around the time that the dinosaurs died off (about 65 million years ago), they found high levels of iridium. So much iridium could not come from earth rocks, they concluded. Could it be extraterrestrial — from outer space? Scientists began to wonder if the impact of a large asteroid caused the disappearance of these prehistoric beasts. If the earth were smacked by a giant asteroid, tons of iridium dust and earth dust would be sent into the air. The sky would grow dark, and much of the sun's light would be blocked off, causing plants and animals to die.

Is this what really happened to the dinosaurs? We may never know for sure, but many scientists now think that's why we don't see giant dinos roaming our streets today.

Element Essentials

IRiDiUM (irr-RiD-ee-um)
* Symbol: Ir
* Number: 77
* Mass: 192.22 amu
* Discovery: In 1803, by Smithson Tennant of England

94

Fizz, Bubble & Flash!

Crater Creator

See how much havoc an asteroid impact could make by creating some craters of your own. But you might want to try this experiment outside!

Materials

- ☻ Ruler
- ☻ Flour
- ☻ Baking pan
- ☻ Small objects (rock, marble, dried bean, puffed cereal, rice)

Make It Happen!

1. Place about 1" (2.5 cm) of flour in the pan. Gently shake the pan from side to side to smooth out the flour.

2. Pick up one of the small objects and hold it 12" (30 cm) above the pan. Drop it into the flour. Carefully pick it up and use the ruler to measure how wide and how deep the crater is.

3. Repeat, trying all the different objects you collected and smoothing the flour between each try. Which matters most, the size, shape, or weight of the "asteroid"?

4. Smooth out the flour again. Repeat the experiment, holding each object about 24" (60 cm) above the pan and then dropping it. How does the size of the crater change?

Curious Minds Want to Know...

Why are the holes different sizes? When the rock, marble, or other object hits the flour, it stops suddenly. All the energy it picked up while falling is transferred into the flour, so the flour sprays out, leaving a hole. The farther the object falls, the more energy it gathers. So the higher you hold the object, and the heavier it is, the bigger the hole!

Having seen what a mess a little rock causes, imagine how much damage would be done by a giant asteroid falling all the way from outer space!

Don't Be Dense!

Iridium is one of the *densest* elements. What does that mean? Well, it *doesn't* mean that it's stupid, first of all! *Density* is a measure of how closely the particles that make up a substance are packed together. A piece of iridium is denser than the same-sized piece of almost any other element. It's 20 times denser than water, for example. If you fill a container with water and it weighs 1 pound (.5 kg), then that same container filled with iridium would weigh 20 pounds (10 kg)! What a difference!

Take It to the SCIENCE FAIR

🎗 **Set up a crater experiment** so others can try it. Make careful measurements of the hole's depth and diameter. Use more than two starting points, and weigh the dropped objects on a food scale. Use a computer to graph your data in different ways — compare weight and hole size, the height from which it's dropped and hole size, hole depth and hole width, or any other combinations you can think of.

🎗 **Compare the density of liquids.** Fill several paper cups to *exactly* the same level with various liquids: water or rubbing alcohol in one, honey or corn syrup in another, and oil in the third. Weigh each cup on a food scale. Which cup is the heaviest? That's the densest liquid!

🎗 **Make liquid lasagna!** Pour corn syrup into a jar until it is one-third full. Gently pour water to fill it another third, then add another third of oil to the top. Don't mix the layers. You have liquid lasagna, thanks to density!

A DENSITY RIDDLE

Q: Which weighs more — a pound (or kg) of iron or a pound (or kg) of feathers?

A: This is a trick — they both weigh one pound (or kg)! Many people confuse the ideas of weight and density. Iron is a lot denser than feathers. One pound (or kg) of iron will take up a lot less space than the feathers, but both weigh the same!

Try this riddle out on some friends! How many give the right answer?

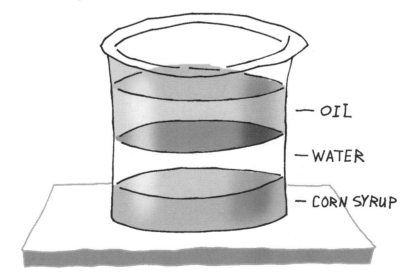

— OIL

— WATER

— CORN SYRUP

GOLD

A valuable element is the one we call gold;
People have treasured it from times of old.
Gold-hungry prospectors called forty-niners
Didn't play football — these guys were all miners!

THE GOLD RUSH

"GOLD!" Few words have been so important in human history! Gold has been used for 4,000 years to make jewelry and coins; wars have been fought the world over for this yellow metal. In the 1800s, gold was found in the mountains of California. Starting in 1849, thousands of prospectors traveled west, dreaming of riches. Today, the San Francisco 49ers football team remembers those "forty-niners" by using their name. Although a few people did become rich during the California Gold Rush, most didn't.

Meet the Transition Metals!

You Can Pan!

Much of the gold in California washed down from the rocks in the mountains and settled on the bottoms of streams where the currents had slowed. It was easy to scoop up, but how could it be separated from all the worthless rocks and dirt? Old-time prospectors used *panning*.

Materials

- 10 small pieces of metal, like washers or nuts
- 1 tablespoon (15 mL) flour
- Round metal pan
- Water

Make It Happen!

1. Place the metal objects and flour into the pan. Add $^1/_2$ cup (125 mL) water.

2. Try to remove the flour by swirling the pan and sloshing the water out. Can you keep the washers in the pan?

Curious Minds Want to Know...

Why don't the metal bits wash out? The pieces of metal are heavy, so they stay at the bottom of the pan. The flour floats on the water, and washes away. In the same way, specks of gold, another heavy metal, stayed in the prospectors' pans, and the dirt floated out.

Fizz, Bubble & Flash!

CARATS, NOT CARROTS!

Did you ever wonder what orange vegetables have to do with gold? You sometimes hear gold jewelry called "24 carat," "14 carat," or some other number. The number of *carats* (pronounced like "carrots") tells you how pure the gold is. Twenty-four carats, or 24K, is all gold, but it's so soft that it bends and scratches easily, so most gold jewelry is 18K, 14K, or 12K. Sometimes other metals are added to the gold to change the color slightly — white gold (with nickel), rose gold (with copper), or green gold (with silver).

Pan for gold! Try panning in a real stream or creek. You may be surprised by what you find! Fill your pan with some dirt and water from the stream, removing any big stones. Then gently shake the pan back and forth so some of the water flows over the sides, carrying away most of the light sand and gravel. Pick through the heavier bits, checking for gold specks and other treasures. Remember, treasures don't need to be valuable to have value to you!

The Value of Gold

Why is gold so valuable? Is it because it's so useful? Can we build strong bridges and cars out of it? Is it an important element for life? Is it the rarest metal? Well, no. As a metal, gold isn't much good. But it sure looks nice! The main reason gold is so valuable is that people have *decided* it is valuable. As long as everyone wants it, the price will stay high!

ALL IN THE (TRANSITION METALS) FAMILY

Vanadium (V) helps steel beat the heat, making engines and tools stronger. Regular steel — which is mostly iron — becomes soft when it gets hot. The addition of vanadium makes steel better able to stand up to rubbing and rough treatment.

That jet overhead is made of a whole lot of **titanium** (Ti)! This strong, lightweight metal is used in jet engines and certain bicycle frames, too!

How much nickel in a nickel? *Not* five cents worth! A nickel does contain some **nickel** (Ni), but most of it is copper!

Can you find anything made of **silver** (Ag) in your home? Because pure silver is very soft, many silver items also contain some copper. This mixture is called *sterling silver*. A thin coating of silver is called *silverplate*. The easiest way to tell the difference? Look at the price tag!

For the transition metals not mentioned in this chapter, see the Periodic Table (page 10).

Fizz, Bubble & Flash!

ALL IN THE (TRANSITION METALS) FAMILY

Look inside a clear household light-bulb, and you'll see a thin wire called a *filament* (FILL-ah-ment) that is made of **tungsten** (W). When an electrical current is passed through it, the tungsten glows — making the bright light!

SMALL, but important.

TUNGSTEN

Cobalt (Co) is found in vitamin B$_{12}$ and is essential for your blood, nerves, and growth. So eat plenty of meat, fish, or dairy products to get your daily dose of B$_{12}$!

COBALT

YTTRIUM

Someday you may zoom along on a train that floats over a magnetic field, thanks to **yttrium** (Y)! When cooled to very low temperatures (-256°F, or -160°C), some yttrium compounds become *superconducting* — electricity keeps flowing through them even after the power is turned off!

MERCURY

This metal shines like silver, but pours like water! **Mercury's** (Hg) Latin name, *hydragyrum*, means "liquid silver." Old-fashioned thermometers used mercury, but most thermometers today are filled with alcohol instead.

Meet the Transition Metals!

Meet the Lanthanides!

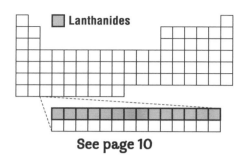

Lanthanides

See page 10

The *lanthanides* (LAN-thuh-nides) really had scientists confused for a while. These elements are all metallic and are almost always found mixed together in certain rocks and minerals. It took many years for scientists to sort them all out. When they finished, they'd found 14 new elements for the Periodic Table! The lanthanides are sometimes called "rare earths," but that's not a very good name for them. There are plenty of elements that are rarer.

The lanthanides include 14 elements starting with lanthanum. They really belong in the next-to-last row of the Periodic Table, following barium (#56), but because that would make the table so wide, they get their own grouping down below. Lanthanides are used to make compact disks, lasers, magnets, computer screens, fiber optics, and more. You might not know they're around, but this family of elements sure makes everyday life more convenient!

LANTHANUM

"Rare earths" like lanthanum are in rocks volcanic,
But if they're nearby, you don't have to panic.
These mountains of fire may well have expired,
They are, you might say, geologically retired.

PARDON ME!

FIRST-CLASS GLASS

Really good glass lenses, like those used in expensive cameras and telescopes, often use a little bit of lanthanum in the glass. The lanthanum changes the *refractive index* of the light. Huh? That just means the light rays bend less when they pass through the glass, so the image is closer to the original.

Element Essentials

LANTHANUM (LAN-tha-num)
* Symbol: La
* Number: 57
* Mass: 138.91 amu
* Discovery: In 1839, by Carl Gustav Mosander of Sweden

Meet the Lanthanides!

103

Refraction Action

Compare the refractive index of three liquids in your kitchen!

Materials

- 3 clear drinking glasses
- Water
- Rubbing alcohol
- Light (clear) corn syrup
- Masking tape
- Marker
- 3 pencils

Make It Happen!

1. Fill each glass about halfway with one of the three liquids. Label each glass.

2. Put a pencil into each glass and let it rest against the side.

3. At eye level with the glass, look through the side. What do you notice about the pencil? Does it look straight or bent? Does it look the same in each liquid?

4. Throw out all the liquids and wash the glasses carefully before using them again.

Why do the pencils look bent? When light rays moving through the air hit the liquid, they slow down. The rays also bend a little, so they fool your eye into thinking that the pencil is bent, too. This is called *refraction* (ree-FRACK-shun). Different liquids make the light rays bend at different angles, so the pencil looks more bent in some liquids and less bent in others. The thicker, or denser (page 96), the liquid, the more bent the pencil will look.

Can you think of another example of refraction that you've seen? (Hint: Think rain.) After a rainstorm, the tiny raindrops left hanging in the air refract the sunlight. White light is really made up of many different colors, so when the rays pass through the raindrops, each color bends a little differently and the colors spread out across the sky. What do you see? That's right — a rainbow!

Curious Minds want to Know...

Take It to the SCIENCE FAIR

🎖 **Experiment with lenses** in magnifying glasses and eyeglasses (get permission first, though!). See if you can tell the difference between glasses for people who are *nearsighted* (can't see things far away) and *farsighted* (can't see things close up). You might even find a pair of bifocals, which have both kinds of lenses! Hold the glasses above a printed page and see what they do to the size and shape of the letters.

🎖 **Check out the index of refraction for other clear liquids.** What can you use? Try vegetable oil, glycerin (from the drugstore), or anything else you can think of!

🎖 **Investigate how a prism or glass crystal** refracts light to form a rainbow of colors. Notice how they're always in the same order? It's good old ROY G. BIV (red, orange, yellow, green, blue, indigo, violet)!

Meet the Lanthanides!

Chemistry Rocks!

Do you know what kinds of rocks are found in your neighborhood? Or how they formed? You may be surprised at what you discover! For example, in many places, the rocks are volcanic, even though today you won't find any active volcanoes for hundreds and hundreds of miles (km). These rocks formed millions of years ago, and pieces of the earth have moved around a lot since then. Sometimes they were carried long distances by *glaciers* (massive "rivers" of ice) during the ice ages. So your local rocks may contain rare earths, or other uncommon elements you wouldn't usually find in your area.

Learn about your local *geology* (GEE-ol-oh-gee) by reading books, searching on the Internet, or visiting a local nature center or science museum. And "rock" on!

Fizz, Bubble & Flash!

NEODYMIUM

Neodymium, boron, and iron combined,
Make magnets of the strongest kind.
Neodymium glass may be purple or blue;
Sunlight or lamplight — that makes the hue.

MAGNET-ICENT!

Neodymium's an element with a magnetic personality! When combined with iron (page 84) and boron (page 42), it makes very small, strong magnets. How strong? Well, if you stick two of these magnets together, it's almost impossible to separate them by hand. These little magnets can be found in all sorts of places. They're used in the door locks and windshield wipers in your car, and they even help to entertain you, in headphones and stereo speakers.

Meet the Lanthanides!

Element Essentials

NEODYMIUM (NEE-oh-dim-ee-um)
* Symbol: Nd
* Number: 60
* Mass: 144.24 amu
* Discovery: In 1885, by Carl Auer von Welsbach of Austria

Dancing Dollars

Did you know that dollar bills are magnetic? Watch them dance!

Materials

- U.S. dollar bill
- Magnet (not the flexible kind)

Make It Happen!

1. Fold the dollar bill in half. Then open it up and place it as shown.

2. Put the magnet very close to the printing on the dollar bill. Move the magnet around. What happens to the dollar bill? Does the magnet have a stronger effect in some places than in others?

Curious Minds Want to Know...

Why does the dollar dance? The ink used to print U.S. dollar bills is magnetic! If you place a magnet near the money, it's attracted to the ink, so the bill "jumps." Can you guess why magnetic ink is used? (Hint: Think like a criminal.) It's part of a plan to keep people from printing *counterfeit* (fake) money! Uncover more of these secrets hidden in money's paper and ink at <www.treas.gov/topics/currency/index.html>.

Fizz, Bubble & Flash!

Feel the Force!

Only a few elements are magnetic — iron, nickel, cobalt, neodymium, and a couple of others. In these elements, the atoms (page 5) act like tiny magnets. If these mini-magnets are jumbled up, then a piece of one of these elements isn't a magnet. But if the magnets all point in the same direction, then the element itself becomes magnetic.

Feel the force around two magnets by playing with them. Try to make them touch each other. Are they pulled together or pushed apart? Turn the magnets around. Does the same thing happen?

One end of a magnet is called the *north pole;* the other is the *south pole.* If you try to bring the north poles (or the south poles) together, the magnets *repel* each other, and you can't make them touch. But bring opposite poles near each other, and it's a different story! The poles *attract,* and the magnets stick together.

Does "north pole" sound familiar? Well, the earth has magnetic poles, too. The "magnetic north pole" is near the top of the globe. (It's in a different spot than the geographic North Pole you see on a map.) Compasses have little magnetized needles that line up with this magnetic pole and point north, so you can always find your way.

The mini-magnets on the left are all mixed up, so this magnet doesn't know which end is up. But the nicely organized mini-magnets on the right will show the way to go!

Meet the Lanthanides!

BIRD BRAINS

Did you know that many birds have small magnets in their brains? Scientists think that they help the birds find their way as they fly south in the fall, and north in the spring. It's as if birds have a built-in compass in their brains!

RAINBOW GLASS

Neodymium isn't just for magnets! Sometimes a little of this element is added to glass to color it. This glass changes color, depending on the kind of light. In the sun, it looks light purple, but under electric lights, it's pink or blue! Some glass figures, bowls, and other decorative pieces are made of this rainbow glass.

Take It to the SCIENCE FAIR

🎗 **Set up an experiment with different kind of money.** Is all U.S. money magnetic? Try other values, like $5, $10, or $20. (Don't forget to return any borrowed bills after you're finished experimenting!)

What about paper money from other countries? Maybe someone you know has kept some foreign bills as a souvenir from a trip. See if any of them are printed with magnetic ink.

🎗 **Build your own compass!** Rub a sewing needle with a magnet until it becomes magnetized. Float the needle in a small dish of water. One end of the needle will point north. Use the position of the sun in the morning to find east, or in the evening to find west. You'll then be able to figure out which end — the eye or the point — of your needle compass points north.

COOL!

Fizz, Bubble & Flash!

PROMETHIUM

Promethium's named for a guy who was Greek,
He stole fire from the heavens — oh, what a sneak!
But you'll not find promethium here,
Even if you searched year after year.

HEY!

THE PROMETHIUM PUZZLE

Promethium had scientists scratching their heads for many years! They knew that there had to be an element between neodymium (#60) and samarium (#62), but, try as they might, they just couldn't find it! Where could #61 be? Then, in 1947, three Tennessee scientists split apart some uranium (#92) atoms and found that they'd made a few atoms of the mysterious #61. That solved the mystery! You see, promethium is a *radioactive* element, which means it is *unstable* — its atoms eventually *decay*, or change into other elements (page 113). Right after the earth formed, there were probably some promethium atoms around, but most of them would have turned into neodymium before 10,000 years had gone by! So any promethium we use today has to be made fresh in the lab!

> ### Element Essentials
>
> **PROMETHIUM** (pro-MEETH-ee-um)
> * Symbol: Pm
> * Number: 61
> * Mass: 144.91 amu
> * Discovery: In 1947, by J. A. Mirinsky, L. E. Glendenin, and C. D. Coryell of the United States

Meet the Lanthanides!

Get a (Half) Life

Imagine that these goodies are radioactive atoms. Watch them "decay" by disappearing into your mouth. Yum!

Materials

- 32 pieces of cereal, raisins, or other bite-sized goodies
- Watch or clock with a second hand

Make It Happen!

Eat the cereal according to the following schedule:

- After 2 minutes, eat 16 pieces
- After a total of 4 minutes, eat 8 more pieces
- After a total of 6 minutes, eat 4 more pieces
- After a total of 8 minutes, eat 2 more pieces
- After a total of 10 minutes, eat 1 more piece
- After a total of 12 minutes, eat any leftover crumbs

Curious Minds Want To Know...

Why can't I eat everything at once? Because you're snacking the way that radioactive atoms decay, that's why. You started with 32 pieces. When did you have half that number left? That answer is the *half-life*, the amount of time it takes for half of a radioactive element to disappear. Sixteen is half of 32, so the half-life of your snack element is two minutes. After two more minutes (another half-life), 8 (half of the leftover 16) pieces go into your mouth. Then, after another two minutes, 4 (half of 8) disappear. And so on … until there's nothing left!

Fizz, Bubble & Flash!

What Is Radioactivity?

In some atoms, the pile of protons and neutrons in the *nucleus* (center) of the atom just can't stick together. So the nucleus breaks into pieces, or picks up some electrons. (For more about these atom adventures, see pages 122–125.) When that happens, everything changes!

When the number of protons in the nucleus changes, the atomic number changes, and the atoms become another element all together. And all these changes give off energy called *radioactivity*. If the energy of these changes is strong — as in radium (page 30) — the elements are very dangerous, and can cause serious diseases. Weak radioactivity, though, can be found almost everywhere. Plenty of rocks and minerals are weakly radioactive, and a little radioactivity can even be found coming from you!

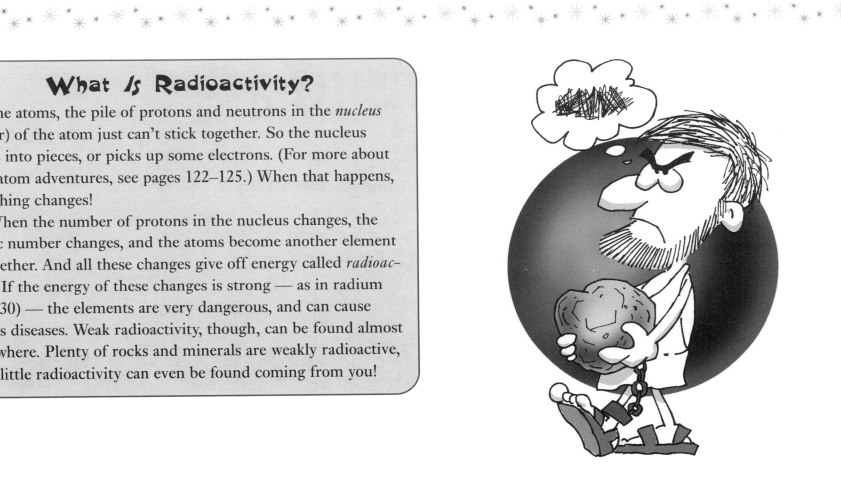

WHAT A MYTH!

Promethium is named for Prometheus, a character from Greek mythology. According to the story, Zeus, the chief god, ordered all the other gods to keep the humans from getting fire. Prometheus didn't think that this was fair, so he gave the cold, hungry people on earth the gift of fire. Not surprisingly, Zeus was really mad, and what do you think he did? He punished Prometheus by chaining him to a rock where eagles bit him all the time! Prometheus was stuck there for many years, until he was rescued by Hercules, a kind of ancient superhero. Even after he was freed, Prometheus still had to carry his chain and part of the rock around with him all the time.

Can you see why the scientists gave this elusive element the name of the chained Prometheus?

Meet the Lanthanides!

TERBIUM

A small Swedish town gave terbium its name;
For three other elements, the story's the same.
Magnetic terbium is found in CDs,
Their beautiful music is certain to please.

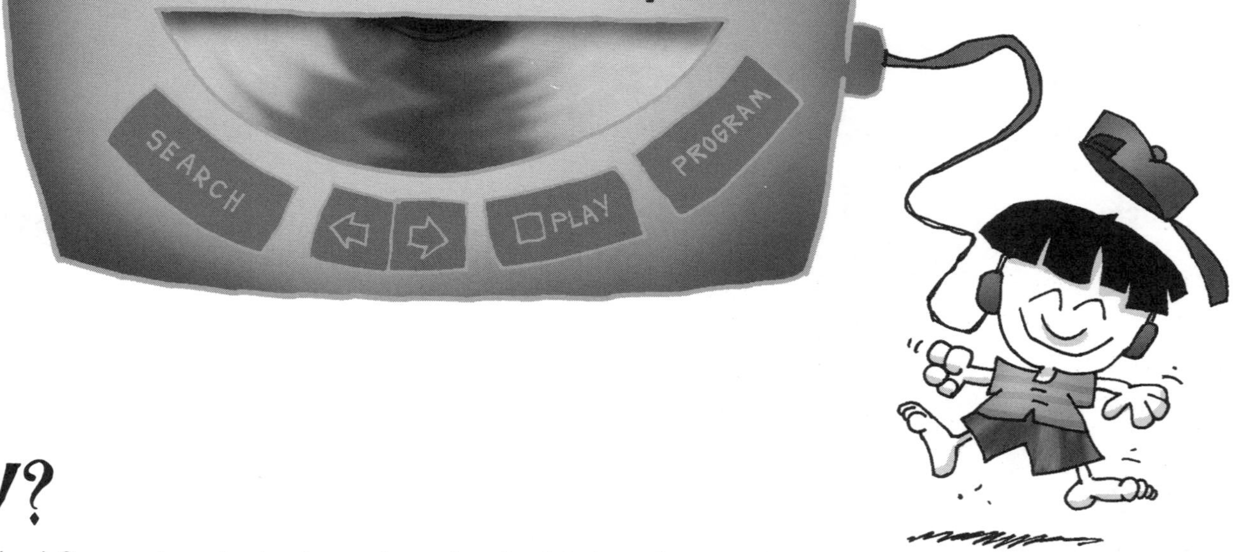

SEARCH ⇦ ⇨ ▢ PLAY PROGRAM

WHAT'S ON TV?

Lanthanides like terbium, that's what! Some chemicals glow when they're hit by a beam of electrons. Terbium is one of these. The green color on a TV screen or computer monitor might just be glowing atoms of terbium.

You can thank terbium for your favorite tunes and computer games, too. A mixture of terbium and some other magnetic elements is used to record music and other information onto compact discs. The CD player or CD-ROM drive then reads the codes from the disc, translating them into sound and pictures!

Element Essentials

TERBIUM (TURB-ee-um)
* Symbol: Tb
* Number: 65
* Mass: 158.93 amu
* Discovery: In 1843, by Carl Gustaf Mosander of Sweden

Fizz, Bubble & Flash!

Rub-a-Bulb

Rub a bulb to scare up some electrons and watch it light up, thanks to terbium!

Materials

- Wool mitten or glove
- Fluorescent bulb

Make It Happen!

In a dark room, quickly rub the wool over the bulb. What do you see?

LUCKY YTTERBY

Terbium is one of four elements named after the village of Ytterby, Sweden. The three others are yttrium (Y), ytterbium (Yb), and erbium (Er). Ytterby is so small that you probably won't find it on a map, but it's near Stockholm, the capital of Sweden. How did a town so small give its name to four elements? They were all eventually discovered in a strange black rock found near Ytterby in 1737.

Another element that starts with the letter T has a city in Colorado named after it. Can you find which element?

CURIOUS MINDS WANT TO KNOW...

Weird! How can the bulb glow without being plugged in? When a fluorescent lightbulb is turned on, electrons smack the inside of the glass tube that's filled with mercury (Hg) gas. This tube is coated with a chemical called a *phosphor* that glows when the electrons hit it. In some bulbs, this coating contains terbium. As you rub the bulb in this experiment, you create *static electricity* (page 50). When you get enough electrons moving around, the bulb starts to shine.

Answer: Tellurium (Te), after which the city of Telluride, Colorado, was named.

ALL IN THE (LANTHANIDES) FAMILY

EUROPIUM

Compounds of **europium** (Eu) glow bright red when they are hit by a beam of electrons, improving the color on TV and computer screens.

Magnets made of **samarium** (Sm) and cobalt are used in headphones and motors. They are much more powerful than iron magnets of the same size.

SAMARIUM

CERIUM

The lenses found in cameras and telescopes are polished with *cerium oxide* (CeO_2) so that they're smooth and shiny.

Erbium (Er) really does make things look rosy. *Erbium oxide* (Er_2O_3) gives glass and ceramics a pretty pink color.

SUSAN'S WELDING SHOPPE

PRASEODYMIUM

Didymium (die-DIM-ee-um) glass contains **praseodymium** (Pr). Welders wear didymium goggles to protect their eyes from the bright torches.

ERBIUM

For the lanthanides not mentioned in this chapter, see the Periodic Table (page 10).

Fizz, Bubble & Flash!

Meet the Actinides!

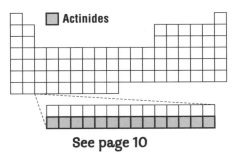

Actinides

See page 10

Watch out for the *actinides* (ACK-tin-ides)! They're a radioactive (pages 9 and 113) family, and only a few of them occur in nature. Named after the first element in the group, actinium, you'll find them below the lanthanides (pages 102 to 116), in the bottom row beneath the main Periodic Table. They really belong up in the last row of the table, between radium (#88) and lawrencium (#103), but they're listed below so that the table isn't so wide.

The first four actinides (actinium through uranium) are found on earth, but all the others were created by scientists. Many of these atoms are so big that they're *unstable*, which means that they don't stay together as that element for very long. Some last only a few seconds, and then — *poof!* — they're gone.

Even though many of the actinides are not naturally found on their own, these elements can still be useful. One of them is probably in your home and could save your life!

Plutonium was very important in exploring the moon.

Pu!

AMERICIUM

In your home, americium helps detect smoke —
An important job, 'cause fire's no joke.
As daylight saving time starts and again when it ends,
Put new batteries in your smoke detector friends.

SNIFF
SNIFF...

SHHHHHH! TOP SECRET!

Element Essentials

AMERICIUM (am-er-REE-shee-um)
* Symbol: Am
* Number: 95
* Mass: 243.06 amu
* Discovery: In 1944, by Glenn T. Seaborg, Ralph A. James, Leon O. Morgan, and Albert Ghiorso of the United States

The discovery of americium was a big secret! In 1944, a group of American scientists working at the University of California in Berkeley made the first atoms of this element. They smashed together atoms of plutonium and some *neutrons* (uncharged atomic particles, page 123) and got a new radioactive element. But World War II was still going on, so this discovery was kept secret. You see, American scientists were trying to build an atomic bomb, and they didn't want others to know that they had the technology to create new elements. So the scientists couldn't tell anyone about their new element until the war ended. They named their discovery americium after America.

Fizz, Bubble & Flash!

I Smell Smoke!

Americium is probably the only artificial element in your home — it's found in smoke detectors. Can a smoke detector detect anything other than smoke? Try this experiment to find out! Just be sure to warn everyone in the house so that they don't think there's a fire!

Materials

- ↻ Hair dryer
- ↻ Smoke detector
- ↻ Bath powder (one that's cornstarch-based) in a container with holes in the lid

Make It Happen!

Important! Ask permission before you try this experiment, and tell all the people in the house what you are doing so no one thinks there's a fire!

1. Turn on the hair dryer and aim it toward the smoke detector. What happens? Does the detector sense heat?

2. Hold the powder container about 6" (15 cm) from the smoke detector. Shake the powder and open the top. Quickly squeeze the container so that some powder "poofs" out. Try this a few times. Does the alarm go off?

My Element, 'Tis of Thee ...

Americium is just one of the elements that is named after a country. Can you find five others in the Periodic Table?

Answer: Francium (Fr), named after France; gallium (Ga), from the Latin word for France; germanium (Ge), named after Germany; polonium (Po), named after Poland; ruthenium (Ru), from the Latin word for Russia.

FIREPROOF YOUR HOME

Is your home fire-safe?

☻ With an adult, inspect your house or apartment. Make sure that there is at least one smoke detector on each floor.

☻ If your detectors are battery-operated, remember to change the batteries at least twice a year. Many people find it easiest to do this when daylight saving time starts and ends.

☻ Do you have fire extinguishers in the kitchen, garage, basement, and other locations where a fire might start? If you do, be sure that they still work. If you don't have any fire extinguishers, visit a hardware or home-improvement store with an adult and buy some.

☻ Does everyone in your family know what to do in case of a fire? Organize a family fire drill.

☻ Call your local fire department, and ask about other fire-safety tips. While you're at it, take a tour of the fire engines and ambulances! Make a poster for your school or other group to show what you've learned.

Curious Minds WANT TO KNOW...

Fires are hot! So why ... does powder set the detector off, but not heat? Not surprisingly, smoke detectors are made to detect smoke! If there's a fire, you smell the smoke before you feel the heat. So smoke is an early warning that you'd better get out of the house!

Smoke is made up of tiny particles of carbon (page 54). They're so lightweight that they can float around in the air. Smoke detectors sense particles of stuff in the air, whatever they're made of — carbon or cornstarch. Here's how it works: The little bit of americium in the detector "charges" nearby air molecules, giving them a little electrical buzz. Pieces of stuff floating through the detector change that charge, causing the alarm to start buzzing.

A word of warning: Smoke detectors are built to protect you from fire *and* from the radioactive americium they contain. So don't ever try to take one apart!

Fizz, Bubble & Flash!

ALL IN THE (ACTINIDES) FAMILY

With the highest atomic mass of all the elements found in nature, **uranium** (U) is the heavyweight champion of the natural elements.

Plutonium (Pu) has been to outer space! Plutonium is radioactive, and the energy it gives off can be used to make batteries that last a long time. Very convenient for powering things that are far away — such as space equipment.

Mendelevium (Md), named for Dmitri Mendeleev, the proud father of the Periodic Table, lasts only a few minutes!

It was here a minute ago!

Scientists at the Nobel Institute in Stockholm, Sweden, thought they had made **nobelium** (No), but were mistaken. A year later, American chemists did create nobelium. The name honors Alfred Nobel (page 50).

I think we made it this time.

No?

Einsteinium (Es) is named in honor of Albert Einstein, one of the most famous scientists who ever lived.

$E = mc^2$... I think...

Fermium (Fm) is named for the Italian physicist Enrico Fermi, who caused the first nuclear chain reaction, in which particles given off by one element crashed into other atoms, shaking loose more particles — producing a huge amount of energy!

For the actinides not mentioned in this chapter, see the Periodic Table (page 10).

Meet the Actinides!

Elements: The Inside Scoop

The Periodic Table (page 10) may help scientists organize all the elements, but it sure is funny-looking. It has steps and skinny parts. Why don't scientists just line up all the elements in nice, neat rows? Keep reading for a strange tale involving chocolate-chip cookies and a chubby twin!

THE CHOCOLATE-CHIP COOKIE CLUES

By the middle of the 1800s, scientists had figured out which elements belonged to which families, but they still didn't understand why the Periodic Table had such a weird shape. They also weren't sure what atoms were actually made of. Were they just little balls made of tiny bits of iron or gold (or whatever the element is)? Or were they something else?

The answer to that puzzle wouldn't come until the early 1900s, when scientists learned to look *inside* atoms so they could see how they're put together. A scientist from England named J. J. Thomson experimented with electricity, and he realized that atoms contained little specks with a negative electric charge, called *electrons*. But the atoms in elements didn't have a charge, so he figured there must also be something positive to balance out the negative electrons. Thomson thought the electrons were just stuck into the positive part of the atom, like chips in a chocolate-chip cookie.

FOILED AGAIN

A few years later, Ernest Rutherford (born in New Zealand, but working in England) proved that this chocolate-chip cookie idea couldn't be right. He shot a powerful beam of helium (He) atoms at a thin piece of gold foil — sort of like throwing a rock at a thin sheet of tissue paper. You'd expect the rock to break through the paper, right? You would be mighty surprised if the rock hit the tissue and bounced back to you!

Well, in Rutherford's experiment, that's exactly what happened. Most of the helium atoms went through, as he expected, but some ricocheted right back! What could this mean? Rutherford realized that each atom in the foil must have a hard center with lots of space around it. Helium atoms that passed through the space around the nucleus kept on going, but the ones that hit the middle bounced back.

We now know that atoms have a hard center called the *nucleus* (NUKE-lee-us). It's filled with the positively charged bits, called *protons*, plus other particles that have no charge, called *neutrons* (they're neutral). The protons and neutrons are stuck together to make the nucleus. Since the proton is positive, and the neutron is neutral, the nucleus has a positive charge.

And what about those electrons? They are really tiny and buzz around the nucleus in fuzzy clouds. (They're so small that they didn't stop any of the helium atoms.)

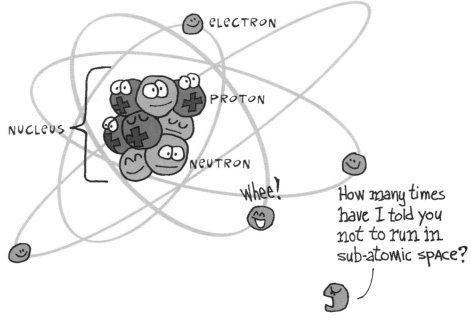

ELECTRON

NUCLEUS

PROTON

NEUTRON

Whee!

How many times have I told you not to run in sub-atomic space?

YOUR BASIC ATOM

ATOMIC FOOTBALL, ANYONE?

So, if all atoms are made up of the same little parts, what makes one atom oxygen, and another one gold? It's the number of protons, called the *atomic number*, that's the key. (Glad we got that straight!) The atomic number is like the player number on the back of a football jersey! But in Atomic Football, #5 isn't the quarterback; it's boron! The number of neutrons and electrons can change, but as long as the atomic number stays the same, it's the same element! So, all atoms with one proton are hydrogen, all oxygens have eight, and all golds, 79.

What about the neutrons? How many are found in each nucleus? You can figure that out from the *atomic mass*. Atoms are really lightweight, so we measure their weight in itty-bitty units called *atomic mass units* (amu). Protons and neutrons each weigh about 1 amu. (Electrons are so lightweight that we just ignore them in figuring out atomic mass.) Hydrogen (atomic number 1) has one proton. Its atomic mass is 1 amu, so there's no neutron in that nucleus. But carbon (atomic number 6, atomic mass 12) has six protons (6 amu) and six neutrons (another 6 amu)!

Can you tell how many neutrons in a calcium atom (atomic number 20, atomic mass 40 amu)?

THE CHUBBY TWIN

Of course, nothing's ever simple in the atomic world. If you look carefully at most elements' atomic masses, you'll see that they're not usually whole numbers like 1, 6, or 19 amu. So what's with chlorine (atomic number 17, atomic mass 35.5 amu)? Some elements can have different combinations of protons and neutrons in their nuclei. These different combinations are called *isotopes* (ICE-oh-topes). Most chlorine atoms have 18 neutrons, for a total mass of 35 amu (17p + 18n). But there are some with 20 neutrons, for a mass of 37 amu (17p +20n). Both of these atoms are chlorine because the number of protons determines what element an atom is. One isotope is just heavier than the other — like twins, with one a little chubbier than the other!

Answer: There are 20 neutrons in a calcium atom.

124

MAKE ROOM FOR ELEMENTS!

OK, now you know about protons and neutrons. But that still doesn't explain the shape of the Periodic Table! That clue is in the electrons, and how they buzz around the nucleus. Electrons in an atom are like people in a building that has several floors. The first floor is just one open space, but the higher floors each have several rooms. When people enter this building, they stand in particular spots, and they have to obey two rules:

1. No one can go to a higher floor, or the next room, until the one before it is filled.

2. There can only be a certain number of people in a room.

So the first person walks into the big room on the first floor and stands there. The second person to enter stands next to her. This room can only hold two people, so now the first floor is full. The third person to enter the building has to climb up to the second floor. The fourth joins him in the same two-person room. There's no more room for anyone else! So the fifth person must go into the other second-floor room. This room can hold six people, so the next five go into this room as well. By this time, there are 10 people in the building, and all the rooms on the first and second floors are full. Where does the next person go? To the third floor, of course, starting the filling process all over again.

Of course, this is a silly way to fill a building, but it's how electrons are arranged in atoms. *Shells* are like the floors, and *orbitals* are like the rooms. Each shell, and the orbitals in it, takes up part of the space around the nucleus. And in each family (or column) of the Periodic Table, *elements in the same column always have the same number of electrons in the highest shell.*

Electrons have a lot to do with how elements act around each other. Sometimes, one atom steals some electrons away from another atom, and that makes a molecule stick together in a kind of tug-of-war over the electrons. In other molecules, the atoms play together nicely, and they share their electrons, just like well-behaved kids!

We're full. Next room please.

Index

More Good Books from Williamson Publishing

Brief Contents

Part IV

Ethnicity and Language   165

Part V

Exceptionality   229

Part VI

School Reform   287

Contents

Part III
Gender   105

Part IV
Ethnicity and Language   165

Preface

Cultural diversity in U.S. schools has deepened considerably during the last two decades. The aging of the mainstream population and the influx of immigrants to the United States since the Immigration Reform Act of 1965 have resulted in a rapid rise in the percentage of ethnic, cultural, language, and religious minorities in the nation's schools. One out of three U.S. students will be an ethnic minority by the turn of the century. The civil rights movement of the 1960s and 1970s and the resulting national legislation have increased cultural diversity within the schools and have also made educators more sensitive to the special educational needs of various groups of students, such as females, the disabled, the poor, and students from various language groups.

Today, most teachers have students in their classrooms from various ethnic, cultural, religious, language, and social-class groups. They are also likely to have one or more exceptional students in their classes. Such students may be handicapped, gifted, or both. Teachers should be aware of the many needs of students from these diverse groups and also sensitive to the special characteristics and needs of female and male students. It is also important for teachers to keep in mind that most students belong to several of these groups. The behavior of each student is influenced by several groups simultaneously.

Although all students belong to several different groups, for many students one group identification is much more important than all the others. Consequently, future and in-service teachers need to study comprehensive multicultural education as conceptualized in *Multicultural Education: Issues and Perspectives* as well as more specialized studies of various cultural and ethnic groups, such as ethnic studies, women's studies, and studies of exceptional groups. *We view comprehensive multicultural education as a supplement to—rather than a replacement for—more specialized studies of ethnic and cultural groups.* A study of comprehensive multicultural education and the specialized study of ethnic and cultural groups are needed for teachers to understand fully the complexity of ethnic, racial, and cultural diversity in the United States and the world.

Multicultural Education: Issues and Perspectives provides future and in-service teachers with the knowledge, insight, and understanding needed to work effectively with students from both gender groups, with exceptional students, and with students from various social-class, religious, ethnic, and cultural groups. A major assumption of *Multicultural Education* is that substantial reforms must be made in schools to give each student from these diverse groups an equal chance to succeed academically. These needed reforms are conceptualized here as an institutional process that involves changes in the total school environment. This process is called multicultural education.

Multicultural Education: Issues and Perspectives is divided into six parts. The three chapters in Part I define the major issues and concepts in multicultural education and discuss the implications of culture for teaching in a pluralistic society. Part I illustrates how such variables as race, gender, class, and exceptionality interact to influence student behavior. Understanding how these variables interact helps us explain and interpret student behavior.

Social class and religion are two of the most important variables that influence student behavior and the educational process. Part II discusses these variables and their effects on education. The influence of social class on the educational process in the United States is increasing as the gap between the haves and the have-nots widens. The strong challenge that some religious groups have made to inquiry teaching in the schools in the last decade is testimony to the continuing influence of religion on education and schooling in the United States.

Part III discusses how educational opportunity differs for female and male students and describes how schools can foster gender equity. Some factors in the schools deny female students an equal chance to succeed. Other factors adversely affect the school experiences of male students, particularly students from certain racial and ethnic groups.

The issues, problems, and opportunities for educating racial, ethnic, and language minorities are treated in the three chapters that constitute Part IV. Ethnicity is the most important identity for an increasing percentage of the nation's students. It has a significant influence on their educational experiences and opportunities.

Public Law 94-142, passed by Congress in 1975, requires that handicapped students be educated in the least restrictive environment. Consequently, most mildly handicapped students are now taught in the regular classroom for part or all of the school day. Part V focuses on exceptionality, describing the issues involved in creating equal educational opportunity for handicapped and gifted students.

The final part of this book, Part VI, focuses on multicultural education as a process of school reform. The two chapters in Part VI discuss some major issues that must be considered in a successful school-reform effort. Using mental-ability tests as a case study, Chapter 15 describes how new paradigms must be embraced and older, restrictive ones eradicated before the schooling process can be substantially reformed. The final chapter describes how parents can and must be involved in order to transform the school and make multicultural education a reality.

The Appendix consists of a list of books for further reading. The Glossary defines some of the key concepts and terms used in the book.

We are grateful to the authors who contributed to *Multicultural Education*. They not only took valuable time from their busy schedules to write original chapters, but they also revised them in response to our comments and suggestions. We would also like to thank our colleagues who reviewed the manuscript, Professors H. Prentice Baptiste, Jr., University of Houston, and Philip T. K. Daniel, Northern Illinois University. We are grateful to Grace

Sheldrick, Wordsworth Associates, for her excellent editorial/production assistance.

We hope you find reading this book as rewarding as we found preparing it and that it helps you accept the challenges and realize the opportunities of multicultural education.

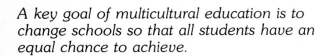

A key goal of multicultural education is to change schools so that all students have an equal chance to achieve.

las toallas de papel

PART I

Issues and Concepts

The chapters in this first part of the book define the major concepts and issues in multicultural education, discuss the meaning of culture, and describe the ways in which variables such as race, class, gender, and exceptionality influence student behavior. A *group* is defined as a collectivity of human beings living together and interacting with their physical, social, and metaphysical environments. *Culture* is a group's program for survival and adaptation to these environments.

Multicultural education is an idea, an educational reform movement, and a process whose major goal is to change the structure of educational institutions so that male and female students, exceptional students, and students who are members of diverse racial, ethnic, and cultural groups will have an equal chance to achieve academically in school. It is necessary to conceptualize the school as a social system to implement multicultural education successfully. Each major variable in the school, such as its culture, power relationships, the curriculum and materials, and the attitudes and beliefs of the staff, must be changed in ways that will allow the school to promote educational equality for students from diverse groups.

To transform the schools, educators must be knowledgeable about the influence of particular groups on student behavior, and they must also be able to understand how influences from several groups interact and intersect to affect student behavior. The chapters in this part of the book describe the nature of culture and groups in the United States as well as the ways in which they interact to influence student behavior.

CHAPTER 1

Multicultural Education: Characteristics and Goals

■ JAMES A. BANKS

The Nature of Multicultural Education

Multicultural education is at least three things: an idea or concept, an educational reform movement, and a process. Multicultural education incorporates the idea that all students—regardless of their gender and social class, and their ethnic, racial, or cultural characteristics—should have an equal opportunity to learn in school. Another important idea in multicultural education is that some students, because of these characteristics, have a better chance to learn in schools as they are currently structured than do students who belong to other groups or have different cultural characteristics.

Some institutional characteristics of schools systematically deny some groups of students equal educational opportunities. For example, in the early grades, girls and boys achieve equally in mathematics and science. However, the achievement test scores of girls fall considerably behind those of boys as children progress through the grades.[1] Girls are less likely than boys to participate in class discussions and to be encouraged by teachers to participate. Girls are more likely than boys to be silent in the classroom. However, not all school practices favor males. As Sadker, Sadker, and Long point out in Chapter 6, boys are more likely to be disciplined than are girls, even when their behavior does not differ from the girls'. They are also more likely than girls to be classified as learning disabled. Ethnic minority males, especially Afro-American males, experience a highly disproportionate rate of disciplinary actions and suspensions in school. Some writers have described the situation of Black males as a ''crisis'' and have called them ''endangered'' in U.S. society.[2]

In the early grades, the academic achievement of such ethnic minorities as Afro-Americans, Hispanics, and American Indians is close to parity with the achievement of White mainstream students. However, the longer these ethnic minority students remain in school, the more their achievement lags behind that of White mainstream students. Social-class status is also strongly related to academic achievement. Persell, in Chapter 4, describes how students from the middle and upper classes are treated more positively in schools than are lower-class students and are given a better chance to learn. Exceptional students, whether they are physically or mentally disabled or gifted and talented, often find that they do not experience equal educational opportunities in the schools. The chapters in Part V of this book describe the problems that such exceptional students experience in schools and suggest ways that teachers and other educators can increase their chances for educational success.

Multicultural education is also a reform movement that is trying to change the schools and other educational institutions so that students from all social-class, gender, racial, and cultural groups will have an equal opportunity to learn. Multicultural education involves changes in the total school or educational environment; it is not limited to curricular changes. The variables in the school environment that multicultural education tries to transform are identified and discussed later in this chapter (see Figure 1.4).

Multicultural education is also a process whose goals will never be fully realized. Educational equality, like liberty and justice, are ideals toward which human beings work but never fully attain. Racism, sexism, and handicapism will exist to some extent no matter how hard we work to eliminate these problems. When prejudice and discrimination are reduced toward one group, they are usually directed toward another group or they take new forms. Because the goals of multicultural education can never be fully attained, we should work continually to increase educational equality for all students.

Multicultural education must be viewed as an ongoing process, and not as something that we "do" and thereby solve the problems that are the targets of multicultural educational reform. When I asked one school administrator what efforts were being taken to implement multicultural education in his school district, he told me that the district had "done" multicultural education last year and that it was now initiating other reforms, such as improving the students' reading scores. This administrator not only misunderstood the nature and scope of multicultural education, but he also did not understand that it could help raise the students' reading scores. A major goal of multicultural education is to improve academic achievement.

Multicultural Education: An International Reform Movement

Since World War II, many immigrant groups have settled in the United Kingdom and in nations on the European continent such as France, the Netherlands, Germany, Sweden, and Switzerland. Some of these immigrants, such as the Asians and West Indians in England and the North Africans and Indochinese in France, have come from former colonies. Many southern and eastern European immigrants have settled in western and northern European nations in search of upward social mobility and other opportunities. Groups such as Italians, Greeks, and Turks have migrated to northern and western European nations in large numbers. Ethnic and immigrant populations have also increased significantly in Australia and Canada since World War II.

Most of the immigrant and ethnic groups in Europe, Australia, and Canada face problems similar to those experienced by ethnic groups in the United States. Groups such as the Jamaicans in England, the Algerians in France, and the aborigines in Australia experience achievement problems in the schools and prejudice and discrimination in both the schools and society at large. The problems that Greeks and Italians experience in Australia indicate that race is not always a factor when ethnic conflict and tension develop.

The United Kingdom, various nations on the European continent, and Australia and Canada have implemented a variety of programs to increase the achievement of ethnic and immigrant students and to help students and teachers develop more positive attitudes toward racial, cultural, ethnic, and language diversity. In the late 1980s, most of the multicultural educational programs in these nations focused on ethnic and language minority groups. Issues related to the rights of women were beginning to develop in educational institutions in these nations. However, the attention focused on women's rights and educational equality for female students was in an early stage of development in most of these nations. The rights of disabled persons were not commonly associated with the multicultural education movement in Europe and Australia in the 1980s.[3]

The Historical Development of Multicultural Education

Multicultural education grew out of the ferment of the civil rights movement of the 1960s. During this decade, Afro-Americans started a quest for their rights that was unprecedented in the United States. A major goal of the civil rights movement of the 1960s was to eliminate discrimination in public accommodations, housing, employment, and education. The consequences of the civil rights movement had a significant influence on educational institutions as ethnic groups—first Afro-Americans and then other groups—demanded that the schools and other educational institutions reform their curricula so that they would reflect their experiences, histories, cultures, and perspectives. Ethnic groups also demanded that the schools hire more Black and Brown teachers and administrators so that their children would have more successful role models. Ethnic groups pushed for community control of schools in their neighborhoods and for the revision of textbooks to make them reflect the diversity of peoples in the United States.

The first responses of schools and educators to the ethnic movements of the 1960s were hurried. Courses and programs were developed without the thought and careful planning needed to make them educationally sound or to institutionalize them within the educational system. Holidays and other special days, ethnic celebrations, and courses that focused on one ethnic group were the dominant characteristics of school reforms related to ethnic and cultural diversity during the 1960s and early 1970s. Grant and Sleeter, in Chapter 3, call this approach *single group studies*. The ethnic studies courses developed and implemented during this period were usually electives and were taken primarily by students who were members of the group that was the subject of the course.

The apparent success of the civil rights movement, plus growing rage and a liberal national atmosphere, stimulated other victimized groups to take actions to eliminate discrimination against them and to demand that the educational system respond to their needs, aspirations, cultures, and histories. The women's rights movement emerged as one of the most significant social reform movements of the late twentieth century. During the 1960s and 1970s, discrimination against women in employment, income, and education was widespread and often blatant. The women's rights movement articulated and publicized how discrimination and institutionalized sexism limited the opportunities of women and adversely affected the nation. The leaders of this movement, such as Betty Friedan and Gloria Steinem, demanded that political, social, economic, and educational institutions act to eliminate sex discrimination and to provide opportunities for women to actualize their talents and realize their ambitions.[4] Major goals of the women's rights movement included equal pay for equal work, the elimination of laws that discriminated against women and made them second-class citizens, the hiring of more women in leadership positions, and greater participation of men in household work and child rearing.

When *feminists* (people who work for the political, social, and economic equality of the sexes) looked at educational institutions, they noted problems similar to those identified by ethnic minority groups. Textbooks and curricula were dominated by men; women were largely invisible. Feminists pointed out that history textbooks were dominated by political and military history—areas in which men had been the main participants.[5] Social and family history and the history of labor and of ordinary people were largely ignored. Feminists pushed for the revision of textbooks to include more history about the important roles of women in the development of the nation and the world. They also demanded that more women be hired for administrative positions in the schools. Although most teachers in the elementary schools were women, most administrators were men.

Other victimized groups, stimulated by the social ferment and the quest for human rights during the 1970s, articulated their grievances and demanded that institutions be reformed so they would face less discrimination and acquire more human rights. Disabled persons, senior citizens, and gay rights advocates were among the groups that organized politically during this period and made significant inroads in changing institutions and laws. Advocates for disabled citizens attained significant legal victories during the 1970s. The Education for All Handicapped Children Act of 1975 (P.L. 94-142), which requires that handicapped students be educated in the least restricted environment and which institutionalized the word *mainstreaming* in education, was perhaps the most significant legal victory of the movement for the rights of the handicapped in education. This act and its teaching implications are discussed in Chapters 12 and 13.

How Multicultural Education Developed

Multicultural education emerged from the diverse courses, programs, and practices that educational institutions devised to respond to the demands, needs, and aspirations of the various groups. Consequently, as Grant and Sleeter point out in Chapter 3, multicultural education is not in actual practice one identifiable course or educational program. Rather, practicing educators use the term *multicultural education* to describe a wide variety of programs and practices related to educational equity, women, ethnic groups, language minorities, low-income groups, and the disabled. In one school district, multicultural education may mean a curriculum that incorporates the experiences of ethnic minority groups; in another, a program may include the experiences of both ethnic groups and women. In a third school district, this term may be used the way it is by me and by other authors, such as Grant and Sleeter and Baptiste,[6] that is, to mean a ***total school reform*** *effort designed to increase educational equity for a range of cultural, ethnic, and economic groups.* This broader and more comprehensive notion of multicultural education is discussed in the last part of this chapter. It differs from the limited concept of multicultural education, in which it is viewed as curriculum reform.

Multicultural Education and Tension among Diverse Groups

The challenge to multicultural educators, in both theory and practice, is how to increase equity for a particular victimized group without further limiting the opportunities of another. Even though the various groups that are targeted for empowerment and equity in multicultural education share many needs and goals, sometimes they perceive their needs as divergent, conflicting, and inconsistent, as some feminist and minority group advocates have in the past.[7] Butler describes this phenomenon in Chapter 8. A major cause of the tension among various victimized groups may be institutionalized practices within society that promote tension, conflict, and divisiveness among them. If this is the case, as some radical scholars suggest,[8] perhaps an important goal of multicultural education should be to help students who are members of particular victimized groups better understand how their fates are tied to those of other powerless groups and the significant benefits that can result from multicultural political coalitions. These coalitions could be cogent vehicles for social change and reform. Jesse Jackson's attempt to form what he called a Rainbow Coalition at the national level in the 1980s had as one of its major goals the formulation of an effective political coalition made up of people from both sex groups and from different racial, ethnic, cultural, and social-class groups.

The Nature of Culture in the United States

The United States, like other Western nation-states such as the United Kingdom, Australia, and Canada, is a multicultural society. The United States consists of a shared core culture as well as many subcultures. In this book, we call the larger shared core culture the *macroculture;* the smaller cultures, which are a part of the core culture, are called *microcultures.* It is important to distinguish the macroculture from the various microcultures because the values, norms, and characteristics of the mainstream (macroculture) are frequently mediated by, as well as interpreted and expressed differently within, various microcultures. These differences often lead to cultural misunderstandings, conflicts, and institutionalized discrimination.

Students who are members of certain cultural, religious, and ethnic groups are sometimes socialized to act and think in certain ways at home but differently at school. One example of this behavior is children who are taught the creation story in the book of Genesis at home but are expected to accept in school the evolutionary explanation of the development and emergence of human beings. A challenge that multicultural education faces is how to help students from diverse groups mediate between their home and community cultures and the school culture. Students should acquire the knowledge, attitudes, and skills needed to function effectively in each cultural setting. They should also be competent to function within and across other microcultures in their society, within the national macroculture, and within the world community.

The Meaning of Culture

In Chapter 2, Bullivant defines *culture* as a group's program for survival in and adaptation to its environment. The cultural program consists of knowledge, concepts, and values shared by group members through systems of communication. Culture also consists of the shared beliefs, symbols, and interpretations within a human group. Most social scientists today view culture as consisting primarily of the symbolic, ideational, and intangible aspects of human societies. The essence of a culture is not its artifacts, tools, or other tangible cultural elements but how the members of the group interpret, use, and perceive them. It is the values, symbols, interpretations, and perspectives that distinguish one people from another in modernized societies; it is not material objects and other tangible aspects of human societies.[9] People within a culture usually interpret the meanings of symbols, artifacts, and behaviors in the same or in similar ways.

Identifying and Describing the
U.S. Core Culture

The United States, like other nation-states, has a shared set of values, ideations, and symbols that constitute the core or overarching culture. This culture is shared to some extent by all the diverse cultural and ethnic groups that make up the nation-state. It is difficult to identify and describe the overarching culture in the United States because it is such a diverse and complex nation. It is easier to identify the core culture within an isolated premodern society, such as the Maoris before the Europeans came to New Zealand, than within highly pluralistic, modernized societies such as the United States, Canada, and Australia.[10]

When trying to identify the distinguishing characteristics of U.S. culture, one should realize that the political institutions within the United States, which reflect some of the nation's core values, were heavily influenced by the British. U.S. political ideals and institutions were also influenced by Native-American political institutions and practices, especially those related to making group decisions, such as in the League of the Iroquois.

Equality

A key component in the U.S. core culture is the idea, expressed in the Declaration of Independence in 1776, that ''all men are created equal, that they are endowed by their Creator with certain unalienable rights, that among these are life, liberty, and the pursuit of happiness.''[11] When this idea was expressed by the nation's founding fathers in 1776, it was considered radical. A common belief in the eighteenth century was that human beings were not born with equal rights; that some had few rights and others, such as kings, had divine rights given by God. When considering the idea that ''all men are created equal'' is a key component of U.S. culture, one should remember to distinguish between a nation's ideals and its actual practices, as well as between the meaning of the idea when it was expressed in 1776 and its meaning today. When the nation's founding fathers expressed this idea in 1776, their conception of men was limited to White males who owned property.[12] White men without property, White women, and all Blacks and Indians were not included in their notion of people who were equal or who had ''certain unalienable rights.''

Although the idea of equality expressed by the founding fathers in 1776 had a very limited meaning at that time, it has proven to be a powerful and important idea in the quest for human rights in the United States. Throughout the nation's history since 1776, victimized and excluded groups such as women, Blacks, Indians, and other cultural and ethnic groups have used this cogent idea to justify and defend the extension of human rights to them and to end institutional discrimination, such as sexism, racism, and handicapism. As a result, human rights have gradually been extended to various groups throughout U.S. history. The extension of these rights has been neither constant nor linear. Rather, periods of extension of rights have often been followed by periods of retrenchment and conservatism. Schlesinger calls these patterns ''cycles of American history.''[13] The United States is still a long way from realizing the ideals expressed in the Declaration of Independence in 1776. However, these ideals remain an important part of U.S. culture and are still used by victimized groups to justify their struggles for human rights and equality.

Individualism and Individual Opportunity

Two other important ideas in the common overarching U.S. culture are individualism and individual social mobility.[14] Individualism as an ideal is extreme in the U.S. core culture. Individual success is more important than commitment to family, community, and nation-state. An individual is expected to experience success by his or her sole efforts. Many Americans believe that a person can go from rags to riches within a generation and that every American boy can, but not necessarily will, become president.

Individuals are expected to experience success by hard work and to pull themselves up by their bootstraps, as the saying goes. This idea was epitomized by fictional characters such as Ragged Dick, one of the heroes created by the popular writer Horatio Alger. Ragged Dick attained success by valiantly overcoming poverty and adversity. A related belief is that if you do not succeed, it is because of your own shortcomings, such as being lazy or unambitious; failure is consequently your own fault. These beliefs are taught in the schools with success stories and myths about such U.S. heroes as George Washington, Thomas Jefferson, and Abraham Lincoln. The beliefs about individualism in American culture are related to the Protestant work ethic. This is the belief that hard work by the individual is morally good and that laziness is sinful. This belief is a legacy of the British Puritan settlers in colonial New England. It has had a powerful and significant influence on U.S. culture.

Groups and Individual Opportunity

The belief in individual opportunity has proven tenacious in U.S. society. It remains strong in American culture despite the fact that individuals' chances for upward social, economic, and educational mobility in the United States are highly related to the social-class, ethnic, gender, and other ascribed groups to which they belong. Social scientists have amply documented the extent of social-class stratification in the United States and the ways in which people's chances in life are affected by the groups to which they belong.[15] Jencks and his associates have documented extensively the extent to which educational opportunity and life chances are related to social class.[16] The chapters in this book on social class, gender, and ethnicity belie the notion that individual opportunity is a dominant characteristic of U.S. society. Yet the belief in individual opportunity remains strong in the United States.

Individualism and Groupism

Although the groups to which people belong have a cogent influence on their life chances in the United States, Americans—particularly those in the main-stream—are highly individualistic in their value orientations and behavior. The strength of the nuclear family reinforces individualism in U.S. culture. One result of the strong individualism is that married children usually expect their older parents to live independently or in homes for senior citizens rather than with them.

The strong individualism in U.S. culture contrasts sharply with the groupism and group commitment found in Asian nations, such as China and Japan.[17] Individualism is viewed rather negatively in these societies. One is expected to be committed first to the family and group and then to oneself. Some U.S. social scientists, such as Lash and Bellah and Bellah's associates, lament the extent of individualism in U.S. society.[18] They believe it is harmful to the common national culture. Some observers believe that groupism is too strong in China and Japan and that individualism should be more valued in those nations. Perhaps modernized, pluralistic nation-states can best benefit from a balance between individualism and groupism, with neither characteristic dominating.

Expansionism and Manifest Destiny

Other overarching U.S. values that social scientists have identified include the desire to conquer or exploit the natural environment, materialism and consumption, and the belief in the nation's inherent superiority. These beliefs justified Manifest Destiny and U.S. expansion to the west and into other nations and the annexation of one-third of Mexico's territory in 1848. These observations, which reveal the less positive side of U.S. national values, have been developed by social scientists interested in understanding the complex nature of American society.[19]

Greenbaum believes that distance is also a key value in U.S. society. He uses this word to describe the formal nature of bureaucratic institutions, as well as unfriendliness and detachment in social relationships.[20] Greenbaum argues that the Anglo-Saxon Protestants, the dominant cultural group in U.S. society, have often used distance in its relationships with other ethnic and cultural groups to keep them confined to their social-class status and group.

In his discussion of the nature of values in U.S. society, Myrdal contends that a major ethical inconsistency exists in U.S. society. He calls this inconsistency "the American dilemma."[21] He states that American Creed values, such as equality and human dignity, exist in U.S. society as ideals. However, they exist alongside the institutionalized discriminatory treatment of Blacks and other ethnic and cultural groups in U.S. society. This variance creates a dilemma in the American mind because Americans try to reconcile their democratic ideals with their treatment of victimized groups. Myrdal states that this dilemma has been an important factor that has enabled ethnic groups to fight discrimination effectively. In their efforts to resolve their dilemma when the inconsistencies between their ideals and actions are pointed out to them by human-rights advocates, Americans, according to Myrdal, often support the elimination of practices that are inconsistent with their democratic ideals or the American Creed. Some writers have refuted Myrdal's hypothesis and contend that most Americans do not experience such a dilemma.[22]

Microcultures in the United States

A nation as culturally diverse as the United States consists of a common overarching culture, as well as of a series of microcultures (see Figure 1.1). These microcultures share most of the core values of the nation-state, but these values are often mediated by the various microcultures and are interpreted differently within them. Microcultures sometimes have values that are somewhat alien to the national core culture. Also, some of the core national values and behaviors may seem somewhat alien in certain microcultures or may take on different forms.

The strong belief in individuality and individualism that exists within the national macroculture is often much less endorsed by some ethnic minority communities and is somewhat alien within them. Afro-Americans and Hispanic Americans who have not experienced high levels of cultural assimilation into the mainstream culture are much more group-oriented than are mainstream Americans. Schools in the United States are highly individualistic in their learning and teaching styles, evaluation procedures, and norms. Many students, particularly Afro-Americans, Hispanics, and American Indians, are group-oriented.[23] These students experience problems in the highly individualistic learning environment of the school. Teachers can enhance the learning

FIGURE 1.1
Microcultures and the National Macroculture The shaded area represents the national macroculture. A, B, C, and D represent microcultures that consist of unique institutions, values, and cultural elements that are nonuniversalized and are shared primarily by members of specific cultural groups. A major goal of the school should be to help students acquire the knowledge, skills, and attitudes needed to function effectively within the national macroculture, their own microcultures, and within and across other microcultures.

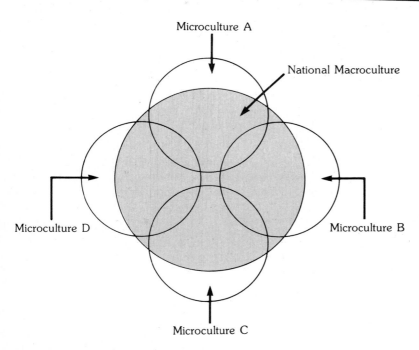

Microculture A

National Macroculture

Microculture D

Microculture B

Microculture C

Reprinted with permission from James A. Banks, *Multiethnic Education: Theory and Practice*, 2nd ed. (Boston: Allyn and Bacon, 1988), Figure 5.1, p. 75.

opportunities of these students, who are also called field-dependent or field-sensitive, by using cooperative teaching strategies that have been developed and field-tested by researchers such as Slavin and Cohen.[24]

Some emerging theories indicate that female students may have preferred ways of knowing, thinking, and learning that differ to some extent from those most often preferred by men.[25] Maher describes the dominant inquiry model used in social science as male constructed and dominated. She contends that it strives for objectivity. "Personal feelings, biases, and prejudices are considered inevitable limitations."[26] Feminist pedagogy is based on different assumptions about the nature of knowledge and results in a different teaching method. According to Maher, feminist pedagogy enhances the learning of females and deepens the insight of males:

> All human experiences are "gendered" or centrally shaped by our being
> either men or women. These experiences are specific and various, not
> generalizable to any single set of universals for interpreting human behavior.
> Therefore, goals, problems in reaching them, and valid solutions to those
> problems all vary; they cannot be reduced or resolved into one best
> answer.[27]

In Chapter 7, Tetreault describes feminist pedagogy techniques she uses to
motivate students and to enhance their understandings.

After completing a major research study on women's ways of knowing,
Belenky and her colleagues concluded that conceptions of knowledge and truth
in the core culture and in educational institutions "have been shaped throughout
history by the male-dominated majority culture. Drawing on their own perspectives and visions, men have constructed the prevailing theories, written history,
and set values that have become the guiding principles for men and women
alike."[28]

These researchers also found an inconsistency between the kind of
knowledge most appealing to women and the kind that was emphasized in most
educational institutions. Most of the women interviewed in their study considered personalized knowledge and knowledge that resulted from first-hand
observation most appealing. However, most educational institutions emphasize
abstract, "out-of-context" knowledge.[29] Ramírez and Castañeda found that
Mexican-American students who were socialized within traditional cultures also
considered personalized and humanized knowledge more appealing than
abstract knowledge.[30] They also responded positively to knowledge that was
presented in a humanized or story format.

Research by Gilligan provides some clues that help us better understand
the findings by Belenky and her colleagues about the kind of knowledge women
find most appealing. Gilligan describes caring, interconnection, and sensitivity to
the needs of other people as dominant values among women and the female
microculture in the United States.[31] By contrast, she found that the values of
men were more characterized by separation and individualism.

A major goal of multicultural education is to change teaching and learning
approaches so that students of both genders and from diverse cultural and
ethnic groups will have equal opportunities to learn in educational institutions.
This goal suggests that major changes ought to be made in the ways that
educational programs are conceptualized, organized, and taught. Educational
approaches need to be transformed.

In her research on identifying and labeling mentally retarded students,
Mercer found that a disproportionate number of Black and Hispanic students
were labeled "mentally retarded" because the testing procedures used in
intelligence tests "reflect the abilities and skills valued by the American core
culture,"[32] which Mercer describes as predominantly White, Anglo-Saxon, and
middle and upper class. She also points out that measures of general intelligence
consist primarily of items related to verbal skills and knowledge. Most Black and
Hispanic students are socialized within microcultures that differ in significant
ways from the U.S. core culture. These students often have not had an equal
opportunity to learn the things that are measured in mental ability tests.
Consequently, a disproportionate percentage of Black and Hispanic students are
labeled as mentally retarded and are placed in classes for slow learners. Mental

retardation, as Mercer points out, is a *socially determined* status. When students are placed in classes for the mentally retarded, the self-fulfilling prophecy develops. Students begin to act and think as though they are mentally retarded.

Groups and Group Identification

Thus far, I have discussed the various microcultures that make up U.S. society. Individuals learn the values, symbols, and other components of their culture from their social group. The group is the social system that carries a culture. As Bullivant points out in Chapter 2, "people belong to, live in and are members of social groups; they are not members of culture." A group is a collectivity of persons who share an identity, a feeling of unity. A group is also a social system that has a social structure of interrelated roles.[33] The group's program for survival, values, ideations, and shared symbols constitutes its culture.

The study of groups is the major focus in sociology. Sociologists believe that the group has a strong influence on the behavior of individuals, that behavior is shaped by group norms, and that the group equips individuals with the behavior patterns they need to adapt to their physical, social, and meta-physical environments (see Chapter 2). Sociologists also assume that groups have independent characteristics; they are more than aggregates of individuals. Groups possess a continuity that transcends the lives of individuals.

Sociologists also assume that knowledge about groups to which an individual belongs provides important clues to and explanations for the individual's behavior. Goodman and Marx write, "Such factors as shared religion, nationality, age, sex, marital status, and education have proved to be important determinants of what people believe, feel, and do."[34] Although membership in a gender, racial, ethnic, social-class, or religious group can provide us with important clues about individuals' behavior, it cannot enable us to predict behavior. Knowing one's group affiliation can enable us to state that a certain type of behavior is probable. *Membership in a particular group does not determine behavior but makes certain types of behavior more probable.*

There are several important reasons that knowledge of group characteristics and modalities can enable us to predict the probability of an individual's behavior but not the precise behavior. This is, in part, because each individual belongs to several groups at the same time (see Figure 1.2). An individual may be White, Catholic, female, and middle class, all at the same time. She might have a strong identification with one of these groups and a very weak or almost nonexistent identification with another. A person can be a member of a particular group, such as the Catholic church, and have a weak identification with the group and a weak commitment to the tenets of the Catholic faith. Religious identification might be another individual's strongest group identification. Identification and attachments to different groups may also conflict. A woman who has a strong Catholic identification but is also a feminist might find it difficult to reconcile her beliefs about equality for women with some positions of the Catholic church, such as its prohibiting women from becoming ordained priests.

The more we know about a student's level of identification with a particular group and the extent to which socialization has taken place within that

FIGURE 1.2
Multiple Group Memberships An individual belongs to several different groups at the same time. This figure shows the major groups discussed in this book.

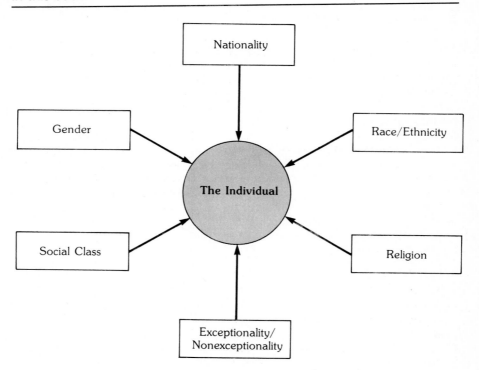

group, the more accurately we can predict, explain, and understand the student's behavior in the classroom. A knowledge of the importance of a group to a student at a particular time of life and within a particular social context will also help us understand the student's behavior. Ethnic identity may become more important to a person who becomes a part of an ethnic minority when he or she previously belonged to the majority. Many Whites who have moved from the U.S. mainland to Hawaii have commented on how their sense of ethnic identity increased and they began to feel marginalized. Group identity may also increase when the group feels threatened, when a social movement arises to promote its rights, or when the group attempts to revitalize its culture.

The Teaching Implications of Group Identification
What are the implications of group membership and group identity for teaching? As you read the chapters in this book that describe the characteristics of the two gender groups and of social class, racial, ethnic, religious, and disabled groups, bear in mind that individuals within these groups manifest these behaviors to various degrees. *Also remember that individual students are members of several of these groups at the same time.* Above I describe the core U.S. culture as having highly individualistic values and beliefs. However, research by Gilligan

indicates that the values of women, as compared with those of men, are more often characterized by caring, interconnection, and sensitivity to the needs of others.[35] This observation indicates how core values within the macroculture are often mediated by microcultures within various gender, ethnic, and cultural groups.

As stated above, researchers have found that some ethnic minority students such as Afro-Americans and Mexican Americans often have field-sensitive learning styles and therefore prefer more personalized learning approaches.[36] Think about what this means. This research describes a group characteristic of these students and not the behavior of a particular Black or Mexican-American child. It suggests that there is a higher probability that these students will have field-sensitive learning styles than will middle-class Anglo-American students. However, students within all ethnic, racial, and social-class groups have different learning styles. Those groups influence students' behavior, such as their learning style, interactively, because they are members of several groups at the same time. *Knowledge of the characteristics of groups to which students belong, about the importance of each of these groups to them, and of the extent to which individuals have been socialized within each group will give the teacher important clues to students' behavior.*

The Interaction of Race, Class, and Gender

When using our knowledge of groups to understand student behavior, we should also consider the ways that such variables as class, race, and gender interact and intersect to influence student behavior. Middle-class and more highly assimilated Mexican-American students tend to be less field-independent than do lower-class and less assimilated Mexican-American students. Black students tend to be more field-dependent (group-oriented) than are White students; females tend to be more field-dependent than are male students. Therefore, it can be hypothesized that Black females would be the most field-dependent when compared to Black and White males and White females. This finding was made by Perney.[37]

Unfortunately, the researcher did not include a social-class measure in the study. After doing a comprehensive review of research on the ways that race, class, and gender influence student behavior in education, Grant and Sleeter concluded that we must look at the ways these variables interact in order to fully understand student behavior.[38]

Figure 1.3 illustrates how the major groups discussed in this book—*gender, race or ethnicity, social class, religion, and exceptionality*—influence student behavior, both singly and interactively. The figure also shows that other variables, such as geographic region and age, also influence an individual's behavior. The ways these variables influence selected student behaviors are described in Table 1.1.

The Social Construction of Categories

The major variables and categories discussed in this book, such as gender, race, ethnicity, class, and exceptionality, are social categories.[39] The criteria for

FIGURE 1.3
The Intersection of Variables The major variables of gender, race or ethnicity, social class, religion, and exceptionality influence student behavior, both singly and interactively. Other variables, such as region and age, also influence student behavior.

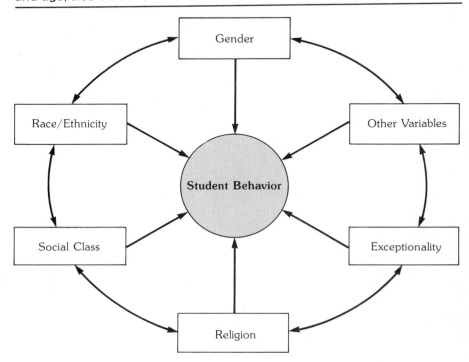

TABLE 1.1
Singular and Combined Effects of Variables

Student Behavior	Gender Effects	Race/Ethnicity Effects	Social-Class Effects	Religious Effects	Combined Effects
Learning Styles (Field Independent/Field Dependent)	X[a]	X			X
Internality/Externality			X		
Fear of Success	X	X			?
Self-Esteem	X	X			?
Individual vs. Group Orientation	X	X	X		?

[a] An X indicates that the variable influences the student behavior described in the far-left column. An X in the far-right column means that research indicates that two or more variables combine to influence the described behavior. A question mark indicates that the research is unclear about the combined effects of the variables.

whether an individual belongs to one of these categories are determined by human beings and consequently are socially constructed. Religion is also a social category. Religious institutions, symbols, and artifacts are created by human beings to satisfy their metaphysical needs.

These categories are usually related to the physical characteristics of individuals. In some cases, as when they have severe or obvious physical disabilities, the relationship between the labels given to individuals and their physical characteristics is direct and would be made in almost any culture or social system. The relationship between categories that are used to classify individuals and their physical characteristics, however, is usually indirect and complex. Even though one's sex is determined primarily by physical characteristics (such as genitalia, chromosome patterns, etc.,), gender is a social construction created and shaped by the society in which individuals and groups function.

Gender

Gender consists of the socially and psychologically appropriate behavior for males and females sanctioned and expected within a society. Gender role expectations vary across cultures and at different times in a society, and within microcultures in the same society. Traditionally, normative behavior for males and females has varied among mainstream Americans, Afro-Americans, Native Americans, and Hispanic Americans. Gender role expectations also vary somewhat across social classes within the same society. In the White mainstream society in the 1940s and 1950s, upper-middle-class women often received negative sanctions when they worked outside the home, whereas women in working-class families were frequently expected to become wage earners.

Race

Race is a socially determined category that is related to physical characteristics in a complex way. Two individuals with nearly identical physical characteristics, or phenotypes, can be classified as members of different races in two different societies. In the United States, where racial categories are well defined and highly inflexible, an individual with any acknowledged or publicly known African ancestry is considered Black. One who looks completely Caucasian but who acknowledges some African ancestry is classified as Black. Such an individual would be considered White in Puerto Rico. In Puerto Rico, hair texture, social status, and degree of eminence in the community are often as important as—if not more important than—physical characteristics in determining an individual's racial group or category. There is a saying in Puerto Rico that "money lightens," which means that upward social mobility considerably enhances an individual's opportunity to be classified as White. There is a strong relationship between race and social class in Puerto Rico and in most other Caribbean and Latin American nations.

Our discussion of race as a social category indicates that the criteria for determining the characteristics of a particular race vary across cultures, that an individual considered Black in one society may be considered White in another, and that racial categories reflect the social, economic, and political characteristics of a society.

Social Class

Social scientists find it difficult to agree on criteria for determining social class. The problem is complicated by the fact that societies are constantly in the throes of change. During the 1950s, social scientists often attributed characteristics to the lower class that are found in the middle class today, such as single-parent and female-headed households, high divorce rates, and substance abuse. Today, these characteristics are no longer rare among the middle class, even though their frequency is still higher among lower-class families. Variables such as income, education, occupation, life-style, and values are among the most frequently used indices to determine social-class status in the United States.[40] However, there is considerable disagreement among social scientists about which variables are the most important in determining the social-class status of an individual or family.

Social-class criteria also vary somewhat among various ethnic and racial groups in the United States. Teachers, preachers, and other service professionals were upper class in many rural Black communities in the South in the 1950s and 1960s but were considered middle class by mainstream White society. The systems of social stratification that exist in the mainstream society and in various microcultures are not necessarily identical.

Exceptionality

Exceptionality is also a social category. Whether a person is considered handicapped or gifted is determined by criteria developed by society. As Shaver and Curtis point out, disabilities are not necessarily handicaps, and the two should be distinguished. They write, "A disability or combination of disabilities becomes a handicap only when the condition limits or impedes the person's ability to function normally."[41] A person with a particular disability, such as having one arm, might have a successful college career, experience no barriers to his achievements in college, and graduate with honors. However, he may find that when he tries to enter the job market, his opportunities are severely limited because potential employers view him as unable to perform well in some situations in which, in fact, he could perform effectively.[42] This individual has a disability but was handicapped in one situation—the job market—but not in another—his university.

Mercer has extensively studied the social *process* by which individuals become labeled retarded. She points out that even though their physical characteristics may increase their chance of being labeled retarded, the two are not perfectly correlated. She writes:

> There are many alternative statuses to which persons with comparable
> biological equipment may be assigned. . . . Mental retardation is not a
> characteristic of the individual, nor a meaning inherent in behavior, but a
> socially determined status, which he may occupy in some social systems and

not in others. It follows that a person may be mentally retarded in one system and not mentally retarded in another. He may change his role by changing his social group.[43]

The highly disproportionate number of Blacks, Hispanics, and particularly males classified as learning disabled by the school indicates the extent to which exceptionality is a social category. Mercer found that the school labeled more people mentally retarded than did any other institution.[44] Many Black and Hispanic students who are labeled mentally retarded function normally and are considered normal in their homes and communities. Boys are more often classified as mentally retarded than are girls. The school, as Mercer and other researchers have pointed out, uses criteria to determine the mental ability of ethnic minorities that conflict with their home and community cultures. Some students in all ethnic and cultural groups are mentally retarded and deserve special instruction, programs, and services, as the authors in Part IV of this book suggest. However, the percentage of ethnic minority students in these programs is too high. The percentage of students in each ethnic group labeled *mentally retarded* should be about the same as the total percentage of that group in school.

Giftedness is also a social category. Important results of the socially constructed nature of giftedness are the considerable disagreement among experts about how the concept should be defined and the often inconsistent views about how to identify gifted students.[45] The highly disproportionate percentage of middle- and upper-middle-class mainstream students who are categorized as gifted compared to lower-class and ethnic minorities such as Blacks, Hispanics, and American Indians is also evidence of the social origin of the category. Many students who are classified as gifted do have special talents and abilities, and they do need special instruction to help them actualize them.

In Chapter 14, Subotnik describes the characteristics of these students and ways in which their needs can be met. However, some students who are classified as gifted by school districts merely have parents with the knowledge, political skills, and power to force the school to classify their children as gifted, which will provide them with special instruction and educational enrichment. In some racially mixed school districts, the gifted programs are made up primarily of middle-class and upper-middle-class mainstream students.

Schools should try to satisfy the needs of students with special gifts; however, they should also make sure that students from all social-class, cultural, and ethnic groups have an equal opportunity to participate in programs for academically and creatively talented students. If schools or districts do not have a population in their gifted programs that represents their various cultural and ethnic groups, steps should be taken to examine the criteria used to identify gifted students and to develop procedures to correct the disproportion. Both excellence and equality should be major goals of education.

The Goals of Multicultural Education

I have discussed the goals of multicultural education throughout this chapter, *the major goal being to transform the school so that male and female students, exceptional students, as well as students from diverse cultural, social-class, racial, and ethnic groups will experience an equal opportunity to learn in school.* Thus, an important goal of multicultural education is to increase the academic achievement of all students. A major assumption of multicultural education is that educators can increase the academic achievement of students from diverse groups if they transform the total school environment and make it more consistent with their cultures, behaviors, and learning styles.

Another major goal of multicultural education is to help all students develop more positive attitudes toward different cultural, racial, ethnic, and religious groups. Researchers have documented the negative attitudes, beliefs, and stereotypes that students have about various groups.[46] Students acquire their attitudes about various groups from people among whom they are socialized and from the mass media. Cortés calls these institutions the "societal curriculum."[47] Children enter kindergarten with many misconceptions, negative beliefs, and stereotypes about people. If the school does not help students develop more positive attitudes about various groups, they will become even more negative as they grow older. Consequently, the school should take steps to help students develop more democratic cultural, ethnic, and racial attitudes, beginning in the earliest grades. Such prejudice-reduction strategies should be consistent, ongoing, and an integral part of the school curriculum.[48] They should not be one-shot interventions that are reserved for special days or for celebrations such as Women's History Week or Black History Month.

Negative misconceptions about groups harm both members of those groups and people outside them. Many women, ethnic minorities, and disabled persons have internalized the negative stereotypes of themselves perpetuated by the larger society. Consequently, they often develop a low self-concept and other characteristics that prevent them from realizing their potentials. Researchers have described how fear of success in women students often prevents them from experiencing high levels of academic success, particularly in such areas as science and mathematics,[49] in which many women tend to have less confidence. Teachers often reinforce this attitude by giving boys more positive feedback in these courses than they give girls. Negative views of groups also harm individuals outside the groups because they develop a false and misleading sense of superiority.

Multicultural education should help empower students from victimized groups and help them develop confidence in their ability to succeed academically and to influence social, political, and economic institutions. Women, ethnic minorities, and people from other victimized groups often lack a sense of control over their environments, are external in orientation, and lack a sense of political and social efficacy. In his massive study in 1966, Coleman found that a sense of control over one's environment is one of the most important correlates of academic success.[50] Schools can help members of marginalized groups become empowered by providing them with opportunities to experience success, by recognizing and giving visibility to their cultures throughout the school, and by teaching them decision-making and social action skills. I describe these skills and ways to teach them in Chapter 10.

Multicultural education should help students to develop perspective-taking skills and to consider the perspectives of different groups. Most of the concepts, events, and issues taught in the school are from the perspective of mainstream middle- and upper-class White males. Students are rarely given the opportunity to view them from the perspectives of women, disabled persons, lower-class people, and ethnic minority groups. Consequently, students gain only a limited conception of the development of the nation and the world. When students are able to view the world from the perspectives of different groups, their views of reality are broadened and they gain important insights into their own behavior. We gain a better view of ourselves when we look at ourselves from the perspectives of other cultures. Students can view a concept such as institutionalized discrimination from the perspectives of several groups and examine how it is manifested in various ways as sexism, racism, and handicapism.

The School as a Social System

To implement multicultural education successfully, we must think of the school as a social system in which all of its major variables are closely interrelated. Thinking of the school as a social system suggests that we must formulate and initiate a change strategy that reforms the total school environment to implement multicultural education. The major school variables that must be reformed are presented in Figure 1.4.

Reforming any one of the variables in Figure 1.4, such as the formalized curriculum or curricular materials, is necessary but not sufficient. Multicultural and sensitive teaching materials are ineffective in the hands of teachers who have negative attitudes toward different cultural groups. Such teachers are rarely likely to use multicultural materials or to use them detrimentally. Thus, helping teachers and other members of the school staff gain knowledge about cultural groups and democratic attitudes and values is essential when implementing multicultural programs.

To implement multicultural education in a school, we must reform its power relationships, the verbal interaction between teachers and students, the culture of the school, the curriculum, extracurricular activities, attitudes toward minority languages, the testing program, and grouping practices. The institutional norms, social structures, cause-belief statements, values, and goals of the school must be transformed and reconstructed.

Major attention should be focused on the school's hidden curriculum and its implicit norms and values. A school has both a manifest and a hidden curriculum. The manifest curriculum consists of such factors as guides, textbooks, bulletin boards, and lesson plans. These aspects of the school environment are important and must be reformed to create a school culture that promotes positive attitudes toward diverse cultural groups and helps students from these groups experience academic success. However, the school's hidden or latent curriculum is often more cogent than its manifest or overt curriculum. The latent curriculum has been defined as the one that no teacher explicitly teaches but that all students learn. It is that powerful part of the school culture that communicates to students the school's attitudes toward a range of issues and problems, including how the school views them as human beings and its attitudes toward males, females, exceptional students, and students from various religious, cultural, racial, and ethnic groups.

FIGURE 1.4
The School as a Social System   The total school environment is a system consisting of a number of major identifiable variables and factors, such as a school culture, school policy and politics, and the formalized curriculum and course of study. Any of these factors may be the focus of initial school reform, but changes must take place in each of them to create and sustain an effective multicultural school environment.

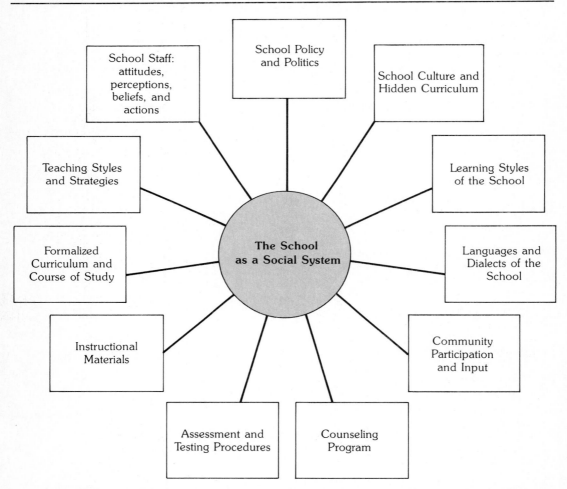

Adapted with permission from James A. Banks (Ed.), *Education in the 80s: Multiethnic Education* (Washington, D.C.: National Education Association, 1981), Figure 2, p. 22.

When formulating plans for multicultural education, educators should conceptualize the school as a microculture that has norms, values, statuses, and goals like other social systems. The school has a dominant culture and a variety of microcultures. Almost all classrooms in the United States are multicultural because White students, as well as Black and Brown students, are socialized within diverse cultures. Teachers also come from many different groups. Many teachers were socialized in cultures other than the Anglo mainstream, although these may be forgotten and repressed. Teachers can get in touch with their own cultures and use the perspectives and insights they acquired as vehicles for helping them relate to and understand the cultures of their students.

The school should be a cultural environment in which acculturation takes place; teachers and students should assimilate some of the views, perspectives, and ethos of each other as they interact. Teachers and students will be enriched by this process, and the academic achievement of students from diverse groups will be enhanced because their perspectives will be legitimized in the school. Both teachers and students will be enriched by this process of cultural sharing and interaction.

Summary

Multicultural education is an idea stating that all students, regardless of the groups to which they belong, such as those related to gender, ethnicity, race, culture, social class, religion, or exceptionality, should experience educational equality in the schools. Some students, because of their particular characteristics, have a better chance to succeed in school as it is currently structured than have students from other groups. Multicultural education is also a reform movement designed to bring about a transformation of the school so that students from both genders and from diverse cultural and ethnic groups will have an equal chance to experience school success. Multicultural education views the school as a social system that consists of highly interrelated parts and variables. Therefore, to transform the school to bring about educational equality, all the major components of the school must be substantially changed. A focus on any one variable in the school, such as the formalized curriculum, will not implement multicultural education.

Multicultural education is a continuing process because the idealized goals it tries to actualize—such as educational equality and the eradication of all forms of discrimination—can never be fully achieved in a human society. Multicultural education, which was born during the social protest of the 1960s and 1970s, is an international movement that exists in various nations on the European continent and in Australia, the United Kingdom, and Canada. A major goal of multicultural education is to help students to develop the knowledge, attitudes, and skills needed to function within their own microcultures, the U.S. macroculture, other microcultures, and within the global community.

Questions and Activities

1. What are the three components or elements of multicultural education?

2. How does the author of this chapter define *multicultural education?*

3. Find other definitions of multicultural education in several books listed under the category "Issues and Concepts" in the Appendix. How are the definitions of multicultural education in these books alike and different from the one presented in this chapter?

4. How is multicultural education in the United States and in nations such as Canada, Australia, and the United Kingdom alike and different?

5. In what ways did the civil rights and women's rights movements of the 1960s and 1970s influence the development of multicultural education?

6. Ask several teachers and other practicing educators to give you their views and definitions of multicultural education. What generalizations can you make about their responses?

7. Visit a local school and, by observing several classes as well as by interviewing several teachers and the principal, describe what curricular and other practices related to multicultural education have been implemented in the school. Share your report with your classmates or workshop colleagues.

8. What major tensions exist among groups such as various racial and ethnic groups and between feminists and ethnic minorities? Can multicultural education help reduce such tensions? If so, how?

9. What is a macroculture? A microculture?

10. How is *culture* defined? What are the most important components of culture in a modernized society?

11. List and define several core or overarching values and characteristics that make up the macroculture in the United States. To what extent are these values and characteristics consistent with practices in U.S. society? To what extent are they ideals that are inconsistent with realities in U.S. society?

12. What problems result when ideals in U.S. society are taught to students as if they were realities? Give examples of this.

13. How is individualism viewed differently in the United States and in nations such as China and Japan? Why? What are the behavioral consequences of these varying notions of individualism?

14. What is the American dilemma defined by Myrdal? To what extent is this concept an accurate description of values in U.S. society? Explain.

15. How do the preferred ways of learning and knowing among women and ethnic minorities often influence their experiences in the schools as they are currently structured? In what ways can school reform help make the school environment more consistent with the learning and cognitive styles of women and ethnic minorities?

16. In what ways does the process of identifying the labeling mentally retarded students discriminate against ethnic minorities such as Blacks and Hispanics?

17. What is a group? What is the relationship between a group and a culture?

18. In what ways can the characteristics of a group help us understand an individual's behavior? In what ways are group characteristics limited in explaining an individual's behavior?

19. How do such variables as race, class, and gender interact to influence the behavior of students? Give examples to support your response.

20. What is meant by the "social construction of categories"? In what ways are concepts such as gender, race, social class, and exceptionality social categories?

21. List several major goals for multicultural education. How can these goals be attained by school reform efforts?

Notes

1. Myra P. Sadker and David M. Sadker, *Sex Equity Handbook for Schools* (New York: Longman, 1982).

2. "The Crisis of the Black Male," *The Black Scholar* 18: 3 (May/June 1987): 2–41. Special issue.

3. James Lynch, *Multicultural Education: Principles and Practice* (Boston: Routledge and Kegan Paul, 1986); James A. Banks and James Lynch, eds., *Multicultural Education in Western Societies* (London: Cassell, 1986).

4. Gloria Steinem, *Outrageous Acts and Everyday Rebellions* (New York: Holt, 1983).

5. Janice Law Trecker, "Teaching the Role of Women in American History," in James A. Banks, ed., *Teaching Ethnic Studies: Concepts and Strategies* (Washington, D.C.: National Council for the Social Studies, 1973), pp. 279–297 (NCSS 43rd Yearbook.)

6. Carl A. Grant and Christine E. Sleeter, *After the School Bell Rings* (Philadelphia: The Falmer Press, 1986); H. Prentice Baptiste, Jr., "Multicultural Education and Urban Schools from a Sociohistorical Perspective: Internalizing Multiculturalism," *Journal of Educational Equity and Leadership* 6 (Winter 1986): 295–312.

7. Angela Y. Davis, *Women, Race and Class* (New York: Vintage Books, 1983).

8. Lee Barton and Stephen Walker, eds., *Race, Class and Education* (London: Croom Helm, 1983).

9. James A. Banks, *Multiethnic Education: Theory and Practice,* 2d ed. (Boston: Allyn and Bacon, 1988), p. 73.

10. Gene Lisitzky, *Four Ways of Being Human: An Introduction to Anthropology* (New York: Viking Press, 1956).

11. "Declaration of Independence," in *The Annals of America,* vol. 2 (Chicago: Encyclopaedia Britannica, 1968), pp. 447–449.

12. Thurgood Marshall, "The Meaning of the Constitution Bicentennial," *Ebony* (September 1987): 62, 64, 68.

13. Arthur M. Schlesinger, Jr., *The Cycles of American History* (Boston: Houghton Mifflin, 1986).

14. Lucy R. Garretson, *American Culture: An Anthropological Perspective* (Dubuque, Ia.: Wm. C. Brown Co., 1976).

15. Philip Green, *The Pursuit of Inequality* (New York: Pantheon Books, 1981); G. William Domhoff, *Who Rules America Now?* (New York: Simon and Schuster, 1983).

16. Christopher Jencks et al., *Inequality: A Reassessment of the Effect of Family and Schooling in America* (New York: Basic Books, 1972).

17. Edwin O. Reischauer, *The Japanese* (Cambridge: Harvard University Press, 1981); Fox Butterfield, *China: Alive in the Bitter Sea* (New York: Bantam Books, 1982).

18. Christopher Lasch, *The Culture of Narcissism* (New York: Norton, 1978); Robert N. Bellah et al., *Habits of the Heart: Individualism and Commitment in American Life* (New York: Harper and Row, 1985).

19. William Greenbaum, "America in Search of a New Ideal: An Essay on the Rise of Pluralism," *Harvard Educational Review* 44 (Au-

gust 1974): 411–440; Aida Negron DeMontilla, *Americanization in Puerto Rico and the Public-School System, 1900–1930* (San Juan: University of Puerto Rico, Editorial Universitaria, 1975).

20. Greenbaum, *America in Search.*

21. Gunnar Myrdal, with the assistance of Richard Sterner and Arnold Rose, *An American Dilemma: The Negro Problem and Modern Democracy* (New York: Harper and Row, 1944, 20th-Anniversary Edition, 1962).

22. Ralph Ellison, "An American Dilemma: A Review," in Joyce A. Ladner, ed., *The Death of White Sociology* (New York: Vintage Books, 1973), pp. 81–95.

23. Manuel Ramírez and Alfredo Castañeda, *Cultural Democracy, Bicognitive Development and Education* (New York: Academic Press, 1974); Janice E. Hale-Benson, *Black Children: Their Roots, Culture, and Learning Styles,* rev. ed. (Baltimore: Johns Hopkins University Press, 1986).

24. Robert E. Slavin, *Cooperative Learning* (New York: Longman, 1983); Elizabeth G. Cohen, *Designing Groupwork: Strategies for Heterogeneous Classrooms* (New York: Teachers College Press, 1986).

25. Carol Gilligan, *In a Different Voice: Psychological Theory and Women's Development* (Cambridge: Harvard University Press, 1982); Mary F. Belenky et al., *Women's Ways of Knowing: The Development of Self, Voice and Mind* (New York: Basic Books, 1986); Diane F. Halpern, *Sex Differences in Cognitive Abilities* (Hillsdale, N.J.: Lawrence Erlbaum Assoc., 1986).

26. Frances A. Maher, "Inquiry Teaching and Feminist Pedagogy," *Social Education* 51 (March 1987): 186.

27. Ibid., 187.

28. Belenky et al., *Women's Ways,* 5.

29. Ibid., 200.

30. Ramírez and Castañeda, *Cultural Democracy.*

31. Gilligan, *Different Voice.*

32. Jane R. Mercer, *Labeling the Mentally Retarded: Clinical and Social System Perspectives on Mental Retardation* (Berkeley: University of California Press, 1973), p. 32.

33. George A. Theodorson and Achilles G. Theodorson, *A Modern Dictionary of Sociology* (New York: Barnes and Noble, 1969), pp. 176, 395.

34. Norman Goodman and Gary T. Marx, *Society Today,* 4th ed. (New York: Random House, 1982), p. 7.

35. Gilligan, *Different Voice.*

36. Ramírez and Castañeda, *Cultural Democracy.*

37. Violet H. Perney, "Effects of Race and Sex on Field Dependence-Independence in Children," *Perceptual and Motor Skills* 42 (1976): 975–980.

38. Carl A. Grant and Christine E. Sleeter, "Race, Class, and Gender in Education Research: An Argument for Integrative Analysis," *Review of Educational Research* 56 (Summer, 1986): 195–211.

39. These two books have greatly influenced my ideas about the social construction of categories: Peter L. Berger and Thomas Luckman, *The Social Construction of Reality: A Treatise in the Sociology of Knowledge* (New York: Doubleday and Co., 1967); Karl Mannheim, *Ideology and Utopia: An Introduction to the Sociology of Knowledge* (New York: Harcourt Brace, 1936).

40. W. Lloyd Warner with Marchia Meeker and Kenneth Eells, *Social Class in America* (New York: Harper Torchbooks, 1949; reissued 1960).

41. James P. Shaver and Charles K. Curtis, *Handicapism and Equal Opportunity: Teaching about the Disabled in Social Studies* (Reston, Va.: The Foundation for Exceptional Children, 1981), p. 1.

42. I adapted this example from one described by Shaver and Curtis, *Handicapism and Equal Opportunity,* 2.

43. Mercer, *Labeling,* 31.

44. Ibid., 96.

45. Dorothy Sisk, *Creative Teaching of the Gifted* (New York: McGraw-Hill Book Co., 1987).

46. John E. Williams and J. Kenneth Morland, *Race, Color and the Young Child* (Chapel Hill: The University of North Carolina Press, 1976).

47. Carlos E. Cortés, "The Societal Curriculum: Implications for Multiethnic Education," in James A. Banks, ed. *Education in the 80s: Multiethnic Education* (Washington, D.C.: National Education Association, 1981), pp. 24–32.

48. James Lynch, *Prejudice Reduction and the Schools* (New York: Nichols Publishing Co., 1987).

49. Matina S. Horner, "Toward an Understanding of Achievement-Related Conflicts in Women," *Journal of Social Issues* 28, No. 2 (1972): 157–175.

50. James A. Coleman et al., *Equality of Educational Opportunity* (Washington, D.C.: U.S. Government Printing Office, 1966).

CHAPTER 2

Culture: Its Nature and Meaning for Educators

■ BRIAN M. BULLIVANT

Culture is a term we all use freely in numerous contexts, and for this reason we tend to take the idea of culture for granted. In many Western societies, the word *culture* has assumed importance because it forms part of the terms *multiculturalism* and *multicultural education*. When used in these two approaches to pluralist education, culture is a defining concept. That is, how we define culture determines the meaning of the term of which it forms a part. Unless we know what culture means, we will find it very difficult to understand the full implications of multiculturalism and multicultural education.

For example, if culture is defined as the heritage and traditions of a social group, then multicultural education means teaching about many (multi-) different heritages and traditions. But if culture is defined as a social group's design for surviving in and adapting to its environment—an approach we favor in this chapter—then one aim of multicultural education is to teach about the many social groups and their different designs for living in our pluralist society.

These are obviously two quite different ways of looking at multicultural education, and they illustrate the necessity to understand the concept of culture. We cannot let the meaning of culture remain vague or take it for granted; thus, this chapter clarifies what culture means and how it can be used in educational programs.

Popular Meanings of Culture

The term *culture* is used in several popular but confusing ways. First, it is commonly associated with such aesthetic pursuits as art, drama, ballet, and literature. These make up what is often called a society's *high culture,* as opposed to its *low culture,* that is, more popular art, pop music, and mass-media

The author would like to thank Barry Troyna for his constructive comments on an earlier version of this chapter.

entertainment. Second, such terms as *hippie culture, adolescent culture,* and *drug culture* imply that distinct groups in society possess these characteristics. Such groups are often termed *subcultures.* A third, scientific use refers to growing material in a chemical laboratory.

A fourth confusing use of culture is as a term for society. Thus, the term *British culture* is often a loose way of referring to British society *and* its culture. When people use the term in this way, they are referring to the people in Britain as being members of British culture or belonging to British culture. The same loose treatment of the term is frequently used to refer to other countries, but as the discussion of culture in this chapter makes clear, this is an invalid use of the term and should be avoided. We cannot emphasize the correct usage enough: People belong to, live in, or are members of social groups; they are not members of culture. Louis Schneider has stressed, "Putting people into culture is a sad maneuver into which social scientists slip time and time again."[1]

Environments Affecting Social Groups

At its most basic, a social group consists of a more or less permanent collectivity of human beings living together and interacting with the varieties of environments that make up its territory. Social groups must survive by adapting to and modifying these environments. The knowledge, ideas, and skills that enable a group to survive can be thought of as its culture or survival program.

The success of a group's survival depends on the kinds of environments the group faces. First, there is the geographical environment, or physical habitat. This provides a variety of natural features that the social group adapts to or modifies through its technology; this constitutes the tools and scientific knowledge used to achieve practical results. Included in these natural features are soil, minerals, climate, topography, vegetation, and such biotic resources as flora and fauna.

Cultural survival programs vary enormously in their levels of technological development, know-how, and sophistication. How much a social group can modify its living conditions and how much it is forced to adapt thus vary widely. A modern society like the United States, with a sophisticated technology, can modify its geographical environment almost at will. On the other hand, a technologically underdeveloped society is more heavily constrained by the difficulties posed by its geographical environment.

Second, members of a social group have to live together and interact. The social group as a whole has other groups as neighbors who make up a *social environment* with which it also has to interact. Some of these other groups are local; others are more distant. On a world scale, major social groups such as nation-states live in regional or global social environments and have to adapt to other nation-states. As we discuss, a major part of culture is made up of all the customs and rules that enable all these different scales of interaction to be carried on smoothly.

Third, there is a kind of environment that we do not usually think about because it cannot be seen or interacted with in this world. Nevertheless it is real for millions of people and strongly influences their lives. Its origin may lie in what is thought to be a basic human drive or universal need to find meaning and explanations in life. One way of satisfying this need for meaning is to develop beliefs that life is governed by a higher order of beings that exist outside humankind, such as a god or gods and other supernatural entities. These are often thought of as living in their own kinds of worlds, such as heaven or paradise. Because they are located outside here-and-now experience or are transcendent, we can refer to these kinds of spiritual worlds as forming a *metaphysical environment.*

Without taking the metaphysical environment into account, it is difficult to understand fully why many social groups live as they do. For example, the lives of traditional Navajo Indians in Arizona would be incomprehensible if one did not know about their beliefs in a dangerous metaphysical environment, populated by sorcerers, witches, and other supernatural beings. The Navajo believe that these beings affect their health and personal well-being; their existence necessitates the adoption of spells to ward off evil influences and the use of ethnomedical practices such as curing ceremonies for people who get sick.

The design of traditional Navajo houses (hogans) and a large body of traditional customs have been developed in response to Navajo views about how to survive in their metaphysical environment. The essential point about these practices and many others in the world is that such metaphysical environments are as "real" to those who believe in them as the Christian God and heaven are to Christians.

Of course, the Navajo interpretations about the causes of illness differ from the ideas of modern Western medicine, and some educational organizations training Navajos to advance in the modern world take account of these differences. For example, the University of Arizona in Tucson offers courses in modern medicine and has also brought in Navajo medicine men to teach students about traditional Indian beliefs. The modern and traditional approaches complement one another.

This sharing of knowledge is an example of one approach adopted to help a group like the Navajo survive in its own environment. It also contains an essential lesson we should learn about living together in a society as pluralistic as the United States. Tolerance and respect for another social group's survival programs are essential ingredients of intercultural understanding.

Institutions and Institutional Agencies

Group life works through *institutions,* major concerns essential for ensuring that a group maintains all the elements needed for its survival. Examples of these elements are food, shelter, and bodily maintenance; procreation and child rearing; defense from external threat; internal law and order; commercial and economic activity; care of the sick, aged, and infirm; and education of the young. Methods of taking care of these concerns are put into operation by *institutional agencies,* or "action systems" according to Talcott Parsons; these terms are used interchangeably in our discussion below.[2]

Each institutional agency or action system is a permanent organization consisting of a structural arrangement of status positions, plus roles, activities, rules or norms, and all the artifacts necessary for smooth operation. For example, the nuclear family is the major Western action system for taking care of procreation and child rearing. Schools, colleges, and universities are the major kinds of action systems we use to educate the young; the institutional agency of law courts takes care of law and order; the army, navy, and air force are action systems that look after defense.

It is important to remember that some of these institutional agencies control people's access to tangible political and economic power, resources, and social rewards. These kinds of agencies are essential for individual and group survival. The legal, political, commercial, business, and bureacratic systems are examples of this type of action system. However, other action systems are less essential to promoting people's physical and material well-being. Action systems such as television companies, movie theaters, sports associations, gambling casinos, and many other recreational and social organizations may provide a certain quality and enjoyment to life but are not essential in the same way as the former kinds of action systems.

The principles that govern a social group's relations with its natural and social environments also apply to those that concern its relationships with the metaphysical environment. The institution of religion is put into operation through institutional agencies or action systems such as churches and syna-gogues, with statuses and roles (priests, pastors, rabbis) together with specified activities such as counseling, worship, ministry, and confession.

Operation of Institutional Agencies

The distinctive pattern or style of an institutional agency's operation is deter-mined by its *charter* or ideology. A charter consists of a collection of beliefs, values, and ideas about what the institutional agency aims at (its ends) and how it will arrange its structure and organization (the means) to carry out its aims. These aspects are all contained in the group's cultural program.

Take the example of a school. Its charter contains ideas and beliefs about the ultimate purpose of education, the kinds of pupils it aims to produce (for example, factory workers or democratically conscious citizens), the need for discipline, the content of the curriculum (whether the emphasis is academic or generalist, for example), how the school should be run, the kind of staff most suitable to employ, the types of equipment and technology required, and many other aspects.

How these can vary becomes obvious if one compares two examples: an ethnic day school serving a group of Hasidic Jews in Williamsburg (part of Brooklyn, New York), such as Chaim Potok describes in his book *The Chosen*, and a local high school that most teachers would know. It quickly becomes apparent that both schools are not only very different action systems, organized with different ends in view, but that they also take very different views of the environments to which they are responding. The Jewish school's ideology is influenced much more by the metaphysical environment. Both schools respond to pressures in their social environments, but in different ways.

This short passage from *The Chosen* illustrates part of the Jewish group's concerns:

> *The sidewalks of Williamsburg were cracked squares of cement, the streets paved with asphalt that softened in the stifling summers and broke apart into*

potholes in the bitter winters. . . . Most of the stores were run by gentiles, but some were owned by Orthodox Jews, members of the Hasidic sects in the area. They could be seen behind their counters, wearing black skullcaps, full beards, and long earlocks, eking out their meager livelihoods and dreaming of Shabbat [Sabbath] and festivals when they could close their stores and turn their attention to their prayers, their rabbi, their God. Every Orthodox Jew sent his male children to a yeshiva, a Jewish parochial school, where they studied from eight or nine in the morning to four or five in the evening. On Fridays the students were let out at about one o'clock to prepare for the Shabbat. Jewish education was compulsory for the Orthodox, and because this was [the United States] and not Europe, English education was compulsory as well—so each student carried a double burden: Hebrew studies in the mornings and English studies in the afternoons. The test of intellectual excellence, however, had been reduced by tradition and unvoiced unanimity to a single area of study: Talmud. Virtuosity in Talmud was the achievement most sought after by every student of a yeshiva, for it was the automatic guarantee of a reputation for brilliance.[3]

Contrast this picture with one most teachers in the United States could paint of a typical high school serving a local community. The metaphysical environment of the school would not figure so prominently in the group's thinking, so the religious emphasis would not be apparent. As the social environment might be more important, more time would be given to sports and social activities. One symbol of a student's success and achievement might be whether he or she made one of the many sports teams. Many extracurricular provisions would be made—in the Jewish school there would be little spare time for them—and the timetable would be arranged in a way that would provide opportunities for students to select a wide variety of courses. A high school student's reputation for brilliance in sports might take the place of the reputation for knowledge of the Talmud aimed at by the yeshiva student.

Other organizational differences would be apparent. The yeshiva would be single-sex, for boys only; the high school would be coed. The students of the yeshiva would be obliged to wear some semblance of a uniform, if only a yarmulke or other head covering, at all times. High school students have won the right to wear what they like to school. Discipline would probably not be as strict in the high school as in the yeshiva. All these and many other contrasts you could list emphasize that the two institutional agencies are trying to implement different aims and values contained in two different charters. Knowing something about their respective social groups' cultures enables us to understand the reasons for these obvious differences.

Cultural Program of an Institutional Agency

Much as a computer is programmed by software containing instructions, so an institutional agency's ideology, organization, structure, and operation are programmed by instructions and information that enable it to function properly. They also provide those in the agency with the necessary knowledge and ideas about what behaviors are appropriate and what are not, together with the rules and routines to follow. All these instructions, knowledge, and information are selected from the society's culture.

Culture defines the meanings of all the things with which the group is concerned. It includes some traditional knowledge and ideas about a whole range of issues and survival problems the society has faced in the past and may want to use in the present without modification. Culture also includes the gradually evolving knowledge and ideas that are accumulating as the society faces new problems or as it develops in anticipation of future survival problems.

It is important to recognize that a group's cultural program is never static, but evolves under new adaptation pressures. As some customs and traditions cease to have adaptive value, they are discarded in time and new ones are adopted to suit changing conditions. Change also results when ideas are brought in from contact with other groups.

One kind of contact that leads to people's acquiring new cultural knowledge and ideas occurs during immigration to another society and consequent exposure to its culture. Immigrants rapidly discover that they have to learn the customary ways of doing things and coping with all sorts of new survival problems and institutional agencies.

This learning is not all one-way, that is, from the receiving society to the immigrants. They bring some new cultural knowledge and ideas into the receiving society because culture is *portable*. That is, once people's behavior and minds are "programmed" with their culture from birth, it is carried around wherever they go. Some parts of this personal culture are retained for a long time; other parts are changed as a result of exposure to new ideas and knowledge.

Maladaptive Culture

This portability of culture has both advantages and disadvantages. When an immigrant group first arrives in a strange receiving society, the traditions and customs in the group's culture provide a source of reassurance and comfort, even though they may not be completely adaptive to its new environments. As time goes on, however, the traditions and customs have increasingly less pragmatic survival value. In other words, they become *maladaptive*. In effect, they are cultural programs that have been frozen as they were when the groups arrived from their countries of origin. Another term for maladaptive cultures is *fossilized cultures*.

Such cultures may provide a source of stability for the original first-generation immigrants, but what of their children, the second generation, who never knew the culture of the "old country" at first hand? This kind of situation can lead to the children of immigrant parents being caught between two cultures, that of their parents and that of the receiving society into which they have been born. A Greek girl in a high school in Melbourne, Australia, talks about her life and the effect on it of her parents' fossilized culture, which has not been significantly changed during the thirty years since they emigrated from a Greek village:

> *Ellie*
> *My mum [mother] was telling me there are two daughters in her family. Her parents couldn't hack it [cope] because there were two daughters, and they always wanted a son, and it makes you feel unwanted.*

It's really hard to know if it's because you're Greek or whether it's because they're like that, and they're just being parents. Is it the way they grew up and the way they were brought up is the way you're being brought up? The thing is the Greeks now in Greece are given so much freedom now that we would not think of having [in Melbourne], and just because our parents came here and they brought their customs here, and that's why it's only the Greeks in Australia. . . . They came with traditions that are really old, and they come to a new country where it's really free. They are really vulnerable so they stick to those things. It's only the Greeks in Australia or Melbourne in particular. They're scared to change.[4]

Misconceptions about Culture

Knowledge and ideas are at the heart of culture, but if this is all culture consists of, then it is very much all in the mind. Social life is more than this, as it consists of behaviors or actions as well as ideas. But when we watch people behaving or carrying out actions in repetitive, patterned ways or customs, we are not seeing bits of a group's culture. Instead, we are seeing the embodiment of a cultural program. In short, behavior is not culture; rather, behavior "contains" it.

Similarly, the thousands of material artifacts a society produces and uses are not strictly culture, even though this is probably one of the commonest ways of thinking about culture. Both behaviors and artifacts contain culture in that ideas and knowledge are embodied or coded in them. They are *cultural forms,* not strictly the program of culture itself. When we want to describe a group's way of life in any detailed way, that is, by giving a "thick description," as anthropologist Clifford Geertz has put it, both the cultural program and cultural forms need to be included.[5]

Culture provides the knowledge and ideas *of* and *for* behavior.[6] That is, people have to know the kinds of knowledge and ideas they must have to carry out a certain kind of behavior properly (*for* behavior) and also to understand what the behavior they see is all about (*of* behavior).

For example, unless we know the meaning of and how to use, say, chopsticks, these implements remain just bits of wood, bone, or ivory. We have to acquire the knowledge and ideas about what they mean and what they are used for that are coded into them. If we are members of the social group that uses such implements, we will know the code by virtue of knowing the culture. A stranger in the group would have to watch chopstick-using behavior or ask for instructions in order to learn the code.

Even then, the stranger might not learn all the subtleties of chopstick use immediately but would have to be acquainted with the social group for a long time before finding out that there are rules of politeness and etiquette surrounding the apparently simple process of eating with chopsticks. This tells us that even the instinctive biological need to satisfy hunger has to be carried out in a culturally programmed way.

The chopsticks example also shows that two kinds of behavior can be involved even in such an everyday routine as eating. The first is *instrumental behavior,* which is used to get things done and is programmed by instrumental knowledge from the culture. The second is *expressive behavior.* This overlaps with instrumental behavior but is more concerned with expressing important beliefs, ideas, and values. Politeness and etiquette are not really needed when eating and when using the relevant instrumental behavior, but they are expressions of preferences about the way to eat, the values placed on the food, and the kinds of surroundings in which to eat.

Expressive behavior is an important part of religious rituals. It may not appear to do anything in the instrumental sense, but it expresses important beliefs and ideas to worshipers. However, even rituals that appear to do nothing concrete may have the important function of bringing psychological comfort to the worshipers. Rituals can be important ways of alleviating feelings of frustration or anxiety in times of crises such as floods, tornadoes, and other natural disasters. In this way, even religious rituals can be said to have instrumental functions.

Finally, it is important to keep in mind that every person in a social group need not follow its cultural program. In most societies, such a program provides a broad range of options, and there will always be those people who modify some of the cultural program and behave independently. Sometimes "doing their own thing" becomes maladaptive for survival, and they can become isolates (remember, culture is primarily a shared program), or even not survive in a very real sense and die. Others who reject the cultural program offend against a society's code of rules and standards and are classed as deviants by the legal institutional agencies and punished.

Distinguishing between Subgroups in Society

All social groups face different survival problems and have to adapt to many kinds of environments. There is a great variety of cultures and cultural forms around the world. Equally, in most pluralist societies, there are different kinds of subgroups, each of which draws on its own survival programs in adapting to and surviving in its environments.

The subgroups within a pluralist society can be distinguished by outsiders, or they can distinguish themselves because of the characteristics their members share. The most common of these characteristics are social class, ethnicity, racial (phenotypical) differences, and possibly even gender differences. Such subgroups are also likely to have evolved distinctive cultures to program their adaptation to the environments in which they live. Thus, it is possible to refer to social-class cultures, ethnic group cultures, racial group cultures, and even to male and female cultures.

The concept of ethnic group has become prominent in recent literature about pluralism and needs to be clarified. A useful definition of an ethnic group has been provided by Theodorson and Theodorson:

> A group with a common cultural tradition and a sense of identity which exists as a subgroup of a larger society. The members of an ethnic group differ with regard to certain cultural characteristics from the other members of their society. They may have their own language and religion as well as certain distinctive customs. Probably most important is their feeling of identification as a traditionally distinct group.[7]

This definition serves for the purposes of this chapter, but it is important to know that some ethnic groups are *culturally* similar to the wider society yet remain separate and distinct because of their *feelings of identification*. In effect, an ethnic group is not invariably a cultural group. Similarly, racial groups are often thought of as ethnic groups because the shared phenotypical characteristics of their members provide the basis of self-identification and identification by those outside the group.

However, a racial group is different from an ethnic group in one important respect. Members of a racial group cannot easily alter the phenotypical characteristics that distinguish them from members of the wider society; in other words, phenotypical characteristics are immutable. In contrast, members of an ethnic group can shed their cultural customs, abandon their language, and even change religion.

No matter how they are distinguished, subgroups have to take part in activities associated with the wider *public domain* of the pluralist society in which they are situated. For example, in the United States, as in most Western societies, there is one system of law, one currency and medium of exchange, one language of commerce and daily interaction, and one system of government, to mention only a few institutions that all members of a society share. However, in the *private domain* of group life, such as ethnic festivals, religious observances, and recreational and sporting activities, there can be many variations. Members of each subgroup need not share such activities with other groups but can take part in their own.

These differences produce a rich variety of cultural forms in cities inhabited by many ethnic groups. In one part of outer Melbourne, Australia, for example, one can come across Italians playing *bocce* (a kind of lawn bowling) in the park, while down on the seafront a Greek Orthodox priest blesses the fishing fleet and Greek boys dive for the cross he tosses into the water. On a nearby playing field, two ethnic teams, Croatia and Hellas, play soccer and are urged on by supporters in their respective languages. A week earlier there would have been a German "Oktoberfest" in another outer suburb, with all the dancing, beer drinking, and festivity one associates with this cultural occasion.

Values in the Cultural Programs

All this variety of cultural forms reflects the respective subgroups' preferences about how to arrange their cultural survival programs. These preferences are termed *values,* and, according to Valentine, "include the ideals, the aims and ends, the ethical and aesthetic standards, and the criteria of knowledge and wisdom embodied within it, taught to and modified by each human generation."[8] A cultural program is a reflection of the values that interpenetrate and lock it together as a unique complex.

Values provide the guidelines that enable individuals and groups to maintain common goals. For example, such democratic values as free speech, equality before the law, justice, freedom, and national pride provide broad standards from which more precise rules (norms) and sanctions (rewards and punishments) can be derived to guide the behavior of all who make up the group.

These broad standards are the kinds of values most social groups would want to maintain. However, people can have strong emotional feelings toward the values of the subgroup to which they belong. This is a normal and healthy feature of social life, but when two or more subgroups have strong emotional attachments to extreme kinds of values, tensions can develop. This occurs because each subgroup maintains that its values alone are correct and should be adopted by all other subgroups. Such a situation can occur in a culturally pluralist society, and to preserve harmony it may be necessary for the common legal system shared by all groups to impose laws that will ensure that conflict does not occur.

Importance of Value Orientations or World Views

A broader category of value concerns a social group's "world views" or value orientations. These are "broad-gauge propositions concerning what people feel positively about: they influence both the means and ends of striving."[9] The following six value orientations were used to study life in an Orthodox Jewish School in Melbourne, Australia.[10]

1. *Human-supernature orientation*—value judgments and existential propositions about the nature of and human relationships with the metaphysical environment. Examples are beliefs in a God, many gods, or atheism.

2. *Human-nature orientation*—value judgments and existential propositions about human relationships with and use of the natural environment. Examples are the value placed on conserving biotic resources and preserving them from damage, as the underlying philosophy of the Greenpeace organization illustrates, as opposed to the exploitation of natural resources by mining or timber companies.

3. *Human-habitat orientation*—value judgments and existential propositions about the way to design and create a human-made environment. Examples are the concrete jungles in many inner-city areas versus the spacious parks and open spaces preserved as green belts around towns. The highly stylized layout of a Japanese garden is an excellent example of the value placed on arranging the immediate human-made habitat to reflect a sense of harmony and control.

4. *Human-relational orientation*—value judgments and existential propositions about the way to conduct relationships in the social environment. Examples are groups that stress the value of communal living in harmony with one another versus groups that are suspicious of outsiders and live within closed areas to guard their privacy, as occurs in some parts of rural Greece.

5. *Human-activity orientation*—value judgments and existential propositions about the kinds of endeavors carried out individually or as a member of a group in the social environment. Examples are valuing work for its own sake more than getting by with minimal effort.

6. *Human-time orientation*—value judgments and existential propositions about how to use time on a micro-scale and on a macro-scale. Examples are the future-time orientation of many Western societies versus the past-time orientation of some peasant communities; the emphasis put on not wasting time versus being able to do nothing and let time slip by.

Influence of Values and World Views on Adaptation

All social groups are able to exercise choices about how they will adapt to environmental pressures. But the range of choices depends on the level of economic, technical, and social development of the social group in question. Choices of *adaptational styles* also reflect the group's value orientations or world views. The following two descriptions illustrate the contrasts between the ways two societies—British settlers and Australian Aborigines—adapted in colonial times.[11] What kinds of values and value orientations can be detected?

The British Style of Adaptation

Land was an economic resource and the basis of considerable social status and power in Britain. Although it also had some sentimental importance, land could be sold and title to the estate transferred to new owners, because it was a possession like any other good. The British were thus able to move away from a piece of land they sold without a great emotional wrench if it was advantageous to do so. While occupying land, they were able to farm it and hunt on it without seeing how these two activities might be incompatible.

Possessions and material goods, of which land formed a part, were at the heart of British culture. Early settlers thus followed a similar pattern of establishing private ownership of land in a tangible way by fencing or tilling it, grazing herds of cattle or flocks of sheep on it, building houses and making equipment to further utilize the land. In this they were exploitative, having little regard for the delicate ecological balance in which the land had existed for centuries. They legitimated this activity by their religious, Christian ideology which can be summed up by the term "Protestant ethic."

The Aboriginal Style of Adaptation

The spiritual importance of the land was as compelling as, or even transcended, the economic importance of the land. Its physical features were often of totemic significance, thus embracing both social and cosmological realms. Land could neither be owned, held in title, nor sold or transferred; such concepts being alien to Aboriginal thinking. One could not be separated from nor leave one's land without being emotionally affected to the very core of one's being. Separation from places meant separation from everything that held the key to Aboriginal understanding of life and regeneration of the world, its natural and social resources. Separation from their land for Aborigines meant losing a vital part of their reason for existence in spiritual terms, if not also in purely physical or temporal terms.

For such a view, the British violated sacred sites and desecrated the land by the exploitative use they made of it. Thus the co-existence of farming and hunting techniques were not possible and could not be condoned. They offended the static conservative approach to land that was basic to Aboriginal thinking, and attempted to preserve resources from excessive exploitation, so maintaining the delicate balance of natural species essential to economic survival and the totemic order of religious life.

Transmission of a Cultural Program

A culture must be transmitted to each new generation of children if the social group is not to collapse and be absorbed into another society or even become extinct. This follows from the way we have thought of culture as a social group's survival program. Without such a culture and the action systems it programs, a group's survival is threatened, so it is necessary for every person in the group to learn as much of the program as possible.

The ultimate aim of the cultural transmission (enculturation) process is to produce a member of a social group who embodies its culture. The following description of a Japanese man describes such a member:

> If you knew of a man named Hashimoto, who spoke only Japanese, ate by preference rice and raw fish, wore a kimono in a home made of bamboo and paper, was enthusiastic about flower arrangements and tea ceremonies, venerated his Emperor as a God, and died by committing suicide because of an insult, you would not only know that he was Japanese, but almost how long ago he lived. . . . You would also know that he had not done all these things out of instinct; that he must have been taught this language, these tastes, these ideas, and for no better reason than that these were the ones the Japanese people happened to have invented, borrowed, and developed before Mr. Hashimoto was born among them.[12]

The key to the cultural transmission process is the language of the social group. This is its system of signs and symbols by which knowledge and meanings are passed on to everyone within the group and particularly to each new generation.

Signs and symbols are not strictly the same but tend to get confused in everyday use. Cultural signs are objects that stand for something else by cultural convention. For example, a red traffic light is a sign for danger. Most languages consist of sets of signs. Natural signs or signals need not have a similar arbitrary meaning; for example, smoke is a sign (signal) of fire.[13]

Symbols are somewhat different. They are able to convey abstract meanings and are often used in expressive and ritual behavior to say something important that cannot be said easily in another way. For example, *flag* is the term for a piece of colored and patterned fabric, but the term can express a symbolic "message." When people salute the flag, they are reacting to a symbolic message that communicates many things to them about the power and glory of their nation.

Because many religious beliefs cannot be expressed directly, symbols are used extensively in that context to convey important ideas to worshipers. Take the "plus" sign (+), which in everyday language stands for a cross. In the different language of the Christian religion it becomes the symbol for a crucifix and expresses a whole cluster of beliefs and sentiments about the crucifixion of Jesus Christ. Symbols are thus important ways of communicating ideas about the metaphysical environment.

The problem with signals, signs, and symbols is that their arbitrary meaning can vary from culture to culture. This becomes apparent when one visits another society and gets involved in cross-cultural communication. Take just two simple examples. In traditional Greek culture, the bodily sign or signal for "no" is a *nod* of the head up and down. The sign or signal for "yes" is a *shake* of the head from side to side. Communication between a Greek and someone from another group can be confusing unless both sides know the cultural conventions for "yes" and "no." Even such a simple action as using a *lift* (English term) or *elevator* (American term) can be confusing unless one knows that "G" stands for "Ground Floor" in a lift and for "Floor 1" in an elevator.

Summary: The Meaning of Culture

We can now bring together all the ideas discussed above in a summary of what culture means:

- The core of a social group's cultural program consists of knowledge and conceptions that are public, in the sense of being shared by most members of the social group.
- The knowledge and conceptions are embodied in the behaviors and artifacts of the social group's members; that is, the cultural program provides the knowledge *for* and *of* behavior and artifacts. Behaviors and artifacts are termed *cultural forms.*
- Another essential component of a cultural program consists of the values a group subscribes to; these broadly control the group's preferences about how its cultural forms should be organized.
- Knowledge, conceptions, and values are transmitted among present members of the social group and to those who are born into it through systems of communication, the most important of which are signs and symbols.
- Part of the cultural program has evolved historically as the social group has adapted to its environments over time. Other parts of the program represent how the social group has modified outdated adaptation strategies to suit its assessment of its present environmental conditions or has added to its own culture by borrowing from other groups and their cultures.
- More parts of the cultural program consist of the knowledge and conceptions that the group devises to anticipate and cope with its assessment of future problems.

The Multicultural Society

As we saw above, pluralist societies are made up of subgroups that differ from each other on various grounds: social class, ethnicity, race, culture, gender. A number of terms have been used to refer to such societies. The most common description is *multicultural,* which implies the existence of many (multi-) cultures within one society.

As we stress from the outset, people in a multicultural society are not members of these different cultures. They are members of the various subgroups making up the society, each of which is programmed by its own culture. Even this is an oversimplification. Subgroup cultures also overlap and interpenetrate each other, so people do not belong exclusively to one subgroup but have to move in and out of several action systems every day and use the appropriate cultural program belonging to each. Members of subgroups also have to participate in the action systems in the public domain of the wider society.

For example, imagine what life might be like for the following family living in a pluralist Western society. (Our portrayal is a stereotype at some points.) The husband and wife start their day by using the culturally patterned behavior and artifacts appropriate to the institutional agency of the family to prepare breakfast and get the children off to school (another institutional agency) and themselves off to work. The husband's job is in the civil service (another institutional agency); the wife works in a firm of lawyers (another institutional agency). In their respective jobs, husband and wife have to adopt the appropriate cultural forms to function effectively.

In the evening, the whole family goes out to eat in a Chinese restaurant and has to adopt ethnic cultural customs for this kind of action system. On Sunday, the family goes to church because another subgroup to which the family belongs believes in the Christian metaphysical environment. The family uses the religious knowledge, ideas, and beliefs appropriate to that action system.

On paper, this sequence looks very complicated. In fact, it is one with which many people cope every day throughout their lives. As a consequence, in a complex Western society everyone needs a great deal of knowledge about the various subcultures and the institutional agencies they program to enable them to cope successfully with daily living.

This also means that teachers cannot rely on the cultural knowledge appropriate to their own social groups if they want to work effectively in the multicultural classroom, in which children from many ethnic groups may be present. For example, in some inner-city high schools in Melbourne, a class may contain children from as many as twenty different ethnic backgrounds.

Dilemmas for Teachers

Teachers need to be aware that sometimes one cultural program interferes with another and poses special problems. For example, girls' gender roles can be influenced by their membership in an ethnic group and by the need to work with boys in class and possibly by boys' and teachers' gender roles. The following conversation about gender relationships took place among a group of year 11 Greek girls in a Melbourne high school in response to the researcher's opening question.

Q. They had a kind of equal opportunity course here didn't they?

A. That was for the teachers so they could become aware of sex discrimination in the form, like letting the boys get away with murder, and not letting the girls because boys are meant to be rowdy and boisterous and the girls are not (first girl).

Q. Do you think they are?

A. Yes [emphatically from most girls in the group], Mrs. H. she lets the boys get away with everything. She lets them swear, sometimes she lets the girls get away with things too. . . . When you think about it the girls don't fool around as much . . . in Greek families it [spoiling boys] exists very much (second girl).

A. When I say things like why can my brother go out they [my parents] say 'he's a boy . . . and can't get pregnant,' and that's it (third girl).

Q. Do girls get resigned to this if they're from migrant backgrounds, or do they fight about it? How strong is the feminist movement?

A. It's quite strong . . . getting stronger. Equal opportunity is quietly strong among Greek women (first girl).

A. Our modern Greek teacher, he's the biggest chauvinist in the school. Last year A____ and myself we were so feminist and sticking up for our rights, we got into so much trouble. He thinks that women should stay at home and have kids every couple of years or so, and do the housework and that's it. I bet if he had a daughter he would probably drown the poor baby (second girl).

A. In Greece, like, they have sons because they don't have to leave them any dowry, and the son can have the second name (fourth girl).[14]

Other kinds of cultural practices can be more extreme. For example, what should a teacher do if he or she comes across a Turkish boy giving his sister a severe beating outside the school gates because he saw her talking to boys during the morning recess? In Turkish culture, a very strong value is placed on a girl's honor, and the boy was putting into effect the norms and sanctions associated with such a value. However, Western societies are not so strict and this kind of situation can place an Anglo teacher in a dilemma of not knowing whether to intervene and criticize such a traditional practice in the interests of the girl, or to ignore it and allow a harmful situation to continue that might even lead to serious injury.

On the one hand, it would be easy and understandable for the teacher to make an *assumption of normative equivalence*. This extension of Tom Wolfe's idea of "moral equivalence" holds that another cultural group's standards, values, and norms are equivalent to one's own.[15] One can then use this assumption as grounds for criticizing what one finds objectionable in the culture of the other group, even though it may be quite permissible to that group's members. However, when teachers do this, they risk being labeled "culturally insensitive" or even "racist."

On the other hand, teachers can adopt a philosophy of *naive* culture relativism. This philosophy maintains that every cultural program is unique and should not be criticized on the basis of another culture's values. Thus teachers may not be able to criticize cultural practices that may be valid in their own cultural context but would not be condoned if they occurred in their own social group.

The basic right of members of minority groups to have the integrity of their cultures respected is stated in the International Covenant on Civil and Political Rights (Article 27):

> In those States in which ethnic, religious or linguistic minorities exist, persons belonging to such minorities shall not be denied the right, in community with other members of their group, to enjoy their own culture, to profess and practice their own religion, or to use their own language.

The phrase "in community with other members of their group" suggests a way out of the teacher's dilemma. Cultural customs could be immune from criticism provided they occur within the action system of an ethnic community. However, when the same customs occur in another action system, such as a school, which is programmed by the public culture shared by many groups, the rules of the public action system must surely apply. We met this problem on a larger scale earlier in this chapter, and the principle was advocated then that the public good should prevail in situations in which group conflict is generated by competing value systems. It seems appropriate that the same principle should be applied, on a smaller scale, to what occurs in a multicultural school.

Teachers working in multicultural classrooms, however, should try to be sensitive to the many cultural variations they are likely to encounter. In particular, they must be aware that children from different cultural backgrounds have been "programmed" with their group's *subjective culture* during their enculturation. *Subjective culture* is defined by Harry Triandis as the characteristic way in which a cultural group perceives and responds to its social environment.[16]

A conscientious teacher thus might make it his or her business to learn something about the subjective cultures of those children from different ethnic groups in the class. This will give the teacher a basis from which to make a value judgment about whether an apparently objectionable cultural custom can be condoned.

Recognition of Issues Involving Power

The example of the Turkish boy involved another factor. This is the power he held over his sister because of her gender, and we could have used the perspective of sexism to analyze what occurred. But the incident was still one that was confined mainly to the private culture of a Turkish community. However, teachers need to be aware that there is a wider issue at stake when working in the multicultural classroom. This is the way multicultural education programs can avoid tackling major differences in ethnic communities' access to socioeconomic power and social rewards in the wider world, and its public culture and action systems.

The distinction we made earlier in this chapter between instrumental and expressive aspects of culture provides a basis for our understanding the wider issue of power. Instrumental culture enables a group to achieve *life chances* in the form of economic gains and rewards from its environment. To do this, the group usually has to compete with other groups and use its instrumental culture to best advantage in the competition that occurs in the public spheres of a pluralist society.

On the other hand, the expressive side of culture need not be employed to gain the same kinds of rewards; it is concerned mainly with enhancing the group's *life-style*. This is usually confined to the private spheres of a pluralist society in the ethnic communities themselves.

It is necessary to recognize that this distinction between life chances and life-styles risks being an oversimplification of what can actually take place. There is always some overlap between private and public spheres of life, but following Melvin Tumin we are using the distinction to make the point that teachers need to be aware of the two sides of the cultures they will meet in the multicultural classroom.[17]

This necessity applies particularly when teachers use multicultural curriculum materials. These can stress life-styles, for example, the history, heritage, traditions, and customs of cultural groups in the society. Or the materials can stress life chances and deal with problems cultural groups face in gaining equal economic opportunity in the wider society.

The latter approach is not common in many multicultural courses, but it is necessary to ensure that young people leaving the school gain a realistic picture of how a pluralist society operates and have some chance of coping effectively in it. In essence, multicultural education programs should be "politicized" and made more radical so that issues of power and control are tackled and are not covered up by teaching only the often-romanticized aspects of ethnic life-styles.[18]

As we saw when describing institutions, pluralism entails members of various subgroups engaging in the power-controlling institutional agencies, such as political organizations, legal systems, and big businesses. Most of these agencies are controlled by the members of the dominant group in society, and a fairer share of power can be gained only by competing with them, using the knowledge and ideas of their appropriate cultural programs.

Many members of other subgroups, such as recent immigrants, lack such knowledge, so it is difficult for them to compete effectively. Unless they are vigilant, ethnic subgroups may find that multiculturalism can be confined largely to encouraging local, recreational, and other kinds of institutional agencies programmed more by the expressive side of culture than by the instrumental side. Such agencies concentrate on the life-styles of subgroups rather than on their life chances. This one-sided approach gives the impression that the agencies are assisting ethnic groups, but in effect they are doing little to overcome the institutionalized ways by which members of subgroups are denied a fair share of economic power and social rewards.

Conclusion

Teachers in multicultural classrooms should be aware of the problems discussed in this chapter. Pluralism is a worldwide phenomenon, and understanding it necessitates the use of appropriate concepts and models. Those of culture, institutional agency or action system, and values provide powerful tools to aid our understanding of the kind of society in which most of us live.

The key concept we discuss in this chapter is culture. We define culture in terms of a group's survival device. This consists of the public knowledge and conceptions embodied in the behavior and artifacts, or cultural forms, that enable the group to adapt to three kinds of environments: the natural, the social, and the metaphysical.

Culture has an expressive side and an instrumental side, and both sides need to be kept in mind when teaching students from diverse cultural backgrounds. The main danger is that a teacher will concentrate only on the expressive side by adopting multicultural programs that stress an ethnic group's customs, heritage, history, and aesthetic aspects. This approach risks ignoring the more sensitive side of ethnic group life, namely, that students must be educated to go out into the pluralist world as adults and make a living in competition with others.

Only by honestly confronting power relationships in a pluralist society will we be able to help students take their places in it. If we can tailor multicultural education programs to this end, perhaps young people will be less inhibited by the frustrations that we ourselves may have experienced in trying to understand why we live as we do. Thus, by being treated honestly in matters of power and control, young people may be encouraged to develop more realistic sets of values rather than suffer the disillusionment and alienation so apparent in many schools.

Questions and Activities

1. How do the teaching implications of multicultural education differ if culture is defined as (a) the heritage and traditions of a social group or (b) a social group's design for surviving in and adapting to its environment?

2. Which definition of culture above (a or b) does Bullivant prefer? Why?

3. What is the difference between *society* and *culture?* How are these concepts related?

4. Name three kinds of environments to which social groups must adapt. How does knowledge about each environment help us understand a particular group and its culture?

5. Spend several days observing in a local public school and in a parochial school in your community or region. Describe how the ideology, that is, the beliefs, values, and ideas, of the two schools differ. In what ways are the two schools alike? Share your observations with your classmates or fellow workshop participants.

6. Interview several teachers who work in a school that has a population of immigrant students. Ask them about special problems these students experience and what the school is doing to ease their adjustment to U.S. society and culture. Talk to some of the immigrant students about their experiences in the school and in U.S. society. Compare the views of the teachers and students. How are they alike? How are they different? Why?

7. What are values? How do they help a group maintain common goals? What problems develop when the values of groups within a multicultural society conflict? Can the schools help solve these problems? Why or why not? If they can, how?

8. How does cultural knowledge about various groups help teachers work more effectively in multicultural classrooms?

9. Bullivant notes that multicultural materials can focus on *life-styles* or on *life chances*. Which approach to multicultural education does he prefer, and why?

10. Spend several days observing boys and girls in the classroom, on the playground, and in other areas of the school. Pay particular attention to the ways boys and girls interact with teachers, especially in different subjects, such as mathematics and social studies. Based on your observations, write a short paper describing whether there are distinct male and female cultures in that school.

Notes

1. Louis Schneider and Charles Bonjean, eds., *The Idea of Culture in the Social Sciences* (Cambridge: Cambridge University Press, 1973), p. 119.

2. Talcott Parsons, *Societies: Evolutionary and Comparative Perspectives* (New York: Prentice-Hall, 1966).

3. Chaim Potok, *The Chosen* (London: Heinemann, 1967), pp. 11–12.

4. Brian M. Bullivant, *Getting a Fair Go: Case Studies of Occupational Socialization and Perceptions of Discrimination in a Sample of Seven Melbourne High Schools* (Canberra: Australian Government Publishing Service, 1986), p. 224. Also in Brian M. Bullivant, *The Ethnic Encounter in the Secondary School* (Lewes: Falmer Press, 1987).

5. Clifford Geertz, *The Interpretation of Cultures: Selected Essays* (New York: Basic Books, 1973).

6. Alfred L. Kroeber and Clyde Kluckhohn, *Culture: A Critical Review of Concepts and Definitions* (Cambridge: Harvard University, Peabody Museum of American Archeology and Ethnology Papers) 47, No. 1 (1952): 181.

7. George A. Theodorson and Achilles G. Theodorson, *A Modern Dictionary of Sociology* (London: Methuen, 1970), p. 135.

8. Charles A. Valentine, *Culture and Poverty: Critique and Counter-Proposals* (Chicago: University of Chicago Press, 1968), p. 7.

9. John J. Honigmann, *Personality in Culture* (New York: Harper and Row, 1967), p. 78.

10. Brian M. Bullivant, *The Way of Tradition: Life in an Orthodox Jewish School* (Melbourne: Australian Council for Educational Research, 1978).

11. Brian M. Bullivant, *Pluralism: Cultural Maintenance and Evolution* (Clevedon, England: Multilingual Matters, 1984), pp. 15–17.

12. Gene Lisitzky, *Four Ways of Being Human: An Introduction to Anthropology* (London: Dobson, 1963), pp. 30–31.

13. John Beattie, *Other Cultures* (London: Cohen & West, 1964), pp. 69–73.

14. Bullivant, *Getting a Fair Go,* 223.

15. Tom Wolfe, "Are the USA and the USSR Morally Equivalent?" "*Quadrant* (October 1985): 10–18.

16. Harry C. Triandis, *The Analysis of Subjective Culture* (New York: John Wiley, 1972).

17. Melvin M. Tumin and W. Plotch, eds., *Pluralism in a Democratic Society* (New York: Praeger, 1977), p. xiv.

18. Brian M. Bullivant, "Towards Radical Multiculturalism: Resolving Tensions in Curriculum and Educational Planning," in Sohan Modgil et al., eds. *Multicultural Education, The Interminable Debate* (Lewes: The Falmer Press, 1986), pp. 33–47.

CHAPTER **3**

Race, Class, Gender, Exceptionality, and Educational Reform

- **CARL A. GRANT and CHRISTINE E. SLEETER**

"Educational reform" is a phrase educators often hear. Educational reform often comes about after a national embarrassment, such as when the Soviets leaped ahead of the United States in the space race by successfully orbiting Sputnik in 1957. The phrase has been used often in recent years by those grappling with the superiority many West German and Japanese firms have demonstrated in several technological areas.

National embarrassments such as these usually lead to severe criticism of public schools. Blue-ribbon committees are appointed by high-ranking government officials (usually the president or the secretary of education) to identify problems in the education system and to recommend change. Observe the statement of the problem in the report *A Nation at Risk* by the National Commission on Excellence in Education, appointed by Secretary of Education Terrell Bell:

> *Our Nation is at risk. Our once unchallenged preeminence in commerce, industry, science, and technological innovation is being overtaken by competitors throughout the world. This report is concerned with only one of the many causes and dimensions of the problem, but it is the one that undergirds American prosperity, security and civility. We report to the American people that while we can take justifiable pride in what our schools and colleges have historically accomplished and contributed to the United States and the well-being of its people, the educational foundations of our society are presently being eroded by a rising tide of mediocrity that threatens our very future as a nation and a people. What was unimaginable a generation ago has begun to occur—others are matching and surpassing our educational attainment.*[1]

The report says that our schools are failing desperately and accuses them of having "squandered the gains in student achievement made in the wake of the Sputnik challenge."[2] The report describes the United States as being "at risk" and recommends as a remedy to this problem a movement to bring excellence into education. "Excellence," the report tells us, means several things.

> At the level of the "individual learner" it means performing on the boundary of individual ability in ways that test and push back personal limits in school and in the workplace. Excellence characterizes a school or college that sets high expectations and goals for all learners, then tries in every way possible to help students reach them. Excellence characterizes a society that has adopted these policies, for it will then be prepared through the education and skill of its people to respond to the challenges of a rapidly changing world.[3]

In recent times, there have been other educational reform movements brought about not because the country has been embarrassed technologically on the world stage, but because certain of its citizens were being treated in a biased way. These reform movements were aimed at improving access to quality education for students of color, students from low-income families, handicapped students, and White female students.

Blacks, for example, started what became an educational reform movement when they protested against racial segregation in U.S. schools. Blacks wanted to eliminate racial segregation, and they wanted to be able to participate more actively in all areas of U.S. society. A statement from the landmark decision in the case of Brown v. Board of Education by Chief Justice Warren explains the school segregation problem:

> The Supreme Court unanimously held that the plaintiffs, by reason of the segregation complained of, were deprived of the equal protection of the laws guaranteed by the Fourteenth Amendment. The "separate but equal" doctrine announced in Plessy v. Ferguson, . . . involving equality in transportation facilities, under which equality of treatment is accorded by providing Negroes and Whites substantially equal, though separate, facilities, was held to have no place in the field of public education.[4]

In other words, the practice of segregating Black and White students in so-called separate but equal schools was declared wrong on Constitutional grounds. This decision led to an educational reform movement that promoted equal educational opportunity. The Civil Rights Act of 1964 aided this reform effort when it prohibited public institutions receiving state and federal funds from assigning students to public school based on their race, color, religion, or national origin. Thus, this reform movement had twin themes, "equal access" and "equal educational opportunity." Other groups such as Hispanics, White women, and Asian-Americans, encouraged by the Black efforts, initiated their own reform effort for equal educational opportunity and equal access.

There are two observable differences between the present reform movement and the reform movement of the recent past. First, the present reform movement is inspired by both international and national concerns, as suggested in A Nation at Risk: "The world is indeed a global village. We live among determined, well-educated, and strongly motivated competitors. We compete with them for international standing and markets, not only with products but also with the ideas of our laboratories and neighborhood workshops."[5]

Second, the present educational reform effort has shifted from improving the quality of education for minorities, the handicapped, the poor, and females, to improving the quality of education for all children. *A Nation at Risk* clearly states, "We must demand the best effort and performance from all students, whether they are gifted or less able, affluent or disadvantaged, whether destined for college, the farm or industry."[6]

Many of the reports and reform proposals inspired by *A Nation at Risk* state twin themes: the pursuit of quality and the assurance of equity. Excellence and equity have stood as giant twin towers to serve as both a vision and a challenge and to provide direction for reform. These twin themes are the kinds of goals needed for education, especially given the student population you will teach. The author of an article in a 1986 issue of *Education Week* pointed out that of the 3.6 million students who began their formal schooling in September of that year:

- One of four were from families who live in poverty;
- 14 percent were children whose mothers were under the age of 18;
- 15 percent were immigrants who spoke little or no English;
- 10 percent had poorly educated or illiterate parents.[7]

According to *Education Week,* these demographic changes are shaping a U.S. society that is "more racially and ethnically diverse than any previous generation in American history." The resulting changes in U.S. schools will mean that teachers will work—and, indeed, are working—"with cohorts of children more ethnically and racially diverse than ever before; and more of whom will bring with them the array of risk factors that bode ill for their development."[8] The *Condition of Education* reports that "the vast majority of pupils classified as handicapped—93 percent—attended regular public school in 1982–1983. More than two-thirds of all handicapped pupils also received the bulk of their instruction in regular classes along with their non-handicapped age mates."[9]

These data suggest that both excellence and equity are needed in the U.S. educational system. Apple[10] and Grant and Sleeter[11] point out that both needs are not being served equally; they argue that the equity theme is being greatly shortchanged. Teachers must ask themselves whether they want to strive for both excellence and equity in the classroom, and if so, how to achieve both goals. These demographic data can be considered depressing, or challenging, depending on one's perspective.

Most students we teach usually give one of three reasons for wanting to become teachers: (1) they love kids, (2) they want to help students, (3) they want to make school more exciting than when they were students. If one of these is the reason you chose to enter the teaching profession, then we hope you will see the demographic data as being challenging and realize that your love and help are needed, not just for some students, but for *all* students.

This chapter discusses the importance of race, class, gender, and exceptionality in classroom life and provides alternative approaches to dealing with these issues in the classroom.

Race, Class, Gender, Exceptionality, and Classroom Life

Ask yourself what you know about race, class, gender, and exceptionality as they apply to classroom life. Could you write one or two good paragraphs about what these words mean? How similar or different would your meanings be from those of your classmates? How much do these ascribed characteristics influence the way you think about teaching? If you and your classmates organize into small discussion groups (try it), and listen closely to each other, you will probably notice some distinct differences in the ways you see the importance of these factors. The point of such an exercise is not to show that you have different ideas and interpretations, but that each of you clearly understands what your ideas and interpretations mean for working with the classroom population described in *Education Week:* How will you bring excellence and equity to your teaching?

Race, social class, and gender are used to construct major groups of people in society. On your college application form, you were probably asked to indicate your race, gender, and parents' place of employment. Most institutions want to know your color, sex, and social-class background. This information provides the institution with the ability to analyze and report data related to any or all of your ascribed characteristics (and to get into your business). Social scientists studying school practices often report results according to race, class, or gender. As a teacher, it is essential for you to understand the importance of how the ascribed characteristics of race, class, and gender can influence your knowledge and understanding of your students. It is also important for you to consider these ascribed characteristics collectively and not separately. Each of your students is a member of all three status groups, and these simultaneous memberships influence their perceptions and actions.

For example, a child in the classroom is not just Asian-American, but also male and middle-class. Thus, he is linked with an oppressed ethnic group, but he is also linked with a gender group and a social class that historically have oppressed others. Therefore his view of reality and his actions based on that view will differ from those of a middle-class Asian-American girl or a lower-class Asian-American boy. A teacher's failure to consider the integration of race, social class, and gender could lead at times to an oversimplified or inaccurate understanding of what occurs in schools, and therefore to an inappropriate or simplistic prescription for educational equity and excellence. You may have noticed, for example, teachers assuming (often mistakenly) that middle- and lower-class Mexican-American students identify strongly with each other and that they view issues in much the same way, or that Black male students have the same goals and views as Black female students.

As you are exposed to the media, be alert to how ascribed characteristics are used or not used. Listen to how other teachers talk among themselves about students. Do the teachers refer to the students' race, gender, or socioeconomic class when discussing their educational performance or social life? Do their comments reflect stereotypes or biases? Do they discuss these ascribed characteristics in an integrated or separate manner? Paying attention to these questions will help you develop a keen understanding of the importance of race, class, and gender in classroom life.

We reviewed most of the multicultural education literature written in the English-speaking world—more than 200 journal articles and 68 books—and discovered that educators often work with students of color, students from low-income backgrounds, and White female students, according to one of five approaches.[12] As we briefly explain these approaches, ask yourself which one you are most comfortable using in your teaching.

Before we begin this discussion, you should understand two important points. First, space does not allow for a complete discussion of each approach; for a thorough discussion, please refer to *Making Choices for Multicultural Education: Five Approaches to Race, Class and Gender.*[13] Second, if you discover that you are a true eclectic or that none of the approaches satisfies your teaching style, that is fine, as long as you are not straddling the fence. Indecision, dissatisfaction, and frustration in teaching style and technique may confuse your students. Also, to be the dynamic teacher you want to be, you need a teaching philosophy that is well thought out and makes learning exciting for your students. Good teaching requires that you have a complete understanding of what you are doing in the classroom and how you are doing it.

Approaches to Multicultural Education

Teaching the Exceptional and Culturally Different

If you believe that a teacher's chief responsibility is to prepare students of color, special-education students, White female students, and low-income students to fit into the existing classroom and later into adult society, this approach may be particularly appealing to you. It may be especially appealing if these students are behind in the main subject areas of the traditional curriculum. The goals of this approach are to equip such students with the cognitive skills, concepts, information, language, and values required by U.S. society and, eventually to enable them to hold a job and function within society's institutions and culture. Teachers using this approach often begin by determining the achievement levels of students who are behind, comparing their achievement to White middle-class students, and then working diligently to help them catch up. Starting where the students are and using instructional techniques and content familiar to the students are important. For example, one teacher who used this approach helped two Black students who had moved from a large urban area to a much smaller college town to catch up on their writing skills by having them write letters to the friends they left in the city. A second teacher grouped the girls in her ninth-grade class who were having problems in algebra, allowing the girls to work together, support one another, and not be intimidated by the boys in the class who had received the kind of socialization that produces good math students. A third teacher provided two learning-disabled students with materials written at their reading level that covered concepts comparable to those the rest of the class was reading about. A fourth teacher placed two Hispanic students with limited English-speaking abilities into a transitional bilingual program. A teacher may believe that only one or two students in the classroom need this approach. Or he or she may decide that all the students in the classroom need it, especially if the school is located in an inner-city community or barrio.

This approach argues that there is a corpus of knowledge to be learned, and that any deviation from that content should be temporary. A content deviation should provide knowledge that students should have acquired in previous grades. For example, an English as a Second Language (ESL) program is designed to provide language learning and some cultural information so that children with limited English proficiency can learn the curriculum that the typical English-speaking student is learning.

Instructional procedures may be changed more than the curriculum when using this approach. The teacher knows what he or she wants to teach but may be uncertain about how to reach the students successfully. Some teachers try to use the student's preferred learning style. For example, Riessman (1976) suggests that "the method of teaching formal communication to inner-city children takes advantage of their communication style by employing teaching techniques that stress the visual, the physical, and the active as much as possible."[14] Fennema and Peterson suggest that girls learn math better when taught through cooperative rather than competitive procedures.[15] In sum, the heart of this approach is building bridges for students to help them acquire the cognitive skills and knowledge expected of the "average" White middle-class student.

Human Relations Approach

If you believe that a major purpose of the school is to help students learn to live together harmoniously in a world that is becoming smaller and smaller, and if you believe that if students learn to respect one another regardless of race, class, gender, or exceptionality the United States will eventually reach its goal of equality for all, then this approach may be of special interest to you. The societal goal is to promote a feeling of unity, tolerance, and acceptance within the existing social structure, "I am okay and you are okay."

The human relations approach teaches positive feelings among all students, promotes group identity and pride for students of color, reduces stereotypes, and works to eliminate prejudice and biases. For example, a teacher of a fourth-grade multiracial, mainstreamed classroom spends considerable time during the first two weeks of each semester, and some time thereafter, doing activities to promote good human relations in the class. Early in the semester he uses a sociogram to learn student friendship patterns and to make certain that every child has a buddy. He also uses this activity to discover how negative or positive the boy-girl relationships are. He uses sentence-completion activities to discover how students are feeling about themselves and their family members. Based on these data, he integrates into his curriculum concepts of social acceptance and humanness for all people, the reduction and elimination of stereotypes, and information to help students feel good about themselves and their people. Also he regularly brings to his classroom speakers who represent the diversity in society to show all students that they too can be successful.

The school's goal is to build good brotherhood and sisterhood relationships between White and non-White people, males and females, and handicapped and nonhandicapped individuals. Advocates of this approach suggest that it should be comprehensive, integrated into several subject areas, and schoolwide. For example, a school attempting to promote gender equality is working at cross-purposes if lessons in language arts teach students to recognize sex stereotypes, while in the science class girls are not expected to perform as well as boys and are thus not pushed to do so. These contradictory attitudes simply reaffirm sex stereotypes.

The curriculum for the human relation approach to teaching addresses individual differences and similarities. It includes contributions of the groups to which the students are members and provides accurate information about various ethnic, handicap, gender, or social-class groups about whom the students hold stereotypes. Instructional procedures include a good deal of cooperative learning, role playing, and vicarious or real experiences to help the students develop appreciation of others. While the "teaching the exceptional and culturally different" approach emphasizes helping students acquire cognitive skills and knowledge in the traditional curriculum, the human relations approach focuses on attitudes and feelings students have about themselves and each other.

Single-Group Studies

We use the phrase "single-group studies" to refer to the study of a particular group of people, for example, Asian-American studies or Native American studies. We wanted to avoid using a phrase such as "ethnic studies," because included in this approach are, for example, women's studies and labor studies; "ethnic studies" would not indicate that inclusion.

The single-group studies approach emphasizes awareness, respect, and acceptance for the group receiving attention. The societal goals are to broaden what counts as mainstream culture and to promote social equality and cultural pluralism. These goals focus on the group as a people, their literature, history, and other culture forms that have not received authentic recognition by mainstream society. They also focus on how they have been and still are oppressed. This approach stresses educating the young to raise the status and respect of the group in society. It works to change negative societal attitudes about the group and provides a basis for social action by providing information about the damaging effects of discrimination on the group. For example, women's studies, according to Westkott, is intended "to change the sexist world."[16] Rutenberg explains that women's studies "rose as a critique to the traditional disciplines."[17] Women's studies corrects history that has been written almost solely by White men about White men. It teaches students about the oppression women face and provides female students with accurate knowledge, purpose, and understanding of themselves. For students of color, single-group studies, according to Cortada, provides the intellectual offensive for the social and political struggle for liberation and cultural integrity.[18] Suzuki describes single-group studies as giving students of color a sense of their history and identity in U.S. society and providing a sense of direction and purpose in their lives.[19] Finally, Nakanishi and Leong argue that single-group studies should help eliminate or reduce White racism.[20]

A school's curriculum for this approach would have units or courses about the history and culture of a group (for example, Asian-American history, labor history, internment of Japanese-Americans during World War II). It would also teach how the group has been victimized and has struggled to gain respect, as well as about current social issues facing the group.

We have seen teachers implement this approach in a number of ways. For example, one high school teacher teaches a course in either Black studies or women's studies every other semester. A seventh-grade social studies teacher spends about two weeks each semester on each of the following ethnic groups: American Indians, Black Americans, Asian-Americans, Hispanic-Americans. She does this by integrating material about the group into the traditional curriculum where possible and by spending some time during each class discussing the group under review.

The single-group studies approach views the student as an active learner, constantly seeking truth and knowledge and committed to reflecting on his or her learning. Instructional practices give special attention to the way members of that group learn best. The student works to develop what Freire calls a "critical consciousness."[21] To summarize, the single group studies approach involves making significant changes in what is normally taught, to provide an in-depth study of specific groups and a critical examination of their oppression.

Multicultural Education Approach

Multicultural education has become the most popular term used by educators to describe working with students who are different because of race, gender, class, or handicap. We use the term to apply to a particular approach, as most advocates of multicultural education prefer.

The societal goals of this approach are to reduce prejudice and discrimination against oppressed groups, to provide equal opportunity and social justice for all groups, and to effect an equitable distribution of power among members of the different cultural groups. The multicultural education approach attempts to reform the total schooling process for all children, regardless of whether the school is an all-White suburban school or a multiracial urban school. The curriculum and instructional program are changed to produce an awareness, acceptance, and affirmation of cultural diversity. The approach helps all students succeed in school and helps them understand and value diverse U.S. cultures and life-styles. To accomplish these goals, a school's staff is reeducated when necessary to ensure the successful implementation of the school's multicultural program. Staff members are hired to reflect the cultural diversity of the nation. The curriculum for this approach includes the perspectives, experiences, and contributions from people of color, low-income people, handicapped people, and White women, as well as White middle- and upper-class males. The curriculum is organized around concepts basic to each discipline, but content elaborating on those concepts is drawn from the experiences of several different cultural groups.

For example, if you are teaching literature, you select literature written by members of different groups. This not only teaches students that groups other than Whites have produced literature; it also enriches the concept of literature because it enables students to experience different literature forms, as well as certain universals that are common to all writing. For example, the universal struggle can be examined by reading about an Alaskan girl in *Julie of the Wolves*[22] and a Polynesian girl in the *Island of the Blue Dolphins*,[23] as well as a White boy in *The Call of the Wild.*[24]

It is also important that the contributions and perspectives you select depict each group as the group would depict itself and show the group as active and dynamic. This requires that you learn about various groups and become aware of what is important and meaningful to them. For example, teachers wishing to teach about famous Native Americans should ask members of different Native American tribes whom they would like to see celebrated, instead of holding up to their students Pocahantas, Kateri Tekakwitha, or Sacajawea. These Native Americans are often thought among their people to have served White interests more than Native American interests. Additionally, Blacks are becoming increasingly concerned because the Black athlete or entertainer (with the exception of Martin Luther King) is held up as the hero and heroine for their group, instead of Blacks who have done well in other areas of life, such as science or literature.

In this approach, instruction starts by assuming that students are capable of learning complex material and performing at a high level of skill. Each student has a personal, unique learning style that teachers discover and build on when teaching. The teacher draws on and uses the conceptual schemes (ways of thinking, knowledge about the world) students bring to school. Cooperative learning is fostered, and both boys and girls are treated equally, in a nonsexist manner. The multicultural education approach, more than the previous three, advocates total school reform to make the school reflect diversity. It also advocates giving equal attention to a variety of cultural groups regardless of whether or not they are represented in the school's student population.

Education That Is Multicultural and Social Reconstructionist

Education that is multicultural and social reconstructionist extends the multicultural education approach by educating students to become analytical and critical thinkers capable of examining their life circumstances and the social stratification that keeps them and their group from fully enjoying the social and financial rewards of this country. Or, if they are members of dominant groups, it helps them become critical thinkers who are capable of examining why their group exclusively enjoys the social and financial rewards of the nation. This approach teaches students how to use social action skills to participate in shaping and controlling their destiny. The phrase "education that is multicultural," Grant explains, means that the entire education program is redesigned to reflect the concerns of diverse (race, class, gender, and handicap) groups.[25] Its orientation and focus are on the whole education process. Social reconstructionism seeks to reform society toward greater equity in race, class, gender, and handicap. It draws on the penetrating vision of George Bernard Shaw, who exclaimed, "You see things, and you say, 'Why?' But I dream things that never were, and I say, 'why not?' "[26]

As we note above, this approach extends the multicultural education approach, in that the curriculum and instruction of these two approaches are very similar. However, there are four practices unique to education that is multicultural and social reconstructionist that should be a part of the program in the schools in which the approach is being implemented. First, democracy must be actively practiced in the schools. Having students read the Constitution and hear lectures on the three branches of government is a passive way to learn about democracy. For students to understand democracy they must *live it*. They must understand the importance of politics, debate, social action, and the acquisition of power. Commenting on this point, Banks says:

> They [oppressed ethnic groups] must also develop a sense of political efficacy, and be given practice in social action strategies which teaches them how to get power without violence and further exclusion. . . . Opportunities for social action, in which students have experience in obtaining and exercising power, should be emphasized within a curriculum that is designed to help liberate excluded ethnic groups.[27]

In the classroom this means that students will be given the opportunity to direct a good deal of their learning and to learn how to be responsible for that direction. This does not mean that teachers abdicate the running of their classroom to the students, but rather that they guide and direct students so they learn how to learn and develop skills for wise decision-making. Shor describes this as helping students become subjects rather than objects in the classroom,[28] and Freire says it will produce women and men "who organize themselves reflectively for action rather than men [and women] who are organized for passivity."[29]

A second practice is that students learn how to analyze their own life circumstances. Anyon tells us that we have a practical consciousness that coexists with a theoretical consciousness. Practical consciousness refers to one's commonsense understanding of one's own life, how "the system" works, and "everyday attempts to resolve the class, race, gender and other contradictions one faces."[30] Theoretical consciousness refers to dominant social ideologies. They are explanations one learns for how the world works, that assume conditions and life in the world are fair and just for everyone.

As you know, these two sets of consciousness do not always mesh; most of us learn to live within the boundaries of both of them. For example, students of color are taught that education is the doorway to success and that if they obey the teacher and do their work they will succeed. However, studies indicate that many students of color who comply with school rules and teachers' requests *still* do not receive the career guidance and school work necessary for becoming successful.[31] Furthermore, education pays off better for Whites than for people of color; for example in 1983, the average White person with four years of high school earned $25,387, whereas the average Black and Hispanic with the same amount of education earned $15,654 and $20,898, respectively.[32] Education that is multicultural and social reconstructionist teaches students to question what they hear about how society works from other sources and to analyze the experiences of people like themselves to understand more fully how society works so they can make informed choices when pursuing their own life goals.

A third practice is that students learn social action skills to increase their chances for success with the first two recommended practices. Bennett describes social action skills as "the knowledge, attitudes and skills needed to help students bring about political, social and economic changes."[33] In this approach the school is seen as a laboratory or training ground for preparing students to be more socially active. For example, some stories that elementary school children read could deal with issues involving discrimination and oppression and could suggest ways to deal with such problems. Students of all ages should be taught to identify sexist advertising of products sold in their community and how to take action to encourage advertisers to stop these types of practices. Advocates of this approach do not expect children to reconstruct the world, but they do expect the schools to teach students how to do their part in helping the nation achieve excellence and equity in all areas of life.

A fourth practice is coalescing, or getting the poor, people of color, and White women to work together for the common good of society. The coalescing of groups across the lines of race, class, gender, and exceptionality is important because it can energize and strengthen the fight against oppression. However, getting groups to work together is difficult because they have their own agendas and believe that they would have to place some of their goals second to those of other groups. For example, Davis has examined the struggle for suffrage for people of color and White women, arguing that White middle-class women distanced themselves from Black people when they feared Black men rather than White women would achieve voting rights.[34] Similarly, Blacks, Hispanics, and Asians find themselves divided along gender and class lines to the extent that middle-class males of all colors fail to take seriously the concerns of women and of lower-class members of their racial groups.

You now have an idea of the approaches used to teach multicultural education. Which one best suits your teaching philosophy and style? An equally important question is, Which approach will best help to bring excellence and equity to education? We next provide an example of how one teacher brings both excellence and equity to her classroom.

Ms. Julie Wilson and Her Approach to Teaching

The following describes a few days in the teaching life of Ms. Julie Wilson, a first-year teacher in a medium-large city. Which approach to multicultural education do you think Ms. Wilson is using? Which of her teaching actions do you agree or disagree with? What would you do if assigned to her class?

May 23

Julie Wilson was happy, but also sad that she had just completed her last exam at State U. As she walked back to her apartment, she wondered where she would be this time next year. She had applied for ten teaching positions and had been interviewed three times. As Julie entered her apartment building, she stopped to check the mail. A large fat white envelope addressed to her was stuffed into the small mailbox. She hurriedly tore it open and quickly read the first sentence. "We are pleased to offer you a teaching position. . . ." Julie leaped up the stairs three at a time. She burst into the apartment, waving the letter at her two roommates. "I've got a job! I got the job at Hoover Elementary. My first teaching job, a fifth-grade class!"

Hoover Elementary had been a part of a desegregation plan that brought together students from several different neighborhoods in the city. Hoover was situated in an urban-renewal area to which city officials were giving a lot of time and attention and on which they were spending a considerable amount of money. The city officials wanted to bring the Whites back into the city from suburbs and to encourage the middle-class people of color to remain in the city. They also wanted to improve the life chances for the poor. Julie had been hired because the principal was looking for teachers who had some record of success in working with diverse students. Julie had a 3.5 grade point average and had worked with a diverse student population in her practicum and student teaching experience. She had strong letters of recommendation from her cooperating teacher and university supervisor. Julie also had spent her last two summers working as a counselor in a camp that enrolled a wide diversity of students.

August 25
Julie was very pleased with the way her classroom looked. She had spent the last three days getting it ready for the first day of school. Plants, posters, goldfish, and an old rocking chair added to the warmth of an attractive classroom. There was also a big sign across the room saying "Welcome Fifth-Graders." Tomorrow was the big day.

August 26
Twenty-eight students entered Julie's classroom: fifteen girls and thirteen boys. There were ten White students, three Hmong students, six Hispanic students, and nine Black students. Three of the students were learning disabled and two were in wheelchairs. Eleven of the students were from middle-class homes, nine were from working-class homes, and the remaining eight were from very poor homes. Julie greeted each student with a big smile and a friendly hello as they entered the room. She asked their names and told them hers. She then asked them to take the seat with their name on the desk.

After the school bell rang, Julie introduced herself to the whole class. She told them that she had spent most of her summer in England, and that while she was there she had often thought about this day—her first day as a teacher. She talked briefly about some of the places she had visited in England as she pointed to the places on a map. She concluded her introduction by telling them a few things about her family. Her mother and father owned a dairy farm in Wisconsin, and she had one older brother, Wayne, and two younger sisters, Mary and Patricia. Julie asked if there were any students new to the school. Michael, a Black male, raised his hand, along with a female Hmong student, Mai-ka. She asked Mai-ka if she would like to tell the class her complete name, how she had spent her summer, and one favorite thing she liked to do. Then she asked the same of Michael. After Mai-ka and Michael finished introducing themselves, Julie invited the other students to do the same. Julie then asked Marie to tell Mai-ka and Michael about Hoover Elementary.

Once the opening greetings were completed, Julie began a discussion about the importance of the fifth grade and how special this grade was. She explained that this is a grade and class where a lot of learning would take place, along with a lot of fun. As Julie spoke, the students were listening intently. Julie radiated warmth and authority. Some of the students glanced at each other unsmilingly as she spoke of the hard work; however, when she mentioned "a lot of fun," the entire class perked up and looked at each other with big grins on their faces.

Julie had begun working on her educational philosophy in the Introduction to Education course at State U. Although she was continually modifying the way she thought about teaching, her basic philosophical beliefs had remained much the same. One of her major beliefs was that the students should actively participate in planning and shaping their own educational experiences. This, she believed, was as important for fifth-graders as twelfth-graders.

Julie asked the class if they were ready to take care of their classroom governance—deciding on rules, helpers, a discipline code, and time for classroom meetings. The class responded enthusiastically. The first thing the students wanted to do was to decide on the class rules. Several began to volunteer rules:

"No stealing."
"No rock throwing on the playground."
"No sharpening pencils after the bell rings."
"No fighting."

As the students offered suggestions, Julie wrote them on the chalkboard. After giving about sixteen suggestions, the class concluded. Julie commented, "All the rules seem very important"; she then asked the class what they should do with the rules. One student, Richard, suggested that they be written on poster board and placed in the upper corner of the room for all to see. Other class members said, "Yes, this is what we did last year in fourth grade." William, however, said, "Yes, we did do this, but we rarely followed the rules after the first day we made them." Julie assured the class this would not be the case this year, and that they would have a weekly classroom meeting, run by an elected official of the class. She then asked if they thought it would be helpful if they wrote their rules using positive statements, instead of "no" or negative statements. The class said yes and began to change statements such as "no stealing" to "always ask before borrowing," and "no rock throwing" to "rock throwing can severely hurt a friend." Once the rules were completed, the class elected their officers.

After the classroom governance was taken care of, Julie asked the students if they would like her to read them a story. An enthusiastic yes followed her question. Julie glanced at the clock as she picked up *To Break the Silence*[35] from the desk. The book is a varied collection of short stories, especially for young readers, written by authors of different ethnic backgrounds. It was 11:35. She could hardly believe the morning had gone by so quickly. She read for twenty minutes. All the students seemed to be enjoying the story, except Lester and Ben, two Black male students. Lester and Ben were drawing pictures, communicating nonverbally between themselves and ignoring the rest of the class members. Julie decided that because they were quiet and not creating a disturbance she would leave them alone.

After lunch, Julie had the class do two activities designed to help her learn about each student both socially and academically. She had the students do a self-concept activity, in which they did sentence completions that asked them to express how they felt about themselves. Then she had them play math and reading games to assess informally their math and reading skills. These activities took the entire afternoon, and Julie was as pleased as the students when the school day came to an end.

When Julie arrived at her apartment, she felt exhausted. She had a quick dinner and shower and then crawled into bed. She set the alarm for 7 P.M., and fell quickly asleep.

By 10:30 that night she had examined the students' self-concept activity and compared the information she had collected from the informal math and reading assessment with the official information from the students' cumulative record cards. She thought about each student's achievement record, social background, race, gender, and exceptionality. She said aloud, "I need to make plans soon to meet every parent. I need to find out about the students' lives at home, the parents' expectations, and if I can get some of them to volunteer."

Julie turned off her desk lamp at 11:45 to retire for the evening. She read a few pages from Richard Wright's *Native Son* and then turned out the light. Tonight she was going to sleep with less tension and nervousness than she had the night before. She felt good about the way things had gone today and was looking forward to tomorrow. As Julie slept, she dreamed of her class. Their faces and most of their names and backgrounds floated through her mind.

Eight of the ten White students were from Briar Creek, a solid middle-class single-unit housing community; these students were performing at grade level or above in all scholastic areas, and each of them was at least a year ahead in some core area subject. Charles, who had used a wheelchair since he was in an automobile accident three years ago, was three years ahead in both reading and math. However, Elaine and Bob had chosen a mixture of positive and negative adjectives when doing the self-concept activity and this concerned Julie. She would keep her eye on them to try to determine the cause of their problems.

Estelle and Todd, the other two White students, were between six months and a year behind in most academic areas. Estelle had been diagnosed as learning disabled, but the information in her personal cumulative file folder seemed ambiguous about the cause of her problem. Julie wondered if Estelle was classified as L.D. based on uncertain reasons. She recalled an article that discussed the learning-disability label as being more socially constructed than based on medical evidence.

All three of the Hmong students were at grade level or very close in their subjects. However, two of them, Mai-ka and Chee, were having some difficulty speaking English. The Kaying family owned a restaurant in the neighborhood. The rumor mill reported that they were doing very well financially, so well that they had recently opened a restaurant in the downtown area of the city. All of the six Hispanic students were Mexican-American, born in the United States. Marie, José, and Lourdes were bilingual, and the other three were monolingual, with English being their primary language. Marie, José, and Lourdes were from working-class homes, and Richard, Jesus, and Carmen were from very poor homes. Lourdes, Carmen, and Richard's achievement scores were at least two years ahead of their grade level. José was working at grade level, and Marie and Jesus were one to two years behind.

The Black students—Lester, Ben, Gloria, Sharon, and Susan—were all performing two years behind grade level in all core area subjects. All five lived in the Wendell Phillips low-rent projects. Two Black students—Shelly and Ernestine—lived in Briar Creek and were performing above grade level in all academic areas. Dolores and Gerard lived in Chatham, a working-class predominantly Black neighborhood; both were performing above grade level in all subjects, except Gerard, who was behind in math. Gerard also had chosen several negative words when doing the self-concept activity.

All students in Julie's class were obedient and came from families that encouraged getting a good education.

May 25, 7:30 A.M.

Julie liked arriving early at school. The engineer, Mike, usually had a pot of coffee perking when she arrived. This was her time to get everything ready for the day. She had been teaching for almost one school year and was proud and pleased with how everything was going. The school principal, Mr. Griffin, had been in her class three times for formal visits and had told others, "Julie is an excellent teacher." He usually offered her one or two minor suggestions, such as "Don't call the roll every day; learn to take your attendance silently," and "The museum has an excellent exhibit on food and the human body your class may enjoy."

Julie had also been surprised by several things. She was surprised at how quickly most of the teachers left school at the end of the day. Out of a staff of twenty classroom teachers, only about five or six came early or stayed late. Even more surprising to her was how she and the other teachers who either came early or stayed late were chided about this behavior. She was surprised at the large number of worksheets and ditto sheets used and at how closely many teachers followed the outline in the books regardless of the needs of students. Also, she noticed, there was a common belief among the staff that her instructional style would not work.

Julie had made several changes in the curriculum. She had adopted a tradebook approach to reading and integrated that with her language arts. She made available to the students a wide assortment of books that featured different races, exceptionalities, and socioeconomic classes. In some stories, both males and females were featured doing traditional as well as nontraditional things. Stories were set in urban and rural settings and some featured children who were handicapped. It had taken Julie several months to get such a diverse collection of books for her students, and she had even spent some of her own money for the books, but the excitement the students had shown about the materials made the expense worthwhile.

She also had several computers in her class. When she discovered that Richard's father owned a computer store, she convinced him to lend the class two computer systems, and she convinced Mr. Griffin to purchase two others at cost. Several of the students from Briar Creek had computers at home. Charles and Elaine, Julie discovered, were wizards at the computer. Julie encouraged them to help the other students (and herself—since she had taken only one computer course at State U). The two students enjoyed this assignment and often had a small group of students remain after school to receive their help. Julie was pleased at how well Charles and Elaine handled this responsibility. Lester and Ben were Charles's favorite students; they liked the computer, but Julie believed they liked Charles and his electric wheelchair even more. Julie had heard them say on several occasion that Charles was "cool." Lester's and Ben's work was showing a steady improvement and Charles enjoyed having two good friends. This friendship, Julie believed, had excellent mutual benefits for all concerned, including herself.

Julie taught most of her math by providing the students with real life opportunities to see the concept in action. She often took her class to the supermarket, to the bank, and to engineering firms. She made certain that she selected firms that employed men and women of color and White women in positions of leadership. She often requested that a representative from these groups spend a few minutes with the students, explaining their role and duties.

Julie took the students on field trips to supermarkets in different areas of town so the students could compare prices and quality of products (e.g., fruit, meat, and vegetables) between the surburban area and the inner-city area. On two occasions this led to a letter-writing campaign to the owner of the food chain to explain their findings. The students also wondered why the cost of gas was cheaper in the suburban areas than in the inner-city area. This became a math, social studies, and language arts lesson. Letters were written and interviews conducted to ascertain the cost of delivering the gas to the inner city as compared to the surburban area of the city, and to ascertain the rental fee for service station property in the inner city in comparison to the surburban areas. Math skills were used to determine if there needed to be a difference in gas prices between the areas after rental fee and delivery charges were taken into consideration.

Julie used advertisements and editorials from newspapers and magazines to help students see the real-life use of such concepts as sexism, justice, and equity. Julie supplemented her social studies curriculum on a regular basis. She found the text biased in several areas. She would integrate into the assigned curriculum information from the history and culture of diffrent ethnic groups. For example, when teaching about the settling of the local community years ago, she invited a Native American female historian and a White historian to give views on how the settling took place and on problems and issues associated with it. She invited a Black historian and a Hispanic historian to discuss what was presently happening in the area.

Students were usually encouraged to undertake different projects to provide a comprehensive perspective on the social studies unit under study. Choices were up to the student, but Julie maintained high expectations and insisted that excellence in every phase of the work was always necessary for each student. She made certain that during the semester each student was a project leader. She also made certain that boys and girls worked together. For example, Julie knew that Ben, Lester, and Charles usually stayed close together and did not have a girl as a member of their project team. She also knew that Carmen was assertive and had useful knowledge about the project on which they were working. She put Carmen on the project term.

Julie did have two problems with her class that she could not figure out. Shelly and Ernestine did not get along well with any of the Black students, especially Ben and Lester. George and Hank, two White boys from Briar Creek, had considerable difficulty getting along with José and went out of their way to be mean to Lourdes and Marie. Julie was puzzled by George's and Hank's behavior; she did not think it was racially motivated because both of the boys got along pretty well with Shelly. She labored over this problem and discussed it with the school counselor. She wondered if she didn't have a problem related to a combination of race, class, and gender in George's and Hank's relationship with José, Lourdes, and Marie. She also concluded that she might have a social-class problem among the Black students. Julie decided to discuss her concerns with the students individually. After some discussion, she discovered that Shelly's and Ernestine's problem with Ben and Lester was related to social class and color. Both Shelly and Ernestine had very fair skin color. They had grown up in a predominantly White middle-class community and had spent very little time around other Black students. Ben and Lester were dark-skinned male students who lived in a very poor neighborhood. Julie felt that if her assumptions were true, she would need help with this problem. She was successful in getting a Black child psychiatrist to talk to her class. She did this in relationship to an art unit that examined "color, attitude, and feelings." His discussion enabled Julie to continue her discussion with Shelly and Ernestine and get them to examine their prejudice.

George and Hank admitted to Julie, after several discussions, that they did not care too much for any girls. But Hispanic girls who wore funny clothes and ate non-American foods were a big bore. It took Julie several months of talking with George and Hank, using different reading materials and having them all work on a group project under her direction, to get George and Hank to reduce some of their prejudices. At the end of the semester, Julie still believed this problem had not been completely resolved. Thus she shared it with the sixth-grade teacher.

At the end of the school year, Julie felt very good about her first year. She knew she had grown as a teacher. She believed her professors at State U, her cooperating teacher, and her university supervisor would give her very high marks. They had encouraged her to become a reflective teacher—committed, responsible, and wholehearted in her teaching effort. Julie believed she was well on her way to becoming a reflective teacher, and she looked forward to her second year with enthusiasm.

From what you know of Julie, what is her approach to multicultural education? Would you be comfortable doing as Julie did? Discuss Julie's teaching with your classmates. How would you change it?

Conclusion

In Julie's classroom, as in yours, race, class, gender, and exceptionality are ascribed characteristics students bring to school that cannot be ignored. To bring excellence into her teaching, Julie had to affirm her students' diversity. Why do we say this?

For one thing, Julie needed to pay attention to her students' identities to help them achieve. She needed to acknowledge the importance of Black males to American life to hold the interest of Lester and Ben; she needed to acknowledge Mai-ka's and Chee's prior learning to help them learn English and school material; she needed to become familiar with her students' learning styles so her teaching would be most effective.

For another thing, Julie needed to pay attention to her students' personal and social needs to help them perceive school as a positive experience. Some of her students disliked other students because of prejudices and stereotypes. Some of her students did not know how to relate to people in wheelchairs or to people who looked or talked differently. Some of her students felt negative about their own abilities. These attitudes interfere not only with achievement, but also with one's quality of life, both as students today and later as adults in a pluralistic society.

Julie also knew that the future of the United States depends on its diverse children. Her students will all be U.S. adults one day, regardless of the quality of their education. But what kind of adults will they become? Julie wanted them all to be skilled in a variety of areas, to be clear and critical thinkers, and to have a sense of social justice and caring for others. Julie had some personal selfish motives for this: She knew her own well-being in old age would depend directly on the ability of today's children to care for older people when they become adults. She also knew her students of today would be shaping the society in which her children would one day grow up. She wanted to make sure they were as well prepared as possible to be productive citizens who had a vision of a better society. She drew from all of the approaches, at one time or another, to address specific problems and needs she saw in the classroom. But the approach she emphasized, and the one that guided her planning, was education that is multicultural and social reconstructionist.

How will you approach excellence and equity in your own classroom? We can guarantee that all your students will have their identities shaped partly by their race, social class, and gender; all of them will notice and respond in one way or another to people who differ from themselves; and all of them will grow up in a society that is still in many ways racist, sexist, and classist. You are the only one who can guarantee what you will do about that.

Questions and Activities

1. Why is it important for teachers to strive to attain both excellence and equity for their students? What can you do to try to achieve both goals in your teaching?

2. What does each of these terms mean to you in relationship to classroom life: *race, class, gender,* and *exceptionality?* How are your notions of these concepts similar to and different from those of your classmates?

3. Give an example of how such variables as race, class, and gender interact to influence the behavior of a particular student.

4. Name the five approaches to multicultural education identified by Grant and Sleeter. What are the assumptions and instructional goals of each approach?

5. In what significant ways does the "education that is multicultural and social reconstructionist" approach differ from the other four approaches? What problems might a teacher experience when trying to implement this approach in the classroom? How might these problems be reduced or solved?

6. Visit a school in your community and interview several teachers and the principal about activities and programs the school has implemented in multicultural education. Using the typology of multicultural education described by the authors, determine what approach or combination of approaches to multicultural education are being used within the school. Share your findings with your classmates or fellow workshop participants.

7. Which approach to multicultural education is Ms. Wilson using? Which aspects of her teaching do you especially like? Which aspects would you change?

8. Which approach to multicultural education described by the authors would you be the most comfortable using? Why?

Notes

1. National Commission on Excellence in Education, *A Nation at Risk* (Washington, D.C.: U.S. Government Printing Office, 1983), p. 5.

2. Ibid.

3. Ibid., p. 12.

4. *Brown* v. *Board of Education,* 347 U.S. 483, 1954.

5. *A Nation at Risk,* p. 6.

6. Ibid., p. 25.

7. "Here They Come, Ready or Not," *Education Week,* 5 (May 14, 1986): 14.

8. Ibid., p. 28.

9. National Center for Education Statistics, *Condition of Education* (Washington, D.C.: U.S. Government Printing Office, 1983), p. 199.

10. Michael W. Apple, "Educational Reports and Economic Realities," in Philip G. Altbach, Gail P. Kelly and Lois Weis, eds., *Excellence in Education* (Buffalo, N.Y.: Prometheus, 1986), pp. 91–106.

11. Carl A. Grant and Christine E. Sleeter, "Equality, Equity, and Excellence: A Critique," in Philip G. Altbach, Gail P. Kelly, and Lois Weis, eds., *Excellence in Education* (Buffalo, N.Y.: Prometheus, 1986), pp. 139–160.

12. Carl Grant, Christine Sleeter, and J. Anderson, "The Literature on Multicultural Education: Review and Analysis," *Educational Studies* 12 (1986): 47–72.

13. Christine E. Sleeter and Carl A. Grant, *Making Choices for Multicultural Education: Five Approaches to Race, Class and Gender* (Columbus, Ohio: Merrill, 1988).

14. Frank Riessman, *The Inner-City Child* (New York: Harper & Row, 1976).

15. Elizabeth Fennema and Penelope L. Peterson, "Effective Teaching for Girls and Boys: The Same or Different?" in David C. Berliner and Barak V. Rosenshine, eds., *Talks to Teachers* (New York: Random House, 1987), pp. 111–125.

16. Marcia Westkott, "Women's Studies as a Strategy for Change: Between Criticism and Vision," in Gloria Bowles and Renate D. Klein, eds., *Theories of Women's Studies* (London: Routledge and Kegan Paul, 1983), pp. 210–218.

17. Taly Rutenberg, "Learning Women's Studies," in Gloria Bowles and Renate D. Klein, eds., *Theories of Women's Studies* (London: Routledge and Kegan Paul, 1983), pp. 72–78.

18. Rafael E. Cortada, *Black Studies: An Urban and Comparative Curriculum* (Greenwich, Conn.: Xerox Publishing Group, 1974).

19. Bob H. Suzuki, "An Asian-American Perspective on Multicultural Education: Implications for Practice and Policy." Paper presented at the Second Annual Conference of the National Association for Asian and Pacific American Education, Washington, D.C., 1980.

20. Don T. Nakanishi and Russell Leong, "Toward the Second Decade, a National Survey of Asian American Studies Programs," *Amerasia Journal* 5 (1978): 1–2.

21. Paulo Freire, *Pedagogy of the Oppressed* (New York: The Seaburg Press, 1970).

22. Jean C. George, *Julie of the Wolves* (New York: Harper and Row, 1972).

23. Scott O'Dell, *Island of the Blue Dolphins* (Boston: Houghton Mifflin, 1960).

24. Jack London, *The Call of the Wild* (New York: Harmony Books, 1977).

25. Carl Grant, "Education That Is Multicultural—Isn't That What We Mean?" *Journal of Teacher Education* 29 (1978): 45–49.

26. George B. Shaw, "Back to Methuselah," in John Bartlett, ed., *Familiar Quotations* (Boston: Little, Brown Co., 1980), p. 681.

27. James A. Banks, *Multiethnic Education: Theory and Practice* (Boston: Allyn and Bacon, 1981), p. 149.

28. Ira Shor, *Critical Teaching and Everyday Life* (Boston: South End Press, 1980).

29. Paulo Freire, *The Politics of Education: Culture, Power, and Liberation,* D. Macedo, trans. (Boston: Bergin and Garvey, 1985).

30. Jean Anyon, "Elementary Schooling and Distinctions of Social Class," *Interchange* 12 (1981): 118–132.

31. Carl A. Grant and Christine E. Sleeter, *After the School Bell Rings* (Barcombe, England: Falmer Press, 1986).

32. U.S. Department of Commerce (Washington, D.C.: Bureau of Census, 1986).

33. Christine E. Bennett, *Comprehensive Multicultural Education* (Boston: Allyn and Bacon, 1986), p. 212.

34. Angela Y. Davis, *Women, Race, and Class* (New York: Random House, 1981).

35. Peter A. Barrett, ed., *To Break the Silence* (New York: Dell Publishing Company, 1986).

Teachers can help create an educational environment that provides equal educational opportunities for students from different social classes and religions.

PART II

Social Class and Religion

The two chapters in Part II of this book discuss the effects of two powerful variables on student behavior, beliefs, and achievement: social class and religion. Social class is a powerful variable in American society despite entrenched beliefs about individual opportunity in the United States. As Persell points out in Chapter 4, three children born at the same time but into different social classes have very unequal educational opportunities. Students from the lower, middle, and upper classes usually attend different kinds of schools and have teachers who have different beliefs and expectations about their academic achievement. The structure of educational institutions also favors middle- and upper-class students. Structure such as tracking, IQ tests, and programs for gifted and mentally retarded students are highly biased in favor of middle- and upper-class students. Structures such as tracking, IQ tests, and programs for tors can create equal educational opportunities for students from different social classes.

Students who are socialized within religious families and communities often have beliefs and behaviors that conflict with those of the school. During the 1980s, religious fundamentalists strongly challenged the scientific theories taught by schools about the origin of human beings. They also attacked textbooks and fictional books assigned by teachers that they felt violated or contradicted their beliefs. Conflicts about the right to pray in the school were also acid during the 1980s. The school should help students mediate between their home culture and the school culture. Uphoff, in Chapter 5, suggests some promising ways in which this can be done.

CHAPTER 4

Social Class and Educational Equality

■ CAROLINE HODGES PERSELL

Picture three babies born at the same time, but to parents of different social-class backgrounds. The first baby is born into a wealthy, well-educated, business or professional family. The second is born into a middle-class family in which both parents attended college and have middle-level managerial jobs. The third is born into a poor family in which neither parent finished high school or has a steady job. Will these children receive the same education in the United States? Although the United States is based on the promise of equal opportunity for all, the educational experiences of these three children are likely to be quite different.

Education in the United States is not a single, uniform system that is available to every child in the same way. Children of different social classes are likely to attend different types of schools, to receive different types of instruction, to study different curricula, and to leave school at different rates and times. As a result, when children end their schooling, they are more different from each other than they were when they entered, and these differences may be seen as legitimating the unequal positions people face in their adult lives. If we understand better how schools may contribute to inequalities, we may be in a better position to try to change them.

The nature and meaning of social class are issues often debated by social scientists. Researchers often measure social class by asking survey questions about a person's or a family's educational level, occupation, rank in an organization, and earnings.[1] However social class is measured, it has been found repeatedly to be related to how well students do in school.[2] Although there are a number of exceptions, students from higher social-class backgrounds tend to get better grades and to stay in school longer than do students from lower-class backgrounds. The question is, why does this happen? Is it determined by the individuals, or does something about the educational system contribute to this result? I argue that three things contribute a great deal to the unequal educational results so often documented by social researchers:

1. The structure of schooling in the United States.
2. The beliefs held by U.S. educators.
3. The curricular and teaching practices in U.S. schools.

By *structure of schooling* I mean such features as differences between urban, rural, and suburban schools, and differences between public and private schools. By *educational beliefs* I mean beliefs about IQ (intelligence quotient) and cultural deprivation, two sets of ideas that have been offered to explain why lower-class children often do less well in school. In *curricular and teaching practices* I include tracking of students into certain curricula, teachers' expectations about what different children can learn, and differences in the quantity and quality of what is taught.

This chapter reviews research showing differences in educational structures, beliefs, and practices; examines how these differences are related to the social-class backgrounds of students; considers the consequences they have for student achievement; and analyzes how they affect individuals' adult lives. Lest this be too depressing an account, at the end of the chapter I suggest some ways that teachers and other educators might work to improve education.

Educational Structures

The three babies described above are not likely to attend the same school, even if they live in the same area. Most students in the United States attend schools that are relatively alike with respect to the social-class backgrounds of the other students. One reason this happens is that people in the United States tend to live in areas that are fairly similar with respect to class and race. If they attend their neighborhood school, they are with students from similar backgrounds. If children grow up in a fairly diverse area such as a large city, mixed suburb, or rural area, they are less likely to attend the same schools. The states with the most private schools, for example, are the states with the largest concentrations of urban areas.[3] If, by chance, students of different backgrounds do attend the same school, they are very likely to experience different programs of study because of tracking and ability grouping.

In older suburbs or cities, children of higher-class families are more likely to attend homogeneous neighborhood schools, selective public schools, or private schools, and to be in higher tracks; lower-class children are also likely to attend school together. Middle-class families try to send their children to special public schools, parochial schools, or private schools if they can afford them.

Private day and boarding schools are also relatively similar with respect to social class, despite the fact that some scholarships are awarded. Researchers who studied elite boarding schools, for example, found that 46 percent of the families had incomes of more than $100,000 per year in the early 1980s.[4]

Let's look more closely at elite private schools and exclusive suburban schools, which are overwhelmingly attended by upper- and upper-middle-class students; at parochial schools, attended by middle-class and working-class students, and at large urban public schools, heavily attended by lower-class pupils. Although these descriptions gloss over many distinctions within each major type of school, they do convey some of the range of differences that exist under the overly broad umbrella we call U.S. education.

Schools of the Upper and Upper-Middle Classes

At most upper- and upper-middle-class high schools, the grounds are spacious and well kept, the computer, laboratory, language, and athletic facilities are extensive, the teachers are well educated and responsive to students and parents, classes are small, nearly every student studies a college preparatory curriculum, and considerable homework is assigned.

At the private schools, these tendencies are often intensified. The schools are quite small, with few having more than 1,200 students. Teachers do not have tenure or belong to unions, so they can be fired by the headmaster or headmistress if they are considered unresponsive to students or parents. Classes are small, often having no more than fifteen students, and sometimes considerably fewer. Numerous advanced placement courses offer the possibility of college credit. Students remark that it is not "cool to be dumb around here."[5] Most students watch very little television during the school week and do a great deal of homework.[6] They have many opportunities for extracurricular activities, such as debate and drama clubs, publications, and music, and the chance to learn sports that colleges value, such as crew, squash, and lacrosse. Students have both academic and personal advisors who monitor their progress, help them solve problems, and try to help them have a successful school experience.

Affluent suburban communities have a robust tax base to support annual costs that in 1987 ran as high as $9,000 per pupil. School board members are elected by members of the community who may know them. Private schools are run by self-perpetuating boards of trustees, many of whom are alumni/ae of the school. The school head is chosen by the board of trustees and may be replaced by them if they are not satisfied.

Private Parochial Schools

Many differences exist among parochial schools, but in general these schools are relatively small. More of these high school students study an academic program and do more homework than do their public-school peers. They also are subjected to somewhat stricter discipline.[7] The classes, however, are often larger than elite private, suburban, or urban school classes, with sometimes as many as forty or fifty pupils per class. Some non-Catholic middle- and working-class parents, especially those in urban areas, send their children to parochial schools.[8]

The costs at parochial schools are relatively low, especially compared to private schools, because these schools are subsidized by religious groups. These schools have relatively low teacher salaries and usually have no teachers' unions. Currently there are more lay teachers and fewer nuns, sisters, priests, and brothers as teachers. The schools are governed by the religious authority that runs them.

Urban Schools

Urban schools are usually quite large, and they are part of an even larger school system that is invariably highly bureaucratic. They usually offer varied courses of study, including academic, vocational, and general curricular tracks. The school systems of large cities and older, larger suburbs tend to lack both political and economic resources. These systems have become highly centralized, with school board members generally elected on a citywide basis.[9] School board members are often concerned members of the community who may send their own children to private schools, and they may have little knowledge about or power over the daily operations of the public system. The authority of professional educators is often buttressed by bureaucratic procedures and by unionization of teachers and administrators. At least one observer[10] has described the system as one of organizational paralysis, rather than governance.

Economically, the large city school systems are also relatively powerless. Their shrinking tax bases make them dependent on nonlocal sources (state and federal monies) to balance their budgets. Moreover, the property tax base of public education in the United States results in vastly unequal resources for urban, suburban, and rural schools, and for major regional variations in educational expenditures.

In general, then, one's social-class background is related to the school one attends, the size of the school, the political and economic resources available to the school, and the curricula offered.

Educational Beliefs

Two educational concepts have been particularly important in influencing educational practices in the twentieth century. These are IQ and *cultural deprivation*. These concepts have also dominated explanations of differences in school achievement among students of different social classes. Considerable attention has been devoted to determining which concept provides the more correct explanation. However, while they seem to be competing explanations, they actually have many common assumptions and share many significant consequences.

A great deal of educational thought and research have been devoted to the study of intelligence quotient, or IQ. The concept of IQ has been used to explain why some children learn more slowly than others, why Black children do less well in school than White children, and why lower-class children do less well than middle- and upper-middle-class children. IQ tests are often used to justify variations in education, achievement, and rewards. The justification usually is that because some people are more intelligent than others, they are entitled to more of these other things as well. Such justification occurs in curricular tracking and in student exposure to different educational programs and resources.

IQ tests, however, were designed to *differentiate* people. This was done by dropping from the final intelligence test those items that everyone answered correctly (about 60 percent of the initial items) and including only those questions that some portion (about 40 to 60 percent) of the respondents answered incorrectly. This was done even when the rejected items represented the best possible measure of achievement or aptitude.

Critics of IQ tests have raised a number of good points about the accuracy of the tests. For example, IQ tests do not measure such important features of intelligence as creative or divergent thinking, logic, and critical reasoning. The idea of multiple intelligences is well developed by Howard Gardner in his book *Frames of Mind.*[11]

IQ tests have good predictive validity for grades in school, which was what Binet designed them for originally. The real question is, how valid are IQ tests or grades for predicting success in life? Many studies find little relationship between educational achievement and performance on the job, in a variety of occupations.[12]

IQ testing, especially at an early age, may be inefficient because it may rule out the late bloomer, the early rebel, or the child whose family does not stress test-taking skills. Yet, those very people may have a great deal to contribute to society.

IQ tests are criticized for being culturally biased. To do well on an IQ test, an individual needs to have learned White middle-class, U.S. English. One section of the WPPSI (Wechsler Preschool-Primary Scale of Intelligence) requires children to repeat sentences verbatim to the examiner. Children who know a different dialect may provide a simultaneous translation of the sentence read and say it in their own dialect, but they are penalized for not repeating the sentence exactly. They have shown a much more advanced skill than rote memory, but in the test scoring it is a handicap. Even nonverbal tasks such as stacking blocks can be culturally loaded, because more middle-class homes have blocks than do lower-class homes. The ideological significance of IQ tests becomes most apparent in the explanations that have been offered for different educational results.

There is a big controversy in the behavioral and social sciences over whether differences in IQ test scores among students of different classes are the result of genetic deficits (nature) or to cultural deprivation (nurture). Advocates of each position take for granted the importance of IQ test scores.

Arthur Jensen rekindled the genetic controversy when he asserted in 1969 that 80 percent of the variation in intelligence is determined by heredity.[13] Even though it is clear that some portion of IQ is transmitted genetically from parent to child, no one knows exactly how much. Nor do we know very much about how heredity and environment interact, except that such interaction is likely and probably very significant. But even if IQ were totally heritable, it could still be influenced by the environment in which the individual was socialized. Traits such as height, which are highly heritable, can change dramatically in different environments.

Economic and social environments facilitate the development of genetic potential. This fact has led to another explanation for differential school achievement, namely, cultural deprivation.

The cultural deprivation explanation sees low-income or minority children as failing to achieve in school because of their deficient home environments, disorganized family structure, inadequate child-rearing patterns, undeveloped language and values, and low self-esteem.

Let us consider the issue of self-esteem, which is related to a person's social status. If cultural deprivation and family deficiencies were the factors that produced low self-esteem in children, we would expect very young children to show the same low self-esteem that older ones do. But the reverse is the case. The older the children and the more time they spend in school, the more their self-esteem plummets.[14] This result suggests that something happens to the initially high self-esteem of lower-class youngsters as they encounter predominantly middle-class institutions. Hence, it is not the so-called pathology of their homes that seems to affect their self-esteem, but something else.

Much of the social science literature has been filled with debates between the IQ and cultural deprivation positions, in what might be today's version of a nature-nurture controversy. But this controversy directs attention away from the common premises and consequences shared by both explanations of differences in test performance and school achievement. These premises include the following:

1. Both genetic and cultural-deficit theorists assume that IQ is important for success in life and appear to agree with the necessity of early testing and selection in schools. They do not question the need for performance on tests designed to differentiate children.

2. Supporters of both theories place the blame for academic failure on children and their families. Thus they divert attention from the entire educational system and how it produces certain outcomes, including failure among certain types of children. (Not every upper-class child has a high IQ, but do you think that those with lower IQs are allowed to fail at the same rate as lower-class and minority children?)

3. Accepting these theories is the same as justifying whatever educators do, because the fault presumably lies with the children.

4. These concepts have self-fulfilling potency; that is, if teachers believe that children *cannot* learn because of their genetic or cultural deficits, they will expect less of them and teach them less, and indeed, it is likely that the children will learn less. Their lower grades tend to confirm the predictions. Hence, the self-fulfilling nature of the prophecy.

5. These theories divert attention from questions about how children learn and what kinds of cognitive skills they have. Such theories make it less likely that effective forms of teaching and learning will happen.

6. Finally, and perhaps most important, the genetic and cultural-deficit theories of differences in school achievement offer compensatory education as the sole solution to poverty, thus diverting attention from structural inequalities of power and wealth. Thus, both views leave existing structures of inequalities unchallenged.

I am not suggesting that intellectual or cultural differences do not exist between individuals. Differences in intelligence or culture may affect the speed at which students can learn certain things, and they also influence the effectiveness of different pedagogical approaches. What is important, however, is how intellectual differences are labeled, regarded, and treated by schools, because those beliefs contribute to the maintenance of educational and social inequalities.

For example, in China and the USSR, where different concepts of individual intellectual abilities prevail, teachers work with slow learners until they learn. As the leaders of a school in Peking said, "Of course people differ in ability. But a student who is weak in one field may be strong in another. And these abilities are not something innate and unchanging. Abilities grow when they are made use of, through practice. . . . As abilities grow by being used they are not constant, and it does not make any sense to say that a given individual has so and so much ability."[15]

The widespread use of IQ testing and the explanations offered for differences in IQ and school achievement are critically important for the curricular and teaching practices in schools.

Curricular and Teaching Practices

As noted earlier, schools attended by children of different social classes vary in terms of what proportion of their students study an academic curriculum. They also vary in terms of how much work they expect and demand of their students. Two curricular and teaching practices in particular highlight how school experiences vary by the students' social class, namely, tracking and teachers' expectations.

Tracking

The first recorded instance of tracking was the Harris plan in St. Louis, begun in 1867. Since then, tracking has followed a curious pattern in the United States of alternate popularity and disuse. In the 1920s and 1930s, when many foreign immigrants settled in the United States, tracking increased greatly. Thereafter it fell into decline until the late 1950s, when it was revived, apparently in response to the USSR's launching of Sputnik and the United States' competitive concern with identifying and educating the gifted.[16] That period was also marked by large migrations of rural southern Blacks to northern cities and by an influx of Puerto Rican and Mexican-American migrants into the United States. Tracking today is widespread, particularly in large, diverse school systems and in schools serving primarily lower-class students.[17] It is less prevalent, and less rigid when it occurs, in upper-middle-class suburban and private schools and in parochial schools.[18]

What exactly is tracking? To address this question, we need to examine the distinction between ability grouping and curriculum differentiation. Proponents of ability grouping stress flexible subject-area assignment. By this they mean that students are assigned to learning groups on the basis of their background and achievement in a subject area at any given moment, and that skills and knowledge are evaluated at relatively frequent intervals. Students showing gains can be shifted readily into another group. They might also be in different ability groups in different subjects, according to their own rate of growth in each subject. This practice suggests a common curriculum shared by all students, with only the mix of student abilities being varied. It also assumes that, within that curriculum, all groups are taught the same material.

In fact, it seems that group placement becomes self-perpetuating, that students are often grouped at the same level in all subjects, and that even a shared curriculum may be taught differently to different groups. This is especially likely to happen in large, bureaucratic, urban public schools. Quite often, different ability groups are assigned to different courses of study, resulting in simultaneous grouping by curriculum and ability. Rosenbaum notes that although ability grouping and curriculum grouping may appear different to educators, in fact they share several social similarities: (1) Students are placed with those defined as similar to themselves and are segregated from those deemed different; (2) group placement is done on the basis of criteria such as ability or postgraduate plans that are unequally esteemed. Thus group membership immediately ranks students in a status hierarchy, formally stating that some students are better than others.[19] Following Rosenbaum, the general term of tracking is applied here to both types of grouping.[20]

On what basis are students assigned to tracks? Three major criteria have been noted in the literature: (1) standardized test scores; (2) teacher grades, recommendations, or opinions about pupils; and (3) pupil race and socioeconomic class. Test scores are usually based on large group-administered aptitude tests, a method considered least valid by test-givers. Teacher opinions about students may be influenced by test scores, pupil social class, or ethnicity, as discussed below. Social class and ethnicity have been found in some research studies to be directly related to track assignments as well, even when ability and teacher recommendations were similar.[21] Thus, the social-class background of students is related to the prevalence of tracking in the schools and to the ways track assignments are made.

Once students are assigned to different tracks, what happens to them? Do they have different educational experiences? The major educational processes that have been observed to vary according to track placement include the unequal allocation of educational resources, the instruction offered, student-teacher interactions, and student-student interactions. Hallinan studied within-class ability grouping in thirty-four elementary school classes. She found that ability grouping affects the learning of students in higher and lower groups because it influences their opportunities for learning, the instructional climate, and the student aptitudes clustered in the different groups. "High-ability" groups spend "more time on tasks" during class; that is, more class time is devoted to actual teaching activities. Also, teachers use more interesting teaching methods and materials. Finally, teachers hold higher expectations, and the other students support learning more in the higher-ability groups. As a result, the aptitude of students in the higher groups tends to develop more than does the aptitude of students in the lower group.[22]

In secondary schools, college-track students consistently receive better teachers, class materials, laboratory facilities, field trips, and visitors than their lower-track counterparts.[23] Oakes observed that teachers of high-track students set aside more time for student learning and devoted more class time to learning activities. Fewer students in these classes engaged in "off-task" activities.[24] Oakes also found that "students are being exposed to knowledge and taught behaviors that differ not only educationally but also in socially important ways. Students at the top are exposed to the knowledge that is highly valued in our culture, knowledge that identifies its possessors as 'educated.'"[25] Similarly, those students are taught critical thinking, creativity, and independence.

Students at the bottom are denied access to these educationally and socially important experiences.[26]

Freiberg found that higher-track students received more empathy, praise, and use of their ideas, as well as less direction and criticism, than did lower-track students.[27] Oakes observed that teachers spent more time in low-track classes on discipline and that students in those classes perceived their teachers as more punitive than did students in high-track classes.[28]

Rosenbaum reported that more than one-third of lower-track (noncollege) students mentioned "blatant insults directed at them by teachers and administrators: 'Teachers are always telling us how dumb we are.'" One articulate general-track student in that study reported that he sought academic help from a teacher but was told that he was not smart enough to learn the material. Several students reported that a lower-track student who asks a guidance counselor for a change of classes is not only prevented from changing but is also insulted for being so presumptuous as to make the request. Rosenbaum was told by one teacher, "You're wasting your time asking these kids for their opinions. There's not an idea in any of their heads." As the researcher notes, "This comment was not expressed in the privacy of the teacher's room; it was said at a normal volume in a quiet classroom full of students!"[29]

Students have been observed to pick up on the negative evaluations associated with lower track placement. They may make fun of lower-track students, call them unflattering names, or stop associating with them.[30] Hence, a major result of tracking is differential respect from peers and teachers, with implications for both instruction and esteem.

Further consequences of tracking include segregation of students by social class and ethnicity,[31] unequal learning by students in different tracks,[32] and unequal chances to attend college.[33]

If tracking has so many negative consequences, why does it persist? Oakes thinks tracking persists because it is "an integral part of the culture of secondary schools: the collection of organizational arrangements, behaviors, relationships, and beliefs that define how things are at a school."[34] She suggests that tracking rests on four unexamined assumptions:

1. Students learn better in groups of those who are academically similar.
2. Slower students develop more positive attitudes about themselves and school when they are not in day-to-day classroom contact with those who are much brighter.
3. Track placements are part of a meritocratic system with assignments 'earned' by students and accorded through fair and accurate means.
4. Teaching is easier when students are grouped homogeneously, and teaching is better when there are not slower students to lower the common denominator.[35]

Oakes's research in 297 classrooms suggests that these assumptions are false. If teachers accept her evidence, they should work to eliminate tracking from schools. However, emerging evidence suggests that educators have not been quick to do so. Finley found that support for the tracking system in the school came from teachers who competed with each other for high-status students.[36]

Teachers' Expectations

Educational structures such as schools that are socioeconomically homoge-neous, concepts such as IQ and cultural deprivation, and practices such as tracking go a long way toward shaping the expectations teachers hold about students. Teacher training and textbooks have tended to attribute educational failures to deficiencies in the children.[37] Often, such deficiencies are social characteristics of the pupils, such as their social-class background, ethnicity, language, or behavior. In a review of relevant research, Persell[38] found that student social class was related to teacher expectations when other factors such as race were not more salient, when expectations were engendered by real children, or when teachers had a chance to draw inferences about a student's social class rather than simply being told his or her background. Sometimes social class was related to teacher expectations even when the child's current IQ and achievement were comparable. That is, teachers held lower expectations for lower-class children than for middle-class children even when those children had similar IQ scores and achievement.

Teachers' expectations may also be influenced by the behavior and physical appearance of the children.[39] Social class may influence teacher expectations directly or indirectly through test scores, appearance, language style, speed of task performance, and behavior. All of these traits are themselves culturally defined and are related to class position. Moreover, teacher expec-tations are influenced more by negative information about pupil character-istics than by positive data.[40] It is important to know this because much of the information teachers gain about low income children seems to be negative.

If teacher expectations are often influenced by the social class of students, do those expectations have significant consequences for students? Research on this question has produced seemingly contradictory results. The controversy began with the publication of *Pygmalion in the Classroom.*[41] That book suggested that the expectations of classroom teachers might powerfully influ-ence the achievement of students. Hundreds of studies on the possibility of "expectancy effects" have been conducted since then.[42] Some of the contra-dictions in research results appear to arise from the answers to three questions: (1) Are teacher expectations natural or induced? (2) Are teacher expectations measured in the research? and (3) Do teacher behaviors vary according to their expectations? In many studies that attempted to induce positive teacher expectations, the researchers did not measure whether the teachers actually adopted the expectations experimenters tried to create. Sometimes when they did measure teacher expectations, they found that the teachers were not convinced. Such teachers are not likely to change their behav-iors. Only expectations that teachers truly believe are likely to affect their behaviors.

When teachers hold higher expectations for pupils, how does this affect their behavior? Their expectations seem to affect the frequency of interaction they have with their pupils and the kinds of behaviors they show toward different children. Teachers spend more time interacting with pupils for whom they have higher expectations.[43] For example, Brophy and Good[44] found that students for whom teachers held high expectations were praised more frequently when correct and were criticized less frequently when wrong or unresponsive than were pupils for whom teachers had low expectations.

Rosenthal[45] believes that teachers convey their expectations in at least four related ways. He bases this judgment on his review of 285 studies of interpersonal influence, including at least 80 in classrooms or other settings. First, he sees a general climate factor, consisting of the overall warmth a teacher shows to children, with more shown to high-expectancy students. Second, he sees students for whom high expectations are held as receiving more praise for doing something right than students for whom low expectations are held. Third, Rosenthal notes that high-expectancy students are taught more than are low-expectancy students. This is consistent with research by others.[46] Fourth, Rosenthal indicates that expectancy may be affected by a response opportunity factor. That is, students for whom the teacher has higher expectations are called on more often and are given more chances to reply, as well as more frequent and more difficult questions.

A fifth way teachers convey their expectations, which Rosenthal does not mention but which has been observed by others, is the different type of curricula teachers may present to children for whom they have different expectations. One study found that teachers report that they present completely different types of economics to students of differently perceived abilities.[47] Another study reported that teachers use more reading texts and more difficult ones with the top reading group.[48] Clearly, there is evidence that at least some teachers behave differently toward students for whom they hold different expectations. The critical question remains: Do these expectations and behaviors actually affect students? Do the students think differently about themselves or learn more as a result of the expectations teachers hold? Therein lies the heart of the "Pygmalion effect" controversy.

When teachers hold definite expectations and when those expectations are reflected in their behavior toward children, these expectations are related to student cognitive changes, even when pupil IQ and achievement are controlled. Moreover, negative expectations, which can be observed only in natural settings because it is unethical to induce negative expectations experimentally, appear to have even more powerful consequences than do positive expectations.[49] Moreover, socially vulnerable children (i.e., younger, lower-class, and minority children) seem to be more susceptible to lower teacher expectations.[50]

Consequences of Social Class and Educational Inequality

This profile of social-class differences in education in the United States is oversimplified, but considerable evidence does suggest that the general patterns described here do exist. Social-class backgrounds affect where students go to school and what happens to them once they are there. Group-administered IQ tests (the least valid kind) are most likely to be used in large, urban, public school systems. Tracking is frequently based on such group-administered tests. As a result, students are less likely to be exposed to valued curricula, are taught less of whatever curricula they do study, and are expected to do less work in the classroom and outside of it. Hence, they learn less and are less well prepared for the next level of education.

Although students have many reasons for dropping out of school or for failing to continue, their experiences in school may contribute to their desire to continue or to quit. Coleman, Hoffer, and Kilgore found that 24 percent of public high school students dropped out, compared to 12 percent of Catholic and 13 percent of other private school students.[51]

Similarly, college attendance depends on a number of factors, including access to the necessary financial resources. Nevertheless, it is striking how differently students at different schools fare. Graduation from a private rather than a public high school is related to attending a four-year (rather than a two-year) college,[52] attending a highly selective college,[53] and earning higher income in adult life.[54] Even within the same school, track placement is related to college attendance.[55] College attendance, in turn, is related to the adult positions and earnings one attains.[56] Thus, educational inequalities help create and legitimate economic and social inequalities.

However, most educators do not want to enhance and legitimate social inequalities. Therefore, it seems reasonable to ask, What can they do to try to change these patterns?

Recommendations for Action

Teachers, educators, and concerned citizens might consider the following actions:

1. Working politically to increase the educational resources available to all children, not just those in wealthy school districts, and not just the gifted and talented. Those concerned might do this by joining a political party that works to advance the interests of the less advantaged members of society, by attending political meetings, and by holding candidates accountable for their positions on education. We can join other people interested in scrutinizing candidates' records of support for education, and contribute time, money, or both to the campaigns of candidates seeking to defeat incumbents who have not supported quality education for all children.

2. Working to reduce economic inequalities in society. This can be done by supporting income-tax reforms at the national level that benefit hard-working low- and middle-income families, by trying to close tax loopholes for the rich, such as oil-depletion allowances, and by supporting aid for impoverished one-parent families.

3. Working to build economically and racially integrated communities. This can be done by choosing to live in such a community, by supporting federal subsidies for low-income housing in mixed-income areas, and by opposing efforts to restrict access to certain communities by members of particular ethnic or income groups. Such restrictions might take the form of zoning that prohibits the construction of high-rise housing for low-income groups or limits housing lots to a large size, such as two acres.

4. Using tests for diagnosing rather than dismissing students. For example, instead of taking a low IQ test score as evidence that a child cannot learn, we can examine what parts of a particular test were difficult for that child. If necessary, we can obtain further, individual testing to identify and analyze what skills the child needs to develop, and devise strategies for teaching those specific skills. We can try alternative teaching strategies with each child until we find one that works. If a child has difficulty learning to read phonetically, for example, we might try teaching that child a different way, perhaps visually. We can help children with various kinds of learning disabilities learn ways to compensate for their difficulties. For example, planning their work in advance, organizing it so that they have enough time to complete the necessary steps, and allowing time for someone else to check their spelling are all compensatory strategies that can be adopted to good effect by children trying to overcome various learning disabilities.

5. Working on finding what abilities students do have, rather than on deciding that they haven't any. For example, if a student has strong artistic, musical, athletic, or auditory talents, but is weaker in the verbal or mathematical areas, we can help that child find ways into the academic subjects through their strengths.

6. Critically examining practices, such as tracking, that may bring teacher and student interests into conflict. Perhaps schools should have someone other than teachers represent the viewpoint and interests of students in the lowest tracks. This role might be filled by community representatives or by university professors who know the research on the negative effects of tracking.

7. Expecting and demanding a lot from students in the way of effort, thought, and work. We can help students take pride in themselves and their work by teaching them what a first-rate job should look like. The written materials students get from teachers and schools and the appearance of the classrooms, hallways, and school should all convey a sense of care, quality, and value. We can carefully check the work students do, suggest constructive ways they might improve it, and expect them to do better the next time.

8. Teaching students content and subject matter. We can show students that we value them and their learning by devoting class time to pedagogically useful tasks, by refusing to waste class time on frivolous activities, and by trying to stick to an annual schedule of curricular coverage.

9. If any form of tracking must be done, we can try to see that it is based on the willingness of students to do more work and on their proficiency in relevant prior areas of study, rather than on general aptitude tests. Systems of grouping should be flexible and easy to change as students progress (or lag behind). They should seek to avoid social evaluation and ranking and should allow students who acquire the necessary competencies to move into more advanced classes.

10. Helping students see how education is relevant and useful for their lives, perhaps by bringing back graduates who have used school as a springboard to better themselves and their worlds. Schools might keep a roster of successful graduates and post pictures and stories about them for current students to see. We can bring in examples that link learning with life accomplishments so students can begin to see connections between school and life.

For example, we might invite people who run their own business to talk about how they use math, or bring in people who work in social service organizations to show how they use writing in their daily work.

Summary

This chapter explores how educational structures, beliefs, and practices contribute to unequal educational outcomes. To achieve greater educational equality, educators must understand what social-class differences presently exist in those structures, beliefs, and practices. If these differences are understood, then the educational experiences of children of all social classes might be made more similar.

The higher one's social-class background, the more likely one is to attend a smaller school with more resources, smaller classes, and an academic curriculum. Achieving greater educational equality means making such school experiences available to more students, regardless of their social-class backgrounds.

Two different educational beliefs exist about why some children learn better than others, namely, beliefs about IQ and beliefs about cultural deprivation. Rather than sinking into the controversy over which one provides a better explanation for educational failure, this chapter considers what these beliefs have in common and examines how they both blame the victims for their failure and divert attention from how the social organization of schools may help to create failures. These beliefs also influence the curricular and teaching practices of schools attended by children of different social classes.

The educational process of tracking refers to the segregation of students into different learning or curriculum groups that are unequally ranked in a prestige hierarchy. Whether based on ability grouping or curricular grouping, such tracking tends to reduce learning opportunities for students in the lower groups, while increasing such opportunities for students in higher groups. As a result, this educational practice contributes to educational inequalities. Efforts to create greater educational equality require that the practice of tracking be changed in major ways.

Teachers may unconsciously form different learning expectations about students of different social-class backgrounds. When teachers hold higher expectations for students, they tend to spend more time interacting with those students, praise them more, teach them more, call on them more often, and offer them a more socially valued curriculum. When teachers hold higher expectations, and when those expectations are evident in their behavior, they increase student learning. Thus, achieving greater educational equality means that teachers' expectations for lower-class students need to be raised.

Because the educational structures, beliefs, and practices examined here are related to unequal educational attainment, and because educational success is related to lifetime occupations and earnings, it is important that educational inequalities be reduced. This chapter recommends a number of steps that concerned educators and citizens can take to promote educational and social equality.

Questions and Activities

1. According to Persell, in what ways do schools contribute to inequality? What evidence does the author give to support her position?

2. Give examples of how each of the following factors contributes to educational inequality: (a) educational structures; (b) beliefs of teachers and administrators; and (c) educational practices.

3. What are the major characteristics of each of the following types of schools: (a) elite private schools and exclusive suburban schools; (b) parochial schools; and (c) large urban public school systems?

4. Why do students from different social-class backgrounds often attend different schools or get assigned to different tracks when they attend the same schools? How does the social-class background of students influence the kind of education they often receive?

5. Visit and observe in (a) a local elite private school; (b) a school in an upper-middle-class suburb; and (c) an inner-city school. How are these schools alike? How are they different? Based on your visits and observations, what tentative generalizations can you make about education, social class, and inequality? To what extent are your generalizations similar to and different from those of Persell?

6. What are some of the major limitations of IQ tests? What cautions should teachers bear in mind when interpreting IQ tests, particularly the scores of lower-class and ethnic minority students?

7. How are the genetic and cultural-deprivation explanations of the low achievement of low-income students alike and different?

8. What is the self-fulfilling prophecy? How does it affect teacher expectations?

9. What is tracking? Why do you think tracking is more widespread in large, diverse school systems and in schools serving primarily lower-class students than in upper-middle-class suburban, private, and parochial schools?

10. How do the school experiences of students in lower and higher tracks differ? How does tracking contribute to educational inequality?

11. How do factors related to social class influence teacher expectations of students?

12. How do teacher expectations influence how teachers and pupils interact, what students are taught, and what students achieve?

Notes

1. Caroline Hodges Persell, *Understanding Society*, 2d ed (New York: Harper & Row, 1987), p. 204.

2. James S. Coleman, Ernest Q. Campbell, Carol J. Hobson, James McPartland, Alexander M. Mood, Frederic D. Weinfeld, and

Robert L. York, *Equality of Educational Opportunity* (Washington, D.C.: U.S. Government Printing Office, 1966); Bernard Goldstein, *Low Income Youth in Urban Areas: A Critical Review of the Literature* (New York: Holt, Rinehart, and Winston, 1967); Torsten Husen, *Social Background and Educational Career* (Paris: Center for Educational Research and Innovation, Organization for Economic Co-Operation and Development, 1972); George W. Mayeske and Carl E. Wisler, *A Study of Our Nation's Schools* (Washington, D.C.: U.S. Government Printing Office, 1972).

3. James S. Coleman, Thomas Hoffer, and Sally Kilgore, *High School Achievement* (New York: Basic Books, 1982), pp. 20–21.

4. Peter W. Cookson, Jr., and Caroline Hodges Persell, *Preparing for Power: America's Elite Boarding Schools* (New York: Basic Books, 1985), p. 58.

5. Ibid., 95.

6. In the Cookson and Persell study, more than half the students at elite boarding schools watched no television during the school week, compared to only 5 percent of public high school students. More than 80 percent of the elite boarding school students did more than 10 hours per week of homework, compared to less than 10 percent of the public high school students.

7. Coleman, Hoffer, and Kilgore, *High School Achievement.*

8. Ibid.

9. David Tyack, *The One Best System* (Cambridge: Harvard University Press, 1974).

10. David Rogers, *110 Livingston Street: Politics and Bureaucracy in the New York City School System* (New York: Random House, 1968).

11. Howard Gardner, *Frames of Mind* (New York: Basic Books, 1983).

12. Ivar E. Berg, *Education and Jobs: The Great Training Robbery* (New York: Praeger, 1970); Randall Collins, *The Credential Society* (New York: Academic Press, 1979), Ch. 1; Donald P. Hoyt, *The Relationship between College Grades and Adult Achievement: A Review of the Literature,* Res. Rep. No. 7 (Iowa City: American College Testing Program, 1965); David C. McClelland, Testing for Competence Rather Than for "Intelligence," in Alan Gartner, Colin Greer, and Frank Riessman, eds. *The New Assault on Equality* (New York: Social Policy, 1974), pp. 163–197; C. Taylor, W. R. Smith, and B. Ghiselin, "The Creative and Other Contributions of One Sample of Research Scientists," in C. W. Taylor and F.

Barron, eds. *Scientific Creativity: Its Recognition and Development* (New York: Wiley, 1963), pp. 53–76.

13. Arthur R. Jensen, "How Much Can We Boost I.Q. and Scholastic Achievement?" *Harvard Educational Review,* 39:No. 1 (Winter 1969): 1–123.

14. Brent Bridgeman and Virginia Shipman, *Predictive Value of Measures of Self-Esteem and Achievement Motivation in Four-to-Nine-Year-Old-Low-Income Children* (ETS-Head Start Longitudinal Study) (Princeton, N.J.: Educational Testing Service, 1975).

15. Quoted in Walter Feinberg, "Educational Equality under Two Conflicting Models of Educational Development, *Theory and Society,* No. 2 (Summer 1975): 183–210.

16. See James B. Conant, *Slums and Suburbs* (New York: McGraw Hill, 1961); Jeannie Oakes, *Keeping Track: How Schools Structure Inequality* (New Haven, Conn.: Yale University Press, 1985).

17. Warren G. Findley and Miriam M. Bryan, *Ability Grouping: 1970–I, Common Practices in the Use of Tests for Grouping Students in Public Schools* (Athens: University of Georgia Center for Educational Improvement, ED 048381, 1970).

18. James D. Jones, Beth E. Vanfossen, and Joan Z. Spade, "Curriculum Placement: Individual and School Effects Using the High School and Beyond Data." Paper presented at the American Sociological Association Annual Meeting, Washington, D.C., 1985.

19. James E. Rosenbaum, *Making Inequality* (New York: Wiley-Interscience, 1976).

20. Rosenbaum, *Making Inequality.*

21. W. B. Brookover, D. J. Leu, R. H. Kariger, *Tracking,* Unpublished manuscript (mimeo) (Western Michigan University, 1965); Roger B. Kariger, "The Relationship of Lane Grouping to the Socioeconomic Status of the Parents of Seventh-Grade Pupils in Three Junior High Schools," Unpublished doctoral dissertation, Michigan State University, *Dissertation Abstracts,* 23: 4586, 1962; Ray C. Rist, "Student Social Class and Teacher Expectations: The Self-Fulfilling Prophecy in Ghetto Education," *Harvard Educational Review,* 40: No. 3 (August 1970): 411–451.

22. Maureen T. Hallinan, "Ability Grouping and Student Learning," in Maureen T. Hallinan, ed. *The Social Organization of Schools: New Conceptualizations of the Learning Process.* (New York: Plenum, 1987), pp. 41–69.

23. Warren G. Findley and Miriam M. Bryan. *The Pros and Cons of Ability Grouping* (Bloomington, Ind: Phi Delta Kappa, 1975); John I. Goodlad, *A Place Called School* (New York: McGraw Hill, 1984) pp. 159–160; Barbara Heyns, "Social Selection and Stratification Within Schools," *American Journal of Sociology,* 79: No. 6 (May 1974): 1434–1451; Oakes, *Keeping Track*; Rosenbaum, *Making Inequality*; Walter E. Schafer, Carol Olexa, and Kenneth Polk, "Programmed for Social Class: Tracking in American High Schools," in Norman K. Denzin, ed. *Children and Their Caretakers* (New Brunswick, N.J.: Transaction Books, 1973), pp. 200–226.

24. Oakes, *Keeping Track,* 111.

25. Ibid., 91–92.

26. Ibid., 92.

27. Jerome Freiberg, *The Effects of Ability Grouping on Interactions in the Classroom* (ED 053194, 1970).

28. Oakes, *Keeping Track*: 133.

29. Rosenbaum, *Making Inequality,* 179–180.

30. Rist, "Student Social Class and Teacher Expectations"; Rosenbaum, *Making Inequality.*

31. D. Esposito, "Homogeneous and Heterogeneous Ability Grouping: Principal Findings and Implications for Evaluating and Designing More Effective Educational Environments," *Review of Educational Research,* 43: No. 2 (Spring 1973): 163–179; *Hobson v. Hansen Congressional Record* (June 21, 1967): 16721–16766; *Racial and Social Isolation in the Schools* (Albany: New York State Education Department, 1969); Oakes, *Keeping Track.*

32. Warren G. Findley and Miriam M. Bryan, *Ability Grouping: 1970-II The Impact of Ability Grouping on School Achievement, Affective Development, Ethnic Separation and Socioeconomic Separation* (Athens: University of Georgia Center for Educational Improvement); ED 048382, 1970; Oakes, *Keeping Track*; Rosenbaum, *Making Inequality*; Schafer, Olexa, and Polk, "Programmed for Social Class."

33. Karl L. Alexander, Martha Cook, and Edward L. McDill "Curriculum Tracking and Educational Stratification: Some Further Evidence," *American Sociological Review* 43 (1978): 47–66; Karl L. Alexander and Bruce K. Eckland, "Contextual Effects in the High School Attainment Process," *American Sociological Review,* 40, No. 3 (June 1975): 402–416; Abraham Jaffe and Walter Adams, *Academic and Socio-economic Factors Related to Entrance and Retention at Two-and Four-Year Colleges in the Late 1960's* (New York: Columbia University Bureau of Applied Social Research, 1970); Rosenbaum, *Making Inequality*; James E. Rosenbaum, "Track Misperceptions and Frustrated College Plans: An Analysis of the Effects of Tracks and Track Perceptions in the National Longitudinal Survey," *Sociology of Education,* 53, No. 2 (April 1980): 74–88; James D. Jones, Joan N. Spade, and Beth E. Vanfossen, "Curriculum Tracking and Status Maintenance," *Sociology of Education,* 60, No. 2 (April 1987): 104–122.

34. Oakes, *Keeping Track,* 191.

35. Ibid., 192.

36. Merrilee K. Finley, "Teachers and Tracking in a Comprehensive High School," *Sociology of Education,* 57, No. 4 (October 1984): 233–243.

37. Sylvia I. B. Hill, *Race, Class and Ethnic Biases in Research on School Performance of Low Income Youth.* Unpublished doctoral dissertation (University of Oregon, 1971); Annie Stein, "Strategies of Failure," *Harvard Educational Review,* 41, No. 2 (May 1971): 158–204.

38. Persell, *Education and Inequality,* 105–107.

39. Gerald R. Adams and Allan S. Cohen, "Children's Physical and Interpersonal Characteristics That Effect [sic] Student-Teacher Interactions," *Journal of Experimental Education,* 43, No. 1 (Fall 1974): 1–5; Gerald R. Adams and Joseph LaVoie, "The Effect of Student's Sex, Conduct, and Facial Attractiveness on Teacher Expectancy, *Education,* 95, No. 1 (Fall 1974): 76–83; M. Clifford and E. Walster, "The Effect of Physical Attractiveness on Teacher Expectation," *Sociology of Education,* 46, No. 2 (Spring 1973): 248–258; F. X. Lawlor and E. Lawlor, "Teacher Expectations: A Study of Their Genesis," *Science Education,* 57, No. 1 (Jan.–Mar. 1973): 9–14.

40. Emanuel J. Mason, "Teachers' Observations and Expectations of Boys and Girls as Influenced by Biased Psychological Reports and Knowledge of the Effects of Bias," *Journal of Educational Psychology,* 65, No. 2 (October 1973): pp. 238–243.

41. Robert Rosenthal and Lenore Jacobson, *Pygmalion in the Classroom* (New York: Holt, Rinehart, and Winston, 1968).

42. See, for example, Harris M. Cooper

and Thomas L. Good, *Pygmalion Grows Up* (New York: Longman, 1983), for a review of some of this research.

43. Jere E. Brophy and Thomas L. Good, "Teachers' Communication of Differential Expectations for Children's Classroom Performance: Some Behavioral Data," *Journal of Educational Psychology,* 61, No. 5 (October 1970): 365–374; Catherine Cornbleth, O. L. Davis, Jr., and Christine Button, "Expectations for Pupil Achievement and Teacher-Pupil Interaction," *Research in Social Studies Education,* Supplement 9, Vol. 38 (January 1974): 54–58, 1974; Barbara K. Given, "Teacher Expectancy and Pupil Performance: Their Relationship to Verbal and Non-Verbal Communications by Teachers of Learning Disabled Children," doctoral dissertation, Catholic University, *Dissertation Abstracts International,* 35: 1529A, 1974; J. T. Jeter, "Can Teacher Expectations Function as Self-Fulfilling Prophecies?" *Contemporary Education,* 46, No. 3 (Spring 1973): 161–165; Patricia L. Kranz, Wilford A. Weber, and Kenneth N. Fishell, "The Relationship between Teacher Perception of Pupils and Teacher Behavior toward Those Pupils." (Paper presented at the American Educational Research Association Annual Meeting, Minneapolis, 1970 ED 038346); Rist, "Student Social Class and Teacher Expectations; P. Rubovits and M. Maehr, "Pygmalion Analyzed: Toward an Explanation of the Rosenthal-Jacobson Findings," *Journal of Personality and Social Psychology,* 19, No. 2 (August 1971): 197–203; Melvin L. Silberman, "Behavioral Expression of Teachers' Attitudes toward Elementary Students," *Journal of Educational Psychology,* 60, No. 5 (October 1969): 402–407; Bill J. Willis, "The Influence of Teacher Expectation on Teachers' Classroom Interaction with Selected Children," doctoral dissertation; George Peabody College, *Dissertation Abstracts International,* 30: 5072A, 1969.

44. Brophy and Good, "Teachers Communication of Differential Expectations."

45. Robert Rosenthal, "The Pygmalion Effect: What You Expect is What You Get," *Psychology Today Library Cassette* 12 (New York: Ziff-Davis, 1974).

46. Walter V. Beez, "Influence of Biased Psychological Reports on Teacher Behavior and Pupil Performance," in Mathew B. Miles and W. W. Charters, Jr., eds. *Learning in Social Settings* (Boston: Allyn and Bacon, 1970), pp. 320–334;

Ronald M. Carter, "Locus of Control and Teacher Expectancy as Related to Achievement of Young School Children," doctoral dissertation, Indiana University, *Dissertation Abstracts International,* 30: 467A, 1969; David H. Martinez, "A Comparison of the Behavior during Reading Instruction, of Teachers of High and Low Achieving in First Grade Classes," doctoral dissertation, University of Oregon, *Dissertation Abstracts International,* 34: 7520A, 1973; William M. McQueen, Jr., "The Effect of Divergent Teacher Expectations on the Performance of Elementary School Children on a Vocabulary Learning Task," doctoral dissertation, University of South Carolina, *Dissertation Abstracts International,* 31: 5206A, 1970; Rist, "Student Social Class and Teacher Expectations."

47. Nell Keddie, ed., "Classroom Knowledge," in Michael F. D. Young, ed., *Knowledge and Control* (London: Collier, MacMillan, 1971), pp. 133–160.

48. Judith Landon Alpert, "Do Teachers Adapt Methods and Materials to Ability Groups in Reading?" *California Journal of Education Research,* 26: 3 (May 1975): 120–123.

49. Damon Floyd Asbury, "The Effects of Teacher Expectancy, Subject Expectancy, and Subject Sex on the Learning Performance of Elementary School Children," doctoral dissertation, Ohio State University, *Dissertation Abstracts International,* 31: 4437A, 1970; Paul M. Kohn, "Relationship between Expectations of Teachers and Performance of Students," *Journal of School Health,* No. 4 (Winter 1973): 498–503; Mason, "Teachers' Observations and Expectations"; William B. Seaver, Jr., "Effects of Naturally Induced Teacher Expectancies, *Journal of Personality and Social Psychology,* 28, No. 3 (December 1973): 333–342.

50. Stephen H. Baker, "Teacher Effectiveness and Social Class as Factors in Teacher Expectancy Effects on Pupils Scholastic Achievement," doctoral dissertation, Clark University, *Dissertation and Abstracts International,* 34:2376A, 1973; William P. Krupczak, "Relationships among Student Self-Concept of Academic Ability, Teacher Perception of Student Academic Ability and Student Achievement," doctoral dissertation, University of Miami, *Dissertation Abstracts International,* 33: 3388A–3389A, 1972; Rosenthal and Jacobson, *Pygmalion In The Classroom*; Albert H. Yee, "Source and Direction Of Casual Influence in Teacher-Pupil Relation-

ships,'' *Journal of Educational Psychology,* 59, No. 4 (August 1968): 275–282.

51. Coleman, Hoffer, and Kilgore, *High School Achievement,* 148.

52. Barbara Falsey and Barbara Heyns, "The College Channel: Private and Public Schools Reconsidered," *Sociology of Education,* 57, No. 2 (April 1984): 111–122.

53. Caroline Hodges Persell and Peter W. Cookson, Jr., "Chartering and Bartering: Elite Education and Social Reproduction," *Social Problem,* 33, No. 2 (December 1985): 114–129.

54. Lionel S. Lewis and Richard A. Wanner, "Private Schooling and the Status Attainment Process," *Sociology of Education,* 52, No. 2, 1979: 99–112.

55. Alexander, Cook, and McDill, "Curriculum Tracking and Educational Stratification: Some Further Evidence"; Karl L. Alexander and Edward L. McDill, "Selection and Allocation within Schools: Some Causes and Consequences of Curriculum Placement," *American Sociological Review,* 41: No. 6 (December 1976): 963–980; Jaffe and Adams, "Academic and Socio-economic Factors Related to Entrance and Retention'';

Rosenbaum, *Making Inequality*; Rosenbaum, "Track Misperceptions and Frustrated College Plans: An Analysis of the Effects of Tracks and Track Perceptions in the National Longitudinal Survey.''

56. Steve Brint, "Intra-Occupational Stratification in Six High-Status Occupations: An Analysis of Status and Status Attainment in Academe, Science, Law, and Corporate Management, Engineering and Medicine,'' Unpublished paper (Yale University, 1985); David Kamens, "Colleges and Elite Formation: The Case of Prestigious American Colleges,'' *Sociology of Education,* 47, No. 3 (Summer 1974): 354–378; Vincent Tinto, "College Origin and Patterns of Status Attainment,'' *Sociology of Work and Occupations,* 7, No. 4 (November 1980): pp. 457–486; Michael Useem, *The Inner Circle: Large Corporations and the Rise of Business Political Activity in the U.S. and U.K.* (New York: Oxford University Press, 1984); Michael Useem and Jerome Karabel, "Educational Pathways to Top Corporate Management,'' *American Sociological Review,* 51, No. 2 (April 1986): 184–200.

CHAPTER 5

Religious Diversity and Education

- ## JAMES K. UPHOFF

Introduction

A beautiful new mosque stands with its center dome and twin minarets vivid against the blue sky. Where in the United States is this religious center located? In Washington, D.C., where many nations of the world send their diplomats? In New York City, the home of the United Nations? In Los Angeles? The answer to each of these questions is no.

The mosque is located on the flat, fertile farmland of northwest Ohio, just south of Toledo, deep in the heart of the midwestern United States. Unusual? Yes, but a vivid sign of the changing times as religions in the United States become more diverse.

Watching local law enforcement officers chain and padlock a church door on the television news recently was unsettling to many people. Yet this scenario did happen in rural Nebraska, when a small independent Protestant church decided to defy a state law requiring all teachers in the state to be certified. This church had recently created its own small school, which met in the church. However, the teaching staff did not meet the qualifications set by the law. The minister made national news as he, on behalf of the congregation, defied the law and all attempts of the authorities to reach a compromise.

In California's San Ramone School District, some parents raised objections to an education curriculum because it called for teachers and students to use decision-making techniques and because it was alleged to be the teaching of "secular humanism," considered by some people to be a type of religion.[1] This example is only the tip of a large iceberg of formal objections that have been made in school districts throughout the nation. More than ever before, school materials and teaching methods, standards, and requirements are being challenged on religious grounds as groups and individuals fight back against what they perceive as the antireligious nature of the public schools.

This chapter helps you better understand the religious element of cultural diversity. If the United States is to function as a cohesive unit, it must be able to accommodate the diversity within it. Teachers have a key role to play, but they can perform it only if they fully understand the play and the audiences who will attend.

To help teachers prepare for this theater, this chapter provides definitions of religion, a glimpse at the importance of religion, a brief review of relevant U.S. history, an examination of constitutional issues involved, facts and figures about the religious diversity within the United States, and a focus on the educational implications of all of these factors.

Definitions of Religion

Before we can discuss religion, we must come to some common agreement about what religion is. The word is a common one that seems easy to define but in fact is difficult to explain. Nearly everyone uses the term, but few have a well-developed idea of what we mean. Wilson contends, "Often, one's definition of 'religion' reveals much more about the point of view or prejudices of the definer than it does about religion itself."[2] He feels that the definition can be either negative or positive depending on the emotions it calls forth in the speaker.

Albanese states, "Everyone knows what religion is—that is, until one tries to define it. It is in the act of defining that religion seems to slip away."[3] She believes that the difficulty exists because religion crosses many boundaries, even though the purpose of most definitions is to establish boundaries.

We provide a definition by describing examples, thus providing each of us with a more common picture on which to build our look at the educational implications of religious diversity. As we focus our camera on this concept, we will need to use both a close-up and a wide-angle lens. These views will give us first the narrow definition most commonly used and then the much broader definition used by the U.S. Supreme Court in several landmark cases regarding church and state.

If we were to play a word-association game using the term *religion*, the responses would probably include at least some of the following: buildings of worship; traditions and festivals; names of organized groups; special objects, symbols, or literature; sets of beliefs; and specific types of persons or roles. Thus, such words as *church, temple, pagoda, shrine, confirmation, bar/bat mitzvah, Hindu, Shinto, Buddhist, Society of Mary, cross, Star of David, clerical collar, Upanishad, Koran, baptism, creed, priest, monk, nun, minister, rabbi, mullah,* and *evangelist* would be commonly stated by people using this narrowly focused view of religion.

The wide-angle view was described by the leaders of the Public Education Religion Studies Center (PERSC) in their 1974 book, *Questions and Answers*[4]:

> The broad definition envisions religion as any faith or set of values to which an individual or group gives ultimate loyalty. . . . Buddhism, Taoism, Ethical Culture, secularism, humanists, scientism, nationalism, money, and power illustrate this concept of religion.

The U.S. Supreme Court has for several decades been using this broader definition as it has made decisions. Thus, Madeline Murray O'Hare, an avowed atheist, has been considered by some to be a very religious person by this broad definition.

Several of the most recent church-state cases currently on appeal in the federal courts involve this broader definition. One federal judge found that secular humanism is a religion, that many textbooks discuss its beliefs, and that other religions such as Christianity do not have their own beliefs included in those same textbooks; thus, more than forty textbooks must be withdrawn from the public schools. Judge William Brevard Hand's ruling in *Smith et al.* v. *Board of School Commissioners of Mobile County et al.* of March 4, 1987, represented a direct use of the broader definition.

One important aspect of this dual definition is that many individuals use and live by both. Often referred to as *crypto* (hidden) religion, these people use a sectarian (narrow definition) mask to hide an ultimate concern. They often use the same symbols as those whose prime belief is a more traditional form of religion. For instance, such groups as the Klu Klux Klan use the Christian cross as a symbol of their "WASP-supremacy ultimate concern religion." Other people "believe" in the acquisition of power or wealth, doing everything they can to obtain them, even though they outwardly profess belief in the giving, sharing, and serving creeds of a particular church.

Thus, the broad definition, because it so clearly includes values and the valuing process, must also be used as we proceed through this chapter. We can understand the many educational implications of religious diversity in the United States and in the world at large only if we use both views. These views include the traditional notion of religion (being Jewish or Christian, for example) and the idea of religion as any strong faith.

Importance of Religion

For what idea, principle, cause, belief, or value would you be willing to give your life? As each of us answers this question of ultimate commitment, we state the importance of our religion. In the history of humanity, millions of people have answered this question through action. Countless lives have been given in defense of religious beliefs. There has been no shortage of examples, from the earliest hunter who believed in the security of family and died while protecting that family, to those who blow themselves up as they conduct holy war.

It is our own system of values and beliefs that makes each example positive or negative. Such emotion-laden terms as *religious fanatic, heroic,* and *martyr* provide clues as to how we perceive a particular event.

If human beings are willing to die for a belief, then they are even more willing to suffer lesser penalties such as ridicule, separation, torture, imprisonment, fines, or restrictions, on behalf of their beliefs. British and American women of the early twentieth century who fought for women's rights certainly suffered as a result of their beliefs. Today, those who decide to school their children at home have often found themselves in court facing state charges for disobeying school-attendance laws.

Religion is an important element in the lives of many people; to some, it is the *most* important element. It has been the source of strength in times of trouble. Certainly this has been the case for Black Americans in their history in the United States. Afro-American historian Barbara Green writes of the relationship between the survival skills and the folklore of Blacks. The spirituals they sang provided them with comfort, hope, and strength. Green states, "The performance of work songs and spirituals was just as important as the songs themselves. Singing them sharpened memory skills; taught language skills, religious values, and survival strategy; and cultivated group identity."[5]

Much of the civil rights movement of the last half of this century had a strong foundation within the churches and synagogues of the United States. People opposed to integration were often placed in the position of being opposed to their own church bodies or to religion in general. Churches became divided, and crypto religions developed.

The public schools often became the battleground for these contrasting belief systems. Governors who stood at the schoolhouse door to prevent integration were endorsed by some ministers and condemned by others. The schools were in the middle. Today, the schools are still in the middle. One example is when laws are passed requiring schools to teach sex education while many individuals and churches object with such vigor that they withdraw their children from school and establish new, private schools.

It should be no wonder, then, that public education as an arm of the state should have found itself frequently at odds with first one religious group and then another, as the United States has become ever more diverse and religiously pluralistic.

We Are What We Were

Historically the United States has always had a number of diferent religions. The similar, yet very different, religions of the Native Americans were well in place when the Europeans arrived. These newcomers brought with them a collection of similar, yet very different, forms of Christianity. Several colonies adopted nearly exclusively a single form of this religion (for example, the Puritans and Congregationalists in Massachusetts, the Catholics in Georgia, and the Anglicans and Episcopalians in Virginia), while others were settled by a variety of groups. Pennsylvania, for instance, became home to Quakers, Lutherans, Baptists, and many others.

Three different types of school systems developed, in part as a result of these patterns of religious settlement. The New England colonies developed public school laws (Massachusetts Laws of 1642 and 1647) that required an elementary school for every 50 families and a grammar school for every 100 families. However, since the government was essentially a *theocracy,* in which the church and state were essentially one, the name of those laws was "Ye Old Deluder Satan Act," and their purpose was to teach the children to read and write so they would be able to read the scriptures on their own and thus "ward off ye old deluder Satan." This *public parochial school* became the model for much of American education.

Because of the geographic size of the Southern colonies and the dominance by the Anglican Church of England, most schooling was done by traveling teachers who would stay for several months, visiting first one plantation and then another. Most children did not attend school; usually only boys from the wealthier families were so privileged. Apprenticeships were widely used for the less well-to-do. Formal education was much more a system of private schooling.

The middle colonies tended to have very diverse settlement patterns. No single religion dominated, but because religion was felt by many people to be a major reason for having formal education, little agreement among the various religious groups was possible. Therefore, a system of parochial schools resulted, with each group establishing its own schools.

Even amid this diversity, however, there was *oneness of religion*, a religious unity among Americans. Albanese says that religious unity refers to the "dominant and public cluster of organizations, ideas, and moral values which, historically and geographically, have characterized this country."[6] Today, this is often referred to as the Judeo-Christian tradition. For some people, this ethic has become a civil religion, in which patriotism and nationalism become an ultimate concern, a cryptoreligion.

As each new wave of immigrants came into the United States, the oneness expanded to accommodate the new arrivals even as the established religions changed and adapted to the new setting. Some geographic areas became closely associated with a particular group, such as the Amish in Pennsylvania. Add to the problems associated with religious differences the difficulties of language, dress, and food, and we can understand the assimilation problems experienced by immigrating groups. Most recently the new immigrants have come from non-Christian lands and are of a different race, thus making for a more difficult assimilation.

The process of assimilation did not always work smoothly. The religious oneness described above was nearly always patterned after the Massachusettes public school model—public parochial schools. Cincinnati's Bible War in 1869–1870 is one example of the assimilation process not working well. The public schools required the reading of the King James version of the Bible, which was objectionable to the large Catholic population, to Jews, and to others. Those in charge argued that the "common schools" were an appropriate place for the "common religion" to be taught. This religion was, however, a generalized Protestant version of Christianity and thus was not acceptable to all students.[7]

From the inception of the United States, the most fundamental question asked about religion and education has been, To what extent should the public schools be an extension of the oneness of religion, an extension of the separateness of the many religions, or no extension of any kind of religion? The many court cases in this century have been part of the process of trying to answer this question. The line separating church and state has always been unclear. Two centuries ago, the framers of the constitution addressed this question; legislative bodies and the courts have tried to clarify it; but it remains an issue very important to many people.

Constitutional Issues

The First Amendment to the U.S. Constitution said clearly: "Congress shall make no law respecting an establishment of religion, or prohibiting the free exercise thereof. . . ." The key word here is *Congress*, because not until the

Fourteenth Amendment was adopted (1868) and gave to the citizens of the states all of the rights they had as citizens of the nation did the federal separation of church and state have any influence on the schools. In fact, not until the 1830s did the Commonwealth of Massachusetts repeal such laws as mandatory church membership as a requirement for holding a public office.

The constitutional separation of church and state has two key elements: no state support to create or maintain a religion (establishment), and no state laws against the practice of a religion (prohibition). Most constitutional cases regarding religion and the schools have dealt with the "establishment clause"; i.e., the state (public school) cannot help to establish a religion by requiring prayer, Bible reading, or devotional moments of silent meditation or by permitting the use of school buildings or funds for religious instruction. Busing children to parochial schools for safety reasons and using public funds to purchase nonreligious textbooks is legal.

The Supreme Court gave strong support to the need for and appropriateness of teaching about religion in the public schools. On June 17, 1963, the Court gave its opinion on the cases of *Abington* v. *Schempp* and *Murray* (son of Madeline Murrary O'Hare) v. *Curlett*, which dealt with required prayer and Bible reading in school. Associate Justice Tom Clark wrote the majority opinion, which included the following statement (emphasis mine):

> It might well be said that one's education is not complete without a *study* of comparative religion or the history of religion and its relationship to the advancement of civilization. It certainly may be said that the Bible is worthy of *study* for its literary and historic qualities. Nothing we have said here indicates that such *study* of the Bible or of religion, when presented objectively as part of a secular program of education, may not be effected consistent with the First Amendment.

Because the headlines following this decision were inaccurate and misleading ("Prayer Banned—Bible Banned"), many educators as well as parents and other citizens were angry, perplexed, and concerned. Almost immediately the school curriculum guides and materials were subjected to "self-censoring," first by educators and then by publishers. So much censorship occurred so rapidly that the American Association of School Administrators published a book in 1964 entitled *Religion in the Public Schools.* The association took a strong and clear position in support of the valid academic study of religion in the public schools when it stated:

> A curriculum which ignored religion would itself have serious implications. It would seem to proclaim that religion has not been as real in men's lives as health, or politics, or economics. By omission it would appear to deny that religion has been and is important in man's history—a denial of the obvious. In day by day practice, the topic cannot be avoided. As an integral part of man's culture, it must be included.

Even though the need for and appropriateness of teaching about religion has been strongly shown since 1963, not everyone in the nation concurs. Problems occur when the public feels that schools are teaching about the religions of other lands but are giving little attention to religions of this land. The emotions schools had hoped to avoid by focusing only on remote and thus less controversial peoples are now in the headlines and in the courts.

Other constitutional issues have addressed how much power the state actually has to regulate religious schools, to require attendance at an approved school (religious or public), and to provide aid (what kind, how much, etc.). A 1980s case, for example, that began in Dayton, Ohio, involved the issue of whether the state civil rights commission had the power to investigate a teacher's charge that she had been dismissed from a private Christian school because she exercised her civil right to question an administrative decision. The school contends that, because the school is a religious institution, civil rights laws do not apply to how it treats its own personnel. This is one of a new type of church-state cases focusing on prohibiting the free exercise thereof clause of the First Amendment.

The founders of the United States had either experienced firsthand or knew about the unwelcome combination of church and state in Europe. Wars, inquisitions, and the absence of freedom were fresh in their minds as they developed the Constitution. The quality of their work is seen today in the fact that in the 200 years that have passed, the United States has become even more religiously diverse but has avoided the major problems of lasting and often violent interreligious conflicts too often found elsewhere in the world.

Religious Diversity in the United States

Lessons from history tell us that religious, ethnic, and language diversity within a nation or other area often lead to many problems. Such examples as Ireland, India, Pakistan, Sri Lanka, and Belgium come to mind. Diversity, however, also exists within particular religions and even within particular denominations of a religion. Conflicts during the 1980s within the Southern Baptist Convention and a split in the Lutheran Church Missouri Synod—both separate Christian denominations—illustrate the point.

If we are to learn from history, we must be more knowledgeable about our own religious diversity and learn how to respond to it more appropriately. This section examines the extent of religious diversity within the United States and within Christianity, the major religious groups.

As a nation, the United States began with a diversity of peoples and their beliefs. The dominant common Western European heritage, although not one of peace and goodwill among themselves, was clearly Christian in a general way. While some early settlers were deeply religious and came to this land in order to practice their religion, others came for different reasons, including economic gain, adventure, and escape from legal or other problems. It must be noted that some of those who sought religious freedom were, in turn, unwilling to grant it to others; Rhode Island was founded by people whose religious beliefs were not welcome in neighboring Massachusetts.

Specific data on religious diversity in the United States are difficult to find. One must turn to a variety of sources and sometimes use information from different studies to gain even a fuzzy picture of how many religions are practiced today in the United States. There is always a danger that comparisons of religions are being made between apples and oranges.

A massive 1980 survey of Judeo-Christian denominations[8] found more than 228 different church groups. A few, 17 out of 111 who returned surveys, reported having more than one million adherents and another 25 church bodies claimed between 100,000 and one million members. After Roman Catholics, who accounted for 42 percent of the total, the figures dropped dramatically to 14.5 percent for Southern Baptists and 10.3 percent for Methodists. A total of 108 'denominations' were listed for the other 31 percent, with no one group claiming more than 2.6 percent of the total.

Add to these data the fact that there are thousands of local churches not affiliated with any larger body, synod, or organization. Many of these independent churches have grown in number of adherents during the 1970s and 1980s. Television evangelists, at least up until their scandals of the late 1980s, experienced large and growing video congregations, which were also outside of the enumerations of the survey cited above.

Still other groups that stand partially or totally outside the Judeo-Christian realm (Unification Church of the Rev. Sun Myung Moon, the Scientologists, and the Hare Krishna movement, for example) experienced growth during the 1970s. Precise numbers for such groups are not available.

Gaustad's data indicate that as the United States has grown over the years, the percentage of the population claiming a religious affiliation has also grown.[9] Another way to say this is that as the United States has become more diverse in the social and religious aspects of its peoples, a larger percentage of people have become affiliated with a religious body. Gaustad reports that in 1865, 26 percent claimed a religious affiliation. This percentage rose over the years to 44 percent in 1930 and 62 percent in 1970, the final year for these data.

Table 5.1, from *Statistical Abstract of the United States,* summarizes data on religious preference, church membership, and attendance from 1957 to 1986 for the noninstitutional population in the United States eighteen years old and over.[10] This table indicates that this population showed the following religious preferences in 1986: Protestant, 59 percent; Catholic, 27 percent; Jewish, 2 percent and other, 4 percent. Although 92 percent of this population expressed a religious preference, only 69 percent were church or synagogue members and only 40 percent actually attended churches or synagogues.

According to the *New Book of American Rankings,* the percentage of Christian-Judaic adherents varies greatly by state. Rhode Island leads the list, with 75.5 percent; Utah follows closely, with 75.2 percent; Alaska, with 30.8 percent, and Nevada, with 29.3 percent, are at the bottom of the rankings. In general, the New England area and the Upper Midwest and Plains states have the highest percentages of adherents, and the West has the lowest.

Data for Christians and Jews are much easier to obtain than is accurate and reliable information for other religions. Only the former tend to maintain records and statistics (many of which are less than complete and current). Most information for other religions is based on informed estimates. What follows, then, should be viewed as general patterns rather than as hard data.

Immigration reports provide a basis for enlightened conjecture as to how many adherents there are for each religion. *The World Almanac and Book of Facts*: 1987 indicates that the total percentage of European immigrants to the United States went down from 33.8 percent in 1961 to only 17.8 percent for the following decade.[11] In sharp contrast is the number of immigrants from Asia. Figures for these immigrants went up dramatically, from 12.9 percent of total

TABLE 5.1
Religious Preference, Church Membership, and Attendance, 1957 to 1986   In percent. Covers civilian noninstitutional population, 18 years old and over. Data represent averages of the combined results of several surveys during year. Data are subject to sampling variability.

Year	Religious Preference					Church/ synagogue members	Persons attending church/ synagogue[1]	Age and Region	Church/ synagogue members, 1986
	Protestant	Catholic	Jewish	Other	None				
1957	66	26	3	1	3	73[2]	47	18–29 years old	63
1967	67	25	3	3	2	73[3]	43	30–49 years old	67
1975	62	27	2	4	6	71	41	50 years and over	75
1980	61	28	2	2	7	69	40		
1984	57	28	2	4	9	68	40	East[4]	70
1985	57	28	2	4	9	71	42	Midwest[5]	71
1986	59	27	2	4	8	69	40	South[6]	74
								West[7]	57

[1] Persons who attended a church or synagogue in the last seven days.
[2] 1952 data.
[3] 1965 data.
[4] ME, NH, RI, NY, CT, VT, MA, NJ, PA, WV, DE, MD, and DC.
[5] OH, IN, IL, MI, MN, WI, IA, ND, SD, KS, NE, and MO.
[6] KY, TN, VA, NC, SC, GA, FL, AL, MS, TX, AR, OK, and LA.
[7] AZ, NM, CO, NV, MT, ID, WY, UT, CA, WA, OR, AK, and HI.

From U.S. Bureau of the Census, *Statistical Abstract of the United States: 1988* (108 edition) (Washington, D.C.: U.S. Government Printing Office), Table 75, p. 52.

immigrants in the 1960s to 35.3 percent in the 1970s. The figures for African immigrants went from 0.9 percent to 1.8 percent, and those for South and Central America and for Australia both declined a little. The continued emigration of the many refugees from Southeast Asia during the 1980s has maintained this pattern and probably has increased the influx of persons from non–Christian-Judaic backgrounds, thus further increasing the religious diversity of the United States.

Other data that support these conclusions indicate that in 1957 there were only 10,000 Buddhists in the United States, but in 1970, 100,000 were here.[12] However, the *Handbook of Denominations in the U.S.,* published in 1985, shows 250,000 Buddhists in the United States.[13]

This same book shows 3,000,000 members of the Muslim faith, but earlier data for comparison purposes are not available. Jewish adherents in 1985 totaled 5,835,000 and made up 2.5 percent of the total United States population, according to *Statistical Abstract of the United States: 1987.*[14] The Jewish numbers in 1960 were 5,367,000,[15] a growth rate of only 8.7 percent over a twenty-five-year span. Thus, although Christianity remains the largest religion in the United States, with Judaism second, some predict that Islam will become the second-largest religion in the United States within another twenty-five or thirty years. Immigration from such areas as Lebanon, Iran, Egypt, India, and Pakistan, as well as the growth of the Black Muslim sect, account for most of the Muslim growth.

Given the fact that American schools and textbooks have paid little attention to the teachings of the Islamic faith, this growth will represent a challenge. According to Uphoff: "William J. Griswold, a key investigator in a thorough study of U.S. textbooks and their treatment of Islam in history, reports that 27 or 45 texts examined either have nothing on the Muslim world, are biased, simplistic, and error-filled, or are scanty and not always dependable in their treatment of Islam."[16]

A report on current languages other than English spoken in the United States is another source of data for our conjecturing about the nation's religious diversity. According to the report, in 1980 the primary languages spoken at home by persons between the ages of five and seventeen were as follows:

- Vietnamese, spoken by 64,000
- Korean, 60,000
- Japanese, 34,000
- Phillipino, 63,000
- Chinese, 114,000
- Other non-European, 544,000

(Spanish was the largest, with 2,952,000 speakers, but most of these children are within the Christian tradition, given their cultural heritage.) Hundreds of thousands of children speaking languages other than English at home and coming from nations where religions other than Christianity and Judaism are practiced are now common in the United States and its schools.

The New Book of World Rankings has developed what it calls a homogeneity index to use when comparing nations on a scale of internal diversity. The book's introduction states:

> *Political stability is often associated with linguistic and ethnic homogeneity. While developed societies in the West are moving toward pluralism and multi-culturalism, traditional societies in Asia and Africa are moving toward monocultures. Many governments are striving to create nations from heterogeneous populations and finding the task difficult. Because the primary loyalty of an individual in traditional societies is to his race, language, and religion, ethnicity becomes the basis for factional and separatist tendencies.*[17]

The index includes 135 countries, with the highest ranking indicating the most homogeneity. North and South Korea are tied for first and second place, with a homogeneity percentage of 100. Others in the top ten include South Yemen, Portugal, Japan, Haiti, Puerto Rico, Hong Kong, East Germany, and West Germany. The United States ranks 82 : 135, with a homogeneity percentage of only 50. These data indicate that the United States is among the most diverse nations in the world in terms of ethnicity, race, language, and religion.

Changes have also taken place within the dominant Christian community of the United States. Membership in many mainline denominations has declined during the past ten to twenty years, while fundamentalist religions have experienced growth. The figures below illustrate these patterns of growth and decline:[18]

Denominations with Their Highest Membership Figures between 1960 and 1970

American Lutheran Church (1970)
Christian Church (Disciples of Christ) (1965)
Church of the Brethren (1960)
Episcopal Church (1965)
Lutheran Church in America (1965)
Lutheran Church—Missouri Synod (1970)
Presbyterian Church (USA) (1960)
Reformed Church in America (1965)
United Church of Christ (1960)
United Methodist Church (1965)

Denominations with Their Highest Membership Figures in 1985

Assemblies of God
Christian and Missionary Alliance
Church of Jesus Christ of Latter-Day Saints
Church of the Nazarene
Jehovah's Witnesses
Roman Catholic Church
Salvation Army
Seventh-Day Adventists
Southern Baptist Convention

Within many mainstream churches, movement also occurred during the 1970s and 1980s. Hill describes it as "the infusion of unfamiliar styles of Christian practice and expression into existing denominations." He talks about many people who remain happily Lutheran or Episcopalian or Roman Catholic "while embracing new forms of spirituality that are more often 'Spirit-filled' than 'pentecostal.' "[19] Hill contends that this movement is away from authority within a church and toward greater individuality. He sees a "moving from tradition to immediacy; from church as authoritative institution to free-form congregations and each individual; from prescribed worship to informal gatherings." Combined with the other growing diversities of religious groups within the United States, schools now face a different public.

This change has given public school leaders many more headaches because they must now deal more frequently with individuals and with individual congregations than with only the local ministerial association. There is now more scrutiny of more aspects of public education by more people than ever before in the nation's history.

Educational Implications

The high level of religious diversity in the United States is a fact. The public schools, which at one time were a public extension of a generalized Protestant belief system, can no longer fill that role. On the other hand, these same schools must be sure that they do not move in the opposite direction, to a position of open hostility to religion.

The mission of the public schools is a broad one and may go beyond what some religious groups deem acceptable. For example, people who object to the teaching of critical-thinking skills (and there are some) will most likely have to find an alternative to public education. Although the public schools cannot be all things to all people—they must be sure to be fair to all, respect all, and be open to all.

Specific implications of this state of diversity are focused on the following eight aspects of education:

1. Curriculum resources such as textbooks, library books, films, and speakers

2. Subject matter to be included in the curriculum, whether elective or required, such as values clarification, sex and health education, and religion

3. School rules of all types, such as teacher qualifications, school attendance, discipline, and dress codes, whether from the federal, state, or local level

4. Student services such as psychological counseling, testing, and health care

5. School calendar decisions, historically tied to Christmas and Easter

6. Scheduling of student activities that interfere with the religious observances of some students (e.g., athletic events on Friday nights)

7. Teaching methods that require student behaviors objectionable to some people, such as value clarification, decision-making, and thinking and debating skills.

8. School financing, especially where local voters must approve new monies for the school budget, but even at the state level, where legislators are subject to intense political pressure

The factors described above have too often caused significant controversies within a community, a state, or the entire nation. Headlines, television cameras, angry protesters, emotional meetings, and court cases have been too common. To avoid such negative situations, every educator must first become better informed about religion in general, and especially about its influence on human beings now and throughout history. The academic study of religion is vital for both teachers and students. Within the public schools, the best place for this type of study to occur is wherever it logically falls in the regular curriculum. In a home economics unit on food preparation, for example, it would be logical to include how some religions have given their adherents rules to follow regarding the handling and consumption of foods in their daily lives. During a unit on the colonial period of U.S. history, students could study the roles of the various churches and how each affected the geographic area in which it was dominant. The effects of beliefs on the decisions of individual leaders could be examined.

Curriculum resources need to be examined carefully. Earlier in this chapter the lack of appropriate treatment of Islamic peoples and beliefs in U.S. history textbooks was cited. An Associated Press story on May 28, 1986, carried the headline "Most High School Texts Neglect Religion, Group Says." The article quotes People for the American Way as follows: "Students aren't learning about America's rich and diverse religious heritage because textbook publishers are still afraid of offending anyone, from moral majoritarians to civil libertarians."[20]

Another report, by the well-respected Association for Supervision and Curriculum Development, refers to the "benign neglect" of religion by textbooks at all levels. It states that "an elementary student can come away from a textbook account of the Crusades, for example, with the notion that these wars to win the Holy Land for Christendom were little more than exotic shopping expeditions."[21]

It is interesting that liberal and conservative political action groups, as well as educational groups, have arrived at the same conclusions regarding the inappropriate treatment of religion in school textbooks. This was exactly the basis used by Judge William Brevard Hand in his decision to ban dozens of books from use in schools.

In addition to becoming better educated about religion, educators must use appropriate teaching methods. The continuing controversy over the teaching of evolution and the call for the balancing inclusion of "creation science" illustrate the need to use effective and sensitive teaching methods. People who accept the story of creation in Genesis and teach it to their children are highly offended when their children are told by teachers that the parents are wrong. The anger of the parents is understandable.

How a teacher handles the teaching of evolution is crucial. Two possible exam questions illustrate how easy it is to avoid a direct confrontation with these children and their parents, and at the same time continue to teach the prescribed curriculum:

> **Poor**   It took millions of years for the earth to evolve to its present state. (True/False)
>
> **Better**   Evolutionists believe that it took millions of years for the earth to evolve to its present state. (True/False)

The first question requires the child to agree with a statement of "fact." The second question allows the child to answer that one group of people has a different set of beliefs than the child has, while at the same time protecting his or her own integrity. The difference is subtle, but powerful. The second question respects diversity of beliefs while teaching scientific information—that is, information about evolutionary theory. No child is forced to go against personal or family beliefs.

Such a change in teaching approaches will help reduce conflict between home and school. However, we need to be aware from the beginning that not everyone will be satisfied. Some people have such a narrow belief system that the public school system will never be able to satisfy them.

Teachers of all subject areas can benefit from the work done on teaching about religion by the National Council for the Social Studies (NCSS). The January 1981 issue of *Social Education* has as its theme "Teaching about Religion: Vistas Unlimited" and includes an article entitled "Instructional Issues in Teaching about Religion." This article calls for teachers to use a wide range of methodologies, including the use of music, skits, art, and role playing.[22] It is next to impossible to teach students to think critically if they are limited to a single source of information, the textbook. A teacher's academic knowledge about religion as distinguished from personal, experiential knowledge is vital. The importance of the teacher's objectivity is also stressed, and specific teacher behaviors to bring this about are presented.

The NCSS in 1984 published its official position, in an article entitled "Including the Study about Religions in the Social Studies Curriculum: A Position Statement and Guidelines."[23] The fourteen guidelines it recommends are specific and helpful. Two guidelines are:

■ Study about religions should stress the influence of religions on history, culture, the arts, and contemporary issues.

■ Study about religions should be descriptive, nonconfessional, and conducted in an environment free of advocacy.

A short booklet entitled *Public Education Religion Studies: Questions and Answers* is available from the National Council on Religion and Public Education (address: % Dept. of Religion, University of Kansas, Lawrence, Kansas 66045). The booklet is organized around eleven different questions, such as "How do you study about religion in public schools?" and "What criteria should be used in selecting teaching materials?" This help for educators is based on the work of a diverse advisory committee that helped the Public Education Religion Studies Center at Wright State University, Dayton, Ohio, in the early 1970s.

Summary

The United States is a religiously diverse nation and is becoming more so every day. If the United States is to avoid the fractionalization and inner turmoil that have destroyed other diverse nations, the public schools must lead the nation in being sensitive to the diversity itself, and by helping students to learn about each other as well as about people in other parts of the world.

The old etiquette guide about not discussing religion or politics in mixed company has done more harm than good. It is not an appropriate policy for the schools of the United States as they prepare citizens for life in the twenty-first century.

Questions and Activities

1. What is the broad definition of religion developed by the Public Education Religious Studies Center? How is this definition of religion similar to and different from other definitions of religion with which you are familiar? With your own personal definition of religion?

2. What are the educational consequences of broad and narrow definitions of religion?

3. Prepare a report indicating the role religion has played in the history and culture of an ethnic group, such as Jewish Americans or Afro-Americans. Helpful references are Irving Howe's *World of Our Fathers: The Journey of the East European Jews to America and the Life They Found and Made* (New York: Simon and Schuster, 1976); E. Franklin Frazier's *The Negro Church in America* and C. Eric Lincoln's *The Black Church Since Frazier* (in one volume) (New York: Schocken Books, 1974).

4. Uphoff points out that an increasing number of children now in U.S. schools have come from nations where religions other than Christianity and Judaism are common. This means that religious diversity is increasing in U.S. schools. What are the educational implications of the increasing religious diversity in U.S. schools?

5. Controversies have developed in many communities about the way Christmas is celebrated in the schools. In some communities, the school boards have established policies that prevent teachers from using religious songs or symbols in holiday celebrations during the Christmas season. What is your opinion of such school board policies? Give reasons to support your position.

6. According to the author, why is it important for students to study religion in the public schools?

7. Why do textbooks tend to ignore religion? How can teachers supplement the textbook treatment of religion? What guidelines should teachers keep in mind when teaching about religion in public schools? What knowledge and sensitivities should they have?

8. To develop a better understanding of religious and cultural diversity in U.S. society, attend services at several religious institutions within your community or region, such as a synagogue, a Catholic church, a Black Baptist church, a Buddhist temple, and a mosque. How are the services and rituals at these institutions alike and different?

Notes

1. "Alleged 'Secular Humanism' Courses Attacked," *Education Week* 5 (October 15, 1986): 12.

2. John F. Wilson, *Religion: A Preface* (Englewood Cliffs, N.J.: Prentice-Hall, 1982), p. 18.

3. Catherine L. Albanese, *America: Religions and Religion* (Belmont, Calif: Wadsworth Publishing Co., 1981), p. 2.

4. Peter Bracher, James V. Panoch, Nicholas Piediscalzi, and James K. Uphoff, *Public Education Religion Studies: Questions and Answers* (Dayton, Ohio: Public Education Religion Studies Center, Wright State University, p. 5.

5. Barbara L. Green, "Solace, Self-Esteem, and Solidarity: The Role of Afro-American Folklore in the Education and Acculturation of Black Americans," *Texas Tech Journal of Education,* 2, No. 1 (Winter 1984): 94.

6. Albanese, p. 10.

7. Robert Michaelsen, *Piety in the Public School* (New York: Macmillan, 1970), pp. 89–98.

8. *The New Book of American Rankings* (New York: Facts on File Publications, 1984), pp. 61–63.

9. Edwin Scott Gaustad, *Historical Atlas of Religion in America,* rev. ed. (New York: Harper & Row, 1976), p. 168.

10. U.S. Bureau of the Census, *Statistical Abstract of the United States: 1988,* 108th ed. (Washington, D.C.: U.S. Government Printing Office, 1988) Table 75, p. 52.

11. *The World Almanac and Book of Facts: 1987* (New York: World Almanac, 1987) p. 226.

12. *Historical Statistics of the United States: Colonial Times to 1970, Part 1,* (Washington, D.C.: U.S. Department of Commerce, Bureau of the Census, 1975), p. 391.

13. Samuel S. Hill, ed., *Handbook of Denominations in the U.S.,* 8th ed., (Nashville, Tenn.: Abington Press, 1985) pp. 70, 176.

14. *Statistical Abstract, 1987.*

15. *Historical Statistics.*

16. James K. Uphoff, "Religious Minorities: In or Out of the Culturally Pluralistic Curriculum?" *Educational Leadership,* 32, No. 3 (December 1974): 199–202.

17. George Thomas Kurian, *New Book of World Rankings* (New York: Facts on File Publications, 1984), pp. 47–49.

18. Constant H. Jacquet, Jr. (ed.), *Yearbook of American and Canadian Churches* (Nashville, Tenn.: Abingdon Press, 1987), pp. 254–255. Used with permission.

19. Hill, "Making Sense of Bewilderment: 262–273.

20. "Most high school texts neglect religion, group says, *The Journal Herald,* Dayton, Ohio (May 28, 1986): 16.

21. *The New York Times,* "Panel of Educators Asks End to 'Neglect' about Religions," (July 2, 1987): 1, 9.

22. James K. Uphoff, "Instructional Issues in Teaching About Religion," *Social Education,* 45, No. 1 (January 1981): 22–27.

23. National Council for the Social Studies, "Including the Study about Religions in the Social Studies Curriculum: A Position Statement and Guidelines," *Social Education,* 49, No. 5 (May 1985): 413–414.

Eliminating sex bias in schools will improve educational opportunities for women.

PART III

Gender

Social, economic, and political conditions for women have improved substantially since the women's rights movement emerged as part of the civil rights movement of the 1960s and 1970s. However, gender discrimination and inequality still exist in schools and in society at large. In 1986, the average earnings for women who were full-time workers were 70 percent of those for men, up from 63 percent in 1979. The status of women in the United States within the last two decades has changed substantially. More women are now working outside the home than ever before, and more women are heads of households. In 1982, nearly 52 percent of women worked outside the home, making up 43 percent of the total work force. In 1984, 16 percent of households in the United States were headed by women. A growing percentage of women and their dependents constitute the nation's poor. Some writers use the term *the feminization of poverty* to describe this development. Nearly half of the nation's population (more than 30 million) living in poverty in the early 1980s were women and their dependent children.

The chapters in this part of the book describe the status of women in the United States, the ways in which schools perpetuate gender discrimination, and strategies that educators can use to create equal educational opportunities for female and male students. As Sadker, Sadker, and Long point out in Chapter 6, both males and females are harmed by sexual stereotypes and gender discrimination. Tetreault describes how school knowledge is dominated by male perspectives and how teachers can infuse their curricula with perspectives from both genders and thereby expand their students' thinking and insights. Butler discusses how women of color have often been ignored by the women's movement, which is predominantly a White, middle-class phenomenon. She describes perspectives and content that will enable teachers to integrate their curricula with the experiences and cultures of women of color.

CHAPTER 6

Gender and Educational Equality

- ## MYRA SADKER, DAVID SADKER, and LYNETTE LONG

Introduction

"Boys are doctors. Girls are nurses," insisted the kindergarten class. Amazed that young children could be so firm in their stereotype, the teacher took the twenty-two youngsters on a field trip to a nearby hospital. She introduced them to a female doctor and a male nurse who talked with them about their jobs and gave them a tour of the hospital.

Upon returning to the classroom, the teacher emphasized her point, "Now you can see that boys can be nurses. Girls can be doctors."

"No they can't," the students insisted.

"What do you mean?" The teacher was stunned. "We visited the hospital and met a man who is a nurse and a woman who is a doctor. You saw them. They talked with you."

"Yes," chorused the children triumphantly, "but they lied."[1]

As this real-life anecdote shows, sometimes it is easier to split an atom than to change an attitude. The past two decades have seen tremendous strides in abolishing sexism, but entrenched resistance remains. From the books they read, to the role models they see, to the way they are treated in classrooms, girls and boys continue to learn subtle yet powerful messages about separate and unequal opportunities based on gender.

This chapter provides an overview of how sexism operates in school, from curriculum and instruction to administration. Through a report card, it also shows the cost of sex bias: its influence on our nation's children. After highlighting current issues, the chapter concludes with strategies educators can use to make sure their classrooms are fair to all students regardless of gender.

Curricular Materials

Central to academic progress are the textbooks, workbooks, tests, encyclopedias, paperbacks, computer software, and a variety of other instructional materials teachers use every day. Administrators and teachers select educational materials based on a variety of criteria, including how well they match the needs of a particular school or group of students, how clearly they present the desired material, and how practical the materials are in terms of affordability and availability. These experts must also consider whether curricular materials reflect equity in their presentation of males and females.

Six Forms of Bias

Below is a description of six forms of sex bias educators can use to evaluate materials for gender equity.[2] The description of each form reviews research and presents historical perspectives on how the form has been manifested in instructional material. Following these six forms of bias, the state of gender equity in curriculum today is assessed.

Linguistic Bias

Referring to the use of masculine terms and pronouns in curriculum materials, linguistic bias is one of the easiest forms of sex bias to detect and eliminate. In history texts, terms such as *caveman, forefathers,* and *mankind* inherently deny the contributions of women. Similarly, masculine occupational titles such as *mailman, policeman,* and *businessman* are labels that deny the participation of women in our society. So does use of the pronoun *he* to refer to all people.

Another form of linguistic bias occurs when women are identified in terms of being someone's wife or possession, as in this sentence: "Winston Williams and his wife and children moved to New York." When this is reworded to read, "The Williams family moved to New York," all members of the family are considered equally.

Stereotyping

Many studies indicate that children and adults have been stereotyped in textbooks. Boys typically are portrayed as exhibiting one set of values, behaviors, and roles, whereas girls are drawn with a different set of characteristics. In reading books, boys routinely have been shown as ingenious, creative, brave, athletic, achieving, and curious. Girls have been portrayed as dependent, passive, fearful, and docile victims. Adults have also been stereotyped in roles and careers. In a study of seventy-seven basal readers published between 1980 and 1982, Britton and Lumpkin found a total of 5,501 careers depicted; 64 percent were attributed to Anglo males, 14 percent to Anglo females, 17 percent to males of color, and 5 percent to females of color. The most common careers shown for Anglo males were soldier, farmer, doctor, and police officer. The most frequently shown role models for males of color were worker, farmer, warrior, Indian chief, and hunter. The most common careers for White women were mother, teacher, author, and princess. For females of color, mother and teacher also headed the list, followed by slave, worker, porter, and artist.[3]

Invisibility

Women have made significant contributions to the growth and development of the United States, yet few have appeared in the history books children are assigned to read. This form of sex bias—invisibility, or omission—has characterized not only history books, but also texts in reading, language arts, mathematics, science, spelling, and vocational education. For example, a 1972 study of science, math, reading, spelling, and social studies textbooks found that only 31 percent of all illustrations included females and that the percentage of females decreased as the grade level increased.[4]

In another study, researchers analyzed 134 elementary readers and found males pictured twice as often as females and portrayed in three times as many occupations.[5] A 1970 study of history texts found that students had to read more than 500 pages before they found one page of information about women.[6] When girls and women are systematically excluded from curricular material, students are deprived of information about half the nation's people. Even though studies in the 1980s show that significant improvement has been made, women and girls are still underrepresented on textbook pages.

Imbalance

Textbooks perpetuate bias by presenting only one interpretation of an issue, situation, or group of people. Often this one-sided view is presented because the author has limited space or decides that it is not feasible to present all sides of an issue in elementary textbooks. History textbooks contain many examples of imbalance, mostly minimizing the role of women. For example, Janice Trecker studied the most widely used history textbooks and found more information on women's skirt lengths than on the suffragist movement.[7] As a result of such imbalanced presentation, millions of students have been given limited perspectives concerning the contributions, struggles, and participation of women in U.S. society. Although more recent textbook studies show improvement, problems remain.

Unreality

Many textbooks have presented an unrealistic portrayal of U.S. history and contemporary life experience by glossing over controversial topics and avoiding discussion of discrimination and prejudice. For example, almost 50 percent of all marriages end in divorce, and one-third of all children will live with a single parent during part of their lives. Yet many textbooks portray the typical American family as one having two adults, two children, a dog, and a house in suburbia. When controversial issues are not presented, students are denied the information they need to confront contemporary problems.

Fragmentation

Textbooks fragment the contributions of women by treating these contributions as unique occurrences rather than integrating them into the main body of the text. In fragmented textbooks, the contributions of important women are often highlighted in separate boxes or are contained in a separate chapter. Fragmentation communicates to readers that women are an interesting diversion but that their contributions do not constitute the mainstream of history and literature. Fragmentation and isolation also occur when women are depicted as interacting only among themselves and as having little or no influence on society as a whole. For example, textbook discussions of feminism often talk about how women are affected by this contemporary movement, but there is little analysis of the effect of the women's movement on other groups and social issues.

Recent Progress

In 1972, Scott, Foresman, the first company to publish nonsexist guidelines, suggested that the achievements of women be recognized, that women and girls be given the same respect as men and boys, that abilities, traits, interests, and activities should not be assigned on the basis of male or female stereotypes, and that sexist language be avoided. Today most textbook publishers edit books for sexist language and produce guidelines for authors to improve the image of women. By following these guidelines and avoiding the six forms of sex bias presented here, authors can develop nonsexist texts and other curricular materials.

Although bias in educational materials still exists, great gains were made in the 1980s. For example, a study of the story problems in mathematics textbooks from the mid-1930s to the late 1980s has found a greater proportion of story problems about women in textbooks used in the 1980s than in the 1970s or before.[8] A study of the Newbery Medal Award books from 1977 through 1984 also found the portrayal of women and girls less stereotypic. Also, compared to a 1971 study, the number of books with girls and women as the main character has increased substantially.[9] Basal science texts are also more sensitive to the issue of sexism. A study of the illustrations of seven elementary science textbook series found that female children are represented with greater frequency than male children.[10] Unfortunately, gains in history have not been as impressive, and a review of thirty-one U.S. history textbooks published in 1986 found that the contributions of women are still minimized.[11] To represent an accurate view of history, textbooks need to portray the role of the average, as well as the exceptional, woman in our nation's history.

The influence of sex bias in curriculum materials is significant. Misrepresentations and omissions can negatively affect the self-image, goals, and philosophy of girls. Children need strong, positive role models for the development of self-esteem. When females are omitted from books, a hidden curriculum is created, one that teaches children that females are less important and less significant in our society than males.

In contrast, studies show that bias-free materials can have a positive influence and can encourage students at various grade levels to change attitudes and behaviors as a result of their reading materials. One researcher found that children in grades 1 through 5 developed less stereotyped attitudes about jobs and activities after reading about people who successfully fought sex discrimination in nontraditional jobs.[12] In a similar study, children who read instructional materials about girls in nontraditional roles were more likely to think that girls could perform the nontraditional activity of the narrative than children who read the same materials with boys as the main characters.[13]

Educators who select gender-fair materials can encourage significant changes in their students. Bias-free materials in literature expand students' knowledge of changing sex roles and encourage greater flexibility in attitudes regarding appropriate behavior for females and males. In science and math, gender-fair materials provide females with encouragement to enter careers in these areas. In history, bias-free materials provide role models and demonstrate contributions of women in the history of this nation.

But gender-fair curricular materials by themselves are not sufficient to create a nonsexist educational environment. Attention must also be paid to the process of instruction.

Instruction

The following scene, a general music class in action, reflects the subtle ways sex bias can permeate the instructional process.[14]

As the bell rings, students take their seats. The girls are clustered in the front and on the right-hand side of the room, while the boys are predominantly on the other side of the room and in the back. This seating arrangement doesn't bother the students—they choose their own seats; and it doesn't seem to bother their teacher, Mrs. Howe, who makes no comment about the segregated arrangement.

Mrs. Howe starts the lesson by playing part of Mozart's *Symphony Concertante* on the record player. After about five minutes, she turns to the class with questions.

Mrs. Howe: Who can tell me the name of this composer?

(A few hands are raised, when John shouts out "Bruce Springsteen." After the laughter dies down, Mrs. Howe calls on Mitch.)

Mitch: Haydn.

Mrs. Howe: Why do you think so?

Mitch: Because yesterday you played Haydn.

Mrs. Howe: Close. Eric what do you think?

Eric: I don't know.

Mrs. Howe: Come on, Eric. During the last two weeks we have been listening to various Classical period composers. Out of those we've listened to, who wrote this piece?

(Silence)

Mrs. Howe: John, can you help Eric out?

John: Beethoven.

Mrs. Howe: No, it's not Beethoven. Beethoven was more a Romantic period composer. Think.

(Mrs. Howe finally calls on Pam, who has had her hand half-raised during this discussion.)

Pam: I'm not sure, but is it Mozart?

Mrs. Howe: Uh-huh. Anyone else agree with Pam?

Mitch (calls out): It's Mozart. It's similar to the Mozart concerto you played yesterday.

Mrs. Howe: Very good. Can you tell us if this is another concerto he wrote?

Mitch: Yes, it's a violin concerto.

Mrs. Howe: That's almost right. It's a special concerto written for two instruments. To help you figure out the other instrument, let's listen to more of the piece.

(Mrs. Howe plays more of the piece and calls on Mitch.)

Mitch: Another violin.

Mrs. Howe: Peter?

Peter: A cello.

Mrs. Howe: You're all close. It's another string instrument, but it's not another violin or a cello.

Ruth (calls out): What about a viola?

Mrs. Howe: Ruth, you know I don't allow shouting out. Raise your hand next time. Peter?

Peter: A viola.

Mrs. Howe: Very good. This is a special kind of concerto Mozart wrote for both the violin and viola called Symphony Concertante. One reason why I want you to listen to it is to notice the difference between the violin and the viola. Let's listen to the melody as played first by the violin then the viola. Listen for the similarities and differences between the two.

This scenario demonstrates several important interaction patterns; in this sex-segregated classroom, Mrs. Howe called on the boys more often than the girls and asked them more higher-order and lower-order questions. She gave male students more specific feedback, including praise, constructive criticism, and remediation. Research shows that from grade school to graduate school, most classrooms demonstrate similar instructional patterns.

One large study conducted in the fourth, sixth, and eighth grades in more than 100 classrooms in four states and the District of Columbia found that teachers gave boys more academic attention than girls. They asked them more questions and gave them more precise and clear feedback concerning the quality of their responses. In contrast, girls were more likely to be ignored or given diffuse evaluation of the academic quality of their work.[15] Other research shows that these same patterns are prevalent at the secondary and post-secondary levels.[16]

One reason boys get more teacher attention is that they demand it. Approximately eight times as likely to shout out questions and answers, they dominate the classroom airwaves. However, when boys call out, teachers accept their comments. In contrast, when girls call out teachers are more likely to reprimand them by saying things like, "In this class, we raise our hands before talking."

Another factor allowing boys to dominate classroom interaction is the widespread sex segregation that characterizes classrooms. Occasionally teachers divide their classrooms into sex-segregated lines, teams, work and play areas, and seating arrangements. More frequently, students sex-segregate themselves. Drawn to the sections of the classroom where the more assertive boys are clustered, the teacher is positioned to keep interacting with male students.

The conclusion of most interaction studies is that teachers give more attention—positive, negative, and neutral—to male students. However, some researchers emphasize that low-achieving males get most of the negative attention, while high-achieving boys get more positive and constructive academic contacts. But no matter whether they are high or low achievers, female students are more likely to be invisible and ignored.[17]

The gender difference in classroom communications is more than a mere counting game of who gets the teacher's attention and who doesn't. Teacher attention is a vote of high expectations and commitment to a student. Decades of research show that students who are actively involved in classroom discussion are more likely to achieve and to express positive attitudes toward schools and learning.[18]

Most teachers do not want to be biased in their treatment of students and are completely unaware of inequitable interaction. On the positive side, studies show that with resources, awareness, and training, teachers can eliminate these patterns and achieve equity in how they teach female and male students. Given the crucial nature of this pervasive problem, it is unfortunate that most schools of education still do not include the issue in their teaching-preparation programs.

School Administration

Effective research on schools has highlighted the crucial role of the principal in encouraging student achievement. When principals become instructional leaders, student performance is enhanced. Student achievement scores rise when the principal is visible throughout the school, especially in classrooms; encourages staff to work as a team in meeting school goals; holds high expectations; and is actively involved in observing and analyzing the instructional process. To accomplish these goals, an effective administrator must have extensive teaching experience, a thorough understanding of the teaching-learning process, and positive human relations skills. Although women excel in these areas, the world of school administration still belongs to men.

Almost 70 percent of teachers in the United States are women, yet women account for less than 30 percent of the administrators. Research shows that women who attain positions in administration are as competent as or more competent than their male counterparts.[19] Female administrators excel at the human relations skills essential to effective leadership. More aware of the problems facing teachers and more supportive of their staffs, female administrators create democratic school climates and are rated high in the areas of productivity and morale.

Women as administrators also have a positive influence on students. They focus more energy on the teaching-learning process and monitor student learning more carefully than their male colleagues do. One study showed that students of all socioeconomic levels achieved more in schools with female principals.[20] Given this research-based demonstration of competence, the question remains, Why are so few women managing schools?

Historical Perspective

During the 1920s, women were well represented as leaders in educational administration. Two-thirds of the nation's superintendents in the West and

Midwest were women. In 1928, 55 percent of all elementary school principals were women. But many of these early small schools served grades 1 through 8, and typically the eighth-grade teacher was also designated as the principal. As schools grew and full-time administrators became the norm, the number of women in administrative positions dropped precipitously. By the mid-1970s only 13 percent of the nation's principalships were filled by women. In terms of school level, only 18 percent of elementary school principals, 3 percent of junior high school principals, and less than 2 percent of senior high principals were female. By the early 1980s, some gains had been achieved, with women comprising 23 percent of elementary principals and 10 percent of secondary principals.[21]

Today women have higher career aspirations and have attained higher levels of education and training than ever before. By 1980, women had earned one-third of all doctorates and one-half of all masters degrees in educational administration. More than 50 percent of female teachers now express interest in educational administration.

Prejudice

Although the 1980s have seen more female principals than the previous decades, problems remain. Women still are not selected as frequently as men: the higher the rung on the ladder, the fewer the women in administration. Study after study has demonstrated that when an equally qualified man and woman apply for the same administrative position, the man is more likely to get the job.[22] Women must be more qualified, more experienced, and more skilled than their male colleagues to secure the administrative appointment. Male superintendents often view women through stereotypic lenses. They see them as too emotional and indecisive for administration, unable to manage budgets and finance, and plagued with problems related to menstruation and pregnancy.

Besides these blatant discriminatory attitudes, other informal barriers inhibit the entrance and promotion of women in educational administration. Job descriptions are often written in sex-stereotyped language that discourages women from applying. Women who decide to apply may find application forms that request personal information, such as marital status or number of children, questions implying that women are too busy with family responsibilities to do an adequate job. Female candidates for administrative positions find themselves facing screening committees comprised primarily of male personnel. Often these committees have a pro-male bias and favor applicants with so-called preadministrative experience, such as coaching.

Women also apply less often than men for administrative positions. Another barrier to administrative advancement is that most women enter teaching not as a stepping-stone to management but rather to work closely with children. Administrative duties away from the classroom are less attractive to these women who view their role primarily as working with children. Some women are also concerned about time commitments that may impinge on home and family responsibilities.

The result of prejudice as well as personal constraint is a dearth of women in administrative roles. Students are denied appropriate role models as well as the opportunity to be led by some of the best talent available to U.S. schools. When politics and prejudice control the selection process, schools and children lose access to the best leadership available.

Report Card: The Cost of Sexism in School

Below is a report card you will not find in any elementary or secondary school.[23] Nevertheless, it is an important evaluation. It reflects the loss that both girls and boys suffer because of sex bias in society and in education. Years after the passage of Title IX of the Education Amendments of 1972, the law that prohibits sex discrimination in schools receiving federal financial assistance, gender inequities continue to permeate schools.

Academic

Girls

■ Girls start out ahead of boys in speaking, reading, and counting. In the early grades, their academic performance is equal to that of boys in math and science. However, as they progress through school, their achievement test scores show significant decline. The scores of boys, on the other hand, continue to rise and eventually reach and surpass those of their female counterparts, particularly in the areas of math and science. Girls are the only group in our society that begins school ahead and ends up behind.

■ Sex differences in mathematics become apparent at the junior high school level. Male superiority increases as the level of mathematics becomes more difficult and is evident even when the number of mathematics courses taken by males and females is the same.

■ Between 1970 and 1984 the National Assessment of Educational Progress conducted three assessments of reading achievement. Although girls continue to outperform boys at the 9-, 14-, and 17-year-old levels, the achievement gap between the sexes has narrowed; as girls' performance has remained stable, boys continue to make achievement gains. A 1985 National Assessment of Educational Progress showed that by ages 21–25, males have caught up with females in reading proficiency and literacy.

■ Males outperform females substantially on all subsections of the Scholastic Aptitude Test (SAT) and the American College Testing Program Examination (ACT). The largest gap is in the math section of the SAT, followed by the ACT natural science reading, the ACT math usage, and the ACT social studies reading.

■ The College Board Achievement Tests are required for admission to more selective colleges and universities. On these achievement tests, males outperform females in European history, American history, biology levels 1 and 2, and mathematics.

■ Girls attain only 36 percent of the more than 6,000 National Merit Scholarships awarded each year. These awards are based on the higher Preliminary Scholastic Aptitude Tests (PSAT) scores attained by boys.

■ On tests for admission to graduate and professional schools, males outperform females on the Graduate Record Exam (GRE), the Medical College

Admissions Test (MCAT), and the Graduate Management Admissions Test (GMAT).

■ In spite of performance decline on standardized achievement tests, girls frequently receive better grades in school. This may be one of the rewards they get for being more quiet and docile in the classroom. However, their silence may be at the cost of achievement, independence, and self-reliance.

■ Girls are more likely to be invisible members of classrooms. They receive fewer academic contacts, less praise and constructive feedback, fewer complex and abstract questions, and less instruction on how to do things for themselves.

■ Girls who are gifted are less likely to be identified than are gifted boys. Those girls who *are* identified as gifted are less likely to participate in special or accelerated programs to develop their talent. Girls who suffer from learning disabilities are also less likely to be identified or to participate in special-education programs than are learning-disabled boys.

Academic

Boys

■ Boys are more likely to be scolded and reprimanded in classrooms, even when the observed conduct and behavior of boys and girls does not differ. Also, boys are more likely to be referred to school authorities for disciplinary action than are girls.

■ Boys are far more likely to be identified as exhibiting learning disabilities, reading problems, and mental retardation.

■ Not only are boys more likely to be identified as having greater learning and reading disabilities, they also receive lower grades, are more likely to be grade repeaters, and are less likely to complete high school.

■ The National Assessment of Educational Progress indicates that males perform significantly below females in writing achievement.

Psychological and Physical

Girls

■ Although women achieve better grades than men, they are less likely to believe they can do college work. Females exhibit lower self-esteem than males during secondary and postsecondary education.

■ Girls have less confidence than boys in their mathematical ability. The sex typing of mathematics as a masculine discipline may also be related to low female confidence and performance.

■ Girls have a less positive attitude toward science than do boys. High school girls view science, especially physical science, as a masculine subject.

■ In athletics, females also suffer from sex bias. For example, although there has been some progress, women's athletic budgets in the nation's colleges are only a modest percentage of men's budgets.

■ One in ten teenage girls becomes pregnant every year. More than 40 percent of all adolescent girls who drop out of school do so because of pregnancy. Teenage pregnancy is related to a constellation of factors, including poverty, low self-esteem, academic failure, and the perception of few life options.

Psychological and Physical

Boys

■ Society socializes boys into an active, independent, and aggressive role. But such behavior is incongruent with school norms and rituals that stress quiet behavior and docility. This results in a pattern of role conflict for boys, particularly during the elementary years.

■ Hyperactivity is estimated to be nine times more prevalent in boys than in girls. Boys are more likely to be identified as having emotional problems, and statistics indicate a higher suicide rate among males.

■ Boys are taught stereotyped behaviors earlier and more harshly than girls; there is a 20 percent greater probability that such stereotyped behavior will stay with them for life.

■ Conforming to the male sex-role stereotype takes a psychological toll. Boys who score high on sex-appropriate behavior tests also score highest on anxiety tests.

■ Males are less likely than females to be close friends with one another. When asked, most men identify women as their closest friends.

■ Until recently, programs focusing on adolescent sexuality and teen pregnancy were directed almost exclusively at females. Males were ignored, and this permissive "boys will be boys" attitude translated into sexual irresponsibility.

■ Family planning experts say that 50 percent of sexually active single males will contract a sexually transmitted disease by the time they are 25. The highest incidence of venereal disease occurs in young men between 15 and 25.

■ Males are more likely to succumb to serious disease and be victims of accidents or violence. The average life expectancy of men is approximately eight years shorter than that of women.

Career and Family Relationships

Girls

■ When elementary school girls are asked to describe what they want to do when they grow up, they are able to identify only a limited number of career options, and these fit stereotypic patterns. Boys, on the other hand, are able to identify many more potential occupations.

■ Starting at the junior high school level, girls say that mathematics are less important and useful to career goals. The majority of girls enter college without completing four years of high school mathematics. This lack of preparation in math serves as a "critical filter" inhibiting or preventing girls from entering many careers in science, math, and technology.

■ Girls from lower socioeconomic backgrounds are less likely to have plans for college than are those from more affluent families. Family finances are less likely to affect the college options of males.

■ Teenagers who become mothers earn only about half the income of females who delay childbearing. When families are headed by young mothers, they are six times as likely to be in poverty. The National Research Council indicates that it costs $18,130 a year to support a 15-year-old mother and her baby.

■ In urban areas, 43 percent of young males who drop out of school are likely to return to school. For young females who drop out, the return rate is only 25 percent.

■ The preparation and counseling girls receive in school contribute to the economic penalties that they encounter in the workplace. Although over 90 percent of the girls in U.S. classrooms will work in the paid labor force for all or part of their lives, the following statistics reveal the cost of the bias they encounter.

■ More than a third of families headed by women live below the poverty level.

■ A woman with a college degree will typically earn less than a male who is a high school dropout.

■ The typical working woman will earn 70 cents for every dollar earned by a male worker.

■ Minority women earn even less, averaging approximately 50 percent of the wages earned by white males.

■ Approximately 77 percent of employed women are in nonprofessional jobs. Only 11 percent are in traditionally male occupations.

■ A majority of women work not for "extra" cash, but because of economic necessity. Nearly two-thirds of all women in the labor force are single, widowed, divorced, or separated, or are married to spouses earning less than $10,000 a year.

Boys

■ Teachers and counselors advise boys to enter sex-stereotyped careers and limit their potential in occupations such as kindergarten teacher, nurse, or secretary.

■ Many boys build career expectations that are higher than their abilities. This results in later compromise, disappointment, and frustration.

■ Both at school and at home, boys are taught to hide or suppress their emotions; as adults, they may find it difficult or impossible to show feelings toward their family and friends.

■ Boys are actively discouraged from playing with dolls (except those that play sports or wage war). Few schools provide programs that encourage boys to learn about the skills of parenting. Many men, through absence and apathy, become not so much parents as "transparents." In fact, the typical father spends only twelve minutes a day interacting with his children.

■ Men and women vary in their beliefs of the important aspects of a father's role. Men emphasize the need for the father to earn a good income and to provide solutions to family problems. Women, on the other hand, stress the need for fathers to assist in caring for children and in responding to the emotional needs of the family. These differing perceptions of fatherhood lead to family strain and anxiety.

■ Scientific advances involving the analysis of blood and other body fluids now make possible genetic testing for paternity. Such testing, along with the passage of stricter laws and enforcement procedures for child support have major implications for the role of males in parenting.

Ongoing Problems and New Issues

The cost of sexism is obvious. As educators and other professionals fight the traditional barriers to female achievement, new issues emerge. Many topics have attracted current attention, including nonsexist parenting and the role of fathers, the potential conflict between cultural background and sex equity, and the impact of sex equity on a potential teacher shortage. However, in this chapter, three issues are explored in greater detail. Since legal decisions in the 1980s have threatened the power and coverage of Title IX, developments surrounding this law, which prohibits sex discrimination in education, are discussed. Another intriguing new problem on the equity horizon is the differential treatment of male and female latchkey children.

Finally, it is important to note current developments related to single-sex schools, since recent research in the late 1980s demonstrates how viable these are for girls' achievement. Even as the evidence mounts in favor of these schools, they are facing extinction.

Latchkey Children

Approximately one-third of all elementary school children come home to an empty house and care for themselves part of each school day while their parents work. These unsupervised children, commonly referred to as latchkey children, spend an average of two to three hours alone daily, and they report high levels of fear, boredom, loneliness, and stress.[24]

Although boys and girls are left alone in approximately equal numbers, their experiences are not the same. Parents worry about the safety of their daughters more, and consequently place greater restrictions on their freedom. Girls as old as 12 are likely to be instructed by their parents to stay inside, while boys as young as 10 are generally allowed to play outside. Because of these restrictions, females experience greater isolation than their male counterparts.[25]

Girls not only experience more restrictions, but they also shoulder more household responsibility, including child care and meal preparation. If there are several children in the family, the oldest girl is generally in charge. Because of these child-care responsibilities, girls are more often required to come straight home from school and are less able to participate in after-school activities. These additional responsibilities further isolate young girls from their peers and force them to assume adult roles early; with less time to spend on their schoolwork, they begin to see their primary responsibility as raising a family rather than attaining an education.

A large percentage of latchkey children of both sexes suffer psychologically because of the long hours they spend alone. Because of the differential treatment they receive from their parents, girls are even more likely to suffer from excessive responsibility, isolation, and stress. After-school programs would provide an alternative for working parents and allow all children, especially girls, a fuller childhood.

Single-Sex Schools

The past decades have witnessed a precipitous decline in U.S. single-sex secondary and postsecondary schools. The number of women's colleges has dwindled from almost 300 to fewer than 100. The widespread belief that single-sex education is an anachronism has caused many schools to become coeducational institutions—or to close their doors. Single-sex high schools, typically private and parochial, are also vanishing. Further, Title IX, with good intention, has encouraged coeducation in all but the most limited public school situations, such as contact sports and sex education.

The transition to coeducation continues on a national scale despite research suggesting the benefits of single-sex schools, especially for female students. These benefits include increased academic achievement, self-esteem, and career salience, as well as a decrease in sex-role stereotyping. A 1986 study found that students in girls' schools in the United States expressed greater interest in both mathematics and English, took more mathematics courses, did more homework, and had more positive attitudes toward academic achievement.[26] Finally, research shows that girls in single-sex schools show more interest in the feminist movement and are less sex-role stereotyped than are their peers in coeducational schools.[27] Despite these impressive findings, single-sex education has become a vanishing option.

Title IX

By the mid-1970s, Title IX of the 1972 Educational Amendments was being implemented, with varying degrees of success in the nation's 16,000 school districts. The Title IX legislation prohibits sex discrimination in all educational programs receiving federal assistance. Widely known for its application to sports, Title IX also prohibits sex discrimination in counseling, discipline, testing, admissions, medical facilities, the treatment of students, financial aid, and a host of educational activities. Although theoretically the vast majority of programs should have eliminated sex bias in the past decade, the reality has been less positive. Too often sexist practices continue because of the unwillingness of parents and students to lodge complaints, or because of the slow pace of federal enforcement practices.

In the 1980s, the *Grove City College* case dealt Title IX a serious blow. The Supreme Court ruled that federal funds must be traced directly to the discriminatory activity before Title IX can be enforced. This decision meant that elementary and secondary schools as well as colleges and vocational programs could practice sex discrimination in all their programs except those directly receiving federal support. If a library was built with federal funds, for example, Title IX would prohibit sex discrimination in the library only. On the same campus or school, however, financial aid could be given legally only to male students without violating federal law. The *Grove City College* case jeopardized not only Title IX, but also much of the civil rights legislation currently on the books. In late 1987, Congress considered the Civil Rights Restoration Act, which would nullify the *Grove City College* case. This new legislation would revitalize Title IX and protect all students and educators from sex discrimination if any school program receives federal assistance.

Creating Gender-Fair Education

Although the struggle against a sexist educational system is long and difficult, change is already taking place. Consider the following:

- Although both girls and boys typically picture sex-stereotyped occupations, girls are beginning to view more prestigious and lucrative professional careers as both attainable and desirable.[28]
- In 1960 women comprised 35 percent of students in higher education. Today they are the majority.[29]
- In 1958 the labor force participation rate of women stood at 33 percent; by 1980 it had reached 50 percent. Although most women are still over-represented in low-paying jobs, barriers are falling as some women are entering higher-level positions previously held only by men.[30]
- More than 600,000 students participated in a *Weekly Reader* national survey on the future. From ten statements describing the future, the largest number of students strongly agreed with the item predicting equal treatment of the sexes. Overwhelmingly, our nation's young people express egalitarian attitudes about roles for women and men.[31]

While change is possible, it takes time, effort, and commitment to break down barriers that have been in place for centuries. Following are ten key steps you can take to build nonsexist classrooms today.[32]

1. If the textbooks you are given to use with students are biased, you may wish to confront this bias rather than ignore it. Discuss the issue directly with your students. It's entirely appropriate to acknowledge that texts are not always perfect. By engaging your students in a discussion about textbook omission and stereotyping, you can introduce them to important social issues, and develop critical reading skills as well.

2. Supplementary materials can offset the influence of unrepresentative textbooks. Often school, university, and local libraries have information on the lives and contributions of women and minority-group members.

3. Have your students help you assemble bulletin boards and other instructional displays. Teach them about the forms of bias and make sure that the displays they assemble are bias free.

4. Analyze your seating chart to determine whether there are pockets of race or gender segregation in your classroom. When your students work in groups, check to see if they are representative of the different populations in the class.

5. When students themselves form segregated groups, you may need to intervene. Establish ground rules to ensure that work and play groups and teams are representative. Explain to students why segregation on any basis—race, religion, national origin, or gender—is harmful to learning and the principles of a democratic society.

6. Reinforcement can be effective for increasing the amount of time boys and girls work and play in coeducational arrangements. In one study, teachers made a consistent effort to praise girls and boys who were working and playing cooperatively together. When teachers praised in this way, the amount of time girls and boys spent working and playing cooperatively increased.

7. Peer tutoring can encourage gender integration. Moreover, this technique increases achievement not only for the students being helped, but for the student tutors as well. While the research shows that peer tutoring is an effective technique, it should be used as a supplement to (not a replacement for) teacher-led instruction. Also, peer tutoring is much more powerful when students receive training in how to tutor others.

8. Most teachers find it difficult to track their own questioning patterns while they are teaching. Try to have someone do this for you. Make arrangements to have a professional whose feedback you value—a supervisor, your principal, another teacher—come into your classroom and observe. Your observer can tally how many questions you ask boys and how many you ask girls, how many questions you ask majority and how many you ask minority students. Then you can consider the race and sex of your involved and silent students and determine whether one sex or race is receiving more than its fair share of your time and attention.

9. Because teachers may find it difficult to have professional observers come into their classrooms on a regular basis, many have found it helpful to have students keep a tally of questioning patterns. Before you do this, you may want to explain to the class how important it is for all students to get involved in classroom discussion.

10. Since research on sex equity in education is occurring at a rapid pace, it is important to continue your reading and professional development in this area. Be alert for articles and other publications on the topic, and be careful that your own rights are not denied because of sex discrimination.

When teachers become aware of the nature and cost of sex bias in schools, they can make an important difference in the lives of their students. Teachers can reduce sexism in schools or even make it obsolete. They can make sex equity a reality for children in our schools. Then tomorrow's children, boys and girls, need not suffer from the limiting effects of sexism in school.

Questions and Activities

1. The authors of this chapter list six forms of gender bias that you can use when evaluating instructional materials: (1) linguistic bias, (2) stereotyping, (3) invisibility, (4) imbalance, (5) unreality, and (6) fragmentation

Define each form of bias. Examine a sample of social studies, language arts, reading, science, or mathematics textbooks (or a combination of two kinds of textbooks) to determine whether they contain any of these forms of gender bias. Share your findings with your classmates or workshop participants.

2. Give some examples of how teachers can supplement textbooks to help to eliminate the six forms of gender bias identified in activity 1 above.

3. What are some of the behavioral and attitudinal consequences for students of gender bias in curriculum materials? Of gender-fair curriculum materials?

4. In what ways do Mrs. Howe's interactions with the boys and girls during the music lesson indicate gender bias? How can Mrs. Howe be helped to change her behavior and to make it more gender fair?

5. Observe lessons being taught in several classrooms that include boys and girls and students from different racial and ethnic groups. Did the ways the teachers interacted with males and female students differ? If so, in what ways? Did the teachers interact with students from different ethnic groups differently? If so, in what ways? Did you notice any ways that gender and ethnicity combined to influence the ways the teachers interacted with particular students? If so, explain.

6. What are the major reasons there are fewer women than men who are educational administrators? Are more women likely to become educational administrators in the future? Why or why not?

7. Girls start out in school ahead of boys in speaking, reading, and counting. Boys surpass girls in math performance by junior high school. Why do you think this happens? Do you think this trend can be changed? Why or why not?

8. In what ways, according to the authors, are single-sex schools beneficial for females? Why do you think all-girls schools are vanishing? Do you think this trend should be halted? Why or why not?

9. After reading this chapter, do you think there are some ways you can change your behavior to make it more gender fair? If yes, in what ways? If no, why not?

Notes

1. Myra Sadker, David Sadker, and Susan Klein, "Abolishing Misperceptions about Sex Equity in Education," *Theory into Practice,* 25 (Autumn 1986): 220–226.

2. Myra Sadker and David Sadker, *Sex Equity Handbook for Schools* (New York: Longman, 1982).

3. Gwyneth Britton and Margaret Lumpkin, "Females and Minorities in Basal Readers," *Interracial Books for Children Bulletin,* 14, No. 6 (1983): 4–7.

4. Lenore Weitzman and Diane Rizzo, *Biased Textbooks* (Washington, D.C.: The Resource Center on Sex Roles in Education, 1974).

5. Women on Words and Images, *Dick and Jane as Victims: Sex Stereotyping in Children's Readers* (Princeton, N.J.: Women on Words and Images, 1975).

6. Janice Law Trecker, "Women in U.S. History High-School Textbooks," in Janice Pottker and Andrew Fishel, eds. *Sex Bias in the Schools: The Research Evidence* (Cranbury, N.J.: Associated University Presses, 1977), pp. 146–161.

7. Ibid.

8. William Nibbelink, Susan Stockdale, and Matadial Mangru, "Sex Role Assignments in Elementary School Mathematics Textbooks," *The Arithmetic Teacher* 34 (October 1986): 19–21.

9. Judith Kinman and Darwin Henderson, "An Analysis of Sexism in Newbery Medal Award Books from 1977 to 1984," *The Reading Teacher* 38 (May 1985): 885–889.

10. Richard Powell and Jesus Garcia, "The Portrayal of Minorities and Women in Selected Elementary Science Series," *Journal of Research in Science Teaching* 22, No. 6 (1985): 519–533.

11. O. L. Davis, Jr., Gerald Ponder, Lynn Burlbaw, Maria Garza-Lubeck, and Alfred Moss, "A Review of U.S. History Textbooks," *Looking at History: A Review of Major U.S. History Textbooks* (Washington, D.C.: People for the American Way, 1986).

12. Kathryn Scott, "Elementary Pupils' Perceptions of Reading and Social Studies Materials: Does the Sex of the Main Character Make a Difference?" *Dissertation Abstracts* 780973 (Ann Arbor: University of Michigan, 1977).

13. Kathryn Scott, "Effects of Sex-Fair Reading Materials on Pupils Attitudes, Comprehension, and Interest, *American Educational Research Journal* 23 (Spring 1986): 105–116.

14. Robin Carter, Unpublished class paper, American University, Washington, D.C., 1987. Used with permission.

15. David Sadker and Myra Sadker, "Is the O.K. Classroom O.K.?" *Phi Delta Kappan* 66 (January 1985): 358–361.

16. Myra Sadker and David Sadker, *Effectiveness and Equity in College Teaching: Final Report* (Washington, D.C.: Fund for the Improvement of Postsecondary Education, 1985).

17. Jere Brophy and Thomas Good, *Teacher-Student Relationships: Causes and Consequences* (New York: Holt Rinehart, and Winston, 1974).

18. Ned Flanders, *Analyzing Teaching Behaviors* (Reading, Mass.: Addison-Wesley, 1970).

19. N. Gross and A. Trask, *Men and Women as Elementary School Principals* (Cambridge, Mass.: Harvard University Press, 1965).

20. Ibid.

21. Myra Sadker, "Women in Educational Administration," (Washington, D.C.: The Mid-Atlantic Center for Sex Equity, 1985).

22. M. Smith, J. Kalvelage, and P. Schmuck, *Women Getting Together and Getting Ahead* (Washington, D.C.: Women's Educational Equity Act Program, 1982).

23. Myra Sadker and David Sadker, adapted from "Cost of Sex Bias in Schools," *Sex Equity Handbook for Schools* (New York: Longman, 1982). Copyright © 1987 David and Myra Sadker. All rights reserved. (pp. 114–117.)

24. Lynette Long and Tom Long, *Handbook for Latchkey Children and Their Parents* (New York: Arbor House, 1982).

25. Ibid.

26. Valerie Lee and Anthony Bryk, "Effects of Single-Sex Secondary Schools on Student Achievement and Attitudes," *Journal of Educational* Psychology 78 No. 5 (October 1986): 381–395.

28. Kathleen Lenerz, "Factors Related to Educational and Occupational Orientations in Early Adolescence." Paper presented at the American Educational Research Association, Washington, D.C., 1987.

29. Karen Bogart, "Improving Sex Equity in Postsecondary Education," in Susan Klein, ed., *Handbook for Achieving Sex Equity through Education* (Baltimore: Johns Hopkins University Press, 1984)

30. National Commission on Working Women, "An Overview of Women in the Workforce," (Washington, D.C., 1986).

31. Lynell Johnson, "Children's Visions of the Future," *The Futurist,* 21, No. 3, (May–June 1987): 36–40.

32. Myra Sadker and David Sadker, *PEPA (Principal Effectiveness—Pupil Achievement): A Training Program for Principals and Other Educational Leaders* (Washington, D.C.: American University, 1986). Ten steps copyright © David and Myra Sadker. All rights reserved.

Integrating Content about Women and Gender into the Curriculum

■ MARY KAY THOMPSON TETREAULT

We are presently in a period of challenging the male dominance over curricular content and over the substance of knowledge itself. Evidence of that challenge is our new understanding of the extent to which the curriculum we learned excluded (or included) women's traditions, history, culture, values, visions, and perspectives. More difficult yet to ascertain is the impression that viewing human experience primarily from a male perspective, with the authority of the school behind it, made on us. We are beginning to envision a curriculum that includes content about women and gender, one that interweaves issues of gender with ethnicity, race, and class. Over time we may be able to see the impression that viewing the human experience from a gender-balanced, multicultural perspective, with the authority of the schools behind it, will make on our students.[1]

Feminist Phase Theory

One of the most effective ways I have found to set a frame for envisioning a gender-balanced, multicultural curriculum, while at the same time capturing the reforms that have occurred over the past twenty years, is feminist phase theory. Conceptually rooted in the scholarship on women, feminist phase theory is a classification system of the evolution in thought during the past fifteen years about the incorporation of women's traditions, history, and experiences into selected disciplines, The model I have developed identifies five common phases of thinking about women: *male-defined curriculum, contribution curriculum, bifocal curriculum, women's curriculum,* and *gender-balanced curriculum.*

The language of this system or schema, particularly the word *phase,* and the description of one phase and then another, suggests a sequential hierarchy, in which one phase supplants another. Before presenting the schema, please refrain from thinking of these phases in a linear fashion and envision them as a series of intersecting circles, or patches on a quilt, or threads in a tapestry, which interact and undergo changes in response to one another. It is more accurate to view the phases as "different emphases that co-exist in feminist research."[2] The important thing is that teachers, scholars, and curriculum developers ask and answer certain questions at each phase. In the section that follows, I identify key concepts and questions articulated initially at each phase, using examples from history, literature, and science, and then discuss how the phases interact and undergo changes in response to one another.[3] The final part of this chapter contains specific objectives, practices, and teaching suggestions for incorporating content about women into the K–12 curriculum in social studies, language arts, and science.

Male-Defined Curriculum

Male-defined curricula rest on the assumption that the male experience is universal, that it is representative of humanity, and that it constitutes a basis for generalizing about all human beings. The knowledge that is researched and taught, the substance of learning, is knowledge articulated by and about men. There is little or no consciousness in it that the existence of women as a group is an anomaly calling for a broader definition of knowledge. The female experience is subsumed under the male experience. For example, a well-known scientist cited methodological problems in some research about sex differences that draws conclusions about females based on experiments done only on males or that uses limited (usually White, middle-class) experimental populations from which scientists draw conclusions about all males and females.[4]

The incorporation of women into the curriculum has not only taught us about women's lives but has led to questions about our lopsided rendition of men's lives, wherein we pay attention primarily to men in the public world and conceal their lives in the private world. Historians, for example, are posing a series of interesting questions about men's history: What do we need to unlearn about men's history? What are the taken-for-granted truths about men's history that we need to rethink? How do we get at the significant masculine truths? Is man's primary sense of self defined in relation to the public sphere only? How does it relate to boyhood, adolescence, family, life, recreation, and love? What does this imply about the teaching of history?[5]

Feminist scholarship, like Black, Native-American, Latino, and Asian scholarship, reveals the systematic and contestable exclusions in the male-defined curriculum. When we examine it through the lens of this scholarship, we are forced to reconsider our understanding of the most fundamental conceptualization of knowledge and social relations within our society. We understand in a new way that knowledge is a social construction, written by individual human beings who live and think at a particular time and within a particular social framework. All works in literature, science, and history, for example, have an author—male or female, White or ethnic or racial minority, elite or middle-class or occasionally poor—with motivations and beliefs. The scientist's questions and activities, for instance, are shaped, often unconsciously, by the great social issues of the day (see Table 7-1). Different perspectives on the same subject will change the patterns discerned.

TABLE 7.1
Male-Defined Curriculum

Characteristics of Phase	Questions Commonly Asked about Women in History*	Questions Commonly Asked about Women in Literature*	Questions Commonly Asked about Women in Science*
The absence of women is not noted. There is no consciousness that the male experience is a "particular knowledge" selected from a wider universe of possible knowledge and experience. It is valued, emphasized, and viewed as the knowledge most worth having.	Who is the author of a particular history? What is her or his race, ethnicity, religion, ideological orientation, social class, place of origin and historical period? How does incorporating women's experiences lead to new understandings of the most fundamental ordering of social relations, institutions, and power arrangements? How can we define the content and methodology of history, so it will be a history of us all?	How is traditional humanism, with an integrated self at its center and an authentic view of life, in effect part of patriarchal ideology? How can the objectivist illusion be dismantled? How can the idea of a literary canon of "great literature" be challenged? How are writing and reading political acts? How do race, class, and gender relate to the conflict, sufferings, and passions that attend these realities? How can we study language as specific *discourse,* that is, specific linquistic strategies in specific situations, rather than as universal language?	How do scientific studies reveal cultural values? What cultural, historical, and gender values are projected onto the physical and natural world? How might gender be a bias that influences choice of questions, hypotheses, subjects, experimented design, or theory formation in science? What is the underlying philosophy of an andocentric science that values objectivity, rationality, and dominance? How can the distance between the subject and the scientific observer be shortened so that the scientist has some feeling or empathy with the organism? How can gender play a crucial role in transforming science?

* New questions generated by feminist scholars.

Contribution Curriculum

Early efforts to reclaim women's rightful place in the curriculum were a search for missing women within a male framework. Although there was the recognition that women were missing, men continued to serve as the norm, the representative, the universal human being. Outstanding women emerged who fit this male norm of excellence or greatness or conformed to implicit assumptions about appropriate roles for women outside the home. In literature, female authors were added who performed well within the masculine tradition, internalizing its standards of art and its views on social roles. Great women of science, who have made it in the male scientific world, most frequently Marie Curie, for example, were added.

Examples of contribution history can be seen in United States history textbooks. They now include the contributions of notable American women who were outstanding in the public sphere as rulers or as contributors to wars or reform movements to a remarkable degree. Queen Liliuokalani, Hawaii's first reigning queen and a nationalist, is included in the story of the kingdom's annexation. Molly Pitcher and Deborah Sampson are depicted as contributors to the Revolutionary War, as is Clara Barton to the Civil War effort. Some authors have also included women who conform to the assumption that it is acceptable for women to engage in activities outside the home if they are an extension of women's nurturing role within the family. Examples of this are Dorothea Dix, Jane Addams, Eleanor Roosevelt, and Mary McLeod Bethune.[6]

The lesson to be learned from understanding these limitations of early contribution history is not to disregard the study of notable women, but to include those who worked to reshape the world according to a feminist reordering of values. This includes efforts to increase women's self-determination through a feminist transformation of the home, increased education, women's rights to control their bodies, to increase their political rights, and to improve their economic status. A history with women at the center moves beyond paying attention to caring for the unfortunate in the public sphere to how exceptional women influenced the lives of women in general (see Table 7.2). Just as Mary McLeod Bethune's role in the New Deal is worth teaching to our students, so is her aggressive work to project a positive image of Black women to the nation through her work in Black women's clubs and the launching of the *Afro-American Woman's Journal*.

Bifocal Curriculum

In bifocal curricula, feminist scholars have made an important shift, from a perspective that views men as the norm to one that opens up the possibility of seeing the world through women's eyes. This dual vision, or bifocal perspective, generated global questions about women and about the differences between women and men. Historians investigated the separation between the public and the private sphere and asked, for example, how the division between them explains women's lives. Some elaborated on the construct by identifying arenas of female power in the domestic sphere. Literary critics aimed to provide a new understanding of a distinctively female literary tradition and a theory of women's

TABLE 7.2
Contribution Curriculum

Characteristics of Phase	Questions Commonly Asked about Women in History	Questions Commonly Asked about Women in Literature	Questions Commonly Asked about Women in Science
The absence of women is noted. There is a search for missing women according to a male norm of greatness, excellence, or humanness. Women are considered exceptional, deviant, or other. Women are added into history, but the content and notions of historical significance are not challenged.	Who are the notable women missing from history and what did they and ordinary women contribute in areas or movements traditionally dominated by men, for example, during major wars or during reform movements like abolitionism or the labor movement? What did notable and ordinary women contribute in areas that are an extension of women's traditional roles, for example, caring for the poor and the sick? How have major economic and political changes like industrialization or extension of the franchise affected women in the public sphere? How did notable and ordinary women respond to their oppression, particularly through women's rights organizations? * Who were outstanding women who advocated a feminist transformation of the home, who contributed to women's greater self-determination	Who are the missing female authors whose subject matter and use of language and form meet the male norm of "masterpiece?" What primary biographical facts and interpretations are missing about major female authors?	Who are the notable women scientists who have made contributions to mainstream science? How is women's different (and inferior) nature related to hormones, brain lateralization, and sociobiology? Where are the missing females in scientific experiments? What is the current status of women within the scientific profession? * How does adding minority women into the history of science reveal patterns of exclusion and recast definitions of what it means to practice science and to be a scientist? * How is the exclusion of women from science related to the way science is done and thought? * What is the usual pattern of women working in science? How is it the same as or different from the pattern of notable women? * How do our definitions of science need to be broadened to evaluate women's

Characteristics of Phase	Questions Commonly Asked about Women in History	Questions Commonly Asked about Women in Literature	Questions Commonly Asked about Women in Science
	through increased education, the right to control their bodies, to increase their political rights, and to improve their economic status? * What did women contribute through the settlement house and labor movements?		contributions to science? Do institutions of science need to be reshaped to accommodate women? If so, how?

* New question generated by feminist scholars

literary creativity. They sought to provide models for understanding the dynamics of female literary response to male literary assertion and coercion.[7] Scientists grapple with definitions of woman's and man's nature by asking how the public and private, biology and culture, and personal and impersonal inform each other and affect men and women, science, and nature.

Scholars have pointed out some of the problems with bifocal knowledge. Thinking about women and men is dualistic and dichotomized. Women and men are thought of as having different spheres, different notions of what is of value in life, different ways of imagining the human condition, and different associations with nature and culture. But both views are valued. In short, women are thought of as a group that is complementary but equal to men; there are some truths for men and there are some truths for women. General analyses of men's and women's experiences often come dangerously close to reiterating the sexual stereotypes scholars are trying to overcome. Because many believe that the public sphere is more valuable than the private sphere, there is a tendency to slip back into thinking of women as inferior and subordinate.

The generalized view of women and men that predominates in the bifocal curriculum often does not allow for distinctions within groups as large and as complex as women and men. Important factors like historical period, geographic location, structural barriers, race, paternity, sexual orientation, and social class, to name a few, clearly make a difference.

Other common emphases in the bifocal curriculum are the oppression of women and exploration of that oppression. Exposés of woman-hating in history and literature are common. Kate Millett's analysis of male writers like Norman Mailer, Arthur Miller, and D. H. Lawrence was one of the first literary exposés.[8] The emphasis in her analysis is on the misogyny (the hatred of women) of the human experience, particularly the means men have used to advance their authority and to assert or imply female inferiority. The paradoxes of women's existence are sometimes overlooked with this emphasis on oppression. For example, although women have been excluded from positions of power, a few of them as wives and daughters in powerful families were often closer to actual power than were men. If some women were dissatisfied with their status and role, most women adjusted and resisted efforts to improve women's lot.[9] Too much emphasis on women's oppression perpetuates a patriarchal framework presenting women as primarily passive, reacting only to the pressures of a sexist society. In the main, it emphasizes men thinking and women being thought about.[10]

The past decade of women's scholarship has helped us see that understanding women's oppression is more complex than we initially thought. We do not yet have adequate concepts to explain gender systems, founded on a division of labor and sexual asymmetry. To understand gender systems, it is necessary to take a structural and experiential perspective that asks from a woman's point of view where we are agents and where we are not; where our relations with men are egalitarian and where they are not. This questioning may lead to explanations of why women's experiences and interpretations of their world can differ significantly from men's.

Further, the concepts with which we approach our analysis need to be questioned. Anthropologists have pointed out that our way of seeing the world—for instance, the idea of complementary spheres for women (the private sphere) and men (the public sphere)—is a product of our experience in a Western, modern, industrial, capitalistic state with a specific history. We distort our understanding of other social systems by imposing our world view on them. Feminist critics are calling for rethinking, not only of categories like the domestic versus the public sphere, and production and reproduction but even of categories like gender itself.[11]

Feminist scholars have helped us see the urgency of probing and analyzing the interactive nature of the oppressions of race, ethnicity, class, and gender. We are reminded that we can no longer take a liberal reformist approach that does not probe the needs of the system that are being satisfied by oppression. We have to take seriously the model of feminist scholarship that analyzes women's status within the social, cultural, historical, political, and economic contexts. Only then will issues of gender be understood in relation to the economic needs of both male dominance and capitalism that undergird such oppressions.[12]

One of the most important things we have learned about a bifocal perspective is the danger of generalizing too much, of longing for women's history, instead of writing histories about women. We must guard against establishing a feminist version of great literature and then resisting any modifications or additions to it. We have also learned that the traditional disciplines are limited in their ability to shed light on gender complexities, and it becomes apparent that there is a need for an interdisciplinary perspective (see Table 7.3).

Women's Curriculum

The most important idea to emerge in women's scholarship is that women's activities, not men's, are the measure of significance. What was formerly devalued, the content of women's everyday lives, assumes new value as scholars investigate female rituals, housework, childbearing, child rearing, female sexuality, female friendship, and studies of the life cycle. For instance, scientists investigate how research on areas of primary interest to women— menstruation, childbirth, and menopause—challenge existing scientific theories. Historians document women's efforts to break out of their traditional sphere of

TABLE 7.3
Bifocal Curriculum

Characteristics of Phase	Questions Commonly Asked about Women In History	Questions Commonly Asked about Women in Literature	Questions Commonly Asked about Women in Science
Human experience is conceptualized primarily in dualist categories: male and female, private and public, agency and communion. Emphasis is on a complementary but equal conceptualization of men's and women's spheres and personal qualities There is a focus on women's oppression and on misogny. Women's efforts to overcome the oppression are presented. Efforts to include women lead to the insight that the traditional content, structure, and methodology of the disciplines are more appropriate to the male experience.	How does the division between the public and the private sphere explain women's lives? Who oppressed women, and how were they oppressed? * What are forms of power and value in women's worlds? * How have women been excluded from and deprived of power and value in men's spheres? * How do gender systems create divisions between the sexes such that experience and interpretations of their world can differ significantly from men's? * How can we rethink categories like public and private, productive and reproductive, sex and gender?	Who are the missing minor female authors whose books are unobtainable, whose lives have never been written, and whose works have been studied casually, if at all? How is literature a record of the collective consciousness of patriarchy? What myths and stereotypes about women are present in male literature? How can we critique the meritocratic pretensions of traditional literary history? How can we pair opposite-sex texts in literature as a way of understanding the differences between women's and men's experiences? How is literature one of the expressive modes of a female subculture that developed with the distinction of separate spheres for women and men? * How can feminist literary critics resist establishing their own great canon of literature and any additions to it?	How have the sciences defined (and misdefined) the nature of women? Why are there so few women scientists? What social and psychological forces have kept women in the lower ranks or out of science entirely? How do women fit into the study of history of science and health care? How do scientific findings, originally carried out on males of a species, change when carried out on the females of the same species? How do the theories and interpretations of sociobiology require constant testing and change to fit the theory for males and females with regard to competition, sexual selection, and infanticide? How does the science/ gender system—the network of associations and disjunctions between public and private, personal and impersonal, and masculine and feminine—inform each other and affect men and women, science and nature? * What are the structural barriers to women in science?

* New questions generted by feminist scholars

the home in a way that uses women's activities, not men's, as the measure of historical significance. These activities include women's education, women's paid work and volunteer work outside the home, particularly in women's clubs and associations. Of equal importance is the development of a collective feminist consciousness, that is, of women's consciousness of their own distinct role in society. Analyses begun in the bifocal phase continue to explore what sex and gender have meant for the majority of women.

As scholars look more closely at the complex patterns of women's lives, they see the need for a pluralistic conceptualization of women. Although thinking of women as a monolithic group provides valuable information about patterns of continuity and change in those areas most central to women's lives, generalizing about a group as vast and diverse as women leads to inaccuracies. The subtle interactions among gender and other variables are investigated. Historians ask how the particulars of race, ethnicity, social class, marital status, and sexual orientation challenge the homogeneity of women's experiences.

Questions about sex and gender are set within historical, ideological, and cultural contexts, including culture's definition of the facts of biological development and what they mean for individuals. Researchers ask, for example, Why are these attitudes toward sexuality prevalent at this time in history? What are the ways in which sexual words, categories, and ideology mirror the organization of society as a whole? What are the socioeconomic factors contributing to them? How do current conceptions of the body reflect social experiences and professional needs?[13]

Life histories and autobiographies shed light on societies' perceptions of women and women's perceptions of themselves. Women's individual experiences are revealed through these stories and contribute to the fashioning of the human experience from the perspective of women.

Scholars find it necessary to draw on other disciplines for a clearer vision of the social structure and culture of societies as individuals encounter them in their daily life. Likewise, there are calls for new unifying frameworks and different ways to think of periods in history and literature to identify concepts that accommodate women's history and traditions. There is also a more complex conceptualization of historical time. The emphasis in much history is on events, a unit of time too brief to afford a sense of structural change, changes in the way people think about their own reality, and the possibilities for other realities. *L'Ecole des Annales* in France (a group of historians who pioneered the use of public records such as birth, marriage, and death certificates in historical analysis) has distinguished between events and what they call the *longue durée*.[14] By the *longue durée* they mean the slow, glacial changes, requiring hundreds of years to complete, that represent significant shifts in the way people think.

Examples of areas of women's history that lend themselves to the concept are the structural change from a male-dominated to an egalitarian perspective, the transformation of women's traditional role in the family to their present roles as wives, mothers, and paid workers outside the home. Also important is the demographic change in the average number of children per woman of childbearing age from seven to fewer than two children between 1800 and 1980 (see Table 7.4).

**TABLE 7.4
Women's Curriculum**

Characteristics of Phase	Questions Commonly Asked about Women in History	Questions Commonly Asked about Women in Literature	Questions Commonly Asked about Women in Science
Scholarly inquiry pursues new questions, new categories, and new notions of significance that illuminate women's traditions, history, culture, values, visions, and perspectives. A pluralistic conception of women emerges which acknowledges diversity and recognizes that variables besides gender shape women's lives, for example, race, ethnicity, and social class. Women's experience is allowed to speak for itself. Feminist history is rooted in the personal and the specific; it builds from that to the general. The public and the private are seen as a continuum in women's experiences. Women's experience is analyzed within the social, cultural, historical, political, and economic contexts. Efforts are made to reconceptualize knowledge to encompass the female experience. The conceptualization of knowledge is not characterized by disciplinary thinking but becomes multidisciplinary.	What were the majority of women doing at a particular time in history? What was the significance of these activities? How can female friendship between kin, mothers, daughters, and friends be analyzed as one aspect of women's overall relations with others? What kind of productive work, paid and unpaid, did women do and under what conditions? What were the reproductive activities of women? How did they reproduce the American family? How did the variables of race, ethnicity, social class, marital status, and sexual preference affect women's experiences? What new categories need to be added to the study of history, for instance, housework, childbearing, and child rearing? How have women of different races and classes interacted throughout history?	What does women's sphere—for example, domesticity and family, education, marriage, sexuality, and love—reveal about our culture? How can we contrast the fictional image of women in literature with the complexity and variety of the roles of individual women in real life as workers, housewives, revolutionaries, mothers, lovers, and so on? How do the particulars of race, ethnicity, social class, marital status, and sexual orientation, as revealed in literature, challenge the thematic homogeneity of women's experiences? How does literature portray what binds women together and what separates them because of race, ethnicity, social class, marital status, and sexual orientation? How does the social and historical context of a work of literature shed light on it?	How do the cultural dualisms associated with masculinity and femininity permeate scientific thought and discourse? How does women's actual experience, as compared to the physician's analysis or scientific theory, challenge the traditional paradigms of science and of the health care system? How does research on areas of primary interest to women, for instance, menopause, childbirth and menstruation/estrus, challenge existing scientific theories? How do variables other than sex and gender, such as age, species, and individual variation challenge current theories? How do the experience of female primates and the variation among species of primates, for example, competition among women, female agency in sexuality, and infanticide, test the traditional paradigms?

TABLE 7.4 *(cont.)*

Characteristics of Phase	Questions Commonly Asked about Women in History	Questions Commonly Asked about Women in Literature	Questions Commonly Asked about Women in Science
	What are appropriate ways of organizing or periodizing women's history? For example, how will examining women's experiences at each stage of the life span help us to understand women's experiences on their own terms?		

Gender-Balanced Curriculum

This phase continues many of the inquiries begun in the women's curriculum phase but articulates questions about how women and men relate to and complement one another. Conscious of the limitations of seeing women in isolation and aware of the relational character of gender, researchers search for the nodal points at which women's and men's experiences intersect. Historians and literary critics ask if the private, as well as the public, aspects of life are presented as a continuum in women's and men's experience.

The pluralistic and multifocal conception of women that emerged in the women's curriculum phase is extended to humans. At every juncture, the variables of race, sex and gender, ethnicity, social class, and sexual orientation, to name a few, are taken into account. Scientists ask explicit questions about male-female relations in animals and inquire about how such variables as age, species, and individual variation challenge current theories. Accompanying this particularistic perspective is attention to the larger context, for example, the interplay among situation, meaning, economic systems, family organization, and political systems. Thus, historians ask how gender inequities are linked to economics, family organization, marriage, ritual, and politics. Research scientists probe how differences between the male and female body have been used to justify a social agenda that privileges men economically, socially, and politically. In this phase, a revolutionary relationship comes to exist between things traditionally treated as serious, primarily the activities of men in the public sphere, and those things formerly perceived as trivial, namely the activities of women in the private sphere.

This new relationship leads to a recentering of knowledge in the disciplines, a shift from a male-centered perspective to one that includes both females and males. This reconceptualization of knowledge works toward a more holistic view of human experience. As in the previous stage, the conceptualization of knowledge is characterized by multidisciplinary thinking.

Feminist scholars have cautioned against moving too quickly from women's curricula to gender-balanced curricula. As the historian Gerda Lerner once observed, our decade-and-a-half-old investigation of women's history is only a speck on the horizon compared to the centuries-old tradition of male-defined history.[15] By turning too quickly to studies of gender, we risk short-circuiting important directions in women's studies and again having women's history and experiences subsumed under those of men. It remains politically important for feminists to defend women as women in order to counteract the male domination that continues to exist. French philosopher Julia Kristeva, however, pushes us to new considerations when she urges women (and men) to recognize the falsifying nature of masculinity and feminity, to explore how the fact of being born male or female determines one's position in relation to power, and to envision more fluid gender identities that have the potential to liberate both women and men to a fuller personhood (see Table 7.5).[16]

A Sampler of Ideas for Incorporating Women and Gender into the Curriculum

Once I began to understand the implications of a multifocal, relational conception of women and men, I also understood the importance of constructing learning so that the diversity among my students would be central to the process.

TABLE 7.5
Gender-Balanced Curriculum

Characteristics of Phase	Questions Commonly Asked about Women in History	Questions Commonly Asked about Women in Literature	Questions Commonly Asked about Women in Science
A multifocal, gender-balanced perspective is sought which weaves together women's and men's experiences into multilayered composites of human experience. At this stage, scholars are conscious of particularity, while at the same time identify common denominators of experience. They must begin to define what binds together	Are the private, as well as the public, aspects of history presented as a continuum in women's and men's experiences? How is gender asymmetry linked to economic systems, family organization, marriage, ritual, and political systems? How can we compare women and men in all	How can we validate the full range of human expression by selecting literature according to its insight into any aspect of human experience rather than according to how it measures up to a predetermined canon? Is the private as well as the public sphere presented as a continuum in women's	What explicit questions need to be raised about male-female relations in animals? How do variables such as age, species, and individual variation challenge current theories? What are the limits to generalizing beyond the data collected on limited samples to other genders, species, and conditions not

TABLE 7.5 (*cont.*)

Characteristics of Phase	Questions Commonly Asked about Women in History	Questions Commonly Asked about Women in Literature	Questions Commonly Asked about Women in Science
and what separates the various segments of humanity.	aspects of their lives to reveal gender as a crucial historical determinant?	and men's experiences?	sampled in the experimental protocol?
Scholars have a deepened understanding of how the private as well as the public form a continuum in individual experience. They search for the nodal points where comparative treatment of men's and women's experience is possible.	How did the variables of race, ethnicity, social class, marital status, and sexual preference affect women's and men's experiences in history?	How can we pair opposite-sex texts in literature as a way of understanding how female and male characters experience "maleness" and "femaleness" as a continuum of "humanness?"	How have sex differences been used to assign men and women to particular roles in the social hierarchy?
Efforts are made to reconceptualize knowledge to reflect this multilayered composite of women's and men's experience. The conceptualization of knowledge is not characterized by disciplinary thinking but becomes multidisciplinary.	How is gender a social construction? What does the particular construction of gender in a society tell us about the society that so constructed gender?	How do the variables of race, ethnicity, social class, marital status, and sexual orientation affect the experience of female and male literary characters?	How have differences between the male and female body been used to justify a social agenda that privileges men economically, socially, and politically?
	What is the intricate relation between the construction of gender and the structure of power?	How can we rethink the concept of periodicity to accentuate the continuity of life and to contain the multitude of previously ignored literary works, for example, instead of Puritanism, the contexts for and consequences of sexuality?	
	How can we expand our conceptualization of historical time to a pluralistic one which conceives of three levels of history: structures, trends, and events?	How can we deconstruct the opposition between masculinity and feminity?	
	How can we unify approaches and types of knowledge of all social sciences and history as a means of investigating specific problems in relational history?		

Whereas previously my purpose in teaching was to set objectives that taught the students predetermined and objective generalizations, I now want to help students recognize, use, and enlarge their own perspectives in relation to the themes of the courses, as well as to present views reflecting a fuller range of male and female lives. My ultimate goal is to construct versions of subject matter that are personally meaningful to students and will make a difference in their feelings, their thinking, and their lives, rather than constructing conclusions that are generally true in some abstract, universal sense.

One of my major teaching goals is to build common understandings inductively from the students' unique experiences combined with and informed by reading. I seek to build a more complex conceptualization of a given issue, one that legitimizes students' voices and puts them in a larger explanatory context. Thus, the significance becomes not the worth of the ideas in and of themselves, but the students' experiences with them. This is different for different students.

Let me give you an example of how this works with older students. I spend my preparation time reading the course material for the questions it raises for me, the way the material connects with my education and experience. Instead of going into class with predetermined generalizations for my students to discover, I now go with my questions, answers, connections, and interpretations for the material that will interact with those of the students. Student writing assignments, particularly journals and short writing assignments, are central to the process. I frequently use students' writing to generate discussion in class. This enables them to take much greater responsibility for their learning. In fact, I find that they prepare for class in much the same way I do. They do not just read the materials; they make their own meaning out of them through the writing process.

I seek to model the idea that discussion and writing are an opportunity to develop ideas not fully formed and to risk thinking new thoughts. Students have to be encouraged to bring the complexities of a situation out into the open, to deal with the so-called mess, to try to build toward better understanding. Feminist phase theory is particularly useful in this respect because it emphasizes the variety of human experience. It has helped my students and me to be suspicious of generalizations in a way I have not seen before. It frees us to be less concerned about the right answer.

A subtle shift has taken place in my classroom. Control shifts from me, the teacher, the arbiter of knowing, to the interactions of students and myself with the subject matter. A learning community is established that, rather than threatening my power, makes me a learner along with the students. Together we build meaning that is multifocal, and we see where there is a common denominator of experience. We also build meaning that is relational by seeing where we are bound together in these ideas and where we separate. The range of inquiry and insight expands.

In the lessons that follow, I attempt to model teaching that is constructed to reveal the particular and the common denominators of human experience. These sample lessons are organized by the subject areas of language arts, science, and social studies, but they can be adapted to other subject areas as well.

Language Arts

Analyzing Children's Literature

SUGGESTED ACTIVITIES   Ask students to locate five of their favorite children's books, to read or reread them, and to keep a written record of their reactions to the books. Either on the chalkboard or on a sheet of newsprint, keep a record of the students' (and your) book choices. Divide the class into small groups according to the same or similar favorite books, and have students share their written reactions to the books. Ask the groups to keep a record of the most noteworthy ideas that emerge from their small-group discussions. When you bring the small groups together, ask each group to present their noteworthy ideas. Ideas that may emerge may be as follows:

How differently they read the book now than at the time of their first reading
The differences and similarities in "girls" books and "boys" books
The importance of multicultural or international perspectives
What the stories reveal about the culture in which the stories are set.

A follow-up activity could be to interview grandparents, parents, teachers, and other adults students about characters and stories they remember from childhood. Questions to ask include, How do they recall feeling about those stories? Have images of female and male behavior or expectations in children's stories changed? Is race or ethnicity treated similarly or differently?

Pairing Female and Male Autobiographies

SUGGESTED ACTIVITIES   Pairings of autobiographies by male and female authors can contribute greatly to students' multifocal, relational understanding of the human experience. Two pairings I have found to be particularly illuminating are *Black Boy*[17] by Richard Wright and *Women Warrior* by Maxine Hong Kingston.[18] Another interesting pairing is Maya Angelou's *I Know Why the Caged Bird Sings*[19] and Mark Twain's *Huckleberry Finn.*[20] When I teach these books, I have students keep journals. I ask several students to write about a particular section of the book or in response to a specific question. I then begin class by asking these students to read from their journals. Their questions and insights thus become a basis for discussion. At other times, I might ask students to build a list of the things we need to talk about in relation to our common reading. I record their list on the chalkboard, adding my own questions and ideas where appropriate. The list we have built together then guides our discussion.[21]

Autobiographies of this nature are a rich stimulus for discussions of the many factors that intersect to shape human experience—time in history, geographic location, social class, gender, race, and ethnicity.

Science

Fear of Science: Fact or Fantasy?

SUGGESTED ACTIVITIES   Fear of science and math contribute to the limited participation of some students, most often female, in math and science classes.

Their inadequate participation limits their choice of most undergraduate majors that depend on a minimum of three years of high school mathematics. The following exercise was designed by the Math and Science Education for Women Project at the Lawrence Hall of Science (University of California, Berkeley).[22] The purpose of the exercise is to decrease female and male students' fear of science by enabling them to function as researchers who define the problem and generate solutions to it.

Ask students to complete the following sentence by writing for about fifteen minutes:

When I think about science, I . . .

When they are finished, divide students into groups of five or six to discuss their responses to the cue. Ask each group to state the most important things they have learned. Discuss fear of science with the class and whether there is a difference in how girls and boys feel about science. What could be some reasons for these differences or similarities? When the findings from this exercise are clear, suggest to students that they broaden their research to include other students and teachers in the school. Have each group brainstorm questions that might appear on a science attitude questionnaire. Put the questions on the chalkboard. Analyze the questions and decide on the ten best questions.

Decide with the class what group of students and teachers you will research and how you will do it; for example, other science classes, all ninth-grade science classes, or the entire school during second period. Obtain permission to conduct the survey from the administration and other teachers or classes involved in your research project. Have the class do the survey or questionnaire as a pilot activity. Analyze the questions for sex differences and make minor revisions before giving the survey and questionnaire to your research group. Distribute the survey or conduct interviews. Have the students decide how to analyze the information. Let each group decide how they will display their findings and information. Have each group give (1) a report to the class on what they found, using graph displays to convey their information; and (2) their recommendations for decreasing science anxiety in their school. Place the entire student research project in the school library, main office, or gymnasium, where the rest of the school population can see the results. Have a student summarize and write an article for the school paper.

Doing Science

SUGGESTED ACTIVITIES   Evelyn Fox Keller's biography of Barbara McClintoch, *A Feeling for the Organism,* allows students to explore the conditions under which dissent in science arises, the function it serves, and the plurality of values and goals it reflects. Questions her story prompts are, What role do interests, individual and collective, play in the evolution of scientific knowledge? Do all scientists seek the same kinds of explanations? Are the kinds of questions they ask the same? Do differences in methodology between different subdisciplines ever permit the same kinds of answers? Do female and male scientists approach their research differently?

This book is difficult reading for high school or college students but is manageable if they read carefully and thoroughly. The best way I have found to help them manage is to ask them to read a chapter or section and to come to class with their questions about the reading and to propose some answers.

Social Studies

My Family's Work History

SUGGESTED ACTIVITIES Women and men of different social classes, ethnic groups, and geographic locations have done various kinds of work inside and outside their homes in agricultural, industrial, and postindustrial economies. Before introducing students to the history of work, I pique their interest by asking them to complete a Family Work Chart (see Table 7.6). When their charts are complete, the students and I build a work chronology from 1890 to the present. Our work chronology contains information gleaned from the textbook and library source about important inventions, laws, demographics, and labor history.

I then reproduce the work chronology on a chart so they can compare their family's history. By seeing their families' histories alongside major events in our collective work history, students can see how their family was related to society. A sample of items from our chart looks like this:[23]

Historical Events		**Your Family History**
1890	Women are 17 percent of labor force	
1815	Telephone connects New York and San Francisco	
1924	Restriction of immigration	

Students conclude this unit by writing about a major theme in their family's work history. They might focus on how the lives of the women in the family differed from the lives of the men. They might focus on how their family's race or ethnicity shaped their work history.

Integrating the Public and Private Spheres

SUGGESTED ACTIVITIES Human life is lived in both the public and the private spheres in wartime as well as in peacetime. By asking students to consciously examine individuals' lives as citizens, workers, family members, friends, members of social groups, and individuals, they learn more about the interaction of these roles in both spheres. War is an extraordinary time when the nation's underlying assumptions about these roles are often put to the test. By having students examine the interaction of these roles in wartime, they can see some of our underlying assumptions about the roles and how they are manipulated for the purposes of war. Through researching the histories of their families, and by reading primary source accounts, viewing films, and reading their textbook, they will see the complexity and variety of human experiences in the United States during World War II.

Students research their family's history during World War II by gathering family documents and artifacts and by interviewing at least one relative who was an adult during World War II. Students draw up questions beforehand to find out how the individual's social roles were affected by the war. During the two

TABLE 7.6
Family Work Chart

	Work Experience			
			After Marriage	
	Year of Birth	Before Marriage	While children were young?	When children were grown?
Your Maternal Side				
Mother				
Grandmother				
Grandfather				
Great-grandmother				
Great-grandfather				
Great-grandmother				
Great-grandfather				
Your Paternal Side				
Father				
Grandmother				
Grandfather				
Great-grandmother				
Great-grandfather				
Great-grandmother				
Great-grandfather				

This activity was developed by Carol Frenier. Reprinted with permission from the Education Development Center from Adeline Naiman, Projector Director, *Sally Garcia Family Resource Guide,* Unit 3 of *The Role of Women in American Society* (Newton, Mass.: Education Development Center, Inc., 1978), p. 62.

weeks they are researching their family's history, two class periods are spent on this project. During the first period, students give oral reports to a small group of fellow students in read-around groups.

Appropriate readings and films on World War II are widely available. Studs Terkel's book *The Good War* is particularly useful because of the variety of people the author interviewed.[24] For instance, students can read about the internment of Japanese-Americans and role-play an account read. Their textbook may provide good background information. My students answer two questions in this unit: World War II has been described as a 'good war.' From the materials you have examined, was it a good war for individuals' lives as citizens, workers, family members, friends, and members of social groups? How were their experiences similar to or different from those of your relatives?

Summary

This chapter has illustrated how women's studies is challenging male domination over curricular content. The evolution of that challenge is illuminated by understanding the different emphases that coexist in male-defined, contribution, bifocal, women's and gender-balanced curricula. We now have a conceptual framework for a curriculum that interweaves issues of gender with ethnicity, race, and class. This framework acknowledges and celebrates a multifocal, relational view of the human experience.

The idea of the phases of feminist scholarship as a series of intersecting circles, or patches on a quilt, or threads on a tapestry suggests parallel ways to think about a class of students. Each student brings to your classroom a particular way of knowing. Your challenge as a teacher is to interweave the individual truths with course content into complex understandings that legitimate students' voices. This relational knowledge, with the authority of the school behind it, has the potential to help students analyze their own social, cultural, historical, political, and economic contexts. The goal of relational knowledge is to build a world in which the oppressions of race, gender, and class, which capitalism and patriarchy depend on, are challenged by critical citizens in a democratic society.

Questions and Activities

1. What is a gender-balanced, multicultural curriculum?

2. What is feminist phase theory?

3. Define and give an example of each of the following phases of the feminist phase theory developed and described by the author: a. male-defined curriculum; b. contribution curriculum; c. bifocal curriculum; d. women's curriculum; e. gender-balanced curriculum

4. What problems do the contribution and bifocal phases have? How do the women's curriculum and gender-balanced curriculum phases help solve these problems?

5. The author states that "knowledge is a social construction." What does this mean? In what ways is the new scholarship on women and ethnic groups alike? In what ways does the new scholarship on women and ethnic groups challenge the dominant knowledge established in the society and presented in textbooks? Give examples.

6. Examine the treatment of women in a sample of social studies, language arts, mathematics, or science textbooks (or a combination of two types of textbooks). Which phase or phases of the feminist phase theory presented by the author best describe the treatment of women in the textbooks you examined?

7. What is the *longue durée*? Why is it important in the study of social history, particularly women's history?

8. The author states that she uses a teaching approach designed to legitimize the voices of her students and put "them in a larger explanatory context." What does she mean by this statement? What are examples of teaching strategies that she believes legitimize the voices of her students?

9. Research your family history, paying particular attention to the roles, careers, and influence of women in your family's saga. Also describe your ethnic heritage and the influence of ethnicity on your family's past and present. Share your family history with a group of your classmates or workshop participants.

Notes

1. A gender-balanced perspective, one that is rooted in feminist scholarship, takes into account the experiences, perspectives, and voices of women as well as men. It examines the similarities and differences between women and men but also considers how gender interacts with such factors as ethnicity and class.

2. Jane Atkinson, "Gender Studies, Women's Studies, and Political Feminism" (unpublished paper, Lewis and Clark College: Portland, Ore.: 1986).

3. My thinking about women, gender, and science was influenced by Sue Rosser's work, particularly "The Relationship between Women's Studies and Women in Science," in Ruth Bleier, ed., *Feminist Approaches to Science* (New York: Pergamon Press, 1986) and Londa Schiebinger, "The History and Philosophy of Women in Science," *Signs* 12, No. 2 (Winter 1987): 276–292.

4. Carole Jacklin, "Methodological Issues in the Study of Sex-Related Differences," *Developmental Review* 1 (1981): 266–273. Cited in Anne Fausto-Sterling, *Myths of Gender* (New York: Basic Books, 1985).

5. Peter Filene, "The Secrets of Men's History." Unpublished Paper (Chapel Hill: University of North Carolina, no date).

6. Mary Kay Thompson Tetreault, "Integrating Women's History: The Case of United States History Textbooks," *The History Teacher*. 19, No. 2 (February 1986): 211–262.

7. Sandra M. Gilbert and Susan Gubar, *The Madwoman in the Attic: The Woman Writer and the Nineteenth-Century Literary Imagination* (New Haven: Yale University Press, 1979).

8. Kate Millett, *Sexual Politics* (London: Virago, 1977).

9. Gerda Lerner, *The Majority Finds Its Past* (New York: Oxford University Press, 1979).

10. Carolyn Lougee, "Women's History and the Humanities: An Argument in Favor of the General Curriculum," *Women's Studies Quarterly* 9 (Spring 1981): 4–7.

11. Atkinson, "Gender Studies," 9–10. See also Sandra Coyner, "The Idea of Mainstreaming: Women's Studies and the Disciplines," *Frontiers* 8, No. 23 (1986): 87–95.

12. I am grateful to Patti Lather for this emphasis. Personal correspondence with Patti Lather, September 10, 1985.

13. Carroll Smith-Rosenberg, *Disorderly Conduct* (New York: Oxford Press, 1985).

14. For an excellent bibliographic review of the Annales School of History, see "Letters to the Editor," *Social Education* (October 1982) Vol. 46: 378, 380.

15. Gerda Lerner is reputed to have said this at a conference on women's history in 1982. Private conversation with Peggy McIntosh.

16. Toril Moi, *Sexual/Textual Politics* (New York: Methuen, 1985).

17. Richard Wright, *Black Boy* (New York: Harper and Brothers, 1945).

18. Maxine Hong-Kingston, *The Woman Warrior* (New York: Alfred Knopf, 1976).

19. Maya Angelou, *I Know Why the Caged Bird Sings* (New York: Bantam Books, 1969).

20. Samuel Clemens, *The Adventures of Huckleberry Finn* (New York: Collier, 1912).

21. These ideas about teaching literature are drawn from my observations of a colleague in the English Department at Lewis and Clark College, Dr. Dorothy Berkson. I observed her classes as part of an ethnographic study of feminist teachers.

22. Reprinted with permission from *Fact or Fantasy* (adapted from *Spaces: Solving Problems of Access to Careers in Engineering and Science*), Sherry Fraser, Project Director. Copyright © 1982 by the Lawrence Hall of Science, Regents of the University of California.

23. This chart appears in *Approaches to Women's History,* Ann Chapman, ed. (Washington, D.C.: American Historical Association, 1979).

24. Studs Terkel, *The Good War: An Oral History of World War II* (New York: Pantheon Books, 1984).

CHAPTER 8

Transforming the Curriculum: Teaching about Women of Color

■ **JOHNNELLA E. BUTLER**

Introduction

Teaching about women of color has been a subject long ignored at every level. The least work seems to have been done in kindergarten and grades 1 through 12. The March 1987 issue of *Social Education,* "Getting Women and Gender into the Curriculum Mainstream," makes reference throughout to women of color. The article that most specifically discusses women of color is about teaching from a global, culturally different perspective.[1] When we deal with cultures in other nations, we seem to grasp that before we can have a proper understanding of the women in these cultures, we must adapt a multicultural perspective. It seems less apparent to us that to understand the lives of women in America, a cross-ethnic, multiethnic perspective is also essential.

This chapter focuses on the teaching of women of color in the United States. It provides information applicable and necessary for this cross-ethnic, multiethnic endeavor. The discussion is rooted in the method of critical pedagogy developing in this country that is influenced, but certainly not totally defined, by Brazilian educator and activist Paulo Friere. I see feminist pedagogy as an evolution of this critical pedagogy, as well as the pedagogy implicit in ethnic studies. Examples are provided throughout to keep the theory from seeming only abstract and unrelated to teaching. Although I do not provide suggested activities for kindergarten and grades 1 through 12, I provide information and a conceptual framework, the appropriate starting point for such activities. Readers are made aware of the teaching process as they convey the content on women of color. The appendix of this book includes bibliographic resources for content about the lives of women of color. They provide a starting point. Much work has yet to be done to make this information available to teachers.

Why "Women of Color"?

The phrase *women of color* has come into use gradually. Its use immediately brings to mind differences of race and culture. It also makes clear that Black women are not the only women of color. In an ostensibly democratically structured society, with a great power imbalance signified by race and class privilege, labels representative of reality for those outside the realm of power are difficult to determine. This form of that power is both cultural and political and consequently further complicates labeling. Selecting the phrase *women of color* by many women of American ethnic groups of color is part of their struggle to be recognized with dignity for their humanity, racial heritage, and cultural heritage as they work within the women's movement of the United States. The effort of women of color to name themselves is similar to attempts by Afro-Americans and other ethnic groups to define with dignity their race and ethnicity and to counter the many stereotypical names bestowed on them. Because we tend to use the word *women* to be all-inclusive and general, we usually obscure both the differences and the similarities among women.

With the decline of the civil rights movement of the 1960s, the women's movement in the second half of the twentieth century got under way. Not long after, Black women began to articulate the differences they experienced as Black women, not only because of the racism within the women's movement or the sexism within the Black community, but also because of their vastly differing historical reality. One major question posed by Toni Cade's pioneering anthology, *The Black Woman*, remains applicable: "How relevant are the truths, the experiences, the findings of White women to Black women? Are women after all simply women?" Cade answers the question then as it might still be answered today: "I don't know that our priorities are the same, that our concerns and methods are the same, or even similar enough so that we can afford to depend on this new field of experts (White, female). It is rather obvious that we do not. It is obvious that we are turning to each other."[2] This anthology served as a turning point in the experience of the Black woman. Previously, White males, for the most part, had interpreted her realities, her activities, and her contributions.[3]

Although we are beyond the point of the complete invisibility of women of color in the academic branch of the women's movement, women's studies, Black women must still demand to be heard, to insist on being dealt with from the perspective of the experiences of women of color, just as they did in 1970, as the blurb in the paperback *The Black Woman* implies: "Black Women Speak Out. A Brilliant and Challenging Assembly of Voices That Demand to Be Heard." By the latter part of the 1970s, the logic of a dialogue among women of color became a matter of course. We find, as in Cade's *The Black Woman*, women of color speaking to one another in publications such as *Conditions: Five, The Black Women's Issue*, and *This Bridge Called My Back: Writings by Radical Women of Color*.[4] The academic community began to recognize

American women of color who identify with the Third World, both for ancestral heritage and for related conditions of colonization; in 1980 we see, for example, the publication of Dexter Fisher's anthology *The Third Woman: Minority Women Writers of the United States.*[5]

While it remains difficult to have American women of color properly represented in the higher education curriculum, the age-old problem of dissemination of the necessary information to elementary and secondary schools also holds true in this instance. The issue of *social education* stands as somewhat of an aberration, as does Peggy McIntosh's first week-long training workshop for leaders of year-long faculty workshops in women's studies, because the woman of color in varying degrees is present and accounted for. While both of these efforts have as their goal the integration or transformation, respectively, of the school curriculum through women's studies, McIntosh, from a multiethnic perspective, insists that the inclusion of women of color is necessary for this transformation to occur.[6]

The most familiar ethnic groups of color are the Asian Americans, Afro-Americans, Hispanic Americans, and Native Americans. Yet within each group there are cultural, class, and racial distinctions. These ethnic groups can be further delineated: Asian Americans consist of Chinese Americans, Japanese Americans, Filipino Americans, Korean Americans, in addition to the more recent immigrants from Southeast Asia. Afro-Americans consist of the U.S. Afro-American and the West Indian or Afro-Caribbean immigrants. The number of African immigrants is most likely too small to consider as a group; however, their presence should be accounted for. Hispanic Americans, or Latino-Americans as some prefer, are largely Puerto Rican, Chicano, and Cuban. The Native American is made up of many tribal groups such as Sioux, Apache, Navajo, and Chicahominy.

The phrase *women of color* helps women of all these groups acknowledge both their individual ethnicity and their racial solidarity as members of groups that are racial minorities in the United States, as well as a majority as people of color in the world. The concept also acknowledges similarity in historical experiences and position in relation to the White American. In addition, the use of the phrase *and* the concept *women of color* implies the existence of the race and ethnicity of White women, for whom the word *women* wrongly indicates a norm for all women or wrongly excludes other women.

What We Learn from Studying Women of Color

When we study women of color, we raise our awareness and understanding of the experiences of all women either implicitly or directly. Quite significantly, because of the imbalanced power relationship between White women and women of color, information about one group tends to make more apparent the experiences of the other group. It is well known, for example, that ideals of beauty in the United States are based on the blond, blue-eyed model. Dialogue about the reactions to that model in the experience of women of color, both within their ethnic groups and as they relate to White women, ultimately reveals that White women often judge themselves by that model of beauty. White women also serve simultaneously as reminders or representatives of that ideal to women of color and, most frequently, to themselves as failures to meet the ideal.

Another way of stating this is that a way of understanding an oppressor is to study the oppressed. Thus, we come to another level of awareness and understanding when we study women of color. We see clearly that White women function both as women who share certain similar experiences with women of color and as oppressors of women of color. This is one of the most difficult realities to cope with while maintaining valuable dialogue among women and conducting scholarship. White women who justifiably see themselves as oppressed by White men find it difficult to separate themselves from the effects of and shared power of White men. White women share with White men an ethnicity, an ancestral heritage, racial dominance, and certain powers and privileges by virtue of class, race, and ethnicity, by race and ethnicity if not class, and always by virtue of White skin privilege.[7]

The growing scholarship on women of color gives us much to teach about women's lives, their joys and celebrations, and their oppressions. I cannot begin to relate the content you must deal with in order to know women's lives. However, the books in the appendix can provide a beginning guide for you to become familiar with the history and culture of women of color. When we study women of color, we raise our awareness and understanding of the experiences of all women either explicity or implicitly.

Once we realize that all women are not White, and once we understand the implications of that realization, we see immediately the importance of race, ethnicity, and class when considering gender. Interestingly, some scholarship that intends to illustrate and analyze class dynamics is blind to racial and ethnic dynamics. In similar fashion, much scholarship that illustrates and analyzes racial dynamics and class dynamics fails to see ethnic dynamics. Other scholarship gives short shrift to, or even ignores, class. We have begun to grapple with the connectedness of the four big "-isms"—racism, sexism, classism, and ethnocentrism. Much scholarship in women's studies, however, fails to work within the context of race, class, ethnicity, and gender and their related "-isms," which modulate each other to a greater or lesser extent. Elizabeth V. Spelman illustrates how the racist equating of Blackness with lustfulness in Western culture modulates sexism toward Black women.[8] One resulting stereotype is that the Black woman has a bestial sexuality and, as such, deserves or expects to be raped. This racism is also modulated by an ethnocentrism that further devalues the Black woman, thereby justifying the sexism. Classism may also modulate this sexism if the perpetrator is of a higher class status than are most Black women. However, if this cannot be claimed, racism, ethnocentrism, or both will suffice. Nonetheless, each is operative to some degree. Lower-class Whites or Whites of the same economic class as Blacks can invoke skin privilege to differentiate within the class common denominator. The categories of race, class, ethnicity, and gender are unified; likewise their related "-isms" and their correctives.

Attention to race makes us aware of the differing perspectives that women have about race and skin color—perceptions of what is beautiful, ugly, attractive, repulsive, what is ordinary or exotic, pure or evil, based on racist stereotypes; the role that color plays in women's lives; and the norms by which women judge themselves physically. Attention to race also brings us to a realization that White women, too, are members of a race with stereotypes about looks and behavior. Attention to race in women's lives, with the particular understanding that race has a function for White women as well, reveals the oppression of racism, both from the point of view of one oppressed and of one who oppresses or participates in oppression by virtue of privilege.

Attention to class reveals, among other things, that because of different historical experiences, class means different things to different groups. Not necessarily measured by financial status, neighborhood, and level of education, class status frequently is measured by various ways in which one approximates the Anglo-American norm of middle to upper class. Our society encourages such behavior to a great extent, as shown by the popularity of the Dynasty model, the Yuppie, and the Buppie. Simultaneously, our society insists on formally measuring class status by economic means. Yet for the woman of color, as for the man of color, the dynamic of social class becoming a measure for success is particularly insidious, threatening to destroy the affirmation of ethnic strengths. Chinese Americans who have reached a high education level may move from Chinatown. Adherence to the Anglo-American norm dictates certain dress, foods, and lifestyle, as well as a sense of superiority of the Anglo values. This, in turn, may threaten the sense of identity of a Chinese American whose family has been in the United States many years without interacting with the more newly arrived Asian immigrants or other Chinese Americans. Ties to family and friends may be questioned, and the very traditions and understandings that provided the source of strength for coping in the White world may be devalued and discarded. Poverty quickly becomes shameful, and the victim is easily blamed for not being a rugged enough individual.

Ethnicity, as a category of analysis, reveals the cultural traditions, perspectives, values, and choices that shape women's lives and their position in society, ranging from hairstyles and jewelry adornment to modes of worship and ways of perceiving a divine force, from values to the perception of women's roles and the roles of men. Ethnicity, our cultural and historical heritage, shapes our perception of race and racism, sex and sexism, class and classism.

The element of power or lack of power has a great deal to do with the benefits or deficits of race and ethnicity. Similar to the example regarding classism, ethnic traditions, kinships, and values that are sustaining in the context of an ethnic group that is a minority, and thus, powerless, may become deficits when interacting with the majority or dominant society. On the other hand, when one becomes secure in one's ethnic identity, deficits of powerlessness and the moves to various levels of success (access to limited power) can be negotiated through variations on those strengths. Kinship networks, for example, are of primary importance to people of color for cultural reasons and for survival. Women's friendships have particular significance, specifically friendships of younger women with elder women. The structure of the larger American society does not make allowances for such friendships. Most of us do not live in extended families or in neighborhoods near relatives. Women of color frequently insist that they maintain such relationships over great distances. Time spent with family, especially extended family, must have priority at various times during the year, not just for tradition's sake, but for maintaining a sense of rootedness, for a dose of shared wisdom, a balanced perspective of who you are, and often, simply for that affirmation that Momma or Aunt Elizabeth loves you. Ethnicity tells us that women of color celebrate who they are and where they come from, that they are not simply victims of ethnocentrism and other "-isms."

Ethnicity is important in women's lives. Most important, ethnicity reveals that besides the usually acknowledged European American ethnic groups, White Anglo-Saxon Protestants are an ethnic group. Even though it is an ethnicity that boasts a defining dominance that makes it unnecessary to name itself, it is an ethnicity. That it is an ethnicity to which many Whites have subscribed, rather than one to which they belong by birth, frequently is cause for confusion. However, it is no less an ethnicity for this reason.

The presence of Anglo-American ethnicity within the ethnicity of ethnic groups of color is often cause for confusion. Nonetheless, American ethnic groups of color manifest ethnicities that constantly balance, integrate, and synthesize the Western European Anglo-American, with what has become, with syncretism over the years, Chinese American, Japanese American, Afro-American, Chicano, Native American, and Puerto Rican American. In a similar fashion, the English who came here syncretized with the values that emanated from being on this continent and became English Americans. They maintained a position of power so that other Europeans syncretized to their English or Colonial American culture eventually resulted in their being called Americans. The assumption that people living in the United States are called Americans and that those living in other nations in the hemisphere are Latin Americans, Caribbean Americans, or Canadians attests to this assumed and enforced position of power.

Religion is closely related to ethnicity. Its values are sometimes indistinguishable from ethnic values. Ethnicity as a category of analysis reveals sources of identity, sources of sustenance and celebration, as well as the cultural dynamics that shape women's experience. It makes apparent the necessity of viewing women pluralistically.

Gender roles may assume differing degrees of importance. By virtue of the modulation of the other categories, women may see gender or sexism to be of lesser or greater importance. Gender roles for women of color are more apparently designated, determined, or modulated by ethnicity, race, and sexism. Therefore, racism may assume primary importance as an oppressive force with which to reckon. The Black woman harassed in the workplace because she wears her hair in intricate braids and wears clothes associated with her African heritage receives harsh treatment because of racism, not sexism. Racism also caused Black women to be denied the right to vote after White women gained suffrage rights.

Women of Color: The Agent of Transformation

In dealing with the commonalities and differences among women, a necessity in teaching about women of color, I am reminded that the title of Paula Gidding's work on Afro-American women is taken from Anna J. Cooper's observation: "When and where I enter, then and there the whole . . . race enters with me."[9] Repeated in many forms by women of color from the nineteenth-century struggle for the vote to the present-day women's movement, this truth ultimately contains the goal of transformation of the curriculum: a curriculum that reflects all of us, egalitarian, communal, nonhierarchical, and pluralistic. Women of color are inextricably related to men of color by virtue of ethnicity and traditions as well as by common conditions of oppression. Therefore, at minimum, their struggle against sexism and racism is waged simultaneously. The experiences and destinies of women and men of color are linked. This reality poses a special problem in the relationship between White women and women of color. Moreover, in emphasizing the commonalities of privilege between White men and women, the oppressive relationship between men of color and White men, women of color and White men, and men of color and White women—all implied in Anna J. Cooper's observation[10]—the teaching about women of color provides the natural pluralistic, multidimensional catalyst for transformation. As such, women of color are agents of transformation.

This section defines transformation and provides the theoretical framework for the pedagogy and methodology of transformation. The final section discusses aspects of the process of teaching about women of color, which, though closely related to the theoretical framework, manifest themselves in very concrete ways.

A review of feminist pedagogy over the past fifteen years or so reveals a call for teaching from multifocal, multidimensional, multicultural, pluralistic, interdisciplinary perspectives. This call, largely consistent with the pedagogy and methodology implied thus far in this chapter, can be accomplished only through transformation. Although many theorists and teachers now see this point, the terminology has still to be corrected to illustrate the process. In fact, we often use the words *mainstreaming, balancing, integration,* and *transformation* interchangeably. Mainstreaming, balancing, and integration imply adding women to an established, accepted body of knowledge. The experience of White, middle-class women has provided a norm in a way that White Anglo-American ethnicity provides a norm. All other women's experience is added to and measured by those racial, class, ethnic, and gender roles and experiences.

Transformation, which does away with the dominance of norms, allows us to see the many aspects of women's lives. Understanding the significance of naming the action of treating women's lives through a pluralistic process— transformation—leads naturally to a convergence between women's studies and ethnic studies. This convergence is necessary to give us the information that illuminates the function and content of race, class, and ethnicity in women's lives and in relation to gender. In similar fashion, treating the lives of people of color through a pluralistic process leads to the same convergence, illuminating the functions and content of race, class, and gender in relation to lives of ethnic Americans and in relation to ethnicity.

We still need to come to grips with exactly what is meant by this pluralistic, multidimensional, interdisciplinary scholarship and pedagogy; much of the scholarship on, about, and even frequently, by, women of color renders them systematically invisible, erasing their experience or part of it. White, middle-class, male, and Anglo-American are the insidious norms corresponding to race, class, gender, and ethnicity. In contrasting and comparing experiences of pioneers, White males and females when dealing with Native Americans, for example, often speak of "the male," "the female," and "the Indian." Somehow, those of a different ethnicity and race are assumed to be male. Therefore, both the female and the male Indian experience is observed and distorted. They must be viewed both separately and together to get a more complete view, just as to have a more complete view of the pioneer experience, the White male and White female experiences must be studied both separately and together. Thus, even in our attempts to correct misinformation resulting from measurement by one norm, we can reinforce measurement by others if we do not see the interaction of the categories, the interaction of the "-isms," as explained in the previous section. This pluralistic process and eye is demanded in order to understand the particulars and the generalities of people's lives.

Why is it so easy to impose these norms, effectively to erase the experience of others? I do not think erasing these experiences is always intentional. I do, however, think that it results from the dominance of the Western cultural norm of individuality, singularity, rationality, masculinity, and Whiteness at the expense of the communal, the plural, the intuitive, the feminine, and people of color. A brief look at Elizabeth Spelman's seminal work, "Theories of Race and Gender: The Erasure of Black Women," explains the important aspects of how this erasure comes about.[11] Then, a consideration of the philosophical makeup of transformation both tells us how our thinking makes it happen and how we can think to prevent it from happening.

Spelman gives examples of erasure of the Black woman, similar to the examples I have provided. She analyzes concepts that assume primacy of sexism over racism. Furthermore, she rejects the additive approach to analyzing sexism, an approach that assumes a sameness of women modeled on the White, middle-class, Anglo-oriented woman. Spelman shows that it is premature to argue that sexism and racism are either mutually exclusive, totally dependent on one another, or in a causal relationship with one another. She discusses how women differ by race, class, and culture or ethnicity. Most important, she demonstrates that Black does not simply indicate victim. Black indicates a culture, in the United States the African-American culture. She suggests, then, that we present women's studies in a way that makes it a given that women are diverse, that their diversity is apparent in their experiences with oppression and in their participation in United States culture. To teach about women in this manner, our goal must not be additive, that is, integrating, mainstreaming or balancing the curriculum. Rather, transformation must be our goal.

Essentially, transformation is the process of revealing unity among human beings and the world, as well as revealing important differences. Transformation implies acknowledging and benefiting from the interaction among sameness and diversity, groups and individuals. The maxim on which transformation rests may be stated as an essential affirmation of the West African proverb, "I am because we are. We are because I am." The communality, the human unity implicit in the proverb, operates in African traditional (philosophical) thought in regard to human beings, other categories of life, categories of knowledge, ways of thinking and being.[12] It is in opposition to the European, Western pivotal axiom, on which integration, balancing, and mainstreaming rest (as expressed through the White, middle-class, Anglo norm in the United States), "I think; therefore, I am," as expressed by Descartes.

The former is in tune with a pluralistic, multidimensional process; the latter with a monolithic, one-dimensional process. Stated succinctly as "I am we," the West African proverb provides the rationale for the interaction and modulation of the categories of race, class, gender, and ethnicity, for the interaction and modulation of their respective "-isms," for the interaction and modulation of the objective and subjective, the rational and the intuitive, the feminine and the masculine, all those things which we, as Westerners, see as either opposite or standing rigidly alone. This is the breakdown of what is called variously critical pedagogy, feminist pedagogy, multifocal teaching, when the end is the comprehension of and involvement with cultural, class, racial, and gender diversity toward the end not of tolerance, but rather of an egalitarian world based on communal relationships within humanity.

To realize this transformation, we must redefine categories and displace criteria that have served as norms in order to bring about the life context (norms and values) as follows:

1. Nonhierarchical terms and contexts for human institutions, rituals, and action

2. A respect for the interaction and existence of both diversity and sameness (a removal of measurement by norms perpetuating otherness, silence, and erasure)

3. A balancing and interaction between the individual and the group

4. A concept of humanity emanating from interdependence of human beings on one another and on the world environment, both natural and human-created

5. A concept of humanity emanating from a sense of self that is not abstract and totally individually defined (I think; therefore, I am), but that is both abstract and concrete, individually and communally defined (I am we; I am because we are; we are because I am)

Such a context applies to pedagogy and scholarship, the dissemination and ordering of knowledge in all disciplines and fields. Within this context (the context in which the world does operate and against which the Western individualistic, singular concept of humanity militates) it becomes possible for us to understand the popular music form "rap" as an Americanized, Westernized version of African praise singing, functioning, obviously, for decidedly different cultural and social reasons. It becomes possible to understand the syncretization of cultures that produced Haitian voudoo, Cuban santería, and Brazilian candomblé from Catholicism and the religion of the Yoruba. It becomes possible to understand what is happening when a Japanese American student is finding it difficult to reconcile traditional Buddhist values with her American life. It becomes possible to understand that Maxine Hong Kingston's *Woman Warrior* is essentially about the struggle to syncretize Chinese ways within the United States whose dominant culture devalues and coerces against syncretization, seeking to impose White, middle-class conformity.

Thinking in this manner is foreign to the mainstream of thought in the United States, although it is alive and well in Native American traditional philosophy, in Taoist philosophy, in African traditional philosophy, and in Afro-American folklore. It is so foreign, in fact, that I realized that in order to bring about this context, we must commit certain "sins." Philosopher Elizabeth Minnich suggested that these "sins" might be more aptly characterized as "heresies," since they are strongly at variance with established modes of thought and values.[13]

The following heresies challenge and ultimately displace the ways in which the Western mind orders the world.[14] They emanate from the experiences of people of color, the nature of their oppression, and the way the world operates. Adopting them is a necessity for teaching about women of color. Using the heresies to teach women's studies, to teach about the lives of all women, becomes natural when we study women of color and leads naturally to the transformation of the curriculum to a pluralistic, egalitarian, multidimensional curriculum.

Heresy #1	The goal of interaction among human beings, action, and ideas must be seen not only as synthesis, but also as the identification of opposites and differences. These opposites and differences may or may not be resolved; they may function together by virtue of the similarities identified.
Heresy #2	We *can* address a multiplicity of concerns, approaches, and subjects, without a neutral or dominant center. Reality reflects opposites as well as overlaps in what are perceived as opposites. There exist no pure, distinct opposites.
Heresy #3	It is not reductive to look at gender, race, class, and culture as part of a complex whole. The more different voices we have, the closer we are to the whole.
Heresy #4	Transformation demands an understanding of ethnicity that takes into account the differing cultural continua (in the United States, Western European, Anglo-American, African, Asian, Native American) and their similarities.
Heresy #5	Transformation demands a relinquishing of the primary definitiveness of gender, race, class or culture and ethnicity as they interact with theory, methodology, pedagogy, institutionalization, and action, both in synthesis and in a dynamic that functions as opposite and same simultaneously.
	A variation on this hersey is that although all ''-isms'' are not the same, they are unified and operate as such; likewise their correctives.
Heresy #6	The Anglo-American, and ultimately the Western norm, must be seen as only one of many norms, and also as one that enjoys privilege and power that has colonized, and may continue to colonize, other norms.
Heresy #7	Feelings are direct lines to better thinking. The intuitive as well as the rational is part of the process of moving from the familiar to the unfamiliar in acquiring knowledge.

Heresy #8   Knowledge is identity and identity is knowledge. All knowledge is explicitly and implicitly related to who we are, both as individuals and as groups.

Teaching about Women of Color

The first six heresies essentially address content and methodology for gathering and interpreting content. They inform decisions such as the following:

1. Not teaching Linda Brent's *Narrative* as the single example of the slave experience of Afro-American women in the nineteenth century, but rather presenting it as a representative example of the slave experience of Afro-American women that occurs within a contradictory, paradoxical world that had free Black women such as Charlotte Forten Grimke and abolitionist women such as Sojourner Truth. The picture of Black women that emerges, then, becomes one that illuminates their complexity of experiences and their differing interactions with White people.

2. Not simply teaching about pioneer women in the West, but teaching about Native American women, perhaps through their stories, which they have "pass(ed) on to their children and their children's children . . . using the word to advance those concepts crucial to cultural survival." The picture of settling the West becomes more balanced, suggesting clearly to students the different perspectives and power relationships.

3. Not choosing biographies for children of a White woman, an Asian American woman, and an Afro-American woman, but rather finding ways through biography, poetry, and storytelling to introduce children to different women's experiences, different according to race, class, ethnicity, and gender roles. The emphases are on the connectedness of experiences and on the differences among experiences, the communality among human beings and the interrelatedness among experiences and ways of learning.

The last two heresies directly address process. After correct content, process is the most important part of teaching. Students who learn in an environment that is sensitive to their feelings and supports and encourages the pursuit of knowledge will consistently meet new knowledge and new situations with the necessary openness and understanding for human development and progress. If this sounds moralistic, we must remember that the stated and implied goal of critical pedagogy and feminist pedagogy, as well as of efforts to transform the curriculum with content about women and ethnicity, is to provide an education that more accurately reflects the history and composition of the world, that demonstrates the relationship of *what* we learn to *how* we live, that implicitly and explicitly reveals the relationship between knowledge and social action. Process is most important, then, in helping students develop ways throughout their education to reach the closest approximation of truth toward the end of bettering the human condition.

The key to understanding the teaching process in any classroom in which teaching about women of color from the perspective of transformation is a goal, is recognizing that the content alters all students' perceptions of themselves.

First, they begin to realize that we can never say *women* to mean all women, that we must particularize the term as appropriate to context and understanding (for example, White, middle-class women, Chinese American, lower-class women, middle-class, Mexican-American women). Next, students begin to understand that using White, middle-class women as the norm will seem distortingly reductive. White women's ethnic, regional, class, and gender commonalities and differences soon become apparent, and the role in oppression of the imposed Anglo-American ethnic conformity stands out. Student reactions may range from surprise, to excitement about learning more, to hostility and anger. In the volume *Gendered Subjects,* Margo Culley details much of what happens. Her opening paragraph summarizes her main thesis:

> *Teaching about gender and race can create classrooms that are charged arenas. Students enter these classrooms imbued with the values of the dominant culture: they believe that success in conventional terms is largely a matter of* will *and that those who do not* have it all *have experienced a failure of will.* Closer and closer ties between corporate America and higher education, as well as the "upscaling" of the student body, make it even harder to hear the voices from the margin within the academy. Bringing those voices to the center of the classroom means disorganizing ideology and disorienting individuals. Sometimes, as suddenly as the fragments in a kaleidoscope rearrange to totally change the picture, our work alters the ground of being for our students (and perhaps even for ourselves). When this happens, classrooms can become explosive, but potentially transformative arenas of dialogue.[15]

"Altering the ground of being" happens to some extent on all levels. The White girl kindergarten pupil's sense of the world is frequently challenged when she discovers that heroines do not necessarily look like her. Awareness of the ways in which the world around children is ordered occurs earlier than most of us may imagine. My niece, barely four years old, told my father in a definitive tone as we entered a church farther from her home than the church to which she belongs, "Gramps, this is the Black church." We had not referred to the church as such, yet clearly that Catholic congregation was predominantly Black and the girl's home congregation predominantly White. Her younger sister, at age three, told her mother that the kids in the day school she attended were "not like me." She then pointed to the brown, back side of her hand. Young children notice difference. We decide what they do with and think of that difference.

Teaching young children about women of color gives male and female children of all backgrounds a sense of the diversity of people, of the various roles in which women function in American culture, of the various joys and sorrows, triumphs and struggles they encounter. Seeds of awareness of the power relationships between male and female, among racial, ethnic, and class groups are sown and nurtured.

Teaching about women of color early in students' academic experience, thereby bringing the voices of the margin to the center, disorganizes ideology and ways of being. Furthermore, however, it encourages an openness to understanding, difference and similarity, the foreign and the commonplace, necessary to the mind-set of curiosity and fascination for knowledge that we all want to inspire in our students no matter what the subject.

Culley also observes that "anger is the energy mediating the transformation from damage to wholeness,'' the damage being the values and perspectives of the dominant culture that have shaped opinions based on a seriously flawed and skewed American history and interpretation of the present.[16] Certain reactions occur and are part of the process of teaching about women of color. Because they can occur at all levels to a greater or lesser extent, it is useful to look for variations on their themes.

It is important to recognize that these reactions occur within the context of student and teacher expectations. Students are concerned about grading, teachers about evaluations by superiors and students. Frequently, fear of, disdain for, or hesitancy about feminist perspectives by some students may create a tense, hostile atmosphere. Similarly, fear of, disdain for, or hesitancy about studying people different from you (particularly by the White student) or people similar to you (particularly by the student of color or of a culture related to people of color) also may create a tense, hostile atmosphere. Student expectations of teachers, expectations modulated by the ethnicity, race, class, and gender of the teacher, may encourage students to presume that a teacher will take a certain position. The teacher's need to inspire students to perform with excellence may become a teacher's priority at the expense of presenting material that may at first confuse the students or challenge their opinions. It is important to treat these reactions as though they are as much a part of the process of teaching as the form of presentation, the exams, and the content, for indeed, they are. Moreover, they can affect the success of the teaching of the material about women of color.

Specifically, these reactions are part of the overall process of moving from the familiar to the unfamiliar. As heresy #7 guides us, ''Feelings are direct lines to better thinking.'' Affective reactions to content, such as anger, guilt, and feelings of displacement, when recognized for what they are, lead to the desired cognitive reaction, the conceptualization of the facts so that knowledge becomes useful as the closest approximation to the truth. As Japanese-American female students first read accounts by Issei women about their picture bride experiences, their reactions might at first be mixed.[17] Raising the issue of Japanese immigration to the United States during the late nineteenth century may challenge the exotic stereotype of the Japanese woman or engender anger toward Japanese males, all results of incomplete access to history. White students may respond with guilt or indifference because of the policy of a government whose composition is essentially White, Anglo-oriented, and with which they identify. Japanese-American male students may become defensive, desirous of hearing Japanese-American men's stories about picture bride marriages. Afro-American male and female students may draw analogies between the Japanese-American experience and the Afro-American experience. Such analogies may be welcomed or resented by other students. Of course, students from varied backgrounds may respond to learning about Issei women with a reinforced or instilled pride in Japanese ancestry or with a newfound interest in immigration history.

Teacher presentation of Issei women's experience as picture brides should include, of course, lectures, readings, audiovisuals about the motivation, the experience, the male–female ratio of Japanese-Americans at the turn of the century, and the tradition of arranged marriage in Japan. Presentations should also anticipate, however, student reaction based on their generally ill-informed or limited knowledge about the subject.[18] Discussion and analysis of the students' initial perspectives on Issei women, of how those perspectives have changed given the historical, cultural, and sociological information, allows for learning about and reading Issei women's accounts to become an occasion, then, for expressing feelings of guilt, shame, anger, pride, interest, and curiosity, and for getting at the reasons for those feelings.

Understanding those feelings and working with them to move the student from damage, misinformation, and even bigotry to wholeness sometimes becomes a major portion of the content, especially when anger or guilt is directed toward a specific group—other students, the teacher, or perhaps even the self. Then it becomes necessary for the teacher to use what I call pressure-release sessions. The need for such sessions may manifest itself in many ways. For example,

> The fear of being regarded by peers or by the professor as racist, sexist or "politically incorrect" can polarize a classroom. If the [teacher] participates unconsciously in this fear and emotional self-protection, the classroom experience will degenerate to hopeless polarization, and even overt hostility. He or she must constantly stand outside the classroom experience and anticipate such dynamics. . . . "Pressure-release" discussions work best when the teacher directly acknowledges and calls attention to the tension in the classroom. The teacher may initiate the discussion or allow it to come about in whatever way he or she feels most comfortable.[19]

The hostility, fear, and hesitancy "can be converted to fertile ground for profound academic experiences . . . 'profound' because the students' knowledge is challenged, expanded, or reinforced"[20] by a subject matter that is simultaneously affective and cognitive, resonant with the humanness of life in both form and content. Students learn from these pressure-release sessions, as they must learn in life, to achieve balance and harmony in whatever pursuits, that paradoxes and contradictions are sometimes resolved and sometimes stand separately yet function together (recall heresy #1).

Teaching about women of color can often spark resistance to the teacher or cause students to question subject veracity. Students often learn that the latter part of the nineteenth century and the turn of the century was a time of expansion for the United States. Learning of the experiences of Native American and Mexican women who were subjected to particular horrors as the United States pushed westward, or reading about Chinese immigrant women whose lives paralleled those of their husbands who provided slave labor for the building of the railroads, students begin to realize that this time was anything but progressive or expansive. Teaching about Ida Wells-Barnett, the Afro-American woman who waged the antilynching campaigns at the end of the nineteenth century and well into the twentieth century, also belies the progress of that time. Ida Wells-Barnett brings to the fore the horror of lynchings of Black men, women, and children, the inhuman practice of castration, the stereotyped ideas of Black men and women, ideas that were, as Giddings reminds us, "older than the Republic itself—for they were rooted in the European minds that shaped America."[21] Furthermore, Wells-Barnett's life work reveals the racism of White women in the suffragist movement of the early twentieth century, a reflection of the racism in that movement's nineteenth-century manifestation.

The ever-present interaction of racism and sexism, the stereotyping of Black men and women as bestial, the unfounded labeling of Black men as rapists in search of White women, and the horrid participation in all of this by White men and women in all stations of life, make for difficult history for any teacher to teach and for any student to study. The threat to the founding fathers and Miss Liberty versions are apparent. Such content is often resisted by Black and White students alike, perhaps for different reasons, including rage, anger, or shame that such atrocities were endured by people like them; indifference in the face of reality because "nothing like that will happen again;" and anger, guilt, or shame that people of their race were responsible for such hideous atrocities. Furthermore, all students may resent the upsetting of their neatly packaged understandings of U.S. history and of their world.

The teacher must know the content and be willing to facilitate the pressure-release sessions that undoubtedly will be needed. Pressure-release sessions must help students sort out facts from feelings, and, most of all, must clarify the relevance of the material to understanding the world in which we live and preventing such atrocities from recurring. Also, in teaching about the Issei women and about the life of Ida Wells-Barnett, teachers must never let the class lose sight of the vision these women had, how they dealt with joy and sorrow, the triumphs and struggles of their lives, the contributions to both their own people and to U.S. life at large.

In addition to variations on anger, guilt, and challenges to credibility, in learning about women of color, students become more aware of the positive aspects of race and ethnicity and frequently begin to take pride in their identities. As heresy #8 states, "Knowledge is identity and identity is knowledge. All knowledge is explicitly and implicitly related to who we are, both as individuals and as groups." The teacher, however, must watch for overzealous pride as well as unadmitted uneasiness with one's ethnic or racial identity. White students, in particular, may react in a generally unexpected manner. Some may predictably claim their Irish ancestry; others may be confused as to their ethnicity, for they may come from German and Scottish ancestry, which early on assumed Anglo-American identity. Students of Anglo-American ancestry, however, may hesitate to embrace that terminology, for it might suggest to them, in the context of the experiences of women and men of color, an abuse of power and "all things horrible in this country," as one upset student once complained to me. Here teachers must be adept not only at conveying facts, but also at explaining the effects of culture, race, gender, and ethnicity in recording and interpreting historical facts. They also must be able to convey to students both the beautiful and the ugly in all of us. Thus, the Black American teacher may find himself or herself explaining the cultural value of Anglo-American or Yankee humor, of Yankee precision in gardening, of Yankee thriftiness, and how we all share, in some way, that heritage. At whatever age this occurs, students must be helped to understand the dichotomous, hierarchical past of that identity and in moving toward expressing their awareness in a pluralistic context.

Now that we have explored the why of the phrase *women of color*, identified the essence of what we learn when we study women of color, discussed the theory of transformation, and identified and discussed the most frequent reactions of students to the subject matter, we will now focus on the teacher.

Conclusion

Teaching about women of color should result in conveying information about a group of people largely invisible in our curricula in a way that encourages students to seek further knowledge and ultimately begin to correct and reorder the flawed perception of the world based on racism, sexism, classism, and ethnocentrism. To do so is no mean feat. Redefining one's world involves not only the inclusion of previously ignored content, but also the revision, deletion, and correction of accepted content in light of missing and ignored content. As such, it might require a redesignation of historical periods, a renaming of literary periods, and a complete reworking of sociological methodology to reflect the ethnic and cultural standards at work. This chapter, then, is essentially an introduction to the journey that teachers must embark on to begin providing for students a curriculum which reflects the reality of the past, which prepares students to deal with and understand the present, and which creates the basis for a more humane, productive, caring future.

The implications of teaching about women of color are far-reaching, involving many people in many different capacities. New texts need to be written for college-level students. Teacher education must be restructured to include not only the transformed content but also the pedagogy that reflects how our nation and the world are multicultural, multiethnic, multiracial, multifocal, and multi-dimensional. College texts, children's books, and other materials need to be devised to help teach this curriculum. School administrators, school boards, parents, and teachers need to participate and contribute to this transformation in all ways that influence what our children learn.

For teachers and those studying to be teachers, the immediate implications of a transformed curriculum can seem overwhelming, for transformation is a process that will take longer than our lifetimes. Presently, we are in the formative stages of understanding what must be done to correct the damage in order to lead to wholeness. I suggest that we begin small. That is, decide to include women of color in your classes this year. Begin adding some aspect of that topic to every unit. Pay close attention to how that addition relates to what you already teach. Does it expand the topic? Does it present material you already cover within that expansion? Can you delete some old material and still meet your objectives? Does the new material conflict with the old? How? Is that conflict a valuable learning resource for your students? Continue to do this each year. Gradually, other central topics will emerge about men of color, White men, White women, class, race, ethnicity, and gender. By beginning with studying women of color, the curriculum then will have evolved to be truly pluralistic.

This chapter pays the most attention to the student. The teacher, who embarks on this long journey, must be determined to succeed. Why? Because all the conflicting emotions, the sometimes painful movement from the familiar to the unfamiliar, are experienced by the teacher as well. We have been shaped by the same damaging, ill-informed view of the world as our students. Often, as we try to resolve their conflicts, we are simultaneously working through our own. Above all, we must demand honesty of ourselves before we can succeed.

The difficulty of the process of transformation is one contributing factor to the maintenance of the status quo. Often we look for the easiest way out. It is easier to work with students who are not puzzled, concerned, or bothered by what they are studying. We, as teachers, must be willing to admit that we do not know everything but that we do know how to go about learning in a way that reaches the closest approximation of the truth. Our reach must always exceed our grasp, and in doing so, we will encourage the excellence, the passion, the curiosity, the respect, and the love needed to create superb scholarship and encourage thinking, open-minded, caring, knowledgeable students.

Questions and Activities

1. When Butler uses the phrase *women of color,* to what specific ethnic groups is she referring? Why did this phrase emerge, and what purpose does it serve?

2. How can a study of women of color help broaden our understanding of White women? Of women in general?

3. In what ways, according to Butler, is ethnicity an important variable in women's lives? Give specific examples from this chapter to support your response.

4. How does racism, combined with sexism, influence the ways in which people view and respond to women of color?

5. What does the author mean by *transformation* and a *transformed curriculum*? How does a transformed curriculum differ from a mainstream or balanced curriculum?

6. How can content about women of color serve as a vehicle for transforming the school curriculum?

7. The author lists eight heresies, or assumptions, about reality that differ fundamentally from dominant modes of thought and values. Why does she believe these heresies are essential when teaching about women of color?

8. The author states that teaching about women of color may spark resistance to the teacher, the subject, or both. What examples of content does she describe that may evoke student resistance? Why, according to Butler, might students resist this content? What tips does she give teachers for handling student resistance?

9. Develop a teaching unit in which you incorporate content about women of color, using the transformation approach described in this chapter. Useful references on women of color are found in the appendix ("Gender" section).

Notes

1. Susan Hill Gross, "Women's History for Global Learning," *Social Education,* 51, No. 3 (March 1987): 194–198.

2. Toni Cade, *The Black Woman: An Anthology* (New York: New American Library, 1970), p. 9.

3. The Moynihan Report of 1965, the most notable of this scholarship, received the widest publicity and acceptance by American society at large. Blaming Black social problems on the Black family, Moynihan argues that Black families, dominated by women, are generally pathological and pathogenic. In attempting to explain the poor social and economic condition of the Black lower class, Moynihan largely ignores the history of racism and ethnocentrism and classism in American life and instead blames their victims. His study directly opposes the scholarship of Billingsley and others, which demonstrates the organizational differences between Black and White family units as well as the existence of a vital Afro-American culture on which to base solutions to the social problems Moynihan identifies. See Daniel Moynihan, *The Negro Family* (Washington, D.C.: U.S. Dept. of Labor, 1965); Joyce Ladner, ed. *The Death of White Sociology* (New York: Vintage, 1973); Andrew Billingsley, *Black Families in White America* (Englewood Cliffs, N.J.: Prentice-Hall, 1968); and Harriet McAdoo, ed., *Black Families* (Beverly Hills, Calif: Sage Publications, 1981).

4. *Conditions, Five: The Black Woman's Issue* 2, No. 3 (Autumn 1979); Cherríe Moraga and Gloria Anzaldúa, eds. *This Bridge Called My Back: Writings by Radical Women of Color* (Watertown, Mass., Persephone Press, 1981).

5. Dexter Fisher, ed. *The Third Woman* (Boston: Houghton Mifflin, 1980).

6. Peggy McIntosh, associate director of the Wellesley Center for Research on Women, directed a training workshop in June 1987 for faculty at participating independent schools to prepare them for running faculty-development workshops in women's studies on their respective campuses. Dr. McIntosh's definition of transformation is similar to mine. I am grateful to work with her periodically, sharing and developing ideas.

7. See "On Being White: Toward a Feminist Understanding of Race and Race Supremacy" in Marilyn Frye's *The Politics of Reality: Essays in Feminist Theory* (Trumansburg, N.Y.: The Crossing Press, 1983), pp. 110–127. Also see "Understanding Correspondence between White Privilege and Male Privilege through Women's Studies Work," unpublished paper presented by Peggy McIntosh at the 1987 National Women's Studies Association Annual Meeting, Atlanta, Ga. Available through Wellesley Center for Research on Women, Washington St., Wellesley, Mass., 02181. These works illuminate race and class power relationships and the difference between race and skin privileges. They emphasize not the rejection of privilege but the awareness of its function in order to work actively against injustice.

8. Elizabeth V. Spelman, "Theories of Gender and Race: The Erasure of Black Women," *Quest: A Feminist Quarterly* 5, No. 4 (1982): 36–62. Also see Renate D. Klein, "The Dynamics of the Women's Studies Classroom: A Review Essay of the Teaching Practice of Women's Studies in Higher Education," *Women's Studies International Forum* 10, No. 2 (1987): 187–206.

9. Paula Giddings, *When and Where I Enter: The Impact of Black Women on Race and Sex in America* (New York: William Morrow, 1984).

10. See Lillian Smith, *Killers of the Dream* (New York: Norton, 1949, 1961). Smith provides a useful and clear description of the interaction between racism and sexism and its legacy.

11. Spelman, *Theories of Gender and Race,* 57–59.

12. See John Mbiti, *Introduction to African Religion* (London: Heinemann, 1975); Basil Davidson, *The African Genius* (Boston: Little, Brown, 1969).

13. I began to conceptualize this framework while doing consulting work with college faculty to include Black studies and women's studies content in their syllabi. They were first presented as heresies at the First Working Conference on Critical Pedagogy at the University of Massachusetts, Amherst, February 1985. The concept of heresy here implies a reworking of the way that Westerners order the world, essentially by replacing individualism with a sense of communality and interdependence.

14. See Paulo Friere, *Pedagogy of the Oppressed* (New York: Seabury, 1969); *Education for Critical Consciousness* (New York: Seabury, 1973).

15. Margo Culley, "Anger and Authority in the Introductory Women's Studies Classroom" in Margo Culley and Catherine Portuges, eds., *Gendered Subjects: The Dynamics of Feminist Teaching* (Boston: Routledge and Kegan Paul, 1985), p. 209.

16. Ibid., 212. Also see in same volume, Butler, "Toward a Pedagogy of Everywoman's Studies," 230–239.

17. *Sei* in Japanese means "generation." The concepts of first-, second-, and third-generation Japanese-Americans are denoted by adding a numerical prefix. Therefore, Issei is first generation, Nisei, second, and Sansei, third. Most

Issei immigrated to the United States during the first quarter of the twentieth century to provide cheap, male manual labor, intending to return to Japan after a few years. However, their low wages did not provide enough money for them to return. In 1900, out of a total of 24,326 in the United States, 983 were women. Through the immigration of picture brides by 1920, women numbered 38,303 out of a population of 111,010. Because of racist, anti-Japanese agitation, the U.S. government helped bring these brides to the United States. For a complete discussion, see the Introduction and "Issei Women" in Nobuya Tsuchida, ed., *Asian and Pacific American Experiences: Women's Perspectives* (Minneapolis: University of Minnesota, 1982).

18. An important rule in the scholarship of critical pedagogy is that the teacher should build on the ideas and feelings that students bring to a subject, helping them understand how they might be useful, in what ways they are flawed, correct, or incorrect. Sometimes this simply means giving the student credit for having thought about an idea, or helping the student become aware that he or she might have encountered the idea, or aspects of material studied elsewhere. Generally this process is referred to as moving the student from the familiar to the unfamiliar.

19. Butler, "Toward a Pedagogy," 236.

20. Ibid.

21. Giddings, *When and Where I Enter,* 31.

las toallas de papel

Language and ethnic diversity can enrich a classroom.

PART IV

Ethnicity and Language

The drastic increase in the percentage of ethnic and language minority students in the nation's public schools is one of the most significant developments in education within the last several decades. The growth in the percentage of ethnic and language minorities in the nation's schools results from several factors, including the new wave of immigration that began after 1968 and the aging of the White population. The nation's classrooms are experiencing the largest influx of immigrant students since the turn of the century. The United States received 808,000 immigrants in 1980, more than in any year up to that time since 1914. Ethnic minorities, such as Afro-Americans and Hispanic Americans, are much younger in terms of median age than are Whites and consequently have more children.

Demographers predict that if current trends continue, one of every three students in the public schools will be an ethnic minority by the year 2000. Ethnic minorities will constitute majorities in the school districts in large cities. In most urban school districts, such as Los Angeles, Washington, D.C., Chicago, and Seattle, ethnic minorities are already majorities. In late 1987, forty-four of the largest urban school districts were members of The Council of Great City Schools. Seventy-five percent of the students enrolled in these schools were ethnic minorities; 45.8 percent were Black, 22.7 percent were Hispanic, and 4.9 percent were Asians. A large percentage of the students who attended these schools were also poor. Thirty-three percent of them came from families that received public assistance. Eighty percent were eligible for free or reduced-price lunches.

While the percentage of ethnic minorities in the nation's schools are increasing greatly, the percentage of ethnic minority teachers is decreasing sharply. In 1980, minority teachers made up 12.5 percent of the nation's teachers. If current declining trends continue, minority teachers will make up only about 5 percent of the nation's teachers by the turn of the century. In the year 2000, most students in the nation's cities will be ethnic minorities, and more of the teachers than today will be White and mainstream. This development underscores the need for all teachers to develop the knowledge, attitudes, and skills needed to work effectively with students from diverse racial, ethnic, and language groups.

Language diversity in the nation's schools is a consequence of the increased number of ethnic minority students. Most immigrants (82 percent) who entered the United States between 1971 and 1980 came from Latin American and Asian nations. Only 18 percent of the nation's immigrants came from European nations during this period. Consequently, most new immigrants to the United States speak Spanish and Asian languages. The array of languages spoken by these groups has had a cogent influence on the schools. In 1987, 110 different languages were spoken by students enrolled in the Great City Schools.

The chapters in this part of the book document the educational inequality that ethnic minority students such as Afro-Americans, Hispanics, and American Indians still experience in the schools and describe steps that educators can take to give these students a better chance to achieve academically. Chapter 10 describes approaches teachers can use to integrate their curricula with ethnic content and explains why doing so is essential. The final chapter in this part, Chapter 11, discusses the problems and challenges of the wide variety of languages spoken by students in U.S. schools.

CHAPTER 9

Ethnic Minorities and Educational Equality

■ **GENEVA GAY**

The most popularly understood meaning of educational equality in the United States is the access of Blacks, Hispanics, Asians, and Indians to the same schools and instructional programs as middle-class Anglo students. The prevailing assumption is that when ethnic minorities become students in majority schools, equal educational opportunity is achieved. Little attention is given to the quality of the content and processes of schooling itself. The possibility that what happens within schools might not be equal or comparable in quality for all students tends to be overlooked.

For those who accept this conception of educational equality, the issue of inequality is largely resolved. After all, they argue, federal and state laws now exist prohibiting educational discrimination on the basis of race, color, creed, gender, nationality, and social class. For these people, the persisting discrepancies between the academic achievement, quality of school life, and other indicators of school success for ethnic minority and majority students are not a result of differences in educational opportunities at all. Rather, these problems are matters of personal and individual abilities. Poor students and ethnic minorities do not do as well in school as their middle-class, Anglo counterparts because of individual deficiencies, not because of some disparities in the experiences and opportunities available to them in schools. Black, Hispanic, and Indian youths drop out and experience school failure at a higher rate because of their own personality traits and family backgrounds, not because aspects within the schooling process function systematically to their detriment.

In addition to being overly simplistic, these notions of what educational equality means for ethnic minorities are culturally chauvinistic. They assume that the education White students are receiving is universally desirable, and that the only way for minority youths to get a comparable education is to imitate Whites. Given the great diversity in quality of the teachers, facilities, resources, and instruction that exists in U.S. schools, including predominantly White ones, these conceptions are inadequate. Any viable definitions of and approaches to educational equality must take into consideration the quality of the opportunities, not merely the presence or absence of opportunity. Legal mandates guaranteeing the accessibility of schooling to all students do not ensure quality unless the opportunities themselves are of equal quality.[1] And under no circumstances can identical educational opportunities for very diverse groups and individuals (whether that diversity stems from class, gender, race, ethnicity, nationality, or personal traits) constitute equality.

Ideas that equate sameness of opportunity and open access to all schools for all students with educational equality ignore some of the more fundamental issues of equality of opportunity and access to the processes of schooling. How can *equality* be understood to mean equity and comparability of treatment based on diagnosed needs as opposed to the misconception of sameness of treatment for all students? What elements of the process of schooling should be considered in a more comprehensive and realistic approach to achieving educational equality for ethnic minority students? In other words, how can we assure that the quality of provision and substance of educational experiences available to ethnic minority youths receive priority over mere access measures of educational equality? Or, as Grant and Sleeter might ask, what happens "after the school bell rings"[2] for ethnic minorities in U.S. schools? These issues are explored in this chapter.

Current Educational Status of Ethnic Minorities

Contrary to the misconceptions of some people, legal access of ethnic minorities to all schools was the mere beginning, not the end, of the resolution of educational inequality. The issue prevails at crisis levels today. In its 1983 report, *Equality and Excellence: the Educational Status of Black Americans,* the College Entrance Examination Board concluded that "although many of the legal barriers to educational opportunity have been removed, education—to a large extent—remains separate and unequal in the United States."[3] This inequality becomes clearer when we analyze the current educational status of ethnic minorities, especially Blacks, Mexican-Americans, Puerto Ricans, and American Indians, and the pervasiveness of the problems these groups encounter in schools. The situation is not quite as serious for Asian Americans, at least on some standardized test measures of school achievements, school attendance, and graduation records.

Unquestionably, some progress has been made in the last twenty years in the social conditions of schooling for and academic achievement of ethnic minorities. During the 1970s through the early 1980s we also saw:

■ The number of high school graduates for all ethnic minority groups increase dramatically.

■ The gap between standardized test scores in reading and mathematics for Hispanics, Blacks, and Whites narrow somewhat. This was a result of the greater relative gains minorities made in academic achievement compared to Whites.

■ The Bilingual Education Act, the Indian Education Act, and Title IX improve educational opportunities for millions of non-English speakers, Indians, and females, respectively.

- The Education for All Handicapped Children Act (PL 94-142), which allows many disabled children to be educated in regular classes.[4]
- The creation of a variety of pullout programs for special needs instruction to help students in basic skills and to aid in the development of the gifted and talented.

During the 1980s, many of these beginnings toward equalizing access to educational resources were minimized by an unsympathetic national administration and a general social climate of conservatism toward social service programs. For instance:

- The cutting of more than 750,000 children from Chapter 1 programs (federal educational assistance for economically deprived children).
- Relaxation of requirements for schools receiving federal funds to comply with antidiscrimination laws.
- New funding arrangements that benefit rural and private schools at the expense of urban and inner-city schools.
- Drastic cuts in bilingual, migrant, Indian, and women's equity educational funding and programs.[5]
- Steady decline during the last ten years in minority college attendance and completion at both the undergraduate and graduate levels.

Other serious problems that negatively affect minority students' educational opportunities and testify to the persistence of educational inequality prevail. Most elementary and secondary schools in the United States continue to be racially segregated. Racial minorities now constitute the majority student population in twenty-three of the nation's twenty-five largest school districts, and that ratio is increasing yearly. In many of these school systems, the minority enrollment exceeds 75 percent. In 1980, 6.8 percent of all Hispanic children attended schools in which 50 percent or more of the total student enrollment was minority, and one-fourth were enrolled in schools with a minority population of 90 to 100 percent.[6]

Yet, the ethnicity of teachers, administrators, and policymakers in these districts is the reverse. Whites far outnumber minorities in all school leadership and instructional positions. In fact, the numbers of ethnic minority teachers and school administrators have been steadily declining in the last fifteen years. The percentage of Black teachers declined from 12 percent in 1970 to 8 percent in 1986 and is projected to be as low as 5 percent in 1990. In 1980, Hispanics represented only 2.6 percent of all the elementary and 1.7 percent of the secondary teachers in the United States.[7] Traditionally, urban schools have had less money, fewer resources and poorer facilities, larger numbers of inexperienced teachers, greater management problems, and higher turnover rates among teachers, administrators, and students (see Chapter 4). Moreover, few systematic and sustained high-quality teacher and leadership training programs exist to prepare educators to work effectively with urban ethnic minorities.

Although the levels of educational attainment of ethnic minorities, as measured by median years of schooling completed, high school graduation, and daily attendance records, are increasing for successive generations, the dropout rates continue to be a major problem. The median years of schooling completed by Blacks increased from 8.0 years in 1970 to 12.0 in 1985. For Whites in the same period, the medians were 10.9 and 12.5, respectively. By 1985 the median years of schooling completed for Hispanics had reached 10.8. The dropout rate for Blacks declined between 1971 and 1981, from 26 to 18 percent, compared to 15 and 12 percent for Whites. Yet the overall average dropout rate for Blacks in 1985 (12.6 percent) was still higher than the national average (10.6 percent), and for Whites (10.3 percent).[8]

The situation is even worse for Hispanics. In 1978, Hispanics between the ages of fourteen and nineteen were more than twice as likely as Whites to drop out of school, and nearly 40 percent of those between the ages of eighteen and twenty-four were dropouts compared to 14 percent of a comparable White population. A 1986 California State University System Advisory Council on Educational Equity reported that Hispanics have the highest dropout rate of all ethnic groups in California. Some school districts indicated that as many as 40 percent of Hispanic students left school before grade 10. Nationwide, approximately 50 percent of Mexican-Americans and Puerto Ricans drop out of high school before graduation. In some urban school districts, such as Chicago and New York, the Puerto Rican high school dropout rates exceed 70 percent.[9]

Another school attendance factor that helps explain educational inequality for ethnic minority students is *school delay*. Defined by Nielsen as "the discrepancy between the educational level reached by students and the normal level corresponding to their age,"[10] school delay rates are substantially greater for Blacks, Hispanics, and Indians than for Whites. These groups repeat grades more often and generally take longer to complete school. This situation is more serious than it might first appear. It may initiate a cumulative process that ultimately results in the child's leaving school completely. Delayed students are likely to be judged academically inadequate and assigned to special category, low academic, or vocational-track curricula. As these students fall behind their age group, they become stigmatized as slow learners and socially isolated in schools, and teachers tend to have low expectations of achievement for delayed students.

Dropout rates for American Indians, Native Alaskans, and Asian Americans are not reported as systematically as for Blacks and Hispanics. But, given the general educational status of American Indians on other measures of school success that indicate that their situation is even worse than that for Blacks and Hispanics, we can assume that the dropout rates for American Indians are as high or higher. The 1980 Bureau of Census data indicate that Asian American students' school enrollment and attendance are at parity with that of Anglo-Americans. At all age levels the percentages of Asian Americans enrolled in schools and colleges exceed those of Anglo-Americans (see Table 9.1).[11] Although the magnitude of the high school dropout problem is far less for Asian Americans than for other racial minority groups, the gender pattern is similar. More Asian males leave school prior to graduation than do females.[12]

Even for minority students who remain in school and attend racially mixed schools, the likelihood of the greater number of them receiving educational equality is dubious. The academic achievement levels of all ethnic minority groups, except Asian Americans, is significantly lower than for Whites. These differences exist on all measures for every age group at all levels of schooling, in every region of the country, and at every socioeconomic level.[13] Despite reports by the National Assessment of Educational Progress (NAEP), the College Board,

TABLE 9.1
Percentage of Persons Enrolled in School by Age for Selected Ethnic Groups in the United States (1980)

	Whites	Chinese	Japanese	Koreans	Vietnamese
Five- and Six-Year-Olds	86.1	91.4	94.6	88.4	—
Sixteen- and Seventeen-Year Olds	89.0	96.0	96.2	94.9	90.2

1980 Census of Population, Volume 1, *Characteristics of the Population,* Chapter C, *"Social and Economic Characteristics,* Part I, *United States Summary,* Report Number PC–80–1–C1 (Washington, D.C.: Bureau of the Census, U.S. Department of Commerce, December, 1983).

and the National Center for Educational Statistics indicating that the reading and mathematics test performance of Blacks and Hispanics improved during the 1970s, their average achievement levels continue to be lower than those of Whites.

On closer inspection, these improvements are not as positive as we might hope, for several reasons. First, the overall performance of all students on standardized tests declined in the 1980s compared to the 1970s. For example, the national averages on SAT scores dropped from 937 in 1972 to 893 in 1985. A 1987 study, based on a nationwide survey of 7,812 high school juniors, funded by the National Endowment for the Humanities and conducted by the National Assessment of Educational Progress, gave failing marks to the nation's seventeen-year-olds in literature and history. More than two-thirds of the students were unable to locate the Civil War within the correct half century, or to identify the Reformation and the *Magna Carta.* The vast majority were unfamiliar with such classic writers as Dante, Chaucer, Dostoevsky, Whitman, and Hawthorne. Even students who performed adequately did not display exemplary performance levels.[14]

Second, the performance patterns across all the subscales of standardized tests are not the same across and within ethnic groups. A case in point is Asian Americans. Often considered the model minority, Asian Americans are commonly considered high achievers who perform well in all aspects of schooling and on all measures of achievement. This positive stereotype overlooks the immense diversity of the Asian-American subgroups, the serious language and adjustment problems that recent Southeast Asian refugees and new immigrants encounter, the disparity between educational attainment and income, and the special educational needs of individual Asian students.

When school performance, income, and employment data are analyzed carefully, a bimodal pattern of achievement for Asian Americans emerges. It suggests that Asian-American students are more likely than other students to enroll in college preparatory programs, to maintain heavier high school course loads, to take more foreign languages and more high-level mathematics and science, to spend more time on homework, and to have higher educational aspirations. Although Japanese, Chinese, Filipino, and Korean Americans equal or surpass White Americans in median number of school years completed, they also have a higher percentage of adult population with less than five years of education. They hold more professional and technical jobs than Anglos, and more low-paying jobs. A larger proportion of Asian Americans have four or more years of college, yet they earn less money and experience higher rates of education-occupation mismatches than do Whites. Some Asian-American students (principally Japanese and Chinese) are high achievers on some aspects of standardized school achievement (science and math), and others (recent immigrants and refugees) are low achievers. Although nationwide the median SAT math scores of Asian-American students exceed those of White students by more than 54 points, their median verbal scores are more than 100 points lower. As family income levels increase, these differences decrease, but the White advantage never disappears. Furthermore, high academic achieving Asian-American students are not necessarily socially and emotionally well adjusted. For instance, they do not feel as positive about their physical features and stature as do their White peers. Other psychological problems they may experience include stress associated with pressure for high performance, learning to cope with failure, the perceptions and expectations teachers have for students they consider model minorities, and ethnic identity[15] conflict.

Third, the improvement pattern on standardized tests is not consistent for all age groups of Blacks and Hispanics. NAEP reports achievement data for nine-, thirteen-, and seventeen-year-olds. The most recent NAEP test scores showed higher increases in math and reading for younger Blacks than for older Blacks. Nine-year-olds increased their average percentage of correct reading responses by ten points compared to a three-point gain for Whites, and Black thirteen-year-olds improved by four percentage points compared to no increase for Whites. The reading scores of Black seventeen-year-olds increased by 0.5 percent, and the scores of their White counterparts declined by 0.7 percent.

Mathematics test scores between 1977 and 1982 showed an increase of 2 percentage points for nine-year-old Blacks and 1 point for Hispanics compared to a 0.7 percent increase for Whites. Test scores for Black and Hispanic thirteen-year-olds each increased by 6.5 points, but only 3.2 for Whites. As with reading, the math performance of seventeen-year-olds was less encouraging. Blacks increased by 1.3 points from 1977 to 1982, and Hispanics by 0.9 points. The math achievement of White seventeen-year-olds over the same period remained stable. Blacks in all three age groups performed better in areas of mathematical knowledge (recalling and recognizing facts) than in areas of mathematical skills (performing computations and manipulations) and applications (reasoning and problem solving). Science achievement showed a decline for all students across all ethnic and age groups.[16]

In its 1986 *Writing Report Card* NAEP reported that writing achievement correlates highly with reading achievement. Better readers also are better writers. In all grades (4, 8, and 11), Blacks and Hispanics and students from disadvantaged urban communities performed at a substantially lower level than did Whites, Asians and advantaged urban students on all writing skills assessed (informative, persuasive, and imaginative). On all measures, Whites and Asians performed identically at grades 4 and 8, but Whites were slightly higher than Asians at grade 11. Writing achievement for Hispanics was slightly higher than for Blacks at grades 4 and 8, but the performance of the two groups was identical at grade 11. Black and Hispanic eleventh-grade writing achievement was lower than that of White and Asian eighth-graders. All students in all ethnic groups and grade levels were deficient in higher-order thinking skills, as evidenced by difficulty in performing adequately on analytical and persuasive writing tasks.[17] No data were reported for American Indians.

These test scores present mixed messages. It is encouraging to see younger minority students making recognizable gains in reading and mathematics achievement, but it is disheartening that this pattern is not true for older students. How can we explain these mixed results? One possible explanation is that teachers and instructional programs are beginning to be more responsive to the educational needs and learning styles of ethnic minorities, and this responsiveness is having effects on students outcomes. Given what we know about patterns of school failure for minority students, a more plausible explanation is that the cumulative negative effects of schooling for these students are not yet fully in force for nine-year-olds. It is in about fourth grade (age nine or ten) that school failure for minority students crystallizes. From that point on, the longer Black, Hispanic, and American Indian youths stay in school, the further they fall behind academically. The decreasing levels of recent improvement on NAEP standardized tests for thirteen- and seventeen-year-olds may be a substantiation of this failure pattern.

Another explanation is that standardized achievement test scores, despite their frequent use, are not valid measures of educational equality. Measures of educational equality need to concentrate more on multidimensional inputs into the schooling process, such as curriculum content and substance, and the quality of classroom instructional interactions. Although recent improvements by ethnic minorities on standardized tests show that they are making some gains on low-level cognitive skills, such as decoding, computation, factual recognition, and recall, they are not developing high-level skills, such as making inferences, critical thinking, analyzing and synthesizing information, logical reasoning, and creative expression. These findings may be a direct result of the curriculum differentiations that exist for ethnic minority and Anglo students in elementary and secondary schools.

An unequal curriculum and instruction system exists in U.S. schools—the substance of education, access to knowledge, classroom climates, and the quality of instructional interactions are qualitatively different for ethnic minority and Anglo students. In its *Mexican-American Education Study,* conducted between 1971 and 1974, the U.S. Civil Rights Commission attributed quality and equality of educational experiences to the opportunities different students receive to participate in classroom interactions with teachers. It found that Mexican Americans were not receiving as many opportunities as Whites to participate in classroom interactions, as evidenced by fewer and lower-level questions asked of them, the time allowed to give responses, and the praise and encouragement teachers gave for students' efforts.

In 1974, Gay's similar findings for Black students' interactions with both Black and White teachers led her to conclude that minority and White teachers act more alike than differently in their classroom treatment of students. All teachers tend to give preferential treatment and more quality opportunities to participate in the substance of instruction to Anglo students. These patterns of interactional and instructional inequalities between ethnic minority and Anglo students have not changed significantly in the years since these studies were conducted.[18]

Minority students are disproportionally enrolled in special-education programs, vocational courses, and low-track classes and are underrepresented in high-track and college preparatory programs (see Chapter 15). Furthermore, the placement of ethnic minorities in vocational courses occurs earlier, and the programs differ substantially in kind and content from those for Whites. Minority students are assigned to vocational programs that train specifically for low-status occupations (e.g., cosmetology, mill and cabinet shop, building maintenance, television repair, retail sales, clerical jobs). By comparison, White students enroll more often in vocational courses that offer managerial training, business finance, and general industrial arts skills. To receive their training, minority youths must leave the school campus more often than Whites, thus isolating them from many of the social activities of the school.[19]

The enrollment of ethnic minority students in academic programs also indicates unequal distributions. Minorities are highly underrepresented in college preparatory and in gifted and talented programs. In its 1985 report on the educational status of Black Americans, the College Entrance Examination Board found that most Black seniors in 1981 had taken fewer years of coursework in mathematics, physical sciences, and social studies than had Whites. Even in subjects in which the years of coursework are similar, the content of the courses differs substantially for Blacks and Whites. Although college-bound Black seniors in 1980 were as likely as Whites to have taken three or more years of mathematics, they were less likely to have taken algebra, geometry, trigonometry, and calculus and were more likely to have taken general and business math. Furthermore, students in low-income and predominantly minority schools have less access to microcomputers, have fewer qualified teachers trained in the use of computers, and tend to use microcomputers more for drill and practice in basic skills than for conceptual knowledge or programming instruction.[20]

The routinely used system of tracking to organize students for instruction is probably the most effective means of denying educational equality to ethnic minority students (see Chapter 4). In general, tracking differentiates access to knowledge, content and quality of instruction, expectations of teachers, and classroom climates for learning between upper and lower tracks. The studies of school tracking conducted by Oakes, Goodlad, Rosenbaum, Morgan, and others present convincing and devastating proof of the extent to which this practice perpetuates educational inequities along race, ethnic, and socioeconomic lines. For example:

■ In low-track classes a greater share of instructional time than in high tracks is devoted to developing compliance-type social behaviors and attitudes, classroom management and discipline, and generally dull, unimaginative teaching strategies. High-track and college preparatory students have better teachers, materials and laboratory equipment, field trips and classroom visitors, information about educational and occupational consequences, validations of personal worth, and self-direction.

■ The quality of knowledge students receive is differentiated by tracks. For example, high-track students get math concepts, low tracks get computational exercises.

■ The fostering of lower self-esteem and lower educational aspirations for low-track students.

■ Differences in the intellectual processes and cognitive levels of learning tasks. High-track students do activities that demand critical thinking, problem solving, making generalizations, drawing inferences, and synthesizing knowledge. Instruction in low-track classes focuses on memory and comprehension tasks.

■ Denial of opportunity for low-track students to learn content and materials that are essential for mobility among tracks.

■ High-track students are exposed to high-value social and academic knowledge—knowledge that permits access to advanced education, upper-level social and economic positions, and leadership roles. Low-track students are exposed to knowledge that is of low status and does not permit special access, and to social skills such as following directions, good work habits, punctuality, compliance to authority, and rules of social decorum.

■ In high-track classes, greater portions of the time allocated for instruction are actually used to engage students in learning tasks.

■ Differences in classroom relationships among students and types of involvement exist between low- and high-track classes. For example, stronger feelings of friendliness, cooperation, involvement, trust and goodwill, and positiveness exist in high tracks than in low tracks.

■ Students enrolled in general track and heterogeneously grouped classes are treated more like those in high and academic tracks than are those in homogeneously grouped low-track and vocational courses.[21]

Blacks, Hispanics, and American Indians are overrepresented in lower-track curriculum programs. Because low-track students do not experience comparable curriculum content, instructional practices, classroom climates, and classroom interactions and relationships as do general (average) and high-track students, these ethnic groups are consistently and systematically denied equal access to the substance of quality education. *In effect, tracking is a process for the legitimation of the social inequalities that exist in the larger society.* It serves the instrumental functions of social selection, creating castes among students, and closing off paths for personal advancement for students in the lower levels.[22] Through this practice, students learn to accept the unequal patterns of social and political participation in society and all its institutions as the natural order of things.

Ethnic minority students' underenrollment in high-track and academic programs exists at every educational attainment level—high school completion, baccalaureate degrees, and graduate degrees. The higher the level of education, the greater is the degree of underrepresentation. Although minority college enrollments increased between 1972 and 1980, they are now declining, and the attrition rates continue to be substantially greater than for Anglos. Minorities also are underrepresented in all fields of college study, except the social sciences and education. The greatest minority underrepresentation is in the areas of engineering, biological sciences, and physical sciences. However, in 1975–1976 and in 1980–1981, there was an increase in the math and science-related degrees granted to minorities and women.[23]

In the final analysis, it is the kinds of access ethnic minority students have to the content and substance of education, and the interactions between students and teachers in individual schools and classrooms that define educational quality and equality, not with whom the students attend school. These processes are what ultimately determine which students are educated for self-determination and social empowerment and which ones are trained for a life of dependency in the economic and social underclass.[24] The current educational status of America's ethnic minorities suggests that too many of them are being trained for the underclass.

Why Educational Inequality Exists for Ethnic Minorities

Wherever ethnic minorities attend school, whether in predominantly minority or racially mixed settings, in urban or suburban environments, in poor or middle-class communities, in the northern, eastern, southern, or western United States, issues of educational inequality prevail. These issues concern access to excellence and equity of educational opportunities and experiences, with the focus of access being the substance of the educational process. The pivotal question is how to make the total educational enterprise more responsive to the histories, heritages, life experiences, and cultural conditioning of ethnic minorities in all of its policy-making, program-planning, and instructional practices.

The quality of the various resources used in the educational process has a direct effect on the level and quality of student achievement. When different groups of students are exposed to qualitatively different resources, their achievements also differ. In the debate on educational equality, a crucial question is whether the resources used in teaching ethnic minority students are comparable to those used with Whites on measures of accuracy, technical quality, relevance, and appropriateness. These resources include facilities, personnel, financing, instructional materials and programs, and environmental settings.

The relative value of instructional resources cannot be determined independently of environmental context, intended users, and expected outcomes. School resources are preferentially allocated to high-track and academic programs and to middle-class, Anglo students. Even when ethnic minority students receive the same educational resources as Anglo students, the effects are not identical. Although they may benefit and facilitate Anglo development they can block or retard the development of ethnic minorities. How is this possible?

We have seen how the overrepresentation of ethnic minorities in low-track programs, vocational courses, and special-education classes minimizes their educational opportunities in several ways. One way is how school systems and personnel generally perceive and treat these program options relative to expected performance and resource allocations. They receive fewer laboratory facilities, fewer out-of-classroom learning experiences, lesser qualified teachers, and less commitment, concern, and effort from teachers.

But not all ethnic minorities are enrolled in these programs. Most are enrolled in regular classrooms and programs across a wide spectrum of curriculum options, including general education, academic, and college preparatory courses. If educational resources are allocated by programs and if these programs receive the best, how is it possible to claim that the ethnic minority students enrolled in them are being denied comparable access to quality resources? Several ways are possible. First, the sameness of educational resources for diverse individuals and groups does not constitute comparability of quality or opportunity. Teachers, materials, and teaching environments that work well for Anglo students do not necessarily work equally well for ethnic minorities. To believe that they do is to assume that Black, Hispanic, American Indian, Asian American, and Anglo students are identical in personal, social, cultural, historical, and family traits.

Second, most graduates of typical teacher-education programs know little about the cultural traits, behaviors, values, and attitudes different ethnic minority groups bring to the classroom, and how they affect the ways these students act and react to instructional situations. They do not know how to understand and use the school behaviors of these students, which differ from their normative expectations, as aides to teaching. Therefore, they tend to misinterpret them as deviant and treat them punitively. Because teachers' cultural backgrounds and value orientations are highly compatible with middle-class and Anglo-American culture, they can use these cultural connections to facilitate learning for Anglo students.

Third, like teacher training, most curriculum designs and instructional materials are Eurocentric. As such they reflect middle-class, Anglo experiences, perspectives, and value priorities. They are likely to be more readily meaningful and to have a greater appeal to the life experiences and aspirations of Anglo students than to ethnic minorities. Thus, when attempting to learn academic tasks, Anglo students may not have the additional burden of working across irrelevant instructional materials and methods. More of their efforts and energies can be directed toward mastering the substance of teaching. Ethnic minority students are often placed in double jeopardy. That is, they must divide their energies and efforts between coping with curriculum materials and instructional methods that are not culturally relevant to their learning styles or reflective of their life experiences and also to mastering the academic knowledge and tasks being taught. Because this division of efforts dissipates their concentration on learning tasks, they do not receive the quality educational opportunities to learn the substance of teaching that Anglo students do.

Fourth, the school environments in which students live and learn are not comparable for Anglo and ethnic students. When students and teachers arrive at school they do not leave their cultural backgrounds at home. This is not a problem for most Anglo students, since school culture and rules of behavior are reflections and extensions of their home cultures. A high degree of cultural congruency exists between middle-class Anglo student culture and school culture. These students do not experience much cultural discontinuity, social-code incompatibility, or need for cultural style shifting to adjust to the behavioral codes expected of them in school. The converse is true for ethnic minority students. Many of the social codes for succeeding in school are unfamiliar to them or are diametrically opposed to the codes they have learned in their home cultures. When learning situations do not reflect the cultures of the students, gaps exist "between the *contexts of learning* and *the contexts of performing*."[25] These gaps are greatest for students from ethnic-group cultures and communities that are not part of the mainstream culture. Many of the inequities that exist between the educational opportunities of Anglo and ethnic minority students are situated in these contextual incompatibilities.

Most educators do not teach ethnic minority students how to survive and succeed in school, for example, how to study across ethnic learning styles, how to adjust talking styles to accommodate school expectations, how to interact appropriately with school administrators and classroom teachers, and how to identify and adjust to the procedural rules for functioning in different instructional classrooms. Educators operate on the assumption that school codes of behavior are common knowledge acquired from living in the broader culture that surrounds schools. What most educators forget is that many ethnic minorities live only marginally in mainstream culture and that they do not have a heritage and tradition of success in predominantly White schools.

The effect of these differences in socialization of Anglo and ethnic minority students in how to survive in school is another example of the differential use of personal energies and efforts. Minority students have to learn how to survive in school while simultaneously learning what is taught. When they fail to master the social codes, they never get a chance to try the academic tasks, because mastery of the social protocols of schooling is a prerequisite to learning itself.

The school failure of ethnic minorities because of their inability to master social codes of behavior is much more frequent than for Whites. In-class success for minorities also is measured by social skill mastery more often than for Anglos. Teachers evaluate minority students more on criteria such as "he is a nice boy," "she is cooperative," "I feel sorry for these students," and "their work is very neat." Anglo students' performance is assessed more on academic criteria ("he studies hard," "she is an overachiever," "they are very attentive in class," "she asks provocative questions"). Inequalities exist in these situations because the bases for determining school success and failure for Anglo and ethnic minority students are frequently not similar. For the former, reasons for failing tend to be academic incompetence; for the latter they are often social incompetence.

Closely related to the issue of comparable quality resources is the role of teacher attitudes, expectations, and competencies in perpetuating educational inequality for ethnic minorities. The essence of this issue is, How can teachers who have grown up in ethnically isolated communities and in a racist society teach ethnic minorities as well as they can Anglos? This question is crucial in equations of educational equality, especially when most teachers are racially White, culturally Eurocentric, middle class, and trained in White, Eurocentric colleges and universities to teach White, Eurocentric students.

Most teachers know little about different ethnic groups' life-styles or learning habits and preferences. They tend to be insecure and uncertain about working with Black, Hispanic, Asian, and American-Indian students and to have low expectations of achievement for these students. Too many teachers still believe that minority students either are culturally deprived and should be remediated by using middle-class Whites as the appropriate norm or do not have the capacity to learn as well as Anglos. "Teachers form expectations about children based directly upon race and social class, . . . pupil test scores, appearance, language style, speed of task performance, and behavior characteristics which are culturally defined. Moreover, teacher expectations are more influenced by *negative* information about pupil characteristics than positive data."[26] Teachers transmit these attitudes and expectations in everything they say and do in the classroom. Ethnic minority students' responses to these expectations become self-fulfilling prophesis. They come to believe that they are destined to fail, and they act accordingly. Anglo students internalize the high expectations teachers have of them and accordingly believe they are destined to succeed.

Educators tend to discriminate their school behaviors according to their performance expectations of different students. For example, teachers who do not have high academic expectations for ethnic minority students ask them low-level memory, recall, and convergent questions, do not praise or encourage them as often as Anglos, use lower standards for judging the quality of their work, and do not call on them as frequently. Guidance counselors who do not believe minority students can master high-level math and science skills do not schedule them into these classes. School administrators who expect greater discipline problems from ethnic minorities tend to treat their rule infractions with harsher punishment. In general, low expectations of educators cause them to feed Blacks, Hispanics, and American Indians academic pablum. They then wonder why these students do not do well on standardized measures of school achievement.

Special-purpose instruction for minorities tends to be remediation; for Anglos, it tends to be enrichment. Minority students for whom educators have low expectations are suspected of dishonesty and cheating when they defy these expectations by performing well. When they live down to these expectations, their teachers make comments such as "What else can you expect?" Presumed high-achieving Anglo students who do not live up to expectations are described as underachievers, and low-performing Anglos who exceed expectation are called overachievers. These attitudes and expectations cause wide disparities in how educators interact with Anglo and minority students in the day-to-day operations of schools and thereby perpetuate educational inequalities among them.

The educational inequities in school resources, teacher attitudes, and classroom interactions are reinforced further by culturally biased tests and procedures used to diagnose students' needs and to evaluate their performance. Whether standardized achievement measures, minimum-competency tests, teacher-made tests, classroom observations, or even criterion-referenced tests, most assessment approaches currently used discriminate against ethnic minorities in content, standardization norms, and administration procedures. By their nature they contribute to the social stratification of students. Because they are designed and used to discriminate differences among and to rank students according to competence, even the most content bias–free tests—especially norm-referenced ones—are tools for sorting students into unequal categories.[27]

Schools prize verbal learning and written demonstrations of achievement. These styles of demonstrating achievement are consistent with mainstream American and Anglo students' cultures, but they are contrary to the performance styles of many ethnic minority groups. For Black Americans, whose cultural socialization emphasizes aural, verbal, and participatory learning, and for American Indians who are accustomed to imitative learning in their home cultures, it is difficult to transform what they know from one performance style to another. When they have to demonstrate their achievement on written tests, the format may be more of a problem for them than are the content and substance of the learning tasks. While they are struggling to translate their knowledge and skill mastery into an unfamiliar expressive style, Anglo students are busy demonstrating their knowledge of the content. These differences in performance starting points mean that ethnic minority students are at a disadvantage from the beginning of formal schooling. Not understanding the problems they are having with performance formats and styles, teachers conclude that their failure is due totally to their failure to master the instructional content and substance. The effects of these misdiagnoses and misevaluations become cumulatively greater for ethnic minority students as they advance in school. Until they receive starting points comparable to those of Anglo students in terms of diagnosis, and until evaluation assessments tools and techniques are more compatible with their cultural and learning styles, inequities in educational opportunities will continue to exist for Blacks, Hispanics, and American Indians.

A similar argument holds for the content and substance of student evaluations. All achievement tests are designed to determine what students know. Presumably they reflect what is taught in schools. This is a reasonable expectation, and there would be no issue of ethnic inequality if schools taught equally relevant curricula equally well to all students. But they do not. Although progress has been made in the last two decades to make school curricula more inclusive of ethnic and cultural diversity, most of the knowledge content taught, and consequently achievement tests, continue to be Eurocentric. Even skill mastery is transmitted through Eurocentric contexts. For instance, achievement tests may embed skills in scenarios about situations that are not relevant to the cultural backgrounds and life experiences of ethnic minorities. These students then have to decipher the contexts in order to extrapolate the skill content. Minority students may know the skill but may be unfamiliar with the contextual scenario. This limitation interferes with the effective demonstration of their knowledge of the skill. Most Anglo students do not have this problem. Both the context and the performance format are familiar to them, and if they know the skill, they have no problem demonstrating their mastery. Thus, ethnic minority students are placed at an unfair disadvantage, and their overall performance on achievement measures reflects this disadvantage.

This is not to say that minority students should not take achievement tests, that their school performance should not be evaluated, or that high levels of achievement should not be expected of them. Rather, it is to suggest that to avoid perpetuating educational inequality through assessment procedures, a wide variety of measures should be used so that no single one that is highly advantageous to one ethnic group over another is used consistently. It is also to suggest that the substance of education, including curriculum, teaching, and testing, should be revised to incorporate more fully the contributions and experiences of the full range of ethnic groups in the United States.

Achieving Educational Equality

The College Entrance Examination Board concluded its report on *Equality and Excellence* with the observation that "excellence for Black students will not become a reality until they receive enriched curricular opportunities in elementary and secondary schools, sufficient financial assistance to pursue higher education opportunities, and instruction from well-qualified teachers."[28] John-Steiner and Leacock state that "when the background of the teacher differs greatly from that of the children she works with, a setting results which is alien and tension-producing for the teacher or the student or both."[29]

To this observation we can add that alien and tension-filled environments substantially reduce the potential for educational equality for students who live and function in them. This is too often the fate of ethnic minorities in U.S. schools. Casso argues that "it is the educational system which needs to be changed and restructured rather than the Mexican-American child . . . lest it keep compounding the crime of attempting to remold every brown child into a cog for the white middle class machine."[30] Fantini proposes that efforts to bring about equality focus on providing equal access to quality education. This can be achieved through institutional reform aimed at creating school structures that respond positively to human diversity and through developing a policy of quality that views learners as educational consumers with some fundamental rights.[31] Two of these rights are educational equality and excellence.

Implicit in these suggestions and the issues of inequality discussed earlier in this chapter is that educational equality for ethnic minority students cannot be achieved without massive schoolwide, institutional reform. The reform efforts should begin with a redefinition of *equality* as equal access to the best-quality substance of schooling for all students. Quality should be determined by the degree to which learning experiences engage minority students' interest and involvement and empower them with personal development. Defining equality as access shifts attention away from evaluating quality and equality primarily in terms of dollar inputs, teacher certifications, test scores, and locations of school attendance to the intrinsic dynamics of the learning process itself. In operational terms, this redefinition of educational equality means affirming that problems or shortcomings in learning are located not so much in shortcomings in ethnic minority students as in inequalities in the schools they attend. It also means refocusing schools toward being more responsive to human variability, spending less time manipulating ethnic students to make them comply to institutional structures, and instituting programs and processes that empower students through access to high-quality knowledge and experiences.[32] This will be a significant departure from most current notions of equality as access to uniform school resources.

Such a concept of educational equality requires reform in all aspects of the schooling enterprise, including teacher training, curriculum design, classroom instruction, grouping of students for instruction, the climates in which students learn, and how students' needs are diagnosed and their achievement assessed. All of these issues cannot be discussed in detail here. Because of the crucial role teachers play in determining the quality of learning opportunities students receive in classrooms, more attention is given to teacher training.

All forms of tracking should be eliminated entirely. Even under the best of circumstances, tracking denies equal educational opportunities to minority students and others who populate the lower levels. It closes rather than opens paths to social and academic advancement and commits some students early to an educational underclass. Tracking should be replaced with flexible and frequently changed groupings of students for specific instructional tasks or skill development purposes only. For example, students grouped together to learn geographical directions should remain together only until that skill is mastered.

All forms of norm-referenced tests for evaluating student achievement also should be eliminated. Instead, students should be evaluated against their own records, with range of improvement between different points of reference being the focus of attention, as opposed to performance at isolated points in time. This means that schools should use multiple techniques and procedures, including academic, social, psychological and emotional measures, as well as verbal, visual, observational, participatory, and kinetic means to assess students' school performance. These approaches should always serve diagnostic and developmental functions. That is, they should be used to determine how and why students are proceeding with specific learning tasks. They should be administered frequently, and instructional programming should be changed according to the results obtained. Thus, ethnic minority students should be put on self-referenced and self-paced programs to complete their schooling. Narrative reports, developmental profiles, student-teacher-parent conferences, and anecdotal records should replace letter and symbol grades for reporting student progress.

School curricula, too, must be reformed if equal educational opportunities are to be assured for all students. However, the emphases of the various commission studies and proposals for greater curriculum quantity as the measure of quality is not the answer. More of the same irrelevant school subjects will not improve the quality of schooling for any students, especially ethnic minorities. This more-of-the-same approach to quality increases the likelihood of school failure and educational inequality by broadening the gap between the kinds of learning opportunities minority and low-achieving students receive compared to Anglo and high-achieving students. If minority students are already failing science, taking more of it means they will have even greater opportunities to fail. If low-track students are already taking substantially different kinds of mathematics courses than high-track students, then the gap in the substantive content they are learning widens as the high-track students take even more advanced courses, and the low-track students take even more remedial math courses.

What schools consider to be essential knowledge and skills for all students to learn and how these are understood and taught—that is, the canons of American education—need to be revised. These revisions should reflect the comprehensive realities of U.S. society and the world, not just the technological and economic sides of life in the United States. This means, first, that school curricula should demonstrate and emulate the interdisciplinary nature of human knowledge, values, and skills. Second, they should teach and model the interdependence of the world, a world in which Whites are a small numerical minority and in which the control of natural resources and social aspirations is gradually shifting from Western to non-Western, non-White nations. Third, a concerted effort should be made to achieve a greater balance between technological developments and humanistic concerns. These curricular reform emphases increase the possibility that the experiences, cultures, and contributions of ethnic minority groups in the United States will be included across the various subject matter content areas; that ethnic minority students will identify with and relate better to the substance of school curricula; that they will have a greater sense of ownership in the schooling enterprise; and that Blacks, Asians, Hispanics, and American Indians will have opportunities comparable to those of Anglo students to establish personally enabling connections with schools and thereby improve their overall academic achievement.

Because teachers play such a central role in the kinds of educational opportunities minority students receive in classrooms, their reeducation and training are fundamental to providing educational equality. This training should have four primary emphases. The first is self-knowledge. Teachers, counselors, and administrators need to become familiar with the attitudes and behaviors they have toward different ethnic groups and with how these are habitually exhibited in their school functions. They also need to understand the effects of these on students, relative to self-concepts, academic abilities, and educational opportunities available to students.

Merely telling teachers about the existence and effects of negative attitudes and low expectations on ethnic minority students' chances for educational equality will not suffice. Nor will reading the impressive body of research that documents these effects. These approaches seem too much like personal indictments and tend to cause teachers to become defensive and alienated. Teachers need to be shown how they behave toward minority students. This can be done by projecting mirror images of or replaying their classroom behaviors back to them, training teachers how to be participant observers of their own classroom dynamics and how to use different techniques to systematically analyze their instructional behaviors. Audio- and videotapes of individual teaching behaviors are invaluable for showing teachers what they actually do in classrooms. They are much better than outside observers, because recorders and cameras do not misrepresent what actually occurs. Training in ethnographic techniques, interactional analysis, questioning strategies, cultural decoding, frame analysis, and feedback mechanisms are very useful for these purposes.

While learning how to see their classroom attitudes and behaviors more clearly, teachers also need to be taught how to analyze these from different cultural perspectives. Without training, most educators cannot see the cultural biases and prejudices of their routine school behaviors. When suggestions are made to the effect that they are not treating ethnic minority and Anglo students equally, they associate these claims with blatant acts of discrimination. They do not understand the subtleties of negative ethnic attitudes and low expectations. For instance, educators need to know how and why treating all students the same can be an effective way to deny ethnic minority students equal educational opportunities.

A second emphasis in teacher reeducation for educational equality is understanding the differences in cultural values and behavioral codes between themselves as middle-class Anglos and ethnic minority students, how these values and codes operate in classrooms, and how instructional processes can be restructured to accommodate them better. Teachers cannot begin to treat Blacks, Hispanics, Indians, and Asians comparable to Anglos until they accept that these students have comparable human worth. This acceptance begins with acquiring knowledge about ethnic groups' cultural backgrounds, life experiences, and interactional styles to replace racial myths and stereotypes. Once they understand the organized structures and motivations behind these cultural behaviors, teachers can begin to design instructional options more compatible with them and thereby improve the quality of the learning experiences ethnic minority students receive.

The third focus of teacher reeducation should be the development of technical instructional skills that are more appropriate for use with ethnic minorities. The point of departure for this training should be understanding the specific traits of different teaching styles and ethnic learning styles. This knowledge should be combined with learning how to diversify teaching strategies ethnically; to create more supportive environments for learning and demonstrating achievement; to reduce stress, tension, and conflict in ethnically pluralistic classrooms; to select materials that have high-quality interest appeal for different ethnic groups; to develop and use learning activities that are meaningful, involving, enabling, and empowering for ethnic minority students; and to integrate ethnically diverse perspectives, aspirations, and experiences into curricula, program planning, and student evaluation. That is, teachers need to learn how to integrate ethnically their structural arrangements for teaching, culturally diversify their instructional strategies, multiculturalize the substance of learning, and democraticize the environments constructed for learning. These general skills can be operationalized by helping teachers learn how to use specific instructional skills with ethnic minority students such as questioning, feedback, and reinforcement, cooperative learning, inductive teaching, social context learning, and auditory and visual learning.

The approaches used in teacher training to develop these skills should be three-dimensional, including diagnosis, design and development, and debriefing, with teachers-in-training actively involved in each aspect. The training process should begin with a careful assessment of the value of and problems associated with using various instructional strategies with ethnic minority students. Examples of actual teaching behaviors should be used for this purpose. The training should then proceed to having teachers develop alternative instructional strategies and try them out in real or simulated teaching situations. Finally, these development efforts should be carefully examined to determine their strengths and weaknesses in terms of design and implementation criteria. That is, teachers should analyze them to assess the quality of the new teaching strategies relative to their ethnic sensitivity and ability to increase educational opportunities for ethnic minority students and to determine how effective they are in presenting the teaching tasks.

A fourth emphasis in the retraining of teachers, counselors, and school administrators for educational equality is public relations skill development. Major reform is needed in how educators are trained to communicate and interact with ethnic parents and to mobilize ethnic community resources to help in the educational process. There is a growing tendency to blame the school failure of ethnic minority students on the lack of involvement of their parents in school affairs. However, this buck-passing is counterproductive. It is another form of educators' blaming the victims and abdicating their responsibility for teaching minority youths.

Certainly minority parents should be more actively involved in their children's education, but it is understandable why they are reluctant or unable to do so. The schools that are failing their children are the same ones that failed them when they were students and that still treat them in paternalistic ways. Educators usually approach parents about their children only when the children get into trouble with the school system. This punitive, adversarial posture is not conducive to cooperation among educators and minority parents. Furthermore, many minority parents do not have the time, the personal resources, or the technical skills to assist in the education of their children in ways educators typically expect. How can parents effectively supervise their children's home-work or come to the schools on demand when they are unfamiliar with the latest pedagogical strategies used in schools and when they are working at hourly wage or low-salaried jobs that do not permit them to take time off without significant cost? Teacher training programs should help educators develop different interactional skills that work well with minority parents and community organizations.

This retraining process should begin with the inclusion of ethnic minority community relations skill building in all levels of professional preparation, undergraduate and graduate, preservice and in-service. It should start with acquiring an accurate knowledge base about the cultural dynamics of different ethnic communities, who the power brokers are in these communities, and how interactions and relationships are negotiated. It should also include specific strategies and skills about how to approach ethnic communities and parents—for instance, identifying and tapping informal networks of influence within the communities, understanding different ethnic interactional decorums, establish-ing consultancy relations with ethnic minority parents and community organiza-tions, and communicating effectively with ethnic parents.

Instead of always expecting parent-school interactions to take place in schools (which often are alien and hostile territory for ethnic minority parents and students), educators need to locate their efforts to increase parental involvement more within ethnic communities, or at least in neutral territory. Where school-parent interactions, discussions, conferences, and consultations occur is important as a symbolic statement of how committed schools are to involving parents in decisions about their children's education. When parents always have to go to the school at the educator's convenience, the implicit messages are that parents must defer to the school's position and that their inputs are not as valuable as those of the school personnel.

All of these are elements of the cultural diplomacy that classroom teachers, guidance counselors, and school administrators need to master in order to develop more constructive and cooperative relations with ethnic minority parents and communities. They, like the components of teacher self-knowledge, understanding ethnic minority cultures, and culturally specific instructional skills, are fundamental to establishing more culturally informed and ethnically sensitive foundations for changing how schools and teachers interact with ethnic minority students and to improving the educational opportunities these students receive.

Conclusion

Many researchers and scholars agree that the quality of student-teacher interactions in instructional situations is the ultimate test of educational equality, and that the central focus of both equality and excellence in education is maximum development of the personal talents of all students. The access of ethnic minority students to high-quality programs, materials, resources, and facilities is necessary for educational equality. But this is not sufficient. These students must also have access to quality knowledge and classroom interactions. As John Goodlad suggests, the central problem of both educational equality and excellence for today and tomorrow is "no longer access to school. It is access to knowledge for all."[33] This means that school reform toward improving educational equality for ethnic minority students needs to concentrate on equalizing the quality and comparability of the day-to-day learning experiences of ethnic minority and Anglo students within schools.

Questions and Activities

1. How do popular conceptions of educational equality differ from the view of this concept presented by Gay, the author of this chapter? What unfortunate assumptions, according to Gay, underlie these popular notions of educational equality?

2. In what ways did the educational status of ethnic minority students improve between the 1970s and the early 1980s? Why did the educational status of ethnic minority students improve during this period?

3. In what ways did the educational status of ethnic minorities decline during the 1980s? What is the reason for the decline?

4. How does the reference to Asian Americans as the "model minority" oversimplify their educational status? Give specific examples from this chapter to support your response.

5. How do school and curriculum practices such as tracking, vocational courses, and special education classes deny ethnic minority students equal educational opportunities?

6. The author argues that ethnic minority students are often placed in double jeopardy in school, in part because of differences between their cultures and the culture of the school. Explain what the author means by this concept. How can teachers help reduce the problems ethnic minority students experience in the schools?

7. How does testing, according to the author, promote educational inequality for lower-class and minority students? How can assessment programs be changed so they will contribute to educational equality for all students?

8. According to the author, how can curriculum reforms related to ethnic diversity contribute to educational equality?

9. Gay contends that educational equality for ethnic minority students cannot be achieved short of "massive schoolwide, institutional reform." What factors in the school environment and in teacher education does she think require reform? What specific recommendations does she make for attaining these reforms?

10. Observe for several days in an inner-city school that has a large percentage of ethnic minority students. In what ways do your observations support the conclusions by Gay about the problems minority students experience in the schools? What programs and efforts are being implemented in the school you observed to improve the educational status of ethnic minority students?

Notes

1. Alexander A. Astin, *Achieving Educational Excellence: A Critical Assessment of Priorities and Practices in Higher Education* (San Francisco: Jossey-Bass, 1985).

2. Carl A. Grant and Christine E. Sleeter, *After the School Bell Rings* (Philadelphia: Falmer Press, 1986).

3. *Equality and Excellence: The Educational Status of Black Americans* (New York: College Entrance Examination Board, 1985), p. vii.

4. *Teachers' Views on Equity and Excellence* (Washington, D.C.: National Education Association, 1983), pp. 3–4; Lori S. Orum, *The Education of Hispanics: Status and Implications* (Washington, D.C.: National Council of La Raza, August 1986, ERIC Document, ED 274753); Evangelina Mangino, David Wilkinson, Richard Battaile, and Wanda Washington, "Student Achievement, 1984–85 in the Austin Independent School District," (ERIC Document, ED 264286).

5. *Teachers' Views on Equity and Excellence,* 4–5.

6. Michael A. Olivas, "Research on Latino College Students: A Theoretical Framework and Inquiry," in Michael A. Olivas, ed., *Latino College Students* (New York: Teachers College Press, 1986), pp. 1–25; Orum, *The Education of Hispanics.*

7. *USA Today,* May 13, 1986, p. 1; Orum, *The Education of Hispanics.*

8. *Statistical Abstract of the United States, 1987,* 107th ed. (Washington, D.C.: U.S. Department of Commerce, Bureau of the Census, 1986).

9. Isaura Santiago Santiago, "The Education of Hispanics in the United States: Inadequacies of the Melting Pot Theory," in Dietmar Rothermund and John Simon, eds., *Education and the Integration of Ethnic Minorities* (New York: St. Martin's Press, 1986), pp. 151–185; The College Entrance Examination Board, *Equality and Excellence;* Orum, *The Education of Hispanics;* Cheryl M. Fields, "Closing the Education Gap for Hispanics: State Aims to Forestall a Divided Society," *Chronicle of Higher Education* 34, No. 3 (September 16, 1987): A1, A36, A38.

10. Francois Nielsen, "Hispanics in High School and Beyond," in Michael A. Olivas, ed., *Latino College Students* (New York: Teachers College Press, 1986), p. 79.

11. *1980 Census of Population, Vol. I, Characteristics of the Population.* Chapter C, *Social and Economic Characteristics, Part I, United States Summary,* Rept. No. PC-80-1-C1 (Washington, D.C.: Bureau of the Census, U.S. Department of Commerce, December 1983).

12. Elena S. H. Yu, Mary Doi, and Ching-Fu Chang, *Asian American Education in Illinois: A Review of the Data* (Springfield: Illinois State Board of Education, November 1986).

13. Reginald A. Gougis, "The Effects of Prejudice and Stress on the Academic Performance of Black-Americans," in Ulric Neisser, ed., *The Achievement of Minority Children: New Perspectives* (Hillsdale, N.J.: Lawrence Erlbaum Associates, 1986), pp. 145–158.

14. Scott Heller, "17-Year-Olds Get 'Failing Marks' in Their Knowledge of Great Works of Literature and Historical Events," *Chronicle of Higher Education,* 34, No. 3 (September 16, 1987): A35, A38; *American Memory: A Report on the Humanities in the Nation's Public Schools* (Washington, D.C.: National Endowment for the Humanities, 1987).

15. Yu et al., *Asian American Education in Illinois;* Valerie O. Pang, Donald T. Mizokawa, James K. Morishima, and Roger G. Olstad, "Self-Concept of Japanese American Children," *Journal of Cross-Cultural Psychology* 16 (March 1985): 99–108.

16. The College Entrance Examination Board, *Equality and Excellence.*

17. Arthur N. Applebee, Judith A. Langer, and Ina V. S. Mullis, *The Writing Report Card: Writing Achievement in American Schools,* Rept.

No. 15–W–02 (Princeton: Educational Testing Service, 1986).

18. U.S. Civil Rights Commission, *Mexican-American Educational Study,* Reports I–VI (Washington, D.C.: Government Printing Service, 1971–1974); Geneva Gay, *Differential Dyadic Interactions of Black and White Teachers with Black and White Pupils in Recently Desegregated Social Studies Classrooms: A Function of Teacher and Pupil Ethnicity* (Wasington, D.C.: Office of Education, National Institute of Education, January 1974); Carl A. Grant and Christine E, Sleeter, "Equality, Equity, and Excellence: A Critique," in Philip G. Altbach, Gail P. Kelly, and Lois Weis, eds. *Excellence in Education: Perspectives on Policy and Practice* (Buffalo, N.Y.: Prometheus Books, 1985), pp. 139–159.

19. Jeannie Oakes, *Keeping Track: How Schools Structure Inequality* (New Haven, Conn.: Yale University Press, 1985).

20. The College Entrance Examination Board, *Equality and Excellence;* John D. Winkler, Richard J. Stravelson, Cathleen Stasz, Abby Robyn, and Werner Fiebel, *How Effective Teachers Use Microcomputers in Instruction* (Santa Monica, Calif.: The Rand Corporation, 1984).

21. Oakes, *Keeping Track;* John I. Goodlad, *A Place Called School: Prospects for the Future* (New York: McGraw-Hill, 1984); James E. Rosenbaum, *Making Equality: The Hidden Curriculum in High School Tracking* (New York: John Wiley & Sons, 1976); Edward P. Morgan, *Inequality in Classroom Learning: Schooling and Democratic Citizenship* (New York: Praeger, 1977); Richard R. Verdugo, "Educational Stratification and Hispanics," in Michael A. Olivas, ed. *Latino College Students* (New York: Teachers College Press, 1986), pp. 325–347; Caroline Hodges Persell, *Education and Inequality: A Theoretical and Empirical Synthesis* (New York: Free Press, 1977).

22. Morgan, *Inequality in Classroom Learning.*

23. The College Entrance Examination Board, *Equality and Excellence;* Astin, *Achieving Educational Excellence.*

24. The College Entrance Examination Board, *Equality and Excellence,* 49.

25. Vera P. John-Steiner and Eleanor Leacock, "Transforming the Structure of Failure," in Doxey A. Wilkerson, ed. *Educating All of Our Children: An Imperative for Democracy* (Westport, Conn.: Mediax, 1979), p. 87.

26. Persell, *Education and Inequality,* 112.

27. Grant and Sleeter, "Equality, Equity, and Excellence, 139–159;" Morgan, *Inequality in Classroom Learning;* Persell, *Education and Inequality.*

28. The College Entrance Examination Board, *Equality and Excellence,* 4.

29. John-Steiner and Leacock, "Transforming the Structure of Failure," 87–88.

30. Henry J. Casso, "Educating the Linguistically and Culturally Different," in Doxey A. Wilkerson, ed. *Educating All of Our Children: An Imperative for Democracy* (Westport, Conn.: Mediax, 1979), p. 121.

31. Mario D. Fantini, "From School System to Educational System: Policy Considerations," in Doxey A. Wilkerson, ed. *Educating All of Our Children: An Imperative for Democracy.* (Westport, Conn.: Mediax, 1979), pp. 134–153.

32. Ibid., 147.

33. Goodlad, *A Place Called School,* 140.

CHAPTER 10

Integrating the Curriculum with Ethnic Content: Approaches and Guidelines

■ JAMES A. BANKS

The Mainstream-Centric Curriculum

The United States is made up of many different racial, ethnic, religious, and cultural groups. In many school curricula, textbooks, and other teaching materials, most of these groups are given scant attention. Rather, most curricula, textbooks, and teaching materials focus on White Anglo-Saxon Protestants. This dominant cultural group in U.S. society is often called mainstream Americans. A curriculum that focuses on the experiences of mainstream Americans and largely ignores the experiences, cultures, and histories of other ethnic, racial, cultural, and religious groups has negative consequences for both mainstream American and cultural and ethnic minority students. A mainstream-centric curriculum is one major way in which racism and ethnocentrism are reinforced and perpetuated in the schools and in society at large.

A mainstream-centric curriculum has negative consequences for mainstream students because it reinforces their false sense of superiority, gives them a misleading conception of their relationship with other racial and ethnic groups, and denies them the opportunity to benefit from the knowledge, perspectives, and frames of reference that can be gained from studying and experiencing other cultures and groups. A mainstream-centric curriculum also denies mainstream American students the opportunity to view their culture from the perspectives of other cultures and groups. When people view their culture from the point of view of another culture, they are able to understand their own culture more fully, to see how it is unique and distinct from other cultures, and to understand better how it relates to and interacts with other cultures.

A mainstream-centric curriculum negatively influences ethnic minority students such as Afro-Americans, Hispanics, and Asian Americans. It marginalizes their experiences and cultures and does not reflect their dreams, hopes, and perspectives. Students learn best and are more highly motivated when the school curriculum reflects their cultures, experiences, and perspectives. Many ethnic minority students are alienated in the school in part because they experience cultural conflict and discontinuities that result from the cultural differences between their school and community. The school can help ethnic minority students mediate between their home and school cultures by implementing a curriculum that reflects the culture of their ethnic groups and communities. As Diaz points out, the school can and should make effective use of the community cultures of ethnic minority students when teaching them such subjects as writing, language arts, science, and mathematics.[1]

In the mainstream-centric approach, events, themes, concepts, and issues are viewed primarily from the perspective of Anglo-Americans and Europeans. Events and cultural developments such as the European explorations in the Americas and the development of American music are viewed from Anglo and European perspectives and are evaluated using mainstream-centric criteria and points of view.

When the European explorations of the Americas are viewed from a Eurocentric perspective, the Americas are perceived as ''discovered'' by the European explorers such as Columbus and Cortés. The view that native peoples in the Americas were discovered by the Europeans subtly suggests that Indian cultures did not exist until they were ''discovered'' by the Europeans and that the lands occupied by the American Indians were rightfully owned by the Europeans after they settled on and claimed them. The Anglocentric view, below, of the settlement of Fort Townsend in the state of Washington appears on a marker in a federal park on the site where a U.S. Army post once stood. With the choice of words such as *settlers* (instead of *invaders*), *restive,* and *rebelled,* the author justifies the taking of the Indian's lands and depicts their resistance as unreasonable.

> **Fort Townsend**
> **A U.S. Army Post was Established on this Site in 1856**
> *In mid-nineteenth century the growth of Port Townsend caused the Indians to become restive. Settlers started a home guard, campaigned wherever called, and defeated the Indians in the Battle of Seattle. Indians rebelled as the government began enforcing the Indian Treaty of 1854, by which the Indians had ceded most of their territory. Port Townsend, a prosperous port of entry on Puget Sound, then asked protection of the U.S. army.*

When the formation and nature of U.S. cultural developments, such as music and dance, are viewed from mainstream-centric perspectives, these art forms become important and significant only when they are recognized or legitimized by mainstream critics and artists. The music of Black musicians such as Chuck Berry and Little Richard were not viewed as significant by the mainstream society until White singers such as the Beatles and Rod Stewart publicly acknowledged the significant ways their own music had been deeply influenced by these Black musicians. It often takes White artists to legitimize ethnic cultural forms and innovations created by Asian Americans, Blacks, Hispanics, and Native Americans.

Efforts to Establish a Multiethnic Curriculum

Since the civil rights movement of the 1960s, educators have been trying, in various ways, to better integrate the school curriculum with ethnic content and to move away from a mainstream-centric and Eurocentric curriculum. These have proven to be difficult goals for schools to attain for many complex reasons. The strong assimilationist ideology embraced by most U.S. educators is one major reason.[2] The assimilationist ideology makes it difficult for educators to think differently about how U.S. society and culture developed and to acquire a commitment to make the curriculum multiethnic. Individuals who have a strong assimilationist ideology believe that most important events and developments in U.S. society are related to the nation's British heritage and that the contributions of other ethnic and cultural groups are not very significant by comparison. When educators acquire a multiethnic ideology and conception of U.S. culture, they are then able to view the experiences and contributions of a wide range of cultural, ethnic, and religious groups as significant to the development of the United States.

Ideological resistance is a major factor that has slowed and is still slowing the development of a multiethnic curriculum, but other factors have also affected its growth and development. Political resistance to a multiethnic curriculum is closely related to ideological resistance. Many people who resist a multiethnic curriculum believe that knowledge is power and that a multiethnic perspective on U.S. society challenges the existing power structure. They believe that the dominant mainstream-centric curriculum supports, reinforces, and justifies the existing social, economic, and political structure. Multiethnic perspectives and points of view, in the opinion of many observers, legitimize and promote social change and social reconstruction.

Other factors that have slowed the institutionalization of a multiethnic curriculum include the low level of knowledge about ethnic cultures that most educators have and the heavy reliance on textbooks for teaching. Teachers must have an in-depth knowledge about ethnic cultures and experiences to integrate ethnic content, experiences, and points of view into the curriculum. Many teachers tell their students that Columbus discovered America and that America is a "new world" because they know little about the diverse Native American cultures that existed in the Americas more than 30,000 years before the Europeans began to settle in the Americas in significant numbers in the sixteenth century.

Many studies have revealed that the textbook is still the main source for teaching, especially in such subjects as the social studies, reading, and language arts.[3] Some significant changes have been made in textbooks since the civil rights movement of the 1960s. More ethnic groups and women appear in textbooks today than in those of yesteryear.[4] However, the content about ethnic groups in textbooks is usually presented from mainstream perspectives, contains information and heroes that are selected using mainstream criteria, and rarely incorporates information about ethnic groups throughout the text in a consistent and totally integrated way. Information about ethnic groups is usually discussed in special units, topics, and parts of the text. Because most teachers rely heavily on the textbook for teaching, they approach the teaching of ethnic content in a fragmented fashion.

Levels of Integration of Ethnic Content

The Contributions Approach

Four approaches to the integration of ethnic content into the curriculum that have evolved since the 1960s can be identified (see Figure 10.1). The *contributions approach* to integration (level 1) is one of the most frequently used and is often used extensively during the first phase of an ethnic revival movement.

The contributions approach is characterized by the insertion of ethnic heroes and discrete cultural artifacts into the curriculum, selected using criteria similar to those used to select mainstream heroes and cultural artifacts. Thus, individuals such as Crispus Attucks, Benjamin Bannaker, Sacajawea, Booker T. Washington, and Cesar Chavez are added to the curriculum. They are discussed

FIGURE 10.1
Levels of Integration of Ethnic Content

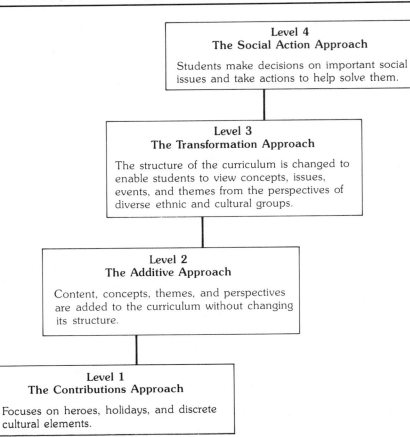

Level 4
The Social Action Approach

Students make decisions on important social issues and take actions to help solve them.

Level 3
The Transformation Approach

The structure of the curriculum is changed to enable students to view concepts, issues, events, and themes from the perspectives of diverse ethnic and cultural groups.

Level 2
The Additive Approach

Content, concepts, themes, and perspectives are added to the curriculum without changing its structure.

Level 1
The Contributions Approach

Focuses on heroes, holidays, and discrete cultural elements.

when mainstream American heroes such as Patrick Henry, George Washington, Thomas Jefferson, and John F. Kennedy are studied in the core curriculum. Discrete cultural elements such as the foods, dances, music, and artifacts of ethnic groups are studied, but little attention is given to their meanings and importance within ethnic communities.

An important characteristic of the contributions approach is that the mainstream curriculum remains unchanged in its basic structure, goals, and salient characteristics. Prerequisites for the implementation of this approach are minimal. They include basic knowledge about U.S. society and knowledge about ethnic heroes and their roles and contributions to U.S. society and culture.

Individuals who challenged the dominant society's ideologies, values, and conceptions and advocated radical social, political, and economic reform are seldom included in the contributions approach. Thus, Booker T. Washington is more likely to be chosen for study than is W. E. B. Du Bois, and Sacajawea is more likely to be chosen than is Geronimo. The criteria used to select ethnic heroes for study and to judge them for success are derived from the mainstream society and not from the ethnic community. Consequently, use of the contributions approach usually results in the study of ethnic heroes who represent only one important perspective within ethnic communities. The more radical and less conformist individuals who are heroes only to the ethnic community tend to be ignored in textbooks, teaching materials, and activities used in the contributions approach.

The heroes and holidays approach is a variant of the contributions approach. In this approach, ethnic content is limited primarily to special days, weeks, and months related to ethnic events and celebrations. Cinco de Mayo, Martin Luther King's Birthday, and Black History Week are examples of ethnic days and weeks celebrated in the schools. During these celebrations, teachers involve students in lessons, experiences, and pageants related to the ethnic group being commemorated. When this approach is used, the class studies little or nothing about the ethnic group before or after the special event or occasion.

The contributions approach (level 2 in Figure 10.1) provides teachers a way to integrate ethnic content into the curriculum quickly, thus giving some recognition to ethnic contributions to U.S. society and culture. Many teachers who are committed to integrating their curricula with ethnic content have little knowledge about ethnic groups and curriculum revision. Consequently, they use the contributions approach when teaching about ethnic groups. These teachers should be encouraged, supported, and given the opportunity to acquire the knowledge and skills needed to reform their curricula by using one of the more effective approaches I describe later.

There are often strong political demands from ethnic communities for the school to put their heroes, contributions, and cultures into the school curriculum. These political forces may take the form of demands for heroes and contributions because mainstream heroes, such as Washington, Jefferson, and Lincoln, are highly visible in the school curriculum. Ethnic minority communities want to see their own heroes and contributions alongside those of the mainstream society. Such contributions may help give them a sense of structural inclusion, validation, and equity. Curriculum inclusion also facilitates the quests of victimized ethnic and cultural groups for a sense of empowerment and efficacy. The school should help ethnic-group students acquire a sense of empowerment and efficacy. These factors are positively correlated with academic achievement.[5]

The contributions approach is also the easiest approach for teachers to use to integrate the curriculum with ethnic content. However, this approach has several serious limitations. When the integration of the curriculum is accomplished primarily through the infusion of ethnic heroes and contributions, students do not attain a global view of the role of ethnic and cultural groups in U.S. society. Rather, they see ethnic issues and events primarily as an addition to the curriculum and consequently as an appendage to the main story of the development of the nation and to the core curriculum in the language arts, the social studies, the arts, and other subject areas.

Teaching ethnic issues with the use of heroes and contributions also tends to gloss over important concepts and issues related to the victimization and oppression of ethnic groups and their struggles against racism and for power. Issues such as racism, poverty, and oppression tend to be avoided in the contributions approach to curriculum integration. The focus tends to be on success and the validation of the Horatio Alger myth that all Americans who are willing to work hard can go from rags to riches and ''pull themselves up by their bootstraps.''

The success stories of ethnic heroes such as Booker T. Washington, George Washington Carver, and Jackie Robinson are usually told with a focus on their success, with little attention to racism and other barriers they encountered and how they succeeded despite the hurdles they faced. Little attention is also devoted to the process by which they become heroes. As Gay points out, students should learn about the process by which people become heroes as well as about their status and role as heroes.[6] Only when students learn the process by which individuals become heroes will they understand fully the way in which individuals, particularly ethnic minority individuals, achieve and maintain hero status and what the process of becoming a hero means for their own lives.

The contributions approach often results in the trivialization of ethnic cultures, the study of their strange and exotic characteristics, and the reinforcement of stereotypes and misconceptions. When the focus is on the contributions and unique aspects of ethnic cultures, students are not helped to view them as complete and dynamic wholes. The contributions approach also tends to focus on the life-styles of ethnic groups rather than on the institutional structures, such as racism and discrimination, that strongly affect their life chances and keep them powerless and marginalized.

The contributions approach to content integration may provide students with a memorable one-time experience with an ethnic hero, but it often fails to help them understand the role and influence of the hero in the total context of U.S. history and society. When ethnic heroes are studied separate and apart from the social and political context in which they lived and worked, students attain only a partial understanding of their roles and significance in society. When Martin Luther King is studied outside the social and political context of institutionalized racism in the U.S. South in the 1940s and 1950s, and without attention to the more subtle forms of institutionalized racism in the North during this period, his full significance as a national social reformer is neither revealed nor understood by students.

The Ethnic Additive Approach

Another important approach to the integration of ethnic content to the curriculum is the addition of content, concepts, themes, and perspectives to the curriculum without changing its basic structure, purposes, and characteristics. The ethnic *additive approach* (level 2 in Figure 10.1) is often accomplished by the addition of a book, a unit, or a course to the curriculum without changing it substantially. Examples of this approach include adding a book such as *The Color Purple* to a unit on the twentieth century in an English class; the use of the film *Miss Jane Pittman* during a unit on the 1960s; and the addition of a unit on the internment of the Japanese-Americans during a study of World War II in a class on U.S. history.

The additive approach allows the teacher to put ethnic content into the curriculum without restructuring it, a process that would take substantial time, effort, training, and rethinking of the curriculum and its purposes, nature, and goals. The additive approach can be the first phase in a more radical curriculum reform effort designed to restructure the total curriculum and to integrate it with ethnic content, perspectives, and frames of reference.

However, this approach shares several disadvantages with the contributions approach. Its most important shortcoming is that it usually results in the viewing of ethnic content from the perspectives of mainstream historians, writers, artists, and scientists because it does not involve a restructuring of the curriculum. The events, concepts, issues, and problems selected for study are selected using mainstream-centric and Eurocentric criteria and perspectives. When teaching a unit such as "The Westward Movement" in a fifth-grade U.S. history class, the teacher may integrate the unit by adding content about the Oglala Sioux Indians. However, the unit remains mainstream-centric and focused because of its perspective and point of view. A unit called "The Westward Movement" is mainstream and Eurocentric because it focuses on the movement of European-Americans from the eastern to the western part of the United States. The Oglala Sioux were already in the West and consequently were not moving westward. The unit might be called "The Invasion from the East," from the point of view of the Oglala Sioux. Black Elk, an Oglala Sioux holy man, lamented the conquering of his people, which culminated in their defeat at Wounded Knee Creek on December 29, 1890. Approximately 200 Sioux men, women, and children were killed by U.S. troops. Black Elk said, "The [Sioux] nation's hoop is broken and scattered. There is no center any longer, and the sacred tree is dead."[7]

Black Elk did not consider his homeland "the West," but rather the center of the world. He viewed the cardinal directions metaphysically. The Great Spirit sent him the cup of living water and the sacred bow from the West. The daybreak star and the sacred pipe originated from the East. The Sioux nation's sacred hoop and the tree that was to bloom came from the South.[8] When teaching about the movement of the Europeans across North America, teachers should help students understand that different cultural, racial, and ethnic groups often have varying and conflicting conceptions and points of view about the same historical events, concepts, issues, and developments. The victors and the vanquished, especially, often have conflicting conceptions of the same historical event. However, it is usually the point of view of the victors that becomes institutionalized within the schools and the mainstream society. This happens because history and textbooks are usually written by people who won the wars and gained control of the society, and not by the losers—the victimized and the powerless. The perspectives of both groups are needed to help us fully understand our history, culture, and society.

The people who are conquered and the people who conquered them have histories and cultures that are intricately interwoven and interconnected. They have to learn each others' histories and cultures to understand their own fully. White Americans cannot fully understand their own history in the western United States and in America without understanding the history of the American Indians and the ways their histories and the histories of the Indians are interconnected. James Baldwin insightfully pointed out that when White Americans distort Black history, they do not learn the truth about their own history because the history of Blacks and Whites in the United States is tightly bound together.[9] This is also true for Black history and Indian history. The history of Blacks and Indians in the United States is closely interconnected, as Katz documents in his book *Black Indians: A Hidden Heritage*.[10] The additive approach fails to help students view society from diverse cultural and ethnic perspectives and understand the ways that the histories and cultures of the nation's diverse ethnic, racial, cultural, and religious groups are interconnected.

Content, materials, and issues that are added to a curriculum as appendages instead of being integral parts of a unit of instruction can become problematic. Problems might result when a book such as *The Color Purple* or a film like *Miss Jane Pittman* is added to a unit when the students lack the concepts, content background, and emotional maturity to deal with the issues and problems in this material. The effective use of such emotion-laden and complex materials usually requires that the teacher help students acquire, in a sequential and developmental fashion, the content background and attitudinal maturity to deal with them effectively. The use of both of these materials in different classes and schools has resulted in major problems for the teachers using them. A community controversy arose in each case. The problems developed because the material was used with students who had neither the content background nor the attitudinal sophistication to respond to them appropriately. Adding ethnic content to the curriculum in a sporadic and segmented way can result in pedagogical problems, trouble for the teacher, student confusion, and community controversy.

The Transformation Approach

The *transformation approach* differs fundamentally from the contributions and additive approaches. In both approaches, ethnic content is added to the mainstream core curriculum without changing its basic assumptions, nature, and structure. The fundamental goals, structure, and perspectives of the curriculum are changed in the transformation approach.

The transformation approach (level 3 in Figure 10.1) changes the basic assumptions of the curriculum and enables students to view concepts, issues, themes, and problems from several ethnic perspectives and points of view. The mainstream-centric perspective is one of only several perspectives from which issues, problems, concepts, and issues are viewed. It is neither possible nor desirable to view every issue, concept, event, or problem from the point of view of every U.S. ethnic group. Rather, the goal should be to enable students to view concepts and issues from more than one perspective and from the point of view of the cultural, ethnic, and racial groups that were the most active participants in, or were most cogently influenced by, the event, issue, or concept being studied.

The key curriculum issues involved in multicultural curriculum reform is not the addition of a long list of ethnic groups, heroes, and contributions, but the infusion of various perspectives, frames of references, and content from various groups that will extend students' understandings of the nature, development, and complexity of U.S. society. When students are studying the revolution in the British colonies, the perspectives of the Anglo revolutionaries, the Anglo loyalists, Afro-Americans, Indians, and the British are essential for them to attain a thorough understanding of this significant event in U.S. history. Students must study the various and sometimes divergent meanings of the revolution to these diverse groups to understand it fully.[11]

In the language arts, when students are studying the nature of U.S. English and proper language use, they should be helped to understand the rich linguistic and language diversity in the United States and the ways that a wide range of regional, cultural, and ethnic groups have influenced the development of U.S. English. Students should also examine how normative language use varies within the social context, the region, and the situation. The use of Black English is appropriate in some social and cultural contexts and inappropriate in others. This is also true of formal U.S. English. The United States is rich in languages and dialects. The nation has more than 17 million Hispanic citizens; Spanish is the first language for most of them. Most of the nation's approximately 30 million Afro-Americans speak both standard English as well as some form of Black English. The rich language diversity in the United States includes more than twenty-five European languages; Asian, African, and Middle Eastern languages; and American Indian languages. Since the 1970s, languages from Indochina, spoken by groups such as the Hmong, Vietnamese, Laotians, and the Cambodians, have further enriched language diversity in the United States.

When subjects such as music, dance, and literature are studied, the teacher should acquaint students with the ways these art forms among U.S. ethnic groups have greatly influenced and enriched the nation's artistic and literary traditions. The ways that Black musicians such as Bessie Smith, W. C. Handy, and Leontyne Price have influenced the nature and development of U.S. music should be examined when the development of U.S. music is studied. Blacks and Puerto Ricans have significantly influenced the development of American dance. Ethnic minority writers, such as Langston Hughes, N. Scott Momaday, Carlos Bulosan, Maxine Hong Kingston, Rudolfo A. Anaya, and Piri Thomas, have not only significantly influenced the development of American literature, but have also provided unique and revealing perspectives on U.S. society and culture.[12]

When studying U.S. history, language, music, arts, science, and mathematics, the emphasis should not be on the ways that various ethnic and cultural groups have contributed to mainstream U.S. society and culture. *The emphasis, rather, should be on how the common U.S. culture and society emerged from a complex synthesis and interaction of the diverse cultural elements that originated within the various cultural, racial, ethnic, and religious groups that make up American society.* I call this process *multiple acculturation* and argue that even though Anglo-Saxon Protestants are the dominant group in the United States—culturally, politically, and economically—it is misleading and inaccurate to describe U.S. culture and society as an Anglo-Saxon Protestant culture.[13] Other U.S. ethnic and cultural groups have deeply influenced, shaped, and participated in the development and formation of U.S. society and culture. Afro-Americans, for example, profoundly influenced the development of the U.S. southern culture, even though they had very little political and economic power.[14] One irony of conquest is that those who are conquered often deeply influence the cultures of the conquerors.

A multiple acculturation conception of U.S. society and culture leads to a perspective that views ethnic events, literature, music, and art as integral parts of the common, shared U.S. culture. Anglo-Saxon Protestant culture is viewed as only a part of this larger cultural whole. Thus, to teach American literature without including significant ethnic minority writers, such as those named above, gives a partial and incomplete view of U.S. literature, culture, and society.

The Social Action Approach

The *social action approach* (level 4 in Figure 10.1) includes all the elements of the transformation approach but adds components that require students to make decisions and take actions related to the concept, issue, or problem studied in the unit. Major goals of instruction in this approach are to educate students for social criticism and social change and to teach them decision-making skills. To empower ethnic students and help them acquire political efficacy, the school must help them become reflective social critics and skilled participants in social change. The traditional goal of schooling has been to socialize students so they would accept unquestioningly the existing ideologies, institutions, and practices within society and the nation-state.[15]

Political education in the United States has traditionally fostered political passivity rather than political action. A major goal of the social action approach is to help students acquire the knowledge, values, and skills they need to participate in social change so that victimized and excluded ethnic and racial groups can become full participants in U.S. society. To participate effectively in social change, students must be taught social criticism and must be helped to understand the inconsistency between our ideals and social realities, the work that must be done to close this gap, and how students can, as individuals and groups, influence the social and political systems in U.S. society. In this approach, teachers are agents of social change who promote democratic values and the empowerment of ethnic students. Teaching units organized using the social action approach have the components described below.

1. *A decision-problem or question.* An example of a question is: What actions should we take to reduce prejudice and discrimination in our school?

2. *An inquiry that provides data related to the decision problem.* The inquiry might consist of these kinds of questions:

    a. What is prejudice?

    b. What is discrimination?

c. What causes prejudice?
d. What causes people to discriminate?
e. What are examples of prejudice and discrimination in our nation, community, and school?
f. How do prejudice and discrimination affect the groups below? How does each group view prejudice? Discrimination? To what extent is each group a victim or a perpetuator of prejudice and discrimination?
g. How has each group dealt with prejudice and discrimination? (Groups: White mainstream Americans, Afro-Americans, Asian Americans, Hispanic Americans, Native Americans.)

The inquiry into the nature of prejudice and discrimination would be interdisciplinary and would include readings and data sources in the various social sciences, biography, fiction, poetry, and drama. Scientific and statistical data would be used when students investigated how discrimination affects the income, occupations, frequency of diseases, and health care within these various groups.

3. *Value inquiry and moral analysis.* Students are given opportunities to examine, clarify, and reflect on their values, attitudes, beliefs, and feelings related to racial prejudice and discrimination. The teacher can provide the students with case studies from various sources, such as newspapers and magazines. The case studies can be used to involve the students in discussions and role-playing situations that enable them to express and to examine their attitudes, beliefs, and feelings about prejudice and discrimination.

Poetry, biography, and powerful fiction are excellent sources for case studies that can be used for both discussion and role playing. Countee Cullen's powerful poem ''Incident'' describes the painful memories of a child who was called ''nigger'' on a trip to Baltimore. Langston Hughes's gripping poem ''I, Too'' poignantly tells how the ''darker brother'' is sent into the kitchen when company comes. The teacher and the students can describe verbally or write about incidents related to prejudice and discrimination they have observed or in which they have participated. The following case, based on a real-life situation, was written by the author for use with his students.[16] After reading the case, the students discuss the question at the end of it.

Trying to Buy a Home in Lakewood Island

About a year ago, Joan and Henry Green, a young Black couple, moved from the West Coast to a large city in the Midwest. They moved because Henry finished his Ph.D. in chemistry and took a job at a big university in Midwestern City. Since they have been in Midwestern City, the Greens have rented an apartment in the central area of the city. However, they have decided that they want to buy a house. Their apartment has become too small for the many books and other things they have accumulated during the year. In addition to wanting more space, they also want a house so that they can receive breaks on their income tax, which they do not receive living in an apartment. The Greens also think that a house will be a good financial investment.

The Greens have decided to move into a suburban community. They want a new house and most of the houses within the city limits are rather old. They also feel that they can obtain a larger house for their money in the suburbs than in the city. They have looked at several suburban communities and decided that they like Lakewood Island better than any of the others. Lakewood Island is an all-White community, which is comprised primarily of lower-middle-class and middle-class residents. There are a few wealthy families in Lakewood Island, but they are exceptions rather than the rule.

Joan and Henry Green have become frustrated because of the problems they have experienced trying to buy a home in Lakewood Island. Before they go out to look at a house, they carefully study the newspaper ads. When they arrived at the first house in which they were interested, the owner told them that his house had just been sold. A week later they decided to work with a realtor. When they tried to close the deal on the next house they wanted, the realtor told them that the owner had raised the price $3,000 because he had the house appraised since he put it on the market and had discovered that his selling price was much too low. When the Greens tried to buy a third house in Lakewood Island, the owner told them that he had decided not to sell because he had not received the job in another city that he was almost sure he would receive when he had put his house up for sale. He explained that the realtor had not removed the ad about his house from the newspaper even though he had told him that he had decided not to sell a week earlier. The realtor the owner had been working with had left the real estate company a few days ago. Henry is bitter and feels that he and his wife are victims of racism and discrimination. Joan believes that Henry is paranoid and that they have been the victims of a series of events that could have happened to anyone, regardless of their race.

Questions: What should the Greens do? Why?

4. *Decision making and social action* (synthesis of knowledge and values). Students acquire knowledge about their decision problem from the activities in 2, above. This interdisciplinary knowledge provides them with the information they need to make reflective decisions about prejudice and discrimination in their communities and schools. The activities in 3 enable them to identify, clarify, and analyze their values, feelings, and beliefs about prejudice and discrimination. The decision-making process enables the students to synthesize their knowledge and values to determine what actions, if any, they should take to reduce prejudice and discrimination in their schools. They can develop a chart in which they list possible actions to take and their possible consequences. They can then decide on a course of action to take and implement it.

Mixing and Blending Approaches

The four approaches for the integration of ethnic content into the curriculum (see Table 10.1) are often mixed and blended in actual teaching situations. One approach, such as the contributions approach, can be used as a vehicle to move to other, more intellectually challenging approaches such as the transformation and social action approaches. It is unrealistic to expect a teacher to move directly from a highly mainstream-centric curriculum to one that focuses on decision making and social action. Rather, the move from the first to higher levels of ethnic content integration is likely to be gradual and cumulative.

A teacher who has a mainstream-centric curriculum might use the school's Martin Luther King's birthday celebration as an opportunity to integrate

TABLE 10.1
Approaches for the Integration of Ethnic Content

Approach	Description	Examples	Strengths	Problems
Contributions	Heroes, cultural components, holidays, and other discrete elements related to ethnic groups are added to the curriculum on special days, occasions, and celebrations.	Famous Mexican-Americans are studied only during the week of Cinco de Mayo (May 5). Black Americans are studied during Black History Month in February but rarely during the rest of the year. Ethnic foods are studied in the first grade with little attention devoted to the cultures in which the foods are embedded.	Provides a quick and relatively easy way to put ethnic content into the curriculum. Gives ethnic heroes visibility in the curriculum alongside mainstream heroes. Is a popular approach among teachers and educators.	Results in a superficial understanding of ethnic cultures. Focuses on the life-styles and artifacts of ethnic groups and reinforces stereotypes and misconceptions. Mainstream criteria are used to select heroes and cultural elements for inclusion in the curriculum.
Additive	This approach consists of the addition of content, concepts, themes, and perspectives to the curriculum without changing its structure	Adding the book *The Color Purple* to a literature unit without reconceptualizing the unit or giving the students the background knowledge to understand the book. Adding a unit on the Japanese-American internment to a U.S. history course without treating the Japanese in any other unit. Leaving the core curriculum intact but adding an ethnic studies course, as an elective, that focuses on a specific ethnic group.	Makes it possible to add ethnic content to the curriculum without changing its structure, which requires substantial curriculum changes and staff development. Can be implemented within the existing curriculum structure.	Reinforces the idea that ethnic history and culture are not integral parts of U.S. mainstream culture. Students view ethnic groups from Anglocentric and Eurocentric perspectives. Fails to help students understand how the dominant culture and ethnic cultures are interconnected and interrelated.
Transformation	The basic goals, structure, and nature of the curriculum is	A unit on the American Revolution describes the	Enables students to understand the complex ways in which diverse racial	The imple-mentation of this approach requires substantial

TABLE 10.1 *(cont.)*

Approach	Description	Examples	Strengths	Problems
	changed to enable students to view concepts, events, issues, problems, and themes from the perspectives of diverse cultural, ethnic, and racial groups.	meaning of the revolution to Anglo revolutionaries, Anglo loyalists, Afro-Americans, Indians, and the British. A unit on 20th-century U.S. literature includes works by William Faulkner, Joyce Carol Oates, Langston Hughes, N. Scott Momoday, Carlos Bulosan, Saul Bellow, Maxine Hong Kingston, Rudolfo A. Anaya, and Piri Thomas.	and cultural groups participated in the formation of U.S. society and culture. Helps reduce racial and ethnic encapsulation. Enables diverse ethnic, racial, and religious groups to see their cultures, ethos, and perspectives in the school curriculum. Gives students a balanced view of the nature and development of U.S. culture and society. Helps to empower victimized racial, ethnic, and cultural groups.	curriculum revision, in-service training, and the identification and development of materials written from the perspectives of various racial and cultural groups. Staff development for the institutionalization of this approach must be continual and ongoing.
Decision Making and Social Action	In this approach, students identify important social problems and issues, gather pertinent data, clarify their values on the issue, make decisions, and take reflective actions to help resolve the issue or problem.	A class studies prejudice and discrimination in their school and decides to take actions to improve race relations in the school. A class studies the treatment of ethnic groups in a local newspaper and writes a letter to the newspaper publisher suggesting ways that the treatment of ethnic minority groups in the newspaper should be improved.	Enables students to improve their thinking, value analysis, decision-making, and social-action skills. Enables students to improve their data-gathering skills. Helps students develop a sense of political efficacy. Helps students improve their skills to work in groups	Requires a considerable amount of curriculum planning and materials identification. May be longer in duration than more traditional teaching units. May focus on problems and issues considered controversial by some members of the school staff and citizens of the community. Students may be able to take few meaningful actions that contribute to the resolution of the social issue or problem.

the curriculum with ethnic content about King, as well as to think seriously about how content about Afro-Americans and other ethnic groups can be integrated into the curriculum in an ongoing fashion. The teacher could explore with the students these kinds of questions during the celebration:

1. What were the conditions of Afro-Americans before the emergence of Martin Luther King as a leader?

2. What has happened to the social, economic, and political condition of Blacks since the civil rights movement of the 1960s?

3. What is the social, economic, and political condition of Afro-Americans today?

To bring in elements of the transformation and social action approaches, the teacher could explore these questions with the students:

1. What were the conditions of other ethnic groups during the time that King was a civil rights leader?

2. How did other ethnic groups participate in and respond to the civil rights movement?

3. How did these groups respond to Martin Luther King, Jr.?

4. What can we do today to improve the civil rights of ethnic minority groups?

5. What can we do to develop more positive racial and ethnic attitudes?

The students will be unable to answer all the questions they have raised about ethnic groups during the celebration of Martin Luther King's birthday. Rather, the questions will enable the students to integrate content about ethnic groups throughout the year as they study such topics as the family, the school, the neighborhood, and the city. As the students study these topics, they can use the questions they have formulated to investigate ethnic families, the ethnic groups in their school and in schools in other parts of the city, ethnic neighborhoods, and various ethnic institutions in the city such as churches, temples, synagogues, schools, restaurants, and community centers. As a culminating activity for the year, the teacher can take the students on a tour of an ethnic community in the city. However, such a tour should be both preceded and followed by activities that enable the students to develop perceptive and compassionate lenses for seeing ethnic and cultural differences and for responding to them with sensitivity. A field trip to an ethnic community or neighborhood might reinforce stereotypes and misconceptions if students lack the knowledge and insights needed to view ethnic cultures in an understanding and caring way. Theory and research indicate that contact with an ethnic group does not necessarily lead to more positive racial and ethnic attitudes.[17] Rather, the conditions under which the contact occurs and the quality of the interaction in the contact situation are the important variables.

GUIDELINES FOR TEACHING ETHNIC CONTENT

The following fourteen guidelines are designed to help you better integrate content about ethnic groups into the school curriculum and to teach effectively in multiethnic environments.

1. You, the teacher, are an extremely important variable in the teaching of ethnic content. If you have the necessary knowledge, attitudes, and skills, when you encounter racist content in materials or observe racism in the statements and behavior of students you can use these situations to teach important lessons about the experiences of ethnic groups in the United States.

2. Knowledge about ethnic groups is needed to teach ethnic content effectively. Read at least one major book that surveys the histories and cultures of U.S. ethnic groups. One book that includes historical overviews of U.S. ethnic groups is James A. Banks, *Teaching Strategies for Ethnic Studies,* 4th ed. (Boston: Allyn and Bacon, 1987).

3. Be sensitive to your own racial attitudes, behavior, and the statements you make about ethnic groups in the classroom. A statement such as "Sit like an Indian" stereotypes Native Americans.

4. Make sure that your classroom conveys positive images of various ethnic groups. You can do this by displaying bulletin boards, posters, and calendars that show the racial and ethnic diversity within U.S. society.

5. Be sensitive to the racial and ethnic attitudes of your students and do not accept the belief, which has been refuted by research, that "kids do not see colors." Since the pioneering research by Lasker in 1929, researchers have known that very young children are aware of racial differences and that they tend to accept the evaluations of various racial groups that are normative within the wider society.[18] Do not try to ignore the racial and ethnic differences that you see; try to respond to these differences positively and sensitively.

6. Be judicious in your choice and use of teaching materials. Teaching materials contain both subtle and blatant sterotypes of ethnic groups. Point out to the students when an ethnic group is stereotyped, omitted from, or described in materials from Anglocentric and Eurocentric points of view. A helpful guide is *Guidelines for Selecting Bias-Free Textbooks and Storybooks* (New York: Council on Interracial Books for Children, n.d.).

7. Use trade books, films, videotapes, and recordings to supplement the textbook treatment of ethnic groups and to present the perspectives of ethnic groups to your students. Many of these sources contain rich and powerful images of the experience of being an ethnic minority member in the United States.

8. Get in touch with your own cultural and ethnic heritage. Sharing your ethnic and cultural story with your students will create a climate for sharing in the classroom, will help motivate students to dig into their ethnic and cultural roots, and will result in powerful learning for your students.

9. Be sensitive to the possible controversial nature of some ethnic studies materials. If you are clear about the teaching objectives you have in mind, you can often use a less controversial book or reading to attain the same objectives. *The Color Purple* by Alice Walker, for example, is a controversial book. A teacher, however, who wants her students to gain insights about Blacks in the South can use *Roll of Thunder, Hear My Cry* by Mildred D. Taylor instead of *The Color Purple.*[19]

10. Be sensitive to the developmental levels of your students when you select concepts, content, and activities related to ethnic groups. Concepts and learning activities for students in kindergarten and the primary grades should be specific and concrete. Students in these grades should study such concepts as *similarities, differences, prejudice,* and *discrimination* rather than higher-level concepts such as *racism* and *oppression.* Fiction and biographies are excellent vehicles for introducing these concepts to students in kindergarten and the primary grades. As students progress through the grades, they can be introduced to more complex concepts, examples, and activities.

If you teach in a racially or ethnically integrated classroom or school you should keep the following guidelines in mind.

11. View your minority students as winners. Many minority students have high academic and career goals. They need teachers who believe they can be successful and are willing to help them succeed. Both research and theory indicate that students are more likely to achieve highly when their teachers have high academic expectations for them.

12. Keep in mind that most minority parents are very interested in education and want their children to be successful academically even though the parents may be alienated from the school.[20] Do not equate education with schooling. Many parents who want their children to succeed have mixed feelings about the schools. Try to gain the support of these parents and make them partners in the education of their children.

13. Use cooperative learning techniques and group work to promote racial and ethnic integration in the school and classroom. Research indicates that when learning groups are racially integrated, students develop more friends from other racial groups, and race relations in the school improve. A helpful guide is Elizabeth G. Cohen's *Designing Groupwork: Strategies for the Heterogenous Classroom* (New York: Teachers College Press, 1986).

14. Make sure that school plays, pageants, cheerleading squads, school publications, and other formal and informal groups are racially integrated. Also make sure that various ethnic and racial groups have equal status in school performances and presentations. In a multiracial school, if all of the leading roles in a school play are filled by White characters, an important message is sent to ethnic students and parents whether such a message was intended or not.

Summary

In this chapter, I describe the nature of the mainstream-centric curriculum and the negative consequences it has for both mainstream and ethnic minority students. This curriculum reinforces the false sense of superiority of mainstream students and fails to reflect, validate, and celebrate the cultures of ethnic minority students. Many factors have slowed the institutionalization of a multiethnic curriculum in the schools, including ideological resistance, lack of teacher knowledge of ethnic groups, and the heavy reliance of teachers on textbooks.

Four approaches to the integration of ethnic content into the curriculum are identified in this chapter. In the *contributions approach,* heroes, cultural components, holidays, and other discrete elements related to ethnic groups are added to the curriculum without changing its structure. The *additive approach* consists of the addition of content, concepts, themes, and perspectives to the curriculum, with its structure remaining unchanged. In the *transformation approach,* the structure, goals, and nature of the curriculum are changed to enable students to view concepts, issues, and problems from diverse ethnic perspectives. The *social action approach* includes all elements of the transformation approach, as well as elements that enable students to identify important social issues, gather data related to them, clarify their values, make reflective decisions, and take actions to implement their decisions. This approach seeks to make students social critics and reflective agents of change. The final part of this chapter presents guidelines to help you teach ethnic content and to function more effectively in multiethnic classrooms and schools.

Questions and Activities

1. What is a mainstream-centric curriculum? What are its major assumptions and goals?

2. Examine several textbooks and find examples of the mainstream-centric approach. Share these examples with colleagues in your class or workshop.

3. How does a mainstream-centric curriculum influence mainstream and ethnic minority students?

4. According to Banks, what factors have slowed the development of a multiethnic curriculum in the schools? What is the best way to overcome these factors?

5. What are the major characteristics of the following approaches to curriculum reform: the contributions approach; the ethnic additive approach; the transformation approach; the social action approach?

6. Why do you think the contributions approach to curriculum reform is so popular and widespread within schools, especially in the primary and elementary grades?

7. In what fundamental way do the transformation and social action approaches differ from the other two approaches identified above?

8. What are the problems and promises of each of the four approaches?

9. What does the author mean by "multiple acculturation"? Do you think this concept is valid? Why or why not?

10. What problems might a teacher encounter when trying to implement the transformation and social action approaches? How might these problems be overcome?

11. Assume that you are teaching a social studies lesson about the Westward Movement in U.S. history and a student makes a racist, sterotypic, or misleading statement about Native Americans, such as, "The Indians were hostile to the White settlers." How would you handle this situation? Give reasons to explain why you would handle it in a particular way.

12. Develop a teaching plan in which you illustrate how you would teach a unit incorporating elements of the transformation and social action approaches to curriculum reform.

Notes

1. Stephen Diaz, "Learning Styles and Teaching Styles," paper presented at the institute *Increasing the Academic Achievement of Minority Students*, sponsored by the Educational Materials and Services Center, Bellevue, Wash., July 1987.

2. James A. Banks, *Multiethnic Education: Theory and Practice*, 2d ed. (Boston: Allyn and Bacon, 1988).

3. John I. Goodlad, *A Place Called School* (New York: McGraw-Hill, 1984); *The Current State of Social Studies: A Report of Project SPAN* (Boulder, Colo.: Social Science Education Consortium, 1982).

4. Jesus Garcia and Julie Goebel, "A Comparative Study of the Portrayal of Black Americans in Selected U.S. History Books," *Negro Educational Review* 36 (1985): 118–127.

5. James S. Coleman, Ernest Q. Campbell, Carol J. Hobson, James McPartland, Alexander M. Mood, Frederic D. Weinfeld, and Robert L. York, *Equality of Educational Opportunity* (Washington, D.C.: U.S. Government Printing Office, 1966).

6. Geneva Gay, "Motivation: An Antecedent to Academic Achievement," paper presented at the institute *Increasing the Academic Achievement of Minority Students*, sponsored by the Educational Materials and Services Center, Bellevue, Wash., July 1987.

7. John G. Neihardt, *Black Elk Speaks* (New York: Pocket Books, 1972), p. 230.

8. "Black Elk's Prayer from a Mountaintop in the Black Hills, 1931," in Jack D. Forbes, ed. *The Indian in America's Past* (Englewood Cliffs, N.J.: Prentice-Hall, 1964), p. 69.

9. James Baldwin, *The Price of the Ticket: Collected Nonfiction 1948–1985* (New York: St. Martin's Press, 1985).

10. William Loren Katz, *Black Indians: A Hidden Heritage* (New York: Atheneum, 1986).

11. Geneva Gay and James A. Banks, "Teaching the American Revolution: A Multiethnic Approach," *Social Education* 39 (November–December 1975): 461–465.

12. Selections by most of these writers are reprinted in Henry Knepler and Myrna Knepler, eds. *Crossing Cultures: Readings for Composition* (New York: Macmillan, 1983).

13. Banks, *Multiethnic Education*, 128–130.

14. See, for example, Dorothy Abbott, ed., *Mississippi Writers: Reflections on Childhood and Youth*, II: *Nonfiction* (Jackson: University Press of Mississippi, 1986).

15. Fred N. Newmann, "Discussion: Political Socialization in the Schools," *Harvard Educational Review* 38 (1968): 536–545.

16. Reprinted with persmission from James A. Banks, *Teaching Strategies for Ethnic Studies*, 4th ed. (Boston: Allyn and Bacon, 1987), pp. 224–226.

17. Gordon W. Allport, *The Nature of Prejudice*, 25th anniversary ed. (Reading, Mass.: Addison-Wesley, 1979).

18. David Milner, *Children and Race* (Beverly Hills, Calif.: Sage, 1983).

19. Alice Walker, *The Color Purple* (New York: Harcourt Brace, 1982); Mildred Taylor, *Roll of Thunder, Hear My Cry* (New York: Dial, 1976).

20. Reginald M. Clark, *Family Life and School Achievement: Why Poor Black Children Succeed or Fail* (Chicago: University of Chicago Press, 1983).

CHAPTER 11

Language Diversity and Education

■ CARLOS J. OVANDO

Language diversity has a strong influence on the content and process of schooling practices for both language minority and majority students in the United States. Language, as a system of communication linking sound, written or visual symbols, and meaning, is an indispensable bridge for accessing knowledge, skills, values, and attitudes within and across cultures. It has tremendous power as the paramount instrument of cognitive development, and it can open or close the door to academic achievement. How, then, is the educational inequality experienced by language minority students related to their inability to understand, speak, read, and write standard English in the curriculum?

To present an overview of how language diversity is related to educational outcomes, this chapter is organized in three sections. In the first section we consider what language is and how children and adults acquire their first and second languages. In the second section we survey varieties of nonstandard English as well as non-English-language diversity in the United States. In the third section we address classroom adaptations to meet the needs of language minority students.

The Sociocultural Nature of Language and Language Acquisition

Language is an important part of culture. As with culture, language is learned, it is shared, and it evolves and changes over time. Language can be analyzed from many different points of view. For instance, at the physical level, it is a system of sounds and movements made by the human body and decoded by the listener's auditory system. From the psychological or cognitive point of view, it is a tool for the expression of thought. From the anthropological point of view, it is an intricate and pervasive component of culture. Language can also be studied as a system of signs and symbols that have socially determined meanings.[1]

Language is much more than a set of words and grammar rules. It is a forceful instrument for giving individuals, groups, institutions, and cultures their identity. Through language we share and exchange our values, attitudes, skills, and aspirations as bearers of culture and as makers of future culture.

From the pedagogical point of view, what has an individual learned when he or she is said to have gained communicative competence in a particular language? To begin with, there are the more familiar domains of language:

1. Phonetics and phonology—learning how to pronounce the language
2. Morphology—the study and description of word formation
3. Syntax—the grammar of sentence formation
4. Lexicon (the vocabulary)

Beyond these, however, are the five culture-related domains to be mastered for communicative competence. These domains illustrate the subtleties and cultural components of the process of learning a language.

1. Discourse: How the language is organized in speech and writing beyond the sentence level (for example, topic sentence and supporting details).
2. Appropriateness: The kind of language use according to the social situation (for example, ''Hit the lights, will ya?'' versus ''Would you mind turning the lights off, please?'').
3. Paralinguistics: Gestures, facial expressions, distance between speakers, intonation, and volume and pitch of speech.
4. Pragmatics: Brings together discourse, appropriateness, and paralinguistics. For example, pragmatics have to do with implicit cultural norms for when it is and is not appropriate to talk, how speech is paced, the correct way to listen, when to be direct and when to be indirect, how to take turns in conversation, and how to adapt language according to roles, social status, attitudes, settings, and topics.
5. Cognitive-academic language proficiency: Mastery of the language skills needed to learn and develop abstract concepts in such areas as mathematics, science, and social studies.[2]

Even such a cursory listing of these skills and domains clearly suggests that language acquisition is a complicated, subtle, and culture-specific process. Educators thus need to realize that the difference between English and Spanish, for example, or even between standard English and Black English, is much more than a difference in pronunciation, grammar, and vocabulary. We could also argue that learning basic communication in one's first language is a simple process—child's play, so to speak. However, when examined carefully, even one's full development of the first language—including literacy skills and knowledge about the structure and function of the language—is a sophisticated endeavor that takes years to master. Knowing this, teachers are more likely to develop respect for and sensitivity to students who arrive in the classroom speaking anything other than standard English. For non-English speakers in particular, teachers should be realistic as to the years of exposure it takes speakers to move from basic communication in English to full communicative competence.

Languages grow and develop as tools of communication within a given environment. In this sense, there is no such thing as "right" or "wrong" language, only language that is appropriate or inappropriate in a given context. Languages and language varieties develop and thrive because they meet the needs of communities. If a given community of speakers finds it necessary to maintain a language because it satisfies spiritual, social, intellectual, technical, scientific, economic, or political needs, then the chances that that particular linguistic community will survive are greatly enhanced. Thus, for example, Yupik (an Eskimo-Aleut language spoken by the Yupik, a group of Eskimos) is alive in Akiachak, Alaska, despite the powerful influence of English, because it fulfills the people's need for continuity with their heritage. Within the domain of English itself, the United States teems with a variety of linguistic microcultures representing a diversity of experiences: American Indian varieties of English, Creoles, Black English, and a broad array of regional accents, vocabularies, and styles.

Because multicultural education seeks to promote equity and excellence across such variables as race, ethnicity, nationality, gender, social class, regional groups, and language background, educators must understand the function language can play in either helping or inhibiting the educational fulfillment of individuals. As Dell Hymes states:

> *The law of the land demands that equal educational opportunity not be denied because of language. "Language" has been understood most readily in terms of "languages," such as Spanish, and structurally definable varieties of a language, such as Black English Vernacular. If one defines "language," as I do, in terms of ways of speaking, as involving both structure and ways of using structure, there are even deeper implications, implications not yet legally explored. One's language affects one's chances in life, not only through accent, but also through action. Access to opportunities in the form of access to schools, jobs, positions, memberships, clubs, homes, may depend on ways of using language that one has no chance to master, or chooses not to master.[3]*

Within and outside the school setting, it becomes important to consider how persons come to acquire and value the particular types of first and second languages they prefer to use in formal and informal situations. Therefore, we now turn to research on first and second language acquisition and its application in classrooms. We focus here on the process by which non-English speakers acquire English language skills.

For the past twenty years, linguists have made considerable progress in understanding first and second language acquisition. The research indicates that language learning is a developmental process that goes through predictable stages. We acquire our first language as children, in the context of a natural, interesting, and meaningful interaction with the social and physical environment. In such an environment, the child is exposed day after day to peer and adult language models in a context that gives meaning to language. Because of this strongly contextualized environment, speakers tend to learn communication shortcuts such as incomplete responses, a limited vocabulary, and many nonverbal cues.

Cummins refers to this type of language as basic interpersonal communicative skills (BICS) and suggests that an average non-English-speaking student can learn to communicate at this level in English after about two years of instruction in an acquisition-rich environment similar to that of a child learning a first language.[4] This ability to get along in the world conversationally enables students limited in English proficiency to make everyday conversational contact with their English-speaking peers. Such contact, in turn, provides a pivotal function in the acculturation of such students, especially to the school culture. In addition, such face-to-face communication serves as an initial platform for building a self-concept in social relationships. In other words, the acquisition of BICS serves a powerful and important sociolinguistic function in the lives of persons learning their second languages.

However, even though a student of limited English proficiency may seem to be making rapid progress in the acquisition of English judging from the informal observations in the social environment of the school setting, such control of BICS does not necessarily equip the student for the curriculum's more cognitively demanding tasks. Cognitive tasks require a second developmental level beyond BICS that consists of the language used in school and many facets of adult life. Here, the context is less clear; instead, communication depends on a speaker's (or writer's) ability to manipulate the vocabulary and syntax with precision.[5] Again, research by Cummins indicates that, as measured in standardized tests, children with little or no prior schooling experience attain nativelike control of English in cognitive-academic language proficiency (CALP) in about five to seven years.[6]

Just as speakers of non-standard varieties of English come to school with a wealth of home experience that can be tapped by the teacher, non-English speakers also come to school not as a blank tablet but with a vast array of skills that can be drawn on. Again, Cummins's research[7] concludes that prior acquired knowledge and skills in the home language transfer automatically to the new language. This is known as the common underlying proficiency (CUP) for both languages. Of importance to language minority educators is Cummins's conclusion on the instructional use of both the home language (L1) and English (L2):

> The results of research on bilingual programs show that minority children's L1 can be promoted in school at no cost to the development of proficiency in the majority language. . . .
> The data clearly show that well-implemented bilingual programs have had remarkable success in developing English academic skills and have proved superior to ESL-only programs in situations where direct comparisons have been carried out.[8]

Thus, using the home language of learners for instructional purposes can provide a base for skills development that is comprehensible to students and can then be applied to their academic and language growth in English.

Language Variety in the United States

As a language laboratory, the United States is truly remarkable. To date, about 206 Native American languages have survived the overwhelming assimilative powers of the English language.[9] Languages other than English used by the colonizers of the United States—such as Spanish and French—continue not only to survive but also to serve as lively communicative and cultural instruments in various regions of the country. The successive waves of immigrants to the United States made the nation linguistically rich. The language assets range from such languages as Navajo—still spoken today in the same communities in which it was spoken hundreds of years ago—to Hmong, spoken by recent refugees from the highlands of Laos and Cambodia.

In addition to the varied mix of languages, language contact in the United States has also produced many indigenous language varieties known as creole, pidgin, and dialect. Creole is the adoption of a pidgin as the accepted language of a community. As Anttila puts it, "this happened often on the plantations of the New World, where slaves from different language backgrounds were forced to use a pidgin among themselves, and between themselves and the masters. After escape, freedom, or revolution the pidgin was all they had, and it had to become the first language of the community."[10] Three examples of creole varieties in the United States are (1) Gullah, an English- and West African–based creole spoken on the Sea Islands, from the Carolinas to northern Florida; (2) Louisiana French Creole, which coexists with two local varieties of French and another local variety of English; and (3) Hawaiian creole, which has been influenced by Hawaiian, Japanese, Chinese, Portuguese, English, and Ilocano. Complementing the rich indigenous creole traditions of the United States is Black English, spoken by a large segment of the Afro-American population.

As noted earlier, Gullah is geographically associated with Afro-Americans who initially settled in South Carolina in the 1700s. Nichols estimates that there are now about 300,000 Afro-Americans who speak Gullah in an area including South Carolina, Georgia, and parts of lower North Carolina and northern Florida.[11] Ties between Gullah and its West African language ancestors include similar vowel sounds and some vocabulary items such as *goober* for "peanut," *cooter* for "turtle," and *buckra* for "White man."[12] Structurally, Gullah also differs from standard English. For example, instead of using *he* and *she*, the neuter pronoun *ee* is used for both male and female. *Fuh* is used to indicate an infinitive clause, as in "I came *fuh* get my coat." Progressive action can be indicated by *duh* plus the verb: "Greg duh hide" instead of "Greg is hiding."[13]

Most members of the Gullah-speaking community are not strictly creole speakers. What is found instead are individuals "who show greater or lesser use of creole features along a continuum of language use ranging from creole to a dialect of English."[14] Not surprisingly, there is a strong association of Gullah use with age and amount of formal schooling. For example, the very old and the very young tend to use Gullah more extensively. Young school-age children tend to switch back and forth between Gullah—referred to as "country talk"—and the prestige variety of standard English, especially for the benefit of teachers, who usually do not understand Gullah.

Gullah has been analyzed extensively by linguists, and much is known about its phonology, grammar, vocabulary, and sociolinguistic usage. Gullah has also been popularized through literature such as the stories of Ambrose Gonzalez[15] and the novels and Gullah sketches of Pulitzer Prize winner Julia Peterkin.[16] Yet the children who speak Gullah have been stigmatized in the schools, and there has not been a vigorous effort to incorporate their language into the curriculum to create bridges to standard English. To date, no curricular materials have been written in Gullah. Although some teachers are addressing literacy development for such children by using the language-experience approach, by and large such creole-speaking children may not be receiving equal educational opportunities in classrooms in which standard English is the accepted medium of instruction.

Like Gullah, Louisiana French Creole reflects a linguistic structure that sets it apart from English. Louisiana Creole speakers may have difficulty understanding English, and vice-versa. Louisiana French Creole, a contemporary of Gullah, supposedly evolved via West African slaves who were introduced by French colonists to southern Louisiana and needed a common language to communicate with each other. Louisiana French Creole has structural similarities with English-related creoles such as Gullah. For example, the pronoun *li* is used for both *he* and *she*. Also, like Gullah, no verb "to be" is used in equative clauses. However, unlike Gullah, most of the Louisiana French Creole vocabulary is derived from French rather than from English, with some use of African vocabulary items.[17]

Although Acadian and standard French are officially affirmed in the school curriculum, Louisiana French Creole does not seem to have the same status. As with Gullah, children who speak Louisiana French Creole therefore run the risk of not receiving equal educational opportunities. Furthermore, they and their parents may interpret the neglect of their primary language as a devaluation of their sociolinguistic background in the eyes of school personnel and society at large.

A recent newcomer into the family of indigenous creoles in American society is Hawaiian Creole, the use of which dates back to the late nineteenth or early twentieth century. Unlike Louisiana Creole, there is considerably more careful scholarly documentation about its origin, structure, and function.[18] Hawaiian Creole evolved as a pidgin during the late nineteenth century when plantations were developed and the Hawaiian Islands came under the influence of English speakers from the United States mainland. Similar to Gullah, Hawaiian Creole is English-related, and its lexicon is predominantly English, with the aforementioned influence from Hawaiian, Japanese, Chinese, Portugese, and Ilocano. This rich linguistic mixture in the Hawaiian Islands has led language scholars to view Hawaiian English "in terms of three coexistent systems—a pidgin, Creole, and dialect of English—none of which occurs in unadulterated forms but only in combinations of different proportions."[19]

Whether Hawaiian English is a dialect of English or a creole language is a complex issue. Somewhat like Gullah, its degree of similarity to English ranges on a continuum depending on the community and the context. For example, linguists note a highly decreolized language variety in the more urbanized population centers like Oahu and more creolized traditional patterns in the more remote islands of Kauai and Hawaii.[20]

In any event, Hawaiian Creole is a lively language that plays a key role in the lives of many Hawaiian children both socially and academically. As with Gullah and Louisiana French Creole, Hawaiian Creole, or Pidgin English, as it is known by island residents, is a highly stigmatized language variety that until the 1970s had been singled out by educational policymakers as a cause of the many academic problems experienced by Hawaiian students. According to Nichols, the policy was to decreolize the students' language. Because such a posture toward Hawaiian Creole did not produce the desired result of eliminating it from the lives of students, education policies since then have tended toward acceptance of the language in the lives of the students. However, there is still a sense that it is a "deficient language" and thus in need of correction.[21] The attempt in Hawaii to eradicate Hawaiian Creole confirms once more that when something as important as a language is threatened, its users tend to protect and defend it. This is what happened in the islands, where Hawaiian Creole speakers began to see their use of creole as an important symbol of solidarity in their community.

Black English, although a dialect of English rather than a creole language, shows parallels in historical development with creole languages. Black English reflects influence from British and American English as well as English-based pidgin from sixteenth-century West Africa. In situations involving language contact, one has to understand the nature of the social relationships within and outside the involved communities. Slave-master relationships were not generally conducive to a trusting and caring communicative process. But it is in this type of socially strained context that Black English and White English coexisted and influenced each other. From the late 1700s until the early 1900s, approximately 90 percent of the United States' Black population lived in the southern states.[22] With such a high concentration of speakers, Black English was able to mature into a highly sophisticated and rule-governed "subsystem within the larger grammar of English."[23]

Unlike Gullah, Louisiana French Creole, and Hawaiian Creole, Black English spread throughout the United States. In the twentieth century, many Blacks began to migrate to the large urban centers of the North. Through this two-way connection between Black communities in the rural South and the industrial North, Black English emerged. As Whatley observes, "Funerals, homecoming celebrations at churches, and family reunions took northerners 'down home' at least annually."[24] Strong regional and familial ties between the rural south and the industrial north generated much cross-fertilization of old and new communication patterns.

On the other hand, de facto segregation in the large urban centers of the north tended to insulate Black and White communities from each other. That meant that, given the social distance created between the speakers of Black English and White English, both languages had minimal influence on one another. Thus Black English tended to continue developing its own set of structures, functional patterns, and styles.

Despite the presence of Black English throughout the United States, the perception of Whites and others as to what Black English is may be highly distorted. As Whatley points out, much of what the nation has come to understand as Black English has come about through Hollywood and the electronic media, with all their distortions and stereotypic tendencies. Thus, the world of entertainment has given White society an opportunity to observe highly stylized Black speech—*jiving, copping, playing the dozens, boasting, preaching, and fussing*—within a family entertainment format. However, the impression television, radio, theater, and musicals have given White audiences regarding Black communities is just the tip of the linguistic iceberg. As Whatley indicates, there are many uses of Black English other than those portrayed in the media.[25]

As with any other language, there is great speech variation among speakers of Black English. Also, speech behavior is highly contextualized. That is, individuals tend to assess the communicative situation and respond accordingly. Most people speak a variety of English in their daily lives, ranging on continua of degrees of formality and social status. Within the Black experience, praising, fussing, teasing, lying, preaching, jiving, boasting, or joking are carefully determined by the age, gender, and status of speakers. For example, the eldest members of the Black community tend to have greater latitude and prestige in language use, and children are the lowest-ranking members of the speech community. This, of course, does not mean that Black children are not allowed to interact with adults in creative and expressive ways. What it does mean, however, is that there is a certain speech protocol that is sensitive to such variables as age, social status, gender, and formal and informal settings.

Because of Black Americans' historical status as an oppressed minority, Whites have tended to perceive Black English not as a valid linguistic system, but rather as "a mass of random errors committed by Blacks trying to speak English."[26] The language variety used by Blacks, however, has an internal linguistic infrastructure and a set of grammar rules just as any other language does. For example, the use of the verb "to be" follows different rules in Black English than in standard English. Speakers of standard English tend to contract forms of the verb "to be," as in the sentence, "She's tall" instead of "She is tall." Black English deletes "is" entirely so that the sentence becomes "She tall." Black English also has a use for "be" that standard English does not. The sentences "He always be walkin' on a desert on TV" and "He jus' be walkin' dere sometime" use what linguists call the "invariant be." This use of the verb refers to action that takes place habitually over a period of time, and for this there is no exact standard English equivalent.[27]

Multiple negation is perhaps one of the most stigmatized aspects of Black English when speakers enter the formal school system. Yet there are no logical bases for such stigmatization. Acceptance or nonacceptance of the double negative as a socially correct form is essentially a historical accident. According to language scholars, multiple negation was an integral part of the English language up to the time of Shakespeare. Also it is useful to know that although Latin is credited for having influenced the single negation in English, other Romance languages such as Spanish, French, and Italian use double negative as part of their respective standard speech patterns.[28]

A fair curricular process is one that builds on whatever sociocultural and linguistic backgrounds the students bring with them. Yet use of Black English has had many negative consequences for Black students. Many Black youth have not prospered in U.S. schools, and in the process of searching for reasons for this, society has singled out their nonstandard communication patterns as an important part of the cause for their academic failure. In the past, a common perception among educators, although not necessarily articulated, has been that speakers of Black English are language deficient. Use of Black English, from this point of view, is seen as being detrimental to the student's cognitive development. However, consider as an example the following conversation between two young speakers of Black English:

A: Do you know 'bout factors and all that stuff?
B: Yea, I know all that.
A: Well, how come you only made a 50 on that test?

B: That test was tough—she ain't no good teacher anyway.

A: But you have been in the other math class, the one dat ain't done factors like we have.

B: Yea, but I can do spelling—and you can't.[29]

Whatley interprets the above playful interaction as follows:

> It is clear in this boasting episode that child A had collected highly specific information to support his boast, and he set child B up to a challenge by a seemingly innocent question. The strategies and information to support these were planned in advance. Child A wins this sequence, because child B must shift topic and begin another boast.[30]

From the above boasting episode, it is apparent that although the children are not using standard English, they are certainly not language deficient. If anything, the pair reflect a high level of creativity and spontaneity with language behavior which is highly desirable for cognitive development. Such children may be linguistically different, but they are not deficient. Their linguistic behavior and vocabulary inventory serve their communication needs extremely well.

Gullah, Louisiana Creole, Hawaiian Creole, and Black English have much in common. They are rule govererned and legitimate linguistic expressions just as standard English is. They are a link to our past and have a birthright to exist and be accepted. Yet they are not given much recognition in the larger society. Rather, they are viewed by many people as aberrant and inferior language varieties. Consequently, a great unfounded fear exists on the part of educators that affirmation of such languages will perpetuate school failure in the lives of such students. Because teaching practices are not always linguistically enlightened, language can become a main source of inequality surrounding the lives of students who come to school marked with a stigmatized speech variety.

Cognitive psychologists, on the other hand, tell us that we build our cognitive repertoire on prior knowledge, experiences, attitudes, and skills.[31] It is a layering process. Educators, therefore, dare not destroy what was there before. The goal should be to build on and add to what is already present in the lives of students. Creative bridges using the early socialization patterns of the home language and culture can be useful in motivating students to learn. This, of course, means that such students will come to see their teachers as professionals who understand the value of their nonstandard languages and use their structure and function to build another layer of linguistic skill that will enable these students to negotiate the prestige variety of English in the larger society and thus to have more options in their lives.

Limited-English-Proficient Students

As a result of shifting demographics, the United States is currently experiencing an increasing representation of limited-English-proficient (LEP) students in its schools. Since the passage of the 1968 Title VII Bilingual Education Act and the landmark U.S. Supreme Court Decision *Lau* v. *Nichols* (1974), which provided a legal basis for equitable treatment of LEP students in U.S. schools, educational policy for non-English-language communities has put non-English-language varieties in the national spotlight. Limited-English-proficient students in U.S. schools come from an astounding variety of backgrounds. For example, foreign-born children come to U.S. schools speaking only their ancestral language. Their families may be voluntary immigrants or involuntarily uprooted refugees, such as the Hmong. They may reside in the U.S. legally or as undocumented workers. There are also aboriginal or native-born language minority students for whom the United States is and has always been their home country. In this group, we place the 206 or so Indian languages used in this country. Within the group of individuals for whom the United States is the homeland are those for whom such colonial languages as Spanish, French, German, Swedish, Dutch, or Russian may be the primary language. All of these students may fall anywhere on a broad continuum of language status, ranging from entirely monolingual in the non-English language to bilingual in the home language and English, to dominant in English, with only a few fragmentary skills in the ancestral language.

As noted earlier, the United States has become an amazing linguistic laboratory. Even in Anchorage, Alaska, more than 100 languages spoken by students have been identified by the local school district's bilingual education program. The Los Angeles School District, whose students spoke about 79 languages, offered bilingual instruction in Spanish, Cantonese, Vietnamese, Korean, Filipino, and Armenian in 1987.

At the national level, the following picture emerges.

Every state [in the United States] has a significant language minority population: in twenty-three states, it constitutes at least 10 percent of the population, and seven states have more than a million language minority persons. People of Spanish background, the largest group, number about 10.6 million, three-fifths of them in the southwestern states of California, Arizona, Colorado, New Mexico, and Texas. The top immigrant languages are Italian and German, then come French and Polish. Nearly two million speakers are of Chinese, Filipino, Japanese, Korean, or Vietnamese language background.[32]

Other data show that during the ten years between 1970 and 1980, U.S. society became increasingly multiracial, multicultural, and multilingual. The demographic trend shows that in these ten years the total population of the United States grew by 11.6 percent. But when separated ethnically and racially, we see a demographic picture of minority groups galloping ahead of the rest of the Caucasian and non-Hispanic population. During that decade, Hispanics increased by 61 percent, Native Americans by 71 percent,[33] and Asian-Americans by 141 percent.[34] Increased immigration from both Latin America and Asia as well as high fertility rates within these populations are the major factors contributing to this recent demographic shift.

California, with its large language minority population, has become the Ellis Island of the 1980s. By the year 2000, the state is projected to have a minority population between 40 and 50 percent.[35] If these figures are examined in relation to school-age populations, it is projected that in the year 2000, 52 percent of students in California will be ethnic minorities. This is not surprising, considering that as recently as 1985 California's minorities represented "47 percent of the 4.15 million students, including more than one-half million limited English proficient students."[36]

Other figures show that as of 1980 there were approximately "3.5 million to 5.3 million such students, representing the range of language minority children who scored respectively, below the 20th percentile and below the 40th percentile in English proficiency."[37] Demographers predict that the numbers of non-English-background students will be about 5 million in the year 2000.[38]

While these figures are useful in giving at least an imperfect glimpse at the numbers of children from language minority homes, they do not begin to scratch the surface when it comes to figuring out who is eligible for bilingual services and how long they are to be served. Thus, as Ulibarri suggests,

> *Differences in estimates of the limited-English-proficient population derive from efforts to count the number of children according to different definitions and interpretations of eligibility for services. At issue are the criteria for determining which language minority children are in need of English and native language related services. Thus, the problem is not simply one of differences in number of eligible children, but one in which the actual definition of who is eligible also varies.[39]*

Although there is great variation depending on the student's background and schooling opportunities, most LEP students do not achieve well academically. In fact, they are overrepresented at the bottom of the test score ladder. Despite the research-based knowledge we have gained over the past twenty years about how individuals learn their first and second languages and about how acculturative and assimilative forces work with immigrants and indigenous groups, there is still a wide gap between theory and practice. Consider, for example, the strong resistance that home language instruction has received in educational circles despite the evidence indicating that LEP students who develop a strong sociocultural, linguistic, and cognitive base in their primary language tend to transfer those attitudes and skills to the other language and culture. Moreover, the poor track record schools have had in schooling American Indians, for example, suggests that schooling not only such Indian students but most language minorities as well has generally been surrounded by a great deal of political and ideological controversy at the expense of sustained and well-founded curricular development.

Addressing Language Needs in the Multicultural Classroom

The basis for the debate surrounding the schooling of language minority students has to do essentially with the kind of citizens we want and need in our society. Should the school curriculum affirm cultural and linguistic pluralism through an additive process? Or should the schools pursue an ideologically conservative agenda of assimilating language minorities into mainstream U.S. society by subtracting their ancestral cultures and languages?

These questions raise some pointed and difficult issues regarding the nature and extent of cultural and linguistic pluralism in U.S. society. However, rather than thinking in terms of pluralism or assimilation, perhaps it would be useful to view U.S. society as a dynamic and complex cultural and linguistic organism that is constantly undergoing evolution, change, and modification according to the nature of circumstances—a constructive pluralism in which maintenance, diversification, and assimilation are taking place simultaneously under varying circumstances. Within such an environment of constructive pluralism, blaming the student's genetic, environmental, cultural, or linguistic background for lack of academic success in the English-dominated classroom cannot be accepted. Programs and practices can be implemented to redress some of the past inequities experienced by both English-background students who come to our schools speaking stigmatized nonstandard versions of English as well as students whose primary language is not English. Implementing such programs, however, can resemble paddling a canoe against a powerful and recurring tide with strong, cold winds buffeting it from the sides. Not to do so, on the other hand, suggests abdicating responsibility of the tenets of multicultural education, which means equity of treatment to all our students regardless of ethnicity or language background.

A good place to start is by examining what constitute effective teaching and learning classroom climates for students in general. Griffin and Barnes, citing investigations of teacher effectiveness, state:

> A composite picture of effective teachers drawn from this body of research findings would give attention to the following: the teacher's establishment of a work orientation while maintaining a warm, supportive environment; a high level of organization with emphasis on management of the class to increase the productive use of time; active involvement with students to prevent misbehavior and prompt interventions to stop misbehavior; clear presentation of new material with opportunities for students to practice new skills; monitoring of student behavior; provision of feedback to students; assignment of individual seatwork; and systematic evaluation of student products.[40]

This research provides an important reminder of certain basic pedagogical practices that may have validity for all students, regardless of language background, and should not be overlooked when trying to create a "special" program for language minority students. Nevertheless, language minority students do need some types of special classroom instruction.

One issue regarding the education of speakers of nonstandard English is whether their language varieties should be used formally in the classroom. Also, should students be trained to be bidialectical, that is, to be able to switch from their home variety of English to standard English according to the situation? Some educators interpret bidialectalism as a waste of educational effort, suggesting that students need to discard their mother dialect and replace it with standard English, preferably by the time they leave kindergarten. And yet most linguists keep reminding us that suppressing such dialects is confusing and detrimental to the academic and social well-being of students. As proven by the repeated attempts to eradicate nonstandard English varieties for the past fifty years in the schools, such efforts have not been positively correlated with the achievement gains of language minority students.[41] The use of nonstandard English itself cannot be singled out as the cause for school failure. As Torrey puts it, "teachers should not judge children's language abilities by their schoolyard grammar."[42] Instead, a more likely source of poor academic performance is the school's reaction and approach to nonstandard English. The pedagogical position taken by Torrey

> *affirms the importance of home dialect and its appropriate use within the community in which it is spoken while at the same time students are taught the standard variety. Affirming home language means that students may produce utterances in the classroom in native dialect without being told that they are wrong or that what they say is vulgar or bad. Instead, the teacher analyzes with the students the differences between their dialect and the standard variety: grammatical patterns, pronunciation, vocabulary items, varying social contexts, and so on.[43]*

Of course, the challenge for LEP students is not that they speak a stigmatized variety of English, but rather that they speak little English at all. Based on teacher effectiveness research, Macias identifies some basic competencies for quality instruction for LEP students regardless of whether the teacher speaks the students' home language:

> *Use of "active" teaching behaviors, including giving directions clearly, describing tasks accurately, specifying how students will know when the tasks are completed correctly, and presenting new information by using appropriate strategies like explaining, outlining and demonstrating, keeping students' engagement in instructional tasks by pacing instruction appropriately, by involving students actively, and by expressing expectations for students' successful task completion, monitoring students' progress and providing immediate feedback when necessary.[44]*

In addition to this, Macias found that significant instructional features for teachers who speak the students' first language included "use of both languages for instruction, assuring not only understandable instruction, but a clear and positive environment and status for each language; the integration of English language development with academic skills development; understanding and appropriate use of the cultural background and diversity of the students to mediate learning, and classroom management."[45]

Shifting focus from teacher behavior to program design, Troike has found the following seven elements to be important for effective bilingual instruction.

1. Emphasis must be given to the development of native language skills, including reading, and the overall amount of English used should not exceed 50 percent;

2. Teachers must be trained and able to teach fluently in the language of the students;

3. The program should extend over at least five grades, and preferably more;

4. The program must be integrated into the basic structure of the school administration and curriculum, and a supportive environment must exist;

5. Materials of comparable quality to those used in English should be available;

6. There should be support from the community and parents;

7. High standards for student achievement should be set and every effort made to maintain them.[46]

Many teachers who work with LEP students are not bilingual, and they provide instruction in English as a Second Language (ESL) rather than bilingual instruction. Among the skills important to their task are a sound knowledge of how languages are naturally acquired and an explicit grasp of the rules of the English language coupled with an ability to convey such things as grammar rules through means other than lectures and drills.[47]

An important principle to keep in mind when working with language minority students—either English or non-English-speaking—is that their cognitive development must be launched from within a given sociolinguistic context. There are no such things as exportable models that work everywhere without adaptation. As Brice-Heath points out, language arts curricula are based on an assumption of a path of language development that is the same for all children, regardless of ethnic origin. Yet the research that establishes such lines of development is predominantly based on middle-class English-speaking families. Only in recent years have ethnographers working in language minority communities begun to identify culturally different patterns of language socialization experienced by children. One implication of this variation in language development is that the academic success that language minority students will experience in school hinges more on how these children are able to manipulate language in a variety of contexts and for different purposes than on the specific language they use.[48] Given this assertion, it follows that the school's responsibility is to provide a wide range of experiences that will facilitate language development for social interaction as well as language for academic prosperity. Given the fact that language mastery and cognitive development in the primary language will transfer to the second language, language minority children should first be exposed to conceptual and language development in the language in which they feel more comfortable.

Beyond the face-to-face language we all need to get along socially with peers, language minority students also need to acquire language they will use in literacy-related activities. In other words, it is insufficient for students to be able to converse with their peers only on the playground or in the halls. They need to be able to use the decontextualized language associated with extracting meaning from the printed word, for synthesizing and evaluating materials, and for writing. The importance of the development of such high-level skills is illustrated in Collier's research on non-English-speaking students who enter school in the United States at seventh grade. Even though they may have a solid academic background in their home language, in the U.S. school system they tend to fall behind in standardized test norms, except in mathematics, by the time they reach the eleventh grade. Collier suggests that

> these students are not being provided any native language content instruction to keep up with grade level skills while they are mastering beginning levels of BICS (Basic Interpersonal Communication Skills) and CALP (Cognitive Academic Language Proficiency) in English. As they master enough BICS and develop a wide enough range of vocabulary in English to move into deeper development of CALP in second language, they have in the meantime lost 2–3 years of CALP development at their age-grade level. This puts them significantly behind in mastery of the complex material required for high school students.[49]

Collier's research supports Cummins's findings that an LEP student may need five to seven years to reach nativelike control of the English language to perform well on academic tasks. Especially in the upper grades, school success is to a large extent developed and measured through lecture and paper-and-pencil tasks, which are largely "context-reduced." In context-reduced situations, the meaning of the lesson is derived or manipulated primarily through linguistic cues and the internal logic of the text rather than from prior knowledge or experience. Therefore, LEP students need to have control of formal English in order to achieve academically.

Mentioned earlier in this chapter are the culturally influenced domains of language beyond phonology, vocabulary, and syntax—such things as body language, degrees of formality, types of organizations and styles of speech, and appropriate speaking and listening etiquette. Related to these domains is Brice Heath's research on genres. Regarding the specific linguistic elements that are essential for academic success in school regardless of language background, Brice Heath has summarized the research on genre, which she defines as the

> kind of organizing unit into which smaller units of language, such as
> conversations, sentences, lists, or directives may fit. Each cultural group has
> fundamental genres that occur in recurrent situations; and each genre is so
> patterned as a whole that listeners can anticipate by the prosody or opening
> formulae what is coming—a joke, a story, or a recounting of shared
> experiences. Moreover, each sociocultural group recognizes and uses only a
> few of the total range of genres that humans are capable of producing.[50]

Brice Heath then argues that in order for students to function well in formal U.S. school settings, they must be able to use a variety of genres typical to American pedagogy, such as label quests, meaning quests, recounts, accounts, eventcasts, and stories. Label quests are activities in which adults ask children to say their name or to identify an item—"What's that?" or "What kind of _____ is that?" Meaning quests are activities in which an unstated or partly stated meaning is inferred from an oral or written language source. For example, a teacher might ask, "What did the author mean when she wrote, 'Andy kicked the book out of his way'?" In recounts, the child retells an experience that is already known to the teller and the listener. The speaker may be prompted with guiding questions by the adult. Accounts are activities in which the child provides new information to the listener. Accounts are often judged by their logical sequence and their truthfulness. Such accounts are the predecessors of research and creative writing assignments in the upper grades. Eventcasts are running narratives of events occurring or about to occur. For example, making a gelatin dessert may be accompanied by the mother's sequenced narrative.[51]

Indicating that such genres exist in mainstream American school-based activities in a predictable and consistent manner but that they may or may not all be consistently present in the same way in language minority contexts, Brice Heath suggests that it is the school's responsibility to access these genres to students by working closely with the ethnolinguistic community. In doing so, teachers can broaden cross-culturally the base of linguistic experiences to maximize their students' opportunities for acquiring such genres, which are critical for their academic success. Language minority students should have access first to these genres in whatever language they are the strongest. Also, parents who have a limited grasp of English should be encouraged to use their primary language rather than English with their children. Given their limited command of the English language, they will not be able to use English across the variety of suggested genres and thus will limit the quality and range of linguistic interaction with their children. Instead, such parents ideally should concentrate on engaging their children in conversations in their home language that are interesting and also representative of the variety of genres—written and oral—that schools require. Teachers in a creative partnership with ethnolinguistic communities should make a sustained and creative effort to expose students to these school-valued genres, at the same time capitalizing on community genres available.

Supportive of the notion that creating bridges between the world of the language minority student and that of the school will produce positive cognitive, linguistic, and cultural outcomes is the following example from California. In 1980, the California Office of Bilingual Education launched the "Case Studies Project," based on leading theories of cognitive development, second-language acquisition, and cross-cultural communication. An integrated curriculum incorporating home language instruction, communication-based sheltered English and mainstream English has produced excellent results in reading, language arts, and mathematics for language minority students. Five principles serve as the pedagogical platform for the Case Studies Project:

1. Language development in the home language as well as in English has positive effects on academic achievement.

2. Language proficiency includes proficiency in academic tasks as well as in basic conversation.

3. An LEP student should be able to perform a certain type of academic task in his or her home language before being expected to perform the task in English.

4. Acquisition of English language skills must be provided in contexts in which the student understands what is being said. Crawford describes such instruction:

(a) Content is based on the students' communicative needs; (b) instruction makes extensive use of contextual clues; (c) the teacher uses only English, but modifies speech to students' level and confirms student comprehension; (d) students are permitted to respond in their native language when necessary; (e) the focus is on language function or content, rather than grammatical form; (f) grammatical accuracy is promoted, not by correcting errors overtly, but by providing more comprehensible instruction; and (g) students are encouraged to respond spontaneously and creatively.[52]

5. The social status implicitly ascribed to students and their languages affects student performance. Therefore, majority and minority students should be in classes together in which cooperative learning strategies are used. English speakers should be provided with opportunities to learn the minority languages, and teachers and administrators should model using the minority languages for some noninstructional as well as instructional purposes.[53]

As noted earlier, there are no instructional panaceas for addressing the cognitive, linguistic, and cultural needs of stigmatized language minority students. But these five principles and their practical implications can help educators who are genuinely interested in putting into practice in their classrooms what we have learned over the past twenty years or so about how people acquire their first and second languages, learn in their primary and secondary languages, and adjust socioculturally to the dominant culture.

Language diversity, as a powerful and ubiquitous ingredient of the U.S. multicultural mosaic, enriches the lives of those who use such languages and the lives of those privileged to come into contact with them. As educators we need to assure that the rich and varied sociolinguistic experiences of language minorities do not continue to be translated into negative cognitive, cultural, and linguistic outcomes. As suggested in this chapter, we now have some of the conceptual, programmatic, and curricular tools with which to begin the job.

Summary

Throughout this chapter I stress the power that language issues have to affect schooling outcomes for language minority students. In the first section I discuss how language is interwoven with cultural styles and values. As such, language comprises more than grammar rules, vocabulary, and a sound system. To have communicative competence in a language requires not only these things but also the appropriate facial and body gestures, use of varying levels of formality in the appropriate contexts, correct styles of conversation, and the ability to express abstract concepts.

By studying how children learn language, linguists have determined that language learning is a developmental process that goes through predictable stages. Cummins has identified two levels of language proficiency that are particularly important when designing educational programs for limited-English-proficient (LEP) students: basic interpersonal communicative skills (BICS), which take approximately two years to obtain; and cognitive-academic language proficiency (CALP), which may take five to seven years to achieve. Equally important is the common underlying proficiency (CUP), the concept that skills learned in the first language will automatically transfer to the second language.

The second section of the chapter surveys the extensive nature of language variety in the United States. An examination of nonstandard English and Creole languages emphasizes that language changes fulfill sociohistorical needs. Likewise, the language varieties resulting from these changes have their own grammatical and phonological rules and appropriate cultural styles. The number of students from non-English-speaking backgrounds continues to increase in the United States, and these students are present in significant numbers in every state.

In the final section of the chapter I describe some principles and methods for instruction of language minority students. In nonstandard English varieties, the home language cannot be blamed for school failure. The more likely cause for language-related school failure is the educator's negating approach toward the home language. Through an additive process, the value of the home language can be affirmed while models are also provided for use of the standard language in appropriate contexts.

For students who come from non-English-speaking backgrounds, an active teaching style rather than a lecture style is needed, with frequent checking for understanding. Skills should continue to be developed in the home language while the students are also studying English as a second language (ESL). Regarding ESL instruction, basic interpersonal communicative skills are not sufficient for academic success. Schools must continue to provide support for limited-English-proficient students to achieve cognitive-academic language proficiency.

Finally, there is a need for the continued development and maintenance of social and cultural bridges between the language minority student's home life and school life. An awareness of how language is used in the home community will enable educators to be sensitive to school genres that are different. Efforts to equalize the social and language status of majority and minority students within the school setting will also yield positive results for all students in the classroom, and ultimately, in society.

Questions and Activities

1. What are some of the major characteristics of a language? What role does language play in the maintenance of a culture?

2. How can teachers draw on the home experiences of non-English speakers and speakers of nonstandard varieties of English to help these students develop competence in standard English?

3. What is creolization? Name three Creole varieties in the United States.

4. What is Black English? What are some of its major characteristics? What common misconceptions about Black English are held by some educators? To what extent is Black English spoken by Afro-Americans? How can a knowledge of the nature of Black English be helpful to teachers of Black students?

5. What are Gullah and Hawaiian Creole? What problems do the speakers of these Creole languages experience in schools? Why?

6. Prepare a report on the 1974 *Lau* v. *Nichols* Supreme Court Decision for presentation in your class or workshop. How has this court decision influenced bilingual education programs in the United States? Why is this decision controversial?

7. Visit an inner-city or suburban school in a nearby school district. Find out how many different languages are spoken by the students in the district when they first come to school and what programs are being implemented to deal with the language diversity of the students.

8. What special problems do limited-English-proficient students experience in schools? What programs and practices can schools implement to help these students experience educational success?

9. Identify some principles the author describes for working effectively with dialect and language minority students. What support and training might teachers need to implement these principles in the classroom?

Notes

1. Sebastian Shaumyan, *A Semiotic Theory of Language* (Bloomington and Indianapolis: Indiana University Press, 1987), pp. 1–2.

2. Carlos J. Ovando and Virginia P. Collier, *Bilingual and ESL Classrooms: Teaching in Multicultural Contexts* (New York: McGraw-Hill, 1985), pp. 229–230.

3. Dell H. Hymes, "Foreword," in Charles A. Ferguson and Shirley Brice Heath, eds., *Language in the USA* (Cambridge, Mass.: Cambridge University Press, 1981), pp. vii–viii.

4. Jim Cummins, "The Role of Primary Language Development in Promoting Educational Success for Language Minority Students," in California State Department of Education, *Schooling and Language Minority Students: A Theoretical Framework* (Los Angeles: National Evaluation, Dissemination, and Assessment Center, California State University, 1981), p. 16.

5. Carlos J. Ovando, "Bilingual/Bicultural Education: Its Legacy and Its Future," *Phi Delta Kappan* 64, No. 8 (April 1983): 566.

6. Cummins, *Schooling and Language Minority Students,* 16.

7. Ibid., 23–25.

8. Ibid., 28.

9. William L. Leap, "American Indian Languages," in Charles A. Ferguson and Shirley Brice Heath, eds., *Language in the USA* (Cambridge, Mass.: Cambridge University Press, 1981), p. 116.

10. Raimo Anttila, *An Introduction to Historical and Comparative Linguistics* (New York: Macmillan, 1972), p. 176.

11. Patricia Nichols, "Creoles of the USA," in Charles A. Ferguson and Shirley Brice Heath, *eds., Language in the USA* (Cambridge, Mass.: Cambridge University Press, 1981), p. 73.

12. Ibid., 75.

13. Ibid., 73–75.

14. Ibid., 73.

15. Ibid., 75.

16. Ibid.

17. Ibid., 79.

18. Ibid., 83.

19. Ibid.

20. Ibid.

21. Ibid., 86.

22. Elizabeth Whatley, "Language among Black Americans," in Charles A. Ferguson and Shirley Brice Heath, eds., *Language in the USA* (Cambridge, Mass.: Cambridge University Press, 1981), p. 104.

23. William Labov, *Language in the Inner City: Studies in the Black English Vernacular* (Philadelphia: University of Pennsylvania Press, 1972), p. 64.

24. Whatley, *Language in the USA,* 94.

25. Ibid., 95.

26. William Labov, Paul Cohen, Clarence Robins, and John Lewis, *A Study of the Non-Standard English of Negro and Puerto Rican Speakers in New York City,* Rept. on Cooperative Research Project 3288 (New York: Columbia University, 1968).

27. Whatley, *Language in the USA,* 102.

28. Ibid., 103.

29. Ibid., 99.

30. Ibid., 30.

31. James V. Wertsch, *Vygotsky and the Social Formation of Mind* (Cambridge, Mass.: Harvard University Press, 1985).

32. Ferguson and Brice Heath, *Language in the USA,* xxxi.

33. Carlos E. Cortes, "The Education of Language Minority Students: A Contextual Interaction Model," in California State Department of Education, *Beyond Language: Social and Cultural Factors in Schooling Language Minority Students* (Los Angeles: Evaluation, Dissemination, and Assessment Center, California State University, 1986), pp. 8–9.

34. James A. Banks, *Teaching Strategies for Ethnic Studies,* 4th ed. (Boston: Allyn and Bacon, 1987), p. 412.

35. Cortes, *Beyond Language,* 9.

36. Ibid., 10.

37. Dorothy Waggoner, "Basic Questions Spur Controversy," *Education Week 6,* 27 (April 1, 1987): 25.

38. Louis G. Pol, Rebecca Oxford-

Carpenter, and Samuel Peng, "Limited English-Proficiency: Analytical Techniques and Projections," in Eugene C. Garcia and Raymond V. Padilla, eds., *Advances in Bilingual Education Research* (Tucson: The University of Arizona Press, 1985), p. 259.

39. Daniel M. Ulibarri, "Issues in Estimates of the Number of Limited English Proficient Students," in *A Report of the Compendium of Papers on the Topic of Bilingual Education of the Committee on Education and Labor House of Representatives,* 99th Congress, 2D Session (Washington, D.C.: U.S. Government Printing Office, 1986), p. 57.

40. Gary A. Griffin and Susan Barnes, "Using Research Findings to Change School and Classroom Practices: Results of an Experimental Study," *American Educational Research Journal* 23, No. 4 (Winter 1986): 573–574.

41. Ovando and Collier, *Bilingual and ESL Classrooms,* 69.

42. Jane W. Torrey, "Black Children's Knowledge of Standard English," *American Educational Research Journal* 20, No. 4 (Winter 1983), p. 627.

43. Ovando and Collier, *Bilingual and ESL Classrooms,* 70.

44. Reynaldo F. Macias, *"Teacher Preparation for Bilingual Education,"* in A Report of the Copendium of Papers on the Topic of Bilingual Education of the Committee on Education and Labor House of Representatives, 99th Congress, 2D Session (Washington, D.C.: U.S. Government Printing Office, 1986), pp. 43–44.

45. Ibid.

46. Rudolph C. Troike, "Improving Conditions for Success in Bilingual Education Programs," in *A Report of the Compendium, 2.*

47. Marianne Celce-Murcia and Diane Larsen-Freeman, *The Grammar Book: An ESL/EFL Teacher's Course* (Rowley, Mass.: Newbury House, 1983), p. 1.

48. Shirley Brice Heath, "Sociocultural Contexts of Language Development," in California State Department of Education, *Beyond Language: Social & Cultural Factors in Schooling Language Minority Students* (Los Angeles: National Evaluation, Dissemination, and Assessment Center, California State University, 1986), p. 145.

49. Virginia P. Collier, "Age and Rate of Acquisition of Cognitive-Academic Second Language Proficiency." Paper presented at the American Educational Research Association Meeting, April 23, 1987), p. 12.

50. Brice-Heath, "Sociocultural Contexts of Language Development," p. 166.

51. Ibid., 168–170.

52. James Crawford, "Bilingual Education: Language, Learning, and Politics," *Education Week: A Special Report* (Arpil 1, 1987): 43.

53. Ibid., 43.

*Teachers must be prepared
to respond to the special
educational needs of
students who are
handicapped and who are
intellectually gifted
and talented.*

PART V

Exceptionality

Expanded rights for handicapped students was one major consequence of the civil rights movement of the 1960s and 1970s. The Supreme Court's *Brown* decision, issued in 1954, established the principle that to segregate students solely because of their race is inherently unequal and unconstitutional. This decision, as well as other legal and social reforms of the 1960s, encouraged advocates for the rights of handicapped students to push for expanded rights for them. If it were unconstitutional to segregate students because of their race, it was reasoned, segregating students because they were disabled could also be challenged.

The advocates for the rights of handicapped students experienced a major victory in 1975 when Congress enacted Public Law 94-142, The Education for All Handicapped Children Act. This act was unprecedented and revolutionary in its implications. It requires free public education for all handicapped children, nondiscriminatory evaluation, and an individualized education program (IEP) for each handicapped student, and it stipulates that each handicapped student should be educated in the least restricted environment. This last requirement has been one of the most controversial provisions of Public Law 94-142. Most students who are classified as handicapped—about 90 percent—are mildly handicapped. Consequently, most handicapped students—about two-thirds—spend at least part of the school day in regular classrooms. Handicapped students who are taught in the regular classroom are *mainstreamed;* this process is called *mainstreaming.*

Exceptionality intersects with factors such as gender and race or ethnicity in interesting and complex ways. Males and ethnic minorities are more frequently classified as special education students than are females and White mainstream students. Nearly twice as many males as females are classified as special education students. Consequently, ethnic minority males are the most likely group to be classified as mentally retarded or learning disabled. The higher proportion of males and ethnic minorities in special education programs is related to the fact that mental retardation is a socially constructed category (see Chapter 1).

Handicapped as well as gifted students are considered *exceptional.* Exceptional students are those who have learning or behavioral characteristics that differ substantially from most other students and that require special attention in instruction. Concern for gifted and talented students in the United States increased after the Soviet Union successfully launched Sputnik in 1957. A Gifted and Talented Children's Education Act was passed by Congress in 1978. However, the nation's concern for the gifted is ambivalent and controversial. In 1982, special funding for gifted education was consolidated with twenty-nine other educational programs. The controversy over gifted education stems in part from the belief by many people that gifted education is elitist. Others argue that gifted education is a way for powerful mainstream parents to acquire a special education for their children in the public schools. The fact that few ethnic minority youths are classified as gifted is another source of controversy. Despite the controversies that surround programs for gifted and talented youths, schools needed to find creative and democratic ways to satisfy the needs of students with special gifts and talents.

The chapters in this section describe the major issues, challenges, and promises involved in creating equal educational opportunities for exceptional students—those who are mentally retarded as well as those who are intellectually gifted and talented.

CHAPTER 12

Educational Equality for Exceptional Students

- **WILLIAM L. HEWARD and MICHAEL D. ORLANSKY**

All children differ from one another in their physical attributes and in their ability to learn. Some are taller, some are stronger, some can run fast, and some cannot run at all. Some children learn quickly and generalize what they have learned to new situations. Other children must be given repeated practice to master a simple task, and then they may have difficulty successfully completing the same task the next day. The differences among most children are relatively small, and most children can benefit from the general education program offered by their school. However, the physical attributes or learning abilities of some children differ from the norm—either below or above—to such an extent that typical school curricula or teaching methods are not appropriate or effective, and individualized programs of special education are required to meet their needs. These are the children called *exceptional students*.

In this chapter, we briefly outline the long history of exclusion and educational inequality experienced by many exceptional students in U.S. schools. We also examine the progress during the past two decades that has led to federal legislation requiring that all children, regardless of the type or severity of their handicap, be provided with appropriate educational opportunity. We look at the key features of a landmark law, the outcomes of its implementation, and the major barriers that still stand in the way of true educational equality for exceptional students. But first, let us take a closer look at the concept of exceptionality and find out how many exceptional students there are.

Who Are Exceptional Students?

To begin to understand exceptionality, one must know the meaning of several related terms.[1] The term *exceptional students* (or *exceptional children*) includes not only children who have difficulty learning but also children whose performance is so advanced that an individualized educational program is necessary to meet their needs. Thus, *exceptional* is an inclusive term that includes both severely disabled students and students who are gifted and talented. The term *disability* refers to the loss or reduced function of a certain body part or organ; *impairment,* although technically referring to defective or diseased tissue, is often used synonymously with disability. A child with a disability cannot perform certain tasks (e.g., walking, speaking, seeing) in the same way in which most nondisabled children do. However, a disabled child is not considered handicapped unless the disability results in educational, personal, social, or other problems. For example, a child with one arm who can function in and out of school without problems is not considered handicapped for educational purposes.

Handicap refers to the difficulties a person with a disability experiences when interacting with the environment. Some disabilities pose a handicap in some environments but not in others. The child with only one arm may be handicapped when playing with nondisabled classmates on the playground, but having the use of only one arm might not pose a handicap in the classroom. Unlike the term *exceptional children,* the term *handicapped children* does not include students who are gifted and talented.

One more term is important to understanding educational equality for exceptional students. Children not currently identified as handicapped but who are considered to have a higher-than-normal chance of developing a handicap are referred to as *at risk* or *high risk.* This term is used with infants and preschoolers who, because of difficulties experienced at birth or conditions in the home environment, may be expected to have developmental problems as they grow older. Some educators also use the term to refer to students who are having learning problems in the regular classroom and are therefore ''at risk'' of being identified as handicapped and in need of special education services. Physicians also use the terms *at risk* or *high risk* to identify pregnancies in which there is a higher-than-usual probability of the baby's being born with a physical or developmental disability.

The physical and behavioral disabilities that adversely affect the learning and development of students can be roughly classified into the following categories of exceptionality.

- Mental retardation or developmental handicaps[2]
- Learning disabilities[3]
- Behavior disorders or emotional disturbance[4]
- Communication (speech and language) disorders[5]
- Hearing impairments[6]
- Visual impairments[7]
- Physical and other health impairments[8]
- Severe and multiple handicaps[9]
- Gifted and talented[10]

It is beyond the purpose and scope of this chapter to describe the defining characteristics and educational implications of each type of exceptionality. Interested readers can refer to the sources identified in the Notes to obtain sound and current information about each area.

Regardless of the terms used to refer to students who experience differences in learning and development, it is incorrect to believe that there are two kinds of students—those who are exceptional and those who are normal. All children differ from one another to some extent; exceptional students are those whose differences are significant enough to require a specially designed program of instruction in order for them to achieve educational equality. We cannot state too strongly that exceptional students are more like other students than they are different from them. All students, whether they are considered exceptional or not, are unique individuals who deserve individual attention and nurturing. Yet *all* students are more like one another than they are different in that *all* students benefit from an education in which carefully selected curriculum content is taught through direct, systematic instruction.

Classification of Exceptional Students

The classification of students according to the various categories of exceptionality is done largely under the presumption that students in each category share certain physical, behavioral, and learning characteristics that hold important implications for planning and delivering educational services. However, it is a mistake to believe that once a child has been identified as belonging to a certain handicapping category, his or her educational needs and how those needs should be met have also been identified.

The classification and labeling of exceptional students have been widely debated for many years. Some educators believe that a workable system of classification is necessary to obtain the special educational services and programs that are prerequisite to educational equality for exceptional students. Others argue that the classification and labeling of exceptional students serve only to exclude them from the mainstream of educational opportunity. The classification of exceptional students is a complex issue affected not only by educational considerations, but by social, political, and emotional concerns as well. Research conducted to assess the effects of labeling has been of little help, with most of the studies contributing inconclusive and contradictory evidence.[11] Here are the most common arguments given for and against the labeling of exceptional students.[12]

Possible Advantages of Labeling
1. Categories can relate diagnosis to specific treatment.
2. Labeling may lead to a protective response in which nonlabeled children accept certain behaviors of their handicapped peers more fully than they would accept those same behaviors in normal children.
3. Labeling helps professionals communicate with one another and to classify and assess research findings.
4. Funding of special education programs is often based on specific categories of exceptionality.
5. Labels allow special-interest groups to promote specific programs and to spur legislative action.
6. Labeling helps make the special needs of exceptional children more visible in the public eye.

Possible Disadvantages of Labeling

1. Labels usually focus on negative aspects of the child, causing others to think about the child only in terms of inadequacies or defects.

2. Labels may cause other people to react to and hold low expectations of a child based on the label, resulting in a self-fulfilling prophecy.

3. Labels that describe a child's performance deficit often mistakenly acquire the role of explanatory constructs (e.g., "Sherry acts that way because she is emotionally disturbed.").

4. Labels used to classify children in special education emphasize that learning problems are primarily the result of something wrong within the child, thereby reducing the likelihood of examining instructional variables as the cause of performance deficits.

5. A label may help cause a child to develop a poor self-concept.

6. Labels may lead peers to reject or ridicule the labeled child.

7. Labels have a certain permanence about them. Once labeled as *retarded* or *learning disabled,* a child has difficulty ever achieving the status of being just like the other kids.

8. Labels often provide a basis for keeping students out of the regular classroom.

9. A disproportionate number of students from culturally diverse groups have been inaccurately labeled *handicapped.*

10. The classification of exceptional children requires the expenditure of much professional and student time that could be better spent in planning and delivering instruction.

As can be seen, there are strong reasons both for and against the classification and labeling of exceptional students. At one level, classification can be seen as a way to organize the funding and administration of special education programs in the schools. In fact, the federal government and most states and school districts allocate money and resources according to the number of students in each category of exceptionality. To receive an individualized program of educational services to meet his or her needs, a student must first be identified as handicapped and then, with few exceptions, be further classified into one of the categories, such as for learning disabilities or visual impairment. So, in practice, being labeled as belonging to a given handicapping category, and therefore being exposed to all of the potential disadvantages that label carries with it, is prerequisite to receiving the special education services necessary to achieve educational equality. Many educators are aware of this problem and argue that the classification and labeling of exceptional students by category of handicapping condition actually interfere with the kind of assessment and instruction most needed by the student. Stainback and Stainback,[13] for example, contend that

> these categories often do not reflect the specific educational needs and interests of students in relation to such services. For example, some students categorized as visually handicapped may not need large print books, while others who are not labeled visually impaired and thus are ineligible for large print books could benefit from their use. Similarly, not all students labeled behaviorally disordered may need self-control training, while some students not so labeled may need self-control training as a part of their educational

*experience. Such categories . . . actually interfere with providing some
students with the services they require to progress toward their individual
educational goals. Eligibility for educational and related services should be
based on the abilities, interests, and needs of each student as they relate to
instructional options and services, rather than on the student's inclusion in a
categorical group.*

One major challenge facing education today lies in determining how to meet the
individualized needs of exceptional students without subjecting them to the
potentially negative outcomes of classification and labeling as it is currently
practiced.

How Many Exceptional Students Are There?

It is impossible to know for certain how many exceptional students there are in
U.S. schools. Six reasons for this uncertainty are:

1. State and local school systems use different criteria for identifying
exceptional students.

2. The identification of exceptional students is not completely systematic
because of the less-than-exact nature of screening and assessment procedures.

3. The significant role played by subjective judgment in interpreting the
results of referral and assessment data makes identification inconsistent from
case to case.

4. The number of exceptional students identified by a given school is
affected by the school's relative success in providing instructional support to the
regular classroom teacher so that an at-risk student does not become a
handicapped student.

5. The relative ability of a school system to provide special education
services for every identified handicapped student (a requirement of federal
legislation) may affect how hard the school system works to identify students
with exceptional needs.

6. A student might be identified as exceptional at one time and as not
exceptional (or included in another exceptional category) at another time.

In spite of the difficulty these and other factors pose in determining the
actual number of exceptional students, data are available showing how many
handicapped students receive special education services in the United States.
Each year the U.S. Department of Education, Office of Special Education and
Rehabilitation Services (OSERS) submits a report to Congress on the education
of handicapped children. At the time this chapter was written, the most recent
information was for the 1984–1985 school year.[14]

Consider these five facts about exceptional students in the United States:

1. More than 4.3 million handicapped children, aged three to twenty-one,
received special education services during the 1984–1985 school year.

2. Handicapped children represent approximately 11 percent of the entire
school-age population.

3. About twice as many males as females receive special education
services.

4. The three largest categories of handicaps are learning disabilities, speech and language impairment, and mental retardation, which account for 42, 26, and 16 percent, respectively, of all students receiving special education.

5. The vast majority—perhaps 90 percent—of school-age students receiving special education are "mildly handicapped."[15]

Figure 12.1 shows the number of children who received special education services during the 1984–1985 school year by the categories of handicapping conditions recognized by the federal government. States are required to provide such "child-count" data in their yearly reports to the U.S. Department of Education. Also included in the figure are data for the 1976–1977 school year, so that comparisons of changes within and across categories can be made.

These data do not include gifted and talented students, for whom special educational services are not presently mandated by federal legislation. One report states that 909,437 gifted students were served by special programs in 1981.[16] This would make gifted and talented children the third-largest group of exceptional students receiving special education services. However, if one uses the often-cited estimate that from 3 to 5 percent of the school-age population is gifted, then there are between 1.5 and 2.5 million gifted children who may require special education services. This means that gifted and talented children are probably the most underserved group of exceptional students.

History of Educational Equality for Exceptional Students

If our society and its institutions were to be judged by how they treat people who are different, our educational system would not be judged very favorably.[17] Students who are different, whether because of race, culture, language, gender, or exceptionality, have often been denied equal access to educational opportunities. For many years, educational opportunity of any kind did not exist for many students with handicaps. Students with severe disabilities were completely excluded from public schools. Before 1970, many states had laws permitting local school districts to deny access to children whose physical or intellectual disability caused them, in the opinion of school officials, to be unable to benefit from typical instruction.

Most students with handicaps were enrolled in school, but perhaps half of the nation's handicapped children were denied an appropriate education through what Turnbull[18] calls "functional exclusion." The students were allowed to come to school but were not participating in an educational program designed to meet their special needs. Students with mild learning and behavior problems remained in the regular classroom but were given no special help. If they failed to make satisfactory progress in the curriculum, they were called "slow learners"; if they acted out in class, they were called "disciplinary problems" and suspended from school.

For students who did receive a program of differentiated curriculum or instruction, special education usually meant a separate education in segregated classrooms and special schools isolated from the mainstream of education. Gifted and talented students seldom received any special attention in the

FIGURE 12.1
Number of children aged three to twenty-years receiving special education services by handicapping condition in the United States during school years 1976–1977 and 1984–1985

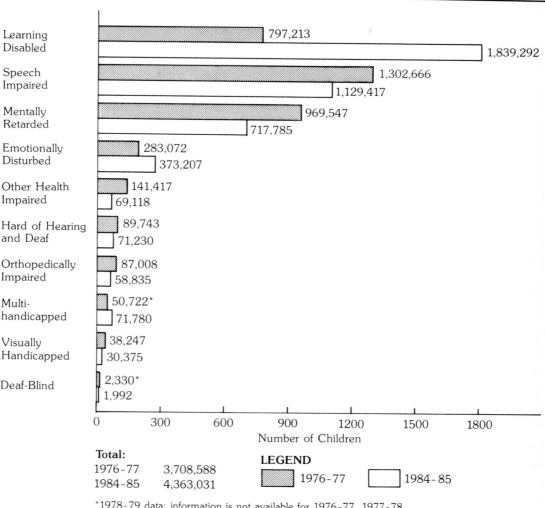

	1976-77	1984-85
Learning Disabled	797,213	1,839,292
Speech Impaired	1,302,666	1,129,417
Mentally Retarded	969,547	717,785
Emotionally Disturbed	283,072	373,207
Other Health Impaired	141,417	69,118
Hard of Hearing and Deaf	89,743	71,230
Orthopedically Impaired	87,008	58,835
Multi-handicapped	50,722*	71,780
Visually Handicapped	38,247	30,375
Deaf-Blind	2,330*	1,992

Number of Children

Total:
1976-77   3,708,588
1984-85   4,363,031

LEGEND
[shaded] 1976-77   [open] 1984-85

*1978-79 data; information is not available for 1976-77, 1977-78

From *Eighth Annual Report to Congress on Implementation of The Education of the Handicapped Act* (Washington, D.C.: Office of Special Education and Rehabilitation Services, United States Department of Education, 1986), p. 4.

schools. Many educators believed (as some still do today) that gifted students can make it on their own without any special programming.

Education's response to exceptional students has changed considerably over the past several decades from a pattern of exclusion and isolation to one of integration and participation. But this change did not come easily, nor did it come by chance. Today's efforts to ensure educational equality for exceptional students can be viewed as an outgrowth of the civil rights movement. All of the issues and events that helped shape society's attitudes during the 1950s and 1960s affected the development of special education for exceptional students, particularly the 1954 landmark case of *Brown* v. *Board of Education of Topeka*. This case challenged the practice, common in 1954, of segregating schools according to the race of the children. The U.S. Supreme Court ruled that education must be available to all children on equal terms and that it is unconstitutional to operate segregated schools under the premise that they are separate but equal.

The *Brown* decision initiated a period of intense questioning by parents of handicapped children who wondered why the same principles of equal access to education did not also apply to their children. Numerous cases challenging the exclusion and isolation of handicapped children by the schools were brought to court by parents and advocacy groups. One of the most influential court cases in the development of educational equality for exceptional students was the 1972 *Pennsylvania Association for Retarded Children* v. *Commonwealth of Pennsylvania*. The association (PARC) brought the class-action suit to challenge a state law that enabled public schools to deny education to children they considered "unable to profit from public school attendance."

The attorneys and parents who represented PARC argued that it was neither rational nor necessary to assume that the children were uneducable. Since the state could neither prove that the children were uneducable nor demonstrate a rational basis for excluding them from public school programs, the court decided that the children were entitled to a free, public education. Other court cases followed with similar rulings—handicapped children, like all other citizens, are entitled to the same rights and protection under the law as guaranteed in the Fourteenth Amendment, which declares that people may not be deprived of their equality or liberty on the basis of any classification such as race, nationality, or religion. Together, all of these developments contributed to the passage of a federal law concerning educational equality for handicapped students.

Public Law 94-142: A Legislative Mandate for Educational Equality for Exceptional Students

In 1975, Public Law 94-142, The Education for All Handicapped Children Act, was reluctantly signed by President Ford, who expressed concern that the federal government was promising more than it could deliver. This landmark bill represents the culmination of the efforts of a great many parents, educators, and legislators to bring together under one comprehensive law the requirements and safeguards deemed necessary if handicapped students are to experience educational equality. Since its passage, P.L. 94-142 has twice been amended slightly. However, the basic rules it originally outlined still govern the education of students with handicaps today.

Major Components of P.L. 94-142

To receive any federal tax dollars to support the cost of educating exceptional students, each state must show evidence that its local school districts comply with each of the following six major components of P.L. 94-142.[19]

Free, Public Education for All Handicapped Children

P.L. 94-142 requires that all handicapped children aged six to twenty-one, regardless of the type or severity of their disabilities, must be provided with a "free, appropriate public education which emphasizes special education and related services designed to meet their unique needs." In addition, incentive funds were made available to states that provided early intervention programs to handicapped preschool children aged three to five. The law clearly mandates a zero reject policy that prohibits schools from excluding any child solely becuase the child is handicapped. This fundamental requirement of the law is based on the proposition that all handicapped children can learn and benefit from an appropriate education, and that schools therefore do not have the right to deny any child access to educational opportunity.

Nondiscriminatory Evaluation

The law requires that exceptional students be evaluated fairly. Assessment must be nondiscriminatory so that it does not wrongly identify as handicapped students who are not. This requirement of P.L. 94-142 is particularly important because of the disproportionate number of children from non-White and non-English-speaking cultural groups who were being identified as handicapped, often solely on the basis of a score from standardized intelligence tests. Both of the intelligence tests that have been used most often in the identification of students with learning problems had been developed based on the performance of White, middle-class children. Because of their Anglo-Centric nature the tests are often considered to be unfairly biased against children from diverse cultural groups who have had less of an opportunity to learn the knowledge sampled by the test items.[20] P.L. 94-142 states clearly that the results of a single test cannot be used as the sole criterion for placement into a special education program.

In addition to the concern for fair identification of exceptional students, multifaceted assessment that includes several tests and observational techniques is necessary to determine the extent of all of a child's special needs so that an appropriate program of individualized education can be developed. The law requires that a child be assessed by a multidisciplinary team in all areas of functioning.

Individualized Education Program

Perhaps the most significant aspect of P.L. 94-142 is the requirement that an individualized education program, or IEP, be developed and implemented for each handicapped child. The law is very specific in identifying the kind of information an IEP must include and who is to be involved in its development. Each IEP must be created by a child study team whose membership consists of at least the child's teacher(s), a representative of the local school district, the child's parents or guardian, and whenever appropriate, the child. In practice, many child study teams include professionals from various disciplines such as school psychology, physical therapy, occupational therapy, and medicine, to name just a few. It is believed that an interdisciplinary team whose members represent varied training, experiences, and points of view is best able to determine the special educational and related services many students with disabilities need.

Although the particular formats vary from school district to school district, all IEPs must include the following nine items:

1. A statement of the child's present level of educational performance.
2. A statement of the annual goals to be achieved by the end of the school year in each area requiring specially designed instruction.
3. Short-term objectives stated in measurable, intermediate steps between the present level of performance and the annual goals.
4. The specific educational and related services (e.g., physical therapy) needed by the child, including the physical education program and any special instructional media and materials that are needed.
5. The date by which those services will begin and the anticipated length of time for which the services will be provided.
6. A description of the extent to which the child will participate in the regular education program of the school.
7. Objective criteria, procedures, and schedules for determining, at least annually, whether the short-term objectives are being achieved.
8. A justification for the type of educational placement being recommended for the child.
9. A list of the individuals responsible for implementing the IEP.

Although the IEP is a written document signed by both school personnel and the child's parents, is is not a legally binding contract. That is, parents cannot take their child's teachers or the school to court if all goals and objectives stated in the IEP are not met. However, schools should be able to document that the services described in the IEP have been provided in a systematic effort to meet those goals. IEPs must be reviewed by the child study team at least annually.

Least Restrictive Environment

As described earlier, the 1972 PARC class-action case had been settled with a ruling that it was neither rational nor necessary to exclude or segregate students from regular education programs solely because of a handicap. P.L. 94-142 made this finding of the PARC case the law by mandating that handicapped students must be educated in the least restrictive environment (LRE). Specifically, the law states that

> to the maximum extent appropriate, handicapped children, including children
> in public or private institutions or other care facilities, are educated with
> children who are not handicapped, and that special classes, separate
> schooling, or other removal of handicapped children from the regular
> educational environment occurs only when the nature or severity of the

handicap is such that education in regular classes with the use of supplementary aids and services cannot be achieved satisfactorily.[21]

The LRE requirement has been one of the most controversial and least understood aspects of P.L. 94-142. During the first couple of years after its passage, the law was erroneously interpreted by some professionals and parents to mean that all handicapped children, regardless of the type or severity of their disabilities, had to be placed in regular classrooms. Instead, the LRE principle requires that each handicapped child be educated in a setting that most closely resembles a regular class placement and in which his or her individual educational needs can be met. Although some people argue that any decision to place a handicapped child in a special class or school is inappropriate, most educators and parents realize that a regular classroom placement can be overly restrictive if the child's academic and social needs are not met. Two different students who have the same disability should not necessarily be placed in the same setting. LRE is a relative concept; the least restrictive environment for one handicapped student would not necessarily be appropriate for another.

To provide an appropriate LRE for each handicapped child, most schools must offer a *continuum of services* made up of a range of placement and instructional options. Figure 12.2 shows a continuum of placement options as it is most often depicted. The least restrictive regular classroom placement is at the bottom of the pyramid and is widest to show that the greatest number of exceptional students should be placed there. Moving up from the bottom of the pyramid, each successive placement option represents an environment in which increasingly more restrictive, specialized, and intensive instructional and related services can be offered. The more severe a child's handicap, the greater the need for specialized services. As we have already noted, however, the majority of exceptional students are mildly handicapped, and hence the pyramid grows smaller at the top to show that more restrictive settings are required for fewer students.

The continuum-of-services concept is meant to be flexible. That is, decisions regarding the placement of exceptional students should not be considered permanent but should be reviewed periodically. A student may be moved to a more restrictive setting for a limited time, but when certain performance objectives have been met, the student should be returned to the more integrated setting as soon as possible.

Note that in the first three placement options, handicapped students spend the entire school day in regular classes with their nonhandicapped peers. In fact, two-thirds of all students with handicaps receive at least part of their education in regular classrooms with their nonhandicapped peers (see Figure 12.3). However, many of these students spend a portion of each school day in a resource room (Level 4 in Figure 12.2), where they receive individualized instruction from a specially trained teacher. Approximately one of every four handicapped students is educated in a separate classroom in a regular public school. Special schools provide the education for about one in twenty handicapped children, usually students with the most severe handicaps.

Due Process Safeguards

P.L. 94-142 acknowledges that handicapped students are people with important legal rights. The law makes it clear that school districts do not have absolute

FIGURE 12.2
Continuum of educational placement alternatives for students with handicaps

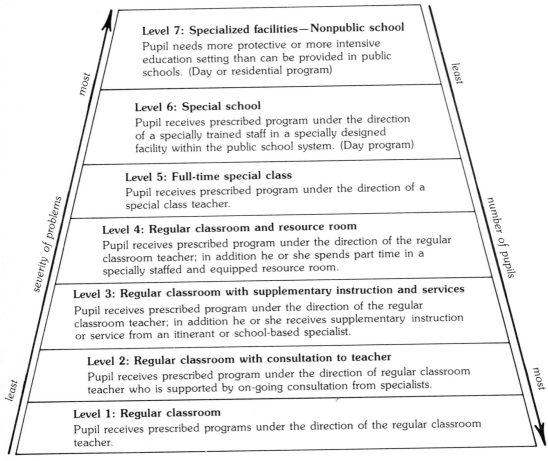

Level 7: Specialized facilities—Nonpublic school
Pupil needs more protective or more intensive education setting than can be provided in public schools. (Day or residential program)

Level 6: Special school
Pupil receives prescribed program under the direction of a specially trained staff in a specially designed facility within the public school system. (Day program)

Level 5: Full-time special class
Pupil receives prescribed program under the direction of a special class teacher.

Level 4: Regular classroom and resource room
Pupil receives prescribed program under the direction of the regular classroom teacher; in addition he or she spends part time in a specially staffed and equipped resource room.

Level 3: Regular classroom with supplementary instruction and services
Pupil receives prescribed program under the direction of the regular classroom teacher; in addition he or she receives supplementary instruction or service from an itinerant or school-based specialist.

Level 2: Regular classroom with consultation to teacher
Pupil receives prescribed program under the direction of regular classroom teacher who is supported by on-going consultation from specialists.

Level 1: Regular classroom
Pupil receives prescribed programs under the direction of the regular classroom teacher.

Used with permission of Montgomery County Public Schools, Rockville, MD, and Maynard D. Reynolds.

authority over exceptional students; schools may not make decisions about the educational programs of handicapped children in a unilateral or arbitrary manner. Due process is a legal concept that is implemented through a series of procedural steps designed to assure fairness of treatment among school systems, parents, and students. Due process requires that parents (1) must be notified whenever the school system wishes to initiate a change in educational placement or services, (2) can protest the school's decision by presenting their case in front of an impartial party, and (3) can appeal a ruling they consider unfavorable.

Turnbull and Turnbull, who are both special educators and the parents of a child with severe handicaps, describe due process in these terms:

FIGURE 12.3
Percentage of all handicapped children served in four educational environments during the 1983–1984 school year

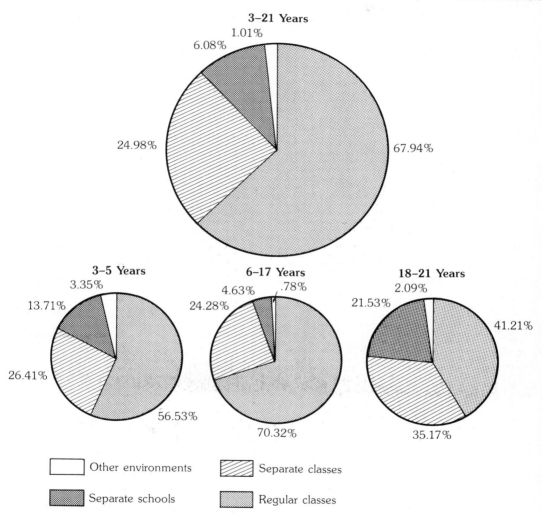

3–21 Years
1.01%
6.08%
24.98%
67.94%

3–5 Years
3.35%
13.71%
26.41%
56.53%

6–17 Years
4.63%   .78%
24.28%
70.32%

18–21 Years
2.09%
21.53%
41.21%
35.17%

☐ Other environments   ▨ Separate classes

▨ Separate schools   ▨ Regular classes

From *Eighth Annual Report to Congress on Implementation of The Education of the Handicapped Act* (Washington, D.C.: Office of Special Education and Rehabilitation Services, United States Department of Education, 1986), p. 59.

Due process is a way to help families and students make schools accountable. The first four principles of the law—zero reject, nondiscriminatory evaluation, appropriate education, and least restrictive placement—are the "inputs" from the school to the student. Due process is a way to ensure the school has done its job under those principles. . . . Due process is a way of changing the balance of power between professionals, who have traditionally wielded power, and families, who have felt they could not affect their children's education.[22]

The due process requirements of P.L. 94-142 do more than just protect the rights of students and their parents. Schools may bring a due process hearing against parents who object to the school's proposed plan for a given child.

Parent Participation

The authors of P.L. 94-142 strongly believed in the benefits of active parent participation. They believed that parents not only have a right to be involved in their child's education, but that parents of exceptional students also can help professionals select appropriate instructional goals and can provide information that will help teachers be more effective in working with their children. As already noted, parents are to take an active role as a full member of the child study team that develops the IEP for their child. Of course, parents cannot be forced to do so and may waive their right to participate. In addition to involving parents in IEP development, P.L. 94-142 requires each state to include parents of exceptional students on their special education advisory panel that is responsible for helping the state education agency develop its overall plan and policies for meeting the needs of students with disabilities.

Legislation Affecting the Education of Gifted Students

P.L. 94-142 mandates that special education and related services be provided to meet the individual needs of all students with handicaps; it does not speak to the educational needs of students who are gifted and talented. Nor is there a comparable federal law that requires states to provide special-education services to gifted students. In 1978, Congress passed P.L. 95-561, the Gifted and Talented Children's Education Act, which provided financial incentives to states and local education agencies for developing special programs for gifted and talented students. The law included special procedures to ensure that gifted and talented students from disadvantaged backgrounds would be identified and served. Money was also appropriated for the funding of inservice teacher training and research.

However, in 1982 the Education Consolidation Act phased out the federal Office of Gifted and Talented created by P.L. 95-561 and merged funding for gifted education with twenty-nine other education programs. States now receive federal dollars to support these thirty wide-ranging K–12 education programs in the form of block grants. Each state must decide what amount of the block grant funding, if any, will be used to develop and support special education programs and services for gifted students. Nevertheless, a national survey reported in 1984 found that forty-seven state departments of education had appointed a state director or consultant in charge of gifted education.[23] This is a significant improvement over a 1972 report that only ten state education agencies had a member of their staff whose primary responsibility was gifted education.

Educational Equality for Exceptional Students: Some Progress and Remaining Challenges

What effects has P.L. 94-142 had? Without question, the law has resulted in many more exceptional students' receiving special education and related services than previously had been served. Data reported in the U.S. Department of Education's *Eighth Annual Report to Congress on the Implementation of The Education of the Handicapped Act* [24] illustrate one extent to which P.L. 94-142 has changed the schools. During the 1983–1984 school year, 247,791 special-education teachers were employed in U.S. schools (up from 179,804 in 1976–1977, the first year after passage of P.L. 94-142). In that same year, an almost equal number of school personnel other than teachers also worked to provide the special education and related services needed by exceptional students (226,505 in 1983–1984, as compared to 151,649 in 1976–1977). These figures reflect not only the increased number of exceptional students being educated in U.S. schools, but also the fact that to meet the wide-ranging and sometimes extensive needs of its students with learning and physical disabilities, today's schools have had to become complex human service agencies. Schools no longer simply provide traditional academic training; they also employ a large number of professionals from such fields as medicine, social work, physical therapy, audiology, occupational therapy, recreational therapy, adaptive physical educators, and mental health.

Perhaps the law has had its most dramatic effect on students with severe disabilities, many of whom had been completely denied the opportunity to benefit from an appropriate education. No longer can schools exclude students with disabilities on the premise that they are ineducable. Indeed, P.L. 94-142 states clearly that all students can benefit from an appropriate education and that it is the local school's responsibility to make the modifications in curriculum content and teaching method dictated by the unique needs of each handicapped student. In essence, the law requires schools to adapt themselves to the needs of students rather than allowing schools to deny educational equality to students who do not fit the school.

Most people would agree that P.L. 94-142 has contributed positively to the education of students with handicaps, but significant barriers remain to full educational equality for exceptional students in the United States. We briefly examine three of these impediments. If a truly appropriate educational opportunity is to be a reality for students with handicaps, U.S. schools must work hard to (1) move beyond simple compliance with the law to effective instruction, (2) provide more and better early intervention programs for young children with handicaps, and (3) increase the success of young adults with disabilities as they make the transition from school to community.

Effective Instruction

The challenge of providing educational equality for exceptional students goes beyond the requirements of any law. Just because a handicapped student has undergone multifactored evaluation, received an IEP, and has been placed with due process in the LRE does not guarantee that he or she will benefit from schooling. For true educational equality to exist, it is imperative that students with handicaps receive effective instruction. Criticizing the manner in which he felt many school districts were implementing P.L. 94-142, a well-known special educator wrote in 1978:

> Without even trying, I have been shown six sets of transparencies, listened to endless audio cassettes on the requirements of P.L. 94-142, and I have been guided through several versions of "sure-fire" forms to satisfy all of the new regulations.
>   What I see and hear seems well designed to keep teachers out of jail—to comply with the law, that is—but usually I sense little vision of how people might come together creatively to design environments for better learning and living by handicapped students.[25]

The design and implementation of effective instruction for exceptional students require much more than maintaining a file drawer full of IEPs. Some educators resent the paperwork requirements of P.L. 94-142 and argue that all the time and resources that must be devoted to the planning and writing of IEPs could be better spent in teaching children with handicaps. Although the legal requirement of IEPs is relatively new, competent teachers of exceptional students conducted systematic assessments and carefully planned educational objectives long before P.L. 94-142 required such procedures.

Today, special and regular educators have both the opportunity and the responsibility to work together to advance beyond mere compliance with the law and to create an educational system that produces positive outcomes for exceptional students. Teachers of exceptional students must take advantage of a large and continually advancing body of research on effective instructional practices.[26] We believe that

> Teachers must demand effectiveness from their instructional approaches. The belief that special educators require unending patience is a disservice to exceptional children and to the teachers whose job it is to help them learn. The special educator should not wait patiently for the exceptional child to learn, attributing his lack of progress to retardation, a learning disability, or some other label. Instead, the special educator should modify the instructional program in an effort to improve its effectiveness, using the information obtained from direct observation of the child's performance of the skills being taught.[27]

Early Intervention

The years from birth to school age are very important to a child's learning and development. The typical child enters school with a large repertoire of intellectual, language, social, and physical skills on which to build. Unfortunately, for many children with handicaps, the preschool years represent a long period of missed opportunities. Without systematic instruction, most young children with handicaps do not acquire many of the basic skills their nonhandicapped peers seemingly learn without effort. Parents concerned about their child's inability to reach important developmental milestones have often been told by professionals, "Don't worry. He'll probably grow out of it before too long." Many handicapped children, as a result, fall further and further behind their non-handicapped peers, and minor delays in development often become major delays by the time the child reaches school age.

Although there were virtually no early intervention programs two decades ago for handicapped children from birth to school age, early childhood special education is today perhaps the fastest-growing area in the field of education. As with special education of school-age exceptional students, federal legislation has played a major role in the development of early intervention programs. By passing Public Law 99-457, the Education of the Handicapped Act Amendments of 1986, Congress reaffirmed the basic principles of P.L. 94-142 and added two major sections concerning early intervention services.

It was estimated that only about 70 percent of the handicapped pre-schoolers aged three to five were being served under the incentive provisions of P.L. 94-142 (which did not require states to provide a free, public education to handicapped children under the age of six years). P.L. 99-457 requires that by the 1990–1991 school year, each state must show evidence of serving all three- to five-year-old handicapped children to receive any preschool funds.

The second major change brought about by P.L. 99-457 is that incentive grants are available to states for developing systems of early identification and intervention for handicapped infants and toddlers from birth to age two. The services must be planned by a multidisciplinary team that includes the child's parents and must be implemented according to an individualized family services plan that is similar in concept to the IEP for school-aged handicapped students.

Nearly every special educator today now realizes the critical importance of early intervention for both handicapped and at-risk children, and most also agree that the earlier intervention is begun, the better. Fortunately, many educators are working to develop the programs and services so desperately needed by young handicapped and at-risk children to give them a fighting chance of experiencing educational equality when they enter school.

Transition from School to Adult Life

If the degree of educational equality afforded to exceptional students is to be judged, as we think it should, by the extent to which students with handicaps can function independently in everyday environments, then we still have a long way to go. Follow-up studies of young adults who have graduated or left public school secondary special education programs have produced disquieting results. Only about 60 percent find work, and much of the work is part time and at or below minimum wage.[28] The probability of a person with moderate or severe disabilities finding real work in the community is much lower. One study of 117 young adults with moderate, severe, or profound mental retardation found an *unemployment* rate of 78.6 percent.[29] Of the twenty-five who had jobs, only fourteen were in the community; eleven were working in sheltered workshops. Only eight of those working earned more than $100 per month.

Employment problems are not the only difficulties faced by adults with handicaps. One recent national survey found that 56 percent of disabled Americans indicated that their handicaps prevented them from doing many everyday activities taken for granted by nondisabled people, such as getting around the community, attending cultural or sporting events, and socializing with friends outside their homes.[30]

Education cannot be held responsible for all of the difficulties faced by adults with handicaps, but the results of these and other studies make it evident that many young people leave public school special education programs without the skills necessary to function in the community. Many educators today see the development of special-education programs that will effectively prepare exceptional students for adjustment and successful integration in the adult community as the ultimate measure of educational equality for students with handicaps.

Summary

The task of providing educational equality for exceptional students is enormous. By embracing the challenge, U.S. schools have made a big promise to exceptional students, to their parents, and to society. Progress has been made, but, as we have seen, significant challenges must still be overcome if the promise is to be kept. The views of our society are changing and continue to be changed by people who believe that our past practice of excluding people with handicaps was primitive and unfair. As an institution, education reflects the attitudes of society.

Providing educational equality to exceptional students does not mean either ignoring a child's handicap or pretending that it does not exist. Children with handicaps do have differences from children who are not handicapped. But, as we state at the beginning of this chapter, exceptional students are more like other students than unlike them. Every exceptional student must be treated first as an individual, not as a member of a labeled group or category.

There is a limit to how much educational equality can be legislated, for in many cases it is possible to meet the letter of the law but not necessarily the spirit of the law. Treating every student with a handicap as a student first and as a handicapped student second may be the most important factor in providing true educational equality. This approach does not diminish the student's exceptionality, but instead it might give us a more objective and positive perspective that allows us to see a handicap as a set of special needs. Viewing exceptional students as individuals with special needs tells us a great deal about how to help them achieve the educational equality they deserve.

Questions and Activities

1. Why are both learning disabled children and gifted students considered exceptional?

2. In what ways are exceptional students similar to and different from other students?

3. Name nine categories of exceptionality. Identify community and school resources from which teachers can receive help when working with exceptional students.

4. What are the advantages and disadvantages of labeling exceptional students? Be sure to consider the views of educators, parents, and students.

5. Interview a local special education school administrator to determine: (a) how many students in the district receive special education services; (b) how many of these students are bilingual, males, females, or members of ethnic minority groups; (c) how many students are in each of the nine categories of exceptionality; (d) how many special education students are mainstreamed, the portion of the school day in which they are mainstreamed, and the classes in which mainstreamed students participate.

6. How did the civil rights movement influence the movement for educational equality for exceptional students?

7. What is an IEP and how can it benefit students with handicapping conditions? Visit a special education classroom and ask to review some of the student IEPs. Talk with the special education teacher about how an IEP may influence regular classroom teachers when students are mainstreamed.

8. Are all students with handicapping conditions mainstreamed? Why or why not? How does the concept of least restrictive environment (LRE) influence alternative placements for students with handicapping conditions?

9. How does your state support special programs and services for gifted students? Are state funds provided for gifted education?

Notes

1. William L. Heward and Michael D. Orlansky, *Exceptional Children: An Introductory Survey of Special Education,* 3d ed. (Columbus, Ohio: Merrill, 1988), pp. 3–4.

2. James R. Patton, James S. Payne, and Mary Beirne-Smith, *Mental Retardation,* 2d ed. (Columbus, Ohio: Merrill, 1986).

3. Cecil D. Mercer, *Students with Learning Disabilities,* 3d ed. (Columbus, Ohio: Merrill, 1987).

4. James M. Kauffman, *Characteristics of Children's Behavior Disorders,* 3d ed. (Columbus, Ohio: Merrill, 1985).

5. J. M. Costello and A. L. Holland, eds., *Handbook of Speech and Language Disorders* (San Diego, Calif.: College Hill, 1987).

6. Donald F. Moores, *Educating the Deaf: Psychology, Principles and Practices,* 3d ed. (Boston: Houghton Mifflin, 1987).

7. G. T. Scholl, ed., *Foundations of Education for Blind and Visually Handicapped Children and Youth: Theory and Practice* (New York: American Foundation for the Blind, 1986).

8. June L. Bigge, *Teaching Individuals with Physical and Multiple Disabilities,* 2d ed. (Columbus, Ohio: Merrill, 1982).

9. Marti E. Snell, ed., *Systematic Instruction of Persons with Severe Handicaps,* 3d ed. (Columbus, Ohio: Merrill, 1987).

10. Barbara Clark, *Growing Up Gifted,* 2d ed. (Columbus, Ohio: Merrill, 1983).

11. Donald L. MacMillan, *Mental Retardation in School and Society,* 2d ed. (Boston: Little, Brown, 1982).

12. Heward and Orlansky, *Exceptional Children,* 11. Used with permission.

13. William Stainback and Susan Stainback, "A Rationale for the Merger of Special and Regular Education," *Exceptional Children* 51 (October 1984): 105.

14. *Eighth Annual Report to Congress on the Implementation of The Education of All Handicapped Children Act* (Washington, D.C.: U.S. Department of Education, 1986), p. xiv.

15. G. J. Hagerty and M. Abramson, "Impediments for Implementing National Policy Change for Mildly Handicapped Students," *Exceptional Children* 53 (January 1987): 317.

16. Bruce M. Mitchell, "An Update on the State of Gifted/Talented Education in the U.S." *Phi Delta Kappan* 63 (January 1982): 357–358.

17. E. B. Fiske, "Special Education Is Now a Matter of Civil Rights," *The New York Times* (April 25, 1967): 14.

18. H. Rutherford Turnbull III, *Free Appropriate Education: The Law and Children with Disabilities* (Denver, Colo.: Love, 1986).

19. H. Rutherford Turnbull III and Ann P. Turnbull, *Free Appropriate Public Education: Law and Implementation* (Denver, Colo.: Love, 1978).

20. Jane R. Mercer, *Labelling the Mentally Retarded* (Berkeley: University of California Press, 1973).

21. *Public Law 94-142: The Education of All Handicapped Children Act,* 1975, Section 612(5)B.

22. Ann P. Turnbull and H. Rutherford Turnbull III, *Families, Professionals, and Exceptionality: A Special Partnership,* (Columbus, Ohio: Merrill, 1986), p. 254.

23. Dorothy Sisk, "A National Survey of Gifted Programs," Presentation to the National Business Consortium for Gifted and Talented (Washington, D.C.: October 1984).

24. *Eighth Annual Report to Congress,* G21–G28.

25. Maynard C. Reynolds, "Staying Out of Jail," *Teaching Exceptional Children* 10 (1978): 60.

26. "In Search of Excellence: Instruction That Works in Special Education Classrooms" (special issue), *Exceptional Children* 52 (April 1986).

27. Heward and Orlansky, *Exceptional Children* 27.

28. Eugene Edgar, "How Do Special Education Students Fare after They Leave School? A Response to Hasazi, Gordon, and Roe," *Exceptional Children* 51 (April 1985): 470–473.

29. Paul Wehman, J. Kregel, and J. Seyfarth, "Employment Outlook for Young Adults with Mental Retardation," *Rehabilitation Counseling Bulletin* 5 (1985): 343–354.

30. *Eighth Annual Report to Congress,* 1986.

CHAPTER 13

Teaching Handicapped Students in the Regular Classroom

■ **JANE B. SCHULZ**

All classrooms are characterized by diversity because society is characterized by diversity. Differences among children may be more obvious in school settings because of the nature of the tasks required of students. Thus, students who are not handicapped in other situations may have difficulty in settings requiring attending skills, reading skills, and problem-solving skills. They may, however, be similar to other students in many ways. For this reason, "students who have a handicap" is a better description than "handicapped students."

A *handicap* may be defined as "a disadvantage that makes achievement unusually difficult." This chapter focuses on the educational implications of handicapping conditions and strategies to be used in facilitating achievement.

It is important to realize that children who are severely handicapped are not usually placed in regular classes. Their needs are generally different from those of most other students, and therefore their learning environment must be different. It is also important to note that students with sensory difficulties, such as visual or auditory impairment, comprise a small segment of the school population. Students who are physically impaired are generally more easily integrated into classroom situations that are students who have learning and behavior problems.

The categories of handicaps most prevalent are communication disorders, mental retardation, learning disabilities, and emotional or behavior disorders. Students exhibiting problems in these areas are likely to be integrated into regular classes. Because their problems make it difficult for them to acquire and maintain academic skills and information, teachers often find that these students add to the ability levels in their classrooms. For example, in a traditional sixth-grade classroom, reading ability may vary from fourth- to seventh-grade levels. With the addition of students who are handicapped, the level may drop to second grade or lower. Teachers may also notice discrepancies in their students' learning; a student may be at an extremely low level in math but be at grade level or above in other subject areas. It is also possible that students will exhibit unusual behavior and emotional immaturity that challenge even the best teachers.

One major component of the Education for All Handicapped Children Act (Public Law 94-142) is the requirement that children and young people identified as handicapped be educated in the least restrictive environment. The concept of least restrictive environment (frequently referred to as *mainstreaming*) provides multiple programming options. The options include enrollment in a regular class for none, part, or all of the day, and enrollment in a special class or resource room for all, part, or none of the day. The many settings available require a different kind of school environment in which all personnel are comfortable with and skilled in working with students who are handicapped. An effective working relationship depends on the development of positive attitudes and professional skills.

Teachers' Attitudes

In a measure of regular classroom teachers' attitudes toward teaching handicapped children, Stephens and Braun[1] identified four variables related to teachers' willingness to accept handicapped students into their classrooms:

1. Teachers who had taken courses in special education were more willing to integrate handicapped students into their classes than were teachers who had not had such courses.

2. Teachers who believed that handicapped students can become useful members of society were more willing to integrate them than were teachers who did not share this belief.

3. Teachers who believed that public schools should educate exceptional students were more willing to integrate them than were teachers who did not endorse this position.

4. Teachers confident of their abilities to teach exceptional children were more willing to integrate them than were teachers who were not confident.

Although willingness is not always equated with success, it seems to be a trait of teachers who are more successful in teaching students who are handicapped. An examination of these four traits serves to pinpoint attitudes for success.

Special Education Courses

Many states now require that all preservice teachers take at least one course in special education. Usually such courses give an overview of different areas of exceptionality and are designed to help teachers develop appropriate teaching strategies. The main purposes of an introductory course are to create an awareness of different handicapping conditions and to develop an attitude of acceptance toward students who exhibit those conditions and characteristics. Certainly it is helpful to have this knowledge; it is not essential. It is essential that teachers recognize that there is a problem, that they know the process of referral, and that they are aware of whom they can call on for help. The most knowledgeable teachers are not familiar with all handicapping conditions. An experienced special education teacher once stated:

> *Although I have taught special education for many years, last year was the first time I had ever had a blind student. My first reaction was panic: Would I have to learn braille? How could I teach him math? To my surprise, I found that there were many resources available to me and to Josh. I found that there was a teacher of braille from Social Services; that the State Division for the Blind would send tapes, talking books, and the necessary equipment; and I even had an offer one day from a retired teacher who was willing to braille any textbook material I needed. Josh taught me how to use an abacus effectively, and together we worked out his mobility problems. I learned to think through problems with him. This was good for both of us.*

Although formal coursework helps, there are many other avenues open to teachers who want to learn about their students who are handicapped. In every school system, there are special education teachers, coordinators of special education programs, parents, and volunteers who can furnish valuable information. Once teachers encounter students with handicaps, they can ask the appropriate questions.

Acceptance of Students

An attitude of openness helps teachers recognize that students who are handicapped are useful members of society. The attitude of acceptance that pervades multicultural education is the same attitude that views all people as worthy citizens. Most students who are mainstreamed into the regular classroom have mild handicaps. This means that they are more like other students than they are different from them. Most of them will finish school, find jobs, and become part of the communities in which they live.

School Responsibility

It is the legal obligation of the school to provide an appropriate education for each student who is handicapped. P.L. 94-142 clearly established the rights of students who are handicapped to be placed in as normal a situation as possible, to have an individualized education program, to be evaluated with nondiscriminatory measures, to have their parents involved in educational decisions, and to receive all the benefits of due process.

Beyond the letter of the law is the belief held by many teachers that students with handicaps are entitled to an excellent education. This belief is necessary if teachers are to develop the appropriate skills for teaching exceptional children and young people.

Teachers' Confidence

Teachers who are confident of their abilities to teach handicapped students are more willing to accept those students and are certainly more successful in meeting their needs. There has been a myth for some time that special-education teachers have some sort of magic that enables them to teach children who have learning problems. The truth is that the same skills are required for teaching all children. A college professor in special education expressed this philosophy in relating the following incident:

> I had been asked to work with a teacher who was seeking certification in special education. She had an initial certification in business education and had been given a position teaching children who were moderately mentally retarded. I decided to visit her class and was amazed to see a class that was totally reading oriented, with phonics charts on the wall and books on every desk. I realized at that point that she didn't know much about the children she was teaching. However, I was amazed to find that the children were reading. I was reluctant to suggest that she take courses in which she would learn that they could not read!

In the same way that good teaching generalizes to many situations, good traditional strategies can be adapted to meet diverse needs of students.

Professional Skills

Attitudinal changes must be accompanied by appropriate changes in instructional strategies. The same principles apply that have been applied to multicultural education: Teachers must become aware that they have to adapt instruction to the students' backgrounds and ability levels. The ability to individualize and adapt instruction to meet the needs of handicapped students depends on the understanding and use of three principles: readiness, relevance, and reinforcement.

Academic Readiness

One of the most difficult concepts to grasp is that academic readiness is not age oriented. Educators have tended to equate readiness with early grade activities and with young children. Readiness, at any age, is a concern of the classroom teacher. Many students with learning problems do not have the basic underlying skills and concepts on which more advanced learning is based. Examples are clear in the areas of reading and math.

Reading Readiness
Poor reading skills are apparent in every school experience. Teachers of social studies, science, and all other content areas frequently see the inability to read as the greatest problem they face in teaching students who are handicapped. Students who are mentally retarded, emotionally handicapped, learning dis-

abled, visually impaired, and hearing impaired may exhibit reading levels far below that expected for their grade placement. The problem is compounded by the fact that textbooks, particularly in social studies and science, vary a great deal in readability range. Matching the content material to the student's reading level is difficult. In art, music, physical education, and vocational education, reading and following directions are essential to mastery of skills. Thus, reading becomes a major factor in all subject areas.

Reading is based on life experiences, skills in listening, and oral language facility. Many students who are disadvantaged because of cultural or learning differences have not had the experiences on which to build communication. Children with physical handicaps, for example, may have had limited opportunities to travel in the community as well as outside the community. A teacher reported that a student in a wheelchair had never been in a grocery store until the class went on a field trip. It is easy to understand his difficulty in relating to some of the stories he encountered in school. Providing a number of experiences may build toward readiness to read.

Listening skills are also an important aspect of reading. Children spend a great proportion of their school day listening, and teachers frequently assume that listening skills are developing. However, they may not be developing for all students. Assessment of listening skills may indicate that a deficiency exists and that specific activities should be developed to build listening skills. Listening behavior can be assessed informally by noting whether the student consistently asks to have directions repeated, appears to be easily distracted during class presentations, frequently completes the wrong pages in assignments, or does not participate in class discussions. Activities designed to improve listening skills are available in a number of language arts books. In addition, teachers should be aware of the following six procedures that promote good listening:

1. Provide a classroom environment that encourages good listening.
2. Listen to the students; model good listening.
3. Use appropriate tone, pitch, volume, and speed in speaking.
4. Vary the classroom program to provide listening experiences, such as films, discussions, debates, and reports.
5. Help students see the purpose for listening in various activities.
6. Build a program in which listening skills are consistently taught and practiced.

Listening is a basic skill; it can be improved through training.

Oral language production and comprehension are essential to the development of successful reading skills. Reading is communication; it begins with talking, listening to others, and understanding the message. Because reading is, as one child put it, "wrote-down talk," if the material is not within the student's language comprehension, it will not be meaningful. Children who are handicapped are frequently lacking in oral language ability. For children who are culturally different, the language patterns learned in the home may be different from those taught in school. For handicapped children, this fact may be complicated by physical, mental, and emotional problems that directly relate to speech and language acquisition. One technique in teaching reading that overcomes this problem is the language experience approach. Although this technique is used for young children in traditional reading programs, it is quite appropriate for older students who are at a readiness level.

The language experience approach is based on the idea that a person's oral language is important, that what is said can be written, and that what is written can be read. Stories can be dictated to the teacher or taped on a cassette recorder, and then written for the student. The story is in the student's language and therefore is a good start toward reading. One of the greatest challenges in teaching older students who are at the readiness level is finding appropriate materials. The language experience approach helps overcome this problem and can be used in any subject area. Other techniques are presented in the section on *relevance*.

Math Readiness

Math presents many examples of the importance of readiness and of building on basic concepts. Students struggling with the processes of multiplication and division can be found in many classrooms. Frequently, close examination reveals that such students may not know addition facts and may not understand that multiplication is a form of addition. If they do not exhibit skill in addition, they are not ready for more advanced concepts. It may be assumed that students have mastered the Piagetian concepts of classification, reversibility, and number concepts associated with numerals. Formal and informal assessment, including error analysis, may reveal some gaps in this learning.

There may also be gaps in math content. The following experience of a special education resource room teacher serves as an example:

> The fifth-grade teacher sent three students to my resource room, asking me to work with them on multiplication and division. As is my custom, I administered the Key Math test to each of the students. I found that although they were good in addition and subtraction, they had no knowledge of money values and did not even recognize different coins. Since money usage was not part of the fifth-grade curriculum, the teacher was not aware of this deficiency.

The same sort of problem may be demonstrated in math language. Children with learning disabilities, in particular, may have trouble with such concepts as *before* and *after* (related to telling time), and *first* and *last* (related to seriation). In these instances, teachers should use shorter, simpler sentences when giving directions and should determine whether the difficulty lies in math skills, math concepts, or language comprehension.

Readiness for math should be presented in concrete, exploratory activities. For example, reversibility can be demonstrated and discovered by depicting equations with poker chips $(4+2=6; 6-4=2)$ and with pictorial representation $(\cdots\cdot + \cdot\cdot = \cdots\cdots\cdot; \cdots\cdots - \cdots\cdot = \cdot\cdot)$. Math readiness activities should proceed from concrete (poker chips) to semiconcrete (dots on cards) to abstract (numerals).

Motoric and sensory readiness are as important as conceptual readiness. Physical education, music, and art require basic abilities related to motor and sensory development. Children who are limited in these areas will need to start at a level below that of their nonhandicapped peers.

Relevance

There are two considerations in assuring that instruction is relevant for students who are handicapped. The first is based on the learning principle that meaningful material is more easily assimilated than is nonmeaningful material. The second relates to priorities. For students limited in the amount and quality of their learning, instructional time is critical. One mother of a child who is mentally retarded stated, "When I visited Mark's classroom and saw that he was learning his colors, I was sick. He had known his colors for years, and there were so *many* things he needed to learn."

Time can be used to greater advantage when the materials, curriculum, and techniques are relevant to students' ability, interests, and needs.

Ability

Assessment is important in determining the ability levels of all students; it is critical for students who are handicapped. Because students' levels of ability may differ across subject areas, assessment should go beyond the survey level, such as group achievement tests. Because this is a time-consuming task, it is logical for teachers to enlist the aid of the special education teacher in administering diagnostic tests. Subject area teachers can use their observational skills to find additional information. All tests, formal and informal, should lead to remediation and learning. Many diagnostic tests in use are criterion-referenced and provide objectives related to the student's ability.

Once the ability level is determined, adaptations need to be made. Although adaptations are challenging, demanding, and sometimes frustrating, there are some rather simple techniques that can be used.

In the elementary grades, materials developed at different reading levels can be used. In the upper elementary grades, there may be some stigma attached to materials, particularly reading books, graded at lower levels. One resourceful teacher, who observed the social implications of this problem, found book covers with motorcycles emblazened on them. With these covers on the primary books, his students were not embarrassed to carry their books on the bus. Language experience stories, referred to in the previous section, can also be used to develop topics at the reading and language levels of the student. Other areas of expression may be found for students who do not read at all. One student who did not speak and did not read was provided with an easel on which he could paint at any time. As he began to express himself in art, his abilities in other areas developed.

Difficulty in reading continues to be a problem at the secondary level. One method of reducing reading difficulty in all subject areas is to rewrite the material to be used. This is time-consuming at the outset, but with practice it becomes easier. Two pointers serve to speed the process:

1. Select a good article, pertinent to topics to be discussed in class, or an important portion of a textbook.
2. Have word lists available to determine grade level of the material. The Dolch list, lower-level books, and spelling lists can be used.

The following five steps simplify the process:

1. Select the concept or the main idea of the passage; write it down.
2. List the specialized vocabulary you feel is necessary to understanding the concept (use no more than 5 specialized vocabulary words per 100 words).
3. Next to the difficult words or concepts, substitute easy words.
4. Use common nouns; underline proper names; use short sentences of 5 or 6 words; turn written numbers into numerals; use simple sentence construction and present-tense verbs when possible.
5. Type, double-spaced, with the largest type available. Make sentences one line long, if possible.

Options include making passages into booklets, tape-recording the booklet so several students can read at a listening station, writing comprehension questions to create discussion, and making up games, activities, or exercises to reinforce the concept. An extra copy should remain in the teacher's files.[2] A format to facilitate organization is presented in Figure 13.1. Peer assistants, adult volunteers, and other teachers can help develop collections of rewritten material. The process is valuable in helping assistants and teachers pinpoint the salient concepts to be developed in a passage.

Another strategy in adapting material for different ability levels and learning styles is to change the format. The change may be as simple as reducing the number of math problems on a page or reducing the reading assignment to a few paragraphs. Sometimes the style of presentation is a problem for the student with learning difficulties. In a home economics class, for instance, sewing directions were written in longhand by the teacher, with instructions and diagrams for three hand stitches on a single page (see Figure 13.2).

One student who had problems with space orientation could not follow the instructions. The perceptive teacher examined her directions and made a simpler presentation, as demonstrated in Figure 13.3. After noting the difference in student comprehension, the teacher decided that this format would be better for all of her students.

In some cases, the reading problem can be circumvented. The use of films, audio programs, filmstrips, and hands-on experiments can replace reading assignments. In social studies, a great deal of information on current events can be learned from television and can enable all students to take part in group discussions.

At the secondary level, instructional adaptation is difficult. Teachers who work with large numbers of students may not have time to devote to individuals who are handicapped. In such cases, peer assistance may prove to be invaluable. Such assistance cannot be haphazard; it must be carefully planned to be successful. However, an investment of time initially may prove to be efficient in the long run. A successful program was demonstrated in a high school resource room by a teacher who had taught English before working with handicapped students. She explained her procedure:

> In the spring of each year, I visit the junior-level English classes. I ask for volunteers for my peer teaching program, explaining that the volunteers will be trained and that they will receive elective credit. During the summer, we

FIGURE 13.1
Textbook Adaptation

Title of Textbook _____

Grade Level of Text _____ Reading Level of Student _____

Chapter or Passage Title _____ Page Number _____

Word List:

Concepts to Be Developed:

Specialized Vocabulary:

Rewritten Passage:

FIGURE 13.2
Sewing Instructions

Running stitch – Basic sewing stitch used for gathering, mending, and tucking. Take several small stitches at a time, draw thread through the fabric, and repeat.

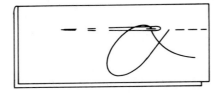

Backstitch — Used to reinforce seams, and make them stronger. Bring needle through the fabric and take a small back stitch, bringing the needle out ahead of the preceding stitch. Take another back stitch, putting the needle in at the end of the preceding stitch.

have sessions in which I explain the program and demonstrate how it works. I teach them the techniques to be used and help them develop materials we will use.

In the fall, I pair a volunteer with a student in the resource room. The volunteer assists the student in writing paragraphs, developing science projects, learning to use the telephone book, or whatever has been determined to be the student's need. Frequently the volunteers prepare

FIGURE 13.3
Adapted Sewing Instructions

RUNNING STITCH

A BASIC HAND SEWING STITCH.

USED FOR GATHERING, MENDING, AND TUCKING.

TO DO: PUT NEEDLE IN FABRIC AND TAKE A FEW SMALL STITCHES.

PULL THE THREAD UP TIGHT.

DO THIS AGAIN UNTIL YOU HAVE GONE ALL THE WAY ACROSS YOUR
    FABRIC.

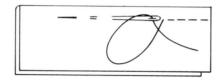

instructional material that is usable in the regular classroom and can extend the learning that has taken place.

Sometimes the volunteers and students ask if they can exchange partners. I ask them to wait for three weeks. Without exception, I find that after three weeks of working together, the pair is inseparable.

This system extends my time and skills. It facilitates skill building for the volunteers and for the resource room students; it also promotes social integration. I could not run my program without it.

Peer helpers can also help teachers in regular classes in the same manner. The key to success is to remember that volunteers should be trained and should be reinforced in some way, either with school credit or with special privileges.

The use of peer assistants is not limited to nonhandicapped students working with those who are handicapped. Sometimes students who have handicaps have developed special skills and strategies. The following example demonstrates this principle:

David, who is blind, is particularly good in math. He has developed his skills through the use of an abacus and other manipulatives. In a discussion of classroom techniques, a fourth-grade teacher was heard to exclaim, "I'm having a real problem getting across the concept of place value to my children. Any suggestions?" David's special education teacher immediately suggested that he visit the fourth-grade class and demonstrate place value with his abacus. The teacher was delighted. David met with the class, related to them at their level, and simplified the process in a way that was totally understandable. The fourth-grade students were enthusiastic, asked a number of questions, and asked him to return one day and show them braille. The experience was successful for everyone.

Cross-age tutoring is another example of handicapped students assisting nonhandicapped students. Students at an intermediate level in a special class were encouraged to read to kindergarten children. In preparation for this experience, they practiced until they could do it well. Another way to develop such a strategy is to have the older students read into a cassette recorder, improving their performance until they are satisfied with it. Both processes benefit everyone.

Interests

Instruction and materials should be relevant to the students' interests. As a start, interest inventories can be developed and used, teachers can observe what students do in their free time, and conversation can reveal major interests. In working with students who are handicapped, teachers may find that interests have to be developed. This can be accomplished by placing the handicapped student into a group of students who are working on projects of interest or with a peer who has status in the eyes of the handicapped student.

When interests are revealed, implications for instruction may follow. For example, a student who is mentally retarded demonstrated an interest in working with wood and wanted to make a table for his family. His shop teacher worked with him and discussed the interest with other teachers. The outcome was that the math teacher worked with the student on using the ruler, and other teachers worked with him on reading and interpreting diagrams and instructions. The resulting table was only part of the learning that took place.

Needs

Skills for living are the ultimate goals of education for handicapped students. Although some students who are mildly handicapped will go to college, many will not. Most students who are mildly mentally retarded leave high school and go directly into the work world. If this probability can be ascertained during the early school years, it helps parents and teachers determine curriculum priorities. Every subject area can be used to prepare students for independent living.

Science teaches students to be aware of their surroundings, to interact with and respect their environment, and to become citizens in a world that depends on science and technology. It is also a valuable vehicle to teach students to solve problems and to make decisions based on facts and consequences. When science includes approaches to everyday problems and situations, it speaks to the future needs of students who are handicapped.

Social studies help students develop positive attitudes toward themselves and others, to develop value systems, and to acquire skills for working in groups. Social studies also provide a unique opportunity to discuss handicapism as a social phenomenon. For students who are handicapped and for those who are not, the history of bias and prejudice includes all disenfranchised people, including those who are handicapped. Understanding the issues raised by handicapism is as important as understanding the issues concerning racism and sexism.

Physical education speaks to the need that handicapped students have for maximum development of their physical potential as well as the acquisition of healthy recreational outlets. Many of the jobs to be filled by students who are handicapped are in the unskilled and semiskilled labor force. These jobs demand physical stamina; physical education can teach proper care and use of the body.

Certainly the aesthetic aspects of life are important. Art and music provide outlets for emotional expression, the development of creativity, interaction with others, and tools for leisure activities. They also provide opportunities for students who are handicapped in academic areas to initiate their own ideas and projects rather than to assume passive roles.

Although it is assumed that vocational education will provide working skills for students who will not pursue advanced education programs, it becomes the responsibility of every teacher to incorporate living skills into the curriculum. This can be accomplished in a number of ways.

Schilit and Caldwell[3] have prepared a word list of 100 essential career and vocational words for mentally retarded students. The list includes such words as *boss, emergency, danger, tools, late,* and *foreman.* Teachers can prepare such lists from their own curriculum areas and teach them as spelling words and sight vocabulary.

Many ordinary materials respond to the needs of handicapped young people. The newspaper, for example, is an ideal instructional device. It is written at a relatively low reading level, it is mature in format and acceptable in an adult world, and it provides for skill building in every area. The importance of reading newspapers is obvious; math skills can be gained from shopping lists, sporting events, and weather reports; scientific information is readily available; and social learning can be acquired not only from the news, but even from the advice columns. Specific vocational information is available from want ads, and guides for living from real estate ads. Other materials relevant to the needs of young people are driver's license manuals, cookbooks, vacation folders, maps, and magazines. Every teacher will find appropriate materials once the need is recognized.

Reinforcement

Although the term *reinforcement* has been used to denote a "payoff" in many cases, a more accurate interpretation would be to think of it in terms of encouragement. Because learning is the strongest reinforcer, encouraging the student to learn is the goal for all teachers. Reinforcement means to encourage, to strengthen, and to support. It applies to students, to teachers, and to parents.

Students
Students are encouraged to learn when the environment is conducive to their learning. If the teacher recognizes that there are different learning styles, for example, learning is strengthened. Students respond differently to various stimuli—visual materials, sound recording, printed media, manipulative materials, or combinations. Some students work best alone, some work best in small task groups, and some do their best work in large teams. Some prefer structured, teacher-directed learning; others work best with open-ended, self-directed assignments.

Students who have attention, behavior, or motivational problems may learn better in a controlled environment in which behavior management techniques and systems are implemented. Students who perform at a low level usually respond to immediate or short-term reinforcement schedules while learning to delay their gratification. For such students, games, music, art activities, and peer interaction serve this function. It is important to remember that the student should be involved in the selection of reinforcing activities, and that the rules for acquiring them should be clear and fair. Teachers who have emotionally handicapped students in their classes will need to work closely with special educators and school counselors to determine the best reinforcement system.

Handicapped students are strongly supported when they are provided with materials and devices to help them learn. In addition to the previous suggestions, specific aids are available for students who need extra help. One obvious device is the calculator. In addition to traditional calculators, talking calculators are also available. Originally designed for visually impaired students, they are also helpful for learning-disabled students who may need auditory as well as visual input. Certainly, computers have opened doors for many students who have not learned in other ways. They are strong motivators.

Teacher-made materials are also effective motivators. The reference dictionary has been used for a number of years for students of all ages. It can take any form, from a notebook of normal size to a pocket-sized booklet. Any information the student needs to refer to from time to time can be entered in the reference dictionary. It could include the student's name, address, telephone number, and Social Security number; it could contain the multiplication tables; it could list words the student finds difficult to spell; it can be changed as the student's needs change.

Teachers facilitate learning when they help students read. When a handicapped learner has not learned to read, several techniques can minimize problems in all subject areas. In addition to alternate materials and rewriting techniques discussed previously, the teacher could use some of the following suggestions:

- Have another student read the assignment, allowing for better comprehension of the material without penalizing the handicapped student for poor reading ability.
- Tape-record passages from the text and have the student listen or follow along in the text.
- Underline words and ideas essential to the reading passage. Key sentences can be highlighted in text material, teacher-made selections, or newspapers.
- Permit the student to have additional time to read, with the opportunity to take the assignment home or to a study hall.
- Separate the reading assignment into parts, having the student concentrate on reading each small section.
- Provide the student with questions to be answered during the reading process. This helps the student know what to look for and to stay on task.

Many students with learning problems encounter a great deal of difficulty in solving math problems. The most obvious problem is identifying the process to be used. One tangible way of assisting is to identify, with the students, different words that relate to different processes and then to list these words in color. For example, such words as *plus, and, sum,* and *together* could be listed in red under the word *add.* As a bridge to understanding the process, the teacher could underline words in the problem in the appropriate color. Color cues can gradually be reduced as students acquire the verbal skills associated.

In addition to instructional reinforcement, students need social reinforcement. Although they need acceptance and approval from the teacher, peer acceptance is even more important. Studies conducted since the implementation of mainstreaming indicate that social integration does not occur spontaneously; it must be planned. The three aspects of socialization that need to be addressed are attitudes toward handicapped people, knowledge about handicapping conditions, and behavior of and toward handicapped people.

Attitudes toward handicapped people have been greatly facilitated by the media, especially television. Situation comedies, adventure series, and news stories frequently highlight people who are handicapped and deal with their differences in a positive way. It is quite different, however, to have a handicapped student enter the classroom, particularly if there has not been any prior preparation.

There are a number of social integration activities that help prepare teachers and students for successful integration. One simple activity aimed at dealing with bias in general is to point out similarities and differences among the class members. Encourage discussion about which differences are important and which are not. Some students may reveal instances in which their differences have proved embarrassing. In classrooms in which openness is encouraged, awareness of bias will become apparent.

Movies and videotapes provide visible stimuli to assist in the acquisition of knowledge and awareness concerning people who are handicapped. An even more powerful tool is the use of simulated handicaps. Teachers who are concerned about social acceptance and integration of handicapped students will find that the time and effort involved in a simulation workshop prove to be a good investment.

A number of situations lend themselves to simulation. In every community there are companies that rent or sell prosthetic devices. Usually they are cooperative in providing wheelchairs, crutches, walkers, and other devices to aid persons with physical handicaps. Visual and auditory handicaps can be simulated with the use of blindfolds and earplugs; learning problems can be experienced through test materials presented in unusual formats and at difficult levels. It is important to talk about the frustrations and difficulties experienced and to remind the students of the difference between simulated, temporary handicaps and permanent handicaps.

Ultimately, a student's attitude toward people who have handicaps is a reflection of the teacher's attitude. Teachers' attitudes provide powerful models of acceptance or rejection.

Knowledge about handicapping conditions is important for students who have handicaps and for those who interact with them. Sometimes people are at a loss to know whether to ask questions about a condition or to ignore the problem. In classrooms in which communication is free and invited, there are many opportunities for knowledge and understanding to develop. It is natural for children to ask questions; such questions need to be answered.

Accurate information about handicaps is necessary to the complete acceptance of them. Guest speakers—both children and adults—are excellent providers of information. Children are frank in asking questions and thus become better informed at their own levels.

Understanding is a gradual process that may never be reached by some children (or adults). It is difficult to understand why some children are handicapped and some are not, as well as why some children receive special consideration because they are handicapped. It has been observed, however, that as children and young people become more aware of differences and the origin of those differences, they grow in empathy.

Behavior of handicapped and nonhandicapped students is an important aspect of social integration.[4] Some students who are handicapped may exhibit poor social skills and should learn appropriate, socially acceptable behavior. Some of these skills are very elementary, such as smiling, greeting, sharing and cooperating, and complimenting others. Classroom teachers should ask special educators and parents to assist in the teaching of social skills.

Some students will laugh, point, and label other students who are handicapped. Such behaviors should be discouraged by teachers as attempts are made to develop positive attitudes. It may be necessary to teach handicapped students some short rebuttals to negative comments. One student, who was called "stupid," learned to respond, "But I'm not rude." The name-calling soon ceased.

Teachers

Classroom teachers are in a difficult position regarding students who are handicapped. For years, they have been told that special educators teach handicapped children and that other teachers need only to be experts in their respective fields. Since the implementation of P.L. 94-142, the situation has changed drastically. Teachers are being asked to individualize instruction, to teach basic skills, and to model attitudes of acceptance.

Parents, administrators, and students should be aware that most teachers are trying to meet the needs of all of their students, including those with handicaps. A first-grade teacher was asked, "How can you accommodate Tommy in your class? He's severely retarded." The teacher replied, "It's no problem; all my children have folders for their work and Tommy has one that suits his ability." There are many caring, capable teachers who are meeting the needs of their students who are handicapped.

Teachers need to reinforce each other. One positive outcome of mainstreaming has been the opportunity for teachers and other professionals to work together. Through understanding the unique problems of each teaching situation, classroom teachers and specialists have gained empathy and respect for each other. Teachers who are experts in biology are not expected to be experts in special education; special educators are not necessarily experts in biology. Respect for each other promotes honesty about skills, responsibilities, and concerns. A harmonious working situation is reinforcing.

Certainly the strongest reinforcer for teachers occurs when their students learn. There is no feeling more rewarding than the knowledge that "this child learned in my class."

Parents

Parents are reinforced through communication and participation. Frequently, parents of handicapped children have not had good experiences in school. They may have been unsuccessful in their own school careers, or they may have had a number of embarrassing and upsetting experiences with their handicapped child. There are many reasons parents may be reluctant to come to school for conferences or meetings of any sort: The time may not fit into their work schedule, they may be reluctant to hear any problems about their child, or they may fear that they will be blamed for those problems.

The best way to build a good relationship with parents is to ensure that the first contact is a positive one. A letter of introduction at the beginning of the year or a note commenting on their child's progress is a good beginning. When the first contact concerns a problem, communication is difficult.

Parent participation is a main component of P.L. 94-142. This principle acknowledges the facts that parents are their child's first teachers, and that their knowledge and experience are valuable to the child's growth and development throughout the school years. Not all parents want or are capable of full participation, and different levels of involvement should be expected. However, all parents should be made to feel welcome and comfortable in the school and should be informed about their child's progress.

Parents, too, are reinforced when their child makes progress. Work samples, criterion-referenced assessment and advancement, and honest compliments let parents know that teachers care about their child and about them. Suggestions for helping their child do better in school are usually welcome. Parents' suggestions may also be sought and used to advantage.

Conclusion

Shortly after the passage of the law for the education of handicapped children, the president of the National Education Association declared that "P.L. 94-142's challenge for the education profession is incalculable, as is its promise for those handicapped students whose educational needs have been neglected or ignored by the public school."[4] Since that time, the challenge has permeated every level of education.

Schools and universities concerned with teacher education have been required to examine their purpose, strategies, and programs. The field of special educations has changed drastically to accommodate the changing population of exceptional children and young people and therefore the changing role and environment of the educator.

Perhaps more challenging has been the changing role of general educators. Teachers and other personnel have been required to change their attitudes and to increase their repertoire of competencies to enable them to understand and teach children whom they may not have expected to teach.

Although the role of the teacher appears to be overwhelming at times, there are also positive changes. Technological advances promise to alleviate some of the paperwork and to expedite communication between home and school. Community resources are becoming involved in schools and providing opportunities to students and teachers for extended experiences. Administrators are discovering the advantages of volunteer programs and the unlimited possibilities that develop through school-community-home interaction.[5]

There are still many unanswered questions: Are teachers and parents fully prepared for the responsibilities they have in educating children and young people who have handicaps? Is the present system working? Are handicapped students leaving school with the skills they need? Concerned, capable teachers will help find answers to these and other questions as they learn to know and to work with students who are handicapped, their parents, and other teachers.

Questions and Activities

1. Why is it more appropriate to call a student with a learning disability a "student with a handicapping condition" rather than a "handicapped student"?

2. Form a discussion group with other members of your class. Use Stephens and Braun's four variables related to teacher's willingness to accept students with handicapping conditions into their classrooms as a departure point to discuss your attitudes toward teaching students with handicapping conditions.

3. Using the guidelines on reducing reading difficulty on pp. 257–258, rewrite an article on a topic you plan to teach or a chapter in a student textbook so that it can be read by students who are having difficulty reading grade-level assignments.

4. Give three examples of "teacher-made" materials and tell why they can be effective motivators for students.

5. Make a chart giving examples of how you can help learning-disabled (LD) students build listening, reading, and math skills.

6. Use a children's book such as *Yellow Bird and Me* by Joyce Hansen (New York: Houghton Mifflin, 1986) to develop a role-playing activity that can give students an opportunity to explore their feelings about people with handicapping conditions.

7. Review several textbooks currently in use to determine how people with handicapping conditions are portrayed. How many times are they mentioned or pictured in illustrations? In what context are they portrayed? What are their ethnic groups and gender? In what ways can you add materials on people with handicapping conditions to supplement textbooks?

Notes

1. T. M. Stephens and B. L. Braun, "Measures of Regular Classroom Teachers' Attitudes toward Handicapped Children," *Exceptional Children* 46, No. 4 (1980): 292–294.

2. L. C. Craig, "If It's Too Difficult for the Kids to Read—Rewrite It!" *Journal of Reading* 21, No. 3 (1977): 213.

3. Jeffrey Schilit and Mary Lou Caldwell, "A Word List of Essential Career/Vocational Words for Mentally Retarded Students," *Education and Training of the Mentally Retarded* 15, No. 2 (1980): 115.

4. John Ryor, "Integrating the Handicapped, *Today's Education* 24 (1977): 24.

5. Jane B. Schulz, *Parents and Professionals in Special Education* (Boston: Allyn and Bacon, 1987), p. 333.

CHAPTER 14

Teaching Gifted Students

■ RENA F. SUBOTNIK

Overview of Gifted Education

Definitions of Giftedness

Meet Amy Smith and Jason Jones. Amy is an entering kindergarten student who reads at the third-grade level. Jason Jones, a sixth-grader from a troubled inner-city school, is the only student in his grade to be reading at grade level. Both of these children need some kind of educational intervention. Whether they would qualify to participate in the local gifted program would depend on the definition of giftedness used in Jason's and Amy's state or local district.

A variety of definitions of the term *gifted* have been proposed by scholars and educators. Definitions promoted by Marland, Meeker, Renzulli, and Sternberg are briefly described in the following paragraphs. All four definitions seek to expand the conception of giftedness beyond the traditional high-IQ mode.

In 1972, Commissioner Sidney Marland entered into the public record the definition of giftedness proposed by United States Office of Education (USOE) for use by state and local agencies in developing policies for serving gifted children.[1] The USOE definition acknowledged that some children exhibit such an exceptional level of ability in certain domains that regular school programs might not adequately address their educational needs. Those domains include general intellectual ability such as critical thinking, problem solving, and recognizing abstract relationships; aptitudes in one or more school subjects; creative or productive thinking (e.g., developing a variety of methods to achieve a solution, or applying a variety of solutions to a given method); leadership ability; and talent in the visual and performing arts. Little emphasis was placed on promoting specific methods of identification to be used with each domain.

Psychologist Mary Meeker applied the work of J. P. Guilford to the development of tests that would identify gifted children in the domains of general intellectual ability and creative and productive thinking. Dr. Guilford was commissioned by the United States government to design an instrument to identify potential candidates for pilot training. As an outgrowth of this assignment, he created a model of human intelligence called the Structure of the Intellect. His model identifies 120 separate functions, including a set associated with creative thinking. According to Guilford, every individual exhibits a profile of strengths and weaknesses among those functions.[2] Meeker translated Guilford's work into instruments that schools could use to individualize their programs.[3] The tests were designed to generate a profile for each student in such areas as problem solving, memory, recognizing relationships, and divergent thinking (coming up with a variety of responses to a given stimulus). Schools employing the Structure of the Intellect definition (SOI) work with Dr. Meeker's institute to determine the range of profiles students need in order to receive gifted programming services.

Joseph Renzulli criticized the USOE for promoting the idea that the five domains of giftedness were independent of one another.[4] He argued that general intellectual abilities, creativity or leadership skills, or a combination of skills are prerequisites to the exhibition of talent in specific academic areas and in the visual and performing arts. In addition, according to Renzulli, other definitions of giftedness, including the USOE and the Structure of the Intellect, ignored the role of motivation in the manifestation of talent. Renzulli described the student exhibiting gifted behavior as one who, given an appropriately stimulating environment, demonstrated above-average ability, creativity, and the motivation to carry out a creative task.

Cognitive psychologist Robert Sternberg has constructed the most recent prominent definition of giftedness.[5] His triarchic theory of intellectual giftedness includes three subtheories. The first subtheory addresses the need for a gifted individual to be skilled at information processing, such as planning, learning and carrying out given tasks. The second subtheory promotes the need for a gifted individual to deal successfully with novel ideas and situations. The third subtheory incorporates practical decision-making abilities, such as knowing when it is better to pursue or drop a project, widen or narrow one's focus, or think reflectively rather than quickly.

In general, Sternberg points to the previously unexplored role of executive abilities as a distinguishing characteristic of the intellectually gifted individual. He does not specifically address the role of motivation. Although the instruments necessary to carry out an identification program based on Sternberg's theories is not yet widely available, his ideas are circulating among people interested in the field of gifted education and are serving as stimuli to renewed discussion of such important questions as What is giftedness? and How is giftedness manifested?

Definitions selected by most American school systems that provide programs for gifted children have thus far focused on serving the gifted children who, because of their exceptional intellectual, creative, or academic abilities, need modification of the regular curriculum. Although recognition is also given to giftedness in leadership and in visual and performing arts, programs and accompanying research in those domains are less numerous. The rationale for this discrepancy is usually attributed to the belief that assessment of talent in leadership and in the visual and performing arts is too subjective, whereas standardized tests are available for use in the identification of intellectual, academic, and creative aptitude. Although the author does not support the belief that talent in leadership or in the visual and performing arts is less important or recognizable, this introductory chapter to a rapidly growing and changing field focuses on the education of intellectually, academically, and creatively talented children and youths.

Background and Rationale for the Gifted Education Movement in the United States

Until the 1920s, most Americans who were not academically oriented did not go to high school, and certainly not to college. Secondary and postsecondary education was therefore geared to the academically able. In addition, exceptional elementary school youngsters were double-promoted (skipped a grade). In this way, they could work with their intellectual, if not their chronological, peers.

In the early 1920s, Lewis Terman and Melita Oden[6] began a pioneering research program that profoundly affected the future course of gifted education. Terman developed a test of intelligence as an American revision of the work of French psychologist Alfred Binet. In honor of Terman's professional assistants at Stanford University, Terman named the test the Stanford-Binet Intelligence Test. To validate its capacity to predict a child's adult productivity on the basis of a test score, he established a longitudinal study of nine- to eleven-year-olds who scored in the ninety-ninth percentile and above on the Stanford-Binet (IQ 140 and higher). These individuals, followed up in adulthood, proved to be exceptionally productive in comparison to a random group of individuals of the same fairly high social and economic background.[7] Most of these individuals became prominent academics, writers, lawyers, and business executives. Several experimental programs, including the Hunter College Elementary School in New York City, were developed in the 1940s using the Stanford-Binet to identify gifted children.

The Soviet launching of Sputnik in 1957 spread concern throughout the United States that its educational system was not preparing young people to compete in science and technology. This factor, along with the positive results associated with Terman's research, led to a series of curriculum development projects and the widespread initiation of special programs for intellectually gifted students.

At the same time, researchers J. P. Guilford and E. P. Torrance[8] continued their investigations into the measurement of creativity. Not until the 1960s, however, were they able to convince the education community that creativity and an extremely high IQ did not necessarily go hand in hand—that, in fact, many creative individuals would be missed if gifted programs catered only to the high-IQ child.

In the 1970s, the impact of the civil rights movement and the advent of special-education legislation led theorists and researchers in the field to focus on the discovery and nurturance of gifted children handicapped by poverty, racism, sexism, and physical and learning disabilities. The trends of the 1980s, however, are difficult to define. Seventeen states presently fund gifted education to the same degree as other categories of special education. Although gifted programs are much more widespread than before, many programs are being conducted without trained personnel and without the necessary attention to the problems of identifying and supporting gifted students outside the U.S. mainstream. Finally, despite the outpouring of policy statements decrying the state of public education, the federal government has not yet provided additional funding to support the special education of gifted and talented children.

As you can see in the previous chapters, some students require modifications of the regular curriculum in order to participate with their age mates in the mainstream classroom. Gifted students, because they tend to learn more quickly and comprehensively, need educational modifications presented at an appropriate speed and level of comprehension.

Unless attended to, gifted students spend many hours in school covering material they already know and answering questions that for them require simplistic responses. A common misconception is that gifted students do not need special attention to be successful in school. Gifted students are therefore sent to the library for unsupervised reading or research, or sent on errands for the teacher. Alternatively, they may be assigned more problems at a level at which they have already demonstrated mastery, or they may be given the opportunity to tutor a fellow student. Although none of these options is innately problematic and can in some cases be rewarding, gifted students deserve to have at least some portion of both the school curriculum and the teacher's attention focused on their educational needs.

Identification of Gifted Students

Identifying students for special programming is integrally tied to the definition adopted by the school district or state. Some kind of standardized test score is almost always included among the requirements for placement in a gifted program. However, other criteria besides high test scores, such as nominations based on behavioral checklists, should always be used to assist in determining eligibility.[9]

Tests

Tests used to identify or consider a child for special programming have been categorized into four types: tests of achievement, individual intelligence, group intelligence, and creativity.

Achievement Tests

Each year, most public school students take a battery of tests used to compare their academic standing with those of students in the same grade throughout the country. Results of these tests can pinpoint students who are significantly above or below the national norm. Raw scores are translated into percentiles or stanines, and children who score above a predetermined cutoff, such as the ninetieth percentile or the ninth stanine, may become candidates for further assessment. A major drawback inherent in the use of achievement tests for the identification of gifted students is their tendency to be too easy for the academically gifted student. If tests are not difficult enough, much useful information about actual student achievement levels is lost.

Individual Intelligence Tests

The WISC-R, Stanford-Binet, and K-ABC are the most commonly used means for determining IQ, or intelligence quotient. The IQ score derived from the individual test as opposed to the group test is considered more reliable, particularly with middle- and upper-middle-class children. Test items draw on students' problem-solving skills (such as reproducing block patterns), as well as on educational and cultural experiences (such as word comprehension). Individual IQ tests are expensive to administer and tend to discriminate against some minority groups by not accurately reflecting their intellectual potential. Test bias can occur in any of the following ways: lack of tester-testee rapport; difficulties resulting from limited standard English proficiency; and variability in exposure to vocabulary and experiences appearing on the test.

Group Intelligence Tests

Group intelligence tests were designed to call on one's abilities to remember concepts learned in school, to make reasonable guesses from context, and to generalize from what is already known. Various instruments such as the Ross Test of Higher Cognitive Processes, Cognitive Abilities Tests, and the Ravens Progressive Matrices Test ask the examinee to solve series, analogies, or logic puzzles based on patterns of recognized words, nonsense words, or drawings.

Group tests are less expensive to administer than individual intelligence tests, but they are less reliable than individual tests in both the very high and the very low ranges. Each error made within the most difficult category of questions has a more significant effect on the total score than an error made in the middle range of the test. This factor penalizes students who are capable of negotiating items in the upper range.[10] In addition, test-takers who tend to answer questions correctly but with fewer completions or guesses are also penalized by the scoring mechanisms of some timed group tests such as the Scholastic Aptitude Test (SAT).[11]

Creativity Tests

Research in the area of creativity has led to the development of tests to identify creative potential. The instruments, such as the Torrance Test of Creative Thinking, use pictures or words to stimulate the examinee to generate a quantity of original and elaborated ideas within a regulated period of time. These tests, like those mentioned above, are not universally valid predictors of later intellectual or creative productivity, but in combination with other sources of information they can provide valuable insights into a student's cognitive functioning.

Behavior Checklists

Useful information can be collected about specific students for assessment purposes from teachers, parents, peers, and the student.

Teachers

Teachers' reliability as identifiers of gifted students is affected by their understanding of the school district's definition of giftedness. Without delineating desired student characteristics, teachers tend to nominate academically able students who are obedient, attractive, bright, and socially adept, while missing students who are shy, bored, less popular, and of a lower socioeconomic level.[12] Given instruction as to the identifying characteristics of gifted students, however, teachers become a good source of referrals.[13] The Renzulli-Hartman Scale is the most widely used checklist of characteristics to guide teachers in the selection of students for gifted programming. The scale is divided into three sections, one for each component of the Renzulli definition of gifted behavior: above-average ability, creativity, and task commitment.

Parents

Depending on the local culture, parents may over- or underrate their children's abilities.[14] A behavior checklist, filled out by parents, however, can provide invaluable assistance to teachers and administrators by describing children's interests and accomplishments outside school. Parents know when their child learned to speak in full sentences or about talents that are expressed before or after the school day. For example, two seventh-grade students being considered for special programming in an urban public school where the author was a gifted specialist never discussed their out-of-school activities with teachers, thinking that those activities had no relationship with their school responsibilities. Parents informed us that one young man was the conductor of the city's youth symphony and the other had amassed a small fortune by investing in the stock market.

Peers

An excellent source of candidates for possible special programming, especially gifted culturally different children, is a peer-nomination instrument. School districts, such as the Seattle Public Schools, have devised instruments that ask for the names of schoolmates who best fit the following categories: (1) who learns quickly and easily, (2) who has creative ideas, (3) who is concerned with fairness, and (4) who tells the wildest stories.[15] To best identify candidates with this method, however, students must have spent a period of time together in school. If school assignments change from year to year, it may be necessary to delay nomination procedures until new students are at least fairly well integrated into the school population.

Self

Some students, because of a reticent personality or a lack of social skills, or because of interests that take place mainly outside both the school and home, will not be noticed by parents, peers, or teachers. Self-nomination provides such individuals with the opportunity to describe their interests and activities to specialists who can use the information for possible placement in a gifted program. One published instrument, the Interest-A-Lyzer (Creative Learning Press, P.O. Box 320, Mansfield Center, Conn. 06520) elicits responses to imaginary situations that reveal students' interests and aspirations. Sample items include imagining the theme of a book one could write if one were a famous author, or the collections one would pursue if money or time were unlimited. Autobiographies, taped or written, may serve the purpose as well.

Work Samples

Direct examples of creative work that go beyond academic expectations are sometimes used to audition for special programs. These products are direct reflections of youngsters' creative ability and motivation and in this way are more valid than tests purported to measure the potential to be creatively productive. This work can take the form of science projects, artwork, dance or music performances, games, or essays. For example, one seven-year-old described by Leta Hollingworth[16] caught an adult's attention by designing and illustrating rules for three- and four-sided checkers and by writing, typing, and editing a popular playground newsletter. To reduce the influence of individual judges' taste and values on the recognition of a quality product, it is important to use *more than one rater* in the evaluation of submitted work.

In conclusion, a responsible and effective identification procedure uses as much information as possible to help raters make decisions about placing students into programs. Generally it is better to err in the direction of placing a possibly unqualified student into a program than to leave out a student who is disqualified only on the basis of an extremely stringent test score cutoff. Most important, identification by itself cannot satisfy a student's educational needs. The goal is to provide a high-quality program designed to foster the intellectual, academic, and creative strengths of the identified students.

Intellectual Characteristics

Not every gifted child exhibits the same set of characteristics. However, the descriptions that follow have appeared regularly in studies of gifted children and adults. The intellectual characteristics include accelerated pace of learning, capacity for seeing relationships and patterns, curiosity, and persistence.[17]

Accelerated Pace of Learning

The primary characteristic of giftedness noticed by classroom teachers is the speed with which these children learn. Many gifted children are already reading when they enter school. Students who learn math concepts, vocabulary, and reading skills after minimal exposure are using their extraordinary ability to memorize, strategize, and concentrate. It is not uncommon, however, for an award-winning mathematics student to be a competent but uncreative writer. In fact, some gifted students have serious academic problems that require special planning and may be caused by learning disabilities. Within the student's area of exceptional strength, however, he or she learns and understands quickly and completely. If a class dwells on a simple concept for too long, the gifted child may become bored and disruptive. Teachers who work with intellectually and academically gifted students learn to make portions of the regular curriculum more compact to increase the pace at which it is presented.

Capacity for Seeing Relationships and Patterns

In the self-contained classroom, or in a team-teaching environment, instructors have the opportunity to draw their students' attention to concepts and patterns that are central to one or more academic disciplines (e.g., power, change, tradition) so that students exercise their capacity to make generalizations, solve complex problems, and devise insights. In addition, students who are skilled at seeing relationships and patterns can be taught two or more concepts from the regular curriculum at once, increasing the complexity of the lesson as well as saving time for enrichment. In the beginning foreign language instruction, for example, both gender notations and tense can be taught together instead of separately.

Curiosity and Persistence

Young gifted students tend to be extremely curious about many topics and concepts to which they are exposed, such as dinosaurs, computer programming, or product invention. Once a child becomes captivated by a project, it may be difficult to tear him or her away to do anything else, even to eat or sleep. Such a child may become disgruntled when an interesting point in class is passed over by classmates who are satisfied with a superficial explanation. Scheduling, when possible, should include blocks of time in the class or resource room for students to pursue discussion or projects in depth.

Creative Characteristics

Until recently, most classrooms did not focus on developing children's creative characteristics. Gifted specialists are now promoting the notion of students as producers rather than as mere consumers of knowledge.[18] Being a producer requires the ability to do more than learn and understand. The student also must be able to see relationships where they did not exist before and translate those insights into products that give pleasure, satisfy a need, or generate new ideas. Creative children want to try different ways to solve problems (e.g., a new way to learn the multiplication tables, take attendance, sell cereal, breed hamsters, end the arms race). Although we may admire our most creative students, their nontraditional approach to classroom life can sometimes be troublesome, particularly in a large heterogeneous class.

Class assignments can be designed to promote the notion of student-as-producer by requiring the inclusion of some original dimension to every major assignment. For example, a research report should not simply describe the history of the scholarship on the topic but should also incorporate the student's reactions to the literature described. Science reports should not only delineate the procedures of the experiment, but should also encompass a section on follow-up questions or alternative hypotheses.

Affective Characteristics

In the past, gifted children were assumed to be more moral, empathic, and honorable than average children. We now know that the quality researchers were trying to describe was really acute sensitivity. Most gifted children have an extraordinary ability to read people and situations. They may not know how to handle what they see or hear, nor will they necessarily use the ability for the benefit of other people. Some of the ways gifted children manifest this sensitivity include high expectations for themselves and others, low tolerance for lags between intellectual and physical development, and concern with inconsistencies between ideal and real behavior. Problematic behavior derived from these attending characteristics (not requiring outside therapy or medication) are best handled in individual or small-group counseling sessions with other gifted students led by counselors familiar with the constellation of problems found most typically among gifted students.

High Expectations of Self and Others

You may be surprised to find one of your students refusing to read his or her A+ paper to the class. In the course of private conversation, you may find that the student is pleased that you liked the paper but that it failed to meet his or her personal standards, particularly for public review. At the elementary school level, many gifted children learn relatively effortlessly, and if not adequately challenged will submit hastily conceived work. High expectations of others gets played out when gifted students, who tend to be extraordinarily concerned with issues of fairness, are devastated when friends fail to live up to the individual's sometimes overly demanding code of behavior.

Impatience with Lags in Physical Development

Although most gifted children are not particularly small for their age, they may try to engage in activities and solve problems normally associated with older children. Primary age gifted children are particularly prone to frustration when they can visualize problem solutions but do not have the agility or vocabulary to carry them out. For example, a first-grader may want to explore the properties of a paper geodesic dome model but may not be able to manage the necessary cutting to carry out this wish. The same holds true for the youngster who dreams up elaborate tales for a book but does not yet have the motor coordination to write them down. A friend from a sixth-grade classroom, the teacher, or teacher assistant can lend a literal helpful hand by doing the necessary cutting or writing. Older students, particularly boys who have been double-promoted, may be much smaller and less physically agile than their age mates. Other gifted adolescents may be extremely interested and well read in topics such as death but do not have the emotional maturity to achieve any more than an intellectual understanding of the topic. Discussing their thoughts on the topic with uninterested age mates or with adults uncomfortable with the youngster's paradoxical intellectual precocity and emotional immaturity can be problematic.

Noticing Inconsistencies between Ideal and Real Behavior

Gifted children can be victims of a phenomenon called existential depression, or carrying the burden of the world on their shoulders.[19] Becoming aware of hypocracies found in everyday life can leave such a child numb or cynical. Activism and idealism modeled by a parent, teacher, or friend can help channel these concerns constructively.

General Suggestions for Curricular and Instructional Modifications

The regular curriculum was designed to be a basic foundation for all students. Differentiating the regular curriculum for use with gifted students requires a combination of acceleration and enrichment and the use of interdisciplinary themes; the proportions should be determined by the individual student's academic and talent profiles.[20]

Acceleration

Although the term *acceleration* is often associated with double promotion, it can also be used to mean moving more rapidly through the year's required curriculum to create more time for higher-level enrichment activities. The teacher must first assess the skill and knowledge levels of the students, allowing those who have already mastered the initial units to begin more advanced units. Continuous monitoring for mastery is, of course, necessary. Some subjects, like mathematics, foreign language, grammar, and reading skills are more conducive to this kind of acceleration because of their sequential nature.

Many school subjects are taught as a series of incremental steps toward the acquisition of a higher goal. Acceleration works best when that goal is presented in the beginning as the object of the upcoming series of lessons, much like pieces of a jigsaw puzzle fit together to create a picture. If the real goal is understanding the picture, and the pieces are simply building blocks to reaching the goal, then the student and teacher can work together to determine the minimum amount of pieces the student needs to see the picture. Another method of acceleration is to reduce the number of practice exercises a student must successfully complete to demonstrate mastery. If, after instruction, a child can do the last ten problems in the unit, he or she should not have to do the first forty.

Enrichment

Curriculum can be enriched for gifted students in a number of ways. One way is to introduce topics that are extensions of the regular curriculum. Some examples include (1) the study of biographies of scientists, mathematicians, or creative writers whose work contributed to the skills and knowledge learned in the regular science, math, and language arts curriculum; (2) the investigation of English-language newspaper stories from other parts of the world covering a historical period under examination in social studies. These ideas are usually derived from the expertise or interest of teachers, available community or parent mentors, or the students themselves.

Developing new skills not taught in the regular curriculum is another enrichment technique. Research topics such as survey development, interviewing, finding primary resources, organizing case studies, and elementary statistics can be introduced to the gifted student for use in becoming a producer of knowledge. The classroom teacher not familiar with these topics can get assistance from subject matter specialists, resource teachers, parents, other members of the community, and books.

Providing enrichment to gifted students in the regular classroom requires that the teacher answer a series of questions:

1. What topics from the regular curriculum are most conducive to extension and enrichment?

2. How much time for enrichment can be derived from acceleration of the regular curriculum?

3. What are the abilities, interests, and time constraints of the students, staff members, parents, and community members who might be involved in independent projects?

Having all of that information in hand allows the teacher to formulate a plan within the constraints of available time and resources.

Contracts with gifted students for time to work on independent projects can then be negotiated with clearly established time limitations and criteria for evaluation. (A sample evaluation form is available from Creative Learning Press; see address on p. 274.) The expected outcome of enrichment is for students to synthesize their newly gained knowledge and skills into the design and completion of an individual or small-group investigation to be evaluated by experts within the school and the community.[21] Students are given a list of criteria that determine successful completion of a project, including a required number of references, a preselected audience, and a positive evaluation by an adult expert.

Interdisciplinary Themes

Interdisciplinary frameworks are rarely used by teachers in planning curricula for the gifted. This is unfortunate because the technique capitalizes on the gifted child's ability to see relationships and make generalizations. The real world, of course, is not divided up into subject areas. When we develop an impression of an event, place, or person, we do not think in terms of subtraction, verbs, spelling, or data-retrieval charts. Instead we find ourselves intrigued because that object, person, or event is, among other things, beautiful, revolutionary, adaptive, changing, traditional, or powerful. Teachers can take advantage of students' ability to organize their thinking around these major themes by pointing them out when they appear in the regular curriculum. For example, the concept of power can be explored in the social studies through the balance of power in the American system of government, in science by the generation of electricity, in language arts by persuasive language, in art by political cartoons or posters, and in mathematics by symbol systems (e.g., powers of 10) that allow us to describe enormously large or small numbers elegantly.

Teachers need to develop good questioning strategies to carry out the interdisciplinary themes component of the curriculum. Become aware of the level of questions you ask and the purposes those questions serve. Tape yourself during a class session. See how many questions you ask students that require a simple yes or no answer. How many questions require an answer you already know? (Ninety percent of teacher's questions generally fall into these two categories.) All students, at the very least, could be challenged to demonstrate comprehension by using analogies from their own lives. Gifted students can be challenged with a regular diet of high-level questions, those requiring the analysis of real-life problems and the creation of new ideas or products based on those explorations. The ultimate goal of this questioning strategy is for students to generate questions that can lead to future individual or small-group projects.

Administrative Options

Once identified, gifted students can be served by the schools in a variety of ways, depending on local policy. The options differ by the degree to which gifted students are segregated from their regular classroom peers.

Specialized Schools

Some states such as North Carolina have instituted residential schools for academically talented students from all over the state. Metropolitan areas with large school-age populations have created schools for intellectually or artistically gifted children. New York City, for example, has five specialized high schools (Bronx High School of Science, Stuyvesant High School, Hunter College High School, Brooklyn Technical High School, and La Guardia High School for Music, Art, and the Performing Arts) and at least three lower schools (Hunter College Elementary School, P.S. 308, and Mark Twain). These schools serve students who have demonstrated their potential through competitive tests or auditions. Cutoff scores are made high enough to avoid draining local high schools of too many of their brighter students. Even students within these special schools have varied profiles of talent and academic strengths. These schools must therefore offer regular to very advanced classes in nearly all academic subjects, as well as make arrangements for individual students to work in their area of strength with community, corporate, or university mentors.

Special Groupings within Schools

When there are enough identified gifted students on a grade level to form a class, they may be grouped together for most of their school subjects: science, mathematics, language arts, foreign language, and social studies. Music, art, industrial arts, and physical education may be shared with other students in the school. Separate classes within a school, like the traditional tracking system, can be either a boon to the school or a divisive force. Gifted classes with appropriately trained teachers, students identified in a nonarbitrary manner, and continuous opportunities for the admission of new members may set a tone throughout the school of discipline and experimentation. When the program is weak, however, staff and students outside the program may see the special class as an excuse for placating powerful parents or politicians.

Pullout Programs

Pullout programs are the more common form of administrative option for gifted children.[22] A trained specialist meets with small groups of identified students for one to five hours per week. This specialist focuses on the unique interests and talents of the individual students rather than on traditional academics. Students generally learn research and intellectual skills needed to conduct small-group and individual investigations and make contact with adults in the community who can serve as mentors. Gifted students remain in contact with their age peers for most of their time in school.

Many regular classroom teachers resent the disruptions caused by children leaving to attend sessions with specialists. Other problems that stem from the pullout arrangement include doubling up of homework from both special and regular classes and the difficulty of maintaining continuity in the special program when there are week-long breaks between sessions.

Regular Classroom with Consulting Teacher

Many school districts and counties hire a gifted specialist to serve the entire system. The specialist arranges in-service courses, organizes curriculum-writing teams, and visits with individual teachers who seek advice. If the person has time to be available and provides quality service, motivated regular classroom teachers can derive help and ideas for meeting the needs of gifted children within their classroom. The strength of this arrangement lies in the social integration of gifted students into the mainstream school culture. The drawbacks include the additional strain on teachers to specialize their curriculum and instructional strategies. Without modification, gifted students are often left to fend for themselves.

Sometimes there is no help at all for the regular classroom teacher. Parents can be an excellent source of assistance in these cases. They can organize Saturday programs, inform each other about museum and university offerings geared to gifted children, and serve as mentors for individual projects. Finally, teachers can suggest to administrators that certain children be double-promoted. Although this option is currently unpopular with administrators and the general public, it was until recently the most common form of gifted education. There is no scientific evidence to show that it is academically or socially detrimental to gifted students when the decision is supported by the child, the parents, and the teachers who will be working with the double-promoted child.[23]

Influences on Productivity

Being identified as gifted and placed in a program is no guarantee that a student will fulfill his or her potential. In addition to the role of task commitment and motivation addressed by Joseph Renzulli, Abraham Tannenbaum,[24] and James Gallagher[25] proposed a set of nonintellective factors that can negatively influence the productivity of a gifted child: lack of support from parents, teachers, peers, or one's subculture; and plain bad luck.

Parents

Parents with high ambitions for their gifted child will ensure that the child receives the highest-quality education possible. However, most parents prefer to have a bright but not gifted child with good social skills. The special child's needs can be intrusive on family life in many ways: reduction of attention to nongifted siblings, parental intimidation by their child's superior intellect, and parental fear that the gifted child will reject the family culture to join the mainstream.[26,27,28] Successful programs must include a parent participation component. Parents, particularly those distrustful of schools as an institution, need to be included in the discussion of program goals and must be convinced of the importance of their emotional support to their child's continuing participation in the gifted program.

Teachers

Teachers can help a gifted child by providing a source of support in a school environment that often rewards athletic and social achievement over intellectual ones. Teachers can excite and stimulate children by modeling intellectual curiosity. They can help students feel comfortable with their intellectual strengths and shore up their weaknesses. Teachers can actively recruit talented culturally different children who may be reluctant to be involved in special programming. However, teachers who are threatened by a student's questions and expertise can transform the student's curiosity and enthusiasm into silent resentment or active rebellion.

Peer Group

A student in a peer group that ridicules academic brilliance has to exhibit extraordinary strength of character in order to withstand derogatory comments and also to pursue intellectual interests. The same individual in the presence of other gifted students is more likely to hear students comparing how long they had toiled over a math puzzle or had worked on a research paper.[29] The strongest argument used by advocates for the segregation of gifted students is the issue of peer culture, particularly in systems where the school culture is nonsupportive of academic brilliance.[30]

Subculture

The more removed a gifted child is from middle- to upper-middle-class mainstream culture, the more difficult it is for the student to be identified and served by the present educational system.[31] To succeed both in school and at home, the student carries the burden of having to become bicultural. This means, for example, that a Black youngster brought up speaking Black English must also learn to operate comfortably in standard English, and most important, to know when each language is most appropriately used. Nonmainstream traditions can serve as a handicap in national competition for jobs, scholarships, and university entrance. The purpose of these comments is not to support the injustice of the system but to ensure children with exceptional intellectual abilities the opportunity to compete on any level they choose.

Reuven Fueuerstein, a pioneering Israeli psychologist, proposed an explanation for the inordinate numbers of non-European Israelis being placed in slower classes. His research showed that in most cases, these children did not know how to approach academic problems.[32] Gifted children facing a baffling school system need to be taught how it works; they need to be taught acceptable behavior and rules for approaching word problems and distinguishing irrelevant facts from relevant facts, and so on. Teachers and school counselors can provide invaluable assistance to children from nonmainstream cultures by alleviating language deficiencies, basic skill deficiencies, or both, by providing opportunities for the children to interact with great works of art, literature, and music associated with both their home culture and mainstream Western culture; and by helping students know when to call on their ethnic ways of speaking, thinking, playing, and learning, and when to call on their proficiency with mainstream resources.[33]

Chance

Chance also plays a role in whether a student fulfills creative and intellectual potential. A child born into a musical family with the coordination, intellect, and aesthetic sensibilities to play a musical instrument skillfully is more likely to have these abilities noticed and supported than is a child born into a family more focused on other interests. Also, in any given year, there may be more gifted children competing for spaces in schools and colleges than during another year. Consequently, a passing score from one year may not be sufficient for admission another year.

Conclusion

Amy Smith and Jason Jones by now have had more information collected about them to assess their eligibility for the gifted program. Amy's parent nomination and individual intelligence test scores and Jason's peer nominations and group intelligence scores were high enough to place them in one of their district's special classes. A teacher working with Amy or Jason analyzes their current standing in the regular curriculum and prepares to accelerate and enrich lessons in their domains of exceptionality. A parent of each child meets with the teachers to devise a support system of monitoring homework and regular trips to the local library. A mentor is found in the community to assist Jason with a project on his neighborhood's history that he has always wanted to pursue.

Continual assessment will take place to monitor the proportions of acceleration and enrichment in each student's course of study. Whenever equilibrium is reached, attention will be focused on a more epistemological approach to learning, like interdisciplinary themes. Jason, and later Amy, will be counseled as to the best available secondary school environment to keep them challenged and on the way to fulfilling their potential. That is, if they're lucky.

Questions and Activities

1. What were some of the social and political factors that led to the development of gifted education in the United States?

2. What methods are used to identify gifted students? Identify some of the problems associated with each method.

3. Form a group with several of your classmates. Research and report on ways students gifted in various areas such as reading, math, and science can be served in the regular classroom.

4. In what ways are gifted and regular students similar and different?

5. What resources and training will you need to teach gifted students?

6. Write a brief paper on how the concept of least restrictive environment (LRE), discussed in Chapter 12, can be applied to teaching gifted students in regular classrooms, in pullout programs, and in specialized schools. What are some benefits and disadvantages of each setting?

7. Using a lesson that you would normally teach, give examples of how the concepts of acceleration and enrichment can be applied in your classroom. What benchmarks would you use to determine when acceleration was appropriate? How would you identify the students who would participate in enrichment activities? Give examples of acceleration and enrichment activities that can be used with the lesson.

8. Do you agree with this statement: "Educators have a special responsibility to identify and provide services to gifted students who are bilingual, culturally diverse, minority, and from low-income homes." Why or why not?

Notes

1. Sidney P. Marland, Jr., *Education of the Gifted and Talented, Vol. 1: Report to the Congress of the United States by the United States Commissioner of Education* (Washington, D.C.: United States Government Printing Office, 1972).

2. J. Paul Guilford, *The Nature of Human Intelligence* (New York: McGraw-Hill, 1967).

3. Mary Meeker, *The SOI: Its Interpretation and Uses* (Columbus, Ohio: Charles E. Merrill, 1969).

4. Joseph Renzulli, "What Makes Giftedness: Reexamining a Definition," *Phi Delta Kappan* 58 (1978): 180–184.

5. Robert J. Sternberg, "A Triarchic Theory of Intellectual Giftedness," in Robert J. Sternberg and Janet E. Davidson, eds., *Conceptions of Giftedness* (Cambridge, England: Cambridge University Press, 1986).

6. Lewis M. Terman and Melita Oden, *Genetic Studies of Genius: Mental and Physical Traits of a Thousand Gifted Children* (Stanford, Calif.: Stanford University Press, 1925).

7. E. Paul Torrance, *Rewarding Creative Behavior: Experiments in Classroom Creativity* (Englewood Cliffs, N.J.: Prentice-Hall, 1965).

8. Lewis M. Terman and Melita Oden, *Genetic Studies of Genius: The Gifted Child Grows Up* (Stanford, Calif.: Stanford University Press, 1947).

9. Edwina D. Pendarvis, "Gifted and Talented Children," in William H. Berdine and A. Edward Blackhurst, eds., *An Introduction to Special Education,* 2d ed. (Boston: Little Brown, 1985).

10. Gary A. Davis and Sylvia B. Rimm, *Education of the Gifted and Talented* (Englewood Cliffs, N.J.: Prentice-Hall, 1985).

11. Phylis Rosser, *Sex Bias in College Admissions Tests: Why Women Lose Out,* 2d ed. (Cambridge, Mass.: National Center for Fair and Open Testing, 1987).

12. James J. Gallagher, *Teaching the Gifted Child,* 3d ed. (Boston, Mass.: Allyn and Bacon, 1985).

13. Gail H. Gear, "Accuracy of Teacher Judgment in Identifying Intellectually Gifted Children: A Review of the Literature," *Gifted Child Quarterly* 20 (1976): 246–261.

14. Davis and Rimm, *Education of the Gifted.*

15. Joseph Renzulli, Sally M. Reis, and Linda H. Smith, *The Revolving Door Identification Model* (Mansfield Center, Conn.: Creative Learning Press, 1981).

16. Leta Hollingworth, *Gifted Children: Their Nature and Nurture* (New York: Macmillan, 1927).

17. Barbara Clark, *Growing Up Gifted,* 3d ed. (Columbus, Ohio: Merrill, 1988).

18. A. Harry Passow, "Intellectual Development of the Gifted," in Frances R. Link, ed., *Essays on the Intellect* (Alexandria, Va.: ASCD, 1985).

19. James T. Webb, Elizabeth A. Meckstroth, and Stephanie S. Tolan, *Guiding the Gifted Child,* 2d ed. (Columbus, Ohio: Ohio Psychology Publishers, 1986),

20. Joyce VanTassel-Baska, "Effective Curriculum and Instruction Models for Talented Students," *Gifted Child Quarterly* 30, No. 4 (1986): 164–169.

21. Joseph Renzulli, *Enrichment Triad Model* (Mansfield Center, Conn.: Creative Learning Press, 1977).

22. June Cox, Neil Daniel, and Bruce Boston, *Educating Able Learners: Programs and Promising Practices* (Austin: University of Texas Press, 1985),

23. James Kulik and Chen-Lin Kulik, "Effects of Accelerated Instruction on Students," *Review of Educational Research* 54, No. 3 (1984): 409–425.

24. Abraham J. Tannenbaum, *Gifted Children: Psychological and Educational Perspectives* (New York: Macmillan, 1983).

25. James J. Gallagher, "The Conservation of Intellectual Resources," in Arthur J. Cropley, Klaus K. Urban, Harold Wagner, and Wilhelm Wieczerkowski, eds. *Giftedness: A Continuing Worldwide Challenge* (New York: Trillium Press, 1986), pp. 21–30.

26. Nicholas Colangelo, "Counseling Needs of Culturally Diverse Gifted Students," *Roeper Review* 8 (1985): 33–35.

27. George Davis, "Bitters in the Brew of Success," *Black Enterprise* 8 (1977): 31–35.

28. Alexinia Baldwin, "Undiscovered Diamonds: The Minority Gifted Child," *Journal for the Education of the Gifted* 10, No. 4 (1987): 271–285.

29. Gallagher, "The Conservation of Intellectual Resources."

30. Mark L. Krueger, ed., *On Being Gifted,* (New York: Walker, 1978).

31. Colangelo, "Counseling Needs of Students," 33–35.

32. Reuven Feuerstein, *Instrumental Enrichment* (Baltimore, Md.: University Park Press, 1973).

33. Thanks to Dr. Evelyn Castro, Cynthia Palmer, and Monique Pauling for their invaluable assistance with this section.

*Students benefit when community leaders like
Governor Booth Gardner are involved
in schools.*

PART VI

School Reform

Reforming schools so that all students will have an opportunity to succeed requires both a new vision of schools and social actors willing to advocate for change. The two chapters constituting this part of the book explore school reform from the perspective of developing new paradigms for assessing students and involving parents in schools. Using testing as a case study, Jane Mercer discusses how the IQ paradigm influences educational decisions and describes alternative paradigms for assessment. Cherry A. McGee Banks discusses the importance of parent involvement as a link to school reform and as a vehicle for increasing student learning.

In her chapter on alternative paradigms for assessment, Mercer defines a *paradigm* as a conceptual model that serves as a cognitive map. Paradigms provide a way to interpret and understand experiences. Paradigms are powerful constructs because they help shape our view of the world and over time tend to be taken for granted. They are accepted as true without question.

Mercer's discussion of paradigms is particularly important in understanding school reform. She examines how the IQ paradigm has become a powerful force in education, influencing access to classes, the development of special programs, and the labeling of students. Special education, tracking, and programs for gifted students stem from the IQ paradigm. Many of the questions Mercer raises related to the school's ability to educate culturally different and low-income students also stem from the IQ paradigm.

Mercer points out that systems of knowledge are socially constructed and provide a rationale for the continued dominance of powerful groups in society. School reform requires an understanding of what paradigms are operating in schools, who benefits from the paradigms, and how old paradigms can be eradicated and new ones embraced. Mercer's chapter helps the reader question the nature of knowledge and its purpose. Answers to these questions can help form the basis for school reform.

Parents, perhaps more than any other group, can legitimize the search for answers to questions raised by Mercer's chapter. They have first-hand knowledge about the school's effectiveness and can be vocal advocates for change. As consumers of educational services, parents can raise questions that are difficult for professional educators and administrators to raise, such as: What is the proportion of males in special-education classes? and What is the ethnic breakdown of students enrolled in higher-level math and science classes? They can also mobilize the community to support educational reform. Parents can be a cogent force in school reform.

Banks argues that parents are more willing to work for school reform if they are involved in schools. Their involvement can lead to a better understanding of the problems and the possibilities for schools. Parents are diverse, with varied interests, skills, and motivations for involvement in schools. Many students come from single-parent homes or from homes with two working parents. The traditional approach to parent involvement with mothers spending time during the day at their children's school will not work for most parents today. Banks suggests ways to expand the traditional ideas about parent involvement and to increase the number and kinds of parents involved in schools.

CHAPTER 15

Alternative Paradigms for Assessment in a Pluralistic Society

■ JANE R. MERCER

Slowly but inevitably the traditional testing paradigm based on standardized tests of intelligence and tests of achievement is being replaced by new paradigms better suited to a multicultural society. The passing of this IQ paradigm has been a battle fought in the courts as well as in scholarly circles.

Many of the nation's largest and most culturally complex school districts—in New York, Chicago, San Francisco, and Los Angeles—no longer use tests that purport to measure intelligence. On September 25, 1986, the United States District Court for the Northern District of California issued its final judgment in *Larry P.* v. *Wilson Riles,* Superintendent of Public Instruction for the State of California. The final order banned the use of all IQ tests for the placement of Blacks in any special-education program, even if there is parental consent for such testing. These tests may not be used to help develop a comprehensive education plan, to gain diagnostic information, to develop goals and objectives, to determine special education needs, to develop a pupil's strength and weaknesses as elicited by the test, or to assess specific learning disabilities.[1] Eventually the ban will be extended to other minority groups, either by the Department of Education or through the courts. Social policy cannot be particularistic in a democratic society.

To comprehend the historic paradigm shift now taking place, it is essential to understand something about the history of public education and testing in the United States and how the IQ paradigm evolved over the past seventy-five years.

Historical Context of Public Education and Testing

During the colonial era, English settlers gradually achieved military and economic dominance over settlers from other linguistic and cultural backgrounds, such as the French, Dutch, and Germans. Faced with linguistic and cultural diversity, the settlers adopted a policy of Anglicization that assumed "the desirability of maintaining English institutions (as modified by the American Revolution), the English language, and English-oriented cultural patterns as dominant and standard in American life."[2] This Americanization policy was first implemented through privately funded free schools established to teach second-generation immigrants the English language and loyalty to Anglo institutions and values.[3] When tax-supported public education was later established, Anglo conformity became a guiding principal. All instruction was in English. The curriculum focused exclusively on Anglo-American institutions, history, literature, and values. Although public schools are officially religiously and politically neutral, they have always been the culture bearer for only one of the many cultural streams brought by immigrants to this continent.

Until 1916, the public schools had no standardized testing as we know it today. Tests were curriculum-based examinations constructed by teachers to determine whether students had mastered materials taught in the school. There was no IQ paradigm.

In 1905 in France, Alfred Binet and his colleagues were commissioned by the French government to design a method for identifying children who would not benefit from the regular school program and should be placed in special schools for the mentally subnormal. They developed a test that contained items covering material that might be learned in school and also included skills and information that they believed all French children would have had an opportunity to acquire outside school from the general "societal curriculum."[4] Items were grouped into age levels based on a sample of normal children three through thirteen years of age. A child's score was expressed as a mental age, the highest age level on the scale at which the child performed successfully.

In 1916, L. M. Terman of Stanford University developed an American version of the Binet scale, the Stanford-Binet Intelligence Test. He translated the test into English, modified the questions to reflect the societal curriculum of the Anglo cultural group, and standardized the scores on White, predominantly middle-class, English-speaking children. Terman formulated the concept of the intelligence quotient (IQ), the ratio between mental age and chronological age, as the standard score for his test. By standardizing for age, he recognized that it would be inappropriate to compare the test performance of a four-year-old with that of a ten-year-old for purposes of inferring intelligence, because they would not have an equal exposure to the material in the test. Following his precedent, subsequent standardized tests have all been standardized by age.

On the 1916 version of the test, girls scored higher than boys. Terman assumed that girls could not be more intelligent than boys and concluded that the test was flawed. To equalize the sexes in his 1937 revision of the test, he took out verbal items, on which girls did better than boys, and replaced them with nonverbal items, on which boys did better than girls.[5] This procedure set a precedent and, subsequently, test-makers have balanced items to achieve sexual equality in total scores.

In 1937, he also discovered that rural children performed less well than did urban children—with IQs of 99.2 compared to 105.7—and that there were large differences by socioeconomic status—116 for children of professional fathers compared to 98 for children of day laborers. Racial differences were also well known by the time of the revision. However, these differences were not interpreted as flaws in the test but as facts about the real world. No adjustments were made.

Although Binet named his test a measure of intelligence, he did not claim that his tests measured innate ability but recognized that they measured what a child had learned, the child's achievement. Lewis Terman and John Goddard, the two men responsible for bringing Binet's test to America, believed the test measured more than learning: they believed it measured innate ability. Furthermore, they believed that innate ability is a highly heritable trait that changes little over the course of a lifetime.[6] Their beliefs are still widely accepted.

Several decades later, test publishers began producing age-standardized tests focused more specifically on the school curriculum—on reading, math, language, grammar, spelling, and so forth—that they called achievement tests. Like intelligence tests, achievement tests were administered in English. They covered curricular materials taught in the Anglicized public school system. As the use of academic achievement tests spread, the belief developed that there are two kinds of tests, intelligence tests, which measure innate ability, and achievement tests, which measure what has been learned. When researchers found high correlations between the scores on these two supposedly different types of tests, correlations between .6 and .8, instead of concluding that the two tests were both simply measures of what a person has learned about the Anglo core culture, they concluded that the correlations proved the IQ tests were valid measures of intelligence.[7] The major elements of the basic IQ paradigm were in place by 1950.

What Is a Paradigm?

A *paradigm* is a conceptual model that serves as a cognitive map to organize experience so that it has meaning and is comprehensible to the observer. Basic paradigms provide the core assumptions about the nature of reality and set the boundaries for intellectual discourse. Their assumptions are usually implicit rather than explicit; that is, persons using the paradigm do not question or examine its basic assumptions. They are passed on to each succeeding generation as truth, as the taken-for-granted reality of everyday life.

Secondary paradigms build on or flow from basic paradigms. They incorporate, implicitly, the basic paradigm but are ancillary models that elaborate the basic structure. If the basic paradigm is faulted, then secondary paradigms built on that basic paradigm will also be faulted, and the entire interrelated structure will require either significant modification or abandonment. The IQ paradigm is a basic paradigm on which an elaborate superstructure of secondary paradigms has been constructed, such as the complex cognitive frameworks surrounding the concepts of *mental retardation* and *learning disability*.

Major paradigms are not simply abstract systems of knowledge. Individuals act on the basis of what they know to be true. Societies create social structures to achieve purposes that make sense within the paradigm. For example, there are categories of disability, such as educable mentally retarded and learning disabled, that are conceptually and operationally dependent on the IQ paradigm. They evolved as categories only after the IQ paradigm was developed, and they owe their existence to concepts and ways of thinking about human behavior made possible by the IQ paradigm. Much of the educational structure of special education has been created to handle the referral, assessment, placement, and treatment of persons defined as disabled on the basis of the IQ paradigm. Teachers and psychologists act according to what they know to be true about disabled students.

Paradigmatic Shifts

There is tremendous social resistance to major paradigmatic shifts. Individuals become disoriented when their habitual ways of making sense of the world are challenged. It is easier to fight the new model than to give up familiar ways of thinking. When a paradigm is useful to socially dominant groups as a mechanism for perpetuating their dominance, self-interest becomes a factor. When a paradigm forms the conceptual basis for large social structures, resistance can be expected from people who have a stake in preserving those structures.

Such is the case with the IQ paradigm. Historically, persons for whom English is a second language and who are not members of the Anglo core culture perform more poorly on both tests of intelligence and tests of achievement than do persons reared in the mainstream culture. This is not surprising, since they are less familiar with the language of the test, have had less opportunity to learn what is in the tests, and may have been less motivated to learn the materials in the test than persons reared in the Anglo core culture. The IQ paradigm, however, interprets these differences as caused by lower inherited ability.[8] Such an interpretation is useful to socially dominant groups. They can justify their own continued social, cultural, and economic dominance on the basis of their presumed superior genetic endowment.

If the IQ paradigm disappears, those disabilities defined solely by that paradigm, such as mental retardation and learning disability, will either die or undergo significant reconceptualization. The structures created to identify those disabilities, such as the whole referral and testing apparatus of public education, will be affected. The social structures created to treat those disabilities, such as the array of placement options available in special education, will necessarily change. Persons who train the psychologists to use the IQ paradigm will face role redefinitions. Paradigmatic shifts are not easy, and the repercussions can be extensive.

Nevertheless, the IQ paradigm is being challenged, and alternative ways of testing and assessment are being proposed. After summarizing the basic elements of the IQ paradigm and presenting the counterarguments to that paradigm, I discuss some alternative assessment paradigms.

Views from the Top and Bottom: The IQ Paradigm

View from the Top

Jensen's exposition and defense of the IQ paradigm contains seven fundamental elements.[9]

1. A fundamental assumption of the IQ paradigm is that IQ tests measure intelligence. The primary evidence presented for this assumption comes from the fact that factor analyses of tests measuring different types of skills yield a general factor, g. The g factor accounts for about 80 percent of the variance in Stanford-Binet items[10] and approximately 50 percent of the variance in the Wechsler Adult Intelligence Scale (WAIS).[11] The universal appearance of the g factor is interpreted as evidence of some type of organic, genetic substrata for g.

2. A second major premise of the IQ paradigm is that intelligence and achievement are separate dimensions; that is, intelligence tests measure something that can be distinguished from achievement.

3. The IQ paradigm holds that intelligence tests are valid because they have predictive validity. They correlate with a variety of criterion measures, such as school grades and academic achievement as measured by achievement tests. "By averaging various IQ and achievement test results over several years, the correlations between and among the tests approach . . . .80 and .90."[12] Therefore, it is concluded that intelligence tests are valid measures of intelligence.

4. Intelligence tests also have concurrent validity. They correlate highly with each other. Correlations among IQ tests average about .67.[13]

5. The IQ paradigm argues that intelligence tests are not culturally biased, because they have similar predictive validity for persons of different cultural backgrounds; that is, they predict achievement test scores of different racial and cultural groups with comparable accuracy. The fact that groups who have less contact with the Anglo core culture score consistently lower on intelligence tests than do core culture groups is *not* considered relevant. Differences in the average performance of different groups are not interpreted as evidence of cultural bias in a test.

6. Furthermore, intelligence tests are not regarded as culturally biased, because they have comparable internal validity for different cultural groups. IQ tests have similar reliability and stability for different groups and similar internal consistency. Factor analyses yield the same factors. Patterns of item difficulty are similar cross-culturally.

7. Finally, defenders of the IQ paradigm contend that there is no need to make allowances for cultural exposure. A single set of norms is appropriate for everyone. America is a culturally homogeneous society based on the English language and the cultural traditions of Western Europe and the British Isles. The amount of cultural loading in IQ tests is small. Differences in test scores of different subpopulations reflect true differences in intelligence.[14]

View from the Bottom

The knowledge created by IQ tests appears quite different when viewed from the perspective of nondominant groups. How can tests administered in English possibly measure the intelligence of someone whose primary language is not English? How can questions drawn from one cultural tradition be used to measure the intelligence of someone reared in another cultural milieu? Do achievement tests really measure anything that is significantly different from what is measured by intelligence tests? Don't both types of tests measure learning? Aren't both simply tests of achievement? Is it a fact that minorities are less intelligent than the dominant group, or is there something wrong with the paradigm?

In the past two decades, such questions have been raised by a significant number of minorities. They have taken their concerns to school boards, to the courts, and to the legislature. In general, they have made the following counterarguments to each of the eight premises of the IQ paradigm.

1. IQ tests do not measure intelligence. There is no known technology for measuring intelligence, mental abilities, aptitudes, mental potential, or other constructs implying genetic, inherited abilities. The g factor yielded by factor analyses of a wide variety of tests cannot be interpreted as evidence that they are measuring intelligence as an entity separate from learning. The g factor simply means that the materials in so-called intelligence tests and achievement tests are all learned and are drawn from the same cultural pool. An individual who has learned a lot about one aspect of a culture is likely to have learned a lot about other aspects of that culture and, consequently, the scores on the tests will be correlated with each other and form a general factor.

2. Intelligence and achievement cannot be distinguished operationally. They are not separate dimensions. All tests are achievement tests in that they measure what a person has learned. The Stanford-Binet and the Wechsler scales are simply individually administered achievement tests.[15]

What a person learns is contingent on many factors, not just intelligence. Learning depends on the opportunity to learn through exposure to the cultural materials to be covered in the test. It depends on the motivation to learn, once the opportunity has been presented. It depends on using effective learning strategies so the materials will be adequately comprehended and retained. It depends on having the sensory equipment needed to learn, primarily adequate vision and hearing. It depends on being in an emotional state that permits learning to take place. High anxiety, stress, depression, grief, and other debilitating emotions interfere with learning. Hence, the score on a test of learned material is the result of multiple influences, not just of an individual's inherited intelligence.

3. Individually administered achievement tests, such as the Wechsler Intelligence Scale for Children-Revised (WISC-R),[16] can reliably measure what a person has learned about the language and cultural materials included in the test. Scores on such tests can validly be used to make first-order inferences about the content of an individual's knowledge and about proficiency in the language and skills covered in the test. Scores earned by different individuals on such tests can be compared, and first-order inferences can be drawn that a person with an appreciably higher score on the test has *learned* more than a person with a lower score. There is no controversy about such first-order inferences.

4. Inferences about intelligence are second-order inferences. Second-order generalizations are those that infer that person A is more intelligent than person B because person A has learned more than person B. Second-order inferences are the crux of the controversy. The central issue in deciding whether it is valid to use achievement tests to infer intelligence lies in the extent to which second-order inferences can properly be made in a particular case. The measurement theory underlying the traditional IQ paradigm fails to distinguish between first-order and second-order inferences.

An achievement test can be used to make second-order inferences about intelligence *if* the persons being compared have had the same opportunity to learn what is in the test, have been similarly motivated to learn what is in the test, have comparable learning strategies, and have no sensory disabilities that might interfere with learning. If all the factors that affect learning other than intelligence are held constant and if one person has learned significantly more than another, then a second-order inference is possible. It can be inferred that the person who has learned more is more intelligent than the person who has learned less. In short, when all the factors other than intelligence that influence learning have been held constant, then any residual difference in scores is attributed to differences in intelligence. If all factors that can affect learning, other than intelligence, are *not* controlled, then second-order inferences are not possible. In such circumstances, it is not legitimate to attribute all residual differences in learning to differences in intelligence, and no inferences about intelligence are possible.

Age is the only factor currently controlled when making second-order inferences in the IQ paradigm. All other factors that can influence learning are ignored. The IQ paradigm is a very fragile measurement model extremely difficult to use in practice because all factors influencing learning except intelligence can never be held constant. This is especially true in a pluralistic society such as the United States. Yet, this requirement *must* be met before practitioners can make valid second-order inferences about intelligence based on tests that measure learning.

5. The validity of second-order inferences is the crucial criterion for test validity. The fact that IQ tests have predictive validity to school grades does not mean that they are valid measures of intelligence. Achievement tests have even higher correlations with school grades. Similarly, the fact that IQ tests correlate with achievement tests in the range of .80–.90 is not evidence for predictive validity; rather, it is evidence that the tests are measuring the same dimensions of performance. Their high covariance means that achievement and IQ tests are statistically indistinguishable. Because both IQ tests and achievement tests are based on the cultural materials taught in the public schools, intercorrelations among the two types of test are inevitable and unremarkable. To argue that those correlations somehow prove that the IQ test is a valid measure of intelligence is highly circular.

6. Similarly, the fact that different IQ tests are highly correlated with each other does not speak to the issue of whether they are valid measures of intelligence. So-called achievement tests are also highly correlated with each other and with intelligence tests.

7. The fact that IQ tests are equally good predictors of school grades and achievement test scores for persons from different linguistic and sociocultural backgrounds is irrelevant to the question of whether the tests can appropriately be used for making second-order inferences about intelligence. What is relevant is the fact that the mean scores on tests that purport to measure intelligence are lower for minority groups than for the majority group. Differences in mean scores clearly indicate that cultural minority groups come from different populations than the majority and that second-order inferences cannot legitimately be made using the average performance of the majority population as the basis for inferring the intelligence of minorities. Clearly, all the factors that influence learning are not the same for the two populations, and differences between the performance of the two populations on the test cannot be interpreted as differences in intelligence.

8. The fact that a test has comparable internal validity for different groups does not speak to the issue of making valid second-order inferences. Research has shown that IQ tests have similar reliability and stability for different groups, similar internal consistency, similar patterns of item difficulty, and similar factor structures. These findings mean that the tests are measuring the cultural knowledge of the persons in different groups in a similar fashion and can appropriately be used as achievement tests to make first-order inferences about what individuals know about that culture. It says nothing whatsoever about the validity of making second-order inferences from those scores.

In general, the courts have been sympathetic to the arguments critical of the IQ paradigm, and the use of intelligence testing is declining in public education. Although there are sizable numbers of persons in academia who still cling to traditional beliefs,[17] others have tried to modify the IQ paradigm to correct its major flaws and still others have abandoned the IQ paradigm completely and are developing alternative assessment paradigms. We turn now to a brief description of these major efforts.

Alternative Assessment Paradigms

Modified IQ Paradigm: Sociocultural Norms

The System of Multicultural Pluralistic Assessment (SOMPA)[18] is based on a modified version of the IQ paradigm. It is a battery of tests that measures the student's adaptive behavior, collects data on the student's health history, includes scales for measuring the sociocultural background of the student's family, and retains the Wechsler Intelligence Scale for Children-Revised (WISC-R).[19] However, it treats the WISC-R as an individually administered achievement test, not as a measure of intelligence. When a student's performance on the WISC-R is compared with the standard, published norms for the test, that score is interpreted simply as a measure of what the student has learned about the dominant Anglo core culture, the student's current functioning level in an Anglo environment. Hence, only first-order inferences are made from the standard norms.

When the diagnostician wishes to make second-order inferences, that is, to make inferences concerning the student's intelligence or learning potential, the diagnostician must first collect information on the sociocultural background of the student's family by asking the parents approximately twenty-five questions concerning the parents' education, the language used in the home, whether the parents were reared in a rural or urban environment, and so forth. Using this information, the diagnostician can determine the sociocultural background of the student and, knowing this, can then compare the student's performance on the test with that of other students from the same sociocultural background. Hence, the test is standardized not only for age but also for sociocultural exposure to the material is in the test.

Sociocultural norms are available for Blacks, Whites, and Hispanics based on probability samples of students attending the California public schools. Using sociocultural as well as age norms, the diagnostician is better able to make valid second-order inferences. By holding constant some of the major sociocultural factors that influence learning, the diagnostician can better interpret residual differences in the performance of students as differences in intelligence.

Criticisms of the modified IQ paradigm have come from both sides in the controversy over intelligence testing. Traditionalists believe that the IQ paradigm is satisfactory as it now exists, that sociocultural norms are not necessary, and that no distinction needs to be made between first- and second-order inferences because intelligence tests measure intelligence, and achievement tests measure achievement.

On the other side, people who have been working to eliminate the IQ paradigm entirely from public education are opposed to any effort to perpetuate that paradigm, even in a modified form. They believe that any attempt to make second-order inferences from any test, even using sociocultural norms, is dangerous because it is not possible to control *all* the environmental factors that influence learning. In their opinion, inferential errors will continue at an unacceptable level even with the sociocultural norms. Therefore, they believe that no second-order inferences from tests should be made.

Furthermore, some critics are convinced that assessment instruments currently used by psychologists, especially IQ tests, have little or no educational utility. They argue that psychometric tests provide little or no information that can guide instruction and are a waste of time and money. Conducting parent interviews to get sociocultural information in order to determine the appropriate sociocultural norm for a particular child not only perpetuates a useless process but also makes it more time-consuming and expensive.[20]

A Cross-Cultural Achievement Testing Paradigm

The cross-cultural achievement testing paradigm retains standardized psychometric tests to assess students' current functioning—linguistically, behaviorally, and academically. It permits first-order inferences about academic performance but would eliminate all attempts to make second-order inferences about intelligence or similar constructs. Those who argue for continued use of psychometric achievement tests assume that information yielded by such tests helps in three ways to make better and more informed decisions about educational programming and instructional procedures than would be possible without them.

Standardized achievement tests provide a wide array of information that is otherwise not available to the individual classroom teacher. A varied battery of achievement tests can provide a richer, fuller understanding of students' many competencies than can curricular-based measures alone, because the latter focus only on academic performance relative to the curriculum of the school. Curricular tests do not include other nonacademic aspects of the student's life that may be equally important or even more important—such as the student's interpersonal skills, spatial and motor abilities, and fluency in more than one language.

A psychometric battery provides a framework beyond the boundaries of the individual school for interpreting students' performances. Without standardized norms based on a larger population, it is easy for the normative expectations of teachers to shift in response to the overall performance level of the students in the school. Psychometric information helps keep educators anchored to the real world in which students will eventually have to compete.

Educators tend to underestimate the capabilities of linguistic and racial minorities and to have low expectations for their academic performance. Seeing them only in the alien culture of a school in which they may be speaking a second language and where much of the cultural knowledge they have gained at home is not valued, it is easy to overlook their areas of competence. A cross-cultural psychometric assessment could provide educators with systematic information on students' linguistic abilities in languages other than English, on their academic competencies when operating in their primary language, and on their knowledge of more than one culture. It could provide information on students' adaptive behavior in nonacademic settings and in the peer group. This information would enhance a teacher's appreciation of students' capabilities by revealing competencies not revealed by typical curricular-based tests.

Following is an example of how such a cross-cultural achievement battery might look for students whose primary language is Spanish. All assessment would be conducted in both English and in Spanish so that two performance profiles for a student would be available (performance in English and performance in Spanish). Multiple normative frameworks would be used to yield varied information about a student's relative performance. There would be both English and Spanish norms and norms for sociocultural groups within each of the language groupings. The person conducting the assessment would use whatever normative frameworks are useful for answering specific questions about a child's relative performance on a particular scale.

A cross-cultural achievement battery would cover the following areas: language development in Spanish and English, mathematical reasoning in Spanish and English, cultural knowledge in Spanish and English, spatial perception, visual-motor coordination, and adaptive behavior in the school and community.

Such a cross-cultural battery would have closer links to curriculum than does the traditional IQ paradigm. For example, the need for instruction to be in Spanish rather than English could be determined by language-development measures. The need for special English as a Second Language (ESL) training could be determined by the student's performance on the English language test. The level of development in mathematical reasoning—whether in English or Spanish—could help educators decide on the appropriate level for mathematics instruction, and so forth. Adaptive behavior measures could provide knowledge of the student's performance in the community and could identify students who, although they are having academic difficulties, are precocious in their interpersonal skills. This information could be used to find ways of motivating students to higher academic performance, to recognize them for competence in nonacademic areas, and to involve them more fully in the life of the school.

If cross-cultural standardized achievement testing were the only psychometric measures used, and if no second-level inferences were permitted, then all special-education categories depending on the IQ paradigm would either have to be eliminated or be completely reconceptualized—categories such as mental retardation and learning disabilities.

The Competency Approach to Assessment

A third alternative paradigm for assessment is to rely entirely on curricular-based competency testing, a policy recommended by the Cantalician Foundation[21] in a study conducted for the U.S. Civil Rights Commission and by a committee of the National Academy of Science.[22] Both groups take the position that all tests should be functionally related to instruction. Those who advocate such an edumetric-only approach argue that standardized tests, both so-called intelligence tests and achievement tests, are irrelevant to the teaching-learning process and consume time and energy that could be better spent securing information about a student's competencies relative to the curriculum of the school. Curricular information helps educators develop an educational plan and directly guides instruction. Educators can implement adequate educational programs for low-achieving children without standardized, norm-referenced tests. Standardized tests administered by psychologists, language specialists, and other diagnosticians do not add any information of significance to the instructional process.

Competency tests directly related to a curriculum are criterion-referenced in terms of levels of performance established in the curriculum for students of various ages. They are, for the most part, teacher-generated. When used as an integral part of the teaching-learning assessment process (as in precision-teaching and mastery-level learning approaches), they are very effective educational devices. In precision-teaching approaches to instruction, curricular-based tests are administered frequently. They are usually scored by the student, and scores are recorded on an individual progress chart. Information yielded by the test is used to determine whether a student is ready to move to the next level in a particular curriculum or needs further work and more instruction at the present level. Although curriculum-focused testing is frequently used in connection with various direct-instruction approaches, such as DISTAR, Exemplary Centers for Reading Instruction (ECRI), and Computer-Assisted Instruction (CAI), it can also be used with other types of curricula.[23]

When competency testing is used effectively as the only testing procedure for evaluating individual students, each student is tested repeatedly, and there is continuous monitoring of his or her academic progress. Individual educational plans in this alternative paradigm are based on direct knowledge of the student's performance level in the curriculum of that particular grade and school. There is no individual psychometric testing of any child for any purpose in this model and no diagnostic labeling by disability category. All educational decisions are based on edumetric test data and on the teacher's professional judgment as an educator.

Once the basic student profile in academic skills has been established, the daily monitoring of student progress quickly identifies students who are progressing at a satisfactory rate and students who are moving more slowly. Additional assistance, such as time with the resource teacher, tutorial assistance from paraprofessionals or peer tutors, or assistance with learning English as a second language, is made available to students who are having difficulty. The type and amount of assistance is continuously adjusted based on edumetric test data showing the student's progress through the curriculum. The need for special assistance is triggered by a teacher request. In this approach, language, per se, is not a major focus, since English proficiency is constantly monitored in the language and reading curriculum, and special assistance needed by those who have limited-English-proficiency is among the special services available in the school.

In this approach, there is no assessment of individual students using any type of IQ test. All educational decisions regarding access to special services are made at the school level by teachers and administrators in the school.

The structural effects of moving to the competency paradigm would be profound. It would eliminate the elaborate referral and assessment system that now consumes a great deal of time, energy, and resources. It would eliminate all special-education categories based on the IQ paradigm and would retain students formerly in those programs in the regular classroom. Special-education personnel would be redeployed to provide support services to the regular classroom teacher in meeting the needs of all children with educational problems.

Assessment of Learning Process Paradigm

A fourth paradigm is just emerging from cognitive psychology. It may someday compete with the modified IQ paradigm, the cross-cultural achievement paradigm, and the competency paradigm for acceptance. It is based on the test-mediate-observe-retest approach to education. This paradigm focuses on teaching the student efficient learning strategies. The rationale for the cognitive paradigm is as follows.

The learner plays an active role in learning and has the potential to exercise control of personal behavior. Most students who have difficulty learning are those who do not use effective learning strategies. They do not know how to learn. If teachers are to help students learn, they need to know what cognitive strategies a student is or is not using so that they can remediate ineffective methods and teach them effective learning procedures.

Edumetric and psychometric testing provides information only on the end products of learning. Alone, such testing yields almost no information on the learning process itself, such as the extent to which a student self-regulates learning, uses different learning strategies for different kinds of intellectual tasks, monitors personal learning, corrects errors, and so forth. Consequently, testing, per se, does not provide the teacher with the primary information needed for effective intervention. Assessment should include an analysis of the learning process being used by the student.

Cognitive processes that go on between the input stimulus and prior to the individual's response can best be studied as the student processes information in a learning situation. These processes become most observable when an intervention is attempted during assessment. The assessor can then determine the student's ability to profit from instruction, can question the student about strategies used in solving different types of problems, and can ascertain the extent to which the student's lack of confidence in the efficacy of employing various strategies may be a factor in failure to learn.

Using findings from the analysis of a student's learning processes, very specific prescriptions for intervention can be developed to teach the student effective strategies for mastering various learning tasks. An important part of the prescription for many students who have been failing academically is attributional retraining, that is, convincing the student that the lack of learning is the result of inefficient learning strategies and low effort rather than low ability. From the viewpoint of this paradigm, psychometric testing, which may convince the student and teacher that failure is the result of low ability, is positively harmful because both student and teacher stop expending the effort needed to learn and to teach the strategies necessary for academic achievement.

Cognitive psychologists have identified many cognitive processes that are important in efficient self-regulated learning. They have been grouped into three major categories: executive control skills, specific strategies, and attributional-motivational characteristics.

Executive control skills are also called *metacognitive* processing skills. These skills include understanding how to evaluate a novel problem and knowing what kind of plan is reasonable, what to do if the plan fails, and how to check one's own performance. They also include awareness of one's own thinking processes, active involvement in identifying various learning options, and modifying one's behavior when a strategy proves to be inefficient.

Knowledge of specific strategies is useful in learning various tasks. For example, the following are effective strategies in reading comprehension: rereading a passage, skimming a passage to study it; paraphrasing a main idea to summarize important points, identifying the topic sentence, writing a topic sentence for paragraphs that have no topic sentence, hypothesizing about what topic will be discussed next, asking oneself questions while reading, deleting trivia and redundancy, and identifying fundamental concepts. In math, checking one's arithmetic and determining whether the answer is within logical limits are valuable strategies. Such strategies can be taught directly rather than expecting students to discover them on their own.

Attributional and motivational characteristics of individual students need to be changed. Because of repeated failures, low-achieving students tend to be inactive learners who do not persist in tasks. Therefore, it is important in the assessment to gain information on a student's attributional characteristics and motivational status. To what does the student attribute success or failure? How important does he or she believe it is to use strategies in learning? What is the probability of success if one expends effort on a task? Most students now labeled mentally retarded and learning disabled have antecedent beliefs they bring to the learning task that impede their learning. These motivational factors must be understood and dealt with as part of the intervention.

The primary technique for learning process assessment is to present the students with a problem or a reading task and ask them to think aloud as they solve the problem or read the passage. It is beyond the scope of this chapter to provide a detailed description of various approaches used to teach students effective cognitive processing, but a special issue of *Exceptional Children*[24] can provide a basic introduction for those seeking further information.

Conclusion

Paradigm shifts are major intellectual and policy events in which the prevailing paradigm is challenged by competing paradigms. The prevailing IQ paradigm has been successfully challenged in the courts, and education is now in a period of transition. It is not clear at this time what paradigm will replace traditional intelligence testing or how long the transition will take. There appear to be four possible alternative paradigms that may supplant the traditional model.

The shift may be minor, such as adopting a modified version of the IQ paradigm using sociocultural norms, as is done in the SOMPA. Diagnosticians would continue to make both first- and second-order inferences from test performance, except that they would use sociocultural norms based on the family background characteristics of the student when making second-order inferences. The modified IQ paradigm would not require major changes in special-education categories. It would be least disruptive of present practice and present thinking in special education.

More drastic changes in present practice would result from adopting a cross-cultural achievement paradigm in which no second-order inferences about intelligence would be permitted, but standardized achievement testing and first-order inferences concerning present performance in different languages and different subject areas would be the focus of assessment. Although special-education categories dependent on the IQ paradigm would probably continue to exist, they would probably be redefined in terms of achievement profiles, without reference to any presumed measure of intelligence. *Mental retardation* might be redefined as a condition in which a student shows very low levels of learning across a variety of academic and nonacademic skills, and *learning disability* might be redefined as a condition in which a student has an erratic achievement profile, one with very low performance in some areas but normal or high levels of performance in others.

If all psychometric testing, including standardized achievement testing, were abandoned, and a pure competency paradigm adopted, there would necessarily be major changes in the structure of special education. Mental retardation and learning disability would disappear as educational categories, and students would be treated on the basis of their functional needs rather than as a diagnostic category. Diagnostic labels would be restricted to students with identifiable physical or sensory problems. All other students would be educated in the regular program of the school, with supplementary services provided by special-education specialists.

The learning process assessment paradigm complements rather than competes with the others. It adds a new perspective to understanding the nature of the learning difficulties encountered by low-achieving students. It can provide valuable new insights when used in conjunction with any of the other models.

It is difficult to know which course education may take. The decision will be hammered out in the political arena. Undoubtedly, the traditional IQ paradigm will persist for a time, especially in the Midwest and other parts of the country where there is greater cultural homogeneity and the limitations of that model are less obvious. Given the vested interest school psychology has in perpetuating the current referral and assessment process, it would be logical for that group to support the modified IQ paradigm. That model still incorporates second-level inferences based on individually administered tests, albeit with sociocultural norms, a task traditionally performed by the school psychologist. Similarly, special educators have a vested interest in perpetuating the present categorical system, a structure that would remain unchanged if a modified IQ paradigm were adopted.

The standardized achievement-testing paradigm would eliminate the role of the school psychologist because only first-order inferences would be required, and achievement tests have traditionally been administered by many different professionals—resource teachers, speech specialists, regular classroom teachers, and so forth. Although the assessment process would be changed, the structure of special education would probably remain relatively unchanged.

A competency-based, edumetric paradigm would be the most radical departure from traditional practice. Not only would standardized tests be eliminated from the assessment process in favor of curricula-based procedures, thus eliminating the need for specialized, assessment personnel, but the basis for defining nonmedically based disabilities also would disappear, requiring a major restructuring of special education.

It is probable that some combination of these paradigms will emerge and become the dominant paradigm in the next two decades. Just what the combination will be and which paradigm will be ascendant is difficult to foresee because public policy is forged in the political arena, and outcomes of political struggles are unpredictable.

Questions and Activities

1. How does Mercer define *paradigm?* Explain how concepts like *learning disability* and *gifted* relate to the IQ paradigm.

2. Why is there resistance to eliminating old paradigms and establishing new ones? Give examples of how resistance occurs.

3. What is a second-order inference? Why is it difficult to make second-order inferences about intelligence?

4. Make a chart identifying the major assumptions of each of the four paradigms discussed in this chapter.

5. Each paradigm discussed in this chapter has implications for classroom teachers. Write a short paper on some of the inferences you can draw from each paradigm as you interpret the test scores of students who are bilingual, members of ethnic minority groups, women, and low income.

6. Compare and contrast criterion-referenced tests and standardized norm-referenced tests. Give examples of each type of test.

7. Identify and discuss some of the social and political reasons for the development of each of the four paradigms discussed in this chapter.

Notes

1. United States District Court for the Northern District of California, *Order Modifying Judgment: Larry P. et al., Plaintiffs* v. *Wilson Riles, Superintendent of Public Instruction for the State of California et al., Defendants,* No. C–71–2270 RFP (September 25, 1986).

2. M. M. Gordon, *Assimilation in American life: The Role of Race, Religion, and National Origins* (New York: Oxford University Press, 1964).

3. Michael B. Katz, *Class, Bureaucracy, and Schools: The Illusion of Educational Change in America* (New York: Praeger, 1971).

4. Carlos E. Cortés, "The Societal Curriculum: Implications for Multiethnic Education," in J. A. Banks, ed., *Education in the 80's: Multiethnic Education* (Washington, D.C.: National Education Association, 1981).

5. L. M. Terman and M. A. Merrill, *Measuring Intelligence: A Guide to the Administration of the New Revised Stanford-Binet Tests of Intelligence* (Boston: Houghton Mifflin, 1937).

6. Leon J. Kamin, *The Science and Politics of I.Q.* (New York: John Wiley and Sons, 1974).

7. Arthur R. Jensen, *Bias in Mental Testing* (New York: The Free Press, 1980).

8. Jensen, *Bias in Mental Testing*; L. M. Dunn, *Bilingual Hispanic Children on the U.S. Mainland: A Review of Research on Their Cognitive, Linguistic, and Scholastic Development* (Circle Pines, Minn.: American Guidance Service 1987).

9. Jensen, *Bias in Mental Testing.*

10. Ibid., 219.

11. Ibid., 216.

12. Ibid., 323.

13. Ibid., 315.

14. Dunn, *Bilingual Hispanic Children.*

15. A. B. Wesman, "Intelligent Testing," *American Psychologist* 23 (4), 1968, 267–274; T. A. Cleary, L. G. Humphreys, S. A. Kendrick, and A. Wesman, "Educational Uses of Tests with Disadvantaged Students." *American Psychologist* 30 (1975), 15–41.

16. D. Wechsler, *Manual for the Wechsler Intelligence Scale for Children-Revised* (New York: Psychological Corporation, 1974).

17. Jensen, 1980; Dunn, 1987.

18. Jane R. Mercer, *SOMPA: Technical and Conceptual Manual* (New York: The Psychological Corporation, 1979).

19. Wechsler, *Manual for the WISC-R.*

20. K. A. Heller, W. H. Holtzman, and S. Messick, *Placing Children in Special Education: A Strategy for Equity* (Washington, D.C.: National Academy Press, 1982).

21. Cantalician Foundation, Inc., *Technical Assistance on Alternative Practices Related to the Problem of the Overrepresentation of Black and Minority Students in Classes for the Educable Mentally Retarded,* Report to the Department of Education, Office of Civil Rights, Contract No. 300–82–0191, (1983).

22. Heller et al., *Placing Children in Special Education.*

23. W. Becker and D. Carnine, "Direct Instruction: An Effective Approach for Educational Intervention with the Disadvantaged and Low Performers," in Benjamin J. Lahey and Alan E. Kadzin, eds., *Advances in Clinical Child Psychology* (New York: Plenum Press, 1980).

24. L. M. Gelheiser and M. J. Shepherd, "Competence and Instruction: Contributions from Cognitive Psychology," *Exceptional Children* 53, No. 2 (October, 1986).

CHAPTER 16

Parents and Teachers: Partners in Multicultural Education

■ CHERRY A. McGEE BANKS

Introduction

A few days after Ms. Jones, a high school science teacher, completed a unit on the origin of the earth, Mr. Evans, one of her student's parents, paid her a visit. Mr. Evans was very polite, but he did not conceal his concern about the unit. "Miss Jones, I know you are a science teacher and naturally you have a scientific perspective on the origin of the earth. I understand your point of view, but I'm not sure you understand mine," he said. Then he opened a Bible and began to read from the book of Genesis. He ended the meeting by giving Ms. Jones a book and saying, "This book will probably explain better than I did what I'm trying to teach my children." The meeting was short and cordial, but it had a tremendous impact on Ms. Jones. She considered herself a good teacher who cared about her students. The last thing she wanted to do was put her students in the middle of a tug-of-war between home and school. Over the next few weeks, Ms. Jones received several notes and calls from parents complimenting her on the unit and telling her how much their children enjoyed going to the planetarium and having a guest speaker from the university. Even though Ms. Jones had every reason to believe the unit was a tremendous success, she could not forget the visit from Mr. Evans. She also knew that similar concerns would surface with some other units she planned to teach.

She decided to discuss the incident with Barbara Woodson, a veteran teacher in her building. In talking with Barbara, she learned that several students in the school were members of a religious group that accepted the teachings of the Bible as literal. She also learned that some of her students were attending public school for the first time. They had attended church schools from kindergarten through eighth grade. Even though the parents wanted their children to make a smooth transition to their new school, they were very concerned about what their children were being taught.

Ms. Jones confronted a serious problem, one with which many teachers will have to grapple. On the surface, her problem seems straightforward. She must try to mediate religious concerns and scientific perspectives. In Chapter 5, Uphoff provides some suggestions for dealing with this problem. He states that teachers can be sensitive to parent concerns about topics that have religious and value implications while continuing to teach the required curriculum.

Ms. Jones's problem deals with religion and education, but it has much broader implications. Education occurs within a social context that partly is shaped by parents.[1] Her experience raises questions about the relationship between education and parents: What role should parents play in their children's education? Is it important to know how parents view what you teach? Can you be an effective teacher without knowing something about your students' home and community life? How important is it for teachers and parents to work together? Is it really necessary to try to work with parents who do not agree with you? This chapter examines these questions and suggests ways you can work with parents to improve student learning.

What Is Parent-Community Involvement?

Parent-community involvement is a dynamic process that encourages, supports, and provides opportunities for parents and educators to cooperate in the education of students. An important goal of parent-community involvement is to improve student learning.

Parent-community involvement is also an important component of school reform. Parents and community groups help form what John Goodlad calls "the necessary coalition of contributing groups."[2] Educational reform needs the support, influence, and activism of parents and community groups. Parents and community leaders can validate the need for educational reform and can provide an appropriate forum for exploring the importance of education. They can also extend the discussion on school improvement issues beyond formal educational networks and help generate interest in educational reform in the community at large.[3] Parents and community leaders can help provide the rationale, motivation, and social action necessary for educational reform.

Why Is Parent-Community Involvement Important?

Students come to school with knowledge, values, and beliefs they have learned from their parents and communities. Parents directly or indirectly help shape their children's value system, orientation toward learning, and view of the world in which they live. Parents can help teachers extend their knowledge and understanding of their students. Through that knowledge and understanding, teachers can improve their teaching effectiveness.

Most parents want their children to succeed in school. Schools can capitalize on the high value most parents put on education by working to create a school environment that reflects an understanding of the students' home and community.[4] When schools conflict with their students' home and community, they can alienate students from their families and communities and cause stress and confusion. For example, many Black low-income children are very verbal. However, there are strict family and community norms dictating when and how children speak. The norms are different from middle-class family and community norms. By understanding those norms, teachers can help students learn the verbal behavior expected in the classroom while preventing potential conflict between the home and the school.[5]

To create a harmonious environment between the school, home, and community, teachers need to know something about their students' community and home life. Teachers need to be knowledgeable about parents' educational expectations for their children, languages spoken at home, family and community values and norms, as well as how children are taught in their homes and communities.[6] Parents also need information about the school. Parents need to know what the school expects their chidren to learn, how they will be taught, and the required books and materials their children will use in school. Parents also need to know how teachers will evaluate their children and how they can support their children's achievement.

Students, parents, and teachers all benefit from parent involvement in schools. When parents help their students at home, students perform better in school.[7] Although we do not know exactly why students show improvements when their parents are involved in their education, we do know that parental involvement increases the number of people who are supporting the child's learning. Such involvement also increases the amount of time the child is involved in learning activities. Parent involvement allows parents and teachers to reinforce skills and provides an environment that has consistent learning expectations and standards. Parents also become more knowledgeable about their child's school, its policies, and the school staff when they are involved in schools. Perhaps most important, it provides an opportunity for parents and children to spend time together. During that time, parents can communicate a high value for education, the importance of effort in achievement, and a high positive regard for their children.

Teachers and principals who know parents treat them with greater respect and show more positive attitudes toward their children.[8] Teachers generally see involved parents as concerned individuals who are willing to work with them. They often believe that parents who are not involved in school do not value education.

Parent involvement helps both parents and teachers become more aware of their need to support student learning. Student improvements that result from parents and teachers working together can increase each teacher's sense of professionalism and each parent's sense of parenting skills. A cooperative relationship between teachers and parents also increases the good will of parents and promotes positive community relations.

Historical Overview

Parent involvement in education is not new, but its importance and purpose have varied at different times in U.S. history. In the early part of the nation's history, families were often solely responsible for educating children. Children learned values and skills by working with their families in their communities.

When formal systems of education were established, parents continued to influence their children's education. During the colonial period, schools were viewed as an extension of the home. Parental and community values and expectations were reinforced in the school. Teachers generally came from the community and often knew their students' parents personally and shared their values.

At the beginning of the twentieth century, when large numbers of immigrants came to the United States, schools were used to compensate for the perceived failures of parents and communities. Schools became a major vehicle to assimilate immigrant children into U.S. society.[9] In general, parents were not welcomed in schools. Students were taught that their parents' ways of speaking, behaving, and thinking were inferior to what they were taught in school. In his 1932 study of the sociology of teaching, Waller concluded that parents and teachers lived in a state of mutual distrust and even hostility.[10]

As society changed, education became more removed from the direct influence of parents. Responsibility for transmitting knowledge from generation to generation was transferred from the home and community to the school. Education was seen as a job for trained professionals. Schools were autonomous institutions staffed by people who were often strangers in the community. Teachers did not necessarily live in their students' neighborhood, know the students' parents, or share their values.

Over time, schools were given more and more duties that traditionally had been the responsibility of the home and community. For example, parental responsibility for sex education was delegated partly to the schools.[11] Schools operated under the assumption of *in loco parentis,* and educators were often asked to assume the role of both teacher and substitute parent.

In a pluralist society, what the school teaches as well as who and how the school teaches, can create tensions between parents and schools. Issues ranging from what the school teaches about the role of women in our society to mainstreaming handicapped students point to the need for educators, parents, and communities to work together. Today, more and more parents, educators, and community leaders are calling for parent involvement in schools. Parents and educators are concerned about parent involvement, and a majority of both groups feel that it is important and necessary.[12] However, parents and educators are unsure about what forms this involvement should take. Often the views of parents and teachers conflict about meaningful ways to involve parents in the educational process.[13]

Parent and Community Diversity

Student diversity mirrors parent and community diversity. Just as teachers are expected to work with students from both genders and from different ethnic groups and social classes, parent involvement challenges teachers to work with a diverse group of parents. Some parents with whom teachers work are from different racial and ethnic groups, single parents, parents with special needs, low-income parents, handicapped parents, or parents who do not speak English. Some parents are members of several of these groups.

Diversity in parent and community groups can be a tremendous asset to the school. However, it can also be a source of potential conflicts and frustrations. Some parents are particularly difficult to involve in their children's education. They resist becoming involved for several reasons. Stress is an important reason for their lack of involvement. The pressures to earn a living and take care of a home and children can put a great deal of stress on parents. At the end of the day, some parents just want to rest. Other parents do not believe they have the necessary educational background to be involved in their children's education. They feel intimidated by educators and believe that education should be left to the schools. Others feel alienated from the school because of negative experiences they have had there or because they believe the school does not support their values.[14] In addition, many parents today are products of the "me" generation. These parents are primarily concerned with narcissistic endeavors. They are involved in self-development and career-advancement activities. They have limited time available for school involvement, and it generally is not a priority in their lives.[15]

Three groups of parents who tend not to be included in school involvement activities are described below. These include parents with special needs, single-parent families, and low-income families. These groups were selected to illustrate particular problem areas for parent involvement. The specific groups of parents discussed should not be interpreted as an indication that only parents from these groups are difficult to involve in schools or that all parents from these groups are difficult to involve in schools. Parents from all groups share many of the concerns discussed here, and there are examples of parents from each group discussed who are actively involved in schools.

Parents with Special Needs

Families with special needs include a wide range of parents. Families with special needs are found in all ethnic, racial, and income groups. Chronically unemployed parents, parents with long-term illness in the family, abusive parents, and parents with substance-abuse problems are examples of parents with special needs. Although parents with special needs have serious problems that cannot be addressed by the school, teachers should not ignore the importance of establishing a relationship with them. Knowing the difficulties students are coping with at home can help teachers create environments that are supportive during the time students are in school. Schools can help compensate for the difficult circumstances students experience at home. The school can be the one place during the day where a student is nurtured.

Abusive parents require special attention from the school. It is important for the school to develop policies on how to treat suspected cases of child neglect or abuse. It is generally helpful for one person to be in charge of receiving reports and other information. All states require schools to report suspected cases of child abuse.

Working with special-needs families generally requires district or building support to develop a list of community outreach agencies for referral. Although some special-needs parents may resist the school's help, they need someone they can trust and turn to for help. Working with these parents can show them that they are not alone. All parents want to feel that they are valued and adequate human beings. They do not want to be embarrassed.[16] Some parents with special needs will be able to be actively involved in schools, but many will be unable to become involved on a regular basis. An important goal for working with parents with special needs is to keep lines of communication open. Try to get to know the parents. Do not accept a stereotypical view of them without ever talking to them. Encourage parents to be involved whenever and however they feel they are able to participate. Be prepared to recommend appropriate community agencies to the family. Try to develop a clear understanding of your student's home environment so that you can provide appropriate intervention at school. Regardless of the circumstances a student confronts at home, teachers have a responsibility to help them perform at their highest level at school.

Single-Parent Families

Almost half of the children in the United States will live in a single-parent home sometime during their childhood. In 1984, 25.7 percent of the families with children under eighteen were single-parent families.[17] Many of the children in these families are from divorced homes or were the children of unwed mothers. In 1984, about half of all recent marriages ended in divorce, and about one-fifth of all children were born to unwed mothers.[18] Both the divorce rate and the number of unwed mothers have increased dramatically since 1970. The number of unwed mothers increased from 5 percent to 18 percent from 1970 to 1980.[19] The divorce rate increased similarly, doubling from 1963 to 1979. Every year, more than one million children experience their parents' divorce.[20] Divorce influences both minority and majority children. Two out of three Black children and one out of three White children experience a divorce in their family before they are sixteen years old.[21]

Most single-parent homes are headed by women. A disproportionate number of these families are poor and minority. Black families are more than twice as likely to be headed by a female as are White families. In 1984, slightly more than 20 percent of White families were headed by a single mother, compared to 59.2 percent of Black families.[22] In 1982, single-parent families represented about 90 percent of the families receiving Aid to Families with Dependent Children.[23]

Single-parent families share many of the hopes, joys, and concerns about their children's education as two-parent families. Because they have limited time and energy to attend school functions, they are sometimes viewed as unsupportive of education. However, when teachers respond sensitively to their needs and limitations, they can be enthusiastic partners with teachers. Some suggestions for working with single parents are listed below. Many of these suggestions apply to other groups of parents as well.

1. Provide flexible times for conferences, such as early mornings, evenings, and weekends.

2. Provide baby-sitting service for activities at the school.

3. Work out procedures for acknowledging and communicating with noncustodial parents. For instance, under what circumstances are noncustodial parents informed about their children's grades, school behavior, or attendance? Problems can occur when information is inappropriately given to or withheld from a noncustodial parent.

4. Use the parents' correct surname. Students will sometimes have different names from their parents.

Low-Income Families

In 1984, a family below the poverty line was defined as a family of four that made less then $10,609.00. About 33.7 million people, or 14.4 percent of the nation's population, were living below the poverty line.[24] Nearly one in every five children in the United States is poor.

The number of people below the poverty level is related to gender and race. In 1984, about 31 percent of Blacks and 25 percent of Hispanic families lived below the poverty line compared to about 9 percent of White families.[25] Approximately 54 percent of the families headed by a female with children under eighteen lived in poverty compared to 12.5 percent of all families.[26] The Children's Defense Fund reported in 1985 that more children die from poverty each year than from traffic fatalities and suicide combined. Twice as many die from poverty than from cancer and heart disease combined.

Low-income parents are generally strong supporters of education. They see education as a means to a better life for their children. However, they are often limited in their ability to buy materials and make financial commitments for activities such as field trips. Many of the suggestions listed for single-parent families also apply to low-income families. Schools can provide workbooks and other study materials for use at home as well as transportation for school activities and conferences. This will increase the ability of low-income families to become more involved in their children's education. The school can offer support to low-income families by establishing a community service program. Students can help clean up neighborhoods and distribute information on available social services. The schools can provide a desk space for voter registration and other services. Perhaps the most important way for schools to work with low-income parents is to recognize that low-income parents can contribute a great deal to their children's education. Although those contributions may not be in the form of traditional parent involvement, they can be very beneficial to teachers and students. The values and attitudes parents communicate to their children and their strong desire for their children to have a better chance in life than they did are important forms of support for the school.

Teacher Concerns with Parent-Community Involvement

Many teachers are ambivalent about parent and community involvement in education. Even though teachers often say they want to involve parents, many are suspicious of parents and are uncertain of what parents expect from them. Some teachers wonder if parents will do more harm than good. They think parents may disrupt their routine, may not have the necessary skills to work with their children, may be inconvenient to have in the classroom, and may show interest only in helping their own child, not the total class. Even teachers who think they would like to involve parents are not sure they have the time to do it or do not know exactly how to involve parents.[27] Many teachers believe that they already have too much to do and working with parents would make their overburdened jobs impossible.

Many of these concerns result from a limited view of the possibilities for parent involvement. When many parents and teachers think of parent involvement, they think it means doing something for the school generally at the school or having the school teach parents how to become better parents. In today's society, a traditional view of parent involvement inhibits rather than encourages parents and teachers to work together. Traditional ideas about parent involvement have a built-in gender and social class bias and are a barrier to most males and low-income parents.

When parent involvement is viewed as a means of getting support for the school, parents are encouraged to bake cookies, raise money, or work at the school as unpaid classroom, playground, library, or office helpers. This form of parent involvement is generally directed to mothers who do not work outside the home. However, the number of mothers available for this form of involvement is decreasing. The number of married mothers in the work force increased from 39.5 percent in 1970 to 54.8 percent in 1984.

When parent involvement is viewed as a means to help deficient parents, the school provides parents with information on how to become better parents. This view of parent involvement is often directed toward culturally different and low-income parents. This approach often makes parents feel they are the cause of their children's failure in school. Teachers are presented as more skilled than parents. Parents and teachers may become rivals for the child's affection.[28]

Cultural perspectives play an important role in the traditional approach to parent involvement. In Chapter 2, Bullivant points out the importance of understanding a social group's cultural program. To be effective, parent and community involvement strategies should reflect what Bullivant calls the core of the social group's cultural program. He states that the core consists of the knowledge and conceptions embodied in the group's behaviors and artifacts and the values subscribed to by the group.

The parent-as-helper idea is geared toward parents who have the skills, time, and resources to become school helpers. Not all parents want to or feel they can or should do things for the school. Whether a parent is willing to come to school is largely dependent on the parent's attitude toward school. This attitude results in part from their own school experiences. The parent in need of parenting skills assumes that there is one appropriate way to parent and that parents want to learn it. Both of these conceptualizations—the parent as helper and the parent in need of parenting skills—are derived from questionable assumptions about the character of contemporary parents and reflect a limited cultural perspective.

Steps to Increase Parent-Community Involvement

Teachers are a key ingredient in parent-community involvement. They play multiple roles, including facilitator, communicator, and resource developer. Their success in implementing an effective parent-community involvement program relates to their skill in communicating and working with parents and community groups. Teacher attitude is also very important. Parents are supportive of the teachers they believe like their children and want them to succeed. Teachers who have a negative attitude toward students will likely have a similar attitude toward the students' parents. Teachers tend to relate to their students as representatives of their parents' perceived status in society. Teachers use such characteristics as class, race, gender, and ethnicity to determine students' prescribed social category.[29]

Below are five steps you can take to increase parent-community involvement in your classroom. These steps involve establishing two-way communication, enlisting support from staff and students, enlisting support from the community, developing resource materials for home use, and broadening the activities included in parent involvement.

Establish Two-Way Communication between the School and Home

Establishing two-way commmunication between the school and home is an important step in involving parents. Most parents are willing to become involved in their children's education if you let them know what you are trying to accomplish and how parents can help. Teachers should be prepared to do some outreach to parents and not to wait for them to become involved. Actively solicit information from parents on their thoughts about classroom goals and activities. When you talk with parents and community members, be an active listener. Listen for their feelings as well as for specific information. Listed below are seven ways you can establish and maintain two-way communication with parents and community members.

1. If possible, have an open-door policy in your classroom. Let parents know they are welcome. When parents visit, make sure they have something to do.

2. Send written information home about school assignments and goals so that parents are aware of what is going on in the classroom. Encourage parents to send notes to you if they have questions or concerns.

3. Talk to parents by phone. Let parents know when they can reach you by phone. Also, call parents periodically and let them know when things are going well. Have something specific to talk about. Leave some time for the parent to ask questions or make comments.

4. Report problems to parents such as failing grades before it is too late for them to take remedial action. Let parents know what improvements you expect from their children and how they can help.

5. Get to know your students' community. Take time to shop in their neighborhoods. Visit community centers and attend religious services. Let parents know when you will be in the community and that you are available to talk to them at their home or at some other location.

6. If you teach in an elementary school, try to have at least two in-person conferences a year with parents. When possible, include the student in the conference. Let the parent know in specific terms how the student is doing in class. Find out how parents feel about their children's level of achievement, and let them know what you think about the students' achievement level. Give parents some suggestions on what the student can do to improve and how they can help.

7. Solicit information from parents on their views on education. Identify their educational goals for their children, ways they would like to support their children's education, and their concerns about the school. There are a number of ways to get information from parents, including sending a questionnaire home and asking parents to complete it and return it to you, conducting a telephone survey, and asking your students to interview their parents.

Enlist the Support of Other Staff Members and Students

Teachers have some flexibility in their classrooms, but they are not able to determine some of the factors that influence their ability to have a strong parent involvement program. For instance, the type and amount of materials available for student use can determine whether a teacher can send home paper, pencils, and other materials for parents to use with their children. If teachers are allowed to modify their schedules, they can find free time to telephone parents, write notes, and hold morning or evening conferences with parents. The school climate also influences parent involvement. However, school climate is not determined by one individual; it is influenced by students, teachers, the principal, and the school secretary. Teachers need support from staff, students, the principal and district level staff to enhance their parent involvement activities.

Your students can help solicit support for parent and community involvement from staff and other students. Take your class on a tour of the school. Ask the class to think about how their parents would feel if they came to the school. Discuss these two questions: Is there a place for visitors to sit? Are there signs asking visitors to go directly to the office? Ask your students to list things they could do to make the school a friendlier place for parents.

Invite your building principal to come to your classroom and discuss the list with your students. Divide the class into small groups and have them discuss how they would like their parents involved in their education. Ask them to talk to their parents and get their views. Have each group write a report on how parents can be involved in their children's education. Each group could make presentations to students in the other classrooms in the building on how they would like to increase parent involvement in their school.

If funds or other support is needed from the district office for your parent involvement activities, have the students draw up a petition and solicit signatures from teachers, students, and parents. When all of the signatures are gathered, they can be delivered to an appropriate district administrator.

Building principals and district administrators can give you the support you need to:

1. Help create and maintain a climate for positive parent-community involvement. This can include supporting flexible hours for teachers who need to be out of the classroom to develop materials or to work with parents. Teachers can be given time out of the classroom without negatively affecting students. Time can be gleaned from the secondary teacher's schedule by combining homerooms one day a week, by team-teaching a class, or by combining different sections of a class for activities such as chapter tests. At the elementary school level, team teaching, released time during periods when students are normally out of the classroom for specialized subjects such as music and art, or having the principal substitute in the classroom are ways to provide flexible hours for teachers.

2. Set up a parent room. The parent room could be used for a number of functions, including serving as a community drop-in center where parents could meet other parents for a cup of coffee, or as a place for parents to work on school activities without infringing on the teachers' lounge. It could also be used as a waiting room for parents who need to see a student or a member of the school staff.

3. Host parent nights during which parents can learn more about the school, the curriculum, and the staff.

4. Send a personal note to students and to their parents when a student makes the honor roll or does something noteworthy.

5. Develop and distribute a handbook that contains student names and phone numbers, PTA or other parent group contact names, and staff names and phone numbers.

6. Ask the school secretary to make sure visitors are welcomed when they come to the school and are given directions as needed.

7. Encourage students to greet visitors and help them find their way around the building.

Enlist Support from the Community

To enlist support from the community, you need to know something about it. The following are some questions you should be able to answer.

1. Are there any drama, musical, dance, or art groups in the community?

2. Is there a senior-citizen group, a public library, or a cooperative extension service in the community?

3. Are employment services such as the state employment security department available in the community?

4. Are civil rights organizations such as the Urban League, Anti-Defamation League, or NAACP active in the community?

5. What is the procedure for referring people to the Salvation Army, Goodwill Industries, or the State Department of Public Assistance for emergency assistance for housing, food, and clothing?

6. Does the community have a mental-health center, family counseling, or crisis clinic?

7. Are programs and activities for youth such as Boys and Girls Clubs, Campfire, Boy Scouts, Girl Scouts, YMCA, and the YWCA available for your students?

As you learn about the community, you can begin developing a list of community resources and contacts that can provide support to families, work with your students, and provide locations for students to perform community service projects. Collecting information about your students' community and developing community contacts should be viewed as a long-term project. You can collect information as your schedule permits and organize it in a notebook. This process can be shortened if several teachers work together. Each teacher could concentrate on a different part of the community and share information and contacts.

Community groups can provide support in several ways. They can develop big sister and big brother programs for students, provide quiet places for students to study after school and on weekends, donate educational supplies, help raise funds for field trips, set up mentor programs, and tutor students.

Community groups can also provide opportunities for students to participate in community-based learning programs. Community-based learning programs provide an opportunity for students to move beyond the textbook and experience real life.[30] Students have an opportunity to see how knowledge is integrated when it is applied to the real world. It puts them in touch with a variety of people and lets them see how people cope with their environment.

Community-based learning also enhances career development. It can help students learn about themselves, gain confidence, and better understand their strengths and weaknesses. Students can learn to plan, make decisions, negotiate, and evaluate their plans. Here are some examples of community work.[31] Students can:

- Paint an apartment for an ill neighbor
- Clean alleys and backyards for the elderly
- Write letters for people who are sick or infirm
- Read to people who are unable to read
- Prepare an empty lot as a play area for young children
- Plant a vegetable garden for the needy
- Collect and recycle newspapers

Develop Learning Resources for Parents to Use at Home

Many of the learning materials teachers use with students at school can be used by parents at home to help students improve their skills. The materials should be in a format suitable for students to take home and should provide clear directions for at-home completion. Parents could let the teacher know how they liked the material by writing a note, giving their child a verbal message for the teacher, or by calling the school. Dr. Reginald M. Clark has written a series of math home-involvement activities for kindergarten through eighth grade. The activities are included in a booklet and are designed to help students increase their math skills. Parents are able to use the creative activities to reinforce the skills their children learn at school.[32] These kinds of materials are convenient for both parents and teachers to use.

It is important for teachers to have resources available for parents to use. This lets parents know that they can help increase their children's learning and that you want their help. Simply telling parents they should work with their children is not sufficient. Parents generally need specific suggestions. Once parents get an idea of what you want them to do, some will develop their own materials. Other parents will be able to purchase materials. You can suggest specific books, games, and other materials for parents to purchase and where these learning materials are available.

Some parents will not have the financial resources, time, or educational background to develop or purchase learning materials. With your principal's help or help from community groups, you can set up a learning center for parents. The learning center could contain paper, pencils, books, games, a portable typewriter, a portable computer, and other appropriate resources. The learning center could also have audiocassettes on such topics as instructional techniques, classroom rules, educational goals for the year, and oral readings from books. Parents could check materials out of the learning center for use at home.

Broaden the Conception of Parent and Community Involvement

Many barriers to parent-community involvement can be eliminated by broadly conceptualizing parent-community involvement. Parents can play many roles, depending on their interests, skills, and resources. It is important to have a variety of roles for parents so that more parents will have an opportunity to be involved. It is also important to make sure that some roles can be performed at home as well as at school. Below are five ways parents and community members can be involved in schools. Some of the roles can be implemented by the classroom teacher. Others need support and resources from building principals or central office administrators.

Parents Working with Their Own Children
Working with their own children is one of the most important roles parents can play in the educational process. Parents can help their children develop a positive self-concept and a positive attitude toward school as well as a better understanding of how their effort affects achievement. Most parents want their children to do well in school and are willing to do whatever they can to help them succeed. Teachers can increase the support they receive from their students' homes by giving parents a better understanding of what is going on in the classroom, by letting parents know what is expected in the classroom, and by suggesting ways they can support their child's learning.

You can work with parents to support the educational process in these three ways:

1. Involve parents in monitoring homework by asking them to sign homework papers.

2. Ask parents to sign a certificate congratulating students for good attendance.

3. Give students extra points if their parents do things such as sign their report card and attend conferences.

Some parents want a more active partnership with the school. These parents want to work with you in teaching their children. Below are three ways you can help parents work with their children to increase their learning.

1. Encourage parents to share hobbies and games, discuss news and television programs, and talk about school problems and events with their children.

2. Send information home on the importance of reading to children and include a reading list. A one-page sheet could be sent home stating, "One of the best ways to help children become better readers is to read to them. Reading aloud is most helpful when you discuss the stories, learn to identify letters and words, and talk about the meaning of the words. Encourage leisure reading. Reading achievement is related to the amount of reading kids do. It increases vocabulary and reading fluency." Then list several books available from the school library for students to check out and take home.

3. You can supply parents with materials they can use to work with their children on skill development. Students can help make math games, crossword puzzles, and other materials that parents can use with them at home.

Professional Support Person for Instruction

Many parent and community members have skills that can be shared with the school. They are willing to work with students as well as teachers. These people are often ignored in parent and community involvement programs. A parent or community member who is a college professor could be asked to talk to teachers about a topic that interests them or to participate in an in-service workshop. A bilingual parent or community member could be asked to help tutor foreign-language students or to share books or magazines written in their language with the class. Parents who enjoy reading or art could be asked to help staff a humanities enrichment course before or after school or to recommend materials for the course. Parents and community members who perform these kinds of duties could also serve as role models for your students and would demonstrate the importance of education in the community. Review the list below and think of how you could involve parents and community members in your classroom. Parents and community members can:

- Serve as instructional assistants
- Correct papers at home or at school
- Use carpentry skills to build things for the school
- Tutor during school hours or after school
- Develop or identify student materials or community resources
- Share their expertise with students or staff
- Expand enrichment programs offered before, after, or during school such as Great Books and art appreciation
- Sew costumes for the school play
- Type and edit a newsletter

General Volunteers

Some parents are willing to volunteer their time but they do not want to do a job that requires specific skills. When thinking of activities for general volunteers, be sure to include activities that can be performed at the school and activities that can be performed at home. Some possible activities include:

- Working on the playground as a helper
- Working in the classroom as a helper
- Working at home preparing cutouts and other materials that will be used in class
- Telephoning other parents to schedule conferences

Decision Makers

Some parents are interested in participating in decision making in the school. They want to help set school policy, select curriculum materials, review budgets, or interview perspective staff members. Roles for these parents and community members include school Board member and advisory council member.

Summary

Parent and community involvement is a dynamic process that encourages, supports, and provides opportunities for teachers, parents, and community members to work together to improve student learning. Parent and community involvement is also an important component of school reform and multicultural education. Parents and community groups help provide the rationale, motivation, and social action necessary for educational reform.

Everyone benefits from parent-community involvement. Students tend to perform better in schools and have more people supporting their learning. Parents know more about what is going on at school, have more opportunities to communicate with their children's teacher, and are able to help their children increase their learning. Teachers gain a partner in education. Teachers learn more about their students through their parent and community contacts and are able to use that information to help increase their students' performance.

Even though research has consistently demonstrated that students have an advantage in school when their parents support and encourage educational activities, not all parents know how they can support their child's education or feel they have the time, energy, or other resources to be involved in schools. Some parents have a particularly difficult time supporting their children's education. Three such groups are parents who have low incomes, single parents, and parents with special needs. Parents from these groups are often dismissed as unsupportive of education, but they want their children to do well in school and are willing to work with the school when the school reaches out to them and responds to their needs.

To establish an effective parent-community involvement program you should establish two-way communication with parents and community groups, enlist support from the community, and have resources available for parents to use in working with their children. Expanding how parent-community involvement is conceptualized can increase the number of parents and community members able to participate. Parents can play many roles. Ways to involve parents and community members include parents working with their own children, parents and community members sharing their professional skills with the school, parents and community groups volunteering in the school, and parents and community members working with educators to make decisions about school.

This chapter opens by describing a problem that deals with religion and education. The problem demonstrates the importance of parents and teachers working together. The chapter concludes by relating how Ms. Jones resolved the problem.

Ms. Jones continued teaching the regular curriculum but made some changes in her teaching methods. She added more discussion activities to the unit and asked students to explore value issues in the topics she covered. When she covered such topics as evolution, she stated that there were other points of view on the origin of human beings. She also encouraged students to talk to their parents about science lessons. Students were assigned specific questions to ask their parents, such as "How do you believe the earth was created?" Ms. Jones wanted parents to know what she was teaching and to have an opportunity to share their views with their children. She gave students extra points for discussing the assigned questions with their parents.

Ms. Jones believes that her new approach to teaching is beneficial for parents, for students, and for her. Parents have an opportunity to make their views on various topics known at the same time the topic is discussed in class. Students learn that scientific knowledge has both a cognitive and affective dimension. Both parents and students are benefiting from the opportunity to communicate with each other. Ms. Jones learned that open discussions on the values implicit in scientific issues increase student interest and help students gain a better understanding of the subject matter. When parent participation in school is effective, students, teachers, and parents are helped and enriched.

Questions and Activities

1. Compare the role of parents in schools during the Colonial period to that of students today. Identify and discuss changes that have occurred and changes you would like to see occur in parent involvement.

2. Consider this statement: Regardless of the circumstances a student experiences at home, teachers have a responsibility to help them perform at their highest level at school. Do you agree? Why or why not?

3. Interview a parent of a bilingual, ethnic minority, religious minority, or low-income student to learn more about the parent's views on schools and the educational goals for his or her children. This information cannot be generalized to all members of these groups, but it can be an important departure point for learning more about diverse groups within our society.

4. Consider this statement: All parents want their children to succeed in school. Do you agree with the statement? Why or why not?

5. Interview a classroom teacher and an administrator to determine his or her perceptions of parent-community involvement.

6. Write a brief paper on your personal views of the benefits and drawbacks of parent-community involvement.

7. Form a group with two other members of your class or workshop. One person in the group will be a teacher, the other a parent, and the third an observer. The teacher and the parent will role play a teacher-parent conference. After role playing the conference, discuss how it felt to be a parent and a teacher. What can be done to make the parent and teacher feel more comfortable? Was the information shared at the conference helpful? The observer can share his or her view of how the parent and teacher interacted.

8. At the beginning of this chapter, you were introduced to a hypothetical teacher, Ms. Jones. If you were Ms. Jones, how would you have responded to Mr. Evans? Discuss what your response would have communicated to Mr. Evans about each of the following:

a. Your views on parent involvement
b. The importance of parents and teachers working together
c. Your willingness to work with parents when you disagree
d. The importance of the school not alienating students from their parents and community.

Notes

1. Nicholas Hobbs, "Families, Schools, and Communities: An Ecosystem for Children," in Hope Jenson Leichter, ed., *Families and Communities as Educators* (New York: Teachers College Press, 1979).

2. John I. Goodlad, *A Place Called School: Prospects for the Future* (New York: McGraw-Hill, 1984), p. 293.

3. David S. Seeley, "Educational Partnership and the Dilemmas of School Reform," *Phi Delta Kappan* 65, No. 6 (February): 383–388.

4. Stephan Díaz, Luis C. Moll, and Hugh Mehan, "Sociocultural Resources in Instruction: A Context-Specific Approach," in *Beyond Language: Social & Cultural Factors in Schooling Language Minority Students* (Los Angeles: California State University, 1986).

5. Diane Scott-Jones, "Mother-as-Teacher in the Families of High- and Low-Achieving Low-Income Black First-Graders," *The Journal of Negro Education* 56, No. 1 (Winter 1987): 21–34. 1987): 21–34.

6. Hobbs, "Families, Schools, and Communities."

7. Reginald M. Clark, *Family Life and School Achievement: Why Poor Black Children Succeed or Fail* (Chicago: University of Chicago Press, 1983).

8. Ibid.

9. James A. Banks, *Teaching Strategies for Ethnic Studies,* 4th ed. (Boston: Allyn and Bacon, 1987).

10. Willard Waller, *The Sociology of Teaching* (New York: Wiley, 1965).

11. James S. Coleman, "Families and Schools," *Educational Researcher* 16, No. 6 (1987), pp. 32–38.

12. D. L. Williams, Jr., "Highlights from a Survey of Parents and Educators Regarding Parent Involvement in Education," Paper presented at the Seventh National Symposium on Building Family Strengths, Lincoln, Nebr., May, 1984.

13. Sara Lawrence Lightfoot, *Worlds Apart: Relationships between Families and Schools* (New York: Basic Books, 1978).

14. Eugenia Hepworth Berger, *Parents as Partners in Education: The School and Home Working Together,* 2d ed. (Columbus, Ohio: Merrill, 1987).

15. Coleman, "Families and Schools."

16. Berger, *Parents as Partners in Education.*

17. U.S. Bureau of the Census, *Statistical Abstract of the United States: 1986,* 106th ed. (Washington, D.C., 1985).

18. Ibid.

19. Ibid.

20. Ibid.

21. Ibid.

22. Ibid.

23. Ibid.

24. Ibid.

25. Ibid.

26. Ibid.

27. David Winkley, "The School's View of Parents," in Cedric Cullingford, ed., *Parents, Teachers and Schools* (London: Robert Royce, 1985).

28. Lightfoot, *World's Apart.*

29. Ibid.

30. Larry McClure, Sue Carol Cook, and Virginia Thompson, *Experience-Based Learning: How to Make the Community Your Classroom* (Portland, Ore.: Northwest Regional Educational Laboratory, 1977).

31. Ibid.

32. Reginald M. Clark, *Home Involvement Activities* (Boston: Houghton Mifflin, 1987).

Appendix: Multicultural Resources

Issues and Concepts

Appleton, Nicholas, *Cultural Pluralism in Education: Theoretical Foundations* (New York: Longman, 1983).

Baker, Gwendolyn C., *Planning and Organizing for Multicultural Instruction* (Reading, Mass.: Addison-Wesley, 1983).

Banks, James A., *Multiethnic Education: Theory and Practice,* 2d ed. Boston: Allyn and Bacon, 1988.

Baptiste, H. Prentice, *Developing the Multicultural Process in Classroom Instruction: Competencies for Teachers* (Washington, D.C.: University Press of America, 1979).

Boyer, James, *Multicultural Education: Product and Process* (Manhattan: Kansas Urban Education Center, 1985).

Bullivant, Brian M., *Pluralism: Cultural Maintenance and Evolution* (Clevedon, Avon, England: Multilingual Matters, 1984).

Cole, Michael, and Sylvia Scribner, *Culture and Thought: A Psychological Introduction* (New York: Wiley, 1974).

Geertz, Clifford, *Local Knowledge: Further Essays in Interpretive Anthropology* (New York: Basic Books, 1983).

Geertz, Clifford, *The Interpretation of Cultures* (New York: Basic Books, 1973).

Gollnick, Donna M., and Philip C. Chinn, *Multicultural Education in a Pluralistic Society,* 2d ed. (Columbus, Ohio: Charles E. Merrill, 1986).

Grant, Carl A., and Christine E. Sleeter, *After the School Bell Rings* (Philadelphia: The Falmer Press, 1986).

Lynch, James, *Multicultural Education: Principles and Practice* (Boston: Routledge and Kegan Paul, 1986).

Lynch, James, *Prejudice Reduction and the Schools* (New York: Nichols, 1987).

McLeod, Keith, A., ed., *Multicultural Education: A Partnership.* (Toronto, Ontario: Canadian Council for Multicultural and Intercultural Education, 1987).

Multicultural Leader, Quarterly newsletter published by the Educational Materials and Services Center, 144 Railroad Avenue, Suite 107, Edmonds, Wash. 98020.

Schniedewind, Nancy, and Ellen Davidson, *Open Minds to Equality: A Sourcebook of Learning Activities to Promote Race, Sex, Class, and Age Equity* (Englewood Cliffs, N.J.: Prentice-Hall, 1983).

Sleeter, Christine E., and Carl A. Grant, *Making Choices for Multicultural Education: Five Approaches to Race, Class and Gender* (Columbus, Ohio: Merrill, 1988).

Social Class

Apple, Michael W., *Education and Power* (Boston: Routledge and Kegan Paul, 1982).

Barton, Len, and Stephan Walker, eds., *Race, Class and Education* (London: Croom Helm, 1983).

Bowles, Samuel, and Herbert Gintis, *Schooling in Capitalist America* (New York: Basic Books, 1976).

Cookson, Peter W., Jr., and Caroline Hodges Persell, *Preparing for Power: America's Elite Boarding Schools* (New York: Basic Books, 1985).

Domhoff, G. Williams, *Who Rules America Now?* (New York: Touchstone Books, 1983).

Jencks, Christopher, Marshall Smith, Henry AcLand, Mary Jo Bane, David Cohen, Herbert Gintis, Barbara Heyns, and Stephen Michelson, *Inequality: A Reassessment of the Effect of Family and Schooling in America* (New York: Basic Books, 1972).

Landry, Bart, *The New Black Middle Class* (Berkeley: University of California Press, 1987).

Katz, Michael B., *Class, Bureaucracy, and Schools: The Illusion of Educational Change in America* (New York: Praeger, 1975).

Oakes, Jeannie, *Keeping Track: How Schools Structure Inequality* (New Haven, Conn.: Yale University Press, 1985).

Persell, Caroline Hodges, *Education and Inequality* (New York: The Free Press, 1977).

Religion

Bullivant, Brian M., *The Way of Tradition: Life in an Orthodox Jewish School* (Hawthorn, Victoria, Australia: The Australian Council for Educational Research, 1978).

Collie, William E., and Lee H. Smith, eds., "Teaching about Religion in the Schools: The Continuing Challenge," *Social Education* 45 (January 1981): 15–34.

Duker, Sam, *The Public School and Religion: The Legal Context* (New York: Harper and Row, 1966).

Ellwood, Robert S., Jr., *Introducing Religion from Inside and Outside* (Englewood Cliffs, N.J.: Prentice-Hall, 1978).

Engel, David E., ed., *Religion in Public Education* (New York: Paulist Press, 1974).

Frazier, E. Franklin, *The Negro Church in America* (New York: Schocken Books, 1964).

Gaustad, Edwin S., *A Religious History of America* (New York: Harper and Row, 1966).

Greeley, Andrew M., *Religion: A Secular Theory* (New York: Free Press, 1982).

Herberg, Will, *Protestant-Catholic-Jew: An Essay in American Religious Sociology* (New York: Anchor Press, 1960).

Lessa, William A., and Evon Z. Vogt, *Reader in Comparative Religion: An Anthropological Approach,* 2d ed. (New York: Harper and Row, 1965).

Michaelsen, Robert S., *Piety in the Public School* (New York: Macmillan, 1970).

Noss, John B., *Man's Religions,* 6th ed. (New York: Macmillan, 1980).

Piediscalzi, Nicholas, and William Collie, eds., *Teaching about Religion in Public Schools* (Niles, Ill.: Argus Communications, 1977).

Gender

Anzaldua, Gloria, and Cherrie Moraga, eds., *This Bridge Called My Back: Writings by Radical Women of Color* (Watertown, Mass.: Persephone Press, 1981).

Baxandall, Rosalyn, Linda Gordon, and Susan Reverby, eds., *America's Working Women: A Documentary History—1600 to the Present* (New York: Vintage Books, 1976).

Belenky, Mary Field, Blythe McVicker Clinchy, Nancy Rule Goldberg, and Fill Mattuck Tarrule, *Women's Ways of Knowing: The Development of Self, Voice, and Mind* (New York: Basic Books, 1986).

Bell, Roseann P., Betty J. Parker, and Beverly Guy-Sheftall, *Sturdy Black Bridges: Visions of Black Women in Literature* (New York: Avon Books, 1979).

Cole, Johnnetta, ed., *All American Women: Lines that Divide, Ties That Bind* (New York: Free Press, 1986).

Davis, Angela, *Women, Race, and Class* (New York: Vintage Books, 1981).

Franklin, Clyde W., *The Changing Definition of Masculinity* (New York: Plenum Press, 1984).

Giddings, Paula, *When and Where I Enter: The Impact of Black Women on Race and Sex in America* (New York: Bantam Books, 1984).

Gilligan, Carol, *In a Different Voice: Psychological Theory and Women's Development* (Cambridge: Harvard University Press, 1982).

Glazer, Nona, and Helen Youngelson Waehrer, eds., *Women in a Man-Made World: A Socioeconomic Handbook,* 2d ed: (Chicago: Rand McNally, 1977).

Halpern, Diane F., *Sex Differences in Cognitive Abilities* (Hillsdale, N.J.: Lawrence Erlbaum Associates, 1986).

Jones, Jacqueline, *Labor of Love, Labor of Sorrow. Black Women, Work and the Family from Slavery to the Present* (New York: Vintage Books, 1985).

Melville, Margarita B., ed., *Twice a Minority: Mexican American Women* (St. Louis: The C. V. Mosby Company, 1980).

Mirande, Alfredo, and Evangelina Enriquez, *La Chicana: The Mexican-American Women* (Chicago: The University of Chicago Press, 1979).

Morales, Aurora Levins, and Rosario Morales, *Getting Home Alive* (New York: Firebrand Books, 1986).

Niethammer, Carolyn, *Daughters of the Earth: The Lives and Legends of American Indian Women* (New York: Collier Books, 1977).

Noddings, Nel, *Caring: A Feminine Approach to Ethnics and Moral Education* (Berkeley: University of California Press, 1984).

Pleck, Joseph H., *The Myth of Masculinity* (Cambridge, Mass.: The MIT Press, 1981).

Rodgers, Harrell R., Jr., *Poor Women, Poor Families: The Economic Plight of America's Female-Headed Households* (New York: M. E. Sharpe, 1986).

Rosen, Raymond, and Linda Reich Rosen, *Human Sexuality* (New York: Knopf, 1981).

Sadker, Myra P., and David M. Sadker, *Sex Equity Handbook for Schools* (New York: Longman, 1982).

Sapiro, Virginia, *The Political Integration of Women: Roles, Socialization, and Politics* (Urbana: University of Illinois Press, 1983).

Spence, Janet T., Kay Deaux, and Robert L. Helmreich, "Sex Roles in Contemporary American Society," in Gardner Lindzey and Elliot Aronson, eds., *The Handbook of Social Psychology,* Vol. 2, 3d ed. (New York: Random House, 1985), pp. 149–178.

Steady, Filomina, ed., *The Black Women Cross-Culturally* (Cambridge, Mass.: Schenkman, 1981).

Tsuchida, Nobuya, ed., *Asian and Pacific American Experiences: Women's Perspectives* (Minneapolis: University of Minnesota, 1982).

Whicker, Marcia Lynn, and Jennie Jacobs Kronenfeld, *Sex Role Changes: Technology, Politics, and Policy* (New York: Praeger, 1986).

Yung, Judy, *Chinese Women of America: A Pictorial History* (Seattle: University of Washington Press, 1986).

Ethnicity and Language

Banks, James A., *Teaching Strategies for Ethnic Studies*, 4th ed. (Boston: Allyn and Bacon, 1987).

Banks, James A., and James Lynch, eds., *Multicultural Education in Western Societies* (London: Cassell, 1986).

Bell, Derrick, *And We Are Not Saved: The Elusive Quest for Racial Justice* (New York: Basic Books, Inc., 1987).

Bennett, Christine I., *Comprehensive Multicultural Education* (Boston: Allyn and Bacon, 1986).

Bilingual Office, California State Department of Education, *Beyond Language: Social and Cultural Factors in Schooling Language Minority Students* (Los Angeles: Evaluation, Dissemination and Assessment Center, California State University, 1986).

Brandt, Godfrey L., *The Realization of Anti-Racist Teaching* (Philadelphia: The Falmer Press, 1986).

Bullivant, Brian, *The Ethnic Encounter in the Secondary School: Ethnocultural Reproduction and Resistance; Theory and Case Studies* (Philadelphia: The Falmer Press, 1987).

Castellanos, Diego, *The Best of Two Worlds: Bilingual-Bicultural Education in the U.S* (Trenton: New Jersey State Department of Education, 1983).

Garcia, Ricardo L., *Teaching in a Pluralistic Society: Concepts, Models, Strategies* (New York: Harper and Row, 1982).

Gay, Geneva, and Willie L. Baber, eds., *Expressively Black: The Cultural Basis of Ethnic Identity* (New York: Praeger, 1988).

Glazer, Nathan, *Ethnic Dilemmas 1964–1982* (Cambridge, Mass.: Harvard University Press, 1983).

Hale-Benson, Janice E., *Black Children: Their Roots, Culture, and Learning Styles*, rev. ed. (Baltimore: The John Hopkins University Press, 1986).

Heath, Shirley Brice, *Ways with Words: Language, Life, and Work in Communities and Classrooms* (New York: Cambridge University Press, 1983).

Longstreet, Wilma S., *Aspects of Ethnicity* (New York: Teachers College Press, 1978).

McAdoo, Harriette P., and John L. McAdoo, eds., *Black Children: Social, Educational, and Parental Environments* (Beverly Hills, Calif.: Sage Publications, 1985).

Neisser, Ulric, ed., *The School Achievement of Minority Children: New Perspectives* (Hillsdale, N.J.: Lawrence Erlbaum Associates, 1986).

Ogbu, John U., *Minority Education and Caste* (New York: Academic Press, 1978).

Olivas, Michael A., *Latino College Students* (New York: Teachers College Press, 1986).

Ovando, Carlos J., and Virginia P. Collier, *Bilingual and ESL Classrooms: Teaching in Multicultural Contexts* (New York: McGraw-Hill, 1985).

Phinney, Jean S., and Mary J. Rotheram, *Children's Ethnic Socialization* (Beverly Hills, Calif.: Sage Publications, 1987).

Prager, Jeffrey, Douglas Longshore, and Melvin Seeman, eds., *School Desegregation Research* (New York: Plenum Press, 1986).

Sollors, Werner, *Beyond Ethnicity: Consent and Descent in American Culture* (New York: Oxford University Press, 1986).

Sue, Derald W., with chapter contributions by Edwin H. Richardson, Rene A. Ruiz, and Elsie J. Smith, *Counseling the Culturally Different: Theory and Practice* (New York: John Wiley, 1981).

Thernstrom, Stephan, Ann Orlov, and Oscar Handlin, *Harvard Encyclopedia of American Ethnic Groups* (Cambridge: Harvard University Press, 1980).

Wilson, William Julius, *The Truly Disadvantaged: The Inner City, the Underclass, and Public Policy* (Chicago: The University of Chicago Press, 1987).

Exceptionality

Goffman, Erving, *Stigma: Notes on the Management of Spoiled Identity* (Englewood Cliffs, N.J.: Prentice-Hall, 1963).

Heward, William L., and Michael D. Orlansky, *Exceptional Children: An Introductory Survey of Special Education*, 2d ed. (Columbus, Ohio: Merrill, 1984).

Mehan, Hugh, Alma Hertweck, and J. Lee Meihls, *Handicapping the Handicapped: Decision Making in Students' Educational Careers* (Stanford, Calif.: Stanford University Press, 1986).

Mercer, Jane R., *Labeling the Mentally Retarded* (Berkeley: University of California Press, 1973).

Morsink, Catherine Voelker, *Teaching Special Needs Students in Regular Classrooms* (Boston: LIttle, Brown, 1984).

Schulz, Jane B., *Parents and Professionals in Special Education* (Boston: Allyn and Bacon, 1987).

Schulz, Jane B., and Ann P. Turnbull, *Mainstreaming Handicapped Students: A Guide for Classroom Teachers,* 2d ed. (Boston: Allyn and Bacon, 1984).

Sisk, Dorothy, *Creative Teaching of the Gifted* (New York: McGraw-Hill, 1987).

Swassing, Raymond H., *Teaching Gifted Children and Adolescents* (Columbus, Ohio: Merrill, 1985).

School Reform

Berger, Eugenia Hepworth, *Parents as Partners in Education: The School and the Home Working Together* (Columbus, Ohio: Merrill, 1987).

Brookover, Wilbur, Charles Beady, Patricia Flood, John Schweitzer and John Wisenbaker, *School Social Systems and Student Achievement: Schools Can Make a Difference* (New York: Praeger, 1979).

Clark, Reginald M., *Family Life and School Achievement: Why Poor Black Children Succeed or Fail* (Chicago: The University of Chicago Press, 1983).

Comer, James P., *School Power: Implications of an Intervention Project* (New York: The Free Press, 1980).

Gardner, Howard, *Frames of Mind: The Theory of Multiple Intelligences* (New York: Basic Books, 1983).

Goodlad, John I., ed., *The Ecology of School Renewal* (Chicago: The University of Chicago Press, 1987).

Goodlad, John I., *A Place Called School: Prospects for the Future* (New York: McGraw-Hill, 1984).

Guthrie, Grace Pung, *A School Divided: An Ethnography of Bilingual Education in a Chinese Community* (Hillside, N.J.: Lawrence Erlbaum Associates, 1985).

Lightfoot, Sara Lawrence, *The Good School: Portraits of Character and Culture* (New York: Basic Books, 1983).

Lightfoot, Sara Lawrence, *Worlds Apart: Relationships between Families and Schools* (New York: Basic Books, 1978).

Mercer, Jane R., *Labeling the Mentally Retarded* (Berkeley: University of California Press, 1973).

Presseisen, Barbara Z., *Unlearned Lessons: Current and Past Reforms for School Improvement* (Philadelphia: The Falmer Press, 1985).

Glossary

Afro-Americans United States citizens who have an African biological and cultural heritage and identity. This term is used synonymously and interchangeably with *Black, Black American,* and *African-American.* These terms are used to describe both a racial and a cultural group. There were about 22 million Afro-Americans in the United States in 1980. They are the nation's largest ethnic minority group.

American Indian *See Native American.*

Anglo-Americans Americans whose biological and cultural heritage originated in England, or Americans with other biological and cultural heritages who have assimilated into the dominant or mainstream culture in the United States. This term is often used to describe the mainstream United States culture or to describe most White Americans.

Asian Americans Americans who have a biological and cultural heritage that originated on the continent of Asia. The largest groups of Asian-Americans in the United States in 1980 were the Chinese, Filipinos, Japanese, Asian Indians, Koreans, and Vietnamese. Other groups included Laotians, Thai, Cambodians, Pakistanis, and Indonesians. Asians are the fasting-growing ethnic group in the United States. They increased 141 percent between 1970 and 1980. There were about 3.5 million Asian-Americans in the United States in 1980.

Cultural assimilation Takes place when one ethnic or cultural group acquires the behavior, values, perspectives, ethos, and characteristics of another ethnic or group and sheds its own cultural characteristics.

Culture The ideations, symbols, behaviors, values, and beliefs that are shared by a human group. *Cultural* can also be defined as a group's program for survival and adaptation to its environment. Pluralistic nation-states such as the United States, Canada, and Australia are made up of an overarching culture, called a macroculture, that all individuals and groups within the nation share. These nation-states also have many smaller cultures, called microcultures, that are in many ways different from the macroculture or that contain cultural components manifested differently than in the macroculture. See Chapters 1 and 2 for further discussions of culture.

Discrimination The differential treatment of individuals or groups based on categories such as race, ethnicity, gender, social class, or exceptionality.

Ethnic group A microcultural group or collectivity that shares a common history and culture, common values, behaviors, and other characteristics that cause members of the group to have a shared identity. A sense of peoplehood is one of the most important characteristics of an ethnic group. An ethnic group also shares economic and political interests. Cultural characteristics, rather than biological traits, are the essential attributes of an ethnic group. An ethnic group is not the same as a racial group. Some ethnic groups, such as Puerto Ricans in the United States, are made up of individuals who belong to several different racial groups. White Anglo Saxon Protestants, Italian Americans, and Irish Americans are examples of ethnic groups.

Individual members of an ethnic group vary considerably in the extent to which they identify with the group. Some individuals have a very strong identity with their particular ethnic group, whereas other members of the group have a very weak identification with it.

Ethnic minority group An ethnic group with several distinguishing characteristics. An ethnic minority group has distinguishing cultural characteristics, racial characteristics, or both, which enable members of other groups to identify its members easily. Some ethnic minority groups, such as Jewish Americans, have unique cultural characteristics. Afro-Americans have unique cultural and physical characteristics. The unique attributes of ethnic minority groups make them convenient targets of racism and discrimination. Ethnic minority groups are usually a numerical minority within their societies. However, the Blacks in South Africa, who are a numerical majority in their naion-state, are often considered a sociological minority group by social scientists because they are politically and economically powerless.

Ethnic studies The scientific and humanistic analysis of behavior influenced by variables related to ethnicity and ethnic-group membership. This term is often used to refer to special school, university, and college courses and programs that focus on specific racial and ethnic groups. However, any aspects of a course or program that includes a study of variables related to ethnicity can accurately be referred to as ethnic studies. In other words, ethnic studies can be integrated within the boundaries of mainstream courses and curricula.

Exceptional   Used to describe students who have learning or behavioral characteristics that differ substantially from most other students and that require special attention in instruction. Students who are intellectually gifted or talented as well as those who have learning disabilities are considered exceptional.

Gender   Consists of behaviors that result from the social, cultural, and psychological factors associated with masculinity and femininity within a society. Appropriate male and female roles result from the socialization of the individual within a group.

Gender identity   An individual's view of the gender to which he or she belongs and his or her shared sense of group attachment with other males or females.

Global education   Concerned with issues and problems related to the survival of human beings in a world community. International studies is a part of global education, but the focus of global education is the interdependence of human beings and their common fate, regardless of the national boundaries within which they live. Many teachers confuse global education and international studies with ethinic studies, which deal with ethnic groups within a national boundary, such as the United States.

Handicapism   The unequal treatment of people who are disabled, and related attitudes and beliefs that reinforce and justify discrimination against people with handicaps.

Hispanic Americans   Americans who share a culture, heritage, and langue that originated in Spain. The word *Latinos* is sometimes used to refer to Hispanic Americans in certain regions of the nation. Most Hispanics in the United States speak Spanish and are mestizos. A *mestizo* is a person of mixed biological heritage. Most Hispanics in the United States have an Indian as well as a Spanish heritage. Many of them also have an African biological and cultural heritage.

The largest group of Hispanics in the United States are Mexican Americans (Chicanos), Puerto Ricans, and Cubans. In 1987, there were about 18.8 million documented Hispanics in the United States. Mexicans made up 63 percent of Hispanics in the United States; Puerto Ricans, 12 percent; Cubans 5 percent; and Central and South Americans, 11 percent. Persons who identified themselves only as *Hispanics* made up 9 percent. Hispanics are one of the nation's fasting-growing ethnic minority groups. They increased 30 percent between 1980 and 1987, from 14.5 to 18.8 million. The nation's non-Hispanic population increased 6 percent during this period. Demographers are predicting that if current growth rates continue, Hispanics will outnumber all ethnic groups in the United States by the year 2000, including Afro-Americans.

It can be misleading to view Hispanics as one ethnic group. Some Hispanics believe that the word *Hispanics* can help to unify the various Latino groups and thus increase their political power. The primary identity of most Hispanics in the United States, however, is with their particular group, such as Mexican American, Puerto Rican, or Cuban.

Mainstream American   A United States citizen who shares most of the characteristics of the dominant ethnic and cultural group in the nation. Such an individual is usually White Anglo Saxon Protestant and belongs to the middle class or a higher social-class status.

Mainstream-centric curriculum   A curriculum that present events, concepts, issues, and problems primarily or exclusively from the points of view and perspectives of the mainstream society and the dominant ethnic and cultural group in the United States, White Anglo Saxon Protestants. The mainstream-centric curriculum is also usually presented from the perspectives of Anglo males.

Mainstreaming   The process that involves placing students with handicaps into the regular classroom for instruction. They might be integrated into the regular classroom for part or all of the school day. This practice was initiated in response to Public Law 94-142 (passed by Congress in 1985), which requires that handicapped students be educated in the least restricted environment.

Multicultural education   A reform movement designed to change the total educational environment so that students from diverse racial and ethnic groups, both gender groups, exceptional students, and students from each social class group will experience equal educational opportunities in schools, colleges, and universities. A major assumption of multicultural education is that some students, because of their particular racial, ethnic, gender, and cultural characteristics, have a better chance to succeed in educational institutions as they are currently structured than do students who belong to other groups or have different cultural and gender characteristics.

Multiethnic education   A reform movement designed to change the total educational environment so that students from diverse racial and ethnic groups will experience equal educational opportunities. Multiethnic education is an important component of multicultural education.

Native American United States citizens who trace their biological and cultural heritage to the original inhabitants in the land that now makes up the United States. *Native American* is used synonymously with *American Indian.*

Prejudice A set of rigid and unfavorable attitudes toward a particular individual or group that is formed without consideration for facts. Prejudice is a set of attitudes that often leads to discrimination, the differential treatment of particular individuals and groups.

Race Refers to the attempt by physical anthropologists to divide human groups according to their physical traits and characteristics. This has proven to be very difficult because human groups in modernized societies are highly mixed physically. Consequently, different and often conflicting race typologies exist.

Racism A belief that human groups can be validly grouped according to their biological traits and that these identifiable groups inherit certain mental, personality, and cultural characteristics that determine their behavior. Racism, however, is not merely a set of beliefs but is practiced when a group has the power to enforce laws, institutions, and norms, based on its beliefs, that oppress and dehumanize another group.

Religion A set of beliefs and values, especially about explanations that concern the cause and nature of the universe, to which an individual or group has a strong loyalty and attachment. A religion usually has a moral code, rituals, and institutions that reinforce and propagate its beliefs.

Sex The biological factors that distinguish males and females, such as chromosomal, hormonal, anatomical, and physiological characteristics.

Social class A collectivity of people who have a similar socioeconomic status based on such criteria as income, occupation, education, values, behaviors, and life chances. *Lower class, working class, middle class,* and *upper class* are common designations of social class in the United States.

Contributors

CHERRY A. McGEE BANKS is president of Educational Materials and Services Center (Edmonds, Washington), an educational initiative that focuses on improving education for special population groups, such as ethnic minorities, women, and exceptional students. She is also editor and publisher of *Multicultural Leader,* a quarterly newsletter. A former teacher in Michigan and specialist in the Seattle Public Schools, she is coauthor of *March toward Freedom: A History of Black Americans* and a contributing author of *Education in the 80's: Multiethnic Education.* She is active in efforts to increase parent participation in education and currently serves on the Board of Directors of the Shoreline (Washington) Community College.

JAMES A. BANKS is professor of education at the University of Washington, Seattle. He is former chairman of Curriculum and Instruction and a past president of the National Council for the Social Studies. He is a specialist in social studies education and multicultural education and has contributed to numerous journals in these fields, including *School Review,* the *Elementary School Journal, Phi Delta Kappan,* and *Social Education.* Professor Banks's books include *Teaching Strategies for Ethnic Studies,* 4th ed.; *Multiethnic Education: Theory and Practice,* 2d ed.; and *We Americans: Our History and People.* He is a former teacher in the Joliet, Illinois, Public Schools and at the Francis W. Parker School in Chicago.

BRIAN M. BULLIVANT is reader in education, Faculty of Education, Monash University (Australia). An anthropologist interested in the influence of culture on education, Dr. Bullivant's books include *The Way of Tradition: Life in an Orthodox Jewish School; The Pluralist Dilemma in Education: Six Case Studies; Race, Ethnicity, and Curriculum; Pluralism: Cultural Maintenance and Evolution;* and *The Ethnic Encounter in the Secondary School.*

JOHNNELLA E. BUTLER is associate professor in the Department of Ethnic Studies at the University of Washington, Seattle. She was formerly on the faculty of Smith College, where she served as chairperson of the Afro-American Studies Department and developed the program in Afro-American Studies. Professor Butler is a specialist in Afro-American literature and women's studies and is particularly interested in how ethnic studies and women's studies can be interrelated. She is the author of *Black Studies: Pedagogy and Revolution* and has contributed to several books, including *Women's Place in the Academy: Transforming the Liberal Arts Curriculum; Feminist Pedagogy;* and *Toward a Balanced Curriculum.*

GENEVA GAY is professor of education at Purdue University. A specialist in curriculum and multicultural education, Professor Gay has contributed to numerous journals and books in these fields. Among the books to which she has contributed are *Teaching Ethnic Studies: Concepts and Strategies; Language and Cultural Diversity in American Education; Teaching American History: The Quest for Relevance; Curriculum Guidelines for Multiethnic Education; Pluralism and the American Teacher: Issues and Case Studies;* and *Considered Action for Curriculum Improvement.* She is the co-editor of *Expressively Black: The Cultural Basis of Ethnic Identity.*

CARL A. GRANT is professor in the Department of Curriculum and Instruction at the University of Wisconsin-Madison. He is a former teacher and assistant principal in the Chicago Public Schools. Since 1972 he has directed a Teacher Corps program to train teachers for urban schools. Professor Grant is a specialist in multicultural education and teacher education. He has contributed to numerous articles and books in these fields. His books include *Multicultural Education: Definitions, Issues, and Applications; Community Participation in Education;* and *Bringing Teaching to Life: An Introduction to Teaching;* and (with Christine E. Sleeter), *After the School Bell Rings.*

WILLIAM L. HEWARD is professor, Department of Human Services Education, at The Ohio State University. A specialist in the education of exceptional children, Professor Heward has contributed to numerous journals, including *Exceptional Children, The Elementary School Journal,* and the *Journal of Applied Behavior Analysis.*

He has coauthored a number of books, including *Exceptional Children: An Introductory Survey of Special Education*, 3d ed.; *Voices: Interviews with Handicapped People*; *Working with Parents of Handicapped Children*; and *Applied Behavior Analysis*.

LYNETTE LONG is associate professor of education at the American University in Washington, D.C. A former high school teacher and university counselor, she has contributed articles to numerous journals and has written or coauthored six books including *Unparented: American Teens on Their Own*; *The Handbook for Latchkey Children and Their Parents*; and *Questioning: Skills for the Helping Process*. Professor Long has done research and training in several areas, including human relations, sex equity, and latchkey children.

JANE R. MERCER is professor of sociology at the University of California, Riverside. Professor Mercer has done extensive research on mental retardation, beginning with her doctoral thesis at the University of Southern California. She is particularly interested in mental retardation as a social construct and in how ethnic minorities are victimized by mental measurement tests that are standardized on the mainstream population. She has written extensively on these issues, developed an alternative assessment, *The System of Multicultural Pluralistic Assessment* (SOMPA), and served as an expert witness in court cases involving the testing of ethnic minorities. She has contributed to numerous books, including *Practical Intelligence: Nature and Origins of Competence in the Everyday World*; *Education in the 80's: Multiethnic Education*; and *Adaptive Behavior: Concepts and Measurement*. She is the author of *Labeling the Mentally Retarded*.

MICHAEL D. ORLANSKY is associate professor and coordinator of Special Education Programs at The Ohio State University. Professor Orlansky taught deaf-blind children at the Perkins School for the Blind and at the Washington State School for the Blind. He has contributed numerous articles to such journals as *Exceptional Children, Child Development,* and the *Journal of Visual Impairment and Blindness*. He is the author of *Mainstreaming the Visually Impaired Child* and coauthor of *Exceptional Children*; and *Voices: Interviews with Handicapped Children*.

CARLOS J. OVANDO is associate professor of Education at Oregon State University, Corvallis. He previously taught at the University of Alaska, Anchorage, and at the University of Southern California. Professor Ovando is a specialist in bilingual and multicultural education and has contributed to numerous publications in these fields. He

has served as guest editor of two special issues of *Educational Research Quarterly* and contributed to the *Phi Delta Kappan*. He is the coauthor of *Bilingual and ESL Classrooms: Teaching in Multicultural Contexts*.

CAROLINE HODGES PERSELL is professor and chair of the Department of Sociology at New York University. Professor Persell is interested in social stratification in education and has examined this issue in two of her books, *Education and Inequality* and *Preparing for Power: America's Elite Boarding Schools*, coauthored with Peter W. Cookson, Jr. Her other books include *Understanding Society: An Introduction to Sociology*, 2d ed.; *Encountering Society* (with others); and *Quality, Careers and Training in Educational and Social Research*.

DAVID A. SADKER is professor of education at The American University in Washington, D.C. He formerly served as director of the Mid-Atlantic Center for Sex Equity and as director of Teacher Education Programs and Undergraduate Studies at The American University. A former social studies teacher, Professor Sadker is a specialist in teacher education and is particularly interested in sex equity. He has contributed to numerous publications and is the coauthor (with Myra Sadker) of *Sex Equity Handbook for Schools*; *Teachers Make the Difference: An Introduction to Education*; and *Now upon a Time: A Contemporary View of Children's Literature*.

MYRA SADKER is professor of education at The American University in Washington, D.C. She was formerly dean of the School of Education and, later, director of the Teacher Preparation Programs. A former language arts teacher, Professor Sadker has contributed to numerous journals and books. She is a specialist in teacher education and has written extensively on sex equity. She is the coauthor (with David Sadker) of *Sex Equity Handbook for Schools*; *Teachers Make the Difference: An Introduction to Education*; and *Now upon a Time: A Contemporary View of Children's Literature*. She is also the coauthor of *Sexism in School and Society*.

JANE B. SCHULZ is professor and coordinator of Special Education at Western Carolina University. A former special education teacher and reading clinician, Professor Schulz has contributed to a number of professional journals, including *Teaching Exceptional Children* and *Exceptional Education Quarterly*. She is the author of *Parents and Professionals in Special Education* and coauthor of *Mainstreaming Handicapped Students: A Guide for the Classroom Teacher*. In 1981, she received the Paul A. Reid Distinguished Service Award at Western Carolina University.

CHRISTINE E. SLEETER is associate professor of education at the University of Wisconsin-Parkside. A former special-education teacher, her research focuses on multicultural education and the ways in which factors such as race, class, gender, and exceptionality influence student behavior. She has contributed to many journals, including the *Review of Educational Research, Educational Policy,* and *Harvard Educational Review.* Her books, with Carl A. Grant, include *After the School Bell Rings, Making Choices,* and *Turning on Learning.*

RENA F. SUBOTNIK is assistant professor of education and coordinator of the Program in Gifted Education at Hunter College of the City University of New York. She was formerly a classroom teacher and a gifted specialist in the Seattle Public Schools. A specialist in gifted education, Professor Subotnik has contributed papers to a number of journals, including the *Questioning Exchange Journal,* the *Journal of Creative Behavior,* and *The Social Studies Teacher.*

MARY KAY THOMPSON TETREAULT is dean and professor of the School of Human Development and Community Service, California State University at Fullerton. A specialist in social studies education and women's studies, Professor Tetreault is particularly interested in how feminist pedagogy can enrich the curriculum for all students and in feminist phase theory. She served as guest editor of a section of *Social Education,* "Getting Women and Gender into the Curriculum Mainstream" (March 1987). She is the author of numerous articles and of the book *Women in America: Half of History.*

JAMES K. UPHOFF is professor of education and human services and director of the Office of Laboratory Experiences in Education at Wright State University, Dayton, Ohio. Professor Uphoff is a specialist in social studies education and has done extensive work on religion and education. He has contributed to journals such as *Educational Leadership* and *Social Education.* He is the coauthor of *Public Education Religion Studies: Questions and Answers; Religion Studies in the Curriculum: Retrospect and Prospect;* and *Summer Children: Ready or Not Ready for School?*

Index